Poets and Singers

Music in Medieval Europe
Series Editor: Thomas Forrest Kelly

Titles in the Series:

Poets and Singers
Elizabeth Aubrey

Chant and its Origins
Thomas Forrest Kelly

Oral and Written Transmission in Chant
Thomas Forrest Kelly

Instruments and their Music in the Middle Ages
Timothy J. McGee

Ars nova
John L. Nádas and Michael Scott Cuthbert

Embellishing the Liturgy
Alejandro Planchart

Ars antiqua
Edward Roesner

Poets and Singers
On Latin and Vernacular Monophonic Song

Edited by

Elizabeth Aubrey
University of Iowa, USA

LONDON AND NEW YORK

First published 2009 by Ashgate Publishing

Published 2016 by Routledge
2 Park Square, Milton Park, Abingdon, Oxon OX14 4RN
52 Vanderbilt Avenue, New York, NY 10017

Routledge is an imprint of the Taylor & Francis Group, an informa business

Copyright © Elizabeth Aubrey 2009. For copyright of individual articles please refer to the Acknowledgments

All rights reserved. No part of this book may be reprinted or reproduced or utilised in any form or by any electronic, mechanical, or other means, now known or hereafter invented, including photocopying and recording, or in any information or storage or retrieval system, without permission in writing from the publishers.

Notice:
Product or corporate names may be trademarks or registered trademarks, and a re used only for identification ans explanation without intent to infringe.

Wherever possible, these reprints are made from a copy of the original printing, but these can themselves be of very variable quality. Whilst the publisher has made every effort to ensure the quality of the reprint, some variability may inevitably remain.

British Library Cataloguing in Publication Data
Poets and Singers: on Latin and vernacular monophonic
    song. - (Music in medieval Europe)
    1. Monophonic chansons - 500-1400 - History and criticism
    2. Trouvere songs - History and criticism 3.Bards and
       bardism 4. Trouveres
    I. Aubrey, Elizabeth, 1951-
    782.4'3

Library of Congress Control Number: 2007943183

ISBN-13: 9780754627074 (hbk)

Contents

Acknowledgements vii
Series Preface ix
Introduction: Poets, Singers, Scribes and Historians xi

PART I   HISTORY AND SOCIETY

1. Christopher Page (1984), 'Music and Chivalric Fiction in France, 1150–1300', *Proceedings of the Royal Musical Association*, **111**, pp. 1–27.   3
2. Ruth E. Harvey (1993), '*Joglars* and the Professional Status of the Early Troubadours', *Medium Aevum*, **62**, pp. 221–41.   31
3. Bryan Gillingham (1994), 'Turtles, Helmets, Parasites and Goliards', *The Music Review*, **55**, pp. 249–75.   53
4. Cyrilla Barr (1988), 'Introduction', in Cyrilla Barr, *The Monophonic Lauda and the Lay Religious Confraternities of Tuscany and Umbria in the Late Middle Ages*, Kalamazoo: Medieval Institute Publications, pp. 1–8; 152–4.   81

PART II   WOMEN

5. Joan Tasker Grimbert (1999), 'Diminishing the *Trobairitz*, Excluding the Women Trouvères', *Tenso: Bulletin of the Société Guilhem IX*, **14**, pp. 23–38.   95
6. Susan Boynton (2002), 'Women's Performance of the Lyric Before 1500', in Anne L. Klinck and Ann Marie Rasmussen (eds), *Medieval Woman's Song: Cross-Cultural Approaches*, Philadelphia: University of Pennsylvania Press, pp. 47–65; 219–23.   111

PART III POETRY AND MUSIC

7. Elizabeth Aubrey (1996), 'Poetics and Music', in Elizabeth Aubrey, *The Music of the Troubadours (Music: Scholarship and Performance)*, Bloomington, Indianapolis: Indiana University Press, pp. 66–79; 285–9.   137
8. Christopher Page (1993), 'Johannes de Grocheio on Secular Music: A Corrected Text and a New Translation', *Plainsong and Medieval Music*, **2**, pp. 17–41.   157
9. Elizabeth Aubrey (2000), 'Genre as a Determinant of Melody in the Songs of the Troubadours and the Trouvères', in William D. Paden (ed.), *Medieval Lyric: Genres in Historical Context*, Urbana: University of Illinois Press, pp. 273–96.   183
10. John Stevens (1974–1975), '"La Grande Chanson Courtoise": The Chansons of Adam de la Halle', *Journal of the Royal Musical Association*, **101**, pp. 11–30.   207

11	Theodore Karp (1977), 'Interrelationships between Poetic and Musical Form in *Trouvère* Song', in Edward H. Clinkscale and Claire Brook (eds), *A Musical Offering: In Honor of Martin Bernstein*, New York: Pendragon, pp. 137–61.	227
12	Manuel Pedro Ferreira (2000), 'Andalusian Music and the *Cantigas de Santa Maria*', in Stephen Parkinson (ed.), *Cobras e Son: Papers on the Text, Music and Manuscripts of the 'Cantigas de Santa Maria'*, Oxford: Legenda, European Humanities Research Centre of the University of Oxford, pp. 7–19.	253
13	Manuel Pedro Ferreira (2004), 'Rondeau and Virelai: The Music of Andalus and the *Cantigas de Santa Maria*', *Plainsong and Medieval Music*, **13**, pp. 127–40.	267

PART IV TRANSMISSION

14	Theodore Karp (1964), 'The Trouvère MS Tradition', in Albert Mell (ed.), *The Twenty-Fifth-Anniversary Festschrift (1937–1962): Queens College of the City University of New York Department of Music*, New York: Queens College, pp. 25–52.	283
15	Hendrik Van der Werf (1965), 'The Trouvère Chansons as Creations of a Notationless Musical Culture', *Current Musicology*, **1**, pp. 61–8.	311
16	Ursula Aarburg (1967), 'Probleme um die Melodien des Minnesangs', *Der Deutschunterricht*, **19**, pp. 98–118.	319

PART V PERFORMANCE

17	Christopher Page (1986), 'The Twelfth Century in the South', in *Voices and Instruments of the Middle Ages: Instrumental Practice and Songs in France 1100–1300*, London: Dent, pp. 12–28; 245–8.	343
18	Sylvia Huot (1989), 'Voices and Instruments in Medieval French Secular Music: On the Use of Literary Texts as Evidence for Performance Practice', *Musica Disciplina*, **43**, pp. 63–113.	363
19	Elizabeth Aubrey (1989), 'References to Music in Old Occitan Literature', *Acta Musicologica*, **61**, pp. 110–49.	415
20	J.E. Maddrell (1970), '*Mensura* and the Rhythm of Medieval Monodic Song', *Current Musicology*, **10**, pp. 64–9 [455–60].	455
21	Hendrik Van der Werf (1970), 'Concerning the Measurability of Medieval Music', *Current Musicology*, **10**, pp. 69–73.	461
22	J.E. Maddrell (1971), 'Grocheo and *The Measurability of Medieval Music*: A Reply to Hendrik Vanderwerf', *Current Musicology*, **11**, pp. 89–90.	467
23	Hans Tischler (1974–76), 'Rhythm, Meter, and Melodic Organization in Medieval Songs', *Revue Belge de Musicologie*, **28–30**, pp. 5–23.	469
24	Hendrik Van der Werf (1988), 'The "Not-so-precisely Measured" Music of the Middle Ages', *Performance Practice Review*, **1**, pp. 42–60.	489

Index	509

Acknowledgements

The editor and publishers wish to thank the following for permission to use copyright material.

American Institute of Musicology for the essay: Sylvia Huot (1989), 'Voices and Instruments in Medieval French Secular Music: On the Use of Literary Texts as Evidence for Performance Practice', *Musica Disciplina*, **43**, pp. 63–113.

Baerenreiter Verlag for the essay: Elizabeth Aubrey (1989), 'References to Music in Old Occitan Literature', *Acta Musicologica*, **61**, pp. 110–49.

Cambridge University Press for the essays: Christopher Page (1993), 'Johannes de Grocheio on Secular Music: A Corrected Text and a New Translation', *Plainsong and Medieval Music*, **2**, pp. 17–41; Manuel Pedro Ferreira (2004), 'Rondeau and Virelai: The Music of Andalus and the *Cantigas de Santa Maria*', *Plainsong and Medieval Music*, **13**, pp. 127–40.

Indiana University Press for the essay: Elizabeth Aubrey (1996), 'Poetics and Music', in Elizabeth Aubrey, *The Music of the Troubadours (Music: Scholarship and Performance)*, Bloomington, Indianapolis: Indiana University Press, pp. 66–79; 285–9.

Manuel Pedro Ferreira for his essay: Manuel Pedro Ferreira (2000), 'Andalusian Music and the *Cantigas de Santa Maria*', in Stephen Parkinson (ed.), *Cobras e Son: Papers on the Text, Music and Manuscripts of the 'Cantigas de Santa Maria'*, Oxford: Legenda, European Humanities Research Centre of the University of Oxford, pp. 7–19.

Medieval Institute Publications for the essay: Cyrilla Barr (1988), 'Introduction', in Cyrilla Barr, *The Monophonic Lauda and the Lay Religious Confraternities of Tuscany and Umbria in the Late Middle Ages*, Kalamazoo: Medieval Institute Publications, pp. 1–8; 151–4.

Oxford University Press for the essays: Christopher Page (1984), 'Music and Chivalric Fiction in France, 1150–1300', *Proceedings of the Royal Musical Association*, **111**, pp. 1–27. Published by Oxford University Press on behalf of the Royal Musical Association; John Stevens (1974), '"La Grande Chanson Courtoise": The Chansons of Adam de la Halle', *Journal of the Royal Musical Association*, **101**, pp. 11–30. Published by Oxford University Press on behalf of the Royal Musical Association.

Pendragon Press for the essay: Theodore Karp (1977), 'Interrelationships between Poetic and Musical Form in *Trouvère* Song', in Edward H. Clinkscale and Claire Brook (eds), *A Musical Offering: In Honor of Martin Bernstein*, New York: Pendragon, pp. 137–61.

Société Guilhem IX for the essay: Joan Tasker Grimbert (1999), 'Diminishing the *Trobairitz*, Excluding the Women Trouvères', *Tenso: Bulletin of the Société Guilhem IX*, **14**, pp. 23–38. Copyright © 1999 by the Société Guilhem IX.

Society for the Study of Medieval Languages and Literature for the essay: Ruth E. Harvey (1993), '*Joglars* and the Professional Status of the Early Troubadours', *Medium Aevum*, **62**, pp. 221–41.

University of Illinois Press for the essay: Elizabeth Aubrey (2000), 'Genre as a Determinant of Melody in the Songs of the Troubadours and the Trouvères', in William D. Paden (ed.), *Medieval Lyric: Genres in Historical Context*, Urbana: University of Illinois Press, pp. 273–96. Copyright © 2000 by the Board of Trustees of the University of Illinois.

University of Pennsylvania Press for the essay: Susan Boynton (2002), 'Women's Performance of the Lyric Before 1500', in Anne L. Klinck and Ann Marie Rasmussen (eds), *Medieval Woman's Song: Cross-Cultural Approaches*, Philadelphia: University of Pennsylvania Press, pp. 47–65; 219–23

Every effort has been made to trace all the copyright holders, but if any have been inadvertently overlooked the publishers will be pleased to make the necessary arrangement at the first opportunity.

Series Preface

This series of volumes provides an overview of the best current scholarship in the study of medieval music. Each volume is edited by a ranking expert, and each presents a selection of writings, mostly in English which, taken together, sketch a picture of the shape of the field and of the nature of current inquiry. The volumes are organized in such a way that readers may go directly to an area that interests them, or they may provide themselves a substantial introduction to the wider field by reading through the entire volume.

There is of course no such thing as the Middle Ages, at least with respect to the history of music. The Middle Ages – if they are plural at all – get their name as the temporal space between the decline of classical antiquity and its rediscovery in the Renaissance. Such a definition might once have been useful in literature and the fine arts, but it makes little sense in music. The history of Western music begins, not with the music of Greece and Rome (about which we know far too little) but with the music of the Latin Christian church. The body of music known as Gregorian chant, and other similar repertories, are the first music that survives to us in Western culture, and is the foundation on which much later music is built, and the basis for describing music in its time and forever after.

We continue to use the term 'medieval' for this music, even though it is the beginning of it all; there is some convenience in this, because historians in other fields continue to find the term useful; what musicians are doing in the twelfth century, however non-medieval it appears to us, is likely to be considered medieval by colleagues in other fields.

The chronological period in question is far from being a single thing. If we consider the Middle Ages as extending from the fall of the Roman Empire, perhaps in 476 when Odoacer deposed Romulus Augustus, into the fifteenth century, we have defined a period of about a millenium, far longer than all subsequent style-periods ('Renaissance', 'Baroque', 'Classical', 'Romantic' etc.) put together; and yet we tend to think of it as one thing.

This is the fallacy of historical parallax, and it owes its existence to two facts; first that things that are nearer to us appear to be larger, so that the history of the twentieth century looms enormous while the distant Middle Ages appear comparatively insignificant. Second, the progressive loss of historical materials over time means that more information survives from recent periods than from more distant ones, leading to the temptation to gauge importance by sheer volume.

There may be those who would have organized these volumes in other ways. One could have presented geographical volumes, for example: Medieval Music in the British Isles, in France, and so on. Or there might have been volumes focused on particular source materials, or individuals. Such materials can be found within some of these volumes, but our organization here is based on the way in which scholars seem in the main to organize and conceptualize the surviving materials. The approach here is largely chronological, with an admixture of stylistic considerations. The result is that changing styles of composition result in volumes focused on different genres – tropes, polyphony, lyric – that are not of course entirely separate in time, or discontinuous in style and usage. There are also volumes – notably those on chant and on instrumental music – that focus on certain aspects of music through the whole period. Instrumental music, of which very little survives from the Middle Ages, is often neglected in favour of music that does survive – for very good reason; but we do wish to consider what we can know about instruments and their music. And liturgical chant, especially the repertory known as Gregorian chant, is present right through our period, and indeed is the only music in Western culture to have been in continuous use from the beginnings of Western music (indeed it could be said to define its beginnings) right through until the present.

The seven volumes collected here, then, have the challenge of introducing readers to an enormous swathe of musical history and style, and of presenting the best of recent musical scholarship. We trust that, taken together, they will increase access to this rich body of music, and provide scholars and students with an authoritative guide to the best of current thinking about the music of the Middle Ages.

THOMAS FORREST KELLY
Series Editor

Introduction

Poets, Singers, Scribes and Historians

Textbooks and surveys of medieval European music conventionally present each repertoire of monophonic songs of the late Middle Ages separately, and for good reasons. The songs of the *trobadors* of Languedoc and Provence, the *trouvères* of France and the *minnesinger* of Germanic regions, the *cantigas* of the Iberian peninsula, the *laude spirituale* of Italy and the Latin monophonic songs that were disseminated throughout Europe are distinguished not only by language, but also by origins and dates, social function, manuscript preservation, genres and performance practices. Each repertoire poses unique hermeneutic and epistemological problems that demand particular approaches. Segregating the repertoires is a lucid way of introducing them to students of medieval music.

This volume, though, is not intended to be an introduction to the repertoires. The essays gathered here represent the principal themes and issues that have occupied scholars of late medieval monophonic songs over the last half century: their place in history and society, the role of women as composers and performers, poetic and musical structures, styles and genres, relationships between poems and melodies, written and oral transmission, and performance practices. Studying how each of these themes is played out across repertoires, cultures, decades and locations offers a rich and variegated panorama of the practice of song in late medieval Europe.

The volume's title implies what the songs have in common: all have texts that were created by poets, and they were sung to monophonic melodies. The poems were not read from books silently, but were sung by the poets themselves and by others. Singers, even when they sang songs composed by someone else, were themselves, in a sense, composers, re-creators of the songs, inventing them anew with each delivery.

A crucial factor that the book's title does not suggest is the matter of the songs' preservation. The extant manuscripts are the principal medieval testimony to the art of monophonic song. Literary texts and archival materials, a few theoretical works and numerous visual representations provide helpful perspective, but our path to the poets and singers lies through the efforts of scribes, and the myriad problems in interpreting what they tell us cast a long shadow over all research on monophonic song.

It will not escape the reader's attention that eight of the twenty-four articles and chapters reprinted here are devoted exclusively to the Old French songs of the *trouvères*, while only one each concerns Latin songs, the Italian *laude* and the Middle High German *minnesinger*; only two essays, both by the same author, focus on the Galician-Portuguese *cantigas* and three (two by the author of this Introduction) are exclusively about the Occitan *trobadors*. This imbalance reflects the state of scholarship as a whole, itself a reflection of the disproportion in the materials that survive for the different repertoires: eighteen major extant manuscripts preserve the music of the *trouvères*, while only two preserve those of the *trobadors*, three record the *cantigas*, two the *laude* and four the *minnesinger*. Latin songs are found mostly in small numbers in many diverse sources, scattered both chronologically and geographically (Gillingham, 1995).

Table 1 provides basic information about each repertoire, offering a snapshot of similarities and differences among the repertoires. While most of the numbers and dates must remain approximate, this table may facilitate navigation through some of the essays in the book.

Language	Location	Dates	Musicians	Genres - Secular	Genres - Sacred	Music Sources	Notation	Preservation - Texts	Preservation - Music
Latin	France, Midi, Germany, Northern Italy, England, Spain	9th century–13th century	'goliards' 'vagantes' clerics scholars	epic eulogy love song satire drinking song ode planctus didactic song	versus prose sequence conductus Marian song	sections in c. 10 mss + scattered fragments	unheighted square	hundreds	c. 200
Occitan	Aquitaine Limousin Auvergne Languedoc Provence Gascony Catalonia	c. 1100–1300	trobadors joglars trobairitz	vers canso sirventes planh descort alba lay pastorela partimen tenso dansa	crusade song Marian song devotional song	2 + sections in two French manuscripts	square Messine mensural	c. 2,600	c. 250
Old French	France Artois Picardy Champagne Lorraine Burgundy	c. 1180–1300	trouvères jongleurs trouveresses	chanson jeu-parti lai pastourelle chanson de femme rondet rondeau soite chanson malmariée rotrouenge refrain song chanson de toile chanson de geste lyric insertion dancing song	crusade song Marian song devotional song	18 + fragments	square mensural	c. 2,130	c. 1,400
Middle High German	Bavaria Swabia Rhineland Franconia Switzerland	c. 1150–c. 1370	minnesinger	minnelied leich spruch wechsel frauenlied tagelied tanzlied	kreuzlied devotional Spruch	4 + fragments	gothic square Messine	c. 1,000	c. 100 early c. 130 late
Galician-Portuguese	Castile León Galicia Navarre	c. 1270–1290	courtly musicians	cantiga d'amor cantiga d'amigo	cantiga de miragres cantiga de loor	3 + fragments	square mensural	c. 435	c. 415
Italian	Tuscany Umbria	c. 1250–c. 1330	laypersons clerics trained musicians		lauda spirituale Marian song hagiographic song devotional song	2 + fragments	square	c. 150	c. 125

Table 1: Repertoires of Medieval Monophonic Song

History and Society

The first four essays reveal the diverse historical and social contexts in which monophonic songs were created and performed, an area in which research has increased over the last twenty years. These essays by Christopher Page, Ruth Harvey, Bryan Gillingham and Cyrilla Barr, and also those in later parts of the book by Susan Boynton, Ursula Aarburg, Manuel Pedro Ferreira, Sylvia Huot and myself, exhibit how important the cultural context of the songs has become to our understanding of their transmission, poetic and melodic style, and performance. Indications from visual, literary, archival and historical, and paleographical materials shed light on who the composers and singers were, what kind of background they may have had (education in the liberal arts, familiarity with literature from the classics to contemporary, instruction in practical skills like reading, writing and music) and venues and occasions for performance. Scholars have become increasingly careful and sophisticated in collecting different kinds of evidence, and bold in their interpretations.

Because research on this topic relies on indirect sources of information, conflicting viewpoints and unresolvable mysteries are inevitable. One matter in particular that remains unclear for many of the songs is the social status of those who composed and performed them. Plentiful accounts attest that aristocrats, clerics, merchants, unpropertied retainers or dependants and members of the lowest classes all engaged in singing songs and hearing them sung. The evidence sometimes, but not always, associates a type of song or activity with one particular class or type of person. Scholars disagree on whether there was a distinction between an unpaid amateur, such as a member of the nobility who would not be dependent for sustenance on composing or singing songs, and a professional singer, who worked for the aristocracy as a long-term or a short-term (that is, itinerant) employee. A variety of terms for composers and performers occurs in many contexts in literary and historical documents, sometimes with reference to specific activities, but sometimes only vaguely associated with music-making. Some texts seem to suggest that composers were distinct from singers and occupied a higher class, singing only for their own amusement, while others forthrightly declare that members of the aristocracy performed or even took up the 'life of a *jongleur*'. Much of the evidence demonstrates a blurred distinction between sacred and secular in medieval society. French clerics composed explicit love songs, Iberian kings produced impassioned prayers to the Virgin, German monks sang ribald drinking songs, Italian merchants sang devout penitential texts, Occitan love-poets issued fervent calls to holy crusade. All told, the picture these documents paint of the composition and performance of monophonic song throughout Europe is not monochromatic across time, place or repertoire.

Women

As for other periods of European history, studies of women in medieval musical life have multiplied in recent years. A bizarre resistance by some literary scholars to the notion of female authorship – what has been called *féminité génétique* – based on a tortured interpretation of a poem's feminine 'voice' – its *féminité textuelle* – has been eloquently answered by Joan Grimbert (Chapter 5) and others with the simple argument that a preconceived theory must not be used to explain away plausible evidence, which includes manuscript attributions, references to women authors in general and to specific women whose lives are attested in archival sources, and the feminine point of view in medieval texts (see also Gaunt, 1995 and Doss-Quinby *et al.*, 2001). The fact that the speaker in a poem is female does not itself prove, of course, that the author of the poem itself was female; but to argue that the poet is male begs for proof. The issue of authorship is not straightforward. Is an attribution in a manuscript rubric ironclad evidence of authorship? How do we reconcile conflicting attributions? Does an attribution apply to the melody as well as to the poem? How do the date and provenance of a manuscript bear on the validity of its attributions? If no source provides an attribution, what other evidence might there be of a song's author? If a woman's song is ascribed to a male author in one source and to a female author in another, is it more reasonable to accept the latter simply because of the text's *féminité textuelle*, or is the former ascription more plausible because – a fact that cannot be denied – there were many more male poets than female, and their songs were more likely to be recorded in writing? While such questions are impossible to answer with absolute certainty in any particular case, the likelihood that women composed songs cannot be rebuffed on a mere theory. Still less reasonable would it be to deny that women performed monophonic songs, for here the mass of evidence is sizeable, as Susan Boynton's essay (Chapter 6) demonstrates. Boynton's work adds depth and colour to the diverse cultural and sociological picture painted by the authors of the first four essays in this book (see also Coldwell, 1986).

Poetry and Music

In this part, essays by the author of this Introduction, Christopher Page, John Stevens, Theodore Karp and Manuel Pedro Ferreira treat various aspects of the poetry and music of monophonic songs and of theoretical constructs that medieval authors used to explain them. Studies by philologists of language, poetic structure and style, and concordant readings of texts have yielded not only editions and valuable reference tools, but also a variety of taxonomies with appropriate vocabularies for describing the poems (see Switten, 1995 and Haines, 2004). Musicologists came somewhat later to the songs, and in the process of carrying out the necessary spadework of recovering the melodies from their medieval notations, they became fixated for decades upon the problem of their rhythm (on this, see further below). The virulent arguments that characterized those early decades have assumed such legendary proportions (see Haines, 1997 and 2001) that they have overshadowed many of the contributions that earlier musicologists made in analysing musical structure and style (see the works by Jean-Baptiste Beck, Pierre Aubry, Hans Spanke and Friedrich Gennrich listed in the Bibliography).

Some of the vocabulary still used to describe the songs comes from the late Middle Ages. Terms such as *frons*, *versus*, *cauda*, *pes* and *diesis* for the parts of a strophe whose metre, rhyme scheme and melody are in some way interrelated, and *oda continua* for a song without musical repetition, come from Dante's well-known *De vulgari eloquentia* (*c.*1302–1305) (Botterill, 1996, pp. 74–79). This treatise continues a centuries-old tradition of analysing human communication through ever-evolving systems of grammar – the art of correct speaking and writing – and rhetoric – the art of persuasion. A poet was a *rhetor*, trained to imitate the masters and to invent persuasive arrangements of words that would move the hearers; he or she was a grammarian who was expected to know the proper disposition of those words so that they could be understood. From these arts come names for the numerous tropes and figures (for example *repetitio*, *conversio*, *exclamatio*, *nominatio*, *translatio*, *coniunctio*), the parts of rhetoric (*inventio*, *dispositio*, *elocutio*, *memoria* and *pronuntiatio*) and the parts of an oration (*exordium*, *narratio*, *partitio*, *confirmatio*, *refutatio* and *conclusio*).

Musical treatises that treat monophonic song are notably lacking; only the late thirteenth-century Parisian Johannes de Grocheio gives serious attention to it, and scholars still debate how to understand much of what he says, a task that has been aided by Christopher Page's translation of the relevant sections of his treatise. While certain aspects of poetry were treated in the context of the discipline of music in the *quadrivium*, it was music as a practical art that brought monophonic songs to life. (Chapter 8)

Scholars continue to appropriate both medieval and modern analytical models and systems to attempt to understand the craft of the poet-musicians whose works are so vast in number and diverse in character. Musicologists and literary scholars lately have made significant forays into one another's territory, and some have produced collaborative studies, breathing life into the idea that poetry and music are equal partners in the composition and performance of the songs.[1]

As Table 1 shows, each of the repertoires of monophonic song comprises several genres. They are distinguished in many ways that seem straightforward, but close inspection reveals ambiguities. A fundamental generic distinction between epic and lyric is clear in differences of structure, theme, content, transmission and social context. Within lyric, genres often are distinguished by the poem's content – love song (*canso*), *alba*, *pastourelle* and so on. But a thematic distinction is not always easy to draw: a dancing song might be about love, for instance. Similarly, differences between genres with sacred content and those with secular themes are not always easy to delineate, an obvious example being the *cantigas de miragres*, ostensibly in honour of the Virgin Mary, but whose humorous, obscene and bawdy tales of miracles obviously were meant to entertain. Elements of structure can be useful in delineating genres, such as the presence or absence of a refrain in a dancing song; yet refrains are not limited to dancing songs: most of the *laude* and *cantigas* have them.

The predominant methodological framework that has emerged in recent years is based on the notion that medieval songs fall into a category of either a 'high style' or a 'low style'. Love songs, serious satire (*sirventes*), laments and the like are considered to be in a 'high', 'courtly' or 'aristocratic' style, while dances, *pastourelles* and other narrative types, and *lais* fall into a 'low', 'popular' or 'jongleuresque' style. The delineation of style according to a song's genre has led scholars to attempt to identify features of the songs such as language, poetic and musical form or melodic complexity as defining characteristics of one style or the other. It has also resulted in broad theories about musical rhythm, the use of instruments and female authorship.[2]

The roots of this bifurcation can be traced to nineteenth-century studies of French Arthurian romances, whose artificially cast theme of adultery was first described by Gaston Paris as *amour courtois* or 'courtly love', a concept that has undergone many permutations in the context of critical analysis and theory, which are far too complex to trace here.[3] The idea soon

---

1 Many authors, including myself, have quoted the phrase 'a verse without music is like a mill without water' with an apocryphal attribution; see the correct attribution in Aubrey (Chapter 9, p. 199, note 1 in this volume).

2 On the argument that the register of women's songs was 'popular' as opposed to the 'high style' associated with songs in the male voice, see Grimbert (2003) and Doss-Quinby et al. (2001, pp. 6–11).

3 'Courtly love' is now recognized as problematic on a number of levels (definition, application, suitability as an analytical tool, consistency). A good summary can be found in Hult (1995). See also Paterson (1999).

was – and continues to be – applied to the lyric love songs of the *trobadors*, *trouvères* and *minnesinger*, building on a proposed affinity between the Occitan expression *fin'amor* (French *amour fine*) that crops up in some lyric texts and a nineteenth-century view of 'love' that implies a refined set of 'rules' governing chivalrous behaviour (see Switten, 1995, pp. 104–109). Scholars began using 'courtly love' as the foundation of a concept of poetic genre and register (see Switten, 1995, p. 122). Roger Dragonetti's 1960 discussion of the quintessential love song of the *trouvères*, which he labelled *le grand chant courtois*, and Paul Zumthor's notion of register – a collection of conventions of language, formulas, syntactic constructions and theme that constitute the 'space' of a poem (1972b, pp. 231–43) – remain profoundly influential. These discussions imply a contrast between *le grand chant courtois* and a type of song that was *not grand* or *courtois*. John Stevens in '"La Grande Chanson Courtoise": The Chansons of Adam de la Halle' (Chapter 10) gave expression to the idea of a 'high' courtly style, and Pierre Bec (1977–78) nuanced the concept of register with the terms 'aristocratisant' and 'popularisant', or 'nobilizing' and 'popularizing'(see Switten, 1995, pp. 122–23), whose formulation as participles implies a difference beyond the content of the song itself, but of a larger social context, wherein the creation and dissemination of a song was associated with one class or another. Christopher Page rendered the dichotomy as 'High Style' and 'Low Style', the capitalization giving a strong implication of authority to the designations. His prolific writings have helped expand the idea to encompass not only a song's subject matter, style and social placement, but also its genre and form (see Switten, 1995, pp. 119ff.). Page's arguments that these are determinative of a historically accurate performance practice have had an enormous impact on musical scholarship of the last two decades.

Yet the duality of 'high style' and 'low style' is a precarious scaffold on which to construct a cogent method for analysing and understanding medieval song. Medieval evidence for the dichotomy, whether theoretical or practical, is at best ambiguous, and most of it can be manipulated to support a particular interpretation.[4] More telling are the difficulties and dangers of applying to melodies a concept defined by literary features – subject matter, genre, linguistic and rhetorical style (most recently O'Neill, 2006). One finds conflicting descriptions of the music of a 'high style' song in some of the essays that follow. In Chapter 10 John Stevens, for instance, summarizes the music of a *grand chant courtois* as 'restrained, traditional, and devoid of personal idiosyncrasy' (p. 226) while for Page it is 'rhapsodic', without 'the conspicuous and short-range patterns that give an easy and instant tunefulness to dance-song', but which 'makes us aware of the voice which is singing to us' (1986, p. 14). It is not difficult to find a melody in the vast repertoire of *trouvère* song (where the high–low contrast is most frequently drawn) that illustrates a particular set of criteria that a critic might devise. It would be a great deal more challenging to analyse a genre or a repertoire of song without presuppositions and to identify features that are unique to that corpus, and then to prove that these features are factors of its genre.

Some musicologists have made valuable contributions to the first of those challenges, cataloguing and analysing musical characteristics without presuppositions. Theodore Karp's work on interrelationships between musical and poetic structure (Chapter 11) provides a sound basis for making some sense out of the vast number of Old French songs that survive,

---

4 Contrary to some assertions, with the exception of sources of the cantigas de Santa Maria, most manuscripts do not group songs according to genre or label them by rubrics.

and my own work with the songs of the *trobadors* is a step in that direction as well (Aubrey, 1996; see also Chapter 23 by Hans Tischler). Research on the German *minnelied*, including that of Ursula Aarburg, is hampered by the deficiencies of its transmission (see below and, for instance, the work of Jammers and Räkel, listed in the Bibliography). On the *cantigas*, Manuel Pedro Ferreira's work joins that of other scholars (including Wulstan, 2000a, 2000b and O'Neill, 1999–2000, 2000) whose new approaches, notably a re-evaluation of how the distinctive mixture of Eastern and Western cultures in the Iberian peninsula affected its literature and music, have offered plausible analyses of not only musico-poetic structure and style, but also origins, interrelations with other monophonic repertoires and performance practices. Yet much remains to be done in defining and describing features of musical style and form in the different bodies of song. Analytical models and tools can include characteristics such as repetition, variation, motives, tonal orientation, contour, range, cadences, intervals, texture; formal descriptors like strophic, through-composed, rounded, formulaic; concepts of unity, diversity, balance, symmetry, regularity, coherence; and subjective judgements like simple or sophisticated, tuneful or rhapsodic, traditional or avant garde, core or peripheral; and many other schemes not yet imagined.

Transmission

It has been only in the last fifty years or so that musicologists have recognized that the difficulties in interpreting the extant manuscripts go far beyond what they do not tell us about the rhythms of the songs; the essays by Theodore Karp, Hendrik Van der Werf and Ursula Aaburg (Chapters 14–16) represent a variety of approaches to the topic. The problems concern issues such as oral and written tradition, whether we can identify a song's 'original' version and to what extent such a formulation is helpful, the literacy of composers and singers, the training of scribes and their interaction with the songs they received and recorded, and relationships among concordant versions of the same melody.

The problems that the surviving sources present are quite complex. Their dates and provenances vary widely from repertoire to repertoire. Only one of the two sources that preserve the music of the *trobadors* is from the Midi; the other was copied in Italy, and both are quite late, from the end of the thirteenth century or beginning of the fourteenth. Several early Latin sources provide small numbers of melodies, but these are in unheighted neumes that are unreadable today. All four of the German music manuscripts were produced much later than the death of the last *minnesinger*, two in the fourteenth century and two in the fifteenth; scholars generally trust the readings of only the two earlier ones. Most of the sources that preserve Old French songs are closer in date to the repertoire, but they are of different types, ranging from anthologies devoted exclusively to monophonic songs, to compendia that also preserve polyphony, to miscellanies that contain non-musical works in other fascicles; and some of the variants are extreme. For all of the repertoires more poems survive than melodies; in sheer numbers, the extant *trouvère* musical corpus is the most abundant, but proportionately, roughly a third of its poems remain unnotated in the manuscripts. In contrast, most of the poems of the *cantigas de Santa Maria*, whose manuscripts appear to be contemporaneous with the composition and performance of the songs at the court of Alfonso X el Sabio, survive with their melodies, while most of the poems of the *trobadors*, the *minnesinger* and Latin songs have reached us with no music.

Some of the broader questions about transmission that have been widely explored and debated include the following.

1) When were the melodies first written down, and how long, if at all, were they transmitted orally? Most extant sources can be dated to within a couple of decades, a few more precisely, and the original provenances of the majority are undisputed. None of the manuscripts appears to have been copied from another that is extant.[5] Some, like Theodore Karp and this author, have argued that scribes of the extant manuscripts of French and Occitan songs for the most part copied texts and melodies from written exemplars (see Aubrey 1982). Others see evidence of oral transmission that persisted up to the moment of their preservation. Certainly when the songs were first written down their scribes were transcribing the melodies by ear, and many songs presumably were still being sung even after their melodies were written down, in which cases oral and written transmission co-existed. The late date of the extant *trobador* musical sources suggests that the earliest songs were transmitted orally for a longer period of time than the later ones, but this is only an assumption, since it is impossible to know when the first written versions were created. The fact that all of the major surviving German music sources postdate the *minnesinger* by many decades can have several explanations, including, as Ursula Aarburg discusses in Chapter 16, the possibility that at some time the texts were spoken and not sung, that a text's *Ton* provided a mere skeleton of a melody that defied written transcription and that the earlier German neumes were unheighted and therefore unreadable. The shorter time frame between composition and preservation of the *laude* and *cantigas* means that there was much less time for an oral transmission process to evolve. But for a melody to change radically could take almost no time at all – it would require but one creative singer or scribe. In all cases we are far from certitude in knowing the processes as well as the effects of either oral or written transmission.

2) What is the meaning of the variant readings of melodies among the sources? These are more substantial in some repertoires than in others. The existence of variants suggests that a melody was not a series of pitches fixed in the course of composition and retained during performance, but that something happened to it during its lifetime. Zumthor (1972b, pp. 65ff.) coined the term *mouvance* to describe this fluidity of a text. It is a daunting task to determine whether changes came about as part of a process of improvisational, oral composition in which a 'melody' was never a stable entity to begin with, as a result of recomposition or recreation during performance (by the composer or subsequent singers) or during the stage of written preservation, or by some combination of all three factors. Many variant readings undoubtedly originated in the process of writing: errors (such as clef misplacement), deliberate scribal intervention (for example the regularization of a melody's structure) or unintended or unconscious but reasonable changes (such as filling in the interval of a third). It might seem reasonable to infer that the longer a melody existed only in oral form, the more likely it was to undergo alteration, but the possibility that a melody remained stable throughout its transmission is not precluded by oral transmission.

---

5 Full descriptions are found in the article 'Sources, MS, §III', with sections by David Fallows, Elizabeth Aubrey et al., in The New Grove Dictionary of Music and Musicians. In none of the repertoires is a stemma codicum possible; if such filiations are to be found, they must be sought for individual songs. For the Occitan, German and Latin repertoires in particular, separate transmissions for texts and melodies renders filiation even of an individual song impossible. On Occitan sources, see Aubrey (1982); on the German songs, see Aarburg (Chapter 16).

3) What were the relationships among composers, singers and scribes? *Trobadors, trouvères* and *minnesinger* were probably the first singers of their songs, so initially there was no separation between the persons who composed and sang, or perhaps even between the actions themselves. The late dates for the sources of the melodies of the Occitan and German songs mean that those scribes never personally knew the earlier authors, although they may have known those who were contemporary; but acquaintance is not the same as collaboration. At least one French manuscript, known as the 'Adam de la Halle' manuscript because it preserves most of his extant works, could well have been copied with his help; likewise, a group of songs by late *trobador* Guiraut Riquier is headed by a rubric that indicates he was responsible for their copying (see Aubrey, 1982, pp. 278–80). Authorship of the *cantigas de Santa Maria* is still in dispute, although most scholars are sceptical that King Alfonso X was himself their composer, although he may well have sung some of them. But he was keen to see that the songs were preserved in writing from perhaps the very beginning, as evidenced in the comprehensive, carefully organized and – in two cases – luxuriously decorated manuscripts that survive. Recent research on Latin songs and the *laude spirituale* has provided a fuller picture of their composition and performance, but the relative paucity of their preservation hampers our understanding of what role scribes played in the lives of the songs. Much more research is needed on the education and literacy of composers and performers, who the notators were and the purposes for which they copied monophonic songs, and when and why the melodies were written down.

Performance

Two issues continue to dominate discussions of performance practices of monophonic songs: 1) whether or not instruments accompanied the singers, and 2) what the rhythms of the notes were. Neither question can be answered with certainty, since the extant evidence is ambiguous. The issue of instruments was not debated until relatively recently, when Hendrik Van der Werf and then Christopher Page published robust challenges to the hitherto universal presumption that singers sang to instrumental accompaniment. The presence of instruments in European culture is well attested in visual, literary, archival and theoretical evidence, from which scholars have gleaned much information about their construction and playing techniques. As the essays by Page, Sylvia Huot and this author (Chapters 17–19) demonstrate, though, the information that these sources provide about the music that instruments played and the circumstances in which instrumentalists performed resists definitive interpretation.

A central thesis of Page's book *Voices and Instruments*, that 'questions of instrumental usage in *trobador* and trouvère song are essentially questions about *genre*' (1986, p. 10), has become widely accepted. The 'High Style ethos' (Page, 1986, p. 25; see p. 356 of this volume) of the songs of these poet-composers, according to the theory, precluded their being sung with instruments, which were more suited to 'low style' songs such as *pastourelles* and dances, as well as narrative *lais*, epics and romances. Page nuances his argument by suggesting that the culture of late thirteenth-century Paris opened the door to a new aesthetic of instrumental usage: 'The emergence of a literate tradition of *trobador* and trouvère song in the second half of the thirteenth century may ... have exerted a profound effect upon performance practice in that repertory, for musical notation enabled songs to be lifted out of the behavioral conventions in which they had become embedded' (1986, p. 52). Thus some late theoretical evidence, notably the writings of Johannes de Grocheio, associates instruments with monophonic song.

Because most of what survives in written form are songs in a 'high style', this theory leaves modern instrumentalists with little music to play. But as suggested above, a division of songs into high and low styles is not without problems, so a theory of performance practice for which it serves as a fundamental premise cannot stand without broad evidentiary support. Information from a wide variety of sources suggests that instruments were ubiquitous, but that many factors besides genre may have influenced whether they accompanied singers of monophonic songs. Other determinants might be date and geographical location, social circumstances, audience and how familiar a song was to performer or audience; and we should not discount sheer serendipity – whether instruments were handy on a given occasion, and whether anyone competent to play them was present. The voluminous evidence denies us the simple or universal answer that we may wish for.

The problem of rhythm also continues to generate heated debate (see Aubrey, 2000b for a brief historiography). For this issue the evidence is meagre. The exchanges reprinted in this volume between J.E. Maddrell and Hendrik Van der Werf (Chapters 20 and 21) and between the former and Hans Tischler (Chapters 22 and 23) typify the disputes that have made this topic so volatile over the last century. Although each author is careful to admit that his interpretations are not certain, he posits them as probable and hastens to defend them against challenge. Because the competing theories – modal (metric-rhythmic patterns), mensural (measurable but not patterned rhythms), declamatory (unmeasurable durations that shift according to the flow of the text), isosyllabic (same duration for each syllable), isotonic (same duration for each note) – are so starkly drawn, it is easy to accept one and dismiss the others wholesale. A close reading of the essays reveals some inaccurate assertions and imperfect reasoning for each theory, but also some valid points and compelling arguments.

The relevant evidence is of three types: 1) the texts, including structure, sound, syntax, style and sense; 2) the melodies, including structure, style, concordant readings and notation; and 3) theoretical and other writings. Poetry is organized by some sort of metre, or measurable units of the verse; in German these units are patterns of accented and unaccented syllables; in the Romance languages the verse is defined by the number of syllables. Greek terms for metre, such as *iambic* and *trochaic*, survived into the late Middle Ages, but whereas the patterns of classical poetry were quantitative, with syllables distinguished by their length, late medieval poetry was qualitative, with syllables distinguished by stress. It would be a mistake to equate stress and duration, and most scholars avoid doing so overtly, but the discussions are not always clear on this point. In French, Occitan, Italian and Galician-Portuguese songs, stress is a metrical factor only at the rhyme and at the *caesura* (a pause in the middle of a longer verse), whereas in German poetry the entire verse proceeds by stress patterns. Rhyme, which is oxytonic (or masculine, accent on the final syllable of a verse), paroxytonic (or feminine, accent on the penultimate syllable) or proparoxytonic (accent on the antepenultimate syllable), helps articulate the structure by defining the end of a line, and it is a prominent sonic attribute of the verse. The words of a poem are arranged according to a coherent syntax. A song's poetic structure, style and sense are factors in determining its genre. Scholars emphasize some of these poetic features more than others in arguing for a particular rhythmic interpretation.

The writings of music theorists provide little useful information about the rhythm of monophonic songs. Melodic features and variants, on the other hand, have a great deal of potential that remains largely untapped. As new studies of the various repertoires reveal their distinctive stylistic and structural characteristics, some insights are emerging about rhythmic practices, while the prospects for one universal theory of rhythm that can be applied to all repertoires or genres are diminishing.

At the heart of the problem is the fact that the notation in most of the manuscripts of secular monophony does not give clear indications of rhythm. Throughout the thirteenth century, when the most important sources of monophonic song were produced, scribes and theorists, especially in Paris, were busy developing more precise ways of capturing rhythm. For the complex new polyphony built on melismatic portions of plainchant, scribes deployed the common neumes of plainchant – *clivis, podatus, torculus, porrectus, scandicus* and *climacus* – in groupings that reflected patterns of rhythm, eventually systematized by theorists into the system of rhythmic modes. For syllables with only one note, notators by the early thirteenth century throughout Europe generally used either the *virga* (a square with a tail descending on the right side) or the *punctum* (without a tail); these symbols in earlier centuries had indicated high and low pitches, a distinction obviously not necessary with the use of the staff, and even though theorists included both symbols in tables of neumes (see Huglo,1954 and Bernhard, 1997, 2001), scribes found the distinction gratuitous and used only one symbol.

The notators of the earliest large modal manuscripts – **W1**, **W2** and **F** (written between about 1230 and 1250) – used the *virga* for all single notes, even in texted motets and *conductus*, except in one special circumstance: where repeated notes precluded the use of a ligature, the scribes often drew them as untailed *puncti*. From the perspective of the later thirteenth century, these look like *breves*, notes that are shorter in duration than tailed notes. But the scribes did not have this in mind. They intended the reader to understand that the repeated notes would have been drawn in ligature if it had been possible; drawing them as *puncti* instead of *virgae* was a signal that they should be grouped together and read according to the prevailing mode. Indeed, often these *puncti* do not signify short notes; many of them must be read as *longae*. For example, here is a short section from the three-voice *organum Sancte Germane*[6] in **F**, fol. 35v, third system:[7]

Example 1
F fol. 35v, 3rd system

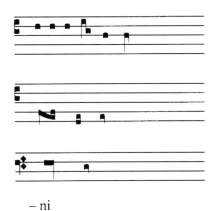

– ni

---

6 Designated O27 in Ludwig (1910).

7 The concordant passage in W1 (fol. 5v, fourth system) is nearly identical, except that the scribe drew the puncti as rhomboid shapes rather than square, in keeping with English fashion.

The *duplum* is in mode 1, and the *triplum* must be as well in order to match. So the rhythms of this passage would be:

Example 2

– ni

Note that the *rhythmic values* of the first and third untailed *puncti* are *longae*, and the second is a *breve*, but the *notation* does not convey that difference unless the three repeated notes are read together as a modal ligature. As they did with the compound neumes, these scribes adapted the single-note neumes to convey modal rhythm patterns.[8] During this period the notators of monophonic song, which do not have long textless passages that would make modal notation possible, used the only notational system appropriate to their needs, that of plainchant, and usually employed the *virga* for single notes.

The notator of the *organum* above in **W2** (fol. 11v, first system), dated c.1250, perhaps a decade later than **F**, drew the three repeated notes of this passage as *virga-punctum-virga*, or tailed-untailed-tailed. This does not appear to be a fluke – he made similar distinctions elsewhere, albeit inconsistently, and still only on repeated notes. But if this scribe (one of several notators of this manuscript) had in mind to convey rhythmic values of single notes by the presence or absence of a tail – here long-short-long – then this is one of the earliest instances of what can only be described as a revolution in the history of music notation, one whose potential began to be realized almost immediately.

The final step toward a truly mensural notation was the use of a square note with a tail and a square note without a tail to signify rhythmic values of long and short on single notes whether they are repeated or not. Scribes of all of the important manuscripts of polyphony (which are outside the scope of this discussion) from the 1270s on clearly and deliberately used these symbols, which can now be called *longa* and *brevis*. They show up as well in scattered places of a few sources of Old French songs from this period, but it was not until about the 1290s that some scribes of monophonic songs fully incorporated the symbols into their notational

---

8 A thorough investigation of these notational developments in manuscripts and theorists of the thirteenth century is forthcoming.

vocabularies, although most did not, and by this time the era of composition and performance was nearing an end.

Scholars legitimately wonder why most scribes of secular monophony did not use mensural symbols once they had been created and adopted into the notational vocabulary of Paris after *c*.1270 (the question is not relevant, of course, for manuscripts produced before then). The most widely accepted answer today is that the rhythms of these songs were not similar to those of polyphony, and thus those notations were not appropriate; this supports a theory of non-measurable rhythms. Another possibility is that in the course of their training scribes of monophonic song had not encountered the mensural notational symbols, plausible certainly for repertoires distant from Paris and its orbit, and indeed few manuscripts of monophonic song were produced there; this does not presuppose anything about the rhythms of the songs. Yet another answer might be that, even knowing about the new symbols, scribes who were copying from written exemplars in non-rhythmic neumes did not wish to expend the effort to change them to mensural symbols, especially for songs with which they were not familiar and thus would not have known what the rhythms should be; this presumes that the melodies had measurable rhythms.

Every scribe had a unique approach to notating music, determined by training and knowledge of notational symbols and their meanings, and doubtless affected by the notation of his or her exemplars. But factors such as familiarity with a melody, an editorial 'programme' such as simplification of unwieldy melodies or interjection of an idiosyncratic rhythmic manner and the purpose of the manuscript – performance, preservation or presentation – could also affect the choice of notational symbols. A striking example of scribal practice that may not have fallen under the sway of a prevailing 'European' aesthetic is that of the *cantigas de Santa Maria*, whose notation includes *longae* and *breves*, but which defy conformity to the Parisian rhythmic modes. It seems difficult to accept that these late thirteenth-century songs did not fall into the clear-cut triple divisions that we associate with late thirteenth-century music, but Manuel Pedro Ferreira's arguments in favour of a culture that was not strongly influenced by a foreign one (French) from north of the Pyrenees is compelling (see Chapters 12 and 13).

The scribe of the late thirteenth-century Burgundian manuscript FPnfr.846 appears to have been attempting to transcribe *trouvère* songs from the non-mensural notation of his exemplars to mensural figures, and in the process he was wildly inconsistent. For two identical musical phrases, often his mensural symbols do not match: where a *longa* falls in the first phrase, he drew a *brevis* in the second, for example. An exhaustive comparison of all such examples reveals two reasons for these inconsistencies: paleographical and melodic. For instance, where a clef change occurs or a chromatic inflection is drawn, the notator often lost track of the rhythm for which he was attempting to create graphic symbols that were not in his exemplar and drew the 'wrong' mensural shape immediately afterwards. Among melodic situations in which his mensural figures are inconsistent are disjunct melodic motion, groups of repeated notes and on the final note of a descending phrase, which also appear to have distracted him from the task of transcription into mensural notation. This manuscript is striking evidence of a creative scribe at work: one who had non-mensural exemplars before him and, for whatever reason, wished to transcribe them into a mensural notation, not always succeeding to the satisfaction of modern editors and performers. Yet his attempt provides insight into how scribes dealt with rapidly changing notational conventions.

In fact, every manuscript has a tale to tell, and much research remains to be done on the notational quirks of the many scribes who wrote down the melodies of monophonic song. Most of the notations will not tell us what rhythms the singers gave the melodies when they sang them. But they do tell us that no single system of either notation or rhythm for all repertoires existed – so much is agreed by most scholars today – and that, whatever the notation of a particular song looks like in a particular source, it may or may not reflect rhythms that a poet might have had in mind when he or she created it. In the end, the notations cannot be trusted to confirm or deny any of the theories of rhythm absolutely.

Modern study of old cultures has produced satisfying insights, but also spectacular blunders and misdirections. The more distant we are from the art of the past, the dimmer the evidence and the less sure our ability to interpret it. But there are ways in which distance in time sharpens our capacity to shed inappropriate assumptions about art and its practitioners. Certainly during the last several decades historians have become more adept at recognizing outdated approaches of previous decades, as well as the fact that our own perspectives are anachronistic filters through which we view the past. The debates about rhythm in monophonic song that dominated the field in earlier decades have given way to new questions and new methodologies. This broadening of the terrain has begun to reveal aspects of the songs that we had not seen before and has given scholars and performers hope that we can better understand and more accurately recreate them today – even while we ourselves are contributing to their evolution and transmission.

Bibliography

Aarburg, Ursula (ed.) (1956), *Singweisen zur Liebeslyrik der deutschen Frühe*, Düsseldorf: Schwann.

Aarburg, Ursula (1957a), 'Walthers Goldene Weise', *Die Musikforschung*, **11**, no. 4, pp. 478–82.

Aarburg, Ursula (1957b), 'Wort und Weise im Wiener Hofton', *Zeitschrift für deutsches Altertum und deutsche Literatur*, **88**, pp. 196–210.

Aarburg, Ursula (1961), 'Melodien zum frühen deutschen Minnesang: eine kritische Bestandsaufnahme mit einem Nachtrag', in Hans Fromm (ed.), *Der deutsche Minnesang: Aufsätze zu seiner Erforschung*, vol. I, Darmstadt: Wisschenschaftliche Buchgesellschaft, pp. 378–423.

Akehurst, F.R.P. and Davis, Judith M. (eds) (1995), *A Handbook of the Troubadours*, Publications of the UCLA Center for Medieval and Renaissance Studies 26, Berkeley: University of California Press.

Anderson, Gordon A. (ed.) (n.d.), *One-Part Conductus, the Latin Rondeau Répertoire, Notre-Dame and Related Conductus: Opera Omnia; Collected Works, X/8*. Henryville, PA: Institute of Mediaeval Music.

Anderson, Gordon A. (1978), 'The Rhythm of the Monophonic Conductus in the Florence Manuscript as indicated in Parallel Sources in Mensural Notation', *Journal of the American Musicological Society*, **31**, pp. 480–89.

Anglès, Higini (ed.) (1943–64), *La musica de las Cantigas de Santa Maria del Rey Alfonso el Sabio, facsimil, transcripcion y estudio critico*, 3 vols, Biblioteca Central, Publicaciones de la Seccion de Musica 15, 18, Barcelona: Diputación Provincial de Barcelona, Biblioteca Central.

Anglès, Higini (1968), 'The Musical Notation and Rhythm of the Italian Laude', in Hans Tischler (ed.), *Essays in Musicology: A Birthday Offering for Willi Apel*, Bloomington: Indiana University Press, pp. 51–60.

Apel, Willi (1954), 'Rondeaux, Virelais, and Ballades in French Thirteenth-Century Song', *Journal of the American Musicological Society*, **7**, pp. 121–30.

Arlt, Wulf (1989), 'Secular Monophony', in Howard Mayer Brown and Stanley Sadie (eds), *Performance Practice: Music Before 1600*, London: Macmillan; New York: Norton, pp. 55–78.

Atchison, Mary (1995), '*Bien me sui aperceuz*: Monophonic Chanson and Motetus', *Plainsong and Medieval Music*, **4**, pp. 1–12.

Aubrey, Elizabeth (1982), 'A Study of the Origins, History, and Notation of the Troubadour Chansonnier Paris, Bibliothèque nationale, f. fr. 22543', Ph.D. dissertation, University of Maryland.

Aubrey, Elizabeth (1987a), 'Forme et formule dans les mélodies des troubadours', in Peter T. Ricketts (ed.), *Actes du premier congrès internationale de l'Association Internationale d'Études Occitanes*, London: Westfield College, University of London, pp. 69–83.

Aubrey, Elizabeth (1987b), 'The Transmission of Troubadour Melodies: The Testimony of Paris, Bibliothèque nationale, f. fr. 22543', *Text: Transactions of the Society for Textual Scholarship*, **3**, pp. 211–50.

Aubrey, Elizabeth (1993 [1997]), 'Literacy, Orality, and the Preservation of French and Occitan Medieval Courtly Songs', *Revista de Musicología: Actas del XV Congreso de la Sociedad Internacional de Musicología, 'Culturas Musicales del Mediterraneo y Sus Ramificaciones,' Madrid 3–10/IV/1992*, **16**, no. 4, pp. 2355–66.

Aubrey, Elizabeth (1994), 'Issues in the Musical Analysis of the Troubadour *Descorts* and *Lays*', in Nancy Van Deusen (ed.), *The Cultural Milieu of the Troubadours and Trouvères*, Ottawa: Institute of Mediaeval Music, pp. 67–98.

Aubrey, Elizabeth (1996), *The Music of the Troubadours. Music: Scholarship and Performance*, Bloomington and Indianapolis: Indiana University Press.

Aubrey, Elizabeth (1997), 'The Dialectic Between Occitania and France in the Thirteenth Century', *Early Music History*, **16**, pp. 1–53.

Aubrey, Elizabeth (1998), 'La Razo trouvée, chantée, écrite et enseignée chez les troubadours', in Jacques Gourc and François Pic (eds), *Toulouse à la croisée des cultures: Actes du Ve Congrès international de l'Association Internationale d'études Occitanes, Toulouse, 19–24 août 1996*, Pau, France: Association Internationale d'Études Occitanes, pp. 297–306.

Aubrey, Elizabeth (2000a), 'Non-liturgical Monophony: French', in Ross W. Duffin (ed.), *A Performer's Guide to Medieval Music*, Bloomington and Indianapolis: Indiana University Press, pp. 134–43.

Aubrey, Elizabeth (2000b), 'Non-liturgical Monophony: Introduction', in Ross W. Duffin (ed.), *A Performer's Guide to Medieval Music*, Bloomington and Indianapolis: Indiana University Press, pp. 105–14.

Aubrey, Elizabeth (2000c), 'Non-liturgical Monophony: Occitan', in Ross W. Duffin (ed.), *A Performer's Guide to Medieval Music*, Bloomington and Indianapolis: Indiana University Press, pp. 122–33.

Aubrey, Elizabeth (2001a), 'Medieval Melodies in the Hands of Bibliophiles of the Ancien Régime', in Barbara Haggh (ed.), *Essays on Music and Culture in Honor of Herbert Kellman*, Paris: Minerve, pp. 17–34.

Aubrey, Elizabeth (2001b), 'Sources, MS, §III, 4: Secular Monophony: French', in Stanley Sadie and John Tyrrell (eds), *The New Grove Dictionary of Music and Musicians*, 24 vols, London: Macmillan, vol. 23, pp. 851–60.

Aubrey, Elizabeth (2001c), 'Sources, MS, §III, 3: Secular Monophony: Occitan', in Stanley Sadie and John Tyrrell (eds), *The New Grove Dictionary of Music and Musicians*, 24 vols, London: Macmillan, vol. 23, pp. 848–51.

Aubry, Pierre (ed.) (1906), *Estampies et danses royales: les plus anciens textes de musique instrumentale du Moyen-Âge*, Paris: Fischbacher.

Aubry, Pierre (1907), *La rythmique musicale des troubadours et des trouvères*, Paris: H. Champion.

Aubry, Pierre (ed.) (1909–12), *Le chansonnier de l'Arsenal (trouvères du XIIe–XIIIe siècle): reproduction phototypique du manuscrit 5198 de la Bibliothèque de l'Arsenal, Publications de la Société Internationale de Musique*, with an introduction by Alfred Jeanroy, Paris.

Aubry, Pierre (1914), *Trouvères and Troubadours: A Popular Treatise* (2nd edn), trans. Claude Aveling, London.

Baltzer, Rebecca A., Cable, Thomas and Wimsatt, James I. (eds) (1991), *The Union of Words and Music in Medieval Poetry*, Austin: University of Texas Press.

Barr, Cyrilla (1978), 'Lauda Singing and the Tradition of the *Disciplinati Mandato*: A Reconstruction of Two Texts of the Office of Tenebrae', in Agostino Ziino (ed.), *L'Ars nova italiana del trecento 4: La musica al tempo del Boccaccio e i suoi rapporti con la letteratura: Siena and Certaldo 1975*, Certaldo: Edizioni Centro di Studi sull' Ars Nova Italiana del Trecento, pp. 21–44.

Barr, Cyrilla (1988), *The Monophonic Lauda and the Lay Religious Confraternities of Tuscany and Umbria in the Late Middle Ages*, Early Drama, Art, and Music Monographs Series 10, Kalamazoo: Medieval Institute, Western Michigan University.

Bec, Pierre (1977–78), *La lyrique française au moyen âge (XIIe–XIIIe siècle): contribution à une typologie des genres poétiques médiévaux*, 2 vols, Centre d'Etudes Supérieures de Civilisation Médiévale de l'Université de Poitiers 6–7, Paris: A. and J. Picard.

Bec, Pierre (1979), '"Trobairitz" et chansons de femme: Contribution à la connaissance du lyrism féminin au moyen âge', *Cahiers de civilisation médiévale*, **22**, pp. 235–62.

Bec, Pierre (1982), 'Le problème des genres chez les premiers troubadours', *Cahiers de civilisation médiévale*, **25**, pp. 31–47.

Beck, Jean-Baptiste (1907), 'Die modale Interpretation der mittelalterliche Melodien der Troubadours und der Trouvères', *Caecilia*, **24**, pp. 97–105.

Beck, Jean-Baptiste (1908), *Die Melodien der Troubadours, nach dem gesamten handschriftlichen Material zum erstenmal bearbeitet und herausgegeben, nebst einer Untersuchung über die Entwicklung der Notenschrift (bis um 1250) und das rhythmisch-metrische Prinzip der mittelalterlich-lyrischen Dichtungen, so wie mit Übertragung in moderne Noten der Melodien der Troubadours und Trouvères*, Straßbourg: K.J. Trübner.

Beck, Jean-Baptiste (ed.) (1927), *Les Chansonniers des Troubadours et des Trouvères: Le Chansonnier Cangé: publiés en facsimilé et transcrits en notation moderne*, vol. 1, pt. 1: *Reproduction phototypique du Chansonnier Cangé, Paris, Bibliothèque Nationale, ms. français no. 846*, vol. 1, pt. 2: *Transcription des chansons du Chansonnier Cangé, notes et commentaires*, Corpus Cantilenarum Medii Aevi I/1, Paris and Philadelphia: Honoré Champion and University of Pennsylvania Press (reprinted New York: Broude Brothers, 1946; Geneva: Slatkine, 1976).

Beck, Jean-Baptiste (1928), *La musique des troubadours: étude critique* (2nd edn), Paris: Henri Laurens.

Beck, Jean-Baptiste and Beck, Louise (eds) (1938), *Les Chansonniers des Troubadours et des Trouvères*, vol. 2, pt. 1: *Le Manuscrit du Roi, fonds français no. 844 de la Bibliothèque nationale*, vol. 2, pt. 2: *Analyse et description raisonnées du manuscrit restauré*, Corpus Cantilenarum Medii Aevi I/2, Philadelphia: University of Pennsylvania Press (reprinted New York: Broude Brothers, 1970).

Bernhard, Michael (1997), 'Die Überlieferung der Neumennamen im lateinischen Mittelalter', in Michael Bernhard (ed.), *Quellen und Studien zur Musiktheorie des Mittelalters*, 2, Munich: Verlag der Bayerischen Akademie der Wissenschaften, pp. 11–91.

Bernhard, Michael (2001), 'Die Überlieferung der Neumennamen im lateinischen Mittelalter,' in Michael Bernhard (ed.), *Quellen und Studien zur Musiktheorie des Mittelalters*, 3, Munich: Verlag der Bayerischen Akademie der Wissenschaften, pp. 175–190.

Bielitz, Mathias (1985), 'Materia und Forma bei Johannes de Grocheo: Zur Verwendung philosophischer Termini in der mittelalterlichen Musiktheorie', *Die Musikforschung*, **38**, pp. 257–77.

Bischoff, Bernhard (ed.) (1967), *Carmina Burana: Facsimile Reproduction of the Manuscript Clm 4660 and Clm 4660a*. Publications of Mediaeval Musical Manuscripts, 9. Brooklyn: Institute of Mediaeval Music.

Boase, R. (1977), *The Origin and Meaning of Courtly Love: A Critical Study of European Scholarship*, Manchester: Manchester University Press.

Botterill, Steven (ed. and trans.) (1996), *Dante: De vulgari eloquentia*, Cambridge: Cambridge University Press.

Boulton, Maureen Barry McCann (1993), *The Song in the Story: Lyric Insertions in French Narrative Fiction, 1200–1400*, Middle Ages Series, Philadelphia: University of Pennsylvania Press.

Brothers, Thomas (1997), *Chromatic Beauty in the Late Medieval Chanson: An Interpretation of Manuscript Accidentals*, Cambridge: Cambridge University Press.

Bruckner, Matilda Tomaryn, Shepard, Laurie and White, Sarah (eds) (1995), *Songs of the Women Troubadours*, Garland Library of Medieval Literature A 97, New York and London: Garland.

Brumana Pascale, Biancamaria (1975–76), 'Le musiche nei jeux-partis francesi', *Annali della Facoltà di Lettere e Filosofia dell'Università di Perugia*, **13**, pp. 509–72.

Brunner, W.-H. (1963–64), 'Walthers von der Vogelweide *Palästinalied* als Kontrafactur', *Zeitschrift für deutsches Altertum und deutsche Literatur*, **92**, pp. 195–211.

Buckley, Ann (2003), 'Abelard's *planctus* and Old French *lais*: Melodic Style and Formal Structure', in Marc Stewart and David Wulstan (eds), *The Poetic and Musical Legacy of Heloise and Abelard: An Anthology of Essays by Various Authors*, Ottawa and Westhumble, Surrey: Institute of Mediaeval Music and Plainsong and Mediaeval Music Society, pp. 49–59.

Burgwinkle, William E. (ed. and trans.) (1990), *Razos and Troubadour Songs*, New York: Garland.

Butterfield, Ardis (1988), 'Interpolated Lyric in Medieval Narrative Poetry', Ph.D. dissertation, University of Cambridge.

Butterfield, Ardis (1990), 'Medieval Genres and Modern Genre Theory', *Paragraph*, **13**, pp. 184–201.

Butterfield, Ardis (1991), 'Repetition and Variation in the Thirteenth-Century Refrain', *Journal of the Royal Musical Association*, **116**, pp. 1–23.

Butterfield, Ardis (2002), *Poetry and Music in Medieval France: From Jean Renart to Guillaume de Machaut*, Cambridge: Cambridge University Press.

Chailley, Jacques (1955), 'Les premiers troubadours et les versus de l'école d'Aquitaine', *Romania*, **76**, pp. 212–39.

Chailley, Jacques (1957), 'Notes sur les troubadours, les versus et la question arabe', in *Mélanges de linguistique et de littérature romanes à la mémoire d'István Frank*, Saarbrucken: Universität des Saarlandes, pp. 118–28.

Cheyette, Fredric L. (2001), *Ermengard of Narbonne and the World of the Troubadours, Conjunctions of Religion and Power in the Medieval Past*, Ithaca, NY: Cornell University Press.

Cohen, Joel (1990), 'Peirol's Vielle: Instrumental Participation in the Troubador [*sic*] Repertory', *Historical Performance*, **3**, pp. 73–77.

Cohen, Judith R. (2002), '*Ca no soe joglaresa*: Women and Music in Medieval Spain's Three Cultures', in Anne L. Klinck and Ann Marie Rasmussen (eds), *Medieval Woman's Song: Cross-Cultural Approaches*, Philadelphia: University of Pennsylvania Press, pp. 66–80.

Coldwell, Maria V. (1981), '*Guillaume de Dole* and Medieval Romances with Musical Interpolations', *Musica Disciplina*, **35**, pp. 55–86.

Coldwell, Maria V. (1986), '*Jougleresses* and *Trobairitz*: Secular Musicians in Medieval France', in Jane Bowers and Judith Tick (eds), *Women Making Music: The Western Art Tradition, 1150–1950*, Urbana: University of Illinois Press, pp. 39–61.

Corral, Esther (2002), 'Feminine Voices in the Galician-Portuguese *cantigas de amigo*', in Anne L. Klinck and Ann Marie Rasmussen (eds), *Medieval Woman's Song: Cross-Cultural Approaches*, Philadelphia: University of Pennsylvania Press, pp. 81–99.

Cummins, Patricia W. (1980), 'The *Chanson de toile*: New Evidence for a Jongleur Genre', *Romance Notes*, **21**, pp. 117–21.

Doss-Quinby, Eglal (1984), *Les refrains chez les trouvères du XIIe siècle au début du XIV*, American University Studies 2, 17, New York: Peter Lang.

Doss-Quinby, Eglal (1994), *The Lyrics of the Trouvères: A Research Guide (1970–1990)*, Garland Medieval Bibliographies 17, Garland Reference Library of the Humanities 1423, New York: Garland.

Doss-Quinby, Eglal, Grimbert, Joan Tasker, Pfeffer, Wendy and Aubrey, Elizabeth (eds) (2001), *Songs of the Women Trouvères*, New Haven and London: Yale University Press.

Dragonetti, Roger (1960), *La technique poétique des trouvères dans la chanson courtoise: contribution à l'étude de la rhétorique médiévale*, Werken uitgegeven door de Faculteit van de Letteren en wijsbegeerte 127° Aflevering, Bruges: Rijksuniversiteit Gent (reprinted Geneva: Slatkine, 1979).

Dronke, Peter (1968), *Medieval Latin and the Rise of European Love-Lyric* (2nd edn), 2 vols, Oxford: Oxford University Press.

Dronke, Peter (1977), *The Medieval Lyric* (2nd edn), London: Cambridge University Press.

Dronke, Peter (1984), *The Medieval Poet and his World*, Rome: Edizioni di Storia e Letteratura.

Duffin, Ross W. (ed.) (2000), *A Performer's Guide to Medieval Music*, Early Music America Performer's Guides to Early Music, Bloomington and Indianapolis: Indiana University Press.

Epstein, Marcia Jenneth (ed. and trans.) (1997), *Prions en chantant: Devotional Songs of the Trouvères*, Toronto Medieval Texts and Translations 11, Toronto: University of Toronto Press.

Evans, Beverly J. (1990), 'The Textual Function of the Refrain Cento in a Thirteenth-Century French Motet', *Music and Letters*, **71**, pp. 187–97.

Everist, Mark (1989), *Polyphonic Music in Thirteenth-century France: Aspects of Sources and Distribution*, Outstanding Dissertations in Music from British Universities, New York: Garland.

Everist, Mark (1992), *Models of Musical Analysis: Music Before 1600*, Oxford: Blackwell.

Fallows, David (2001), 'Sources, MS, §III, 1: Secular Monophony: General', in Stanley Sadie and John Tyrrell (eds), *The New Grove Dictionary of Music and Musicians*, 24 vols, London: Macmillan, vol. 23, pp. 846–47.

Fallows, David and Ferreira, Manuel Pedro (2001), 'Sources, MS, §III, 6: Secular Monophony: Galego-Portuguese', in Stanley Sadie and John Tyrrell (eds), *The New Grove Dictionary of Music and Musicians*, 24 vols, London: Macmillan, vol. 23, pp. 865–66.

Fallows, David and Payne, Thomas B. (2001), 'Sources, MS, §III, 2: Secular Monophony: Latin', in Stanley Sadie and John Tyrrell (eds), *The New Grove Dictionary of Music and Musicians*, 24 vols, London: Macmillan, vol. 23, pp. 847–48.

Fallows, David and Welker, Lorenz (2001), 'Sources, MS, §III, 5: Secular Monophony: German', in Stanley Sadie and John Tyrrell (eds), *The New Grove Dictionary of Music and Musicians*, 24 vols, London: Macmillan, vol. 23, pp. 860–65.

Fernández de la Cuesta, Ismael (1987), 'La música en la lírica castellana durante la Edad Media', in *España en la Música de Occidente. Actas del Congreso Internacional celebrado en Salamanca [Oct. 29–Nov. 5, 1983]*, Madrid: Ministerio de Cultura, vol. 1, pp. 33–43.

Fernández de la Cuesta, Ismael (1993 [1997]), 'El canto viejo-hispánico y el canto viejo-galicano', *Revista de Musicología: Actas del XV Congreso de la Sociedad Internacional de Musicolgía, 'Culturas Musicales del Mediterraneo y Sus Ramificaciones,' Madrid 3–10/IV/1992*, **16**, pp. 438–56.

Ferreira, Manuel Pedro (1986), *Martin Codax [O Som de Martin Codax]*, Lisbon: Unisys Imprensa Nacional–Casa de Moeda.

Ferreira, Manuel Pedro (1987), 'Spania *versus* Spain in the *Cantigas de Santa Maria*', in *España en la Música de Occidente. Actas del Congreso Internacional celebrado en Salamanca [Oct. 29–Nov. 5, 1983]*, Madrid: Ministerio de Cultura, vol. 1, pp. 109–11.

Ferreira, Manuel Pedro (1993a), 'Bases for Transcription: Gregorian Chant and the Notation of the Cantigas de Santa Maria', in José López-Calo (ed.), *Los instrumentos del Pórtico de la Gloria: su reconstrucción y la musica de su tiempo*, La Coruña: Fundación Pedro Barrié de la Maza, Conde de Fenosa, vol. 2, pp. 595–621.

Ferreira, Manuel Pedro (1993b), 'The *Stemma* of the Marian Cantigas: Philological and Musical Evidence', *Bulletin of the Cantigueiros de Santa Maria*, **5**, pp. 49–84.

Ferreira, Manuel Pedro (1998), 'The Layout of the Cantigas: A Musicological Overview', *Galician Review*, **2**, pp. 47–61.

Ferreira, Manuel Pedro (2005), *Cantus coronatus: 7 Cantigas d'El-Rei Dom Dinis/by King Dinis of Portugal*, trans. David Cranmer and Rip Cohen, DeMusica 10, Kassel: Reichenberger.

Filios, Denise K. (2005), *Performing Women in the Middle Ages: Sex, Gender, and the Iberian Lyric*, The New Middle Ages, New York: Palgrave Macmillan.

Gaunt, Simon (1995), *Gender and Genre in Medieval French Literature*, Cambridge: Cambridge University Press.

Gaunt, Simon and Kay, Sarah (eds) (1999), *The Troubadours: An Introduction*, Cambridge and New York: Cambridge University Press.

Gennrich, Friedrich (1921, 1927), *Rondeaux, Virelais und Balladen aus dem Ende des XII., dem XIII. und dem ersten Drittel des XIV. Jahrhunderts, mit den überlieferten Melodien*, vol. 1: *Texte*; vol. 2: *Materialien, Literaturnachweise, Refrainverzeichnis*, Gesellschaft für romanische Literatur, 43, 47, Dresden and Göttingen: Gedruckt für die Gesellschaft für romanische Literatur.

Gennrich, Friedrich (1925), *Die altfranzösische Rotrouenge*, Literarhistorisch-musikwissenschaftliche Studie 2, Halle: Max Niemeyer.

Gennrich, Friedrich (1928–29), 'Internationale mittelalterliche Melodien', *Zeitschrift für Musikwissenschaft*, **11**, pp. 259–96, 321–48.

Gennrich, Friedrich (1930), 'Lateinische Kontrafaktur altfranzösischer Lieder', *Zeitschrift für romanische Philologie*, **50**, pp. 180–207.

Gennrich, Friedrich (1931), 'Das Formproblem des Minnesangs: Ein Beitrag zur Erforschung des Strophenbaues der mittelalterliche Lyrik', *Deutsche Vierteljahrschrift für Literaturwissenschaft und Geistesgeschichte*, **9**, pp. 285–349.

Gennrich, Friedrich (1932), *Grundriß einer Formenlehre des mittelalterlichen Liedes als Grundlage einer musikalischen Formenlehre des Liedes*, Halle: Max Niemeyer (reprinted Tübingen: Niemeyer, 1970, with introduction by Werner Bittinger).

Gennrich, Friedrich (1963a), *Das altfranzösische Rondeau und Virelai im 12. und 13. Jahrhundert*, Summa Musicae Medii Aevi 10, Langen bei Frankfurt: Published by the author.

Gennrich, Friedrich (ed.) (1963b), *Die Jenaer Liederhandschrift: Faksimile-Ausgabe ihrer Melodien*, Summa Musicae Medii Aevi 11, Langen-bei-Frankfurt: Published by the author.

Gennrich, Friedrich (1964), *Bibliographisches Verzeichnis des französischen Refrains des 12. und 13. Jahrhunderts*, Summa Musica Medii Aevi 14, Langen bei Frankfurt: Published by the author.

Gennrich, Friedrich (1965), *Die Kontrafaktur im Liedschaffen des Mittelalters*, Summa Musicae Medii Aevi 12, Langen-bei-Frankfurt: Published by the author.

Gennrich, Friedrich (ed.) (1967), *Die Colmarer Handschrift: Faksimile-Ausgabe ihrer Melodien*, Summa Musicae Medii Aevi 18, Langen-bei-Frankfurt: Published by the author.

Gillingham, Bryan (1993), *Secular Medieval Latin Song: An Anthology*, Musicological Studies 60/1, Ottawa: The Institute of Mediaeval Music.

Gillingham, Bryan (1995), *A Critical Study of Secular Medieval Latin Song*, Musicological Studies 60/2, Ottawa: The Institute of Mediaeval Music.

Gillingham, Bryan (1998), *The Social Background to Secular Medieval Latin Song*, Musicological Studies, 60/3, Ottawa: Institute of Mediaeval Music.

Grimbert, Joan Tasker (2003), 'Songs by Women and Women's Songs: How Useful Is the Concept of Register?', in Barbara K. Altmann and Carleton W. Carroll (eds), *The Court Reconvenes: Courtly Literature Across the Disciplines: Selected Papers from the Ninth Triennial Congress of the International Courtly Literature Society, University of British Columbia, 25–31 July, 1998*, Cambridge: D.S. Brewer, pp. 117–24.

Gushee, Lawrence (1973), 'Questions of Genre in Medieval Treatises on Music', in Wulf Arlt, E. Lichtenhahn and H. Oesch (eds), *Gattungen der Musik in Einzeldarstellungen: Gedenkschrift Leo Schrade*, Bern and Munich: Francke, pp. 365–433.

Haines, John (1997), 'The "Modal Theory," Fencing and the Death of Pierre Aubry', *Plainsong and Medieval Music*, **6**, pp. 143–50.

Haines, John (1998–2002), 'The Transformations of the *Manuscrit du Roi*', *Musica Disciplina*, **52**, pp. 5–43.

Haines, John (2001), 'The Footnote Quarrels of the Modal Theory: A Remarkable Episode in the Reception of Medieval Music', *Early Music History*, **20**, pp. 87–120.

Haines, John (2004), *Eight Centuries of Troubadours and Trouvères: The Changing Identity of Medieval Music*, Cambridge: Cambridge University Press.

Heinen, Hubert (1969), 'Minnesang: Some Metrical Problems', in Stanley N. Werbow (ed.), *Formal Aspects of Medieval German Poetry: A Symposium*, Austin: University of Texas, pp. 79–92.

Heinen, Hubert (1972), 'Walther's "Owe hovelichez singen": A Re-examination', in John Weinstock (ed.), *Saga og språk: Festschrift for Lee Hollander*, Austin: Pemberton, pp. 273–86.

Heinen, Hubert (1984), 'Ulrich von Lichtenstein: Homo (il)litteratus or Poet/Performer?', *Journal of English and German Philology*, **83**, pp. 159–72.

Hibberd, Lloyd (1944), 'Estampie and Stantipes', *Speculum*, **19**, pp. 222–49.

Huglo, Michel (1954), 'Les noms des neumes et leur origine', *Études grégoriennes*, **1**, pp. 53–67.

Huglo, Michel (1982), 'La chanson d'amour en latin à l'époque des troubadours et trouvères', *Cahiers de civilisation médiévale*, **25**, pp. 197–203.

Hult, David F. (1995), 'Courtly Love', in William W. Kibler and Grover A. Zinn (eds), *Medieval France: An Encyclopedia*, New York and London: Garland, pp. 267–69.

Huot, Sylvia (1987a), *From Song to Book: The Poetics of Writing in Old French Lyric and Lyrical Narrative Poetry*, Ithaca and London: Cornell University Press.

Huot, Sylvia (1987b), 'Transformations of Lyric Voice in the Songs, Motets and Plays of Adam de la Halle', *Romanic Review*, **78**, pp. 148–64.

Huseby, Gerardo V. (1983), 'Musical Analysis and Poetic Structure in the Cantigas de Santa María', in J.S. Geary *et al.* (eds), *Florilegium Hispanicum: Medieval and Golden Age Studies Presented to Dorothy Clotelle Clarke*, Madison, WI: Hispanic Seminary of Medieval Studies, pp. 81–101.

Huseby, Gerardo V. (1987), 'The Common Melodic Background of "Ondas do mar de Vigo" and *Cantiga 73*', in Israel J. Katz, John E. Keller, Samuel G. Armistead and Joseph T. Snow (eds), *Studies on the 'Cantigas de Santa Maria'; Art, Music, and Poetry: Proceedings of the International Symposium on the 'Cantigas De Santa Maria' of Alfonso X, El Sabio (1221–1284) in Commemoration of its 700th Anniversary Year, 1981 (New York, November 19–21)*, Madison, WI: Hispanic Seminary of Medieval Studies, pp. 189–201.

Husmann, Heinrich (1952), 'Zur Rhythmik des Trouvèregesanges', *Die Musikforschung*, **5**, pp. 110–31.

Husmann, Heinrich (1954), 'Das System der modalen Rhythmik', *Archiv für Musikwissenschaft*, **11**, pp. 1–38.

Jammers, Ewald (1956), 'Die Melodien Hugos von Montfort', *Archiv für Musikwissenschaft*, **13**, pp. 217–35.

Jammers, Ewald (1960), 'Der Vers der Trobadors und Trouvères und die deutschen Kontrafakten', in *Medium aevum vivum: Festschrift für Walther Bulst*, Heidelberg, pp. 147–160.

Jammers, Ewald (1963), *Ausgewählte Melodien des Minnesangs: Einführung, Erläuterungen und Übertragung*, Altdeutsche Textbibliothek, Ergänzungsreihe 1, Tübingen: Max Niemeyer.

Jammers, Ewald (1965), *Das königliche Liederbuch des deutschen Minnesangs: eine Einführung in die sogenannte Manessische Handschrift*, Heidelberg: Lambert-Schneider.

Jammers, Ewald (1975), *Aufzeichnungsweisen der einstimmigen ausserliturgischen Musik des Mittelalters*, Paleographie der Musik I/4, Cologne: Arno Volk-Verlag.

Jammers, Ewald and Salowsky, Helmut (eds) (1979), *Die Sangbaren Melodien zu Dichtungen der Manessischen Liederhandschrift*, Wiesbaden: L. Reichert.

Jeanroy, Alfred (ed.) (1925), *Le chansonnier d'Arras: reproduction en phototypie*, Société des anciens textes français, Paris: Droz (reprinted New York: Johnson Reprint, 1968).

Karp, Theodore (1960), 'A Lost Medieval Chansonnier', *The Musical Quarterly*, **48**, pp. 50–67.

Karp, Theodore (1962), 'Borrowed Material in Trouvère Music', *Acta Musicologica*, **34**, pp. 87–101.

Karp, Theodore (1965), 'Modal Variants in Medieval Secular Monophony', in Gustave Reese and R. Brandel (eds), *The Commonwealth of Music: In Honor of Curt Sachs*, New York: Free Press, pp. 118–29.

Karp, Theodore (1984), 'Three Trouvère Chansons in Mensural Notation', in Luther Dittmer (ed.), *Gordon Athol Anderson (1921–1981). In Memoriam von seinem Studenten, Freunden und Kollegen*, 2 vols, Henryville, PA: Institute of Mediaeval Music, vol. 2, pp. 474–94.

Karp, Theodore (1993), 'Editing the Cortona Laudario', *Journal of Musicology*, **11**, pp. 73–105.

Karp, Theodore (1998), 'Measurability in Medieval Music Before 1300', *Orbis musicae*, **12**, pp. 107–39.

Katz, Israel J., Keller, John E., Armistead, Samuel G. and Snow, Joseph T. (eds) (1987), *Studies on the 'Cantigas de Santa Maria': Art, Music, and Poetry: Proceedings of the International Symposium on the 'Cantigas De Santa Maria' of Alfonso X, El Sabio (1221–1284) in Commemoration of its 700th Anniversary Year, 1981 (New York, November 19–21)*, Madison, WI: Hispanic Seminary of Medieval Studies.

Kuhn, Hugo (1969), '*Minnesang* and the Form of Performance', in Stanley N. Werbow (ed.), *Formal Aspects of Medieval German Poetry: A Symposium*, Austin: University of Texas, pp. 27–41.

Kulp-Hill, Kathleen (trans.) (2000), *Songs of Holy Mary of Alfonso X, the Wise: A Translation of the Cantigas de Santa Maria*, intro. Connie L. Scarborough, Tempe, AZ: Medieval and Renaissance Texts and Studies.

Labaree, Robert Ridgley (1989), '"Finding" Troubadour Song: Melodic Variability and Melodic Idiom in Three Monophonic Traditions', Ph.D. dissertation, Wesleyan University.

Le Vot, Gérard (1982), 'Notation, mesure et rythme dans la *canso* troubadouresque', *Cahiers de civilisation médiévale*, **25**, pp. 205–17.

Le Vot, Gérard (1985), 'Pour une problématique à l'interprétation musicale des troubadours et des trouvères', *Studia musicologica*, **27**, pp. 239–65.

Linker, Robert White (1970), *Music of the Minnesinger and Early Meistersinger: A Bibliography*, University of North Carolina Studies in the Germanic Languages and Literatures 32, New York: AMS Press.

Linker, Robert White (1979), *A Bibliography of Old French Lyrics*, Romance Monographs 3, University, MS: Romance Monographs.

Ludwig, Friedrich (1910), *Repertorium organorum recentioris et motetorum vetustissimi stili*, I/A, *Handschriften in Quadrat-Notation*, Halle: Max Niemeyer (reprinted rev. edn by Luther A. Dittmer, 2 vols in 3, New York: Institute of Mediaeval Music, 1964–78).

Lug, Robert (1985), 'Melismen-Untersuchungen am Chansonnier de St.-Germain-des-Prés', *Studia musicologica*, **27**, pp. 209–21.

Lug, Robert (1991), 'Minnesang und Spielmannskunst', in Hartmut Möller and Rudolf Stephan (eds), *Neues Handbuch der Musikwissenschaft*, vol. 2: *Die Musik des Mittelalters*, Laaber: Laaber Verlag, pp. 294–332.

Lug, Robert (1993), 'Minne, Medien, Mündlichkeit: Mittelalter-Musik und ihre Wissenschaft im Zeitalter', *Zeitschrift für Literaturwissenschaft und Linguistik*, **90/91**, pp. 71–87.

Lug, Robert (1995), 'Das "vormodale" Zeichensystem des Chansonnier de Saint-Germain-des-Prés', *Archiv für Musikwissenschaft*, **52**, no. 1, pp. 19–65.

Lug, Robert (2000), 'Drei Quadratnotationen in der Jenaer Liederhandschrift', *Die Musikforschung*, **53**, no. 1, pp. 4–40.
Maillard, Jean (1956), 'Le lai lyrique et la tradition celtique', *Ar Falz*, **18**, pp. 58–61.
Maillard, Jean (1957), 'Problèmes musicaux et littéraires du descort', in *Mélanges de linguistique et de littérature romanes à la mémoire d'István Frank*, Saarbrucken: Universität des Saarlandes, pp. 388–409.
Maillard, Jean (1958), 'Problèmes musicaux et littéraires du lai', *Quadrivium*, **2**, pp. 32–44.
Maillard, Jean (1959), 'Le *Lai* et la *Note* du Chèvrefeuille', *Musica Disciplina*, **13**, pp. 3–13.
Maillard, Jean (1963), *Evolution et esthétique du lai lyrique des origines à la fin du XIV siècle*, Paris: Centre de Documentation Universitaire et SEDES.
Maillard, Jean (1973), 'Structures mélodiques complexes au moyen âge', in Jean Dufournet and Daniel Poirion (eds), *Mélanges de langue et de littérature médiévales offerts à Pierre Le Gentil*, Paris, pp. 523–39.
Monterosso, Raffaello (1956), *Musica e ritmica dei trovatori (con i tavola fuori testo e 28 esempi musicali)*, Collezione di studi, testi e manuali a cura della Scuola di Paleografia Musicale-Cremona, Milan: Giuffrè.
Mullally, Robert (1986), 'Cançon de carole', *Acta Musicologica*, **58**, pp. 224–31.
Mullally, Robert (1998), 'Johannes de Grocheo's "Musica vulgaris"', *Music and Letters*, **79**, pp. 1–26.
Müller-Blattau, Joseph (1957), 'Zur Erforschung des einstimmigen deutschen Liedes im Mittelalter', *Die Musikforschung*, **10**, pp. 107–13.
Müller-Blattau, Joseph (1966), 'Die ältesten deutschen geistlichen Lieder', in *Von der Vielfalt der Musik*, Freiburg im Breisgau: Rombach, pp. 9–36.
O'Neill, Mary (1999–2000), 'Oral and Literate Processes in Galician-Portuguese Song', *Galician Review*, **3–4**, pp. 8–18.
O'Neill, Mary (2000), 'Problems of Genre Definition: The Cantigas de Santa Maria in the Context of the Romance Lyric Tradition', in Stephen Parkinson (ed.), *Cobras e Son: Papers on the Text, Music, and Manuscripts of the 'Cantigas de Santa Maria'*, Oxford: Legenda, pp. 20–30.
O'Neill, Mary (2006), *Courtly Love Songs of Medieval France: Transmission and Style in the Trouvère Repertoire*, Oxford: Oxford University Press.
Paden, William D. (ed.) (2000), *Medieval Lyric: Genres in Historical Context*, Illinois Medieval Studies, Urbana and Chicago: University of Illinois Press.
Paganuzzi, Enrico (1955), 'Sulla notazione neumatica della monodia trobadorica', *Rivista musicale italiana*, **57**, pp. 23–47.
Page, Christopher (1986), *Voices and Instruments of the Middle Ages: Instrumental Practice and Songs in France 1100–1300*, Berkeley: University of California Press.
Page, Christopher (1989), *The Owl and the Nightingale: Musical Life and Ideas in France, 1100–1300*, Berkeley: University of California Press.
Page, Christopher (1990), 'Court and City in France, 1100–1300', in James McKinnon (ed.), *Antiquity and the Middle Ages: From Ancient Greece to the 15th Century*, London: Macmillan, pp. 197–217.
Page, Christopher (1997), *Latin Poetry and Conductus Rhythm in Medieval France*, Royal Musical Association Monographs 8, London: Royal Musical Association.
Parker, Ian (1977a), 'The Performance of Troubadour and Trouvère Songs: Some Facts and Conjectures', *Early Music*, **5**, pp. 185–207.
Parker, Ian (1977b), 'Troubadour and Trouvère Songs: Problems in Modal Analysis', *Revue Belge de Musicologie*, **31**, pp. 20–37.
Parker, Ian (1978), 'A propos de la tradition manuscrite des chansons de trouvères', *Revue de musicologie*, **64**, pp. 181–202.
Parker, Ian (1979), 'Notes on the Chansonnier Saint-Germain-des-Prés', *Music and Letters*, **60**, pp. 261–80.

Parkinson, Stephen (ed.) (2000), *Cobras e Son: Papers on the Text, Music and Manuscripts of the 'Cantigas de Santa Maria'*, Oxford: Legenda.
Paterson, Linda M. (1993), *The World of the Troubadours: Medieval Occitan Society, c. 1100 – c. 1300*, Cambridge: Cambridge University Press.
Paterson, Linda (1999), '*Fin'amor* and the Development of the Courtly "*Canso*"', in Simon Gaunt and Sarah Kay (eds), *The Troubadours: An Introduction*, Cambridge and New York: Cambridge University Press, pp. 28–46.
Perrin, Robert H. (1956), 'Some Notes on the Troubadour Melodic Types', *Journal of the American Musicological Society*, **9**, pp. 12–18.
Perrin, Robert H. (1963), 'Descant and Troubadour Melodies: A Problem in Terms', *Journal of the American Musicological Society*, **16**, pp. 313–24.
Phan, Chantal (1987), 'Le style poético-musical de Guiraut Riquier', *Romania*, **108**, pp. 66–78.
Phan, Chantal (1996), 'Structures poético-musicales du chant mélismatique chez Guiraut Riquier et Alphonse le Sage', *Tenso: Bulletin of the Societe Guilhem IX*, **11**, pp. 163–78.
Pillet, Alfred and Carstens, Henry (1933), *Bibliographie der Troubadours*, Schriften der Königsberger Gelehrten Gesellschaft, Halle: Max Niemeyer.
Pollina, Vincent (1985), 'Troubadours dans le nord: Observations sur la transmission des mélodies occitanes dans les manuscrits septentrionaux', *Romanistische Zeitschrift für Literaturgeschichte*, **9**, pp. 263–78.
Räkel, Hans-Herbert (1968), 'Liedkontrafaktur im frühen Minnesang', in *Probleme mittelalterlicher Überlieferung und Textkritik, Oxforder Colloquium, 1966*, Berlin: E. Schmidt, pp. 96–117.
Räkel, Hans-Herbert (1977), *Die musikalische Erscheinungsform der Trouvèrepoesie: Untersuchungen zur mittelalterlichen höfischen Lyrik in Frankreich und Deutschland*, Publikationen der schweizerischen musikforschenden Gesellschaft, Serie II, vol. 27, Bern: Paul Haupt.
Räkel, Hans-Herbert (1982), 'Höfische Strophenkunst', *Zeitschrift für deutsches Altertum und deutsche Literatur*, **111**, pp. 193–219.
Räkel, Hans-Herbert (1986), *Der deutsche Minnesang: Eine Einführung mit Texten und Materialen*, Munich: Beck.
Rohloff, Ernst (ed.) (1967), *Die Quellenhandschriften zum Musiktraktat des Johannes de Grocheio, im Faksimile herausgegeben nebst Übertragung des Textes und Übersetzung ins Deutsche, dazu Bericht, Literaturschau, Tabellen und Indices*. Leipzig: Deutscher Verlag für Musik.
Rosenberg, Samuel N., Switten, Margaret L. and Le Vot, Gerard (eds) (1998), *Songs of the Troubadours and Trouvères: An Anthology of Poems and Melodies*, Garland Reference Library of the Humanities 1740, New York: Garland.
Salmen, Walter (1983), 'The Social Status of the Musician in the Middle Ages', in Walter Salmen (ed.), *The Social Status of the Professional Musician from the Middle Ages to the 19th Century*, New York: Pendragon Press, pp. 1–29.
Sanders, Ernest H. (1985), 'Conductus and Modal Rhythm', *Journal of the American Musicological Society*, **38**, pp. 439–69.
Sawa, George (1981), 'The Survival of Some Aspects of Medieval Arabic Performance Practice', *Ethnomusicology*, **25**, pp. 73–86.
Sawa, George (2004a) 'Baghdadi Rhythmic Theories and Practices in Twelfth-Century Andalusia', in John Haines and Randall Rosenfeld (eds), *Music and Medieval Manuscripts: Paleography and Performance; Essays Dedicated to Andrew Hughes*, Aldershot and Burlington, VT: Ashgate, pp. 151–81.
Sawa, George (2004b), *Music Performance Practice in the Early 'Abbasid Era 132–320 AH/750–932 AD* (2nd edn), Musicological Studies 80, Ottawa: Institute of Mediaeval Music.
Seagrave, Barbara Garvey and Thomas, Wesley (eds) (1966), *The Songs of the Minnesingers*, Urbana: University of Illinois Press.

Sharrer, Harvey L. (1991), 'The Discovery of Seven *cantigas d'amor* by Dom Dinis with Musical Notation', *Hispania*, **74**, pp. 459–61.
Snow, Joseph T. (1977), *The Poetry of Alfonso X, el Sabio: A Critical Bibliography*, London: Grant and Cutler.
Spanke, Hans (1928), 'Das öftere Auftreten von Strophenformen und Melodien in der altfranzösischen Lyrik', *Zeitschrift für französische Sprache und Literatur*, **51**, pp. 73–117.
Spanke, Hans (1929), 'Zur Geschichte des altfranzösischen Jeu-parti', *Zeitschrift für französische Sprache und Literatur*, **52**, pp. 39–63.
Spanke, Hans (1929–30), 'Das lateinische Rondeau', *Zeitschrift für französische Sprache und Literatur*, **53**, pp. 113–48.
Spanke, Hans (1934), 'Zur Formenkunst der ältesten Troubadours', *Studi medievali*, **7**, pp. 72–84.
Spanke, Hans (ed.) (1955), *G. Raynauds Bibliographie des altfranzösischen Liedes. Musicologica 1*, Leiden: Brill (reprinted 1980).
Spiewok, Wolfgang (1995), 'Walther von der Vogelweide: Leben–Dichtung–Wirkung', in Danielle Buschinger and Wolfgang Spiewok (eds), *Walther von der Vogelweide: Actes du Colloque du Centre d'études médiévales de l'Université de Picardie Jules Verne 15 et 16 janvier 1995*, Greifswald: Reineke-Verlag, pp. 15–30.
Stäblein, Bruno (1966), 'Zur Stilistik der Troubadour-Melodien', *Acta Musicologica*, **38**, no. 1, pp. 27–46.
Steel, Matthew C. (1989), 'A Reappraisal of the Role of Music in Adam de la Halle's *Jeu de Robin et de Marion*', in Carmelo Comberiati and Matthew Steel (eds), *Music from the Middle Ages Through the Twentieth Century: Essays in Honor of Gwynn S. McPeek*, New York: Gordon and Breach Science Publishers.
Steiner, Ruth (1966), 'Some Monophonic Latin Songs Composed Around 1300', *The Musical Quarterly*, **52**, pp. 56–70.
Stevens, John (1968), 'Dante and Music', *Italian Studies*, **23**, pp. 1–18.
Stevens, John (1981), 'The Manuscript Presentation and Notation of Adam de la Halle's Courtly Chansons', in Ian Bent (ed.), *Source Materials and the Interpretation of Music: A Memorial Volume to Thurston Dart*, London: Stainer and Bell, pp. 29–64.
Stevens, John (1986), *Words and Music in the Middle Ages: Song, Narrative, Dance and Drama, 1050–1350*, Cambridge Studies in Music, Cambridge: Cambridge University Press.
Stevens, John (2000), 'Reflections on the Music of Medieval Narrative Poetry', in Karl Reichl (ed.), *The Oral Epic: Performance and Music*, Berlin: VWB, Verlag für Wissenschaft und Bildung, pp. 233–248.
Stevens, John (2005), *The Later Cambridge Songs: An English Song Collection of the Twelfth Century*, Oxford: Oxford University Press.
Stewart, Michelle F. (1979), 'The Melodic Structure of Thirteenth-Century *jeux-partis*', *Acta Musicologica*, **51**, pp. 86–107.
Stockmann, Doris (1983), '*Musica vulgaris* bei Johannes de Grocheio (Grocheo)', *Beiträge zur Musikwissenschaft*, **25**, pp. 3–56.
Suchla, Beate Regina (1979), 'Zu Notation, Metrum und Rhythmus des altfranzösischen Liedes. Dargestellt an einem Melodienachtrag zu dem Lied "Pour le tens qui verdoie" im Chansonnier de Saint-Germain, Paris, BN, f. fr. 20050', *Archiv für Musikwissenschaft*, **36**, pp. 159–82.
Sühring, Peter (2003), *Der Rhythmus der Trobadors: zur Archäologie einer Interpretationsgeschichte*, Berliner Arbeiten zur Erziehungs- und Kulturwissenschaft, Bd. 16, Berlin: Logos.
Switten, Margaret L. (1992), 'Modèle et variations: Saint Martial de Limoges et les troubadours', in Gérard Gouiran (ed.), *Contacts de langues, de civilisations et intertextualité, Actes du IIIème Congrès International de l'Association Internationale d'Études Occitanes*, Montpellier: Université Paul Valéry, vol. 2, pp. 679–96.

Switten, Margaret L. (1995), *Music and Poetry in the Middle Ages: A Guide to Research on French and Occitan Song, 1100–1400*, Garland Medieval Bibliographies 19, New York and London: Garland.
Taylor, Ronald J. (1968), *The Art of the Minnesinger: Songs of the Thirteenth Century Transcribed and Edited with Textual and Musical Commentaries*, 2 vols, Cardiff: University of Wales Press.
Tervooren, Helmut, and Müller, Ulrich (eds.) (1972), *Die Jenaer Liederhandschrift in Abbildung, mit einem Anhang: die Basler und Wolfenbüttler Fragmente*, Litterae 10. Göppingen: A Kümmerle.
Thomas, Wesley and Seagrave, Barbara Garvey (eds) (1968), *Songs of the Minnesinger: Prince Wizlaw of Rügen*, Studies in Germanic Languages and Literature 59, Chapel Hill: University of North Carolina Press.
Tischler, Hans (1986), 'Trouvère Songs: The Evolution of Their Poetic and Musical Styles', *The Musical Quarterly*, **72**, pp. 329–40.
Tischler, Hans (ed.) (1997), *Trouvère Lyrics with Melodies: Complete Comparative Edition*, 15 vols, Corpus Mensurabilis Musicæ 107, Neuhausen: American Institute of Musicology and Hänssler-Verlag.
Treitler, Leo (1991), 'The Troubadours Singing Their Poems', in Rebecca A. Baltzer, Thomas Cable and James I. Wimsatt (eds), *The Union of Words and Music in Medieval Poetry*, Austin: University of Texas Press, pp. 15–48.
Treitler, Leo (1992), 'Medieval Lyric', in Mark Everist (ed.), *Models of Musical Analysis: Music Before 1600*, Oxford: Blackwell, pp. 1–19.
Van der Werf, Hendrik (1967a), 'Deklamatorischer Rhythmus in den Chansons der Trouvères', *Die Musikforschung*, **20**, no. 2, pp. 122–44.
Van der Werf, Hendrik (1967b), 'Recitative Melodies in Trouvère Chansons', in Ludwig Finscher and Christoph-Helmut Mahling (eds), *Festschrift für Walter Wiora*, Kassel: Bärenreiter, pp. 231–40.
Van der Werf, Hendrik (1972), *The Chansons of the Troubadours and Trouvères: A Study of the Melodies and Their Relation to the Poems*, Utrecht: A. Oosthoek's Uitgeversmaatschapij.
Van der Werf, Hendrik (ed.) (1977, 1979), *Trouvère-Melodien*, 2 vols, Monumenta Monodica Medii Aevi 11 and 12, Kassel: Bärenreiter.
Van der Werf, Hendrik (1984), *The Extant Troubadour Melodies: Transcriptions and Essays for Performers and Scholars*, Rochester, NY: Published by the author.
Van der Werf, Hendrik (1987), 'Accentuation and Duration in the Music of the Cantigas de Santa Maria', in Israel J. Katz, John E. Keller, Samuel G. Armistead and Joseph T. Snow (eds), *Studies on the 'Cantigas de Santa Maria': Art, Music, and Poetry: Proceedings of the International Symposium on the 'Cantigas De Santa Maria' of Alfonso X, El Sabio (1221–1284) in Commemoration of its 700th Anniversary Year, 1981 (New York, November 19–21)*, Madison, WI: Hispanic Seminary of Medieval Studies, pp. 223–34.
Welker, Lorenz (1984), 'Das Taghorn des Mönchs von Salzburg: Zur frühen Mehrstimmigkeit im deutschen Lied', *Schweizer Jahrbuch für Musikwissenschaft*, **4–5**, pp. 41–61.
Wilkins, Nigel (1989), *The Lyric Art of Medieval France* (2nd edn), Fulbourn: The New Press.
Wilson, Blake (ed.) (1995), *The Florence Laudario: An Edition of Florence, Biblioteca Nazionale, Banco Rari 18*, Recent Researches in the Music of the Middle Ages and Early Renaissance 29–30, Madison, WI: A-R Editions.
Wilson, Blake (1997), 'Madrigal, Lauda, and Local Style in Trecento Florence', *Journal of Musicology*, **15**, pp. 137–77.
Wulstan, David (2000a), 'The Compilation of the *Cantigas* of Alfonso el Sabio', in Stephen Parkinson (ed.), *Cobras e Son: Papers on the Text, Music and Manuscripts of the 'Cantigas de Santa Maria'*, Oxford: Legenda, pp. 154–85.
Wulstan, David (2000b), 'The Rhythmic Organization of the *Cantigas de Santa Maria*', in Stephen Parkinson (ed.), *Cobras e Son: Papers on the Text, Music and Manuscripts of the 'Cantigas de Santa Maria'*, Oxford: Legenda, pp. 31–65.

Zumthor, Paul (1972a), 'Classes and Genres in Medieval Literature', in Norris J. Lacy (ed.), *A Medieval French Miscellany: Papers of the 1970 Kansas Conference on Medieval Literature*, Lawrence: University of Kansas Press, pp. 27–36.
Zumthor, Paul (1972b), *Essai de poétique médiévale*, Paris: Editions du Seuil.
Zumthor, Paul (1983), *Introduction à la poésie orale*, Paris: Seuil (trans. Kathryn Murphy-Judy as *Oral Poetry: An Introduction*, Minneapolis: University of Minnesota Press, 1990).
Zumthor, Paul (1984), 'The Text and the Voice', *New Literary History*, **16**, pp. 67–92.
Zumthor, Paul (1987), *La lettre et la voix: de la 'littérature' médiévale*, Paris: Editions du Seuil.

Part I
History and Society

[1]

Music and Chivalric Fiction in France, 1150–1300

CHRISTOPHER PAGE

> When the meal drew to a close the lady who had served the wine produced a harp and began to play it so sweetly that it was a wondrous thing to hear. So Sir Gawayn listened to her very willingly for a while until he began to feel the cold, for his tunic was not at all well dried. And when the cold got to him he rose up and went to the great fire which was in the middle of the Hall and took a stool and sat down before the fire, turning his shoulder and his back [to the flames] and warmed himself until he slept, as one who had been afflicted the whole day with the rain and the wind.[1]

I TAKE this artless description of harping in a Great Hall to be a depiction of life in the castles of thirteenth-century France and as lifelike as the wicked draught which tortures Sir Gawayn. Like many similar passages in Old French fiction, it seems to transport us directly into a realm of domestic and amateur music-making which, at this date, can barely be glimpsed upon the horizon of other sources such as manuscript paintings and archives.[2]

A lady plays a harp and her music is 'a wondrous thing to hear'. This balance of objective detail and subjective assessment accounts for the special interest of many references to music in Old French fiction; there are no other sources from the twelfth and thirteenth centuries which

---

1 H.O. Sommer, ed., *The Vulgate Version of the Arthurian Romances*, 8 vols. (Washington, 1909–16), 7, Supplement, *Le Livre d'Artus* (Washington, 1913), pp. 173–4. I retain Sommer's orthography:
Qvant uint en la fin du mengier si traist la damoisele cele qui auoit serui du uin une harpe et comenca a harper tant do[l]cement que ce estoit merueilles a oir et a escouter . si lescouta messires Gauuain une piece molt uolentiers tant quil comenca a refroidier que sa robe nestoit mie bien essuiee . et quant il senti la froidure si se leua et uint au feu que granz estoit en mi la sale et prent il meismes un quarrel et sa[s]iet desus deuant le feu et li torne lespaule et le dos et se chaufe tant quil si endort come cil qui toz estoit debatuz tot le ior entier de pluie et de uent. Compare the episode in E. Stengel, ed., *Li Romans de Durmart le Galois* (Tübingen, 1873), lines 3217ff.
2 On thirteenth-century French pictorial sources see G. Foster, *The iconology of musical instruments and musical performance in thirteenth-century French manuscript illuminations* (diss. City University of New York, 1977). Foster concludes, quite rightly in my view, that pictorial material of this date has considerable limitations as a source of information about musical life and performance practice. As for archival sources, relevant documents are not plentiful from the thirteenth-century (and are extremely scarse for the twelfth). Furthermore there are very few documentary sources from any period of the Middle Ages which shed light upon the musical activities of courtly amateurs. Most financial records, for example, bear upon secular music only insofar as they record various kinds of transactions involving the services of minstrels. For some thirteenth-century examples, see A. Henry, ed., *Les Ouvres d'Ardenet le Roi*, 1 (Bruges, 1951), *passim*, but especially p. 65ff.

engage so often and so candidly with the aesthetic pleasure given by music. Nor, perhaps, is there anywhere else to go for a sense of that most elusive quality of life in the past: atmosphere. The lady who plays the harp has previously served wine and now she offers after-dinner music to the guests in the Hall. These narrative details define the ambience of the musical scene: the entertainment is being offered in a casual but courteous spirit. Like the wine, it is a garnish to the meal which the guests are free to accept or to decline according to their pleasure.

The real focus of the passage is not the lady but Sir Gawayn. Even so, every movement which this famous knight makes defines the atmosphere of the musical event a little further:

> So Sir Gawayn listened to her very willingly . . . and when the cold got to him he rose up and went to the great fire which was in the middle of the hall . . . turning his shoulder and his back [to the flames] and warmed himself until he slept.

This is a glimpse of the reality beneath the metal plates of chivalry. Without his armour, and exhausted after a long journey, one of the greatest knights of Christendom is as vulnerable as a tortoise without a shell. Gawayn rises to warm his tired body by the fire but there is no suggestion that this inattentiveness to a lady's harping will damage his reputation as one of Camelot's most amorous knights. This is presumably because the performance (if that is the right word) takes place in a Great Hall, a place whose characteristic ambience can be recovered from a wealth of literary references to its appearance and function. A Great Hall was usually a wide, open space where a large fire sent smoke into the rafters; it was the usual setting for festive minstrel-music[3] and a thoroughfare which echoed to the clatter of trestle-tables being set up for meals. The 'feel' of life in the Great Hall was therefore quite unlike that of inner rooms and chambers – places where more scrupulous behaviour might have been expected of Sir Gawayn. Thus it seems that the lady harpist in our extract is one who, by virtue of her sex and tender age, may be asked to leave her chamber and play in this public and minstrellish space.[4]

'The past is another country', wrote L.P. Hartley; 'they do things differently there'. The passage we have just examined suggests that

---

3   For examples see the texts gathered in E. Faral, *Les jongleurs en France au moyen age*, 2nd edition (Paris, 1971), Appendix 3, items 60, 63, 68, 113, *et passim*, and E. Bowles, 'Musical Instruments at the Medieval Banquet', *Revue Belge de Musicologie*, 12 (1958), pp. 41–51.

4   There are many indications in medieval literature that musical accomplishments were regarded as particularly appropriate to young girls (much as they were in nineteenth-century England). The evidence of didactic literature addressed to women is particularly revealing here. See A. Hentsch, *De la littérature didactique du moyen age s'addressant spécialement aux femmes* (Cahors, 1903), pp. 89 and 107, and J. Ulrich, ed., *Robert von Blois sämmtliche Werke*. 3 vols., (Berlin, 1889–95), 3, p. 70, lines 453–68.

chivalric fiction may sometimes enhance our awareness of how musical things were done in the medieval past. Yet it is *fiction*; surely medieval storytellers were free to wield the power of Merlin's sorcery and to distort life as they pleased? How may the more reliable references to music in their tales be distinguished from their less reliable ones?

One thing can be conceded at once: it is impossible to prove anything about musical life in the Middle Ages on the basis of chivalric fiction alone. Our description of a lady's harping in a Great Hall is believable in the simple sense that it does not strain our credibility, but we would surely be on firmer ground with an archival record of some kind or perhaps a passing reference in a sober historical chronicle? I am sure that we would, but I am also convinced that nothing like the harping-scene of the *Livre d'Artus* is to be found in the known archives and chronicles of the twelfth and thirteenth centuries. This observation can be widened into a claim that (as far as musical life is concerned) the testimony of chivalric fiction is mostly unsupported with regard to exactly the details likely to interest us most.

Yet what gradually happens during a reading of these tales is that passages emerge whose veracity there seems no good reason to doubt:[5]

> Quant il orent mangié a grant plente tant comme il leur plot, li rois escoute et ot en une chambre qui estoit encoste de lui touz les diuers estrumenz dont il eüst onques oï parler en sa vie; si sonoient tout ensamble li vn avec les autres si tres doucement qu'il n'avoit onques oïe melodie que tant li-fust douce ne plesanz a oïr.

> When they had eaten their fill as much as they wished, the king [Arthur] listened to and heard in an adjacent chamber all the various instruments that he had ever heard speak of in his life; they played all together, each one with the others, so very sweetly that he had never encountered music which seems to him so sweet or pleasant to hear.

This passage has obviously been gilded with hyperbole to give it a heraldic brilliance. Arthur listens to 'all the various instruments that he had ever heard speak of in his entire life' and he 'had never encountered music so sweet or pleasant to hear'. Yet hyperbole is not a particularly

---

5 J. Frappier, ed., *La Mort le Roi Artu* (Geneva and Paris, 1936), pp. 46–7. This is an exceptional reference; it seems that musicians have been gathered together to provide concerted instrumental music, for listening, in a chamber specially set aside for the purpose. I do not know of any directly comparable reference in Old French fiction. It may be that the anonymous author of *La Mort le Roi Artu* is recording some thirteenth-century antecedent of a practice recorded in association with King Charles V of France by both Froissart and Christine de Pisan. Froissart describes an occasion when after-dinner music is provided for Gaston Phébus and Charles by players of *bas* instruments in the *chambre de parement* of the castle of Toulouse; Christine de Pisan recounts a very similar event at Paris in 1377 (once again the music is played by *bas* instruments, this time in the *chambre de parlement*). See Kervyn de Lettenhove, ed., *Oeuvres de Froissart*, 25 vols. (Brussels, 1870–7), 14, p. 75, and S. Solente, ed., *Le livre des fais et bonnes meurs du sage Roy Charles V*, 2 vols. (Paris, 1936 and 1940), 2, pp. 108–109.

sophisticated literary strategy. Old French narrators often apply it like paint and it is easy to strip away. In this passage a simple grain of sober and almost domestic description lies beneath the gilt. In the events leading up to this musical scene Arthur arrives at Morgan's castle and is received in the Great Hall (the usual place for a ceremonial reception). Next, he is led into a private chamber to take his meal (again, an accepted custom in the thirteenth and fourteenth centuries).[6] These details evoke a narrator attentive to patterns of use within a castle complex and suggest that the 'concert' arranged for Arthur in a nearby chamber is another example of his scrupulosity. It is also striking that the music is not performed *before* Arthur but is played in an adjacent room – a detail which the author is perhaps unlikely to have invented. It is tempting to regard this passage as a record of contemporary practice.[7]

6 For a superb account of this custom, this time in the most sophisticated of all Middle English Arthurian romances, see J.R.R. Tolkien and E.V. Gordon, eds., *Sir Gawayn and the Green Knight*, second edition, ed. N. Davis (Oxford, 1967), line 853ff.

7 The question of whether medieval romances do, or do not, incorporate verisimilar references to social customs and practices reduces to a matter of faith: when reading these texts one either chooses to believe in the realism of details which seem credible and consonant with external evidence, or one does not choose to believe in them. It would be possible to present very sophisticated arguments in favour of atheism in this regard, for modern developments in literary theory have opened the study of literature to profound philosophical issues that turn upon how words mean, whether they mean what we take them to mean when we use them, and whether they mean anything; immersion in such questions will not fill us with confidence that medieval literature can reveal much about contemporary reality. Yet neither will it reassure us that we know, or can reasonably say, anything about the external world of objects and actions. On moral and humanitarian grounds I dissent from the sceptical view that imaginative literature in general, and medieval romance in particular, cannot reveal objective truths about the past; such scepticism ultimately deposes the notion of objective truth and leaves no basis for rational enquiry.

A more traditional ground for atheism would be to argue, in the best positivist tradition, that medieval romances, being 'literature', must be sharply distinguished from the objective records of fact (especially archives) which are the proper materials of the historian. This argument can be met in two ways.

Firstly, any historian who wishes to adopt this rigorously positivist line will need to base his historical credo almost entirely upon archival sources, yet 'literary' works (especially chronicles and saints' Lives) have long been exploited by historians. Indeed, a distinction between 'factual' writing and 'fictional' writing is hard to maintain in the contexts of the thirteenth century when the biography of a historical figure such as William Marshall could be written in verse and dressed out with many of the conventions of chivalric romance, and when a prose chronicle, such as Villehardouin's *La Conquete de Constantinople*, is strewn with verbal tags and hyperboles drawn from vernacular epics such as *The Song of Roland*.

Secondly, it is simplistic to draw a firm distinction between *history* and *story*. The modern historian does not write in a scientifically objective language which is devoid of rhetorical colouring and transparent to its object, for such writing is not possible to achieve. This is not to deny that historians may make objective statements about the external world; it is merely to urge that a firm distinction between the language of historical fact and the language of literary fiction is not possible and there is therefore no

So far I have suggested that chivalric fiction embodies details of musical life which may be reasonably assumed to be realistic. That is a simple claim, of course, and in the contexts of both literary studies and musicology it is nothing new.[8] Now I wish to go further and to maintain that these tales can supply us with complexes of detail and judgment which help to frame a history of music in medieval France.

Let us glance first at the things which such a history will *not* contain. It will not have much to say about polyphony; organum, motet and conductus rarely appear in the world of Gawayn or Galahad.[9] Nor will it reveal much about specific troubadours and trouvères and the reception of their works.[10] On the other hand a history of music based on chivalric fiction would be directly concerned with performance practice in the most comprehensive sense (who performed for whom, where, to what effect, and so on); it would also be closely involved with the activities of courtly amateurs (whose doings can barely be documented from any other kind of source) and with the life and work of minstrels. On a deeper level chivalric fiction helps to interpret the ideals of the aristocratic class from which many troubadours and trouvères sprang (and to which most courtly monody, of whatever origin, ostensibly refers for its moral and aesthetic values). Indeed these narratives may be our only guide to the place where

cause for the historian to disdain imaginative literature *per se* on the grounds that it may sully the nature of his discourse. See, for example, H. White, *Metahistory: The Historical Imagination in Nineteenth Century Europe* (1974) and S. Bann, *The Clothing of Clio : A Study of the Representation of History in Nineteenth Century Britain and France* (Cambridge, 1984).

8   Old French fiction has been mined for its information about medieval music since at least the late sixteenth century. See, for example, C. Fauchet. *Recueil de l'Origine de la langue et poesie francoise, ryme et romans* (Paris, 1581), pp. 72–3. Modern works which exploit medieval literature in this way are too numerous to mention.

9   Of the tiny handful of references to polyphony in Old French literature the most striking is to be found in Wace's *Brut* of 1155, in a passage describing the festivities at Arthur's coronation. See I. Arnold, ed., *Le Roman de Brut de Wace*. 2 vols., Société des Anciens Textes Français (Paris, 1938 and 1940), 2, lines 10421–4. However, Wace is following his source closely at this point, Geoffrey of Monmouth's *Historia Regum Britannie*, completed at Oxford c. 1136. See A. Griscom and R.E. Jones., eds., *The Historia Regum Britanniae of Geoffrey of Monmouth* (London etc., 1929), p. 456. For other passages which probably refer to polyphony see L. Wright, '*Chanter a gresillon(s)* and *chanter es gresillons*', *Medium Aevum*, 35 (1966), pp. 231–5, and Y. Rokseth, *Polyphonies du XIIIe Siècle*, 4 vols., (Paris, 1935, 1936 and 1939), 4, pp. 65–7, 84, 219–220. There is a terminological problem with some of the texts cited by Rokseth, however. It is far from certain, for example, whether Old French *motet* customarily refers to a polyphonic genre when used in the non-specialist contexts of vernacular poetry and prose.

10 The most famous references to trouvères (complete with citations of songs) in Old French fiction are in Jean Renart's romance of *Guillaume de Dole* (ed F. Lecoy, Classiques Français du Moyen Age (Paris, 1962), lines 844ff, 1451ff, 3620ff, 4120ff and 5228ff). See also P.B. Fay and J.L. Grigsby, eds., *Joufroi de Poitiers* (Geneva, 1972), lines 3601–3692 (the troubadour Marcabrun), and J.E. Matzke and M. Delbouille, eds., *Le Roman du Castelain de Couci et de la Dame de Fayel par Jakemes*, Société des Anciens Textes Français (Paris, 1936), *passim*.

music lay in the minds of secular magnates – men who knew more of the stable, the fencing-yard and the tournament field than they knew of masses, motets and modal rhythms. It is this last, deeper level of reference that I wish to pursue in the first half of this paper by focusing upon chivalric ideology and the rise of the troubadours and trouvères.

1 EPIC AND ROMANCE

To open the earliest and most famous of the French epics, *The Song of Roland* (c. 1080), is to be transported into a world where companies of knights do combat for a communal and aggressively Christian purpose: Charlemagne's crusade against the Saracens in Spain. Roland has his being in the army of Charlemagne; he does nothing alone, and there is little sense in the poem that his (or anybody's) life is a journey of private conflict and conscience.

When we leave Roland at Roncesvals and turn to Arthur at Camelot the world has changed. The epic community of knights, bound together by a common struggle, has vanished; the age of Abelard, and of the new luxurious castles with their individually heated chambers, required a new kind of knight. In contrast to Roland who rides with the army of Charlemagne, the romance knight travels alone in search of some testing adventure or some material advancement in the world. Leaving the court, he journeys along forest paths and tracks where he is tried by mortal and faery enemies. In this scheme of things the court is a secure place where the knight's values are shared and endorsed; it is the point from which he departs to be tested and to which he usually returns when the test has brought him either success or failure.[11] The walls of the court are therefore built against the challenge of the outside world; they enclose a luxurious hostelry whose significance is sustained by a realistic and hyperbolical portrayal of its luxuries, including music. This is why there is much more musical activity in romance than in epic and why the romancers are generally committed to presentations of musical life which may be idealized or gilded with hyperbole but which are generally plausible and charged with the significance of music in courtly civilization.

A glance at the world of Arthur, Gawayn or Galahad is enough to show that chivalric fiction mirrors the key place of music in the social and intellectual revolution which accompanied the second feudal age (roughly

11 The Middle English *Sir Gawayn and the Green Knight* (see note 6) is a Romance plot of classic design. Sir Gawayn must leave Arthur's court and journey through wild country to have his valour and constancy tested in the wilderness at the Green Chapel; he then returns to Camelot where the community of knights is strengthened by his success in the test. In the text this scheme is playfully varied (the real test is over by the time Gawayn reaches the Green Chapel; what he receives there is only his 'result'); yet the outlines of the archetypal Romance plot are clear and lucid throughout the tale.

1050–1300). From our distance it seems that the greatest achievement of these centuries in the West was to widen the range of human experience judged to be consequential. In Romance it is not merely the heroes' deportment in council or combat that matters, although that was virtually all that mattered in the world of Roland; the Romance knight lives in a place where adventures are often solitary and where a measure of freedom from sudden summons to war has enlarged the scope of intimate and private life; he reflects the new stability and security of Western Christendom which found itself largely free of external enemies by the end of the eleventh century. A Gawayn or a Galahad must know how to talk with ladies in a chamber or at a castle window-seat; he must converse elegantly and play the harp if asked.

Within secular aristocratic society the fountainhead of these changes lay with an idea without parallel in the history of warriorhood: that the male's ardour for honour and his ardour for erotic experience are conjunct and almost indistinguishable impulses.[12] Music, always the food of love, was intimately involved with this new sexuality.

The earliest verse-romance of the Middle Ages reveals the link between self-awareness, music and love in a most revealing way. The south-German *Ruodlieb* of c. 1050 recounts the career of a young noble warrior (*miles*) who is forced to leave his homeland. At one point in the narrative Ruodlieb stays at a castle where a young girl lives with her mother; he is entertained with music there but he is far from satisfied with the playing of the castle harpers:[13]

> Meanwhile Ruodlieb and his nephew go with the mistress to where the harpers are playing. When Ruodlieb heard how badly he played the melody (though that harpist was the best pupil of the art among them) he said to the mistress: 'If there had been another harp here. . .'. 'There is', she said, 'a harp here and there is no better; my lord played upon it whilst he lived. Through its music my thoughts languished in love. No one has touched it since he died'.
>
> . . . [two lines of text missing here] . . .
>
> Plucking now with two fingers of the left hand, and now with the right, he renders very

---

12 This is the most distinctive contribution of medieval chivalry to the ethic of warriorhood and the bibliography devoted to it, both by historians of literature and historians of chivalry, is enormous. For a guide through the maze of theories which have been offered to explain it see R. Boase, *The Origin and Meaning of Courtly Love* (Manchester, 1977). Among the works which have been devoted to the subject since the appearance of Boase's book one of the most impressive is R.H. Bloch, *Medieval French Literature and Law* (University of California Press, 1977).

13 For the original see E.H. Zeydel, ed., *Ruodlieb* (Chapel Hill, 1959), p. 110. The translation is mine, though I have drawn extensively on the facing-page version offered by Zeydel. On the *Ruodlieb* as the first surviving example of a medieval verse-romance see P. Dronke, 'Ruodlieb : The Emergence of Romance', in *Poetic Individuality in the Middle Ages : New Departures in Poetry 1000–1150* (Oxford, 1970), pp. 24–6 and 33–65.

sweet melodies as he touches the strings, producing many variations with great distinctness. He who was entirely unversed in moving his feet in a dance or in beating time with his hands learned both of those things quickly. The harpists, who formerly had boldly struck the strings in minstrel fashion, listened silently and did not dare play.

Once Ruodlieb has played three melodies the mistress of the castle asks him to play so that her daughter may dance with Ruodlieb's nephew:[14]

> He carries this out, performing refrains now pausing one note away from the final, now pausing upon the final, in an admirable and decorous way.

A noble string-player who performs so well that he eclipses professionals, with everything which that implies about the strength of the hero's commitment to polite, social skills: this is a new figure in medieval literature. It is not only Ruodlieb's warriorhood which is consequential in this poem but also the courtliness of his behaviour; epic heroes do not often deal in the delicacy of sentiment which prompts Ruodlieb to ask for a harp with a scrupulously unassuming subjunctive: 'If there had been another harp here...' (*Ibi si plus harpa fuisset*);[15] the poet knows that his hero can put the professionals to shame, but he also believes (and here he anticipates Castiglione by five centuries) that the courtier should maintain a nonchalent modesty at all times.

Rudlieb plays for a small company in which there are ladies. There is nothing amorous in his own conduct but a close association between string-playing and passion runs through this musical episode. The *harpa* which Ruodlieb plays is no minstrel's instrument; it was once the private possession of a castellan and it is powerfully associated with the sexual longing of his widow. Her thoughts 'languished in love' every time her lord played upon it and the instrument continues to cast its spell; once

---

14 Zeydel, op. cit., p. 110: *Quem per sistema siue diastema dando responsa/Dum mirabiliter operaretur ue decenter*. It is particularly striking that the author seems to be describing the performance of something closely akin to the later-medieval *estampie*: (1) Ruodlieb's music is danced to, (2) it has a reprise or refrain of some kind (*responsa*) and (3) it appears to have open and closed endings. With respect to this last detail, which is perhaps the most interesting of all, my translation of the words *sistema siue diastema* ('now pausing on a note away from the final, now pausing upon the final...') is based upon the definitions of these terms given in the *De Musica* of John 'of Afflighem': 'diastema... occurs when the chant makes a suitable pause, not on the final, but elsewhere... systema... [occurs] whenever a suitable pause in the melody comes on the final...'. I borrow the translation from W. Babb and C.V. Palisca, *Hucbald, Guido and John on Music* (Yale University Press, 1978), p. 117; for the original, see J. Smits van Waesberghe, ed., *Johannis Affligemensis De Musica cum Tonario*, American Institute of Musicology, Corpus Scriptorum de Musica, 1 (Rome 1950), p. 80. If, as seems likely, John wrote in southern Germany around 1100, then he is well placed to be our intepreter of musical terminology in the south-German *Ruodlieb* which may have been composed during his lifetime.

15 I owe this point to Dronke, '*Ruodlieb*', p. 54.

Ruodlieb's nephew and the lady's daughter have danced to the hero's playing they are 'strongly aglow' for one another.[16]

2 NARCISSISM

By following through the conceptions of male talent to be found in chivalric fiction it is possible to establish a social context for the art of the troubadours and trouvères. Two central themes emerge: narcissism and eloquence.

We have already glimpsed the revolution in warrior-ethics whereby the warrior's ardour for honour merged with his erotic ardour. As I interpret it, the cause of this revolution was the emergence in the aristocratic societies of the eleventh and twelfth centuries of male sexual narcissism. An epic knight may have a magnificent physique, but he is always seen through the eyes of his admiring male peers in the banqueting hall, in the council chamber or on the battlefield. Women barely figure in these places and therefore the epic hero's magnificence is without any sexual nuance. Here, for example, is Ganelon before the war-council of Charlemagne in *The Song of Roland*:[17]

> De sun col getet ses grandes pels de martre
> E est remes en sun blialt de palie;
> Vairs out [les oilx] e mult fier lu visage.
> Gent out le cors e les costez out larges
> Tant par fut bels tuit si per l'en esguardent.
>
> He has thrown back his great marten-fur from his neck and is left standing in his under-tunic of silk; his eyes are flashing and his face is haughty. His body is fair and his sides are broad. He was so fine that all his peers watch him.

'He was so fine that all his peers watch him'; this is a man seen by men. What a difference, then, if we move forward a century to encounter one of the earliest French romances, the *Roman de Horn* of c. 1170. Here is a man whose beauty is seen through the eyes of a woman who desires him to distraction:[18]

> [Rigmel] pense de Horn, ki ele tient trop fier,
> . . . .
> 'Cheveus ad lungs e blois, que nul n'en est sun per;
> Oilz veirs, gros, duz, rianz, pur dames esgarder;
> Nies e buche bien faite pur duz beisiers prester . . .'

---

16 Zeydel, op. cit., pp. 110-3.
17 F. Whitehead, ed., *La Chanson de Roland* (Basil Blackwell, 1970), lines 281-5.
18 M.K. Pope, ec., *The Romance of Horn by Thomas*, 2 vols., Anglo-Norman Text Society (Oxford 1955 and 1964), 1, lines 1250, 1255-7. Compare lines 1050ff where Horn's beauty is described as radiant and angelic. On the presentation of the hero in this poem see J.D. Burnley, 'The *Roman de Horn* and its ethos', *French Studies*, 32 (1978), pp.385-97.

Lady Rigmel thinks of Horn, whom she thinks too proud,
....
'He has long blonde hair so that none can equal him; he has blue eyes, large, sweet and laughing to look upon ladies; he has a fine nose and mouth to give kisses...'

We have become so accustomed to regard 'courtly love' as a male idealization of female beauty that it may come as a surprise to find, here in the first generation of French romance, an idealization of male beauty as seen by a woman. Yet it is this new awareness of male sexuality and narcissism which underlies the courtly cult of love.

And, of course, the courtly cult of music. For the musicologist the most striking aspect of Horn is not his physical beauty but the way in which his sexual attractiveness centres upon his musical accomplishments. Horn is a skilled harpist.

The author of the *Roman de Horn* builds an extended episode around his hero's musical abilities. In a royal chamber, 'strewn with flowers, yellow, indigo and vermillion', Horn gathers with some other young courtiers for entertainments. He is travelling incognito. At one point a harp is called for and Lenburc, the Irish princess, begins to play. Having performed several pieces, she remarks that she has heard a magnificent *lai* but that she only knows half of it. Eventually the harp passes to Horn; needless to say he knows the song and to the astonishment of all the company he begins to sing and play it with surpassing mastery:[19]

```
Lors prent la harpe a sei,        qu'il la veut atemprer.
Deus! ki dunc l'esgardast         cum la sout manïer,
Cum ces cordes tuchout,           cum les feseit trembler,
Asquantes feiz chanter            asquantes organer,
De l'armonie del ciel             li poüst remembrer!
Sur tuz homes k'i sunt            fet cist a merveiller.
Quant ses notes ot fait           si la prent a munter
E tut par autres tuns             les cordes fait soner:
Mut se merveillent tuit           qu'il la sout si bailler.
Et quant il out (is)si fait,      si cummence a noter
Le lai dont or ains dis,          de Baltof, haut e cler,
Si cum sunt cil bretun            d'itiel fait costumier.
Apres en l'esturment              fet les cordes suner,
Tut issi cum en voiz              l'aveit dit tut premier...
Tut le lai lur ad fait,           n'i vout rien retailler.
```

Then he took the harp to tune it. God! whoever saw how well he handled it, touching the strings and making them vibrate, sometimes causing them to sing a melody and at other times join in harmonies, he would have been reminded of the heavenly harmony. This man, of all those that are there, causes most wonder. When he had played his notes he made the harp go up so that the strings gave out completely different notes. All those present marvelled that he could play thus. And when he had done all this he began to play the aforesaid lai of Baltof, in a loud and clear voice, just as the Bretons are versed in

---

19 Pope, op. cit., lines 2830–44.

such performances. Afterwards he made the strings of the instrument play exactly the same melody as he had just sung; he performed the whole lai for he wished to omit nothing.

The problem of what the author means by a *lai* need not concern us here;[20] what matters is that it is clearly a song (Horn both sings and plays during the performance) inspired by love (Horn's love for Rigmel) and composed by a nobleman. The whole episode seems to assume a milieu where there is an intense interest in new songs and their composers. When the Irish princess Lenburc announces that she has heard a marvellous *lai* the response from the young courtiers gathered in the chamber is immediate: 'God! If I might only hear it', exclaims one; 'who composed it, fair sister?'[21]

The *Roman de Horn* was composed around 1170. It is surely no coincidence that this is almost exactly the period of the first trouvères? The story of Horn – and there are others like it – seems to mediate a contemporary interest in the composition of love-songs by well-born composers – we immediately think of trouvères such as Conon de Béthune and the Chastelain de Couci. These tales show how closely their lyric art must have been involved with the male narcissism which lies at the root of chivalry and 'courtly love'. They are an unexplored deposit of the art of the trouvères.

3 ELOQUENCE

We have glanced at the theme of narcissism; in the twelfth century, or so I have suggested, the revolutionary notion of the warrior as one whose ardour for honour was embroiled with his sexual allure brought musical skills, and particularly love-song, within the scope of warrior accomplishment. This brings us to our second theme: eloquence. How did the new cult of song-making and courtesy grow out of the old martial ethos of epic?

Part of the answer may lie in the cult of eloquence. Here we must retrace our steps to *The Song of Roland* and the threshold of the twelfth century. If we turn back to the years around 1080 and to the most famous of the French epics we find that Roland is *proz*, headstrong and brave, whilst his friend Oliver is *sage*, wise and circumspect. Now it is almost exactly at this time – the end of the eleventh century – that the adjective *prudens*, 'wise', becomes by far the most popular epithet to join to the word *miles* in Latin narrative texts.[22] In other words the ideal knight of c. 1100 was closer to Oliver the *sage* than to Roland the *proz*.

How did the knight develop and display his *sagesse*? Above all, I suspect,

---

20 I deal with this question at length in *Voices and Instruments in the Middle Ages* (forthcoming).
21 Pope, op. cit., lines 2788–9.
22 This contrast is discussed in Alexander Murray's richly discursive book *Reason and Society in the Middle Ages* (Oxford, 1978), pp. 125–7.

in the soundness and the eloquence of the counsel which he gave his feudal lord. In *The Song of Roland* the pagan king Marsilie calls upon his dukes and counts for counsel:[23]

> Cunseilez mei ... mi savie hume

and the poet dwells upon the *sagesse* of the pagan warrior Blancandrins: 'He was one of the wisest pagans; he was a knight well-endowed with the qualities of a vassal; he was a man of valour to serve his lord'.[24]

In some measure, I suggest, the lyric art of the troubadours and trouvères began as a transference of the chivalric eloquence which a knight was expected to display before his male peers into the realm of leisure passed in mixed company. In some chivalric narratives both kinds of eloquence are associated. In the epic of *Folque de Candie*, for example, Thibaut is said to be *amez de dames et sages de plaidier*: 'loved by ladies and wise in pleading a case'.[25] And why is Thibaut loved by the ladies? Because, as the author explains elsewhere, of his *beles paroles*, his attractive eloquence.[26]

The fictional figure of Thibaut is given some historical dress in Conon de Béthune, the knightly trouvère who was active in the late twelfth and early thirteenth centuries. In 1203 we find him conducting delicate negotiations at Constantinople on behalf of the Crusaders; he was chosen, it seems, because he was *sage ... et bein emparlez*; 'wise ... and most eloquent'.[27]

4 A NEW SONG ARRIVES AT COURT

It is time to manoeuvre a little closer to the milieux where the songs in the troubadour and trouvère chansonniers flourished. As we turn the pages of those manuscripts we are left with a puzzling sense of being close to the world in which the songs thrived and yet far away from it. They leave us wondering about the circumstances in which courtly interest in lyric art was fostered and maintained. Did minstrels and trouvères take these songs from court to court? Did the arrival of a new song create a stir of anticipation and lead to a flurry of questions about its composer? If so, has all this activity left any imprint outside of the chansonniers? I believe it has left a marked impression upon chivalric romance.

A striking example is provided by the prose romance of *Guiron le courtois*, composed in the first half of the thirteenth century. An extensive episode

---

23 Whitehead, *La Chanson de Roland*, line 20.
24 Ibid., lines 24–6.
25 O. Schultz–Gora, ed., *Folque de Candie*, 3 vols. (Dresden etc. 1909, 1915 and 1936), 2, p. 2 line 9899.
26 Ibid., line 12512.
27 J.E. White Jr. ed., *La Conqueste de Constantinople* (New York, 1968), p. 90. Cf. p. 69.

in this romance relates how Meliadus, the father of Tristan, composes the first *lai* that was ever made (again, the precise meaning of this term does not matter here) in honour of the queen of Scotland whom he loves. Meliadus reveals his plight to one of his knights, a friend since childhood and the most gifted harpist in the world after himself. The knight immediately offers to learn the *lai* and then to travel to Arthur's plenary court and perform it to the queen of Scotland as a confession of love. Meliadus agrees to this plan and the knight learns the *lai*.[28]

Here, surely, is a literary mediation of the jongleurs who sometimes learned and transmitted the songs composed by troudadours and trouvères?[29]

The story then relates how the knight travels to the court of King Arthur. Once there he begins to stir up excitement over the arrival of a new song at court. First, he tells the queen of Scotland that Meliadus has composed a song in her honour; 'tomorrow I will harp it myself before you', he assures her, 'in the full court'.[30] Next, he seeks out Sir Gawayn, a connoisseur of *noveax chant*:[31]

---

28 London, British Library, MS Add. 12228, ff.218–219. *Guiron le courtois* has not been published in modern times and the early printed editions are not adequate for the present purposes. The surviving manuscripts of the work are fully catalogued in R. Lathuillère, *Guiron le Courtois* (Geneva, 1966). MS Add. 12228 is of special interest in that the musical scenes of the romance are lavishly illustrated with coloured miniatures. For an example see *The New Grove* sv. 'Performing practice'.

29 The best-known examples of such minstrels are those mentioned in the (mainly thirteenth-century) *Vidas* or 'Lives' of the troubadours. See J. Boutière and A.H. Schutz, eds., *Biographies de Troubadours*, 2nd edition (Paris, 1973), including pp. 39 (Guiraut de Borneill), 68 (Bertran de Born). For a striking northern example see J.E. Matzke and M. Delbouille, eds., *Le Roman de Castelain de Couci et de la Dame de Fayel par Jakemes*, Société des Anciens Textes Français (Paris, 1936), lines 356–420.

There is a similar episode to this one from *Guiron le Courtois* in the hitherto unpublished section of the *Roman de Perceforest*, probably composed between 1330 and 1350. Lionnel, a knight, composes the words of a *lai* which he wishes all *vrays amans* should know. A minstrel-harpist approaches Lionnel and offers to compose music for it so that it may be sung 'in many assemblies and in many a noble celebration'. Lionnel agrees, requesting that the music should match the *pitoiable* mood of the poetry. This the minstrel does: '*Sire*' [says the minstrel] '*vous promets que se vous le me voulez aprendre, au plaisir du dieu souverain, je le feray ancores jouer en mainte assemblee et en mainte noble feste*'.

'*Par ma foy, mon amy*', dist Lionnel, '*je te diray voulentiers les motz mais il n'a point de chant, et se tu en vouloies faire ung pitoiable comme est le dit, je t'en scauroie bon gre*'.

'*Certes, sire*', dist le menestrel, '*je le feray voulentiers*'. *Adont le preu Lionnel lui dist les moz du lay tant de fois qu'il le sceut par coeur. Ce fait, le menestrel tira sa harpe hors du fourreau et fist dessus ung chant . . . pitaux*, . . . British Library, MS Royal 19 E. iii, f. 139v.

30 *Demain le harperai ge devant vos meesmes en pleine cort*. British Library, MS Add. 12228, f. 220v.

31 '*Missire Yvayn, vos qui tant vos alez delytant en noveax chant, ge vos promet que vos porriez demain oir un chant novel tout le meillor et le plus dolz et le mielz acordant que vos onques oissiez jor de vostre vie*'.

'*Ha! por Deu*', *fait missire Yvayn*, '*quant il est si bons, or me dites qui le fist, se Dex vos doint bone aventure*'.

'*Certes*', *fet il*, '*le meillor chevalier del monde le fist, ce est li rois Melyadus de Loenoys . . . demain le porriez vos oir apres hore de manger*'. Ibid., ff. 220v–221.

> 'Sir Gawayn, you who delight in newly-composed songs, I promise you that you may hear one tomorrow, the best and the sweetest that you have ever heard in your life.'
> 'By God', cried Gawayn, 'since it is so good, tell me who composed it'.
> 'Certainly', said the knight, 'the best knight in the world composed it, that is to say Meliadus of Leonnois . . . you may hear it tomorrow'.

Sir Gawayn is so excited by the arrival of a new song at court that he goes directly to a lady gifted with a fine voice and takes her aside to give her the news:[32]

> He said to her, smiling: 'Tomorrow a new poem and a new melody will come to court, the best and the finest that has ever been brought here . . . the best knight in the world composed it. If you could hear it first and teach it to me I would be your knight, so God help me!'
> 'Tell me', said she, 'who has brought it to court? Is he a knight or a minstrel or a harper?'
> 'Indeed', he replied, 'it is a knight of Leonnois, a knight of King Meliadus who sings extremely well'.

We are deep in the realm of Arthurian fiction here and yet the world of the contemporary trouvères could scarcely be closer. These passages provide a literary image of 'grass-roots' activity in the world that nourished the art of courtly monody in France. They show us the great appetite for *noveax chant* (the phrase recalls countless trouvère poems); the aristocratic trouvère; the emissary who learns the song and carries it to a court and stirs up excitement over its arrival; the eagerness to know who composed the new piece; the impatience to acquire the song for one's own repertory ('if you could hear it first and teach it to me I would be your knight, so God help me!'); the careful distinction between words and music ('tomorrow a new poem and a new melody will come to court') implying a connoisseurship of each; the interest in the social condition of the singer who brings the song ('Is he a knight or a minstrel'?); the keen sense that the performance of the song is a forthcoming attraction that will be performed at an appointed time before 'the full court'. We are looking through the chansonniers here to the chambers, corridors and galleries of thirteenth-century France where the art of the aristocratic trouvères was cultivated and enjoyed.

* * *

So far I have been treating Old French fiction as if it were an enormous stained-glass window with panels of clear glass revealing the world

---

32 . . . *li dit tout en riant: 'Demain vendra a cort un dit novel et un son novel tout le meillor et le plus mielz dit que onques fust aportez a cort . . . le plus meillor chevalier del monde le fist. Se tu puissiez ore faire que tu la preissez premierement et puis la me feisses savoir, ge seroie ton chevalier, se Dex me doint bone aventure'.*
'Or me dites', fet ele, 'qui est cil qui la porte a cort, est il chevaliers ou jugleor ou harpeor?'
'Certes', fait il, 'il est chevaliers et est de Leonoys, et est chevaliers del roi Melyadus et chante molt bien, se sai ge bien veraiement car je l'ay oi'. Ibid., f. 221.

beyond. Now it is time to step back and consider the pattern which all the panels form. I wish to suggest that many passages from chivalric fiction are closely akin to one-another, both on the level of narrative content and of verbal technique. In other words there are certain genres of musical reference in Old French fiction and each individual passage may be seen as a mobilization of the conventions of the genre.[33] By identifying these genres we are able to deal with this narrative material in a systematic way and to answer precise questions about individual passages: are there other passages like this one? how does this one differ from its fellows? and so on. The search for these motifs leads into as dense a forest as ever beset Sir Gawayn, strewn with more than a million lines of verse and prose. I can only hope to reach a high vantage-point and to discern where the tracks lie.

The main path seems to divide references which offer a generalized view of a multifarious activity from references which offer a more particularized view of a specific activity. An example of the generalized view might be a list of musical entertainments offered at a feast, and examples of the more particularized view would include descriptions of solo minstrels performing. These two types of 'view' – the generalizing and the particularizing – are not watertight categories; indeed, they are not really categories at all but only expressions of the two most fundamental patterns in the material.

We are in the depths of the forest already and it is time to go hunting for examples. The Appendix presents a typology of some principal genres of musical reference in epic and romance setting them out in relation to what I call the 'Reviewing Register' (a generalized view of a multifarious activity) and the 'Focusing Register' (a more particularized view of a specific activity). The list opens with a genre which offers the most common and stable manifestation of the generalized view, THE FEAST. Here is a characteristic and influential example, from Chrestien's romance of *Erec*, probably composed in the 1170s:[34]

> Quant la corz fu tote asanblee,
> ...
> An la sale grant joie ot;
> chascuns servi de ce qu'il sot;
> cil saut, cil tunbe, cil anchante
> li uns sifle, li autres chante,
> cil flaüte, cil chalemele,
> cil gigue, li autres vïele...

---

33 I am steering close here to some of the work on formulaic and oral-formulaic composition in medieval literature. See particularly D.H. Fry, 'Old English Formulaic Themes and Type-Scenes', *Neophilologus*, 52 (1968), pp. 48–54.
34 M. Roques, ed., *Erec et Enide* (Paris, 1952–3), lines 1983, 1987–1992.

> When the court was assembled ... there was great celebration in the hall; each [minstrel] offered what he knew how to do; he leaps, he tumbles, he conjures, one whistles, the other sings, he flutes, he plays the reed-pipes, he plays the *gigue*, another fiddles ...

There is implicit hyperbole here, for although Chrestien does not exaggerate at the level of the individual phrase the cumulative effect of the passage is to evoke a feast so abundant and so luxurious that it almost defies description in discursive terms. Therefore Chrestien declines to describe it and contents himself with listing its parts. His use of asyndeton ('he leaps, he tumbles, he conjures') evokes a narrator who is so delighted with what he sees on every side that a more circumstantial description is beyond his powers, and this sense of multifarious grandeur is heightened by parataxis; when Chrestien records that 'he leaps, he tumbles, he conjures', without indicating the sense relations between the three phrases, we cannot tell whether the actions of leaping, tumbling and conjuring happen together and at the same time, or happen apart and at different times; our minds resolve the problem in favour of a vague sense that everything is happening in a single, magnificent moment, which is exactly what Chrestien wants. He also reinforces our sense of vague splendour by declining to name anyone; the entertainers are evoked by distributive pronouns ('he does X ... he does Y' and so on) in another deliberate evasion of detail.

Chrestien's aim seems to be to reinforce the association between lavish entertainment, including music, and the excellence of courtly civilization – an association which is so fundamental to the place of music in romance that the language of FEAST passages (and there are very many of them)[35] tends to settle into a series of signals and formulas. The relation between the narrative voice and what is being described, for example, usually resolves into a direct relation between spectator and spectacle; formulas such as 'there you might have heard ...' sustain the fictional implication that the narrator is only reporting what he experienced and that his account of the feast is therefore an authentic one. In the same way the lists of musical entertainments usually adhere to a consistent plan: they generally follow a meal and are therefore often signalled by some such formula as 'when the meal was over ...', or 'when the table cloths were lifted away ...' (see Appendix, 1:3).

The majority of musical references in Old French fiction follow some broadly similar pattern to the lines from *Erec* which we have just examined: they provide a general picture of some splendid or admirable event; they evade giving precise details in an attempt to evoke a magnificence which defies discursive description; their language is in some measure formulaic and cannot be tacitly assumed to record a fresh perception of contemporary reality.

---

35 For examples see Faral, op. cit., Appendix 3, numbers 60, 63, 92, etc.

In contrast to such passages there are others of a different order which can be more quickly described in that they focus upon some particularized action. Some examples are provided by section 4 of the Appendix, SINGING ON HORSEBACK. This is a common genre of reference in both epics and romances, and the example quoted at the head of section 4 is a representative one:[36]

> Thus Boefs mounts his swift palfrey ... all a-singing he begins to ride.

These two lines focus upon a single, closely-defined sequence of actions. There is no time for the pervasive hyperbole of Feast passages and the veil of anonymity, so impenetrable in passages of the Feast type, is lifted; the protagonist is named in the first line (as in five other references in this set; see Appendix, 4:9). There is little sign of stereotyped diction or syntax.

Those lines about Boefs de Haumtone – 'Thus Boefs mounts his swift palfrey ... all a-singing he begins to ride' – are not particularly interesting (save in that they suggest, as do many other passages, that a great deal of musical life was lived on horseback during the twelfth and thirteenth centuries). Yet by laying the reference to Boefs alongside similar passages we are able to isolate the ones which *are* interesting. This is what I have attempted to do in the Appendix under the number 4:9. As we compare the extracts assembled there it becomes clear that one of them takes a decisive step beyond the conventional boundaries of its genre: the lines from the epic of *Les Quatre Fils Aymon*:[37]

> Aallars and Guichars begin a *son*, the words were from Gascony and the music from the Limousin, and Richars provides a fine *bordon* beneath. One can hear them from a long way off. There is no *rote, viele* or *psalterion* that would have pleased you as much as these three barons.

We are prepared for the idea of a band of men singing together as they ride: we encounter it in *Les Narbonnais* and in *Claris et Laris*. We are also prepared for the music they sing to be called a *son*. But the author breaks the mould of the genre when he reveals that the words of the song are from Gascony, that the music is from the Limousin (the lands around Limoges), and that one of the three men accompanies the other two by singing a *bordon* underneath their melody. If the epic of *Les Quatre Fils Aymon* dates from the late twelfth-century, as is commonly believed, then this would seem to be the earliest known reference to concerted singing involving the term *bordon* (here in verbal form).[38] Presumably the author is describing some kind of unwritten polyphonic practice?

36 A. Stimmung. ed., *Der Anglonormannische Boeve de Haumtone*, (Halle, 1899), lines 863 and 865.
37 F. Castets, ed., *La Chanson des Quatre Fils Aymon* (Montpellier, 1909), lines 6599–6604.
38 For a comprehensive collection of literary references in which the term *bordon* (in various forms and spellings) appears, see B. Trowell, 'Faburden – New Sources, New Evidence; a Preliminary Survey', in E. Olleson, ed., *Modern Musical Scholarship* (Stocksfield etc, 1980), pp. 28–78.

A second example of a reference which reaches beyond the confines of its genre carries us forward to written repertory. Section 6 of the Appendix embraces performances by solo minstrels. Often there is some passing reference to what is performed in these contexts,[39] but a passage from the thirteenth-century romance of *Claris et Laris* is exceptional for the way it describe's the minstrel's performance routine. At one point in this romance knights and ladies listen to a minstrel in the open air:[40]

> La escoutoient bonement
> .I. conteor, qui lor contoit
> Une chançon et si notoit
> Ses refrez en une viele,
> Qui assez iert et bonne et bele.

> There they listened attentively to a minstrel, who sang them a song and performed the refrains on his fiddle which was both good and beautiful.

This *chançon* with its refrains may be a rondeau (or some similar form), and this deduction seems to be reinforced by certain features in the poet's description of the scene. The minstrel performs *En mi* . . . *d'une praierie* which is near *la rive de mer*, and both of these phrases are key registral terms in the thirteenth-century repertory of rondeaux and simple refrain songs. Compare the following incipits of lyrics quoted in Jean Renart's *Guillaume de Dole*:[41]

> C'est la jus *en la praele*
> C'est la gieus *en mi les prez*
> Sor la *rive de mer*
> Mignotement alez
> Tout la gieus, *sor rive mer*

This is not to claim that the author has scattered clues to the nature of the minstrel's song here and there in his account of its performance, only that his imaginative apprehension of this musical scene is impregnated with poetic formulae which suggest that the *chançon* is a monophonic rondeau or virelai such as *C'est la gieus en mi les préz*, whose music has survived (Ex. 1).[42] These few lines may be our only guide to the way in which such songs were performed with instruments during the thirteenth century. I take it that the fiddler is singing the song and doubling the refrains upon his fiddle (perhaps sustaining a drone all the way through; some such technique is

---

39 For some examples of references belonging to this genre see Faral, op. cit., Appendix 3, numbers 59a, 109, 172c etc.
40 J. Alton, ed., *Li Romans de Claris et Laris* (Tübingen, 1884), lines 9940–3.
41 F. Lecoy, op. cit., lines 1846ff; 5440ff; 2523ff;
42 F. Gennrich, *Rondeaux, Virelais und Balladen*, 2 vols., Gesellschaft für Romanische Literatur, 43 (Dresden, 1921 and Göttingen, 1927), 1, p. 10.

Ex. 1: C'est la gieus en mi les préz

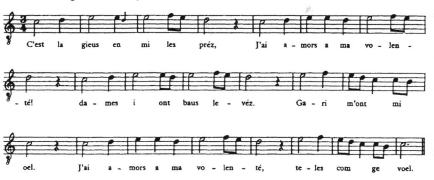

implied by Jerome of Moravia's account of the tuning of the fiddle in his *Tractatus de Musica*).[43]

As they are inventoried in the Appendix, each of these genres of musical reference comprises a set of universal conditions: 'if X then Y, but not Z': if a courtly amateur plays an instrument in public then, if male, he will often be travelling incognito or about some subterfuge, and so on. In other words the presentation of musical life in chivalric fiction is subject to a complex set of rules. How are we to read these patterns, and what is their deep structure? I would like to close with three themes which seem to me to run deeply through the whole corpus of material assembled in the Appendix.

A monophonic universe. In recent years musicologists have repeatedly stressed that monophonic music was the staple fare in both secular and sacred contexts throughout the Middle Ages.[44] Chivalric fiction bears this out, for in more than a million lines of narrative material the existence of polyphony is scarcely even acknowledged.[45]

Chivalric integrity. In many ways the position of any *chevalier* who was not a great lord was akin to that of the *jongleur*: both relied upon the generosity of their masters and were in competition for their surplus spending power.[46] The *chevaliers* were thus inclined to insist upon their social superiority and to avoid any taint of minstrelsy in their own behaviour. Chivalric fiction seems to embody an anxiety within the knightly class that the musical

---

43 C. Page, 'Jerome of Moravia on the *rubeba* and *viella*', *Galpin Society Journal*, 32 (1979), pp. 77–98.
44 See D. Fallows, 'Specific Information on the Ensembles for Composed Polyphony' in S. Boorman, ed., *Studies in the Performance of Late-Medieval Music* (Cambridge, 1983), p. 109.
34 See note 9.
46 This point emerges with some clarity in certain Old Provençal narratives where liberal patrons are mentioned who are generous to both *cavayers* and *joglars*. See, for example, *Jaufre* (?c. 1170) in R. Lavaud and R. Nelli, eds., *Les Troubadours*, 2 vols. (Bruges, 1960–66), 1, p. 44, lines 79–84.

accomplishments proper to a courteous knight should not appear to diminish the gap between *chevalier* and *jongleur*. Thus there is often some kind of distance placed between the knight and the display of his musical powers. In the *Roman de Horn*, for example, the hero is travelling incognito and under an assumed name when he sings and plays the harp at court. In *Guiron le Courtois* we are not allowed to see King Meliadus performing his own *lai* to the harp; this is done by a knight on his behalf. In this same romance Gawayn is presented as a fine singer, but we do not see him perform; he only sings as he rides, expressing his fine state of physical and mental health in an un-selfconscious way. Women, on the other hand, frequently perform 'on stage' in *Guiron le Courtois*.[47]

Modesty, or rather something akin to Castiglione's cult of nonchalance, emerges as a crucial element in the knight's bearing when he shows his musical skills. In contrast to the minstrel who needed to vaunt his abilities, the knight required to be asked to perform. Horn does not play until he is asked, while the knight in *Guiron le Courtois* who performs Meliadus' *lai* makes a great show of modesty and will not consent to play until he is almost overwhelmed with requests to do so:[48]

> [The lady Orgayne] said to the knight: 'I have been told that you know how to sing and to play the harp; I beseech you, seeing these ladies present, that you show a little of the skill that you have acquired.'
> The knight, who wished that there should be more requests than that of the lady alone, replied that he no longer had any skill in singing. Then all the ladies entreated him, and when he saw that they asked him so earnestly, and that even the knights who were there did the same, he replied: 'then pass me the harp . . .'

Anti-intellectualism. On the whole, chivalric fiction looks askance upon the Liberal Arts, so important in contemporary clerical tradition. When they are mentioned they may be surrounded by an unmasculine, unchristian and even unnatural aura, being studied by women, by Saracen children, or by visitors from the seductive and dangerous world of faery. Such is the reflection which clerical learning and the Islamic contribution to Western science finds in the mirror of chivalric narrative.

As for reading and writing as accomplishments of the *chevalier*, they are hardly ever mentioned. There is a striking passage in *Maugis d'Aigremont*, an epic of the first half of the thirteenth century, where the hero is taught to *lire e chanter*, the pair of verbs habitually associated with the distinctive skills of the cleric.[49] I have no doubt that this poet wishes to present his

---

47 British Library, MS Add. 12228, ff.221v–222.
48 *[Orgayne] li dist: 'Sire chevalier, l'en m'a fait entendant que vos savez chanter et harper; ge vos pri que vos voiant cestes dames en faiciez partie de ce que vos en savez'.*
Li chevalier, qui voloit qu'il en eust autre priere que de la damoisele solement, respont qu'il navoit ore talent de chanter, et toutes les dames le prient adonc, et quant il voit qu'eles le prioient si ententivement, et li chevaliers meesmes qui illuec estoient le prient autresint, respont: 'Or me faites baillier cele harpe . . .'. Ibid., f. 222r.
49 P. Vernay, ed., *Maugis d'Aigremont* (Berne, 1980, lines 4361ff.

hero as a literate musician, for he even reinforces the idea with some technical terminology derived from music theory: Maugis can sing *par ordre de game*, 'according to the form of the gamut'.[50] Such terminology is almost unknown to chivalric fiction and it is no surprise to find that Maugis is taught these exotic skills by an inhabitant of the faery realm.

I end with a relatively modern writer, Gerard Manley Hopkins:

> Oh the mind, mind has mountains, cliffs of fall
> Frightful, sheer, no-man-fathomed.

The chivalric narratives of medieval France may sometimes reveal how music was performed: where, when, by whom and to what effect. As such they have some value as a record of performance-practice in the broadest sense of the term. But they are also a door into a vanished country of the mind, frightful in some ways and no-man-fathomed in many: the mind of the secular aristocrat whose thinking was not closely touched by the seven Liberal Arts of clerical tradition and still less by the Renaissance humanism that is our heritage. His was a mentality in which music was embroiled with a generous and extravagant ethic which, after salvation, was the greatest preoccupation of every twelfth and thirteenth-century magnate: the ethic of chivalry.

---

50 Ibid., line 637.
   I am grateful to Professor J.H. Marshall, Professor J. Stevens, Dr David Fallows, Laurence Wright, Régine Page and Ann Lewis for their comments upon the first draft of this paper.

APPENDIX

SELECTIVE TYPOLOGY OF MUSICAL REFERENCES IN FRENCH NARRATIVE FICTION TO 1300

The following typology describes some of the most important genres of musical reference in Old French fiction. It is based upon the following texts:

ROMANCES

Amadas et Ydoine
Athis et Prophilias
Attila
Beaudous
Le bel inconnu
Blancandrin et l'orgueilleuse d'Amour
La Chastelaine de Vergi
Le chevalier au lion (Yvain)
Le chevalier de la Charrete
Li chevaliers as deus espees
Claris et Laris
Cligés
La Confrere d'amours
Le conte du Graal (Perceval)
Le court d'amours
Durmart le Gallois
Eledus et Serene
Eracle
Erec et Enide
Escanor
L'estoire del Saint Graal
L'estoire de Merlin
Fergus
Floire et Blancheflor
Floriant et Florete
Galeran de Bretagne
Gautier d'Aupais
Guillaume de Dole
Gille de Chyn
Gligois

Guillaume d'Angleterre
Guillaume de Palerne
Guiron le Courtois
Hunbaut
Ille et Galeron
Ipomedon
Jehan et Blonde
Joufroi de Poitiers
Kanor
Le lai d'Aristote
Le livre d'Artus
Le livre de Lancelot del Lac
La manekine
Meraugis de Portlesguez
Les mervelles de Rigomer
La mort le roy Artu
Narcisus
Partonopeu de Blois
Peliarmenus
Philomena
Piramus et Tisbé
Prose Tristan (read in Vienna 2542)
Protheslaus
Robert le Diable
Le roman d'Auberon
Le roman de Laurin
Le roman de Silence
Le roman de Thèbes
Le roman de Troie
Le roman de la Violette

EPICS

Aiol
Aliscans
Ami et Amile
Anseïs de Carthage
Anseÿs de Metz
Auberi le Bourgoin
Aye d'Avignon
Aymeri de Narbonne
Boeve de Haumtone
La bataille Loquifer

Garin le Loheren
Gaufrey
Gaydon
Gerbert de Mez
Girart de Roussillon
Girart de Vienne
Godefroid de Bouillon
Gormont et Isembart
Gui de Bourgogne
Hervis de Metz

Brun de la Montagne
La chanson d'Aspremont
La chanson de Godin
La chanson de Guillaume
La chanson des quatre fils Aymon
Le charroi de Nimes
La chevalerie d'Ogier de Danemarche
La chevalerie Vivien
Couronnement de Louis (verse redations)
Doon de Maience
Doon de Nanteuil
Doon de la Roche
Les enfances Guillaume
Les enfances Renier
Les enfances Vivien
L'entree d'Espagne
Fierebras
Floovant
Florence de Rome
Folque de Candie

Hugues Capet
Huon de Bordeaux
Jehan de Lanson
Jourdain de Blaye
Maugis d'Aigremont
Moniage Guillaume (verse redactions)
La mort Garin le Loherain
Les Narbonnais
Otinel
La prise de Cordres et de Sebille
Macaire
Prise d'Orange (verse redactions)
Raoul de Cambrai
Le siége de Barbastre
Tristan de Nanteuil
Voyage de Charlemagne
Yon

THE 'REVIEWING' REGISTER

1 THE FEAST

1.1 Essentially a listing of the musical (and other) entertainments offered at some courtly function,
1.2 usually a feast, and therefore in the hall,
1.3 and in this context often clearly signalled by some formulaic reference to the termination of the meal, often with *Quant* . . . or *Apres* . . .

> Quant les tables furent levees . . .
> Quant les tables ostees furent . . .
> Quant cho vint apres mangier . . .
> Apres disner i eut . . .
> Apres mengier . . .

1.4 The occasion of the feast is often a royal marriage (under the influence of *Brut* lines 10543ff and *Erec et Enide*, lines 1983ff)
1.5 The doings of professional entertainers, especially instrumentalists and singers, loom very large in these lists of entertainments at feasts. Many such lists are mainly strings of instrument-names (a rhetorical procedure acknowledged in Geoffrey de Vinsauf's *Ars Poetica* (c. 1200)).
1.6 However, many lists also include references to the doings of courtiers, primarily dancing (see 2.1–13), tale-telling, and (for the men) the playing of chivalric sports (such as fencing and jumping). In this case there may be moments of focus on specific activities.
1.7 There is a single, stable literary purpose for almost all such material: it emphasizes the luxury and abundance of the scene whilst reinforcing the image of the court as a stable point of departure and point of return for all 'romance experience'.
1.8 In accordance with this fixity of purpose there is a fixity of technique. Syntax is highly stereotyped and built of paratactic formulae, including the following, where (in the first four examples) a cultivated vagueness of sense – suggesting a feast so magnificent

24   that it all but defies description in discursive terms – is intensified by anaphora and asyndeton:

    li uns   VERB   li autres VERB
    cil   VERB   cil   VERB
    li alquant VERB   li plusor VERB

    la ot . . . . .   (la ot . . . . .)

    la oïssiez . . .
    la peüssies oïr . . .

1.9   The total effect of the entertainment and its music is often expressed by the formula

    grant joi/noise (de)mener

1.10 The formulae listed in 1:8 may introduce references ranging from a couplet to a dozen lines. There are other formulae allowing narrators to signal the presence of music in a single line, including:

    (et) VERB et VERB (et) VERB cil jongler

    Cantent et notent, vïelent chil jongler   Hervis de Metz 569
    Cantent et harpent, vïelent cil jongler   Hervis de Metz 7929
    e cantent et vïelent et rotent cil gugler   Voyage de Charlemagne 413
    e cantent et vïelent et rotent cil geugler   Voyage de Charlemagne 837

2 THE CAROLE

    Après disner i eut vïeles,
    Muses et harpes et freteles,
    Qui font si douces melodies,
    Plus douces ne furent oïes.
    Après coururent as caroles
    Ou eut canté maintes paroles.

                                            Jehan et Blonde 4761–4766

2.1 A dance performed by courtly amateurs and often mentioned in FEAST passages (1.1–10), often as an entertainment taken up when the company tires of the music offered by minstrels, or when the celebrations are carried beyond the hall and into the open air.
2.2 *Carole* references therefore often follow the material inventoried in 1.1–10 (as in the example from *Jehan et Blonde* quoted above).
2.3 The dance is often performed outdoors
2.4 to songs which the courtiers sing for themselves
2.5 and which may be accompanied by the instrumental music of minstrels.
2.6 Sometimes, but not frequently, the *caroles* seem to be purely instrumental and provided by minstrels (few texts can be securely interpreted to have this meaning).
2.7 The *caroles* are performed by a mixed company of men and women
2.8 or by women alone
2.9 and are especially associated with young girls (in numerous references the young girls

are said to dance *caroles* while the young men indulge in chivalric sports such as fencing).

2.10 As implied by 2.3, the ethos of the *carole* is predominantly 'pastoral', and it is associated with the freshness and candour of youth. Whence *caroles* are particularly associated with the younger (and perhaps probationary) members of courtly society and are often danced by *puceles, puceletes jouvenceles, meschines, escuiers, bachelers* and *vallets*.

2.11 *Carole* (verb *caroler*) is the most common word for dancing, although *danser, treschier* and *baler* are also used.

2.12 In the tradition of lyric-insertion established by Jean Renart's *Guillaume de Dole* some thirteenth-century romances give the texts (and occasionally the music) of these *caroles*, a degree of explicitness that carries such references away from the Reviewing Register towards the Focusing Register.

2.13 Occasionally the *carole* seems to take the form of a joyous train of courtiers, both male and female, moving across open country. Here the genre blends with the SINGING PARTY genre (3.1–6).

3 THE SINGING PARTY

A genre embracing several classes of reference where courtiers entertain themselves, often as part of a feast when the meal is over and some (or all) of the courtiers have either tired of the minstrels or have chosen this form of entertainment from the first.

3.1 In a group, indoors (in hall or chamber), or outdoors, courtiers sing
3.2 and dance *caroles* (never in the chamber)
3.3 and perhaps tell stories or read romances (the key verb being *conter*).
3.4 The entertainment may be mixed with references to chivalric sports
3.5 and may take place indoors or (perhaps more often) outdoors.
3.6 Large *caroles* danced outdoors to the singing of courtiers often blend with the motif of the journey or formal progress enlivened by instrumental music.

THE 'FOCUSING' REGISTER

4 SINGING ON HORSEBACK

> Boefs si en mounte le palefrei corser . . .
> Tretot en chantaunt comence a chivacher
>
> *Boeve de Haumtone* 863–5

4.1 Outside the *carole* (2.1–13) and the singing party (3.1–6) the courtly amateur rarely sings except when riding (for the singing of *lais* to the *harpe* see 5.1–10). The hero or some other important character (generally male) sings having just mounted his horse, or
4.2 sings during the course of a journey on horseback.
4.3 His song is commonly described as a *son*.
4.4 He may be holding a hunting bird.
4.5 Sometimes he is alone
4.6 and sometimes with others who sing with him (in which case the genre may blend with the SINGING PARTY 3.1–6).
4.7 By singing, the hero expresses his fine state of mental and physical health (in epics before the late 12th century)
4.8 and also his courtliness and amorousness of bearing (in romance, and in many of the later epics).

4.9 There may also be a powerful suggestion (at least in epic) that the singing protagonist is enjoying his last moments of light-heartedness before some disaster, and even that his singing is an expression of a false sense of security.

> Quant Gui l'entent, si ist de son donjon,
> En sa compengne son senechal Milon,
> Ostes et Dreues, que sont si compangnon.
> Es mulez montent, qui furent au perron,
> A l'ostel vindrent trestuit chantant un son,
> Et li frere se drecent.
>
> *Les Narbonnais* 1000–5

> Ferraus repaire et vait nontant .I. son,
> Et Amaufrois disoit .I. lay breton.
>
> *Gaydon* 7778–9

> Jolyvement chauntaunt comence a chevacher.
>
> *Boeve de Haumtone* 1144

> Parmi .I. bois s'en vont [no baron] chantant
> Et molt grant joie demenant.
>
> *Claris et Laris* 15319–20

> Gilles et tout si compeignon
> Vienent cantant une canchon.
>
> *Gille de Chyn* 533–4

> . . . vient [.i. chevalier] .i. esprevier paisant
> Et .i. noviel sonet cantant.
>
> *Mervelles de Rigomer* 15199–200

> Aallars et Guichars commenceront .i. son,
> Gasconois fu li dis et limosins li ton,
> Et Richars lor bordone belement par desos;
> D'une grande huchie entendre les puet on.
> Ainc rote ne viele ne nul psalterion
> Ne vos pleüst si bien comme li troi baron.
>
> *Les Quatre Fils Aymon* 6699–6604.

5 THE LAI/HARP COMPLEX

5.1 A courtly amateur
5.2 who is generally a protagonist or an important character in the narrative, is a gifted harpist
5.4 and harps pieces, in public, called *lais*,
5.5 and can usually compose them,
5.6 and often sings them to his/her own accompaniment.
5.7 There is a slot for some technical description of the performance, usually a tuning procedure.
5.8 The tale in which the courtly harper appears will normally have a 'Celtic' setting (Brittany, Cornwall, Wales; Arthurian Britain is a particular favourite)
5.9 and the harpist will often be in disguise when he performs (or be travelling incognito). This does not usually apply if the character is female.
5.10 If not a major protagonist of the tale the harpist will often be the messenger and ally of a protagonist, carrying his *lai* as a message or commemoration on the protagonist's behalf to one in a foreign realm for whom the *lai* has some special meaning.

6 THE SOLO PERFORMANCE

6.1 A solo musican, often a minstrel, performs. If a courtly amateur, then he/she is usually

6.2   a courtly amateur disguised as a minstrel for some purpose
6.3   or a character wrongly brought up as a minstrel following some tragedy, subterfuge or treachery following his birth,
6.4   or a character within the lai/harp complex (see 5.1–10).
6.5   If the solo performer is an instrumentalist, or a singer/instrumentalist, then the instrument will generally be a *viele* unless the reference falls within 5.1–10.
6.6   If the solo musician is a vocal performer without an instrument then he is usually a narrator of saints' lives or epic tales.
6.7   The genre provides a slot for some passing reference to what the musician plays (which may or may not be filled), and narrators seem to have been free to fill the slot as they wished.
6.8   A special sub-genre of references to courtly, amateur instrumentalists centres upon the private musician/retainer of Charlemagne in epic tradition (*Chanson de Guillaume* and *Aye d'Avignon*).

7 COURTLY ACCOMPLISHMENT

Many epic and romance heroes are praised for their accomplishments which are often itemized in detail.

7.1   In both Epic and Romance chivalric skills and sports (jousting, fencing, leaping etc) predominate in the lists of male accomplishments, and the main arts of peace are chess and draughts.
7.2   It is exceptionally rare for a male to be praised for an ability to sing or to read. References to a hero having mastered the 'vii ars' are also very rare, though rather more frequent in connection with women.
7.3   Outside of 5.1–10 (and of texts relating to Aristotle's education of Alexander) it is almost unknown for a male to be praised for instrumental skills; exceptions are *Florimont*, which is related to the Alexander material, the *Roman de Horn* and *Eracle* where, in both cases, the ability to play the harp is presented as a skill cultivated by the nobility of the past.
7.5   In accounts of female education and accomplishment both singing and playing are sometimes mentioned, and perhaps the seven Liberal Arts.

[2]

JOGLARS AND THE PROFESSIONAL STATUS OF THE EARLY TROUBADOURS

RUTH E. HARVEY

It has long been an accepted critical commonplace that there were two main types of troubadour: the talented, aristocratic amateurs for whom the art of *trobar* was a serious hobby, but additional to their mission in life, as Martin de Riquer puts it; and the vast majority of poets who 'had to make a living by their profession'.[1] The latter, in Occitan sources, are usually referred to as *joglars*, and a number of poets of the early twelfth century have, as a result of their association with this term, been described as 'professional performers'. Moreover, social considerations of rank, wealth, security and status, all of which are linked to the amateur–professional distinction, have played an important role in the modern interpretation of troubadour lyric poetry.[2] However, recent studies of what may be termed the 'cultural context' of the troubadour lyric indicate that a number of changes affecting the material existence of the troubadours may have taken place in the second half of the twelfth century, with the result that general conclusions which have been drawn regarding the professional status of twelfth- and thirteenth-century troubadours as a group may need to be refined and modified as far as the early generation is concerned.[3]

The purpose of this study is to re-examine the distinctions traditionally drawn between troubadour and *joglar*, with a view to nuancing current views of the earlier poets.[4] In particular, attention will be paid to the arguments and evidence underpinning the notion that men like Cercamon, Marcabru and Bernart Marti were full-time professionals, entirely dependent on artistic *mécénat*, and that they earned their livelihoods solely by composition and performance. The corresponding assumption, that Duke William IX of Aquitaine and Jaufre Rudel, prince of Blaye (or, later, Raimbaut d'Aurenga) were not professionals in this sense seems beyond dispute. Historical evidence indicates that these individuals were not dependent on rewards and gifts obtained through their songs, but, as cultivated, gifted amateurs who patronized other poets, they composed their own songs and sometimes performed them as well. However, as will be suggested later, this very knowledge of the troubadours who were also great lords may well be part of the problem facing modern interpreters.

In their studies of this question, scholars have drawn on the four principal types of evidence available to us regarding the status of the troubadours: (1) information supplied by the later *vidas*; (2) evidence from the compositions of the troubadours themselves and (3) from works (mostly songs) by other poets; (4) information garnered from historical documentation such as chronicles, charters, abbey necrologies and letters. The inferences which have been drawn from it may be summarized as follows. Although it is known that William IX sometimes performed his own songs himself and played the *histrio*, he was a great lord and therefore should be viewed as an amateur poet, as should Jaufre Rudel.[5] Both Marcabru and Cercamon were regarded by contemporaries as *joglars*: Aldric del Vilar calls Marcabru a *joglar* and Cercamon is thus described in his *vida*.[6] Cercamon can be and has been taken as a sort of *cas-témoin*: his name, itself seen as an indication that he was a *Spielmann*, showed, for his biographer, that he followed the wandering lifestyle of all *joglars*, and his dependence on rewards and the patronage of a powerful lord is expressed in his own songs, especially the *tenso* in which he laments the death of William X of Aquitaine.[7] Peire de Valeria was of unknown social origins, and his two surviving compositions contain no clue to his professional status, but his *vida* describes him as a *joglar*.[8] Although Alegret has no biography, his status as a professional is confirmed by his jongleuresque name and by Marcabru's attack on him for replacing, or attempting to replace, him in the favour of Emperor Alfonso VII.[9] Similarly, Bernart Marti has no *vida*. He refers to himself as 'lo pintor': while this could indicate his means of livelihood, it has been thought more likely to evoke Bernart's mastery of the *colores rhetorici*.[10] This poet is perhaps to be identified with the Bernart de Saissac to whom Peire d'Alvernha devotes a stanza of his literary satire, but no manuscript attributes any songs to Bernart de Saissac, and the suggestion remains a hypothesis.[11] It is not clear whether or not Marti was a 'professional'. Peire d'Alvernha was, according to his *vida*, the son of a *borges* and, while this is unverifiable, we have it from Bernart Marti that Peire had been a canon but abandoned this calling for *joglaria*.[12] Bernart de Ventadorn's two biographies present him as a man 'de paubre generacion', information which Uc de Saint-Circ claims originated with the viscount of Ventadour himself, and Peire mocks him for the same reasons in his 'galerie littéraire'.[13] Although Bernart's *vidas* do not employ the term *joglar*, critics have agreed in understanding him to have been of lowly birth and a poet who earned his living by his art.[14]

These conclusions are not atypical of received opinion on the matter of the troubadours' rank and status, and several critics have gone further in their interpretation of the terms. Marcabru and Cercamon are thought to have belonged to the generally despised class of itinerant *joglars*, and it has been suggested that they therefore sought to distinguish themselves from the mass of mere professional players. Some have considered the term 'troubadour' to be significant in this connection and suggested that its appearance implied the beginning of a process of differentiation, the singling-out of a particular type of *joglar*.[15] This type may have been a specialist in the noble art of *trobar* and, like 'Maïstre' Cercamon, would have received a clerical education which would have taught him to master the rules and norms of lyric composition.[16] While he may be distinguished by his training, the troubadour's songs are thought to show that he was still obliged to lead the same sort of life as the generality of *joglars*, one characterized by insecurity, impecuniosity and dependence on crumbs from the lordly table. These similarities have been cited to prove that there was little essential difference between a troubadour and a *joglar*. As Faral remarked many years ago:

> le trouveur, c'est simplement le jongleur considéré comme auteur. Aussi ne faut-il pas s'étonner que les deux titres aient bientôt pu s'employer indifféremment l'un pour l'autre. Tout trouveur qui faisait métier de poésie était jongleur et tout jongleur qui composait était trouveur.[17]

More recently, however, Ingrid Kasten has proposed a refinement to Faral's synthesis. On the basis that *joglars* were artists who made their living from their performances, irrespective of their social origins, their training, the content of their art or the place in which they performed, she concludes: 'Deshalb ist jeder Trobador, der seine Tätigkeit als Beruf ausübt, zugleich *joglar*'.[18] The term 'troubadour', in this context, would have artistic rather than social connotations.

Thus two categories of troubadour, conforming to the old amateur–professional division, have again been established. The second, *Berufsliterat*, type is identifiable because the *vidas* and/or songs include, in addition to an evocation of his ability to compose, a reference to him as a *joglar*, or one or more motifs which we are accustomed to associate closely with the figure of the professional player, such as attacks on other poets or references to gifts and rewards. This reasoning has enabled scholars to conclude that the second generation of troubadours already featured a number of 'professional poets'.[19]

This interpretation rests on a number of assumptions, however, not all of them very secure. First among these is the belief that, as was argued by Stroński, although the *vidas*' anecdotes concerning the poets' amorous adventures are purely fictional inventions, the data they contain regarding the origins and *état civil* of the troubadours are fairly accurate.[20] It has therefore been thought to follow that the biographers' references to their subjects as *joglars* are reliable indications of their status as professional poets and performers. That this assumption is unsafe, at least as far as the early troubadours are concerned, can be shown by the example of Peire de Valeria. His very short biography presents him as a contemporary of Marcabru ('el temps et en la sason que fo Marcabrus'), and says that he composed mediocre *vers* 'de foillas e de flors, e de cans e d'ausels'.[21] However, the two songs of reasonably certain attribution which have been preserved by the manuscripts do not feature any of these lyric elements. As de Riquer shows, the *vida* – found in MSS I and K – was based on a song by Arnaut de Tintinhac which I and K wrongly attribute to Peire.[22] This considerably reduces the weight which can be attached to the biography's other assertion that Peire was a *joglar*.

The case of Bernart de Ventadorn shows that neither is it safe to rely on the evidence of the *vidas* when their information is apparently supported by indications in the songs of other poets of the time. Peire d'Alvernha might have alluded to Bernart's father as a 'bon sirven' and said of his mother that she 'escaldava. l forn', but this is a humorous literalization of images of poverty and passion which Bernart employs in his own songs, and much the same process – that of reading literally what was not intended as factual reportage – was followed by the later biographers.[23] As Sarah Kay notes, the lyric motif of the *requête d'amour* induces all troubadours, whatever their social rank, to abase themselves before their *domna*, and Rita Lejeune has even uncovered the existence of a historical *Bernardus*, son of the viscount Eble III de Ventadour (1147–69), who was the cousin of Raimbaut d'Aurenga.[24] While it cannot be proved that this is the same person as the troubadour, it certainly indicates that Bernart should not be confidently classed among the base-born *Berufsdichter*.[25]

Of the other early troubadours under consideration here, Alegret and Bernart Marti do not have surviving biographies; that of Jaufre Rudel mythologizes the motif of the *amor de lonh*; Cercamon's is constructed almost entirely on the basis of his name; both Marcabru's biographies are based largely on material drawn from two of his songs; and William IX's *vida* contains a major genealogical mistake, although not much else in the way of information.[26] As Meneghetti has pointed out, this last, short biography may reflect the moralizing disapproval of the duke of Aquitaine expressed by many ecclesiastical sources, in that it describes William as an immoral deceiver. Interestingly, it includes the phrase 'he travelled through the world' ('anet per lo mon'), which is often applied to other poets, but this element is most probably intended to prepare the audience for William's 'red cat' poem.[27] In the *vidas* of other poets, however, scholars have been prepared to accept the statement 'anet pel mon' as a safe indication of an itinerant *joglar*'s lifestyle.

Increasingly studied as literary creations in their own right, the *vidas* and their relationship to the early poets are more profitably seen as elucidating the reception of their works by later generations. Eliza Ghil, for example, detects in the thirteenth-century *vidas* and *razos* expressions of a 'projet idéologico-littéraire' at the time of the Albigensian Crusade and the French occupation of the Midi: its aim was to draw all classes into identifying with the Occitan aristocratic *milieu* and values and to encourage the belief that, through the goodwill of the native, *lay* powers, even the most lowly born but talented poet could rise to a position of wealth, prestige and influence.[28] Such a political programme of social inclusiveness sheds a different light on the numbers of troubadours of supposedly humble origins who appear in the *vidas*. These short texts would be better considered as attempts to 'définir un statut du troubadour apte à traduire socialement la singularité de l'acte de *trobar*'.[29]

A second assumption involves the meaning of the word *joglar*. It is clear that this term, like *ioculator*, covered a multitude of different types of entertainer, and various authorities have attempted to establish sub-categories of *joglars*. One much-quoted subdivision was developed in the thirteenth century by Thomas of Chobham, who distinguished the more respectable, edifying singers and musicians from the disreputable rabble of rootless entertainers, whose dubious morals and deplorable associates were repeatedly condemned by the Church. Both Léon Gautier, in the nineteenth century, and Edmond Faral, in the twentieth, took this distinction as the basis for their influential studies of jongleurs.[30] Within the 'more respectable' group, Menendez Pidal differentiated those specializing in lyric minstrelsy from the jongleurs whose main strength lay in the performance of epic narratives.[31] While this has met with general critical accept-

JOGLARS AND THE STATUS OF THE EARLY TROUBADOURS

ance, there may be a number of exceptions or anomalies, such as Guiraut de Calanson's *joglar*, Fadet: he is urged to specialize in narratives, but is also enjoined to master a variety of musical instruments (stanzas 5–8), to know how to *trobar* (line 13) and, amongst other skills, to juggle and be a *simïer* (stanzas 4 and 11). Is this a serious portrait of a *joglar* hoping for entry to the royal court of Aragon (stanza 39), or rather a humorous exaggeration of what could be expected from an entertainer – like Guerau de Cabrera's earlier, immense list of all the works his ignorant minstrel ought to know?[32]

The lyric *joglar* is thought to be exemplified by the subject of Raimon Vidal's *Abril issia*, a work which illustrates the refinements, the general cultivation and the degree of social skills required of a courtly *joglar* at the beginning of the thirteenth century, and which thereby brings correctives to the image of the jongleurs, obtained from ecclesiastical sources, as vulgar, dishonest and damnable.[33] Although not explicitly credited with the ability to compose, this *joglar* is a singer of troubadour lyrics and also a courtier–companion. Part of what was expected of him was the ability to oil the wheels of cultivated social intercourse in the *familia* of a great lord and to contribute to the reputation of the court as a place of gracious living: it is his *saber* and *sen* in this connection that distinguish this character from the 'joglar volpil' (line 1054).[34] The tips the narrator gives him on how to conduct himself well and get on in court society involve observing discretion, good manners and developing a courtly shrewdness in managing the sensibilities of competitive, dependent *familiares*, for, as the narrator says:

> Dieu no fes segle tan ver
> vas malvestatz, c'us homs curos,
> adreitz e francx no.n traisses dos
> a se pujar e far valer
> si.n saup genh ni manieir'aver. (1195–9)

> God did not make this age so consistently bad that an ambitious, clever and frank man could not get gifts out of it in order to rise and make himself noticed, if he knew how to be clever and had the right manner.[35]

Smooth eloquence, clever manipulation of others and, ultimately, self-interest are also manifest in descriptions of Henry II's court given by the likes of Walter Map and Peter of Blois. *Curiales* and this *joglar* were subject to the same strains and deployed the same skills in pursuit of broadly the same aim of securing advancement at court.[36]

Raimon Vidal's *joglar* journeys from one seigneurial court to another across the Midi, and the narrator describes troubadours as having made their living by doing the same (755–61); but this detail, also mentioned in the *vidas* of Giraut de Borneil and Gaucelm Faidit, is presented essentially as a feature of the past.[37] The suggestion that, by *c.* 1210, this Golden Age of travelling troubadours and lavish patronage was gone forever is brought out by the *joglar*'s own words (188–221) and supported by the work of Maria-Luisa Meneghetti, who argues that the heyday was of short duration, lasting only for the last quarter of the twelfth century.[38] Thus, although *Abril issia* provides a view of the courtly experience of an itinerant *joglar* 'from the inside', as it were, it does so with reference primarily to the early thirteenth century and it sheds a retrospective, perhaps rosy, light on the circumstances of peripatetic troubadours of the *third* generation.

The term *joglar* also covers the eighty-one named specialists, identified by W. D. Paden, who, according to the evidence of the songs, were entrusted with conveying that song, mostly to a particular recipient. It would seem from this analysis that the majority of these *joglars* were associated with one poet only and that they received at best only a couple of songs from him during that poet's career. Their lyric minstrelsy should therefore be seen as a form of occasional service, one which brought the *joglar* rewards and remuneration, but not enough for him to live on.[39]

Joglar, then, is applied both to the despised, uncouth masses of entertainers and to specialized, occasional singers who served one troubadour, mostly only once, and who can thus be regarded as distinct from the poet–composer.[40] It includes the few men in this group, such as Cardalhac, who appear to have been literate, and it is also used of a number of troubadours. Some 34 of the surviving 101 *vidas* refer to their subjects as *joglars*, and this whether or not the poets are described as educated, or of knightly descent or background.[41] Some would like to see a different usage of *joglar* in the biographies: 'il est évident qu'ici l'antique *ioculator* n'entre pas en ligne de compte';[42] but it is clear from the above that, in itself, the term does not allow us to distinguish the skilled, respectable courtly performer from the dissolute riff-raff castigated by Matfre Ermengaud, or to differentiate between performers who made a living from minstrelsy and occasional, part-time artists.[43]

It seems unlikely, therefore, that the term can bear the weight which some scholars have tried to attach to its presence in the *vidas*. A figure described there as a *joglar* need not be a professional performer who made his living by his art. Even in the 1270s, as Guiraut Riquier's 'Supplication' to the King of Aragon shows, not enough of a terminological distinction was made between *joglars* and worthy troubadours.[44] Rather, *joglar* would seem to be a general, 'catch-all' term which could carry pejorative connotations, and this is probably the way in which it is used by some poets of their fellows.[45] Marcabru, for example, is called a *joglar* by Aldric del Vilar, and also by Uc Catola, in the poetic exchanges he carried on with these two men:[46]

> Quan tornaras
> segurs seras
> de seignor, et ieu de joglar, (xx, 40–2)[47]

says Aldric, at the end of a piece in which he has hurled insults at Marcabru. In his riposte, Marcabru is hardly any more reticent than his interlocutor, but how seriously were these exchanges intended? Surely they were just as likely to be games, staged to entertain an audience who knew how relaxed and close was the relationship between the two participants.[48] Marquis Lanza and Peire Vidal also exchanged vitriolic *coblas*: Lanza begins by calling Peire an ignorant, untalented, drunken fool, and opines that never did a greater coward carry a

JOGLARS AND THE STATUS OF THE EARLY TROUBADOURS

lance, nor a baser man put on spurs, but he does so using the metre of one of Peire's best-known songs, 'undercutting the show of hostility and transforming it instead into a public poetic tribute'.[49] Attacks such as these could be intended seriously and spitefully, as is probably the case in Guilhem de Berguedan's tirades against the bishop of Urgel, or Bertran de Born's slander of Alfonso II of Aragon: perhaps this is also true of Bernart Marti's charge that Peire d'Alvernha was false to God when he abandoned the canonical life to become a 'fols joglares', but the polemic context of these sorts of accusation hardly guarantees the factual reliability of their content.[50] The information they contain may be accurate, but should be treated with caution by the modern reader.

Equally, we should treat with caution Marcabru's attack upon Alegret in *Bel m'es quan la rana chanta* (poem XI). Recent work indicates that the interpretation of this passage is far less straightforward than was previously thought. Very close intertextual links between this song and Alegret's *Ara pareisson ll'aubre sec* suggest rather that Marcabru was wickedly parodying Alegret's composition, and these two men may have been involved, together with Bernart de Ventadorn and Raimbaut d'Aurenga, in a literary polemic concerning the Tristran legend.[51] This lyric context does not point exclusively to the conclusion that Alegret was nothing but a vulgar *joglar*.

The evidence from the Angevin realm indicates that jongleurs, while vulgar entertainers, could achieve a measure of security, even prosperity. Roland le Pettour was a *ioculator* who held of Henry II, by sergeanty, thirty acres of land, in return for the service of performing, every Christmas Day in the presence of the king, 'a leap, a whistle and a fart' ('saltum, siffletum et pettum' or 'bumbulum').[52] Should he be classed among the respectable or the disreputable entertainers? Like a number of Anglo-Norman or Angevin *ioculatores* mentioned in historical records, Roland was a landholder, therefore not of 'no fixed abode', and he thus possessed some degree of stability and status. Traces exist, from the Norman Conquest onwards, to suggest that 'minstrels had a recognised standing at court' and that some were established members of the household, rather than despised itinerants.[53] Peter of Blois, a disgruntled royal functionary writing gloomily to fellow-clerics, sheds further light on the composition of the travelling court of Henry II. He lumps together as court-followers, with entertainers such as singers, *histriones* and *mimi*, many people who had a recognized and useful position in the royal household, including heralds, barbers and waferers, who performed a function and also sang:[54]

> Quod si princeps praedixerit, se ad certum locum summo mane in crastino profecturum, sententia procul dubio mutabitur: ideoque scias eum usque ad meridiem dormiturum. Videbis summarios, sub oneribus exspectantes, silere quadrigas, dormitare praeambulos, mercatores curiae anxiari, omnesque invicem mussitantes. Curritur ad meretrices et tabernacularios curiales, ut inquiratur ab eis, quo princeps profecturus sit. Iloc enim genus curialium arcana palatii frequenter novit. Regis enim curiam sequuntur assidue histriones, candidatrices, aleatores, dulcorarii, caupones, nebulatores, mimi, barbatores – balatrones, hoc genus omne.

The distinction between *curiales*, clerks and troubadours would seem to be far from clear-cut. These groups had much in common. One of the most stimulating aspects of recent studies such as Kasten's is that they provide a survey of the court as the context of poetic activity, using the relatively well-documented Anglo-Norman and Angevin royal households as a model.[55] The abundant primary and secondary sources demonstrate that the *familia* 'd'un grand – sans parler du roi – était recherchée par toutes sortes de gens, laïcs ou clercs', direct vassals, poor knights, intellectuals, poets, ecclesiastics and simple clerks.[56] As the administrative machinery of government became more sophisticated, the need for literate, numerate servants increased and this provided many openings for educated, clever men, anxious to improve their prospects of material security and advance their careers. Some certainly were absorbed into the inner *familia privata* of the lord's household servants and confidants; others, maybe like Raimbaut de Vaqueiras later, became the close knightly companions of their masters.[57] What a troubadour could offer in addition to these services was that he composed and sang as well – surely an advantage in the search to obtain lordly favour.[58]

It has been suggested that educated men such as Marcabru and Cercamon may have exercised some administrative function in the households of the lords with whom they were associated, and the same may well apply to Bernart Marti.[59] Marcabru and Cercamon align themselves explicitly with the *soudadiers*, court dependants or retainers, and in their songs all three poets supply insights into the inner seethings of a seigneurial *familia*.[60] In Bernart Marti's case, he uses terms, topoi and motifs very similar to those employed by Latin court satirists. All apparently focus on the seamy side of the court as a 'theatre of intrigue and villainy, swarming with ruthless, fawning flatterers', and in his song *A, senhor, qui so cuges* Marti highlights the same kind of abuses: false eloquence and flattery; the scramble to acquire influence; unscrupulous, deceitful dealings; and grasping self-interest.[61] It has been suggested that the wicked *lengua-forcat* who are attacked here are untrained, amateur poets whose activities threaten the status and livelihood of 'full-time' professional troubadours, but the evidence for this is rather thin and it is more likely that Marti is criticizing successful *curiales* who certainly exercise some influence and perhaps even hold an office at a court which he frequented.[62] While it is not impossible that Bernart Marti and the others could have acquired their familiarity with the intrigues and workings of a magnate's household in the course of a career as a wandering *Berufsdichter*, they do not seem to have wandered very frequently, they themselves do not mention many patrons and, given Meneghetti's research on the relatively small number of centres of lyric patronage at this time, they would not have had many places to go to.[63] It is probably unnecessary to explain their contact with court life purely in terms of their poetic activity.

Since Cercamon's circumstances are so often held to exemplify the major characteristics of the life of a 'professional poet', it is worth examining his case in a little more depth.[64] It seems clear from his *tenso* with Guilhalmi that he was associated with the Church, for he begins his lament with an enigmatic complaint that the *clerzia* do not come to his aid, and Guilhalmi agrees that 'li clerc' (line 13) are no help to him.[65] It would be difficult to see why the clergy should be expected to extend their support to a professional poet who had just lost his secular patron, but if Cercamon were himself a *clerc*, his disappointment becomes more understandable. Guilhalmi addresses him repeatedly as 'Maïstre', and further indications that he received a clerical education are contained in his songs, but it is unwise to group him with or compare him too closely to the so-called wandering goliards who scraped a precarious living composing satirical Latin verses for a public of *litterati*.[66] In the first place, what evidence there is concerning the authors of this secular Latin poetry suggests that it was composed by 'hard-working, intellectually distinguished professional men', teachers, administrators and holders of posts who nevertheless portrayed themselves in their songs as wretched vagabonds.[67] Secondly, Faral describes a crisis in the clerical world, lasting throughout the Middle Ages and 'venant d'un développement exagéré de la classe cléricale, d'une diffusion d'une instruction qui ne trouvait pas son emploi',[68] but he was incorrect to see this as beginning as early as the eleventh century. The very late eleventh century and the first half of the twelfth may have witnessed a rapid expansion in the numbers of schools and educated clerks, but both Southern and Duby draw attention to the fact that this 'was because more and more careers were opening up for those who had finished their studies'.[69] In the generation following Cercamon, Peter of Blois may not have achieved the ambitious heights his training should have fitted him for, but he was not without a position.[70] It would not be before the end of the century that 'graduate unemployment' could be described as a problem. 'Maïstre' Cercamon, on the other hand, was in approximately the right place at the right time to profit from the early expansion in court administration which has been termed 'the managerial revolution' in twelfth-century Church and State.[71] Thirdly, the parallel between the early troubadours and goliards depends upon the evidence of ecclesiastical condemnations of the *clericus vagus, joculator* and goliard, and the problems involved in interpreting these pronouncements are considerable. While ecclesiastics' use of these Latin terms is not precise, *clericus vagus* and *joculator* are not synonymous, as Waddell's Appendix E seems to imply.[72] Moreover, sufficient attention is not always paid to the purpose and style of these condemnations: many display concern mainly for the decorum of the religious and clerical life, and the notion of the *joculator* introduced here can often serve as a symbol of instability, transgression of the norms and licence and can be applied to those who 'err' only figuratively, not literally.[73] Such condemnations become much more detailed and explicit in the thirteenth century and more clearly concern clerks who turned themselves into disreputable entertainers, but this dating is consonant with the indications of a crisis of graduates and jobs already noted. Furthermore, it can be no coincidence that this development also corresponds to the period of the earliest known *vidas* which assert of their subject that he abandoned his 'letras' or clerical calling and 'fetz se joglars', so that it could equally well be argued that the biographers are depicting a contemporary, thirteenth-century phenomenon and applying it to the early twelfth-century troubadours.[74]

Furthermore, to interpret the destitution implied in Cercamon's dialogue with Guilhalmi as uniquely the expression of a professional poet's loss of a reliable patron is to take too narrow a view, for nothing in the song demonstrates that the two men were discussing patronage of *trobar*. Given the all-important role of a personal relationship with the lord in mediaeval society, one could equally well ask who, of all William X's *maisnada*, agents, servants, household clerks and officials, would have felt sanguine about their future prospects in the April/May of 1137. The death of one's lord, especially one without a suitably 'adult' and male heir, spelled uncertainty if not disaster for all his followers, removing protection and security from everyone.[75] In a song devoted to his inability to get on in a harsh, competitive world, where only money and contacts count, Bernart Marti observes:

> Un non vey tan ric ni tan belh,
> No.s camge de tot son afar,
> Quan trop joves pert son capdelh
> Per qui deuria melhurar. (IV, 7–10)[76]

For the same reasons, it would be imprudent to interpret the references to gifts and rewards in this song as the remuneration a 'professional poet' could expect in return for his artistic services. In an attempt to cheer Cercamon up, Guilhalmi says:

> Car lo bos temps ve, so cre,
> Qe auretz aital guazalha,
> Qe vos dara palafre
> O renda qe mais vos valha,
> Car lo coms de Pieitieus ve. (VIII, 14–18)[77]

A horse, or income from land were indeed gifts made to *joglars*, along with riding-tackle, money, food, clothing and even appointment to an office, but these rewards were precisely those given by lords to all their retainers, agents, servants and officials, great or small.[78]

By virtue of his education, Cercamon may be different from the generality of untrained *joglars*, but this song does not prove that he shares their way of life. All that these lines indicate is that Cercamon seems to lead the life of any court dependant, including some *joglars*, but also including large numbers of other people. Cercamon can thus be described as a troubadour, in that he composed songs, *and* as a dependant, but it has not been clearly demonstrated that the gifts he hopes to receive are rewards given solely for his *trobar* performances.[79]

It must also be recognized that, as Kasten points out, there is no firm evidence that such 'professional poets' performed other functions, such as scribe, tutor, servant or messenger, which could secure their positions at court and enable them to survive through the 'morte saison' of winter, when few feasts were held and when there would presumably be little demand for their artistic services.[80] On the other hand, it is legitimate to ask how we would know if the troubadours did in fact hold such positions. Evidence of this kind would probably be supplied from non-literary sources, such as court records, charters and accounts.[81] Gérard Gouiran remarks of Bertran de Born, 'si on n'avait pour témoins que les écrits de Bertran, on resterait persuadé qu'il vivait dans un état proche de la pauvreté'; 'whereas in reality he was a baron holding fief directly from the Plantagenets'.[82] It is the historical sources that supply this corrective, complementary view of the lord of Hautfort and, of the hundred references to him in charters and chronicles, not one mentions his poetic activity.[83] It is therefore hard to see how one would start to look for traces of Marcabru, Cercamon and Alegret in the documentary records that have survived, since the use of pseudonyms would seem to doom such searches to failure, and very common first names make it unlikely that one would be able to identify one of the plethora of 'Bernardi' as Bernart Marti, or a 'Petrus' as Peire d'Alvernha.[84] Moreover, the documentary evidence is patchy, even for those figures one would have thought would have left some mark. Jaufre Rudel, for example, was a feudal lord of some importance, and yet hardly any historical trace of him survives.[85] If one turns to the songs themselves for enlightenment, two difficulties arise. First, it is not reasonable to expect the troubadours regularly or systematically to include such information about their non-lyric occupations in their songs; and, secondly, we would probably not believe them even if they did claim to have other resources or employment. Bernart Marti describes himself as 'lo pintor', but few critics have shown any inclination to give this credence, and it is not even known for sure whether his name was Bernart Marti or Bernart de Saissac.[86]

While it might be overstating the case to explain Bernart Marti's marginal position in the troubadour tradition and his small surviving corpus in terms of the time taken up by his 'day-job', his claim that he composes two or three songs a year strengthens the case for supposing that these troubadours had some other function or office at court.[87] The insistent reiteration of their stage-names by Marcabru, Cercamon and Alegret more than hints that these figures had other, 'real' names, another identity and a position in society other than the one to which their artistic roles allowed them to accede.[88] More is known of the aristocratic troubadours of this period, so we can be more confident that they had other functions in life, but it might well be that scholars have supposed that the little that is known of the Alegrets of that world was all that there ever was to know. The picture of Alegret as no more than a professional poet fits in with – because it has been determined by – a conception of the *joglar* which has been derived from sources spread throughout the centuries which constitute the 'Middle Ages' and which, at the time that the first influential research was done, may well have been influenced by an anachronistic, Romantic notion that the art of poetry was a Vocation, a noble and full-time calling which left no place for more mundane, bread-winning occupations.[89] As Vigny remarked of Chatterton, '[le poète] a besoin de *ne rien faire* pour faire quelque chose en son art. Il faut qu'il ne fasse rien d'utile et de journalier.'[90] A feudal seigneur may have had the leisure to indulge in lyric composition *en amateur*, rather as the gentlemen-scholars of the nineteenth century studied and published, but perhaps it has been too readily assumed that any other person must have been devoted to their art to the exclusion of all else. The rhetorical ploys exploited by the troubadours themselves encourage this view, for *chanter* equals *aimer*, and *aimer*, to be worth anything at all, has to engage 'cor e cors e saber e sen / e fors'e poder'.[91]

In this connection, it is worth noting that Martin Aurell has detected 'une professionnalisation de la poésie provençale' in the mid-thirteenth century, at the court of Raimon Berenguer V at Aix.[92] While he follows Köhler in seeing the troubadours of the first half of the twelfth century as belonging primarily to the knightly classes, from *c.* 1200 onwards 'des professionnels de la chanson, des jongleurs travaillant auprès du prince, remplacent des chevaliers dans la création de la lyrique occitane'.[93] While some scholars are arguing for the existence of professional poets from the beginning of the twelfth century, others consider their appearance to be a phenomenon specific to thirteenth-century Provence. The significant factor in the second case may be that prolific documentary sources exist to support Aurell's contention that those troubadours, 'comparés pour la plupart à des jongleurs, appartiennent au personnel subalterne de la cour',[94] whereas nothing of the kind assists enquiry into the status of the poets of the early twelfth century. Nevertheless, in the absence of any contemporary evidence either way, the phrase 'poets *and* professionals' might be a more prudent formulation to apply to the troubadours of the second generation.

It seems unlikely that the composers of the early troubadours' *vidas* were using the term *joglar* with quite the informed precision that scholars such as Stroński, Panvini and Kasten imply. The nobly born poets may not have been described as *joglars*,[95] but if the later biographers had some such important information about their subjects' social and political position, they could be expected to build on that to identify and characterize the poet in his *vida*, and only then to add that this lord also composed pleasing songs. It is very probable that, in the case of Marcabru, whatever his real rank may originally have been, all such data had been lost by the time the biographers came to compose his 'life': in their eyes, he was best known for his poetic activity and so that was how he was represented.[96] *Joglar* in such cases may have been merely a convenient general label, representing no more than an attempt to plug a gap in the biographer's knowledge. In other words, the way in which the early troubadours were seen by later generations, and by scholars today, is probably more a result of the understandably patchy survival of factual knowledge about these men, combined with a selective emphasis in the way in which they were subsequently depicted. An educated son of a rather unimportant family who held some undistinguished position in the household or in the budding bureaucracy of the counts of Poitou or Toulouse but who also had talents as a poet and performer would be likely to be remembered for his lyric achievements alone. To draw a perhaps inappropriate modern analogy: even in an age of ready access to information about individuals, posterity is not going to remember Philip Larkin primarily as the librarian of the University of Hull.

Dept of French and Bedford New College, RUTH E. HARVEY
University of London

JOGLARS AND THE STATUS OF THE EARLY TROUBADOURS

NOTES

This article is based on earlier papers read at the London Medieval Society and at the Sixth National Conference on Medieval Occitan Literature and Language (Girton College, 1991). I should like to thank the participants, particularly Dr Linda Paterson, for their helpful comments and suggestions.

[1] P. Dronke, *The Medieval Lyric*, 2nd edn (London, 1978), p. 20; M. de Riquer, *Los trovadores: historia literaria y textos*, 3 vols. (Barcelona, 1975), I, 23.

[2] See esp. the seminal studies by E. Köhler, selected and translated into Italian by M. Mancini, *Sociologia della 'fin'amor': saggi trobadorici*, 2nd edn (Padua, 1987), in particular the introduction (pp. xi–lvii); and, for revisions and reassessments, Simon B. Gaunt, 'Marginal men, Marcabru and orthodoxy: the early troubadours and adultery', MÆ, LXIX (1990), 55–72; S. Kay, *Subjectivity in Troubadour Poetry* (Cambridge, 1990), pp. 111–27, 132–70 (esp. pp. 112–15); I. Kasten, *Frauendienst bei Trobadors und Minnesängern im 12. Jahrhundert* (Heidelberg, 1986), pp. 88–141.

[3] See, e.g., M. L. Meneghetti, *Il pubblico dei trovatori: ricezione e riuso dei testi lirici cortesi fino al XIV secolo* (Modena, 1984), pp. 60–5, on the very limited number of courts associated with lyric poetry in the early twelfth century and the rapid expansion of centres of patronage and of numbers of poets from the 1170s onwards; and L. M. Paterson, *Medieval Occitan Society* (Cambridge, forthcoming), chapter on 'Courts and courtiers', who identifies signs of activity in various areas before 1160, but does not change Meneghetti's overall conclusions. I am very grateful to Dr Paterson for allowing me to read her work in advance of publication.

[4] The principal early poets to be considered here are: William IX, Cercamon, Marcabru, Jaufre Rudel, Alegret, Peire de Valeria, Bernart Marti, and, since their careers are thought to have overlapped with those of the 'second generation' of troubadours, reference will also be made to Peire d'Alvernha and Bernart de Ventadorn (see De Riquer, *Los trovadores*, I, 310, 342). Given the doubts which still subsist over the dating of Rigaut de Berbezilh, I have preferred not to include him in this study (see *ibid.*, I, 281–5; and the studies by Lejeune and Varvaro referred to there).

[5] For William IX, see the sources quoted in De Riquer, *Los trovadores*, I, 108 nn. 14 and 16; for Jaufre, see, e.g., Edmond Faral, *Les Jongleurs en France au moyen âge* (Paris, 1964), p. 75.

[6] See *Poésies complètes du troubadour Marcabru*, ed. by J. M. L. Dejeanne (Toulouse, 1909), poem xx, line 42; *Biographies des troubadours: Textes provençaux des XIIIe et XIVe Siècles*, ed. by J. Boutière and A. H. Schutz, 2nd edn (Paris, 1971), p. 9: 'E cerquet tot lo mon lai on el poc anar, e per so fez se dire Cercamons.'

[7] See *Il trovatore Cercamon*, ed. by V. Tortoreto (Modena, 1981), poem VIII (PC 112, 1); Kasten, *Frauendienst*, pp. 88–9. On jongleurs' names, see, e.g., Dronke, *The Medieval Lyric*, p. 20.

[8] See *Biographies*, ed. Boutière & Schutz, pp. 14–15.

[9] *Poésies ... Marcabru*, ed. Dejeanne, poem XI, lines 65–7, and see De Riquer, *Los trovadores*, I, 236–7; and, for the traditional interpretation of Marcabru's attack, see U. Mölk, *Trobar clus, trobar leu* (Munich, 1968), pp. 92–3.

[10] *Les Poésies de Bernart Marti*, ed. by E. Hoepffner (Paris, 1929), poem IV, line 38. See Kasten, *Frauendienst*, p. 101; and cf. De Riquer, *Los trovadores*, I, 246, and *Il trovatore Bernart Marti*, ed. by F. Beggiato (Modena, 1984), pp. 39–40.

[11] See A. Roncaglia, 'Due postille alla "galleria letteraria" di Peire d'Alvernha', *Marche romane*, XIX (1969), 71–5 (pp. 72–5).

[12] *Biographies*, ed. Boutière & Schutz, p. 263. See Kasten, *Frauendienst*, p. 102; and *Poésies ... Marti*, ed. Hoepffner, poem V, lines 31–6:

> E quan canorgues si mes
> Pey d'Alvernh'en canorgia,
> A Dieu per que.s prometia
> Entiers que pueys si fraysses?
> Quar si feys fols joglares,
> Per que l'entier pretz cambïa.

('And when Peire d'Alvernha became a canon in a monastery, why did he promise his whole self to God, then break (his vows)? For he became a jongleuresque fool, thereby losing the integrity of his reputation.')

[13] See *Biographies*, ed. Boutière & Schutz, p. 21. Kasten, *Frauendienst*, p. 102, takes this reference to an authority as evidence of the *vida*'s reliability; but see W. D. Paden, 'Bernart de Ventadour le troubadour, devint-il abbé de Tulle?', in *Mélanges de langue et de littérature occitanes en hommage à Pierre Bec* (Poitiers, 1991), pp. 401–41 (p. 409), who points out that Uc was writing in 1253, some sixty-nine years after the death of Eble IV, the viscount in question. See De Riquer, *Los trovadores*, I, poem XLIX, lines 19–24:

> E.l tertz, Bernartz de Ventedorn,
> q'es menre de Borneill un dorn;
> en son paire ac bon sirven
> per trair'ab arc manal d'alborn,
> e sa mair'escaldava.l forn
> et amassava issermen.

('And the third, Bernart de Ventadorn, who is a handspan less than Borneil, had in his father a good sergeant to shoot with a bow of laburnum, and his mother heated the oven and gathered vine-shoots.')

[14] See *Biographies*, ed. Boutière & Schutz, pp. 20–8; De Riquer, *Los trovadores*, I, 342–3; Kasten, *Frauendienst*, p. 103.

[15] See, e.g., M. Dumitrescu, '"L'escola N'Eblon" et ses représentants', in *Mélanges offerts à Rita Lejeune*, 2 vols. (Gembloux, 1969), I, 107–18, who sees the term 'troubadour' in the early lyrics as designating poets associated with Eble. See also Kasten, *Frauendienst*, pp. 90–1.

[16] See Kasten, *Fraundienst*, p. 90.

[17] Faral, *Les Jongleurs*, p. 79.

[18] Kasten, *Fraundienst*, p. 91.

[19] See *ibid.*, p. 100. For much of what follows, see the summary *ibid.*, pp. 100–5. I do not intend to examine the same wealth of material as Kasten does, nor am I concerned with the troubadours' treatment of *fin'amor*, but I have taken her chapter 'Der trobadoreske Berufsliterat' as the basis for the first part of this article, because her procedure exemplifies established methods of enquiry and her study is the most recent and thorough synthesis of these issues.

[20] See S. Stroński, *La Poésie et la réalité au temps des troubadours* (Oxford, 1943), pp. 22–3; also A. Jeanroy, *La Poésie lyrique des troubadours*, 2 vols. (Toulouse, 1934), I, 132, and De Riquer, *Los trovadores*, I, 29. I cannot agree with Panvini that the laconic *vidas* of the early troubadours demonstrate the biographer's caution and reluctance to invent: B. Panvini, *Le biografie provenzali: valore e attendibilità* (Florence, 1952), p. 21.

[21] *Biographies*, ed. Boutière & Schutz, p. 14.

[22] PC 34,2. Arnaut names himself in a *tornada* which is not transmitted by MSS I and K: see De Riquer, *Los trovadores*, I, 241; *Biographies*, ed. Boutière & Schutz, p. 15 n. 3; *Le Troubadour Arnaut de Tintinhac*, ed. by J. Mouzat (Tulle, [n.d.]), p. 6 (articles published in *Bulletin de la Société des Lettres, Sciences et Arts de la Corrèze*, 1954–6, later reprinted in a fascicule of 35 pages, referred to here).

²³ See R. Lejeune, 'Le nom de Bernart de Ventadorn', in *Mittelalterstudien. Erich Köhler zum Gedenken* (Heidelberg, 1984), pp. 157–65 (pp. 157–60). Cf. also Dronke, *The Medieval Lyric*, p. 21; and see pp. 231–2 below.

²⁴ Kay, *Subjectivity*, p. 112; Lejeune, 'Le nom', p. 163; and cf. De Riquer, *Los trovadores*, I, 343 (on Bernart): 'Sin duda, si hubiera pertenecido a una clase superior, aparercería su nombre en documentos de archivo.'

²⁵ See also Paden, 'Bernart de Ventadorn', who brings a number of important corrections and clarifications to Lejeune's argument. He suggests that it may be possible to identify the *Bernardus*, abbot of Tulle, with the troubadour, provided that several references in his songs are reinterpreted, that the stanza Peire d'Alvernha devotes to him is taken to refer to a very young man, and that Bernart's poetic career is redated, from 1147–70 (De Riquer, *Los trovadores*, I, 342) to the last third of the twelfth century ...

²⁶ See D. Monson, 'Jaufre Rudel et l'amour lointain: les origines d'une légende', *Romania*, CVI (1987), 36–56; R. E. Harvey, 'The troubadour Marcabru and his public', *Reading Medieval Studies*, XIV (1988), 47–76 (pp. 55–6 for a summary of studies of the two *vidas*); and, on William IX, De Riquer, *Los trovadores*, I, 112. Cercamon, it should be noted, is described as *joglar* in his own *vida*, but as a *trobador* in one of Marcabru's (*Biographies*, ed. Boutière & Schutz, p. 12).

²⁷ Meneghetti, *Il pubblico del trovatori*, pp. 53–4; and see De Riquer, *Los trovadores*, I, poem VII (PC 183,12).

²⁸ E. M. Ghil, *L'Age de parage: Essai sur le poétique et le politique en Occitanie au XIIIe siècle* (New York, 1989), pp. 38–56: 'Il est inutile de demander à ces textes ce qu'ils n'ont jamais eu l'intention de nous donner (à savoir, de rapporter avec les techniques de l'érudition historique positiviste la réalité soi-disant objective du XIIIe siècle' (p. 38).

²⁹ J. C. Huchet, 'L'écrivain au miroir dans les *vidas* et le roman occitan', *Le moyen âge*, XCVI (1990), 81–92 (pp. 83–4). See also E. Wilson Poe, 'Old Provençal *vidas* as literary commentary', *Romance Philology*, XXXIII (1980), 510–18; M. Egan, 'Commentary, *vita poetae* and *vida*: Latin and Old Provençal "lives of poets"', *Romance Philology*, XXXVI (1983), 36–48.

³⁰ On Thomas of Chobham's *Summa Confessorum*, see C. Page, *The Owl and the Nightingale: Musical Life and Ideas in France, 1100–1300* (London, 1989), pp. 23–4, 212 n. 37; Faral, *Les Jongleurs*, pp. 67–70, who also comments on and modifies L. Gautier, *Les Epopées françaises*, 2nd edn, 4 vols. (Paris, 1878–92), II, 21–101, and E. K. Chambers, *The Medieval Stage*, 2 vols. (Oxford, 1903), I, 42–69. On the identity of Thomas of Chobham (*not* the archbishop of Canterbury, as many literary scholars have asserted), see *Thomae de Chobham: 'Summa Confessorum'*, ed. by F. Broomfield, Analecta Medievalia Namurcensia, 25 (Paris; Louvain, 1968), p. xxvi n. 54, pp. xxviii–xxxix.

³¹ R. Menéndez Pidal, *Poesia juglaresca y origines de las literaturas romanicas*, 6th edn (Madrid, 1957), pp. 37–9, 53; and see P. Zumthor, *La Lettre et la voix* (Paris, 1987), p. 63, on jongleurs, specialization and genres.

³² Ed. in F. Pirot, *Recherches sur les connaissances littéraires des troubadours occitans et catalans des XIIe et XIIIe siècles* (Barcelona, 1972), pp. 564–95 ('Fadet joglar', s. xii *ex*) and pp. 546–62 ('Cabra juglar', s. xii *med*.). Menéndez Pidal, *Poesia juglaresca*, p. 37, thought these were idealized portraits; cf. Meneghetti, *Il pubblico del trovatori*, pp. 72–3, on these texts as evidence for specialized repertoires; and see D. Monson, *Les 'Ensenhamens' occitans: Essai de définition et de délimitation du genre* (Paris, 1981), pp. 160–1, and W. D. Paden, 'The role of the joglar in troubadour lyric poetry', in *Chrétien de Troyes and the Troubadours: Essays in Memory of Leslie Topsfield* (Cambridge, 1984), pp. 90–111 (pp. 94–5) on their satirical tone.

³³ *Raimon Vidal, Poetry and Prose 2: 'Abril issia'*, ed. and trans. by W. H. W. Field (Chapel Hill, NC, 1971); and see Page, *The Owl and the Nightingale*, pp. 59–60.

[34] See Page, *The Owl and the Nightingale*, pp. 45–6, 53–6; Meneghetti, *Il pubblico del trovatori*, pp. 74–5.
[35] Translation from Field, *Raimon Vidal*, p. 79. See Page, *The Owl and the Nightingale*, pp. 45–6.
[36] See E. Türk, *Nugae Curialium: Le règne d'Henri II Plantagenêt et l'éthique politique* (Geneva, 1977), pp. 40–2; C. S. Jaeger, *The Origins of Courtliness* (Philadelphia, 1985), pp. 54–66; R. E. Harvey, 'Allusions intertextuelles et les *lengua-forcat* de Bernart Marti', in *Contacte de langues, de civvilisations et intertextualité: Actes du IIIe Congrès international de l'Association Internationale d'Etudes Occitanes*, ed. by G. Gouiran, 3 vols. (Montpellier, 1992), III, 927–42.
[37] See Page, *The Owl and the Nightingale*, p. 47; *Biographies*, ed. Boutière & Schutz, pp. 39, 167:

> ... auziratz, si com yeu fi,
> als trobadors dir e comtar
> si com vivion per anar
> e par sercar terras e locx;
> e viras lay selas ab flocx
> e tans autres valens arnes
> e fres dauratz, e palafres. (755–61)

('And you would hear, as I did, the troubadours tell and relate how they lived by travelling and making the rounds of lands and places; and you would see there tasseled saddles and much other costly harness and gilded bridles and palfreys.') (Field, *Raimon Vidal*, p. 72)

[38] See Page, *The Owl and the Nightingale*, p. 56; Meneghetti, *Il pubblico del trovatori*, pp. 60–5; and n. 3 above.
[39] Paden, 'The role of the joglar', pp. 94–5.
[40] Kay, *Subjectivity*, pp. 145, 247 n. 19.
[41] Paden 'The role of the joglar', pp. 92–3, 97–8.
[42] A. H. Schutz, '*Joglar, borges, cavalier* dans les biographies provençales: essai d'évaluation sémantique', in *Mélanges de linguistique et de littérature romanes offerts à la mémoire d'István Frank* (Saarbruck, 1957), pp. 672–7 (p. 672).
[43] *Le Breviari d'amor de Matfre Ermengaud*, ed. by G. Azaïs, 2 vols. (Béziers, 1862–81), lines 18,426–97.
[44] See V. Bertolucci Pizzorusso, 'La supplica di Guiraut Riquier e la risposta di Alfonso X di Castiglia', *Studi mediolatini e volgari*, XIV (1966), 9–135 (lines 554–863).
[45] This seems to be the implication also of *Abril issia*:

> e s'eratz filh d'emperador
> no seriatz mas can joglar
> mentr'aissi . eus sapcha bo l'anar
> ni.l venir bos e saboros. (1694–7)

See also R. Morgan, 'Old French *jogleor* and kindred terms', *Romance Philology*, VII (1954), 279–325 (pp. 291–2, 317); L. Wright, 'Misconceptions concerning the troubadours, trouvères and minstrels', *Music and Letters*, XLVIII (1967), 35–9.
[46] If Uc Catola is the same man as Hugh Catula, knight, intended monk and recipient of a letter by Peter the Venerable, then this early troubadour is whisked out of the category of lowly *joglar* into which Jeanroy, *La Poésie lyrique*, I, 433, had arbitrarily placed him: see A. Roncaglia, 'La tenzone tra Ugo Catola e Marcabruno', in *Linguistica e filologia: omaggio a Benvenuto Terracini* (Milan, 1968), pp. 203–54 (pp. 208–9 for the letter, and pp. 244–5 on 'joglars esbaluiz', line 44).
[47] 'When you return, you will be assured of a lord, and I of a *joglar*.'
[48] See Stroński, *La Poésie et la réalité*, p. 7; Harvey, 'Public', p. 53 and n. 83; S. B. Gaunt,

JOGLARS AND THE STATUS OF THE EARLY TROUBADOURS

Troubadours and Irony (Cambridge, 1989), pp. 72–3 and nn. 49–53.

[49] Kay, *Subjectivity*, p. 146. See *Les Poésies de Peire Vidal*, ed. by J. Anglade, 2nd edn (Paris, 1966), poem XXI, lines 1–6:
> Emperador avem de tal maniera,
> Que non a sen ni saber, ni membransa:
> Plus ebrics no s'assec en cadeira
> Ni plus volpilhs no port'escut ni lansa,
> Ni plus avols non causset esperos
> Ni plus malvatz no fetz vers ni chansos.

[50] See *Guillem de Berguedà*, ed. by M. de Riquer, 2 vols. (Abadía de Poblet, 1971), poems VI–IX; *L'Amour et la guerre: L'oeuvre de Bertran de Born*, ed. by G. Gouiran, 2 vols. (Aix-en-Provence, 1985), poem XXIII; and see n. 13 above. Cf. Jeanroy, *La Poésie lyrique*, I, 141–2 on *sirventes joglaresc*.

[51] See De Riquer, *Los trovadores*, I, poem XXVIII (PC 17,2), Simon B. Gaunt, 'Did Marcabru know the Tristran legend?', *MÆ*, LV (1986), 108–13; Gaunt, *Irony*, pp. 127–34; and L. Rossi, 'La "chemise" d'Iseut et l'amour tristanien chez les troubadours et les trouvères', in *Contactes de langues*, ed. Gouiran, III, 1119–32. The problems were summarized by Dr Linda Paterson in a paper circulated to the Sixth National Conference on Medieval Occitan Literature and Language (Girton College, April 1991), as part of work in progress towards a new critical edition of Marcabru's works.

[52] See J. Southworth, *The English Medieval Minstrel* (Woodbridge, 1989), p. 47; *Rotuli di Dominibus et Pueris et Puellis de XII Comitatibus (1185)*, ed. by J. H. Round, Pipe Roll Society (London, 1913), p. 62 and n. 3.

[53] On *ioculatores* and sergeanty, see Southworth, *The English Medieval Minstrel*, p. 35; cf. also A. L. Poole, *Obligations of Society in the XII and XIII Centuries* (Oxford, 1946), pp. 57–76. See Southworth, *The English Medieval Minstrel*, pp. 35, 39 and 45–9, for other examples of such landholders; Menéndez Pidal, *Poesia juglaresca*, p. 104, for the example of the landholding (Occitan) *Poncius, ioculatoris regis*, in Aragon, 1122. Cf. C. Casagrande and S. Vecchio, 'Clercs et jongleurs dans la société médiévale (XIIe et XIIIe siècles)', *Annales, economies, sociétés, civilisations*, XXXIV (1979), 913–28 (p. 914), on itinerant, landless jongleurs escaping the social ties of feudal obligations and loyalties; and see Page's nuances (*The Owl and the Nightingale*, p. 43).

[54] *PL*, CCVII, col. 49. See Southworth, *The English Medieval Minstrel*, pp. 46–7; L. Wright, 'The role of musicians at court in twelfth-century Britain', in *Art and Patronage in the English Romanesque*, ed. by S. Macready and F. H. Thompson (London, 1986), pp. 97–106 (pp. 98–9 for the translation):
> If the king has announced that he will go early next morning to a certain place, the decision is sure to be changed: and so you will know he will sleep till midday. You will see pack-animals waiting under their loads, teams of horses standing in silence, heralds sleeping, court traders fretting, and everyone in turn grumbling. One runs to whores and pavilioners of the court to ask them where the king is going. For this breed of courtier often knows the palace secrets. For the king's court has an assiduous following of entertainers (*histriones*), female singers, dice-players, flatterers, taverners (*caupones*), waferers (*nebulatores*), actors (*mimi*), barbers – gluttons the whole lot of them!

Southworth, *The English Medieval Minstrel*, p. 47, notes that 'nearly all these people – even the waferers and barbers – are listed as *ministrelli* in later, wardrobe accounts'. See Wright, 'The role of musicians', who concludes that some musicians also 'performed secondary functions' (p. 105), although the evidence cited is not always entirely persuasive.

⁵⁵ The 'type même de toute cour' (Zumthor, *La Lettre et la voix*, p. 79). See Kasten, *Frauendienst*, pp. 92–9; J. M. Ferrante, 'The court in medieval literature: the center of the problem', in *The Medieval Court in Europe*, ed. by E. R. Haymes (Munich, 1986), pp. 1–25 (pp. 2–4); A. Murray, *Reason and Society in the Middle Ages*, new edn (Oxford, 1986), p. 85.

⁵⁶ Türk, *Nugae Curialium*, p. 4, and cf. pp. 40–1.

⁵⁷ See Murray, *Reason and Society*, pp. 84–6: 'The risers: social ascent through service'. See R. V. Turner, *Men Raised from the Dust: Administrative Service and Upward Mobility in Angevin England* (Philadelphia, 1988), pp. 14–15; E. Bournazel and J. Poly, *The Feudal Transformation, 900–1300*, trans. by C. Higgit (New York, 1991), pp. 187–94; *The Poems of the Troubadour Raimbaut de Vaqueiras*, ed. by J. Linskill (The Hague, 1964), pp. 4–37. Cf. the *joglar* Daurel in *Daurel et Beton*, ed. by A. S. Kimmel (Chapel Hill, NC, 1971) (see Faral, *Les Jongleurs*, p. 83, and, on the dating, L. M. Paterson, 'Knights and the concept of knighthood in the twelfth-century Occitan epic', in *Knighthood in Medieval Literature*, ed. by W. T. H. Jackson (Woodbridge, 1981), pp. 23–38 (p. 35 n. 11)); *The Life and Works of the Troubadour Raimbaut d'Orange*, ed. by W. T. Pattison (Minneapolis, Minn., 1952), pp. 18, 37 on Levet; and, on Guilhelm Mita, pp. 139–40 and L. M. Paterson, 'Great court festivals in the south of France and Catalonia in the twelfth and thirteenth centuries', *MÆ*, LI (1982), pp. 213–24 (pp. 213–14).

⁵⁸ According to John of Salisbury, many frivolous courtiers endeavour by the help of music to advance their own interests (see the discussion in Page, *The Owl and the Nightingale*, p. 220 n. 6 and the references given there). See *ibid.*, pp. 92–101 on members of a lordly household (servants, pages, *vallets*) being trained and expected to sing for their master. See also Zumthor, *La Lettre et la voix*, p. 64; Wright, 'Misconceptions', p. 38.

⁵⁹ See R. N. B. Goddard, 'The early troubadours and the Latin tradition' (unpubl. D.Phil. diss., University of Oxford, 1985), pp. 72–5; Gaunt, 'Marginal men', p. 67.

⁶⁰ See Goddard, 'The early troubadours', pp. 67–9; Harvey, 'Public', pp. 53–7 and nn. 29–37; and, e.g., *Poésies ... Marcabru*, ed. Dejeanne, poems II, IV and XXXIX; *Il trovatore Cercamon*, ed. Tortoreto, poems VI and VIII; *Poésies ... Marti*, ed. Hoepffner, poems II, VI. Kasten, *Frauendienst*, p. 134, restricts the sense of *soudadier* too much when she attributes to it the meaning 'professional poet'.

⁶¹ Jaeger, *The Origins of Courtliness*, p. 58; *Poésies ... Marti*, ed. Hoepffner, poem II (PC 63,2). See also Murray, *Reason and Society*, ch. IV ('Ambition'); Ferrante, 'The court in medieval literature'.

⁶² See *Il trovatore Bernart Marti*, ed. Beggiato, pp. 22–9; and cf. Harvey, 'Allusions'.

⁶³ See nn. 3 and 38 above; Kay, *Subjectivity*, p. 146; Paterson, 'Great court festivals', p. 221. Cercamon's possible patrons were William X, Eble II de Ventadorn, and an Alfonso (?VII of Castile); Bernart Marti may have been associated with Eble III (see F. Pirot, 'Le troubadour Eble de Saignes (avec des notes sur Eble de Ventadour et Eble d'Ussel)', in *Mélanges de langue et de littérature médiévales offerts à Pierre Le Gentil* (Paris, 1973), pp. 641–61 (pp. 658–9); but cf. Roncaglia, 'Due postille', pp. 74–5, who sees this Eble as probably Eble de Saignes); on Marcabru, see R. E. Harvey, 'Aspects of the poetic representation of love and female figures in the works of Marcabru' (unpubl. Ph.D. diss., University of London, 1986), Appendix (although this analysis will need to be revised in the light of the new edition of Marcabru in progress).

⁶⁴ See, e.g., Kasten, *Frauendienst*, p. 89.

⁶⁵ 'E no.m socor la clerzia' (poem VIII, line 3). The sense of *clerzia* 'knowledge, learning' is excluded here by line 13 (*Il trovatore Cercamon*, ed. Tortoreto, p. 204).

⁶⁶ See Goddard, 'The early troubadours', pp. 62–76, on Cercamon's education and style, and see also Part III of his thesis, 'Reflections of basic schooling'; cf. Kasten, *Frauendienst*,

JOGLARS AND THE STATUS OF THE EARLY TROUBADOURS

p. 90, on the comparison with the goliards 'die zu gleicher Zeit bezeugt sind', with reference to Faral, *Les Jongleurs*, pp. 33–43: 'Les Vagants'.

[67] On the Archpoet and Hugh Primas, see Dronke, *The Medieval Lyric*, pp. 21–2; L. Kendrick, *The Game of Love: Troubadour Word-Play* (Berkeley, Calif., 1988), p. 59; F. J. E. Raby, *A History of Secular Latin Poetry in the Middle Ages*, 2 vols. (Oxford, 1934), II, 189.

[68] Faral, *Les Jongleurs*, p. 35.

[69] G. Duby, 'The culture of the knightly class: audience and patronage', in *Renaissance and Renewal in the Twelfth Century*, ed. by R. L. Benson and G. Constable (Oxford, 1982), pp. 248–62 (p. 257); R. W. Southern, 'The schools of Paris and the school of Chartres', *ibid.*, pp. 113–37; R. W. Southern, *The Making of the Middle Ages* (London, 1953), pp. 87–8; Murray, *Reason and Society*, p. 220 and nn. 18–20.

[70] See R. W. Southern, 'Peter of Blois: a twelfth-century humanist?', in *Medieval Humanism and Other Studies* (Oxford, 1970), pp. 105–32 (pp. 108–12, on Peter's ultimately disappointing career), and *The Making of the Middle Ages*, pp. 200–3.

[71] C. Morris, *The Discovery of the Individual: 1050–1200* (London, 1972), pp. 124–5. See Paterson, 'Courts and courtiers', on the early twelfth-century court bureaucracies of Provence, Catalonia and Castile; also Turner, *Men Raised from the Dust*, pp. 9–12; Murray, *Reason and Society*, pp. 302–9, on 'Graduates and jobs' (1250–1450); and Joachim Bumke, *Courtly Culture: Literature and Society in the High Middle Ages*, trans. by T. Dunlop (Berkeley, Calif., 1991), p. 502, on *clerici vagi* in Germany in the thirteenth and fourteenth centuries.

[72] See Morgan, 'Old French *jogleor*', pp. 287–8; Casagrande & Vecchio, 'Clercs et jongleurs' pp. 923–4 n. 1; H. Waddell, *The Wandering Scholars*, 6th edn (Harmondsworth, 1932), Appendix E: 'Councils relating to the *clericus vagus* or *joculator*'. Many of these pronouncements concern apostates and fugitives from justice, and have no connection with entertainers.

[73] Kendrick's happy phrase (*The Game of Love*, p. 59). See Casagrande and Vecchio's important analysis ('Clercs et jongleurs', pp. 916–17 and nn. 17, 22–3); J. D. A. Ogilvy, '*Mimi, scurrae histriones*: entertainers of the early Middle Ages', *Speculum*, XXXVIII (1963), pp. 603–19 (p. 611 on Capitulum XIII of the Canons of Mainz for 843).

[74] Cf. Kendrick, *The Game of Love*, pp. 59–60, 201 n. 12, who cites the Councils of Trèves (1227), Cahors, Rodez and Tulle (1287) and a tenth-century Gautier of Sens, all from Faral, *Les Jongleurs*, p. 43 n. 1. (This last is spurious and should be assigned to 1239: see Waddell, *The Wandering Scholars*, p. 273; Ogilvy, '*Mimi*', p. 613). Cf. also n. 28 above.

[75] See Cercamon's *planh* for William X (*Il trovatore Cercamon*, ed. Tortoreto, poem VII (PC 112,2a), D. Rieger, 'Klagelied', in *Grundriss der romanischen Literaturen des Mittelalters*, ed. E. Köhler, Vol. II, t. 1, fasc. 4 (Heidelberg, 1980), pp. 83–92 (pp. 85–6); Kasten, *Frauendienst*, p. 127; and, for a summary of work on a lord's dependent *familia*, Harvey, 'Public', p. 54 and nn. 34–6. See also nn. 59 and 60 above.

[76] 'I do not see anyone, however rich or handsome he is, whose fortunes do not change completely when, too young, he loses his protector through whom his lot should be improved.'

[77] 'For, I believe, the good times are coming when you will have such a reward, when you will be given a palfrey or rents, which will be worth more to you, for the count of Poitiers is coming.'

[78] See Paden, 'The role of the joglar', p. 94 and n. 24; the sources and examples mentioned in Harvey, 'Allusions', n. 23; and cf. also C. Bullock-Davies, *Menestrellorum Multitudo: Minstrels at a Royal Feast* (Cardiff, 1978), p. 23, on types of payment in kind, over and above wages.

[79] See Murray, *Reason and Society*, ch. iv, esp. pp. 107–9 on 'Dependency'; C. S. Haskins, 'Henry II as a patron of literature', in *Essays in Medieval History presented to T. F. Tout* (Manchester, 1925), pp. 71–7 (pp. 71–3).

⁸⁰ Kasten, *Frauendienst*, pp. 117, 126; but cf. Haskins, 'Henry II', p. 73, on the Angevin court: 'literature was often only a subordinate element in the services the king rewarded'; and Bumke, *Courtly Culture*, pp. 503–4: 'In France it was customary by the twelfth century for art-loving princes to take individual minstrels into their service and give them a secure position at court', but he gives only three references, all to literary sources, one of them German and another from the thirteenth century. It is odd that the *joglar*'s tour in *Abril issia* is undertaken in winter (Page, *The Owl and the Nightingale*, p. 53).

⁸¹ See, e.g., the sources consulted by Haskins, 'Henry II'; Bullock-Davies, *Menstrellorum Multitudo*; and Southworth, *The English Medieval Minstrel*.

⁸² Gouiran, *L'Amour et la guerre*, I, xxxii; Kay, *Subjectivity*, p. 111.

⁸³ Paden, 'Bernart de Ventadour', p. 412.

⁸⁴ See the difficulties over *Bernardus* experienced by Lejeune, 'Le nom', and Paden, 'Bernart de Ventadour'; and cf. *The Life and Works of ... Raimbaut d'Orange*, ed. Pattison, p. 140, on Guilhem Mita ('Big-Nose') and the presence of a *Guillelmus Nason* among the witnesses to Raimbaut d'Aurenga's will. If this identification is correct, it indicates that (some?) scribes latinized vernacular forms such as nicknames.

⁸⁵ See P. Cravayat, 'Les origines du troubadour Jaufré Rudel', *Romania*, LXXI (1950), 166–79 (pp. 174–5); *The Poetry of Cercamon and Jaufre Rudel*, ed. by R. Rosenstein and G. Wolf (New York; London, 1983), pp. 95–7.

⁸⁶ See *Il trovatore Bernart Marti*, ed. Beggiato, pp. 39–40, and the discussion in Goddard, 'The early troubadours', pp. 72–4.

⁸⁷   E si fatz vers tota via
     En l'an un o dos o tres. (ed. Hoepffner, poem v, lines 3–4)
Cf. *Il trovatore Bernart Marti*, ed. Beggiato, pp. 39–40.

⁸⁸ See Kay, *Subjectivity*, pp. 138, 246 n. 15. Kendrick's arguments (*The Game of Love*, pp. 166–7) on lyric performance as a suspension of the rules and norms of everyday social intercourse, opening up a theatrical space and allowing the creation of multiple voices and *personae*, also support this interpretation.

⁸⁹ Cf. Zumthor, *La Lettre et la voix*, p. 77: 'Mieux vaut écarter d'emblée ... certaines obsessions héritées du romantisme et dont les médiévistes ont du mal à s'affranchir: celle, ainsi, qui pousse au classement en *populaire* et *savant*, *clercs* ou *jongleurs*, ou d'autres semblables.' Gautier's fundamental study draws on an enormous variety of sources, Latin and vernacular, and, while he distinguishes pre- and post-eleventh century, what emerges is a composite picture, both chronologically and socio-geographically: his portrait of jongleurs in service at a court (pp. 50–5) and of 'A day in the life of a jongleur' (pp. 102–42) are compiled from sources ranging from twelfth-century Occitan to late fourteenth-century Artesian and Burgundian evidence. Faral brings a number of important corrections to Gautier (see especially *Les Jongleurs*, pp. 66–86: 'Classification des jongleurs'), but his study, which remains the basic work of reference, concerns mainly *northern* France (see Paden, 'Bernart de Ventadorn', p. 106 n. 2). Morgan's lexicological and semantic analysis takes account of nuances and of chronology, but he also assumes a close parallel between the Old French and Occitan ('Old French *jogleor*', p. 292). Paden's valuable work combines study of homogeneous sources with chronological analysis. On the circularity of the consequences of this picture for literary interpretation, see, for example, Pattison's discussion of Levet, member of the *familia* of Raimbaut d'Aurenga: 'What we know of the footloose existence of minstrels makes it improbable that he lived under Raimbaut's protection for many years' (*The Life and Works of ... Raimbaut d'Orange*, ed. Pattison, p. 37), but if it is not assumed that all minstrels were (i) never anything but minstrels and (ii) always footloose, the improbability is considerably reduced.

⁹⁰ *Alfred de Vigny. Oeuvres complètes, I: Poésie et théâtre*, ed. by F. Germain and A. Jarry, Bibliothèque de la Pléïade (Paris, 1986), 'Dernière nuit de travail', p. 753.
⁹¹ 'Heart and body, knowledge and judgement, strength and might': Bernart de Ventadorn, *Non es meravelha s'eu chan* (PC 70,31), in De Riquer, *Los trovadores*, I, poem LXVII, lines 5–6.
⁹² M. Aurell, *La Vielle et l'épée: Troubadours et politique en Provence au XIIIe siècle* (Paris, 1989), p. 126, although he does assert that professional *joglar*-poets had always existed, and cites Marcabru and Cercamon as examples (p. 312 n. 58).
⁹³ *Ibid.*, pp. 126–9, referring to E. Köhler, 'Observations historiques et sociologiques sur la poésie des troubadours', *Cahiers de civilisation médiévale*, VII (1964), pp. 27–51 (in *Sociologia*, pp. 1–38). The poets he studies 'ont des origines fort modestes. Fils de vilains, clercs défroqués, personnages sans patronyme dont on ne connaît qu'un soubriquet burlesque, ce sont des jongleurs dont les compositions deviennent la seule source de revenus' (p. 126).
⁹⁴ Aurell, *La Vielle et l'épée*, p. 127.
⁹⁵ Kasten, *Frauendienst*, p. 92.
⁹⁶ See Harvey, 'Public', pp. 62–3.

[3]

Turtles, Helmets, Parasites and Goliards[1]

BY

BRYAN GILLINGHAM

Long before the post-modernist or even modernist advances in cultural studies and the frequent accusations levelled against the former as "revisionist", some of the very positivists upon whose work we now depend created a potential historical distortion. Philologists working on the rich corpus of mediaeval Latin poetry formulated the notion that, since in many cases the works were scurrilous or satyrical, yet written in the tongue of the Church, they must have emerged from the periphery of the ecclesiastical and societal order. As it was easy to demonstrate that there was extensive wandering in the high Middle Ages, often by poor scholars and disenchanted clerics, and since the behaviour of such individuals was not beyond reproach, this nebulous group was eagerly and confidently claimed as the source for the daring exploitation of lyric verse. The quasi-derisory terms "goliard" and "Vaganten", both of which can be found in mediaeval documents,[2] were the common labels suggested for the supposed brotherhood of wandering minstrels. The travel and wandering in the Middle Ages have been extensively documented by Helen Waddell,[3] and it is a commonplace that behaviour in the period from the eleventh to the fifteenth century was coloured by crusades, pilgrimages and military campaigns. The blind leap of faith, taken by Waddell and many others, which almost invariably lacks documentary support, is that the wandering rascals were indeed the poet-musicians. Some articles even invert the process, seeking out incidents of gluttony, rudeness, satire, drunkenness, moral laxity and travel, in order to prove "goliardedness". Travel, considering that members from every level of mediaeval society engaged in it, would seem to be an unexceptional act, irrelevant to the matter of identifying the poet-musicians, and will largely be set aside here.[4]

It cannot be established that the writers of the poems were any less moral than most authors in the Middle Ages. In fact, much of the supposed "goliardic" song survives in monastic libraries, and the few poets who have been identified, such as Philip the Chancellor, were not ragamuffins. Furthermore, the word "goliard" is never used in the most impressive monument of the supposed brotherhood, *Carmina Burana*. As for the poems,

---

[1] The author is grateful to the Social Sciences and Humanities Research Council of Canada for financial support towards the preparation of this article. Also, Terence Bailey must be thanked for carefully reading a draft of this paper and for many useful suggestions. Thanks, too, to Corey Mulvihill for checking the Latin.

[2] In a recent article, A. G. Rigg suggests that the term "goliardic" is a non-mediaeval adjective, but the noun "goliardus" (and variants) can be found fairly often in the extensive proceedings of Mansi (see examples below) and elsewhere, particularly from the end of the twelfth century onwards. See A. G. Rigg, "Golias and Other Pseudonyms", *Studi Medievali*, 18 (1977), 65 and 68.

[3] *The Wandering Scholars* (New York: Houghton-Mifflin, 1927 [there have been various later editions and reprints]).

[4] One could distinguish between "travel" and "wandering" (aimless travel), but to prove or disprove goal orientation in such phenomena would often be impossible.

> Leur caractère "profane" pose un problème délicat. Jamais au Moyen Age il n'y eut de poètes qui ne fissent que des rythmes "profanes". Le sacré et le profane se sont trouvés toujours mêlés dans leur œuvre.[5]

Articles and books continue (up to the present) to explain the "goliardic" phenomenon by replicating the old ideas, although in many cases the authors admit to a certain discomfort with the conventional wisdom.[6] Back in 1923, James Westfall Thompson suggested that ". . . the origin, meaning and relation of the terms *Golias* and *Goliard* have not yet been precisely ascertained . . . ";[7] the statement is still true. Since the Middle Ages, history has passed through various cultural and social filters (such as the Reformation), which allowed us, on the one hand, to consolidate disparate phenomena and, on the other, to see the component parts of what were formerly seen as uniform processes. We like to think now of the composers, performers and poets as separate individuals, working in specialized fields, when in fact a mediaeval musician may have assumed other functions as an entertainer, worked in different languages and adapted to varying social circumstances. *Goliards* (in the established sense of the word) might also have been *jongleurs, Spielleute, ioculatores* or *histriones*. When some of the wonderful philologists of the last century, such as Schmeller and Wright, produced their important editions of secular lyric, there was, for example, a general assumption that the dramatic arts were entirely lacking in the Middle Ages. We are only now beginning to understand mediaeval drama and the ways in which it was closely allied to other entertainments.

In the interest of correcting the record, two lines of argument need to be reviewed in the light of recent findings: first, the true etymology of the word "goliard", and second (given that etymology), the extent to which the goliards were the real composers of the lyric poetry/song. It is the thesis of this article that the current notion of the word "goliard" and its derivatives is entirely incorrect. Redress of this misconception is long overdue.

There is a wealth of literature, which presents a succession of definitions doubtless fuelled by their understandable inadequacies, on the subject of the word "goliard". A useful first step here is to review the major theories concerning the etymology of "goliard", then to establish how such concepts were formulated, replicated and modified and, finally, to isolate the concomitant problems. One of the oldest, yet still one of the best, discussions of the subject is that of Thomas Wright dating from 1841.[8] Wright, like so many other scholars since, relies heavily on the *Speculum Ecclesiae* of Giraldus Cambrensis,[9] not only for information on Walter Mapes, but for some of his interpretative material on the word "goliard".[10] As the material in Wright's book is of seminal importance, often quoted by later scholars, it deserves a fuller explication than

---

[5] Olga Dobiache-Rojdestvensky, *Les Poésies des Goliards* (Paris: Les Éditions Rieder, 1931), p. 16.

[6] There is no shortage of material surveying the question of "goliardic" etymology. Most of the important articles are listed *passim* in the notes below and need not be duplicated at this point.

[7] "The Origin of the Word 'Goliardi'", *Studies in Philology*, XX (1923), 83.

[8] *The Latin Poems Commonly Attributed to Walter Mapes* (London: Camden Society, 1841).

[9] See J. S. Brewer, ed., *Speculum Ecclesiae*, in *Giraldi Cambrensis Opera* (Rerum Britannicarum Medii Aevi Scriptores), 21/4 (1857) (London: Her Majesty's Stationery Office, 1857), Cap. xv, pp. 291–93. This passage is frequently quoted and/or paraphrased in the studies cited later.

[10] Wright cites the passage from Giraldus in his Appendix V, as well as other information from *Speculum Ecclesiae* in his other appendices.

some of the works that followed. Wright acknowledges the importance of Giraldus Cambrensis and quotes the following well-known account:

> [I]tem parasitus quidam Golias nomine nostris diebus gulositate pariter et lecacitate famosissimus . qui Golias melius quia gule et crapule per omnia deditus! dici potuit. litteratus tamen affatim sed nec bene morigeratus . nec bonis disciplinis informatus in papam et curiam Romanam carmina famosa pluries et plurima tam metrica quam ridmica non minus impudenter quam imprudenter evomuit. De quibus invectionem ridmicam temere nimis et indiscrete . | compositam casualiter incideas clausulas aliquot inde ad detestandum quidem et condemnandum; non approbandum aut imitandum. has scilicet hic apposui: *Roma mundi caput est* . . .[11]
>
> [Likewise in our time a certain parasite, Golias by name, renowned equally for his gluttony and wantonness, who, it may be said, was aptly called Golias because he was given in everything to gluttony and inebriation, who was nevertheless sufficiently literate, but neither overly obliging nor informed by good disciplines, and who vomited forth, not less impudently than imprudently, oftentimes and copiously, famous songs, so metrical as to be rhythmic. Concerning which, [it is said that] the rhythmic invective was altogether thoughtless and indiscreetly composed, casually cut into some little phrases [*clausulae*], some for execrating and condemning rather than approving or imitating, that is to say, like these which I have added here: *Roma mundi caput est* [various other examples given].][12]

This is one of the few texts to bring together the words *gula* and *Golias* in the same passage. Both words are commonly cited as etymological roots of the word "goliard". Wright deduces (not unreasonably) from the passage that Giraldus was referring to a real person by the name of "Golias" but adds that "Giraldus himself was so far deceived as to believe Golias to have been the real name. . ."[13] The conventional wisdom, authorized by Wright, is that the name is a "mere fanciful appellation"[14] applied to the mythical leader of the goliardic order. Wright further explains (as did Du Cange in a similar way) the nature of the goliardic class under Bishop Golias:

> At the end of the twelfth and during the thirteenth century we meet with frequent mention of a class of persons distinguished by the jocular name of Goliards. In Latin they were termed

---

[11] *Speculum Ecclesiae*, Cap. XV, p. 291. The original, from which the above has been edited anew, is found in British Library, Cotton Tiberius B.XIII, f. 126r/v. In his edition, Brewer made various silent emendations; in this passage, for example, he substituted the words "ridicula" and "ridiculam" for "ridmica" and "ridmicam". He also quietly inserted punctuation and classical spelling. We have retained above the original spelling and punctuation. At the top of f. 126v (after the word "indiscrete" above, the manuscript has been damaged; the reading at that point is not certain. This passage has been quoted and/or discussed in many other studies of goliardic literature, among them the following: Charles du Fresne Du Cange, *Glossarium Mediae et Infimae Latinitatis* (Graz: Akademische Druck-u. Verlagsanstalt, 1954 [reprint of the 1883–87 edition]), IV, 85; Helen Waddell, *The Wandering Scholars*, p. 160; A. G. Rigg, "Golias and Other Pseudonyms", p. 82; James H. Hanford, "The Progenitors of Golias", *Speculum*, I (1926), 38; John Addington Symonds, *Wine Women and Song* (New York: Cooper Square Publishers, 1966 [reprint of the 1884 edition]), pp. 25–26; "Goliards", in *The Dictionary of the Middle Ages*, V, 574; P. G. Walsh. "Golias' and Goliardic Poetry", *Medium Aevum*, LII/1 (1983), 2; F. J. E. Raby, *A History of Secular Latin Poetry in the Middle Ages* (Oxford: Clarendon Press, 1957), p. 340; Vincenzo Crescini, "Appunti su l'etimologia di 'goliardo'", *Atti del Reale Istituto Veneto di Scienze ed Arti*, LXXIX (1920), 1113; Olga Dobiache-Rojdestvensky, *Les Poésies des Goliards* (Paris: Les Éditions Rieder, 1931), p. 21; Alfredo Straccali, *I Goliardi* (Firenze: Tipografia Editrice Dell Gazzetta d'Italia, 1880), pp. 32–3; Barthélemy Hauréau, "Notice sur un manuscrit de la Reine Christine à la Bibliothèque du Vatican", *Notices et Extraits* (Paris: Imprimerie Nationale, 1891), Vol. 29, part 2, pp. 257–58. Unless otherwise specified, all translations in this article are mine.

[12] For another paraphrase, see Waddell, *The Wandering Scholars*, p. 160. As mentioned in note 11, most scholars have accepted the words "ridicula" and "ridiculam" for "ridmica" and "ridmicam" respectively. This has unnecessarily skewed the meaning of the passage and is clearly incorrect when compared with the original.

[13] Wright, *The Latin Poems*, p. ix. Also, on p. xix, referring to the *Confessio Goliae*, he mentions that ". . . it is quoted by Giraldus as if it were a real *bona fide* confession of the person who wrote it . . . ".

[14] *Ibid.*, p. x.

goliardi and *goliardenses*; their profession was termed *goliardia*: the verb *goliardizare* was used to signify *goliardorum more agere*. So in the French of the same period we have the terms *goliard, golliard, goulard, gouliard, gouliardois* (explained by Roquefort as signifying *bouffon, gourmand, glouton, mauvais sujet*), *gouliardie, gouliardise* (explained by *raillerie, plaisanterie*), *gouliarder, gouliardeusement*. The explanations of Roquefort are inaccurate, because the word was not used in any of the general meanings which he gives to it. The *goliardi*, in the original sense of the word, appear to have been in the clerical order somewhat the same class as the jongleurs and minstrels among the laity, riotous and unthrifty scholars who attended on the tables of the richer ecclesiastics, and gained their living and clothing by practising the profession of buffoons and jesters. . . . The name (derived apparently from *gula*, and having nothing in common with the French *gaillard*, as has been supposed), was probably given to them on account of their gluttony and intemperance. The name appears to have originated towards the end of the twelfth century, and, in the documents of that time and of the next century, is always connected with the clerical order.[15]

Wright, then, unlike many succeeding scholars, believed the word "goliard" to be derived from *gula*, rather than *Golias*, which is the other accepted etymological root. He failed to establish, other than by the ascriptions to Golias attached to some of the poems he edited, that the goliards were in fact the creators of the lyric song. This is a basic problem that continued to plague the work of later scholars. The notion of a goliardic brotherhood, with Golias as "the *pater* and the *magister goliardorum*; while the latter were the *pueri* and *discipuli Goliae*",[16] is well established by Wright and becomes a chief dialectical issue down to present-day scholarship, with opinions swinging back and forth as to whether "goliard" owes its origins to *Golias* or *gula*. In spite of Wright's apparent preference for *gula* as the root word for "goliard", he does entitle nineteen of the poems in his book with phrases including the name of Golias, such as *Praedicatio Golias, Golias de suo infortunio* and the like, many of these having been drawn from rubrics in the original manuscripts. We shall return to this crucial passage later in the study with a different interpretation.

In Wright's book, then, two etymological explanations are inaugurated according to root words: "the Golias theory" and "the *gula* theory". On the surface, both of these appear to offer promise but, after Wright, opinion swings more to the "Golias theory". A third common approach seeks to bring together the two. Proponents of the *gula* theory point to the citation from Giraldus, particularly to the supposed "intemperance and wantonness"[17] of Golias himself, and, in so doing, establish the conventional notion of the wandering, morally depraved, indulgent goliard. Scholars have very gingerly pointed to the word *gula* and its potential links to the word under investigation. Over a century ago, John Addington Symonds phrased the possibility in terms of a question:

Was Golias a real person? Did he give his own name to the goliardi; or was he invented after the Goliardi had already acquired their designation? In either case, ought we to connect both words with the Latin *gula*, and so regard the Goliardi as noble gluttons. . . .[18]

---

[15] *Ibid.*, pp. x–xii.
[16] *Ibid.*, p. xiii.
[17] Waddell, *The Wandering Scholars*, p. 160. Also see James W. Thompson, "The Origin of the word 'Goliardi' ", p. 83.
[18] *Wine Women and Song* (New York: Cooper Square Publishers, 1966 [reprint of the 1884 edition]), p. 24.

Likewise, this tentative suggestion:

> The origin of the term *goliard* is far from clear. Perhaps *gula*, gluttony, was the germ from which it sprang. But it must soon have gathered to itself, snowball fashion, various other associations. Among these were implications derived from the Philistine giant Goliath, whose name in the Latin of the Vulgate appears as Golias.[19]

The latest explanations are also very tentative on the word *gula*, suggesting that "goliard" is simply "associated" with both *gula* and Golias.[20] Some suggest that the word *gula* was absorbed by the vernacular, particularly in France, that it was supplied with the suffix *-hard* or *-art* with perhaps an intervening "i" inserted, *viz.*, *gol-i-art*.[21] But others have pointed out that this is problematic:

> ... the word *gula* plus the suffix *-ard, -art*, should, according to the usual patterns of phonological development, yield *goulart* in Medieval French; presumably one would expect to find *gulardus*, or at most, *golardus* in Medieval Latin.[22]

But *gula* lacks an "i" and is thus suspect as the etymological root of "goliard". In any case, there is no reason to think that the goliards were special devotees of the sin of gluttony—the *gula* theory does not make much semantic sense.

The manuscript sources sometimes use the root *gul* (often with a crossed "l") in rubrics and texts. For example, in British Library, Harley 2851, we find *Rithmus guleardi* (f. 12v), *Item Gul.* (ff. 13, 14v, 15), and *Incipit missa Gulonis* (f. 151); in British Library, Add. 21243, we find *De vicio gule* (f. 44) and *Invectio contra guliardos* (f. 46); in British Library, Cotton Titus A.XX, there is *Apocalipsis Guliardi* (f. 156), but the poem ends *Hic explicit apocalipsis episcopi Golie* (f. 158); and in Vatican, Reg. lat. 344 there is a *Ridmus episcopi Gulii* (f. 30). Such instances only confirm a less than rigorous attitude to spelling in the Middle Ages, when one vowel could occasionally be substituted for another; such arguments do not prove that *gula* is the root of *goliard*. Then too, *gula*, the sixth deadly sin of gluttony, is sometimes described in mediaeval treatises, as in these two cases from the thirteenth century:

> Sextus latro est gula qua auferit homini cingulum sum [?] corrigiam solis etatis per quam deberet ventrem a superflui cibi que potest restringere. Et iste latro vulnerat in visceribus et intestinis illa quasi perforando nam viscera gulosi venter esse quasi perforata quis per vult imponere . et cum numquam impletur qui aut esurit cibum aut esuriem cibum que ad ventrem tales cepe vulnerantur infirmitatibus.
>
> [The sixth sin is gluttony by which the belt of a man is born away. The correction of this singular estate is that one ought to restrict the belly as is possible from a superfluity of food. This sin causes wounds in the organs and intestines as if perforating them, for the belly wishes to burden the innards of the glutton as if perforated. And when he who either craves food or is starving hungry is never filled, such [bodily parts?] are often wounded by infirmities.]

* * *

---

[19] George F. Whicher, *The Goliard Poets* (New York: New Directions Publishing, 1949), pp. 2–3.
[20] Gordon Anderson, "Goliards", *The New Grove*, VII, 508. Also see "Goliards", *The Dictionary of the Middle Ages*, Vol. 5, 574.
[21] Vincenzo Crescini, "Appunti su l'etimologia di 'goliardo'", *Atti del Reale Istituto Veneto di Scienze ed Arti*, LXXIX (1920), 1091 and 1127. This is an exhaustive survey of the problem.
[22] E. G. Fichtner, "The Etymology of *Goliard*", *Neophilologus*, LI (1967), 231.

De Gula

Ventri vicina est regio genitalibus apta .
Sordentis que gule est filia; seda Venus .
In vererem venter despumat quam falerno .
Estuat ha multis copia magna nocet .
Proth dolor evertit musos sol Jerusalem Nabuzardin .
Nonne pudicitie sepe nociva gula est;
Ex spuma maris est Saturni testibus ortam;
Dans venerem ventres . quid mare; venter erit .
Saturni testes; luna temporis adite spumam;
Scilicet ingluviem . Nascitur inde Venus .
Cuidam tempestatum vicit gula . vendidit Esau .
Ius pro lenticula premiciale suum .
Non cibum in culpa est . sed vix contenta voluntas;
Limitibus certis . certa . proterva . vaga .
Viro quem Cleopatra sibi traiecit in esum .
Testis erat luxus indicium que gule .
Fame venatrix . dictans sibi iura potensque;
Quid non presumat femina pulcra . decens .[23]

[*Concerning Gluttony*

Near to the belly is the right region for the genitals .
And filthy Venus is the daughter of foul gluttony .
In love how obscenely the womb foams .
It rages, harming many in great abundance .
For grief Nabuzardin, the Jerusalem sun, overturned the muses .
Is not the evil belly often shameful!
From the testes of Saturn is the spume of the sea descended .
Giving bellies love, what a sea the belly will be,
The testes of Saturn. The moon in time approaches a froth,
Just as in gluttony; thence is born Venus.
For whom the stomach overcame a storm. Esau sold
his birthright for a mixture of lentils .
Not in the food is the guilt but in desire scarcely contained!
In fixed limits, personable, shameless, roving
Cleopatra cast down a man into hunger.
Excess was the witness and proof of this gluttony.
The famous huntress, dictating her own laws and power,
Which is not presumed fitting in a beautiful woman.]

The evils ascribed to gluttony and the stomach are several, including stomach ulcers and discomfort described in the one account and the associations with female wiles in

---

[23] The first of these excerpts is from Paris, B. N., fonds latin 15129, f. 271v. The manuscript, from St. Victor, is a miscellaneous compilation of treatises on metre, calendars, sermons, and *summae* from the thirteenth and fourteenth centuries. The second is from Paris, B. N., fonds latin 11867, f. 233v. The latter is from the late thirteenth century and contains letters of Peter of Blois, diverse poetry by Serlo of Wilton, Neckham, and others, passages of Cicero, and hymns to the Virgin. In both of these sources the Latin is heavily abbreviated, difficult to read and apparently corrupt. In the second passage, there are several marginal "corrections" in a hand contemporary with the manuscript. The translations, therefore, can only be rough approximations. The point is that such passages do not, even in their incoherence and twisted mythology, seem to shed any light on the etymology of Goliard. For other accounts of "gula" and the seven sins, see Siegfried Wenzel, *Verses in Sermons. Fasciculus Morum and its Middle English Poems* (Cambridge, Mass.: The Mediaeval Academy of America, 1978), pp. 207–8; and *ibid., Fasciculus Morum: A Fourteenth-Century Preacher's Handbook* (University Park: Pennsylvania State University Press, 1989). "Gula" is discussed over ff. 130v–132 of Oxford, Bodleian Library, MS Rawlinson 670.

the second. But there is little in either account to help us in our explanation of the word *goliard*. The first, drawn from a whole treatise *de vitio gule*, makes use of the following forms of the word: *gula, gule, gulosis, gulosorum*,[24] but it has no overt connection to the word "goliard". The second, with its sexist remarks, also does not seem remotely connected to the word "goliard", though it draws attention to some of those nasty qualities usually associated with the Vaganten. In one of the major creations attributed to Golias, the *Apocalypsis*, there is little to do with gluttony or, indeed, vagabondage or other features often associated with the goliards, nor is the word "goliard" itself used. There is one occurrence of the word *gula* in the poem, but it is not applied to wandering scholars, but rather to a monk:

> 96. Quisque de monacho fit demoniacus
> et cuique monacho congarrit monachus
> ut pica pice vel psittaco psittacus
> cui dat ingenium magister stomachus.
> 97. His mola cencium tumorem faucium
> lagena gutturis ventris diluvium,
> oris aculeus dat flammas licium
> et fratrum malleus calorem noxium.
> 98. Cum inter fabulas et Bachi pocula
> modum et regulam suspendit crapula,
> dicunt, quod dicitur favor a fabula,
> modus a modio, a **gula regula**.[25]
> [96. Of monke a monkey monstrous each becomes;
> Monke sounds to monke just like two sounding drums;
> As pye to pye, parret to parret prates,
> Whose wit their master stomacke arbitrates.
> 97. Some teare with teeth untill their jawes doe swell;
> Others drinke drunke, their belly makes a well.
> The sting of tongues the aflaming fire doth feed;
> The fryers clacke the heate of strife doth feed.
> 98. Among theire fables and their pots of wine,
> The meane and rule doth drunkennes resigne.
> They say that favour is from fable tane,
> The meane from much wine, rule from revel drawne.][26]

The author, clearly well educated and familiar with the Church, subjects the monastic orders to scathing criticism, while he is silent on the collective *penchant* of the goliardic class. If the disciples of Golias were guilty of gluttony, there is little evidence of this in one of his chief poems or in any of the others.

The word *gula*, though it rolls off the tongue a little like "goliard", could at best have been a connotative influence on the word "goliard", not its etymological root. Though "the association between the word *gula* and the *vagantes* appears to have existed from the very beginning of the Western monastic tradition . . . ",[27] it is tenuous

---

[24] See B. N., fonds latin 15129, ff. 271–73.
[25] Karl Strecker, *Die Apokalypse des Golias* (Rome: W. Regenberg, 1928), p. 35.
[26] Translation from *The Revelation of Golias the Bisshoppe* (from Oxford, Bodley 538, c. 1623). While this may not be the most rigorous of translations, the sense of the original is well captured in the seventeenth-century paraphrase. The "gula regula" is perhaps better literally translated "rule from gluttony" or "rule from the belly". The passage is given in Wright, *The Latin Poems Commonly Attributed to Walter Mapes*, p. 291.
[27] Fichtner, "The Etymology of *Goliard*", p. 230.

to consider it much more than a distant homonym to the word "goliard". Giraldus Cambrensis seems to have used it as an off-colour pun in association with "Golias", and it is perhaps in this sense that the words are semantically related.

The most common theory of origin for the word "goliard" rests on the word "Golias", the Vulgate's form for Goliath, the great Philistine. But this derivation is very complex and difficult to establish with any assurance; interpretations of the word "Golias" are numerous, with different shades of meaning according to proponent. While the term "goliard" seems not to have been much used before the thirteenth century, "Golias" does appear at various times before then. Generally in sacred accounts of the David and Goliath story, in mediaeval script, "Golias" ends with an "s" rather than a "th", declined like a normal Greek-derived masculine (*e.g.*, Aeneas). The account of David and Goliath (with revised spelling) from the modern edition of the Vulgate is as follows:

> Et egressus est vir spurius de castris Philisthinorum, nomine Goliath, de Geth, altitudinis sex cubitorum et palmi. Et cassis aerea super caput ejus, et lorica squamata induebatur; porro pondus loricae ejus quinque millia siclorum aeris erat. Et ocreas aereas habebat in cruribus; et clypeus aereus tegebat humeros ejus. Hastile autem hastae ejus erat quasi liciatorium texentium; ipsum autem ferrum hastae ejus sexcentos siclos habebat ferri; et armiger ejus antecedebat eum[28]

> [And there came out from the camp of the Philistines a champion named Goliath, of Gath, whose height was six cubits and a span. He had an helmet of bronze upon his head, and he was armed with a coat of mail; the weight of the coat was five thousand shekels of bronze. He had greaves of bronze upon his legs and a javelin of bronze between his shoulders. The shaft of his spear was like a weaver's beam; and his spear's head weighed six hundred shekels of iron, and his shield-bearer went before him.][29]

This account of Goliath was well known and circulated in western Europe at least from the fourth century when Jerome compiled the *Biblia vulgata*. Augustine (or perhaps Cesarius of Arles (469-542)) preached on the Goliath story, equating Goliath with titanic and ruthless power and spiritual wickedness. This doubtless helped to establish Goliath as a symbolic figure of importance within Church circles.[30] "Goliath" and/or "Golias" share their first five letters with "goliard", which would require only a minor adjustment to create the latter word. It is quite understandable why the name of the Philistine giant is considered a likely root for the later word, but clearly, to judge from the many discussions of this possibility in the scholarly literature, one that is not entirely convincing.

There have been attempts to trace the extra-biblical use of the word "Golias" back to the time it purportedly became the foundation of a new word. A Council under Walter, Archbishop of Sens in 913, which berated ribald clerks who were "vulgarly called the family of Golias", is sometimes singled out as an early instance of this use but, as Waddell and others have rightly pointed out, "the authenticity of the council has been justly disputed: Golias makes that one meteoric appearance, and darkness

---

[28] "Liber Primus Samuelis", Pars Tertia, Cap. XVII, 4–7, *Biblia Sacra* (Rome: Desclée et Socii, 1956), p. 275.
[29] *The New Oxford Annotated Bible*, rev. edn. Edited by B. M. Metzger and Roland E. Murphy (Oxford: Oxford University Press, 1994), p. 364.
[30] John M. Manly, "Familia Golia", *Modern Philology*, V (1907–08), 203 and 208.

swallows him until the first decade of the thirteenth century; his presence in the text is almost certainly a clerical error".[31] Other writers have taken this discussion back a little earlier, attempting unsuccessfully (because the arguments are circular) to entrench the scandals of the goliards three or four centuries earlier than should be done: "So wären die goliarden schon im IX. jahrhundert mit den späteren vaganten identisch, und bei Sedulius fänden wir die *älteste erwähnung* dieser kaste". In his study, Jarcho makes claims for the *gens Goliae* being known as early as 848.[32] The discussion appears to extend almost to absurdity when claims such as this are made as to the anteriority of the word "goliard":

> . . . I think it is certain that the word Goliard is anterior to the appellative Goliath . . . it seems to me to be inverting the order of things to believe that Golias is anterior to *goliard*, or that *goliard* is derived from Golias. Men's minds work from particulars to generals, from concrete things to abstract personifications.[33]

It is, of course, possible that "goliard" was used but never written down, but this seems extremely unlikely.

Inextricably confused with the attempt to establish the root of "Golias" are issues relating to the personality of that individual. The late mediaeval Golias, in addition perhaps to being an *antitype* of the *type* represented by the biblical Goliath,[34] may have been a real person, a shadowy literary convention or, perhaps, some sort of amalgam of the two. One theory suggests that it was no less a figure than Peter Abelard who was the Golias who gave his name to an order of goliards. Peter Abelard (d. *c.* 1142) in his own day was referred to as "Golias",[35] as an intellectual giant and purveyor of heresies. The term may well have arisen in the disputes that culminated in the humiliation of Abelard at the hands of Bernard of Clairvaux. An English presence, often linked to the goliardic phenomenon, is understandable in view of the numbers of students from all parts of Europe who studied with Abelard. A poem such as the *Apocalypse* in its culminating lines viciously attacks gluttony, lechery and drunkenness—allegedly widespread in monasteries in the mid-twelfth century. Nor is the dispute between Bernard and Peter isolated; Goswin also compares Abelard to Goliath, "the Philistine bastard".[36] Unfortunately, there is insufficient evidence to claim that Abelard and his followers were the famed Bishop Golias and his *familia*. There are no goliardic poems that can confidently be ascribed to Abelard. The dispute, the name and the circumstances possibly played some part in colouring the meaning of the word

---

[31] Helen Waddell, *The Wandering Scholars*, p. 183; the original text is quoted in her Appendix E, p. 254, from Joannes Dominicus Mansi, *Sacrorum Conciliorum, Nova et Amplissima Collectio* (Venetis: Apud Antonium Zatta, 1773), xviii, 324. Also see Boris I. Jarcho, "Die Vorläufer des Golias", *Speculum*, III (1928), 525; James W. Thompson, "The Origin of the word '*Goliardi*'", p. 84; Armand Machabey, "Remarques sur les mélodies goliardiques", *Cahiers de civilisation médiévale*, VII (1964), 258 [he also feels that the introduction of the word *goliardi* is suspect in the ninth or tenth centuries]; P. G. Walsh, "'Golias' and goliardic Poetry", *Medium Aevum*, LII/1 (1983), 3; and Vincenzo Crescini, "Appunti su l'etimologia di 'goliardo'", *Atti del Reale Istituto Veneto di Scienze ed Arti*, LXXIX (1920), 1083–86; Straccali, *I Goliardi*, p. 7.

[32] "Die Vorläufer des Golias", pp. 524–25.

[33] Thompson, "The Origin of the Word '*Goliardi*'", p. 97.

[34] For a fascinating account of this general phenomenon in literature, see Northrop Frye, *The Great Code* (Toronto: Academic Press, 1982), p. 78 ff.

[35] See Waddell, *The Wandering Scholars*, pp. 107–08; Whicher, *The Goliard Poets*, p. 3; Crescini, "Appunti su l'etimologia di 'goliardo'", p. 1102; and Hanford, *The Progenitors of Golias*, p. 55.

[36] For an excellent discussion of this matter, see P. G. Walsh, "Golias' and Goliardic Poetry", pp. 3–5.

"goliard". The associations with Abelard and his circle could have been a starting-point for the satire often found in goliardic poetry. But none of the known goliardic poets can be connected definitely with Abelard or Golias.

Giraldus Cambrensis, the main witness for a "goliardic family", was born probably in 1146 or 1147—a little late to have observed at first hand the Abelardian revolt; his friend Walter Map was born a little earlier (c. 1135) but would have been a young boy when Abelard died. Extravagant claims concerning the family of Golias have been based on the passage from *Speculum Ecclesiae*:

> Golias, the jovial shepherd of so many black sheep, is the archtype of the loose-living prelate.[37]
>
> *Golias* was the *pater* and the *magister goliardorum*; while the latter were the *pueri* and *discipuli Goliae*.[38]
>
> By the beginning of the thirteenth century they have actually a burlesque order, with Golias for its legendary Grand-master.[39]
>
> We can hardly avoid the conclusion that by Golias Episcopus, Primas and Archipoeta one and the same person, occupying a prominent post in the Order, was denoted. He was the head of the Goliardic family, the Primate of the Wandering Students' Order, the Archpoet of these lettered minstrels. . . . Though we seem frequently upon the point of touching the real man, he constantly eludes our grasp. Who he was, whether he was one or many, remains a mystery.[40]
>
> It seems likely, since so few goliardic authors are known by name, that the fictional company was used to mask the identities of poets who feared that their works, whether parodic, satirical, or just outrageous, would get them into trouble.[41]

Then there are more circumspect suggestions, such as this:

> Titular author of a score of satirical and humorous compositions in Latin accentual verse, noticed early in the thirteenth century by Giraldus Cambrensis as a certain *parasitus, gulositate et leccacitate famossissimus*, of his own day, associated with the term "goliard" as the chief or patron of a kind of international *Bund*, the so called *ordo vagorum*, he is one of the focal points of an important field of mediaeval enquiry and, as such, has provoked much scholarly curiosity. The net result of all discussion thus far has been a disputed etymology and the verdict that Golias, in spite of the veracious Gerald, must be accounted a medieval myth . . . a grotesque creation of the mediaeval mind.[42]

The notion that Golias is a mythical individual, a mediaeval shadow, ". . . the ghost par exellence",[43] is one that seems to have gained pre-eminence in our own time. The vaporous characters, such as the Archpoet, Primas, Golias and Gauterus, are confused

---

[37] Waddell, *The Wandering Scholars*, p. 187.
[38] Wright, *The Latin Poems Commonly Attributed to Walter Mapes*, p. xiii.
[39] Waddell, *The Wandering Scholars*, p. 185.
[40] John Addington Symonds, *Wine Women and Song*, pp. 201–02. The frequent allusion to bishops in the context of secular Latin poetry perhaps has something to do with the obviously prominent place they held in the Middle Ages but also might reflect the original Greek meaning of the word as "an overseer" or "superintendent". In this latter sense the term "episcopus" is closer to the sense of an *arch-mime* as discussed below.
[41] "Goliards", *Dictionary of the Middle Ages*, V, 575–76.
[42] J. H. Hanford, "The Progenitors of Golias", p. 38.
[43] A. G. Rigg, "Golias and Other Pseudonyms", p. 68. Most of the poems bearing the name of Golias in the sources have been determined to be the works of other known mediaeval poets.

in the literature,[44] and some feel that it is perhaps best to consider them literary conventions with some interchangeability.[45]

It is far from clear that the *familia Golias* existed at all; and, if it did, whether it was an identifiable group; whether the compound term was a kind of collective descriptor for a variety of such groups active in Europe in the twelfth and thirteenth centuries; or, finally, whether or not it was simply a literary allusion. There is some scanty evidence that there were other groups active that were not unlike the *familia Golias*. Another group apparently set up with a mock ecclesiastical organization was named the "Eberhardini" (perhaps after Eberhard, Archbishop of Salzburg), which Waddell characterizes as "an alternate name for the *goliardi*".[46] The account books of Wolfger of Ellenbrechstkirchen (active between 1190 and 1210) and the proceedings of a Council in Mainz in 1261 include these comments (respectively):

> *In pascha* Florentiam cuidam Ebberardinorum episcopo et cuidam alii mimo dim. tal. veron. domino episcopo .xij. den. frisac. Aput Senas cuidam cantatrici et duobus ioculatoribus .vij. sol, et .vj. den sen.[47]
>
> [At Easter in Florence to a certain bishop of the Eberhardini and to another actor (mime) [was given] half a Veronese talent [and] to the lord bishop twelve denarii of Freisingen. At Siena to a certain female singer and two *ioculatores* (jongleurs?) seven soldi and six denarii Sienese.]

* * *

> De Quaestuariis et Clericis vagabundis: Clerici et vagabundi, quos vulgus Eberhardinos vocat, quorum vita Deo odibilis, etiam Laicos scandalizat, priori inhaerentes Concilio, a Clericis vel Personis Ecclesiasticis recipi prohibemus, firmiter statuentes: ne aliquid dent iisdem ... adjicientes, quod Eberhardini qui vitam ducunt reprobam et infamem ...[48]
>
> [Concerning mercenaries and vagabond clerks: clerks and vagabonds, which the vulgar call Eberhardini, whose life is hateful to God and also scandalizes the laity, in accordance with a prior council, we prohibit them to be received by clerics or Ecclesiastical persons, firmly decreeing that they not give them anything ... adding that, Eberhardini who lead a life of shame and infamy. ...]

In the first citation, the bishop of the Eberhardini appears to be equated with other actors, singers and entertainers—a point that we will pick up later.[49] This may be the *ordo vagorum*, the "... hobo poets' guild as a kind of burlesque of the religious brotherhoods",[50] but there can be no certainty that there was only one of its type. If wandering scholars were the members, it is unclear, in spite of the rise of mendicant orders in the thirteenth century, how they might have developed an organized brotherhood of this type. There is evidence that a mock order of monks functioned in

---

[44] See, for example, Nic Spiegel, *Die Vaganten und ihr 'Orden'* (Speyer: Jäger'sche Buchdruckerei, 1892), p. 42.
[45] For more on this, see Rigg, "Golias and Other Pseudonyms", *passim*; Hennig Brinkmann, "Anfänge lateinischer Liebesdichtung im Mittelalter", *Neophilologus*, 9 (1924), 208; Raby, *Secular Latin Poetry*, p. 339; Boris Jarcho, "Die Vorläufer des Golias", p. 525.
[46] *The Wandering Scholars*, p. 216.
[47] Ignaz V. Zingerle, *Reiserechnungen Wolfger's von Ellenbrechtskirchen* (Heilbronn: Verlag von Gebr. Henninger, 1877), p. 26.
[48] Quoted in J. Frantzen, "Zur Vagantendichtung", *Neophilologus*, V (1920), 63.
[49] In Mansi, *Sacrorum Conciliorum*, xxii, cols. 293–94, in the proceedings from Lateran Council III of 1179, there is an "Eberardino Paduano" (Eberhard of Padua) mentioned, but without passages which would link him to travelling actors.
[50] Whicher, *The Goliard Poets*, p. 5.

a theatrical environment at Exeter as late as 1348–1352.[51] The accounts of the Eberhardini and, indeed, of the Golias family, say little of the actual activities carried out by its members, other than travel and scandalous behaviour. They do not say that these men were poets or musicians; this is a leap of faith taken by scholars from Wright down to the present day. The shadowy figure of the Archpoet, often equated with Golias, may actually be another similar figure with a following centred near Cologne but, in the absence of clear documentation, further speculation could do more harm than good.[52]

The diffuse and uncertain nature of the so-called "Order of Goliards" and its ephemeral leader do not help to sort out the etymology of the word "goliard", nor does its existence bring us much closer to what a goliard was. In addition to the *gula* and *Golias* theories mentioned above, there are several hybrid and alternative suggestions for the etymology of "goliard" that have been formulated. Some of these may seem, at least, influencing factors in the shaping of the word; others are perhaps more outlandish. One theory, first developed by Jakob Grimm,[53] is that the word "Goliardi" is derived from the vernacular, in particular, from the Provençal *gualiar* ("to deceive") or through the form *gualiador* ("deceiver"). This is reflected by Symonds in 1884 in the suggestion that it is connected with the Provençal *goliar, gualiar, gualiardor*—words that carry the significance of deceit. The obvious problem with this is that we have a rather bankrupt definition if we describe a goliard simply as a "deceiver"—there are better words for that in Latin. Crescini adds the Provençal *galiador, galiar, galiamen* and *galiairitz* to the list.[54] Wright, himself, explored a variety of French words as the possible etymological roots, such as *golliard, goulard, gouliard, gouliardie, gouliardise, gouliarder, gouliardeusement* and the like, and Crescini various others.[55] Some see the vernacular as an interactive factor with the Latin, such as Rigg: ". . . I would agree with Crescini's conclusions, that the words *gula* and *Golias* (Goliath) interacted on each other via the form *golart*".[56] Another combinative formula is that the rare Latin word *ardalio* or *ardelio* was joined with *gula*: "From these two words, *gula* + *ardelio*, plural, *gula* + *ardeliones*, the derivation of the word *goliardi* becomes clear. Hence *goliardenses* or *goliardi*, meaning "busy-bodies in or devotees of gluttony", *gula* being an ablative of specification".[57] This *gula*-based theory concludes with even more far-fetched suggestions that "Old King Cole" was somehow related to Golias.[58] Another theory links a nickname for Peter Abelard, that is, *baiolardus* (lard-licker), with *Golias* and *goliardus*.[59]

Another investigation, using the techniques of linguistics and phonology, reaches some individual notions as to how the word "goliard" emerged. According to patterns of phonological development, *gula* plus the suffix *-ard, -art* should yield *goulart* in

---

[51] See Roger S. Loomis and Gustave Cohen, "Were there Theatres in the Twelfth and Thirteenth Centuries?" *Speculum*, XX (1945), 92.
[52] For an excellent discussion of the Archpoet, see Rigg, "Golias and Other Pseudonyms", pp. 70–72.
[53] *Kleinere Schriften*, III, p. 46. This point is replicated in Manly, "*Familia Goliae*", p. 201 and Thompson "The Origin of the Word 'Goliardi'", p. 83.
[54] "Appunti su l'etimologia di 'goliardo'", p. 1080.
[55] *The Latin Poems Commonly Attributed to Walter Mapes*, pp. x–xii and "Appunti su l'etimologia d 'goliardo'", p. 1091 (respectively).
[56] "Golias and Other Pseudonyms", 66n.
[57] Thompson, "The Origin of the word '*Goliardi* ' ", p. 96.
[58] *Ibid.*, pp. 97–98.
[59] P. G. Walsh, "'Golias' and Goliardic Poetry", p. 5.

French and *gulardus* or *golardus* in Mediaeval Latin. The absent "i" makes *gula* an unlikely root, although it may have had connotative links with the longer word. Endings such as *-ard* and *-hard* were becoming common in twelfth and thirteenth-century Europe, especially in the Rhineland and Netherlands. The ending of "goliard" is just another example of this phenomenon, according to E. G. Fichtner, the one who developed this theory:

> The stem *goli-* is, I submit, the stem of the verb PrGmc. *gōljan*, reflexes of which are present in all branches of the Germanic language family. From the morphological standpoint, it is a *-j-* expansion of the second principal part of the verb PrGmc. *galan/gōl* of the sixth Ablaut series. Both verbs, *galan* and *gōljan*, are present in the various Germanic dialects, though not necessarily both in every one.... The word *goliard*, a compound of *goli-* plus *-(h)ard*, probably originated in the mediaeval German dialects of the Rhine as a derogatory term for wandering clerics who constituted part of the floating population of "Spilleute" and minstrels. In Germany the meaning of the term was probably fairly clear to anyone using it....[60]

Although the theory has some merit, it is more likely that the Angevin empire to the west, where much of the poetry originated and more poets were active, was the real location of the most pertinent etymological development.

Thus far, we have observed a bewildering variety of speculations mixed with scant hard information in support of what should be a relatively simple etymological problem. Most of the theories already expressed are troublesome in one way or another; none can be singled out as even the most probable. The unsettling nature of the "goliardic problem" has led writers such as Rigg to revisit the sources, the ascriptions and colophons themselves, in search of primary information that may have been misconstrued or neglected.[61] But, partly because the literature surveyed thus far did not neglect these very sources, and partly because of the nature of those ascriptions, the return to the sources does not resolve the issues. In the interests of thoroughness, however, at least some of the rubrics should be examined once again; they cannot be neglected in any etymological theory of the word "goliard".

As has been mentioned, Wright (while suggesting that they be ascribed to Walter Map) supplied at least nineteen titles for the poems he edited that included some form of the name "Golias". Not all of these are to be found in the source manuscripts, but some of them are, and Rigg has added many more to the list.[62] The excellent work of Rigg need not be duplicated here, but some notion of the problems that stem from the rubrics is useful. Typically they are associated with particular poems, are indeed written in red ink (or in some other prominent way) at the beginnings, ends and, sometimes marginally, in the middle of the poetry. The descriptors can vary in length from single words (usually names or their abbreviations) to rather extended phrases. For identical poems, the rubrics can change in different versions; for example, the *Apocalypsis* is attributed not only to Primas and Golias, but simply qualified by the

---

[60] "The Etymology of Goliard", *Neophilologus*, LI (1967), 232–33.
[61] "Golias and Other Pseudonyms", p. 69.
[62] *The Latin Poems Commonly Attributed to Walter Mapes, passim*. Wright often indicates the manuscripts, such as Harley 978, Cot. Vesp. A.XIX, and Harley 2851, where these rubrics are found. In other cases, he has simply suggested the titles. For an exhaustive listing, see Rigg, "Golias and Other Pseudonyms", 81ff.

genitive *galiardorum*.⁶³ In the ascriptions, spelling is very casually handled. We encounter such renditions as *guleardi, galiardorum, goliardus, Gula, Golias* and various other related words. Apparent names are often abbreviated, such as *Gul.*, which raises yet another problem of interpretational subjectivity to be dealt with. Does the just-mentioned abbreviation mean *Gulias, Gula, Guola* or *Gualterus*? It has, for unknown reasons, also been assumed that the cryptic single names attached to poems signify the poet. This is a crucial matter, but one that long ago seems to have degenerated into thoughtless dogma on the part of philologists. As we shall see, there is at least the possibility that some of these indicate the performer (actor, singer) who delivered the poem rather than the individual who created it. In liturgical dramas and chants, there are rubrics supplied indicating which person, either a character, cantor, priest or lesser church official, should actually deliver the lines in question. As many of the manuscripts containing secular song were compiled and stored at monasteries, the contingency that certain performers were indicated is distinctly possible. The latter possibility may help to explain the variety of multiple authorships ascribed to goliardic poems and cannot be ruled out as a potential explanation of the rubrics. In any case, the rubrics are not particularly helpful in solving the etymological problem.

A few examples should suffice to indicate why this is so. In British Library, Harley 2851, there is a series of poems on ff. 13, 14v and 15 respectively, which bear the following rubrics attached to poems (in parentheses): *Item Gul de vite* ("Estuans intrinsecus . . ."); *Item Gul. de equo pontificie* ("Pontificalis equus est"); *Item Gul de???* ("Et Leo pontifex . . ."). There is also a *Rithmus guleardi . . .* on f. 12v and a *Missa Gulonis*, a parody of the Mass, on f. 151. In each case when the abbreviation *Gul* appears it has an abbreviatory slash through it and could mean *guleardus, Gulias, Gualterus* or several other things. The term *guleardi* might seem to suggest a link with the *gula* root. Or is it simply a manifestation of casual spelling practices where vowels "a", "u" and "o" are interchanged? Do the rubrics refer to Golias, Gualo, an unknown goliard or, indeed, perhaps Walter Mapes (Gualterus) himself? In British Library, Add. 21243, f. 46, we have an *Invecto contra guliardos* ("Rura tibi mannus . domus . . ."); this presents a similar problem. In Vatican, Reg. lat. 344, f. 30, we encounter the *Ridmus episcopi Gulii* ("Estuans intrinsicus . . .") again. In British Library, Cotton Titus A.XX, f. 156, we find the rubric *Apocalipsis Guliardi* in the side margin in the original hand with a later editorial script above it reading *Goliae pontificis*, yet at the end of the poem in the original hand we see *Hic explicit apocalipsis episcopi Golie*. Moreover, some of the rubrics are clearly later additions, sometimes inserted centuries after the original poems were written. The casual attitude of the scribes makes it unsafe to employ such indications as evidence in the etymological debate.

If the goliards, whoever they were, really wrote the lyrics attributed to them and were indeed organized into some sort of brotherhood, one would expect to find, in the poems themselves, references at the least, and probably various insights into, the social fabric of the creators. Self-references are almost entirely lacking in the large corpus of secular Latin songs. There are just a few song texts that are explicitly connected to the word "goliard", and they are disappointing indicators of the serious creative activities

---

⁶³ This latter in the lost fourteenth-century Herdringen (Louvain UB G. 65) manuscript. See Rigg, "Golias and Other Pseudonyms", p. 93.

of the class. Nevertheless, these poems deserve a close look for what they do tell us. The most frequently cited is that of the aspiring goliard Richard, which begins as follows:

> Omnibus in Gallia angelus **Goliardus**,
> obediens et humilis . frater non bastardus .
> **Goliae** discipulis dolens quod tam tardus .
> mandat salutem fratribus . nomine Ricardus.
>
> Scribo vobis timide . tanquam vir ignotus .
> qui tamen dum vixero . vester ero totus
> deprecor attentius supplex et devotus .
> **Goliardus** fieri non vilis harlotus .
>
> Accedit ad vos nuncius vir magne probitatis .
> magister et dominus . Willelmus de Conflatis .
> **Goliardus** optimus . hoc non timeatis .
> sicut decet socium ipsum admittatis .
>
> quicquid de me dixerit . verum teneatis .
> et quod volueritis . per eum rescribatis .
> que mihi scripseritis . vel ore mandatis .
> pro posse meo faciam certissime sciatis.
>
> * * *
>
> Summa salus omnium filius Marie
> pascat . potet . vestiat pueros **Golye**
> et conservet socios sanctae confratrie .
> ad dies usque ultimos Enohc et Helye . Amen.[64]

[To all brothers in Gaul, an English[65] goliard,
an obedient and humble brother, not a bastard,
a disciple of Golias, grieving for being so slow,
I, Richard by name, entrust a greeting.

I write to you timidly as a humble man,
who nevertheless while I live shall be totally yours;
I pray attentively, suppliant and devoted,
That I might be a goliard, not a vile harlot[66]

A messenger approaches you, a man of great probity,
master and lord William de Conflatus,
a very fine goliard, this you must not fear;
just as it is also fitting that you should accept his friend.

Whatever he will say of me you should consider the truth,
and you may reply whatever you wish through him;
whatever you might write to me or send by word of mouth,
you will know most assuredly what I can do.

* * *

---

[64] Published in Wright, *The Latin Poems Commonly Attributed to Walter Mapes*, p. 69 and found in British Library, Harley 978, f. 58v [38v] (unique source). The spelling and punctuation have been restored to their original form.

[65] Wright gives us the form "Anglus", which would mean "English", but the original manuscript reads "angelus", which could mean either "English" or "angelic". The word "bastardus" at the end of the next line is also problematic. It could designate "a bastard" or it could simply be an adjective meaning "impure". The first two lines could be rendered: "To all brothers in Gaul, an angelic goliard, an obedient and humble brother, not impure . . .".

[66] "Harlotus" can also mean "vagabond" or "beggar".

The high salvation of all, the Son of Mary,
may he feed, provide drink for, and clothe the boys of Golias!
and save the friends of the holy confraternity
to the last days of Enoc and Elias! Amen!]

The term *goliardus* is used three times in the poem and *Goliae* (spelt in two ways) twice. After the first four stanzas there is a passage of 26 lines (omitted above) in which the author, departing from his humble opening and pious postscript, eagerly anticipates the pleasures of the table, drink and the flesh. Waddell interprets the passage (including the stanzas missing above) in this way:

> An English goliard, writing like Mr. Verdant Green, to headquarters in France, propounds a series of points on which he would be resolved, such as whether it is better to make love to Rose or Agnes: to eat boiled beef or little fishes driven into the net....[67]

This English or angelic goliard expresses his sincere aspirations to join like-minded people on the Continent and documents the kinds of activities that he is interested in; but the main point is that these are not specified as poetic or musical pursuits, rather the extra-curricular activities that may be expected in the life-style of the goliard, not the professional pursuits. In wishing to join a group of goliards, which could in fact be a troupe of actors, he is patient, willing to be co-operative and to join in the acceptable activities and revelries of the group. Another poem records a dialogue between a "Goliardus" and "Episcopus" and begins in this way:

> *Goliardus*
> Si dederis vestes que possunt pellere pestes
> dii michi sunt testes erimus Pillades et Horestes
>
> ["If you should be given clothes which can turn away plagues,
> the gods are my witnesses, we will be Pillades and Orestes."]
>
> *Episcopus*
> Si post hoc dictum nummos quaeras vel amictum,
> non est delictum si quis tibi praebeat ictum....
>
> ["If after this speech you seek money or a mantle,
> it is not a fault if anyone offers you a blow...."][68]

From the reference to the tragedy of Euripides based on the Orestes story (Orestes was the son of Agamemnon and Clytemnestra—his faithful friend is Pylades), we can gather that the goliard was familiar with classical drama. The goliard appears to be an aspiring actor, given the chance, rather than a poet or musician. The bishop counsels modesty and to be satisfied with what one is given rather than to seek after things that are difficult to attain. There is no reference in the poem to creating lyric song.

The following excerpt (first two of seven verses) bears the rubric *Rithmus guleardi de pilleo furato ab episcopo dato* (in a different hand from that of the main text) in Harley 2851:

> Raptor mei pillei morte moriatur .
> mors sit subitanea . nec prevideatur [preiudicatur] .

---

[67] Waddell, *The Wandering Scholars*, p. 185.
[68] The poem is published in Wright, *ibid.*, p. 86 and appears in manuscripts British Library, Arundel 334, f. 2 and Harley 978, f. 103v. The former manuscript bears dates 1326 and 1399 on f. 6.

> et pena continua post mortem sequatur .
> nec campis Helysiis post Lethen fruatur [feratur] .
>
> Raptor mei pillei seva morte cadat .
> illum febris . rabies . et tabes invadat
> hunc de libro Dominus vite sancte radat!
> hunc tormentis Eacus cruciandum tradat.[69]
>
> [May the robber of my headgear perish in death,
> may that death be sudden, nor foreseen,
> and may continual torment follow after death,
> nor let him enjoy the Elysean fields after Lethe.
>
> May the robber of my headgear be felled in savage death,
> may fevers, madness and putrefaction invade him,
> may the Lord raze him from the holy book of life;
> may Aeacus deliver him to the torments of crucifixion!]

In classical Latin, the *pilleus* (*pileus*) was a felt cap or hat made to fit close and shaped like half of an egg. It was often worn at the Saturnalia, entertainments and other festivals in ancient Rome. It was also donned by Roman slaves at their manumission. The poet, here designated a goliard by the rubric, twice bitterly reproaches the robber of his hat or *pilleus*, condemning him to the torments of Hell and perdition. Why should the loss of a cap, albeit a later mediaeval version of the *pilleus*, be a matter for such severe condemnation? The answer to this question, I would propose, brings us very close to a reasonable definition of the word "goliard", much more convincing, and consistent with the evidence than previous definitions have been.

We have seen that the word "goliard" may have been related to *gula* and/or *Golia*, although these are not particularly convincing roots, and that spellings for "goliard" can be casual, with "a", "u" and "o" being used for the first syllable of the word. In other words, since the word is spelt *goliardus, guleardus* or *galiardus*, it seems reasonable to broaden the search for a root to allow for these contingencies.[70] Since there are several other possible roots using different combinations of vowels, it is informative to return briefly to dictionaries and lexicons for the word "goliard"[71] and its potential relatives. The word "goliard" itself is not new to such studies and has appeared at various times over the past few centuries. In order to save space, the different possibilities, with sources noted, can be summarized thus:

1. *Goliardus (goliardia, goliardenses)*—(*a*) "Goliardi, bufones, joculatores iidem sunt"; "histrionia, professio Goliardi, seu histrionis"; "Monetae species";[72] (*b*) "jongleur, farceur, juggler, buffoon";[73] (*c*) "reveller, 'goliard' ".[74] The general

---

[69] Wright, *The Latin Poems* . . ., pp. 75–76. The poem appears in British Library, Harley 978, f. 103 (83) and Harley 2851, f. 12v. The original punctuation and spelling have been restored. In addition to the two variants in brackets above, there are several other minor ones between the two sources.

[70] For some of these spellings, see "guleardus" from Harley 2851 (mentioned above); "galiardos" in Mansi, *Sacrorum Conciliorum*, xxv, col. 227; Nic Spiegel, *Die Vaganten und ihr 'Orden'* (Speyer: Jäger'sche Buchdruckerei, 1892), p. 37 (he cites a Salzburg source of 1310); and in the lost Herdringen Manuscript (Louvain UB G. 65), f. 114, we have the designation "Apocalypsis galiardorum".

[71] It should be remembered that various Latin dictionaries and lexicons are classically oriented and do not include the mediaeval word "goliardus".

[72] Du Cange, *Glossarium* . . ., IV, 85.

[73] J. F. Niermeyer, *Mediae Latinitatis Lexicon Minus* (Leiden: E. J. Brill, 1976), p. 471.

[74] R. E. Latham, *Revised Medieval Latin Word-List* (London: Oxford University Press, 1965), p. 214.

argument, vague and sometimes circular, is that the goliard was a type of entertainer with acting capabilities, but these definitions do not really penetrate to the etymological question; they function more from associations and contextual statements. The use of the term as a species of money (Du Cange) is curious but perhaps not unrelated when it is remembered that the "crown" became a unit of currency in various countries. This brings us again to links with the word "hat" or "helmet", which was alluded to earlier.

2. *Golia (golaia, golatia, golola, golora)*—(*a*) "Nomen vulgaris animalis, quod testudo appellatur"; "Testudo, quam vulgo testudinem, alii golaiam dicunt"; "Testudo, animal quod testam gerit, idest golola";[75] (*b*) "Testudo, quam vulgo Guolatiam vocant. Testudo, quam vulgo Golia dicunt";[76] (*c*) "testudo, id est galapago marino sive riano"; ". . . testudo, quam vulgo guleram vocant".[77] Aside from the sense discussed earlier (Golias = Goliath), the term *golia* seems to have indicated a tortoise or turtle. *Testudo* also could mean a lyre (primitively fashioned from a tortoise shell), an arch, the covering of a hedgehog, the collective protection taken by soldiers in putting shields over their heads, or a head-dress in imitation of a lyre.[78]

3. *Galea (galerus, galeo-areatus)*—(*a*) "Nomen, quod videtur esse γαλέη; mustela vel mustellina pellis: quod ex eius corio galea olim fieri, ut eadem a Graecis etiam Χυγέη vocatur, quod e canis corio fieri soleret: ita quoque Itali celata appellant";[79] (*b*) "helmet; helmeted warrior";[80] (*c*) "leather helmet. Commonly taken as . . . weasel skin";[81] (*d*) "A soldier's helmet";[82] (*e*) "Munimentum capitis est, e corio quondam fieri solitum";[83] (*f*) "Cassis de lamina est, galea de corio", "Apex est, quod in summa galea eminet, quo figitur crista";[84] (*g*) "Seu caput abdiderat cristata casside pennis, in galea formosus erat;[85] (*h*) "a helmet (usually of leather), head-piece, morion [crested helmet];" "the crest of the guinea fowl".[86] It might be added that the term is used in the biblical account of David and Goliath.[87] The Greek root of the Latin word may be one source of spelling variation for the first vowel of "goliard". The consensus seems to be that a *galea* was a helmet of leather, often with a plume or crest.

The short words *golia* and *galea* documented above seem to have strong connections to headgear (hats, helmets, even masks). In viewing the rich assortment of pictorial material in books on mediaeval theatre, it is clear that the acting community included individuals who wore hats, often with preposterous shapes and plumes of

---

[75] Aegidii Forcellini & Iosepho Furlanetto, *Totius Latinitatis Lexicon* (Prati: Typis Aldinianis, 1865), iii, 223. Also see *Thesaurus Linguae Latinae* (Lipsia: B. G. Teubneri, 1925–34), vi, col. 2125.
[76] Du Cange, *Glossarium*, IV, 85.
[77] Monks of Vindobensis, *Thesaurus Linguae Latinae* (Lipsia: B. G. Teubneri, 1924), VI, col. 2125.
[78] Lewis and Short, *A Latin Dictionary*, p. 1864.
[79] Forcellini & Furlanetto, *Totius Latinitatis Lexicon*, iii, 180–81.
[80] Latham, *Revised Medieval Latin Word-List*, p. 206.
[81] T. G. Tucker, *A Concise Etymological Dictionary of Latin* (Halle: Max Niemeyer, 1931), p. 107.
[82] P. G. W. Glare, ed., *Oxford Latin Dictionary* (Oxford: Clarendon Press, 1982), p. 752.
[83] Roberti Stephani, *Thesaurus Linguae Latinae* (Basel: E. and J. R. Thurnisiorum, 1740 [reprinted 1964]), II, 440.
[84] Isidore, *Etymologiarum* in Migne, *Patrologia Latina*, 82, Lib. xviii, Caput xiv, Col. 649.
[85] Ovid, *Metamorphoses* (New York: Garland, 1976), p. 250 (the quotation is from the story of Nisus and Scylla).
[86] Lewis and Short, *A Latin Dictionary*, p. 800.
[87] "Et induit Saul David vestimentis suis, et imposuit galeam aeream super caput ejus, et vestivit eum lorica". *Liber Primus Samuelis*, Cap. xvii, 38.

various sorts.[88] To be sure, headgear must also have figured largely in other strata of mediaeval society (*e.g.*, bishop's mitre, regal crowns), but the conspicuously grotesque nature it seems to have displayed in the theatrical world could well have elicited special attention. The *galeae* worn in the Middle Ages must have changed from the military gear worn in the ancient world. It is the thesis of this article that the etymological root of "goliard" ("galiard") is to be found, not in Goliath or the gut, but in the headgear that must have been worn by some members of the acting profession. Not unlike the English term "masker", the term "galiardus" must have sprung from the prominent attire worn by certain actors of the day. This would explain why the "goliard" mentioned above, having lost a key piece of dramatic equipment, should be so incensed at the robbery of his "headgear" or hat.

There is strong evidence that, rather than being poets or poet/musicians, the goliards were members of the acting community. Mediaeval actors, of course, functioned in a very different way from that of actors of today, or even those of Shakespeare's time. It is highly probable that, in addition to drama or quasi-dramatic entertainments, their duties extended to mime (as we know it, and also in the more classical sense of "acting" or imitating reality), elocution (poetry), singing, dancing and any other *ad hoc* entertainment that might have been called for by their fickle patrons. The council proceedings investigated by so many scholars support such a theory overwhelmingly. A brief sampling from twelfth and thirteenth-century church conciliar documents (generally negative towards performers) will suffice to show that the goliards, far from being marginal, were included among the actor-entertainers of the Middle Ages (my bold type) and quite possibly included in monastic life:

Statuimus etiam, ut in mensa, saltem in principio et fine, coram eis sacra lectio recitetur: **et ne in mensa histriones, vel mimos, vel eorum audiant instrumenta**. (Mansi, xxii, col. 840—Council of Paris, 1212 A.D.)

[We also decree, that at table, at least at the beginning and end [of the meal], that in their presence a sacred reading should be recited: and this in order that at table they not listen to actors, mimes, or their instruments.]

Item prohibemus, ne clerici exerceant negotia turpia, et officia inhonesta, quae non decent clericos, qualia sunt haec . . . officium cambitoris, carnificis tabernarii, procenetae, fullonis, sutoris, textoris, nec sint **histriones, joculatores, ballivi, forestarii saeculares, goliardi, thelonarii, unguentarii, triparii, molendinarii**. Si vero clerici aliqui officia talia exercuerint, a suo prelato super hoc puniantur. (Mansi, xxiv, col. 910–911—Synod at Liège, 1287 A.D.)

[Likewise we prohibit clerks from engaging in shameful business, and dishonest occupations which are not suitable for clerks such as . . . money changers, flesh dealers, procurors, fullers, cobblers, weavers, nor are these [suitable occupations]: actors, minstrels, dancers, secular foresters, goliards, thelonaries [?], masseurs, tripe-sellers, millers. If any clerks exercise themselves in such offices, upon this they must be punished by their prelate.]

Item praecipimus quod clerici non sint **joculatores, goliardi, seu bufones**, declarantes quod si per annum illam artem diffamatoriam exercuerint omni prifilegio ecclesiastico sunt nudati. . . . **Item si in goliardia, vel histrionatu** per annum fuerint vel breviori tempore, et ter moniti non desistunt. (Mansi, xxiv, cols. 1017, 1019—Cahors, Rodez, and Toul, 1289 A.D.)

---

[88] See the many photos in Allardyce Nicoll, *Masks Mimes and Miracles* (New York: Cooper Square Publishers, 1963), especially pp. 74, 79, 150, 161, 193. It is abundantly clear from this book that headgear and masks played a fundamental role in mediaeval dramatic presentatons. See also, E. K. Chambers, *The Medieval Stage* (Oxford: Oxford University Press, 1903), frontispiece and *passim*.

[Likewise we enjoin that clerks not be minstrels, goliards or buffoons, declaring that if through a year they shall exercise their defamatory art, they are stripped of all ecclesiastical privileges. . . . Likewise if they do not desist in the activities of goliards or actors through a year or shorter time, and after three warnings.]

De clerics **ioculatoribus**. . . . Clerici qui clericali ordini non modicum detrahentes, se **ioculatores seu galiardos** [*sic*] faciunt, aut **buffones**, si per annum artem illam ignominiosam exercuerint ipso jure. . . . (Mansi, xxv, Col. 227—Salzburg, 1310 A.D.)

[Concerning minstrel clerks. . . . Clerks who not following the precepts of the clerical order, who become minstrels or goliards or buffoons, if through a year they exercise their shameless art by the very law. . . .]

It should be noted that these passages, and others like them,[89] do not claim that goliards (or the other kinds of entertainers) are clerks, but the reverse: as proceedings of the Church, the councils express concern that clerks have been led to serve as actors—that they have been led astray. More such listings can be found in Mansi, sometimes including the word "goliardus" (or a variant) and sometimes not. Occasionally, there seem to be allusions to the "familia Golias", as in this statement by Matthew Paris in 1229: "Quidam famuli, vel mancipia, velilli, quos solemus Goliardenses appellare, versus ridiculosus componebant". In this case, a group, perhaps a troupe of actors, is accused of writing silly verses.[90] And it seems that goliards were capable of singing, judging from the Provincial Council at Trèves in 1227: "Item praecipimus ut omnes sacerdotes non permittant trutannos aut alios vagos scholares aut goliardos cantare versus super *Sanctus* et *Agnus Dei* aut alis in missis vel in divinis officiis".[91] That the actors should move in troupes or sing, even in church (or a parody thereof), is entirely consistent with the kinds of actions that would probably have been expected of travelling Thespians. Rather than thinking of goliards as "poet-musicians", as is usually done, they are better considered as players (perhaps often with mute or visually captivating parts) in mediaeval entertainments or dramas.

At one time, the Middle Ages was considered a dramatic wasteland, a time after the great Classical plays had withered and died and before the blossoming of the rich Renaissance dramatic tradition. Although there may not have been established theatres or professional troupes in the modern sense, nor the twentieth-century aesthetic values, it is now clear that, beyond the numerous mediaeval liturgical dramas, there were many secular plays and quasi-dramatic productions in courts and even in monastic institutions. From the twelfth to the fourteenth century there are about 300 references to non-religious plays, though most of them (assuming they were written down) have not survived.[92] Hrotsvitha (*c.* 935–1000) wrote six Latin *comedia* in imitation of

---

[89] Many more of these citations are to be found in the appendices of Waddell, *The Wandering Scholars*.
[90] Du Cange, *Glossarium*, IV, 85.
[91] "Likewise it is advised that all priests are not to allow rogues, other wandering scholars or goliards to sing verses upon the Sanctus and Agnus Dei, or elsewhere in masses or the divine offices". (Mansi, xxiii, col. 33). Note that there is a distinction made between the wandering scholars and the goliards; this passage has been used to prove that the two are one and the same.
[92] See the various excellent articles under "Drama" in *The Dictionary of the Middle Ages*, IV, 264–289. The existence of secular drama is documented over 266 ff. See also the excellent history of drama from the ancient world to the Middle Ages by Allardyce Nicoll, *Masks Mimes and Miracles, passim*. There is also useful material in J. D. A. Ogilvy, "*Mimi, Scurrae, Histriones*: Entertainers of the Early Middle Ages", *Speculum*, 38 (1963), 603–619. For a presentation of nine passages from seven authors supporting the existence of theatre or theatrical activity, see Roger Loomis and Gustave Cohen, "Were there theatres in the Twelfth and Thirteenth Centuries?" *Speculum*, XX (1945), 92–98.

Terence; Roman plays were commonly studied as a part of scholarly activities.[93] There existed in the ancient world troupes of actors with arch-mimes in charge who sound suspiciously like Golias and his alleged flock[94] and who could easily have functioned as types for the later mediaeval antitypes. In the Middle Ages, there were various names for the performers, some of which had their origins in the ancient world: *histriones* (actors), *ioculatores* (jesters, *jongleurs*, or minstrels), *lusores* (players in games or amusements), *scurrae* (buffoons, jesters) and a host of other words, often vague in their mediaeval meaning, such as *mimi*,[95] *scenici, tragoedi, comoedi, comici, jocistae, corali, thymelci, buffones* and *saltator*. Mediaeval authors sometimes appear to delight in supplying their own lists of such terms:

> Vita talum et tesseram, theatrum et tabernam. . . . Histriones, scurrae, glabriones, garamantes, palpones, pusiones, molles mascularii, ambubjae, pharmacopolae, crissoriae, phitonissae, vultuariae, noctivagae, magi, mimi, mendici, balatrones, hoc genus omne totas replevere domos.[96]
>
> [The life of dice and gaming, theatre and tavern. . . . The actors, jesters, strippers, jewellers, flatterers, pretty boys, gays, immoral singing girls, quacks, exhibitionists, phitons, vultures, night wanderers, magicians, actors, wanderers, babblers, every one of this kind fills all the homes.]
>
> Hinc mimi, salii vel saliares, balatrones, emiliani, gladiatores, palestritae, gignadii, praestigiatores, malefici quoque multi, et tota ioculatorum scena procedit.[97]
>
> [Hence actors, jumpers or acrobats, jesters, combatants, gladiators, wrestlers, producers, magicians, and also many evils, and the whole array proceeds from the minstrels.]

At times it is not clear whether these lists reflect practices in the late Middle Ages or are simply revels in the Latin classics, for ". . . a certain breath of paganism, wafting perfumes from the old mythology . . . was never wholly absent during the darkest periods of the Middle Ages".[98] Whatever the case, some of these entertainers were employed at monasteries and churches from time to time as well as at court.[99] Wolfger's *Reiserechnungen*, from the late twelfth century, cites various cases of *istrioni* and *ioculatori* being paid.[100]

The mediaeval writers themselves do not seem to hesitate in placing those involved in musical activity in the class of actors and entertainers. In the thirteenth-century confessor's manual (or *penitential*) we find some confirmation of this:

> Tria sunt histrionum genera. Quidam transformant et transfigurant corpora sua per turpes saltus et per turpes gestus, vel denudando se turpiter, vel induendo horribiles larvas, et omnes tales damnabiles sunt, nisi reliquerint officia sua. Sunt etiam alii qui nihil operantur, sed criminose agunt, non habentes certum domicilium, sed sequuntur curias magnatum et dicunt

---

[93] "Drama", *Dictionary of the Middle Ages*, IV, 282.
[94] See Nicoll, *ibid*., 85 ff. The *arch-mime* appears to have functioned much like the irreverent *episcopus* of the secular mediaeval lyric.
[95] The word *mimus* in both the classical and mediaeval world did not mean "mime" in the modern sense but referred to an actor, one who mimicked on the stages the various traits of human nature.
[96] Richard of Devizes, *Chronicles*, Rolls Series II, 437.
[97] John of Salisbury, *Policraticus*, ed. C. Webb (Oxford: Clarendon Press, 1909), Vol. I, 47–48. For similar lists by John, see I, 245 and II, 250.
[98] John Addington Symonds, *Wine Women and Song*, p. 14.
[99] See Ogilvy, "*Mimi, Scurrae, Histriones*", pp. 606 and 615 and Loomis and Cohen, "Were there theatres in the Twelfth and Thirteenth Centuries?", p. 93.
[100] See pp. 12, 15, 21, 26, 29, 31 and 57 of the previously cited Zingerle edition.

opprobria et ignominias de absentibus ut placeant aliis. Tales etiam damnabiles sunt, quia prohibet Apostolus cum talibus cibum sumere, et dicuntur tales scurrae vagi, quia ad nihil utiles sunt, nisi ad devorandum et maledicendum. Est etiam tertium genus histrionum qui habent instrumenta musica ad delectandum homines, et talium sunt duo genera. Quidam enim frequentant publicas potationes et lascivas congregationes, et cantant ibi diversas cantilenus ut moveant homines ad lasciviam, et tales sunt damnabiles sicut alii. Sunt autem alii, qui dicuntur ioculatores, qui cantant gesta principum et vitam sanctorum, et faciunt solatia hominibus vel in aegritudinibus suis vel in angustiis, et non faciunt innumeras turpitudines sicut faciunt saltatores et saltatrices et alii qui ludunt in imaginibus inhonestis et faciunt videri quasi quaedam fantasmata per incantationes vel alio modo. Si autem non faciunt talia, sed cantant in instrumentis suis gesta principum et alia talia utilia ut faciant solatia hominibus, sicut supradictum est, bene possunt sustineri tales, sicut ait Alexander papa. Cum quidam ioculator quaereret ab eo utrum posset salvare animam suam in officio suo, quaesivit Papa ab eo utrum sciret aliquod aliud opus unde vivere posset: respondit ioculator quod non. Permisit igitur Papa quod ipse viveret de officio suo, dummodo abstineret a praedictis lasciviis et turpitudinibus. Notandum est quod omnes peccant mortaliter qui dant scurris vel leccatoribus vel praedictis histrionibus aliquid de suo. Histrionibus dare nichil aliud est quam perdere.[101]

[There are three kinds of actors. Certain of these transform and transfigure their bodies through shameful leaps and foul gestures, or by shamefully stripping themselves, or by putting on horrible masks, and all of these types are damnable, unless they give up their practices. There are also those who do nothing, but behave criminally, not having a fixed home, yet who attend the courts of the mighty and relate scandals and dishonours that they might amuse others. Such people are also damnable, for the Apostle forbids us to take food with them; such are said to be droll wanderers, because they are useful for nothing, except for gluttony and foul language. There is also a third class of actors who have musical instruments for delighting men, and these [in turn] are of two kinds. There are those who frequent public drinking-houses and lascivious gatherings: there they sing various songs in order to move men to lust, and they are as damnable as the others. There are those, however, who are called minstrels [*jongleurs*] who sing the deeds of the great men and the life of saints, and give comfort to men either in their illness or in griefs; these latter do not make countless shamefulnesses such as the dancers and dancing girls and those who act in impure spectacles and create phantastic images through their incantations, or in another way. If, however, they do not do these [evil] things, but play on [sing with?] their instruments the deeds of the great and are useful in giving solace to men, just as was said above, they are well able to be lifted up, just as Pope Alexander says. When a certain minstrel asked whether he might save his soul by his work, the Pope asked whether he knew any other kind of work by which he might live: the minstrel answered that he did not. Therefore the Pope permitted him to live by his practice only if he abstained from the above-mentioned lasciviousness and turpitude. It must be noted that all sin mortally who give anything to jokers, orators or the above-mentioned actors. There is nothing to give actors other than perdition.]

It is certainly far from clear that the goliards are of the third type of actor; in view of what has been said earlier, they seem more associated with the first type, those who wear horrible masks and make foul gestures.

At this point, it is appropriate to return to that most important evidence furnished by Giraldus Cambrensis; his passage, cited in the original Latin (p. 251), is susceptible

---

[101] Quoted in E. K. Chambers, *The Mediaeval Stage*, II, 262–63. Versions are to be found in Bibliothèque Nationale, fonds latin 3218 and 3529a. The passage above has been variously attributed to John of Salisbury, Thomas Cabham (Thomas Cobham) and Thomas of Chobham. For an edition of the latter's works edited by the Rev. F. Broomfield, see *Analecta mediaevalia Namurcensia*, 25 (1968). Various other sources are given by Chambers on p. 262.

to a new interpretation on the basis of the findings presented. In translation, the excerpt from *Speculum Ecclesiae* runs like this, with key words highlighted:

> Likewise in our time a certain **parasite, Golias** by name, renowned equally for his **gluttony and wantonness**, who, it may be said, was aptly called Golias because he was given in everything to gluttony and inebriation, who was nevertheless sufficiently literate, but neither overly obliging nor informed by good disciplines, and who **vomited forth**, not less impudently than imprudently, oftentimes and copiously, famous songs, so **metrical** as to be rhythmic. Concerning which, [it is said that] the **rhythmic invective** was altogether thoughtless and indiscreetly composed, casually cut into some little phrases [*clausulae*], some for execrating and condemning rather than approving or imitating, that is to say, like these which I have added here: *Roma mundi caput est* [various other examples given].[102]

There are several obvious points that first need to be made about this passage. First, Giraldus speaks as if Golias is a real person alive in his own time; he ". . . writes as if he knew Golias in the flesh".[103] Second, he does not claim that "Golias" comes from "gula" but, being a wordsmith himself, Giraldus notices the pun and mentions that Golias is appropriately named. Third, he really gives us no indication of Golias's profession. He suggests that Golias was reasonably literate (is this sufficient for the creator of a poem lke the *Apocalypsis*?)[104] but not well trained in letters. Giraldus mentions that he "vomited forth famous songs", not that he composed all of them. "Famous songs" presumably would be those that were widely circulated, perhaps created by a variety of poets, not necessarily written by Golias. He seems to have been renowned (albeit negatively) for singing the songs, though be dabbled in the making of *clausulae* (probably "little verses" or "clauses" rather than the musical *genre*), which were rather clumsily constructed. Giraldus then gives a few examples of lyrics *like* the ones Golias might have constructed—he does not claim that Golias is the poet responsible for the words. In short, the passage is not clear evidence that Golias was distinguished mainly as a poet or even that he was a "goliard".

One word that has been overlooked in all of the commentaries on this passage is the word **parasitus**, yet it may well be the key to the true nature of this ghostly figure, Golias. The word "parasitus" had at least three meanings in the classical world, and it is likely that these continued into the Middle Ages:
  (1) One who partakes of another's hospitality, or a guest [not pejorative];
  (2) One who makes a living from others, metaphorically similar to that which gets pulled from the hair of animals [pejorative];
  (3) In the ancient world, a member of the college of mimes (actors) dedicated to Apollo.[105]

It is, of course, impossible to know in which sense Giraldus was using the word, but the second and third meanings seem the most likely. The usual meaning taken by those who have discussed the passage is the second of these.

It is not difficult, however, to argue the case for the third meaning of the word, with perhaps some expansion to a new mediaeval meaning. Given the *penchant* for listing

---

[102] As mentioned in note 11, most scholars have accepted the words "ridicula" and "ridiculam" for "ridmica" and "ridmicam", respectively.
[103] Hanford, "The Progenitors of Golias", p. 41.
[104] Nobody seems to have suggested that the *Apocalypsis* may be *about* Golias rather than by him.
[105] See Glare, *The Oxford Latin Dictionary*, p. 1294; Tucker, *A Concise Etymological Dictionary of Latin*, p. 179; Du Cange, *Glossarium*, VI, 163; Lewis and Short, *A Latin Dictionary*, p. 1301.

different names for actors and the classical perfumes wafting through mediaeval Europe, it is not surprising to find the word in the works of various twelfth and thirteenth-century writers. Giraldus and his alleged friend, Walter Map, were connected intimately to the Angevin court of Henry II and travelled with the monarch on more than one occasion to the Continent.[106] Nowhere ". . . did the classics receive a warmer welcome than in the valley of the Loire, in the cities of Angers, Tours, Orléans and Fleury",[107] places that Henry and his *entourage* were known to have frequented. While the ancient world yields a few examples of the word "parasitus" in inscriptions and other arcane places,[108] it is perhaps through the dramas of Plautus and particularly the comedies of Terence, whose plays were well known in the Loire valley,[109] that the word was entrenched in mediaeval thinking. In his play *Eunuchus*, for example, one of the *personae* is GNATHO PARASITUS; in *Phormio*, another character is listed as PHORMIO PARASITUS. Within his plays we find the word used a few times:

Colacem esse Naevi, et Plauti veterem fabulam;
parasiti personam inde ablatam et militis .
si id est peccatum, peccatum inprudentiast
poetae, non quo furtum facere studuerit (*Eunuchus*, lines 25–28)

[He lifted the leech [parasite] and the major straight from that antique farce by Naevius and Plautus, *The Yes-Man*. If our author slipped, it was ignorance, void of any attempt to steal.]

si potis est, famquam philosophorum habent disciplinae ex ipsis
vocabula, **parasiti** ita ut **Gnathonici** vocentur. (*Eunuchus*, lines 263–64)

[I'm rather thinking of founding a professional school of sponging. Named after me, of course—just like the philosophers: Plato, Platonists. Gnatho, Gnathonists.]

ne semper servo' currens, iratus senex,
edax **parasitu'**, sycophanta autem inpudens . (*Heauton Timorumenos*, lines 37–38)

[(Let me act a play for you) so that the Running Slave, or The Old Grouch, Or Greedy Parasite, Or Sharp Con Man, or Pimp, do not have to be played by me . . .]

quid fiat? est **parasitu'** quidam Phormio,
homo confidens: qui illum di omnes perduint! (*Phormio*, lines 122–23)[110]

[The upshot? Well, there's a fellow called Phormio. Profession, sponger. Character, cocky. Deserves to be damned by every god who can spare the time.]

---

[106] A. K. Bate, "Walter Map and Giraldus Cambrensis", *Latomus*, 31 (1972), 861.

[107] Christopher McDonough, "Orpheus, Ulysses and Penelope in a Twelfth-Century Setting", *Studi Medievali*, 31 (1990), 85.

[108] Such as "l. AVRELio APOLOVSTO HIERONICO . BIS . CORONATO ET . DIA PANTON . PARASITO ET . SACERDOTI . APOLLINIS AVGVST . CAPVAE MAXIMO". See Theodorus Mommsen, ed. *Corpus Inscriptionum Latinarum* (Berolini: Georgium Reimerum, 1883), X/1, No. 3716, p. 357.

[109] Keith Bate, *Three Latin Comedies* (Toronto: Pontifical Institute of Mediaeval Studies, 1976), p. 4. For a recent anthology of Latin plays in which music is prominent, see Peter Dronke, *Nine medieval Latin plays* (Cambridge: Cambridge University Press, 1994).

[110] For a convenient anthology of Terence's dramas, from which the above are taken, see Robert Kauer and Wallace M. Lindsay, *P. Terenti Afri Comoediae* (Oxford: Clarendon Press, 1958). The translations are from Palmer Bovie, Constance Carrier and Douglass Parker, *The Complete Comedies of Terence* (New Brunswick, NJ: Rutgers University Press) [the lines of the plays are cued into the translations]. These translations are rather colloquial and reflect more the spirit of the lines than their strict meanings. The featuring of a "parasitus" in several plays used extensively in the Middle Ages for study purposes must have helped to define the nature of a parasite among the literate.

And there are other representations by parasites in his plays; the parasite seems to be a stock type, a conventional trickster figure. The sense in which the word is used varies somewhat in the context of each play, but it is not difficult to see how the much later mediaeval theatrical buffs could take this stock figure and turn it into an archetypical name for a sort of actor. It could be added, that the term "Gnatho", here used as a name almost synonymous with "parasite", comes from the Greek meaning an illness of the stomach—that is, it is associated with gluttony.[111] The parasite in *Eunuchus* appears to be a witty "fifth business" character-type rather than a depraved rogue, or even a "sponger", as the word "parasite" is sometimes translated—he was perhaps a parasite in the sense that he was not a main character.

Just to what extent mediaeval writers such as Giraldus may have gleaned information from the plays of Terence is not clear, nor does it matter: it is enough merely that the interchange of the term "parasitus" with actor was possible at the time. Learned writers such as John of Salisbury, also an intimate at the court of Henry II, frequently refers to Terence—sometimes as "nostri Terentii" (our Terence).[112] John of Salisbury was born between 1115 and 1120, studied with Abelard in Paris, was known in the court circles of Henry II, became secretary to two Archbishops of Canterbury (the second of these, Thomas Becket) and completed his *Policraticus* in 1159. In that book, John uses some of the words under investigation in a more mediaeval way that brings us again right back to the acting community:

> Qui ad spectacula confluunt aut euocant ad se spectacula inhonesta aut se ipsos affectatis nugis uolunt esse spectaculo insipientium, quoniam haec lenocinia uanitatis recte sapienti placere non possunt, oculorum capiuntur illecebris et, licet mitius elidantur, corruunt tamen a dignitate conditionis suae et ad eam quam diffitentur seruilem relabuntur. Quid ergo aliud faciunt **mimi, histriones, parasiti, et huiusmodi monstra hominum**, nisi quod ineptam conuincunt felicium seruitutem? Sed et illi qui voculis capiuntur (licet aurium sensus purissimus et defecatissimus sit) seruiunt quidem, iugo tamen premuntur mitiori, si alias non praeualeant uitia. Nam ab olfactu uix aliquis omnino capitur, nisi forte Lotofagum uiuat. Non aliquid aduersus cantores aut musicos struo, cum (teste Quintiliano, Valerio, Flauiano, et aliis multis). Socrates etiam in senectute didicerit musicam credens, si musica defore, sibi cumulum sapientiae defuturum. In ea tamen nimium occupari citra philosophicam grauitatem est.[113]

* * *

> Nolo, inquit sapiens, ab his laudari quorum laus uituperium est, nec ab his culpari uereor quorum criminatio laus est. Cum ergo **histriones, mimi, parasiti** et huiusmodi ineptiae hominum, ni cui indice uita laudabilium, probent, nonne perspicuae desipientiae est illorum, ut quis fulgeat, aucupari fauorem qui sordibus obsiti sunt et quorum gratia nisi per turpia adquiri non potest?[114]

[They who rush to spectacles or give unseemly ones at their own homes, or themselves wish to entertain the foolish with their frivolities (since the enticements of vanity do not attract the truly wise), are captivated by the allurement of the eye. Although they do not come crashing down, they fall just the same from the dignity of their station and degenerate into that state of slavery which they disavow. What other function has the **mimic, actor, parasite**, and

---

[111] Patricius McGlynn, *Lexicon Terentianum* (London: Blackie & Son, 1963), I, 219. For information on "parasitus" see II, 3.
[112] The familiarity with Terence is frequently demonstrated by John. See Loomis and Cohen, "Were there theatres in the Twelfth and Thirteenth Centuries?" p. 96.
[113] *Policraticus*, Vol. 2, Liber VIII, Chapter 12, pp. 309-310.
[114] *Ibid.*, VIII, xiv, p. 328. Translations for the two passages may be found in Joseph B. Pike, ed., *Frivolities of Courtiers and Footprints of Philosophers* (New York: Octagon Books, 1972), pp. 367 and 384.

monstrosities of the sort [Terence, *Eunuchus*, 696] except that of impugning the stupid slavery of the well-to-do? Those who are captivated by melodious tones (granted that hearing is the purest and most refined of the senses) are slaves as well but under a lighter yoke, if no vices prevail in other fields. Scarcely anyone is enslaved by the sense of smell unless perchance he lives the life of a lotus-eater. I have no charges to make against singers or musicians since (on the testimony of Quintilian, Valerius, Flavianus, and many others) Socrates even in old age studied music, for he believed that if music were lacking he would be without that which was the capstone of wisdom. Yet to occupy oneself overmuch with this displays lack of philosophic seriousness.

* * *

The wise man says "I do not desire to be praised by those whose accusation is praise, nor do I fear to be blamed by those whose blame is praise". When therefore **actors, mimics, parasites** and riff-raff of that sort approve, except in the case of one of those who deserves praise on the evidence of his life, is it not palpable folly to curry favour with those who are quite sordid, whose support can be acquired only by base means?]

John conjoins the term "parasitus" with those other dramatical labels associated with acting and mediaeval entertainment. He then seems to distinguish between those actors and musicians. It does not seem too far-fetched to suggest that he is using the word to mean a kind of entertainer, rather than a metaphorical tick or flea.[115] The term could even be substituted without much difference in meaning for the term "goliardus". Perhaps "parasitus", by the Middle Ages, meant a supporting actor who functioned more in the realm of visual effects (costumes, masks, elaborate hats), rather than in the field of oral delivery or singing, just as goliards might have done. However, the figure of Golias, perhaps merely denigrated by Giraldus through the word "parasitus", seems a more prominent figure. In any case, Giraldus may have meant simply that Golias was an **actor** well known in his own day.

If true for John of Salisbury, then the use of the word "parasitus" by Giraldus may have been in the same spirit. Golias the parasite is not just an insect preying on courtly society, although that connotation would not be inappropriate; he is some sort of actor or *ioculator*. If so, the much vaunted society or brotherhood of Golias emerges as a troupe of actors and entertainers who were inclined to be crude and satyrical in their entertainments. It is probably inappropriate to consider him exclusively a poet-musician, though he and his troupe doubtless would have made their own contributions from time to time. Their focus, however, would be the production of drama (and peripheral elements such as music), not composition or poesie. Such a band would have used good material wherever they could find it, including perhaps the works of Walter Map and Hugh Primas, but extending far beyond mere lyric song to the other stage arts. The rubrics in the manuscripts, which seem to indicate poets, may actually indicate entertainers—we cannot know for certain. This would help to explain the multiple, contradictory ascriptions to various lyric songs that survive in the source manuscripts.

What is the etymology of the word "goliard"? It probably stems from the realms of costuming, helmets and masks—the smoke and grease-paint of the stage! And what did goliards do? It seems that they were essentially entertainers, part of the array of

---

[115] In an earlier account that discusses some of the exploits of William the Conqueror and his son Robert, we read of gifts given "histrionibus et parasitis ac meretricibus"—to actors, "parasites" and harlots. See O. Holder-Egger, "Ex monumentis Lemovicensibus", *Monumenta Germaniae Historica. Scriptores*, XXVI (1882), 19.

diversified types involved in the productions at court, church and monastery intended to amuse those who could pay. Bishop Golias seems to have been a well-known actor who also dabbled in poetry and attracted a following, like the *arch-mimes* of the ancient world. Though the synonym "Vaganten" is a misguided term for mediaeval poets, goliards in many cases must have been itinerant opportunists. They could wear grotesque headgear as part of their dramatic presentations and probably would have been adept at other matters to do with entertainment. Were they poets or musicians? They may well have been capable at elocution and singing. Certainly their compatriot *ioculatores* must have been; or perhaps they worked, in the strictest sense of the term goliard, more in the realm of gesture and mime. Their role in the creation, the composition of lyric song, was surely much less important than that of various schoolmen, courtiers, clerics and monks, some of whom can be identified. Nor is there any direct evidence that goliards were poet-musicians at all, though they might have dabbled in the lyric art. The richly diversified secular song of the high Middle Ages was not, as far as can be determined, ever referred to as "goliardic song" in its own period. We, over the last two centuries, have entrenched this appellation and, in so doing, doubtless have contributed to the historical distortion.

[4]
Introduction

Cyrilla Barr

The phenomenon of popular hymnody may in many ways seem remote from present-day experience, and the investigation of its manifestations in medieval Italy is necessarily complicated by the ambiguity of the origins of this important genre, which deserves to be of interest to a broad range of scholars. Popular religious forms of the thirteenth, fourteenth, and fifteenth centuries are now at last becoming the focus of the scholarly attention which they deserve, and the current study is designed to provide insight into one such form. Nevertheless, the popular religious music of Italy, despite various theories and considerable speculation concerning its antecedents, remains in some respects as obscure today as the unrecorded names of those men who cut and carried stones for the cathedrals and churches or who lost their lives in the crusades--men whose immortality in stone and poetry is real, albeit anonymous. This problem is caused in some measure by the tendency of medieval persons toward the anonymity of a communitarian life.

In the realm of the spiritual, medieval communitarianism expressed itself in part in the formation of numerous lay confraternities, which were known by various terms such as 'guilds,' 'societies,' 'companies,' 'brotherhoods,' and 'schools.' In spite of the differing terms used to describe them, they were alike in their pursuit of personal piety through prayer and charitable works, and each followed a rule which required the members to gather at regular intervals for their devotions. They have been characterized by John Henderson as "'lay' inasmuch as the vast majority of their members were laymen, and 'religious' because their practices were loosely adapted

INTRODUCTION

from a monastic rule."[1]

The singing of popular hymns in the vernacular became an important part of the confraternities' way of life, and in time many of these groups were instrumental in disseminating a vast literature of religious lyric poetry and song known as the *lauda*. There is evidence that singing had already been incorporated into religious societies as early as the tenth century in Italy; however, nothing is known of the manner in which this occurred.[2] But by the thirteenth century Florentine chronicles in particular began to mention groups of lay people, *popolo bordone*, who gathered before the figure of the Madonna at the end of the day's work and addressed to her their prayers and songs. Because of the nature of the "praise songs" which they sang, the groups came to be called *laudesi* and their songs *laude*.[3]

The earliest *laude* were simple lyrical hymns in the vernacular. Unfortunately, their music was seldom notated since the *lauda* represents an oral tradition of singing--a tradition which may be one of the longest in the history of Western music. Nevertheless, there are two surviving manuscripts containing *laude* from the Middle Ages which do contain musical notation. The sumptuous fourteenth-century Magliabechiano manuscript (Mgl[1]) seems very likely to have been a votive work rather than a performance score, in contrast to the plain and unpretentious Cortona *laudario* of the previous century. With the exception of clerics, few of those who sang the *laude* contained in the latter were likely able to read, and especially few would be able to read either the newly emerging vernacular in which the manuscript is written or its musical notation. Hence it may be argued that, in spite of the existence of these two collections of *laude* with notation, oral transmission must necessarily have remained the principal practical mode of dissemination.

It has been suggested that the *lauda* was the invention of St. Francis of Assisi whose *Cantico delle creature*, written in

INTRODUCTION

1225,[4] marked the beginning of a long tradition of Italian lyric poetry.[5] Though such speculation must be regarded with suspicion, it is not therefore surprising that the mendicants, especially Franciscans and Dominicans, should recognize this genre as a practical tool for their apostolate, to be used to teach, edify, exhort, and perhaps also to entertain in a language comprehensible even to the illiterate. The Franciscan chronicler Salimbene in fact speaks of several friars in his acquaintance who were gifted in singing and composition.[6] An old pedagogical principle was at work here: large doses of religious dogma could more easily be administered in simple rhymes and sweet tunes which possibly also, like a kind of spiritual nostrum, helped to mitigate the austerities of medieval life. Perhaps more importantly, the form helped to induce a devotional mood which was very important in the life of the confraternity. Further, in much the same way that folk music chronicles the existence of a people--their living, working, loving, and dying--so too the *lauda* reflects certain changes taking place in the confraternities themselves as well as in the larger world outside the brotherhood.

Although the first half of the thirteenth century saw the multiplication of various religious groups, both canonical and lay, the third quarter of that century was marked by a curious phenomenon which to the modern mind might be characterized as religious aberration, a manifestation of "psychic disorientation."[7] This phenomenon was the flagellant mania of 1260 which was initiated in Perugia at the instigation of Raniero Fasani. In its wake there followed the numerous penitential processions that soon spread over nearly all of northern Italy.[8]

The foundation of flagellant confraternities known as *disciplinati* or *battuti* has often been linked to the events of 1260, but in fact the phenomenon should be considered within the broader context of contemporary piety that placed great emphasis upon the incarnate life of Christ. This theme was characteristic of the preaching of the mendicants, who stressed imitation of the God-man from the cradle to the cross.[9] Thus

INTRODUCTION

the Mass became a visual re-enactment of the Passion, and the admonition to penance in the form of flagellation was viewed as the ultimate imitation of Christ. Because these outbursts of fervor were frequently precipitated by disasters, either real or prophesied, they appear to have been motivated by fear of an angry God whose wrath could only be appeased by the expiation of Christ's sufferings through the physical act of self-flagellation.[10]

Reports of these penitential activities around 1260 are found in the accounts of the processions contained in various medieval chronicles, which, to be sure, tend to repeat each other in many details. The story grows to a climax with the statement that the hermit's cry of *penitenza* was sufficient to incite the populace to such extremes of self-inflicted scourging that "in those days Italian blood flowed like water."[11] Medieval fondness for hyperbole notwithstanding, the occurrence was an important factor in the development of the confraternities after 1260. Hence it is appropriate to consider how certain of the political events of mid-thirteenth-century Italy may have contributed to the success of the flagellant movement.

Historians have indeed demonstrated that the events leading up to 1260 provided the proper setting for the outbreak of penitential fervor. Italy had suffered under the scourge of Frederick II, who was regarded by some as the Antichrist, and of his son-in-law Ezzelino da Romano. The already baleful political climate was exacerbated by the preaching of various heretical sects--the Waldenses, Cathari, and other assorted evangelizers. To these must be added the Joachites, who styled themselves the spiritual progeny of Joachim of Fiore (1135-1202).[12] Although the enigmatic figure of Joachim properly belongs to the twelfth century, his influence reached far beyond his own time and his native province of Calabria. His life as a Cistercian, and later as founder of his own order, was exemplary. Apparently even in his own lifetime he was thought to possess prophetic powers, for Pope Lucius III engaged him to interpret sibylline prophecies and subsequently

INTRODUCTION

commissioned him to write the *Liber Concordiae Novi et Veteris Testamenti*.[13] Dante, who placed him in the company of Hugh of St.-Victor, Rabanus Maurus, and Anselm, claimed for him a prophetic spirit (*Paradiso,* Canto 13). Likewise, the Bollandists found fit to include his life in the *Acta Sanctorum*.[14] In justice to Joachim it must be emphasized that the extent of his influence was mainly due to those, most notably the Spiritual Franciscans, who enlarged upon his theses.[15] These followers eagerly seized upon the notion of an evangelical band of barefoot scholars as prefiguring their mission and justifying their attitude toward the rigid observance of the rule of St. Francis.

Joachim believed in an organically developing Church as opposed to what he considered a static foundation. His concept of history was symbolically trinitarian, and, according to his concordance of events in the Old and New Testaments, the Age of the Father had been enlightened by the Old Testament with Adam as the herald of Abraham. Similarly John the Baptist was the precursor of Christ and as such ushered in the era of the New Testament. He devised a system of apocalyptic calculations whereby he determined that the second age was to consist of forty-two generations of thirty years each, or 1,260 years. Thus the year 1260 was to mark the beginning of the Age of the Spirit.[16] According to the interpretation of Gerard of San Donnino, the herald of this new era was Benedict, and the coming of the hero was to be preceded by troubled times in which war, famine, and ecclesiastical corruption would abound. The era would be announced by a new religious order which would cleanse the Church of its impurities and restore it to its pristine state. The Spiritual Franciscans were certain that they were the chosen ones to announce this gospel. Gerard then proclaimed that the third period, the Age of the Spirit, was to be enlightened by the *Eternal Evangel,* a book containing three of Joachim's works with an introduction and gloss written by himself. This book was to supersede the Old and New Testaments which had been viable during the first

INTRODUCTION

two ages in succession. Scholars at the University of Paris were quick to alert the pope, Alexander IV, whereupon the matter was examined by Vatican theologians. Ultimately Gerard was censured (in 1256), and from that time until his death eighteen years later he was kept in detention by the Franciscan Order.[17] Furthermore, the reputation which Joachim's works had accrued eventually resulted in their condemnation at the Provincial Council of Arles.

It would, however, be simplistic to interpret the events summarized above as a *mise en scène* for the drama enacted in Perugia when the hermit Raniero emerged from solitude and began to preach the message of penitence which according to legend had been revealed to him in a vision of the Blessed Virgin Mary. Modern historians have pointed out that, while many chroniclers relate the story of the penitential processions instigated by Raniero, there is a curious silence about the question of Joachim's possible association with the origin of the movement.[18] As Henderson indicates in his study of the flagellants of 1260, the only contemporary chronicler to mention Joachim in this context was Salimbene, whose writings are the chief source for our knowledge of the spread of Joachimism among the Franciscans.[19] But even Salimbene seems to suggest that it was merely coincidental that the occurrence should have taken place in 1260. Perhaps it is typical of the medieval mind to interpret natural phenomena and disasters as signs of an irate God meting out justice and punishment. Thus, according to Henderson, Joachimism probably "helped to generate a mood rather than provide any specific influences to lead to the outbreak of fervor."[20]

Several accounts of Raniero's preaching exist, and there are various theories concerning his identity though these are of little significance to the present study.[21] Far more important is the fact that he was responsible at least indirectly for the formation of the first *disciplinati* society, that of Gesù Cristo in Perugia which was to be the model for many others, some of which would also even assume its name.

INTRODUCTION

Response to the example of the zealous penitents was not, however, universally positive, though their effect on the Italian confraternities was widespread. Some individuals were repelled by their fanaticism, and rulers in certain regions denied the flagellants entrance into their towns.[22] In the face of opposition and censure, the more fanatic element fled from Italy to the North, and soon they were found along with their followers in the Midi and as far north as Poland. Within Italy, the influence of the flagellant movement on the character of the confraternities and consequently also upon the *lauda* is of the greatest significance for our study. Groups of *laudesi* already existed, of course, and now penitential confraternities calling themselves *disciplinati* came into being and espoused the custom of singing *laude* along with their practice of flagellation. Both the earlier type of confraternity and the *disciplinati* continued to exist side-by-side, and at times these two types are difficult to distinguish from each other.[23]

In view of the continued association of *lauda*-singing with the brotherhoods, it is not surprising that the changes which occurred in the structure and practice of the confraternities should have been reflected in the *laude* themselves. The *laude* of the pre-flagellant period had been lyrical in character, and in subject matter leaned heavily upon Marian themes as well as upon laments of the Passion. The suddenness of the outbreak in 1260 would have precluded the composition of an entirely new repertoire for the use of penitents, however. Furthermore, the penitential processions which developed are described by the chroniclers in a manner that seems to indicate only a very simple kind of chanting, perhaps in litany fashion, repeating invocations over and over.[24] Later manuscripts of *laude* belonging to *disciplinati* societies contain considerable evidence of their penitential devotion and manifest a preoccupation with death, judgment, and punishment. The later *laude* are indeed markedly realistic at times in their descriptions of dying or the decomposition of the body and bear comparison with such pictorial representations as the *Trionfo*

INTRODUCTION

della morte at the Campo santo in Pisa.[25]

Documentation of the activities, particularly the musical practices, of the confraternities depends upon examination of two kinds of manuscript sources: (1) manuscripts containing texts of *laude* with musical notation, and (2) the official writings and records of the brotherhoods--in other words, documents not primarily of a musical nature. The former category, as noted above, is unfortunately very limited, whereas the confraternity records are very extensive indeed, though these will have only scattered references of interest to the musicologist among the notations of items relating primarily to life within the organization. Such sources, however, are vital in providing the necessary context within which the musical activities of the confraternities may be understood, and hence they will receive consideration in this study before we turn to the musical sources themselves.

References

[1]John Henderson, "Piety and Charity in Late Medieval Florence: Religious Confraternities from the Middle of the Thirteenth to the Late Fifteenth Century," diss. (Univ. of London, 1983), p. 2.

NOTES

²Ludovico Muratori, *Antiquitates Italicae Medii Aevi sive Dissertationes*, 2nd ed. (Arezzo: Belloti, 1773-80), p. 16, col. 41.

³Johannes Villani, *Historia universalis a condita Florentia*, in *Rerum Italicarum Scriptores*, XIII (Milan: Tipographia Societatis Palatinae in Regia Curia, 1728), p. 342.

⁴Following the chronology of Omer Engelbert, *Vita di San Francesco d'Assisi*, trans. Gino Rampani (1958; rpt. Milan: Mursia, 1976), p. 338.

⁵Although some works of the Sicilian school pre-date the *Cantico del sole*, that school was greatly affected by foreign influence.

⁶See chap. 3, p. 71.

⁷Ronald F. E. Weissman, *Ritual Brotherhood in Renaissance Florence* (New York: Academic Press, 1982), p. 54.

⁸On the geographical diffusion of the flagellants, see Pier Lorenzo Meloni, "Topografia, diffuzione e aspetti delle confraternite," in *Risultati e prospettive della ricerca sul movimento dei disciplinati* (Perugia: Bolletino della R. Deputazione di Storia Patria per l'Umbria, 1972), pp. 15-63. On Raniero, see Raffaelo Morghen, "Raniero Fasani e il movimento dei disciplinati del 1260," in *Il movimento dei disciplinati nel settimo centenario del suo inizio* (Perugia: Bottelino della R. Deputazione di Storia Patria per l'Umbria, 1960), pp. 29-42.

⁹Devotions to the *presepio* as well as to the sufferings of Christ are common in the *Meditations* formerly attributed to St. Bonaventure. See *Meditations on the Life of the Christ: An Illustrated Manuscript of the Fourteenth Century*, trans. Isa Ragusa and Rosalie B. Green (Princeton: Princeton Univ. Press, 1961). On the theory of relationship between this affective type of devotion disseminated by the Friars Minor and the affective quality found more prominently in painting of the time, see Émile Mâle, *L'Art religieux de la fin du moyen âge en France* (Paris: Armand Colin, 1925), p. 34.

¹⁰Henderson, "Piety and Charity," p. 77.

¹¹Monachi Patavini, *Chronicon de Rebus Gestis in Lombardia*

NOTES

Praecipue et Marchia Tarvisina, in *Rerum Italicarum Scriptores,* VIII (Milan: Tipographia Societas Palatinae in Regia Curia, 1726), col. 699.

[12]For extensive treatment of Joachim's life and influence in the Middle Ages, see Marjorie Reeves' *Influence of Prophecy in the Later Middle Ages* (Oxford: Clarendon Press, 1969) and her *Joachim of Fiore and the Prophetic Future* (London: SPCK, 1976); see also Marjorie Reeves and Beatrice Hirsch-Reich, *The Figure of Joachim of Fiore* (Oxford: Clarendon Press, 1972).

[13]Reeves, *Influence of Prophecy,* p. 3.

[14]*Acta Sanctorum,* May, VII, 87-144.

[15]On Joachim's influence on the Franciscan Order, see Angelo Messini, "Profetismo e profezia ritmiche italiane d'ispirazione gioachimito-francescana nei secoli XIII, XIV, e XV," *Miscellanea Francescana,* 41 (1941), 50-73, and "San Francesco e i francescani nella letteratura profetica gioachimita," *Miscellanea Francescana,* 45 (1946), 232-42.

[16]On Joachim's number theory see Reeves, *Influence of Prophecy,* chap. 1, and Raoul Manselli, "L'anno 1260 fu anno Gioachimitico?" *Il movimento,* pp. 99-108.

[17]Reeves, *Influence of Prophecy,* p. 34.

[18]Henderson, "The Flagellant Movement and Flagellant Confraternities in Central Italy, 1260-1400," *Studies in Church History,* 15 (1978), 51.

[19]Ibid., p. 152; see also Reeves, *Influence of Prophecy,* pp. 32ff.

[20]Henderson, "The Flagellant Movement and Flagellant Confraternities," p. 51.

[21]For further information about Raniero's identity and preaching, see Emilio Ardu, "Frater Raynerius Faxanus de Perusio," *Il movimento,* pp. 84-92.

[22]Henderson, "The Flagellant Movement and Flagellant Confraternities," p. 153.

NOTES

[23]On the difficulty of distinguishing betwen the two, see Weissman, p. 58.

[24]See chap. 2.

[25]For an example of an altered text, see chap. 1, pp. 15-16.

Part II
Women

[5]

Diminishing the *Trobairitz*, Excluding the Women Trouvères

Joan Tasker Grimbert

In 1979 appeared an article that has attained seminal status among *trobairitz* scholars: Pierre Bec's "'Trobairitz' et chansons de femme. Contribution à la connaissance du lyrisme féminin au moyen âge." It was written largely in reaction to Meg Bogin's pioneering book on the women troubadours,[1] for Bec reproved Bogin's "philogynie primesautière" and believed justifiably that there was room, between the rhapsodic admiration of some critics and the harsh misogyny of others, for a more rigorous and systematic study (235). Perceived at the time as an important contribution to the understanding of the poetics of the women troubadours, Bec's study continues to exercise considerable influence: Occitanists routinely cite it for its main thesis that the *trobairitz* adapted the *système socio-poétique* of their male counterparts by drawing on themes characteristic of the *chansons de femme*.[2] If Bec's contribution to *trobairitz* studies has generally seemed solid, it is no doubt because his adeptness at structural analysis is legendary, and his analytical skills convey a sense of objectivity that inspires confidence. I believe, however, that this confidence is not always justified, and the purpose of the present study is to demonstrate how, in Bec's celebrated 1979 article, his systematic, cleverly-wrought arguments conceal a bias that has unfairly oriented how scholars assess the contribution of women to medieval poetry.

The key to Bec's orientation is clear from the outset in his arresting formulation of what he calls two apparent paradoxes: "1) des femmes (les *trobairitz*) ont écrit des chansons troubadouresques, c'est-à-dire en conformité avec un système lyrique à dominance masculine; et des hommes ont écrit des 'chansons de femme'; 2) dans le cadre de la seule lyrique gallo-romane, on a curieusement: du côté occitan, des *trobairitz*, mais pas (ou presque) de 'chansons de femme', et du côté français, un certain nombre de 'chansons de femme', mais pas de *trobairitz* [= women trouvères]" (236). If Occitanists have not been troubled by this striking assertion, it may be that they care more about Bec's willingness to admit women troubadours to the pantheon of medieval poets than his determination to exclude women trouvères. For scholars who are already well-disposed to Bec, the appearance of his 1995 anthology, *Chants d'amour des femmes-troubadours. Trobairitz et "chansons de femme,"* featuring a long introduction which owes a large, acknowledged debt to recent work done by Occitanists (especially Angelica Rieger and Katharina Städtler) can only reinforce the impulse to see him as an ally. But those who are tempted to do so, I would suggest, fail to appreciate the rhetorical strategies used by Bec throughout his 1979 article to diminish the contribution of the *trobairitz*, particularly the tissue of erroneous statements woven together in the fourth part of the article to document the assertion that the *chansons de femme* on which the *trobairitz*' originality supposedly depends were all male-authored. This claim and the faulty arguments that underpin it may have raised no eyebrows in 1979, but recent scholarship, particularly by feminists, has made us more sensitive readers.

Bec's contention that there were no women trouvères was challenged by Madeleine Tyssens in 1992 and, more recently, by Eglal Doss-Quinby and Wendy Pfeffer. As early as 1986, Coldwell had devoted a section of her study on secular musicians in medieval France to the women trouvères and published the music to three songs and a *jeu-parti* (50-54).[3] The cause of the women trouvères has also been taken up by William D. Paden, who has actually called for a critical edition of all extant texts and music (117, n. 24). Although the question raised by these scholars, the authorship of the *chansons de femme*, may once have seemed peripheral to *trobairitz* studies, it should not seem so in light of current studies. Under these circumstances and given the publication of Bec's 1995 anthology—which, as the subtitle suggests, reprises in its introduction large segments of the 1979 article—this may be an opportune time to reconsider the value of the earlier study and to examine the corresponding portions of the introduction to the 1995 anthology.[4]

In work focused specifically on the *trobairitz*, two feminist scholars, Kathryn Gravdal and Simon Gaunt, have explicitly questioned Bec's objectivity. Gravdal's article, "Metaphor, Metonymy, and the Medieval

DIMINISHING THE *TROBAIRITZ*

Women Trobairitz," is of particular interest in that it both presents a feminist's complex reaction to Bec's main thesis and, in view of the points Gravdal accepts and rejects, underscores the importance of revisiting the 1979 article:

> For Bec, the fact that the women drew on a male literary tradition for their female persona appears to reduce his estimation of the writerly contribution of the *trobairitz* and to prove that their work is but a pastiche of poetic clichés drawn willy nilly from images of women throughout the medieval lyric, thus closing the question of the female signature.
>
> I would argue on the contrary that the women's typological choice of the feminine lyric voice from *chansons de femme* is a deliberate strategy. (Bruckner 1992, 857-76) The fact that the character comes from a male-authored genre (what genres from which the *trobairitz* could choose were not male-authored?) does not lessen the shrewdness of the choice (114).

Unlike most scholars who cite Bec's article, Gravdal recognizes how Bec's insistence that the *chansons de femme* were male-authored has a negative impact on his assessment of the *trobairitz*. She also understands that he closes "the question of the female signature" and excludes the women trouvères. However, she does not challenge his statements about the women trouvères. Concerned only with the *trobairitz*, she tries merely to present their strategy in a positive light. Unfortunately, in lauding the "shrewdness of [their] choice," she actually reinforces Bec's contention that there were no women trouvères.

Simon Gaunt's critique in *Gender and Genre in Medieval French Literature* scrutinizes an oft-cited distinction that Bec introduces at the beginning of his article. As noted, Bec promises at the outset "une étude plus ponctuelle, plus rigoureuse, plus systématique" (235) than Bogin's. In 1979, the studied objectivity of his approach must have seemed enhanced by his insistence on the need, when speaking of texts, to distinguish between "*féminité génétique* (avec un auteur dont on sait pertinemment qu'il est une femme)" and "*féminité textuelle*, à savoir une pièce, dans la très grande majorité des cas amoureuse, et dont le 'je' lyrique est une femme (l'auteur pouvant être assez fréquemment un homme)" (235-36). But as Gaunt observes, this apparently useful distinction has been exploited by some scholars to deny the existence of a genuine female voice in the *trobairitz* corpus:

> Huchet and Bec's articles on the *trobairitz* highlight a serious theoretical problem for the reader of the corpus, but in some ways (unintentionally, one must assume) they offer a more sophisticated basis for denying that the songs attributed to the *trobairitz* were written by women. The implication of their approach is that it is irrelevant whether the songs were written by women or not because the first-person position the female voices occupy is constructed by the dominant discourse (160).[5]

Gaunt offers an excellent insight into the effect of using this distinction, but that effect hardly seems unintentional in Bec's case. In his 1995 anthology Bec responds to Huchet's claim that "à l'intérieur du texte, il n'est d'autre féminité que celle inscrite par la langue poétique" (73) by asserting that "le texte lui-même implique un *hors-texte* qui le soutienne et le dynamise, sinon un corps réel dans une réalité historique précise, du moins un ensemble de présupposés socioculturels et de connivences collectives qui rendent ce texte parlant" (24, n. 1). If this statement is an objection, it is couched in such opaque terms that it too seems to rob the *trobairitz* of any historical reality.

Bec himself exploits the *féminité génétique/féminité textuelle* distinction in his studies on Occitan and Old French lyric poetry[6] in a way that seems calculated to diminish the contribution of medieval women poets both in Occitania and in northern France. Indeed, in his 1979 article he will remind us frequently of the remarkably small number of Occitan *cansos*

DIMINISHING THE *TROBAIRITZ*

whose author is clearly known to be a woman (*féminité génétique*), while putting great emphasis on the male authorship of the *chansons de femme* (*féminité textuelle*). Moreover, as we shall see, in his 1995 anthology, Bec covers these points (*féminité génétique/féminité textuelle* and male authorship of the *chansons de femme*) in essentially the same terms (48-49). Yet even as he stubbornly continues to deny women a role in the composition of the *chansons de femme*, he graciously allows that "la femme (beaucoup plus que l'homme) a dû jouer un rôle important dans la conservation et la propagation de cette lyrique popularisante où elle demeure le personnage essentiel, autour duquel le texte s'articule" (49).

The section devoted to the *chansons de femme* in Bec's article is actually the last stage in a systematic analysis of the poetics of the women troubadours. In the first three sections of his article, Bec focuses on the *trobairitz*, stressing time and again the minimal size of that corpus. He opens his discussion of the *trobairitz* by saying: "Le corpus des pièces des *trobairitz* est, on le sait, très modeste" (236). The second paragraph begins: "C'est fort peu de chose on le voit" and ends: "Quoi qu'il en soit, le corpus est effectivement minime et, lorsqu'on veut tenter une analyse un peu fine, il faut faire feu de tout bois" (236). Of course, he was dealing in 1979 with Bogin's corpus of twenty-three poems and eighteen names, and since Rieger was able to compile a larger corpus (forty-six pieces and twenty names), Bec puts somewhat less emphasis on this point in his 1995 anthology: he seems content to observe that the corpus is "assez élastique" (20).

Bec also strives in the three earlier sections to depreciate the *trobairitz*' originality. He is pleased to belittle the quality of their accomplishment by underscoring incessantly the dominance of male poets in a poetic system used by both men and women rather than seeing the women as equal partners in the creation and development of that system. For example, he identifies as *spécificités négatives* every characteristic of the male corpus that is absent in the *trobairitz* corpus. Bec would no doubt argue that the use of the term *spécificité négative* is justified in a

Greimasian context, but since his analysis is not explicitly structuralist, the term is out of place and needlessly denigrating. He may have come to the same realization when he opted in his anthology to replace it by *spécificité* (or *trait*) *par défaut* (22), a curious expression that is hardly more positive. Another *spécificité négative* noted in 1979 was that the *trobairitz* had not composed any *sirventes* or *planhs*, a statement that he was forced to modify in 1995 when working with Rieger's larger corpus of songs. Bec's concept of *trobairitz* poetics has, however, remained unchanged: he portrays the women as working to insert themselves into a socio-poetic system dominated by the male troubadours and exploiting themes (especially the *malmariée*) found in the *chansons de femme*, which he claims—and as he will attempt to prove in the fourth and final section of his article—were all authored by men.

Bec's claim that the *trobairitz* drew on themes found in the *chansons de femme* would not seem troubling, or at least suspect, were it not for his dogged insistence on male authorship of these songs, despite evidence to the contrary. He refuses to consider seriously female authorship of any of these songs, even though most of them are anonymous and, as Bec admits more than once in this section—boldly entitled "Les 'chansons de femme' à auteur masculin"—could conceivably have been composed by either sex. After discussing a number of *chansons de femme* or *d'ami* in various Romance languages (the majority by men, admittedly, but some by women), he ends with a few examples in French, and it is here that his determination to exclude women from the corpus is most flagrant. He begins by citing *La froidor ne la jalee* (RS 517)[7] which he characterizes as "la belle 'chanson de femme' anonyme." This song, though indeed anonymous, is attributed in the manuscript (*C* 136) to "une dame," but Bec does not convey this interesting bit of information; after reproducing the first strophe, he repeats: "La pièce est malheureusement anonyme," adding: "Mais comment dire si son auteur est un homme ou une femme?" (258). The second song Bec mentions is also anonymous, *Jherusalem, grant damage me fais* (RS 191); again he asks: "Son auteur est-il un homme ou une femme?" (258). The uncertainty feigned by Bec in these two rhetorical questions is unquestionably a pose designed to un-

DIMINISHING THE *TROBAIRITZ*

derscore the "androgynous" nature of the genesis of a lyric type that is a clear example of *féminité textuelle*, for he leaves no doubt that he believes the author of each of these *chansons* was male. As we remember, he had stated at the beginning of his article that there were no women poets in the North, and his belief is restated in the title he chooses for this section of his study. Moreover, he ends his discussion by citing three *chansons de femme* "dont les auteurs, cette fois-ci, sont connus pour être des hommes" (258): *Chanterai por mon corage* (RS 1287), attributed to Guiot de Dijon, *Onques n'amai tant que jou fui amee* (RS 21), attributed to Richard de Fournival, and *Amors me fait renvoisier et chanter* (RS 498), attributed to Moniot d'Arras. He does not bother to specify that the first two attributions have been questioned by some scholars (including himself),[8] nor does he see fit to mention that a few women's songs bear rubrics ascribing them to women.

For, contrary to what Bec would have us believe, there are a few *chansons* that are attributed to named women in at least some manuscripts, as Madeleine Tyssens has recently reminded us: *Mout m'abelist quant je voi revenir* (RS 145), ascribed to Maroie de Diergnau in both manuscripts that preserve it (*M* and *T*); *Un petit devant le jor* (RS 1995), ascribed to the Duchesse de Lorraine in *C* 247, though ascribed to men in two other manuscripts and anonymous in five more; and *Par maintes fois aurai estei requise* (RS 1640), ascribed to the Duchesse de Lorraine in *C* 182, anonymous in *U* 97.[9] Although Tyssens' article appeared too late to inform Bec's 1979 article, Bec certainly knew about these attributions, because earlier scholars such as Jeanroy (96) had noted them and had been quick to marshal arguments to reject them as fanciful. There is no disputing Bec's right to accept these arguments, but his failure to mention the attributions is troubling. This failure is compounded when one sees that by the time of his 1995 anthology he knew of Tyssens' article (it is cited in his bibliography) but made no reference to it in his introduction and thus no attempt to respond to Tyssens' challenge.

Bec's determination to erase all traces of the women trouvères from Old French poetry can be seen as well in his analysis of the Old

JOAN TASKER GRIMBERT

French medieval lyric, and specifically the *chanson de femme*, in the first volume of *La Lyrique française au moyen âge (XIIe-XIIIe)*, which appeared two years before his article on the *trobairitz*. Although he published a number of examples of this lyric type in the anthology volume ("Textes") of this work, he records not a single woman author, even in cases where there exist manuscript attributions to women. If at least one of the manuscripts containing a particular song attributes it to a male poet, he adopts that attribution. More disturbing still, he does not even mention cases of contradictory manuscript attributions, unlike Samuel Rosenberg, who in his 1981, 1995, and 1998 anthologies preserves the feminine attribution of some of the love lyrics and debate poems and duly notes cases of conflicting attribution.

The last subject broached by Bec in the fourth section of his *trobairitz* article is the existence within the *trobairitz* corpus of eleven *tensos*—nine between a man and a woman, he specifies, and "only two" between two women. The *tenso aristocratisante* of the troubadours belongs to a more general type, the debate poem, and Bec notes that the conflict or contrast is naturally heightened when both sexes are given voice. The implication is that the *tensos* in which the women appear were authored by men who used the female voice for contrast. To support his unstated belief, Bec goes on to note analogies in other languages, including Galician-Portuguese, where all the *tensos* "—il n'y a pas de doute—" were written by men (260). He dutifully records the existence of similar pieces in Old French but mentions only the anonymous ones transcribed by Jeanroy before concluding: "Toutes ces tensons—un peu marginales il est vrai—ont *visiblement* été écrites par des hommes" (261; my emphasis). This statement, like so many in this section, is hardly an argument, and Bec clearly believes that his authority is sufficient to convince us. In reality, although the majority of the Old French *jeux-partis* are attributed to male poets, there are thirteen in which women play an active role as participants (usually against male poets, but in three instances against each other) and fifteen more in which they are named as judges. It is entirely possible that many of the women composed their own parts, as some manuscript attributions indicate.[10]

30

DIMINISHING THE *TROBAIRITZ*

In the second of two "notes additionnelles" appended to his article, Bec claims that after completing his study he became aware of "une dizaine de tensons homme/femme, toutes attribuées à des hommes, mais sans qu'on ait jamais songé à lier automatiquement la 'voix' féminine à la créativité d'une femme réelle, co-auteur de la pièce. Cela nous confirme dans notre suspicion relative à la réalité du personnage féminin de certaines tensons mixtes" (262). It is not clear whether the poems to which Bec is referring are in Occitan or in French, but in either case he would not be inclined to consider women as authors of the feminine voice. In his 1995 anthology, Bec devotes a whole section of his introduction to the Occitan *tensos* in which women participate (43-46). However, he excludes them from his published corpus—entitled *Chants d'amour des femmes-troubadours*—on the grounds that they are not technically "chants d'amour" (although love is clearly the main subject) and also because he believes that the women's parts were invented by the male troubadours.

The last example of a debate poem that Bec mentions in his 1979 article is relegated to a footnote: two *coblas* exchanged between the woman poet Na Tecla de Borja and the Catalan poet Auziàs March.[11] It is curious indeed that although Bec seems willing to admit that women composed poetry in Occitania and Catalonia, he refuses to consider (or even mention) the evidence we have that there were women trouvères in France. Truly, *nulle n'est poète dans son propre pays*!

We might well ask what purpose this fourth section on the "*chansons de femme* à auteur masculin" serves in an article devoted to the *trobairitz*, just as we might wonder what purpose Bec's remarks on the debate poems serve in a section supposedly devoted to the *chansons de femme*. Surely, we cannot fail to see now that it is the final stage in Bec's effort to debase the *trobairitz*. Since one of Bec's main theses is that the *trobairitz* adapted the troubadour system by exploiting material from the *chansons de femme*, and since there exist very few extant Occitan *chansons de femme*, he is obliged to touch on the larger corpus of women's songs in Old French, which gives him the opportunity to assert that they were all male-authored. Moreover, by excluding women in the North from the pantheon of medieval poets, he is able to depreciate still further the contribution of women in the South.

This same strategy is evident in the 1995 anthology where Bec, after asserting that *chansons de femme* are most often anonymous but can also be the work of male troubadours, attempts to justify his decision to include a few of these songs in a collection devoted to "femmes-troubadours clairement reconnues comme telles" (48). It is, he explains, because it is important to distinguish between *féminité génétique* and *féminité textuelle*, and he adds: "Or il se trouve que la situation textuelle de la chanson courtoise écrite par une *trobairitz* est par bien des points la même que celle des *chansons de femme*: à savoir un 'je' lyrique féminin (inversant par là la situation classique de la *canso* troubadouresque) chantant (ou déplorant) son amour pour un *ami*" (49). Here we have the confirmation that Bec still holds fast to his conviction that there were no women trouvères and uses this belief to diminish the *trobairitz*. Indeed, if we accept Gaunt's criticism of the *féminité génétique/féminité textuelle* distinction, it would appear that Bec cannot help undermining the existence of the *trobairitz*, even while he is cashing in on the renewed interest in them.

In conclusion: we recall that Bec had stated at the beginning of his article his determination to inject a large dose of objectivity into the discussion of the *trobairitz* by offering "une étude plus ponctuelle, plus rigoureuse, plus systématique" (235), but as we have seen, his rhetoric belies the desire, conscious or unconscious, to diminish the women troubadours. If further proof of Bec's hidden agenda is needed, it can be seen at the end of his article when he returns to the *trobairitz* and formulates his conclusions concerning their contribution to Occitan poetry. After restating his thesis that the *féminité* observed by Bogin in the poems of the *trobairitz* is a function of the dialectic between two registers—the *registre aristocratisant* (specifically, the troubadour *canso*) and the *registre popularisant* (especially the *chanson de femme*)— he concedes that the access women gained to the closed world of the *trobar* is already an indication of a certain liberation. But he cannot refrain from issuing a final

DIMINISHING THE *TROBAIRITZ*

salvo. In an apparently gracious gesture he determines to give Bogin the last word, but at what price we can only appreciate by examining his closing assertion: "C'est dans ce sens, mais dans ce sens uniquement, que l'on peut dire sans doute, avec Meg Bogin, que les *trobairitz* occitanes nous offrent le premier témoignage—*encore que balbutiant et contingent à notre sens*—'d'une culture que nous n'avions approchée jusqu'ici qu'au travers des hommes'" (262; my emphasis). In this final sentence, he has found occasion to remind us yet again of the limited nature of the corpus, and his characterization of that corpus as testimony that is "balbutiant et contingent" could hardly be more deprecating.[12]

Joan Tasker Grimbert
Catholic University of America

NOTES

[1] *Les Femmes Troubadours* (1978), the French translation of Bogin's book, had just appeared.

[2] Numerous studies published in the past ten years bear witness to this influence. Bruckner's recent work on the *trobairitz* contains multiple references to it. In "Fictions of the Female Voice," she refers to it as "an important article" (872); she cites it repeatedly in her edition of the *trobairitz* and in her entry in *A Handbook of the Troubadours*. See also Blakeslee, Earnshaw, Gaunt (*Gender and Genre*), Gravdal, Kay (who cites Bec's article in a footnote listing the major *trobairitz* articles; 239, n. 45), and Nappholz. Gaunt and Gravdal both have reservations regarding Bec's ideas (see below) but do not treat the specific subject—the authorship of the *chansons de femme*—discussed in the present article.

[3] Coldwell knew Bec's article, since she cites it in reference to the transformation that the trobairitz wrought within the troubadouresque tradition (n. 55). Curiously, though, she passes over Bec's assertion that there were

JOAN TASKER GRIMBERT

no women trouvères! This is symptomatic of the way Bec's article has been perceived by many scholars.

[4] At the beginning of his introduction, Bec himself calls for a *mise-au-point*. Noting that although much work has been done on the *trobairitz* in the past two decades in the United States and Germany, little has been published in French since the French translation of Bogin's book: "Le moment était donc venu, profitant des derniers travaux sur la matière, notamment les deux thèses allemandes d'Angelica Rieger et de Katharina Städtler et dans l'attente d'études à venir, de tenter à la fois de faire le point sur la question et de présenter au médiéviste, et surtout au 'lecteur moyen,' une synthèse suffisamment éclairante qui puisse leur permettre de pénétrer dans le monde somme toute assez clos du grand chant troubadouresque et, plus spécialement, de sa face féminine" (7).

[5] "Jean-Charles Huchet, for instance, suggests that the *trobairitz* are a *fiction littéraire*, while Bec parallels this by insisting that we are dealing less with authentic women poets than with what he calls *textualité féminine*" (159).

[6] In my analysis below I will have occasion to cite his two-volume study/anthology, *La Lyrique française au moyen âge (XIIe - XIIIe siècles)*.

[7] All Old French lyrics are designated by the numbers assigned to them in Spanke 1955.

[8] Just a year before this article was published, Bec himself had found the attribution to Richard de Fournival questionable: in his 1978 anthology of Old French lyrics, he had noted the author as "(Richard de Fournival ?)," both on the page containing the lyric and in the index. Rosenberg appears to accept all three of these attributions, but notes that the crusade song "cannot be attributed with certainty to Guiot de Dijon, who is not known to have composed any other songs touching on a crusade or voicing the sentiments of a woman" (*Songs of the Troubadours and Trouvères*,

DIMINISHING THE *TROBAIRITZ*

289). In a recent book, Michel Zink follows Bec's lead and attributes this song to Guiot de Dijon (143, 147).

[9] Although Tyssens accepts the attribution of RS 1640, she rejects it for RS 1995 on the grounds that it gives voice in the frame to a male narrator (380). No doubt for the same reason (and because she has resolved to limit herself to examples of *féminité textuelle*), she does not mention the prayer to the Virgin, *Amours, u trop tart me sui pris* (RS 1604a) attributed to "Li roïne Blance" (Blanche de Castile). However, if men were able to create fictive women, there is no reason to doubt that women were capable of creating fictive men.

[10] See Tyssens (382-84) and Doss-Quinby. The three *jeux-partis* in which women debate against each other are RS 1112 (*Dame de la Chaucie & Sainte des Prez*), RS 1744 (*Dame Margot & Dame Maroie [Marote]*), and RS 1962 (*Lorete & Suer*). On the lack of objectivity shown by critics when assessing the status of anonymous voices (real vs. fictional) in Occitan male/female debate poems, see Gaunt ("Sexual Difference," 302) and Nappholz (7-8).

[11] Published by Massó i Torrents, who devotes a section of his article to Na Tecla de Borja (411-14); cited in Bec's article (261, n. 94).

[12] Cf. Blakeslee's much more upbeat conclusion assessing the *trobairitz*' accomplishment in an article that details a theory remarkably similar to Bec's (75).

WORKS CITED

Bec, Pierre. *Chants d'amour des femmes-troubadours. Trobairitz et "chansons de femme."* Paris: Stock, 1995.
———. *La Lyrique française au moyen âge (XIIe - XIIIe siècles)*. 2 vol. Paris: Picard, 1977-78.

JOAN TASKER GRIMBERT

———. "'Trobairitz' et chansons de femme. Contribution à la connaissance du lyrisme féminin au moyen âge." *Cahiers de Civilisation médiévale* 22 (1979): 235-62.

Blakeslee, Merritt R. "La chanson de femme, les *Héroïdes*, et la *canso* occitane à voix de femme: Considérations sur l'originalité des *trobairitz*." In *Hommage à Jean-Charles Payen: "Farai chansoneta novela." Essais sur la liberté créatrice au Moyen Âge*. Caen: Université de Caen, 1989: 67-75.

Bogin, Meg. *The Women Troubadours*. 1976; New York and London: W.W. Norton, 1980. [French version: *Les Femmes Troubadours*, trans. Jeanne Faure-Cousin. Paris: Denoël/Gonthier, 1978.]

Bruckner, Matilda Tomaryn. "Fictions of the Female Voice: The Women Troubadours." *Speculum* 67 (1992): 865-91.
———. "The Trobairitz." In F.R.P. Akehurst and Judith Davis, eds. *Handbook of the Troubadours*. Berkeley-Los Angeles-London: University of California Press, 1995: 201-33.
———, Laurie Shepard, and Sarah White, eds. and trans. *Songs of the Women Troubadours*. New York and London: Garland Publishing, 1995.

Coldwell, Maria V. "*Jougleresses* and *Trobairitz*: Secular Musicians in Medieval France." In *Women Making Music: The Western Art Tradition 1150-1950,"* ed. Jane Bowers and Judith Tick. Urbana and Chicago: University of Illinois Press, 1986: 39-61.

Doss-Quinby, Eglal. "*Rolans, de ceu ke m'avez / Parti dirai mon samblant:* The Feminine Voice in the Old French *jeu-parti*." Forthcoming in *Neophilologus*.

Earnshaw, Doris. *The Female Voice in Medieval Romance Lyric*. New York, Bern, Frankfurt, and Paris: Peter Lang, 1988.

DIMINISHING THE *TROBAIRITZ*

Gaunt, Simon. *Gender and Genre in Medieval French Literature*. Cambridge: Cambridge University Press, 1995.

———. "Sexual Difference and the Metaphor of Language in a Troubadour Poem." *Modern Language Review* 83 (1990): 310-29.

Gravdal, Kathryn. "Metaphor, Metonymy, and the Medieval Women Trobairitz." *Romanic Review* 83.4 (1992): 411-26.

Huchet, Jean-Charles. "Les Femmes troubadours ou la Voix critique." *Littérature* 51 (1983): 59-90.

Jeanroy, Alfred. *Les Origines de la poésie lyrique en France au moyen âge*. 4th ed. Paris: Champion, 1965.

Kay, Sarah. *Subjectivity in Troubadour Poetry*. Cambridge: Cambridge University Press, 1990.

Massó i Torrents, Jaume. "Poetesses i dames intellectuals." In *Homenatge a Antoni Rubió i Lluch*. Barcelona, 1936: 405-17.

Nappholz, Carol Jane. *Unsung Women. The Anonymous Female Voice in Troubadour Poetry*. New York: Peter Lang, 1994.

Paden, William D. "Some Recent Studies of Women in the Middle Ages, Especially in France." *TENSO* 7 (1992): 94-124.

———, ed. *The Voice of the Trobairitz: Perspectives on the Women Troubadours*. Philadelphia: University of Pennsylvania Press, 1989.

Pfeffer, Wendy. "Women in the *Jeux-Partis*." Paper presented at the 30th International Congress on Medieval Studies, Western Michigan University, Kalamazoo, Michigan, May 5, 1995.

Rieger, Angelica, ed. *Trobairitz: Der Beitrag der Frau in der altokzitanischen höfischen Lyrik; Edition des Gesamtkorpus*. Tübingen: Niemeyer, 1991.

JOAN TASKER GRIMBERT

Rosenberg, Samuel N., ed.; music ed. Hans Tischler. *Chanter m'estuet; Songs of the Trouvères*. Bloomington: Indiana UP, 1981.

Rosenberg, Samuel N. and Hans Tischler, eds., with the collaboration of Marie-Geneviève Grossel, *Chansons des trouvères: Chanter m'estuet*. Paris: Librairie Générale Française, 1995.

Rosenberg, Samuel N., Margaret Switten, and Gérard Le Vot, eds. *Songs of the Troubadours and Trouvères*. New York and London: Garland Publishing, 1998.

Spanke, Hans. *G. Raynauds Bibliographie des altfranzösischen Liedes*. Musicologica 1. Leiden: Brill, 1955; rpt. 1980.

Städtler, Katharina. *Altprovenzalische Frauendichtung (1150-1250): Historisch-soziologische Untersuchungen und Interpretationen*. Heidelberg: Carl Winter, 1990.

Tyssens, Madeleine. "Voix de femme dans la lyrique d'oïl." In *Femmes-Mariages-Lignages. XIIe-XIVe. Mélanges offerts à Georges Duby*. Bruxelles: De Boeck Université, 1992: 373-87.

Zink, Michel. *Le Moyen âge et ses chansons, ou un Passé en trompe-l'œil*. Paris: Éditions de Fallois, 1996.

[6]

Women's Performance of the Lyric Before 1500

Susan Boynton

The diverse evidence for the performance of lyric poetry by women before 1500 raises several questions related to the context and transmission of medieval music. Did women create the songs they performed? What kinds of women sang, what music, and in what settings? How did the gendered voice of a song affect its performance? In this essay, I will examine these questions in light of the evidence for women's performance of the lyric in various medieval societies. Both literary and historical accounts suggest that women played an important role in the creation, performance, and transmission of lyric poetry. Until recently, however, music historians have rarely addressed the place of gender in the composition and performance of secular song, thus eliding an important dimension of the production and reception of lyric poetry. Women's performance of the lyric is an elusive subject, both because of the fluidity of gender categories as they apply to performance, and because of the flexible relationship between the performance and composition of medieval music.

Since composition was not entirely distinct from performance until the later Middle Ages, the existence of female performers automatically implies the existence of female composers. The creation of medieval music depended on a wide variety of skills and procedures in which performance, composition, and improvisation are not easily separated. Thus the fact that little surviving secular music from before 1500 is attributed to women does not mean that women did not create music. Like other medieval musicians, women performed their own music or adapted the music of others to their own taste and requirements. Every musical performance was inherently an act of composition or recomposition. The music that has survived in manuscript sources is only a small part of the larger tradition, which was usually transmitted orally and routinely included improvisation. Since the predominantly oral transmission of song caused the loss of most melodies in the medieval lyric corpus, the written record reflects a relatively small proportion of the songs that were actually performed. Given the limited survival of melodies for lyric poetry and the prevalence of anonymity among extant works, the lack of attested compositions firmly attributed to women is unsurprising. Investigating women's performance of the medieval lyric entails broadening the scope of the evidence beyond the musical score, rejecting the author function, and placing performance, and thus performers, at the center of the inquiry.

Medieval song was first and foremost a performer's art. Working within a predominantly oral tradition, singers determined many aspects of their songs, including tempo and dynamics; these are among the elements which can be found in many modern scores, but which are not specified in medieval music manuscripts. Moreover, before the late thirteenth century, the rhythm of secular monophony was not clearly represented by musical notation, apparently because the oral tradition was sufficient. Sources vary widely on the role of instrumental accompaniment in song, implying that medieval practices were diverse and flexible. All the evidence suggests that singers learned songs orally and were free to appropriate and alter them for their own purposes; they were not expected to perform a song the same way twice, or to produce a version similar to that of another musician. Contrafacting (the practice of singing a song text to the melody of a different song) was a common procedure, as it is in performances of medieval music today. Mastery of improvisation and ornamentation was central to the craft of both singers and instrumentalists. Composition and performance were thus closely intertwined.

Variants in the manuscript traditions of medieval song reflect the variation and adaptation that took place from performance to performance, and descriptions of performance in literary narrative corroborate the flexibility suggested by the patterns of written transmission. For instance, a group of aristocrats in Jean Renart's early thirteenth-century romance *Guillaume de Dole* simultaneously create and perform a series of related songs by repeating the same verses in a different order and recombining standard formulas, showing "the fluidity of the oral medium, in which singers draw on a repertoire of lyric motifs and refrains that can be pieced together according to conventions of form and decorum."[1] Two scenes near the beginning of the romance exemplify the informality, inventiveness, and playfulness of such musico-poetic exchanges between various singers. In the first passage, a group of men and women walk through the forest singing; three different ladies sing generic refrains and *rondets de carole*, each beginning before the previous one has finished. Three more singers continue, two with short songs on a different subject (fair Aeliz); the third returns to the *rondet* genre.[2] While these songs differ ostensibly in content, several of them share one or two verses, and the two about fair Aeliz are almost identical; the singing constitutes a game of invention and recombination in which singers use formulaic verses to create short new pieces. The second passage also describes a mixed group of individuals, but this time they sing songs to accompany a round-dance (*carole*).[3] In this scene, the singers do not interrupt one another, as those in the previous passage did; the contents of their songs are more closely related, as if they were listening carefully to one another in order to take up the thread of the previous song. Several of the verses used in *Guillaume de Dole* are transmitted within longer pieces of music in thirteenth-century manuscripts; the processes employed by the singers in the romance may reflect procedures of contemporary musicians.[4] As the informal music-making in *Guillaume de Dole* shows, the creation of medieval music was more varied than is communicated by the modern word "composer," with its associated notions of artistic autonomy. The distinction between composer and performer, implying a division of labor into creation and interpretation, has only limited relevance to medieval music.

Historians of music have often assumed that medieval women performed music created by others, resulting in a pervasive historiographic tendency to classify female musicians as "amateurs" whose craft depends on the art of professional men. In this context, definitions of professionalism tend to conform to a model established by the careers of nineteenth-century male musicians; the enduring link between the idea of professionalism and Western cultural notions of musical creativity has led historians to deny agency in the creative process to women deemed nonprofessional, such as aristocratic patrons.[5] In the case of medieval song, however, a radical separation of performer from composer makes little sense. Literary accounts of women singing abound in the Middle Ages, and extensive evidence indicates that they played an important role in their musical cultures.

Female singers in the Middle Ages came from all classes, including slaves, rustic women, urban women, professional minstrels, and aristocratic girls and women. While there is little evidence for women's performance of secular poetry in Latin Europe during the early Middle Ages, an intriguing Carolingian decree from 789 forbids nuns to compose or send love-songs.[6] Much more extensive information exists regarding women musicians in the early medieval Arab world. Female servant-musicians or courtesans are attested in the Iberian peninsula beginning in the eighth century; both Muslims and Mozarabs had dancing and singing slaves in their households. The prominence of women musicians in the Arab world was at its apex during the

'Abbāsid period (750–1258 C.E.).⁷ The tradition of medieval Arabic lyric includes numerous women singers and poet-composers ranging across the social scale from slaves to princesses.⁸ Slave-singers were referred to as *jāriyah* or *qaynat*; *jāqriyah* were generally musicians, but could also be female slaves of any kind. A *qayna* was usually a talented slave who learned and memorized quickly; she was trained not only to sing and play instruments, but also to improvise poetry and generally to entertain guests.⁹ Some female singers were *nadīm*, highly educated boon companions of the ruler. In the early Islamic period, some accomplished singers and instrumentalists were *mawālī* (freemen); after being freed, several of the best-known female *mawālī* had musical salons in their homes, and taught their repertoire to other musicians.¹⁰

Female singers were essential to the performance, creation, and transmission of medieval Arab music. Usually among the most prized musicians in a court, they participated in all types of performances, often singing behind a curtain.¹¹ As in other traditions of medieval music, performers of Arab lyric were in some sense composers as well, because they made songs their own by means of ornamentation and other forms of alteration. In order to maintain a monopoly over their repertoire, musicians sometimes intentionally distorted songs so that rivals would be unable to recreate them exactly. *Jāriyah* are known to have engaged in this practice, implying that they enjoyed a significant amount of control and authority over their musical repertoire.¹² Women musicians in the Arab world were renowned as composers in the strict sense as well: both slaves and princesses are known to have composed their own songs.¹³ Women were also instrumental in passing music on to others: *jāriyah* taught their repertoire to other *jāriyah*, their owners, *mawālī*, or male musicians.¹⁴ They were valued for their ability to memorize large numbers of songs and thus to preserve musical traditions.

As elsewhere in the Arab world, female musicians were central to the musical traditions of the Arab-dominated Iberian peninsula. Singing, dancing, and proficiency in instrumental performance were among the many accomplishments expected of the most valued female slaves, who were given an extensive education before being sold. According to contemporary accounts, innovations in Andalusian musical genres were accomplished with the aid of singing slave-girls.¹⁵ Arab music may have exercised significant influence in Occitania by the later eleventh century, when slave women captured in raids on Arab towns in the Iberian peninsula were present in Occitanian courts.¹⁶ At the same time, female poets flourished in Al-Andalus, leaving behind them a significant literary corpus.¹⁷

It may be no coincidence that the following century saw the emergence in

Occitania of the *trobairitz*, a group of women poet-composers unparalleled elsewhere outside the Arab world. The legacy of the *trobairitz*, for all its richness, exemplifies the difficulties inherent in discussing the musical aspects of medieval women's song. For the entire corpus of Occitan lyric texts attributable to women or written in a woman's voice,[18] only one melody survives, that of "A chantar" by the Comtessa de Dia. In order to reconstruct musical performances of other *trobairitz* lyrics, it is necessary to apply the technique of contrafact, singing a poem with a melody taken from a structurally similar poem.[19] (The recordings of *trobairitz* songs listed in the appended discography employ this method.) Scattered textual references suggest that further melodies by *trobairitz* have been lost or that they survive without attribution. A prose *vida* states that the *trobairitz* Azalais de Porcairagues knew how to compose (*sabet trobar*),[20] but this intriguing comment must be interpreted with caution, since it could refer to the composition of verse without implying the creation of music. The *vidas* were composed significantly later than the poetry of the troubadours and *trobairitz*, and are based as much on fiction (in the form of the poetic corpus) as on fact.[21] A reference to the *son de n'Alamanda* in a poem by Bertran de Born may refer to a composition by Alamanda.[22] Little information is available on the *trobairitz*' performance of their songs; their terse *vidas*, unlike those of the troubadours, do not refer to singing, but several Occitan poems by both men and women refer to women singing. Despite the meager written transmission of their melodies, the *trobairitz* seem to have played an important role in Occitan musical culture, as both performers and composers. Conduct literature such as the *Ensenhamens* of Garin le Brun, which recommends that women sing for their guests, supports this idea.[23] Furthermore, the active participation of Occitan noblewomen in rule and conflict confirms that their voices were meant to be heard. In an important study, Fredric Cheyette and Margaret Switten argue that the well-documented political power of high-born women in Occitan society should be taken into account in evaluating the status of the woman's voice in Occitan lyric. Contrary to much recent criticism that assumes the exclusion of women from power in Occitan society, and thus from troubadour song, Cheyette and Switten demonstrate that "[i]n this society, women were expected to have a role and a voice."[24]

Women could also have performed the female voices in Occitan debate poems; the large proportion of debate poems in the *trobairitz* corpus is suggestive in this regard. Moreover, although the influence of Arabic lyric on that of Occitania is outside the scope of this essay, it is intriguing to speculate that literary dialogue between male and female poets in the Arab world could have inspired similar interactions in Occitan poetry. The mid-eleventh-century exchange of love poems between Wallāda and her lover, Ibn Zaidun, bears general comparison with the lively interchange between men and women in the *tenso* tradition a century later. Wallada and Ibn Zaidun carried on a poetic correspondence that can be likened to a debate,[25] although their poems are separate units not exactly comparable to the exchanges of *coblas* between men and women in the Occitan lyric corpus. While this analogy might seem strained, given the universality of debate poetry in medieval literature, the Occitan *tenso* shares with the exchange between Wallada and Ibn Zaidun the presence of two autonomous voices. Some debates between a troubadour and a lady appear artificial; their dual voicing, which heightens the artifice, is brought out effectively in performance by two singers, such as the male-female *tensos* by Raimbaut de Vaqueiras and Guiraut de Bornelh performed by two singers on the recordings *Cansós de Trobairitz* and *Lo Gai Saber* (see discography). Although the female interlocutors in these poems are fictional (a Genovese lady speaking in her dialect; Alamanda, the maidservant of Giraut's beloved), their colorful depictions of women's voices could lend themselves to female vocal performance.[26] Cheyette and Switten point out that another fictional interlocutor, the *vilana* in Marcabru's *pastorela* "L'autrier jost'una sebissa," "might indeed reflect a taste for works in which powerful women figure prominently."[27]

The effective representation of an articulate female subject in these male-authored debate poems reminds us that the *trobairitz* themselves composed debate poems with men. One example is "Vos que.m semblatz dels corals amadors," an exchange of *coblas* between Garsenda and Gui de Cavaillon; another is a *tenso* between Maria de Ventadorn and Gui d'Ussel, "Gui d'Ussel, be.m pesa de vos."[28] We can only speculate that male-female *tensones* were intended for performance by two people; as in all Occitan poetry, singers must decide how to perform songs without clear, consistent indications of their medieval performance practice.[29] However, Angelica Rieger has pointed out the significance of a miniature representing the troubadour Gaucelm Faidit with his wife, the entertainer Guilelma Monja, standing with her hands on her hips as Gaucelm speaks; she seems to be waiting to respond to Gaucelm's speech with her own half of a dialogue. This image may depict a performance of one of the "mixed" *tensos*; in any case, it represents two known singers at work together, which suggests collaborative performance practice.[30] Guilelma Monja is the only Occitan female minstrel whose name is known to us; narrative sources refer to her as a *soldadeira* (or *soudadeira*), which scholars have often considered equivalent to "prostitute," but Rieger has shown that the term is synonymous with *joglaressa*, a female minstrel who usually worked with a male counterpart. The Occitan *joglaressa* had a distinctive role and image as a professional entertainer who danced, juggled, tumbled, and sang; manuscript illuminations of the thirteenth and fourteenth centuries clearly differentiate between the aristocratic *trobairitz* and the lower-class *joglaressa*.[31] Guilelma Monja thus represents a larger class of female performers.

Female minstrels and trouvères are also attested in northern France during the high and late Middle Ages. In the thirteenth century, female singers and jugglers are mentioned among the entertainers of French and Castilian royalty. Documents from noble and royal households in the fourteenth century list female instrumentalists as well as singers, and several literary texts from this period mention traveling female minstrels.[32] Two heroines, Nicolette (in *Aucassin et Nicolette*) and Fresne (in *Galeran de Bretagne*), disguise themselves successfully as minstrels, perhaps suggesting that a female *jongleur* was not entirely out of the ordinary at the time. Extant songs attributed to female trouvères show that women could compose as well as perform in the high style associated with the male troubadours and trouvères.[33]

Although no significant group of aristocratic composer-poets analogous to the *trobairitz* seems to have flourished in northern France, both literary and didactic sources show that music was considered a desirable accomplishment for noblewomen. Heroines in Chrétien de Troyes's *Philomena* and in Gerbert de Montreuil's *Roman de la Violette* know how to sing, and conduct literature such as the *Chastoiment des Dames* of Robert de Blois instructs women to sing "in the company of worthy people."[34] In the noble society depicted in romances, women sang as often as men.[35] The lyric insertions in Jean Renart's *Guillaume de Dole* represent a microcosm of lyric genres performed by women of diverse status. The heroine and her mother perform *chansons de toile*, a genre typically associated with women.[36] Although the oldest surviving *chansons de toile* are actually from the early thirteenth century, the aura of antiquity surrounding these poems apparently enhanced the charm of the genre for medieval audiences. The ambiguous character of the *chansons de toile*, as a purportedly popular lyric genre preserved in a stylized form, makes them a paradigm for the association of woman's song with archaic lyric poetry.[37]

Guillaume de Dole contains one of the earliest appearances of the *chanson de toile*. The mother of the heroine introduces her song as an ancient genre performed by women in a domestic environment. She and her daughter, Lienor, present a "command performance" of *chansons de toile*, at the request of a family member, to entertain a visitor in their home. This public performance of a private genre is itself an antiquarian gesture reflecting a taste for old-fashioned song, as well as the kind of music-making for guests prescribed in contemporary conduct literature. While distancing the *chanson de toile* from the fictional present, the scene is constructed around the typical characters and situations associated with the genre. Throughout the romance, Jean Renart aligns Lienor with the popular genres of woman's songs, such as the *chansons de toile*, while the hero, Conrad, consistently sings trouvère lyrics; their marriage thus represents the union of woman's song and courtly song.[38] The performance of the *chanson de toile* constitutes a self-conscious performance of womanhood itself. However, later in the romance a knight also sings a *chanson de toile* accompanied by a minstrel; thus a man performs for an audience a genre presented elsewhere in the romance as a song for women's private singing. This section of the text is remarkable for many reasons; it is the longest *chanson de toile* in the entire romance, and the presence of a minstrel implies an unexpected variety in performance practices of the genre.[39] If, as Michel Zink argues, the knight's performance is a parody, it tells us little about medieval performance practice, but the disjunction between the protagonist of the song and the identity of the singer, typical of the lyric insertions in the romance, shows a flexible relationship between performer and author.[40]

Guillaume de Dole also contains numerous and varied descriptions of performances by minor characters. A jongleur's sister sings a section from a *chanson de geste* (62–64; lines 1332–67), the typical repertoire of minstrels and jongleurs.[41] At the beginning of the romance, noblewomen as well as men sing *refrains* and *rondets de caroles* during dances. The *rondet de carole* crossed class lines, however; an innkeeper's daughter sings one to the accompaniment of a minstrel. As if to distinguish her from the other singers of *rondets*, she is rewarded for her performance with a gift:

The maiden received as a token his belt with the silver buckle to thank her
for singing this new little song with Jouglet and his *vielle*:
Down there in the little meadow — now I have a fine new love! —
Perronelle was washing clothes. I should indeed be happy:
now I have a fine new love just to my taste.

> (Ladamoisele ot paramor / Sa ceinture dargent ferree / Deloier carel a chantee / ovoec iouglet enla viele / Ceste chanconete novele. / Cest laius en la praele / orai bone amor novele / dras i gaoit perronele. Bien doi ioie avoir / orai bon amor novele a mon voloir) (86–87; lines 1841–51)

Like the payment for the performance, the reference to washing clothes in the song seems to indicate the nonelite status of the singer. Perhaps it is this allusion to a practical aspect of everyday life, which contrasts with the pastoral conventions used in the other *rondets*, that causes Jean Renart to describe the song as "new."

Later in the romance, two ladies sing a *rondet* together, and a character identified as Bele Doete de Troyes, apparently a female jongleur, sings a *pastourelle*.[42] Thus the songs performed by women in the romance include a generic dance-song (*rondet de carole*), a popularizing trouvère form (the *pastourelle*), and an epic; the singers include noblewomen, a working-class woman, and a professional entertainer. If the music-making in *Guillaume de Dole* is realistic, as some scholars have asserted,[43] the romance indicates what kind of woman performed what sort of song, and also shows the flexibility of the associations between social class and lyric genre.

While both amateur and professional musicians performed courtly lyric, the *carole* was the predominant genre associated with singing by women of all classes in medieval Europe. The multiple genres grouped under the heading *caroles* were characterized by performance during a round-dance; they were "performed by a mixed company of men and women, or by women alone, and are especially associated with young girls."[44] Although women's popular dance-songs were already an ancient custom in the Middle Ages, *caroles* became increasingly prevalent in both rural and urban settings during the twelfth and thirteenth centuries, consequently occupying a significant place in French literature of the period.[45] Theologians also concerned themselves with *caroles*, often condemning young women who danced in them. Christopher Page's suggestion that the *carole* was "the principal point of contact between the musical culture of the villages, towns, and courts" could explain the blending of elite and popular culture in the poetry of songs sung during *caroles*.[46]

While *caroles* are usually presented in a narrative framework as simple dance-songs, authors of romances often exploit their innocent surface to deliver a hidden message. For example, a passage from the thirteenth-century Old Occitan *Roman de Flamenca* describes girls performing a spring dance-song: "The maidens had already brought out may-garlands they had made the night before, and they sang their may-songs. They all passed right in front of Guillem singing a maying-song that goes: 'May the lady be rewarded who does not make her lover anguish.'"[47] Even this apparently artless *kalenda maia* is carefully crafted to fit the narrative context of the romance, for it highlights the fact that Guillem, the hero, is in love with Flamenca, and hopes that she reciprocates his feelings. Similarly, the conventional opening of a *rondet de carole* in *Sone de Nansay* is altered to reflect the name of the heroine; in another *rondet*, the heroine conveys her emotions to her lover.[48] Like the passage from

Flamenca, this episode cannot be regarded simply as direct evidence of women's music-making or of contemporary social practice.

While fictional accounts of performance must be treated with caution as historical evidence, details in the descriptions they contain often provide an example of customary activities that were so common as to seem unremarkable to the writer. A passage in Chrétien de Troyes's *Chevalier au Lion* provides an instructive example, demonstrating the flexibility of descriptions of music-making in medieval narrative. Seven different manuscript readings of these verses variously describe maidens dancing to the accompaniment of instruments.[49] They may be playing or singing at the same time: "whether the maidens are singing, dancing, or playing instruments, scribes may have been inattentive to this distinction because it would be assumed that maidens would be doing all of these things."[50] This example effectively evokes the flexibility of performance practice that seems to be behind the instability of some textual traditions.

The medieval romances of Tristan and Iseut (in German, Isolde) provide numerous descriptions of performances by Isolde, whose musical accomplishment is an integral part of her character. The thirteenth-century Tristan romance by Thomas describes Iseut singing a *lai*: "One day, she sat in her chamber and made a sad lay of love . . . the queen sings sweetly, fits her voice to the instrument; her hands are beautiful, the lay good, her voice sweet and her tone low."[51] The word *fait* probably indicates that Iseut did not just perform the *lai*, but improvised or invented the text and music herself; the related Old Occitan verb *far* can signify both "to compose" and "to perform."[52] In *Guillaume de Dole*, Renart establishes an equivalence between writing and composing (*faire* and *trover*) supporting the idea that *fait* in Thomas's *Tristan* refers to the creation of a text: "and it will seem to everyone that he who wrote the romance also composed all the words of the songs" ("Sest avis a chascun et samble / Q[ue] cil qui a fet les romans / Q[ui]l trovast toz les moz des chans," 2–3; lines 26–28).

Unlike most descriptions of music-making in medieval narrative, this scene in Thomas's romance depicts a private performance, without any intended audience; Cariado's unannounced arrival while Iseut sings is all the more disruptive because he intrudes upon her privacy. Iseut is not restricted to performance alone in her chamber; on the contrary, she generally sings and plays for the court. Her performance of the *lai* is particularly private because it expresses her secret feelings and is not intended to be heard by others; given the personal nature of the song, it is all the more likely that Iseut is supposed to have composed the *lai* herself. The idea of Iseut as composer of *lais* is made explicit in the later development of the legend, the *Roman de Tristan en Prose*; in several manuscripts of this work, narrative *lais* of the type Iseut sings in Thomas's *Tristan* are transmitted with music and attributed to her as author.[53] In the *Roman de Tristan en Prose*, several of the songs are in the form of letters, including one that Iseut composes and sings: "Then she begins to compose a letter as well and as cleverly as she could. She sang so well and so joyously that one could not find a lady who sang better than she" ("Lors conmence .i. brief a trouver au mieulz et au plus soutillement qu'elle onques pout . . . elle chantoit si bien et si envoisieement que l'en ne pouist a celui point trouver nulle dame mieulz chantant de lui").[54] One of the manuscripts of the *Roman de Tristan en Prose* containing musical notation contains the *lai* text corresponding to the passage above:

To you, Tristan, true friend,
Whom I love and will love
All the days of my life,
I send this letter that I have made with my heart.
To you, Tristan, fair sweet friend,
In place of my heart have I sent
This letter, where I have put
That you have wrongly made me your enemy.

> (A vous, Tristran, amis verai / Que je amai et amerai / Tous les jours que je duerrai, / Mant mon brief que fait de cuer ai. / Vous Tristran, biaus dous amis, / En lieu de mon cuer ai tramis / Mon brief, ou je ai dedens mis / Qu'a tort m'estes fais anemis.)[55]

In other parts of the prose *Tristan*, *lais* are sung by several different characters, including young girls who perform *lais* composed by Tristan, at his request.[56] The survival of music for the *lais* indicates that they were intended for performance, presumably by women.

Gottfried von Strassburg's thirteenth-century German romance, *Tristan*, describes Isolde's musical accomplishments in remarkable detail:

She fiddled her "estampie," her lays, and her strange tunes in the French style, about Sanze and St. Denis (than which nothing could be rarer), and knew an extraordinary number. . . . She sang her "pastourelle," her "rotruenge" and "rondeau," "chanson," "refloit," and "folate" well, and well, and all too well. . . . Of love-songs she could make both the words and the airs and polish them beautifully. She was able to read and write.

> (Si videlte ir stampenîe, / leiche und sô vremediu notelîn, / diu niemer vremeder kunden sîn, / in franzoiser wîse / von Sanze und San Dinîse. / Der kunde s'ûzer mâze

vil. . . . / Si sang ir pastureˆle, / ir rotruwange und ir rundate, / schanzûne, refloit und folate / wol unde wol und alze wol . . . / Brieve und schanzûne tihten, / ir getihte schône slihten, / si kunde schríben unde lesen.)[57]

This description of an ideal thirteenth-century courtly musician is informative on several levels. It shows that Gottfried's audience would be impressed by Isolde's mastery of several French vocal and instrumental genres. Gottfried presents the composition of love-songs as a particular accomplishment, and implicitly distinguishes between the creation of texts and melodies. It is significant that Isolde's literacy is mentioned after her ability to compose songs; most secular monody of the high Middle Ages was not written down by the composer, but rather transmitted orally and recorded in manuscripts long after the time of composition. Isolde is presented as both an interpreter and a creator of music, a skilled composer-performer who has reached the summit of artistic achievement.

While the evidence from the twelfth and thirteenth centuries for women's performance of the lyric comes primarily from literary sources, we know significantly more about historical women musicians of the fourteenth and fifteenth centuries. The first Italian text to address the education of women, Francesco da Barberino's *Reggimento e costumi di donna*, can be used as a source of information on the musical experience of women in the early Trecento, with the qualification that it is a prescriptive document.[58] In this text, written in the first two decades of the fourteenth century, Barberino set down restrictions on musical performance by young women of various social classes, from princesses down to peasants. According to Barberino, the lower a woman's status, the more freedom she has to sing; girls and women of the lower classes have the greatest liberty to dance and sing. The daughter of an emperor or a king may perform for guests only at the request of a parent; she can sing songs when in her room with her teacher or with other women, and to pass the time, she may also be permitted to study an instrument. Barberino's treatise contains the earliest reference to singing for a private audience as *camerale*, "of the chamber"; music is thus presented as a form of discipline for women who were essentially confined to their rooms.[59] As conduct literature, the *Reggimento* presents an idealized schema of female socialization, but historical documents show that "most elite women of the fifteenth century had a musical education something like that prescribed by Barberino."[60] Since a great deal of Italian fourteenth-century music was improvised or orally transmitted and was not written down, we know little of the music women performed, but, given the fluid boundary between composer and performer in this period, it is likely that women created at least some of the music they performed. Eleonora Beck remarks cautiously that "women, as described in Barberino's treatise, surely played, sang, and performed music; we can only hypothesize, however, that they did indeed compose music."[61]

In addition to amateur performers, professional women musicians (a category not mentioned by Barberino) performed secular music in northern Italian courts during the fifteenth century.[62] Highly skilled female professional singers are known to have existed in northern Europe in this period as well. In a treatise written around 1400 (possibly in Hainaut), Arnulf of St. Ghislain praised female virtuosos for their vocal technique: "There is a second group among the fourth category, evidently of the favoured female sex, which is so much the more valuable the more it is rare; who in the epiglottis of the sweet-sounding throat divide tones with equipose into semitones, and articulate semitones into indivisible microtones with an indescribable melody that you would think more angelic than human."[63] This unusually specific passage emphasizes the rarity of highly skilled female singers and describes their agility in fast ornamentation. Since decoration of melodic lines was a form of improvisation cultivated by all medieval singers, Arnulf finds the singers remarkable not for the mere fact that they know how to ornament, but rather for their mastery of the art.

In the fifteenth century, the musical literacy of elite women seems to have increased, to judge from the large number of music manuscripts intended for women.[64] Several fifteenth-century women best known as patrons were both prolific poets and active musicians, making it probable that they composed music for their own performance. Margaret of Austria, a skilled poet and performer of music, probably created some of the musical settings of her poetry; Martin Picker argues that Margaret composed the lament for her brother, Philip the Fair.[65] While no extant compositions are attributed to fifteenth-century women, the documented activities of noblewomen and their ladies-in-waiting suggests that they created music and poetry which is lost, or extant but anonymous. The question of voice is central: Paula Higgins argues that much fifteenth-century anonymous lyric poetry in a neutral voice may have been written by women.[66]

In addition to creating new works, much "invisible" compositional activity in the late Middle Ages and Renaissance took the form of arranging well-known songs for instrumental performance. Thus Bianca de' Medici, who sang and played French chansons for the entourage of Pope Pius II at Florence in 1460, may herself have made the arrangements of the vocal works she performed on the organ.[67] Patronage can be seen as another "invisible" musical activity; many noblewomen promoted the composition of works they could perform themselves, and received instruction in performance from musicians in their employ. It is possible that they also learned to improvise in the style of the compositions they commissioned, and thus were creators to some extent as well as performers. That their agency in musical composition took the form of patronage does not diminish their importance as female performers of lyric poetry. To cite one particularly well-known example, Isabella d'Este's patronage of Italian vocal music had a significant effect on music history, contributing to the "shift in taste away from the French chanson and toward native Italian forms and styles."[68]

This essay has tended to separate amateur (elite) from professional (non-elite) performances, dividing them into categories that correspond roughly to the modern designations of private and public. Recent work by ethnomusicologists shows how problematic this distinction is with regard to women's performance, however. Jennifer Post has revealed the ethnocentric bias in scholars' assumptions of a rigid division between public and private performance; in many cultures, such boundaries are not manifested clearly and do not correspond to the experience of the musicians within their society.[69] In the effort to connect the corpus of woman's song to performers of the past, historical musicologists stand to benefit from ethnomusicologists' studies of women's performance traditions in diverse cultures. Peter Jeffery, in a study advocating the application of ethnomusicological methods to medieval Western chant, points out the relevance of cross-cultural study to women's laments, a universal oral tradition that must have influenced more formal liturgical laments in medieval Western music.[70]

Unlike a traditional musicological approach based on written works, an approach to woman's song drawing upon ideas from ethnomusicology has the advantage of treating the medieval lyric as a predominantly oral art in which women played a central role, despite their limited representation as "authors" in the written record. By focusing on the social roles of women musicians and on the social context of their performances, we may better understand the musical dimensions of these traditions while bracketing the problematic questions of authorship and attribution that play a major role in many discussions of woman's song. Pierre Bec has pointed out that, paradoxically, many of the known "woman's songs" were written by men, while the *trobairitz*, who were women, wrote poetry in the genres of the male-voiced troubadour tradition.[71] Critics usually take as given that anonymous songs in a woman's voice were written by male court poets evoking an older tradition of popular poetry. Dance-songs and refrains are often considered to be man-made texts that preserve only a secondary impression of a woman's voice.[72] For example, the following statement in a recent monograph on the *alba* radically separates voice from authorship: "The alba lady's voice is, presumably, *man*-made: all the albas for which authorship is known are by men. Although we cannot rule out the possibility that, in the case of the ten anonymous albas, anonymous was a woman, scholars have found no evidence to suggest that a significant number of anonymous vernacular lyrics were composed by women."[73] Such an approach to the attribution of anonymous woman's songs does not take into account the dynamics of musical performance; the intersection of authorship and voice in the performance of medieval lyric significantly weakens the distinction between songs written by women and anonymous ones written in a woman's voice.

The "authorship" of much medieval song can be seen as at least partly collective, since successive performers or copyists of works altered and adapted them; the transformations to which medieval songs were subject, in both written and oral transmission, thus lessen the extent to which a song's essence is purely a product of the author. A medieval singer essentially recreated a song in performance, and could take on the identity of its poetic "I." Some genres (such as the *canso*) could be performed by women or men, without any inherent link between the voice of the poem and the sex of the singer. Even genres closely associated with performance by women, such as the *chanson de toile* and the *rondet de carole*, could apparently be sung by men or women, as seen above in *Guillaume de Dole*. The appropriation of a song's voice by a singer seems often to have been considered an integral part of the song, which was then interpreted as a personal statement by the performer.

Literary sources suggest that medieval audiences perceived female singers both as interpreting preexisting music and as expressing their own emotions. The performance of well-known songs by characters in some French romances reminds us of medieval singers' readiness to adapt preexisting music to their purposes. In Gerbert de Montreuil's thirteenth-century *Roman de la Violette* the heroine, Euriaut, sings a stanza from a *canso* by Bernart de Ventadorn to express her defiance of the challenge to her love presented by an envious courtier.[74] While Euriaut's choice of song may be a purely literary conceit, it is noteworthy that the narrative depicts a woman singing a song attributed to a male poet, while adapting it to her own situation. The second lyric Euriaut sings falls into the category of traditional woman's song (a *chanson de mal-mariée*), but while the song itself is about marital infidelity, Euriaut uses it to profess loyalty; she alters her songs to express her own feelings.[75] Fresne, in the thirteenth-century romance *Galeran de Bretagne*, also communicates her emotions through song, but is able to conceal her message from everyone but her lover because she is disguised as a minstrel; minstrels, as professional entertainers, are not assumed to express their personal sentiments through their art.[76]

Descriptions of music-making in Boccaccio's *Decameron* also reflect a perception of multiple meanings embedded in songs performed by women. Each evening of the ten days they spend in the country outside Florence, the three men and seven women of the *brigata* dance and sing after dinner, and each of the characters sings one solo *ballata*. During most of the performances, the audience reflects on the meaning of the song, and often aligns the lyric "I" of the song with the persona of the singer, whether man or woman. On the sixth, seventh, and tenth day, the listeners attribute the emotions expressed in the songs to the female performers themselves. They assume that the *ballata* sung by Elissa on the sixth day refers to rejection by her own unidentified lover: "Then, with a rather pitiful sigh, Elissa finished her song, and while all wondered at her words, no one could figure out who was the reason for such singing" ("Poi che con un sospiro assai pietoso Elissa ebbe alla sua canzon fatta fine, ancor che tutti si maravigliasser di tali parole, niuno per ciò ve n'ebbe che potesse avvisare chi di cosí cantar le fosse cagione").[77] Likewise, the members of the *brigata* conclude from Filomena's *ballata* on the seventh day that she is enjoying a new love: "This song made the whole *brigata* think that Filomena was embracing a new and pleasing love, and since her words made it seem that she had experienced more than just the view of this love, some were envious of her, considering her luckier than they" ("Estimar fece questa canzone a tutta la brigata che nuovo e piacevole amore Filomena strignesse; e per ciò che per le parole di quella pareva che ella piú avanti che la vista sola n'avesse sentito, tenendonela piú felice, invidia per tali vi furono le ne fu avuta," *Decameron*, 885–86). Finally, Dioneo explicitly links Fiammetta's song on the tenth day to her private feelings: "When Fiammetta had finished her song, Dioneo, who was next to her, said laughingly: my lady, you would do us a great kindness to tell everyone who he is, so that ownership of him is not accidentally taken away from you through ignorance, since it would make you so angry" ("Come la Fiammetta ebbe la sua canzon finita, cosí Dioneo, che allato l'era, ridendo disse: — Madonna, voi fareste una gran cortesia a farlo cognoscere a tutte, acciò che per ignoranzia non vi fosse tolta la possessione, poi che cosí ve ne dovete adirare," *Decameron*, 1252–53). In each case, a woman's song is interpreted as a direct expression of her own experience, albeit stated in the form of a highly conventional poem. The *brigata*'s literal interpretation of these songs suggests that the singers themselves are the composers, and indeed all the *ballate* are of unspecified authorship. The description of Lauretta's singing at the end of the third day, however, could indicate that the other singers had not all composed their own songs: "Filostrato . . . asked Lauretta to begin a dance and sing a song; she said, 'My lord, I don't know songs by other people, nor can I remember any of my own that would be fitting for such a happy group; if you want one of mine, I will willingly sing one'" ("Filostrato . . . comandò che la Lauretta una danza prendesse e dicesse una canzone; la qual disse; — Signor mio, dell' altrui canzoni io non so, né delle mie alcuna n'ho alla mente che sia assai convenevole a cosí lieta brigata; se voi di quelle che' io so volete, io ne dirò volentierí," *Decameron*, 453). The distinction Lauretta makes between her own songs and "those by other people" may indicate, in addition to modesty, a concern for privacy; like the songs of the other women in the *brigata*, her sad song is closely analyzed by the audience: "noticed by all, it was understood differently by different people" ("la quale notata da tutti, diversamente da diversi fu intesa," *Decameron*, 456). The fact that Lauretta's song is subject to interpretation by the other members of the *brigata* confirms that their collaborative music-making represents interrelationships within the group on both a literal and a figurative level. Nora Beck has aptly characterized the social and ethical function of music in the *Decameron*: "the inclusion of music serves as a multifaceted metaphor relating to the establishment of well-being and good government among the members of the *brigata*."[78] The women dancing *caroles* in the *Decameron*, like those depicted in Lorenzetti's fresco of the *Effects of Good Government* in the Palazzo Pubblico in Siena, combine realism with symbolism; *caroles* were a feature of late-medieval town life, and they also represent the harmony established by good government.[79] The metaphorical dimension of the *carole* can be extended to the *ballate* in the *Decameron*; Jeremy Yudkin has suggested that Boccaccio's depiction of the *ballata* as a simple dance-song, at a time when the genre had already developed into a more complex musical form, is intended to enhance the "idyllic nature of the *cornice*."[80]

The central place of music in the world of the *Decameron* shows the extent to which medieval song was an integral part of its social context and functioned as a metaphor for community. Given the documentary evidence available, it seems more productive to study women's performance of medieval song within its cultural and historical context than to pursue a traditional musicological approach based on the analysis of musical scores. Literary sources suggest that medieval singers consciously engaged in the interplay of different voices created by a performance of poetry, producing the interaction, so prominent in traditions of woman's song, between poetic artifice and the naturalism of the personal.[81]

64 Chapter 3

Selected Discography

"A chantar": Lieder der Frauen-Minne im Mittelalter (Songs of Women—Courtly Love in the Middle Ages). Estampie. Christophorus, 1990. Christophorus 74583. [Comtessa de Dia, "A chantar"; an anonymous *chanson de malmariée*, "Por coi me bait mes maris," a *chanson de toile*, "Bele Ysabiauz."]

Ave Eva: Chansons de Femmes, XIIe et XIIIe siècles. Brigitte Lesne. Opus, 1995. OPS 30-134. [Secular songs include *Cantigas de amigo*, a *lai*, and *chansons de malmariée*.]

Bella Domna. The Medieval Woman: Lover, Poet, Patroness and Saint. Sinfonye. Hyperion, 1988. Hyperion CDA 66283. [Comtessa de Dia, "A chantar"; anonymous *chanson de femme*, "Lasse pour quoi refusai," and a *tenso*, "Domna, pos vos ay chausida," as well as some *cantigas de amigo* and "Onques n'amai," a song in a woman's voice by Richard de Fournival.]

Calamus: Medieval Women's Songs. Eduardo Paniagua. Pneuma, 1995. Pneuma CD-PN 050. [Arabo-Andalusian songs and *cantigas de amigo*.]

Cansós de trobairitz. Hespèrion XX. EMI, 1978, reissued 1990. EMI CDM 7 63417 2. [Performances of five *trobairitz* poems, as well as of a *tenso* by Giraut de Bornelh with Alamanda, and a *canso* in a woman's voice by Cadenet.]

"La chanson d'ami": Chansons de femme, XIIe et XIIIe siècles. Katia Caré, voice, and Perceval. Arion, 1994. ARN 68290. [Several anonymous songs in a woman's voice, including a *rondet de carole*; "Molt m'abellist quant je voi revenir" by the female trouvère Maroie de Diergnau.]

Chansons de Toile au temps du Roman de la rose. Esther Lamandier. Aliénor, 1983, reissued 1987. Aliénor CD AL 1011. [Several *chansons de toile* performed from thirteenth-century manuscripts.]

The Courts of Love: Music from the Time of Eleanor of Aquitaine. Sinfonye. Hyperion, 1990. Hyperion CDA66367. ["L'on dit q'amors est dolce chose," anonymous *chanson de femme*; "S'anc fuy belha ni prezada," *alba* by Cadenet; "S'ie-us quier conseilh, bell'ami' Alamanda," *tenso* by Giraut de Bornelh.]

Lo Gai Saber: Troubadours et Jongleurs 1100–1300/Troubadours and Minstrels/Troubadoure und Spielmänner. Camerata Mediterranea. Erato, 1991. Erato 2292-45647-2. [Contrafacts of a *canso* by the Comtessa de Dia, *Ab joi et ab joven*; and a *tenso* by Raimbaut de Vaqueiras, *Domna, tant vos ai preiada*, performed by a man and woman.]

Le Jeu d'Amour: Chants courtois et à danser du Moyen-Age français. Anne Azéma. Erato, 1997. Erato 0630-17072-2. [*Chansons de malmariée*, dance songs, other *chansons de femme*.]

Le manuscrit du Roi: Trouvères et troubadours. Gérard Zuchetto and Katia Caré. Arion, 1993. ARN 68225. [Includes "Bele Emmelos," a *chanson de toile*.]

The Romance of the Rose: Feminine Voices from Medieval France. Heliotrope. Koch International, 1995. Koch 3-7103-2H1. [Songs from *Guillaume de Dole*, trobairitz *cansos*, *chansons de toile*; anonymous *chansons de femme*.]

Sweet is the Song. Catherine Bott. L'Oiseau-Lyre, Decca 448999-2 [A *chanson de toile* and "A chantar" of the Comtessa de Dia.]

"The sweet look and the loving manner": Trobairitz love lyrics and chansons de femme *from*

Women's Performance of the Lyric

medieval France. Sinfonye. Hyperion, 1993. Hyperion CDA 66625. [Monophony and polyphony, with several instrumental realizations.]

Le Tournoi des Dames: La femme dans la lyrique française (XIIe et XIIIe) siècles. Perceval et Sanacore. Arion, 1997. Arion 68350. [Polyphonic and monophic songs, mostly written in a woman's voice.]

Tristan et Iseult. The Boston Camerata. Erato, 1989. Erato CD 2292-45348-2. [Includes contrafact of Comtessa de Dia, "Estat en greu cossirier," and a *lai* sung by Iseut in the *Roman de Tristan en prose*. The *lai* is intended to illustrate the scene in Thomas' *Tristan* where Isolde sings a *lai*; this scene is discussed above.]

Trouvères à la cour de Champagne. Ensemble Venance Fortunat. Harmonia Mundi, 1995. ED 13045. [Two *chansons de toile*.]

The Unicorn: Chants médiévaux français/Medieval French Songs. Anne Azéma. Erato, 1994. Erato 4509-94830-2. [Includes "Bele Doette."]

Chapter 3

I gratefully acknowledge the support of the Oregon Humanities Center in the preparation of this study. I would like to thank one of the anonymous readers for the University of Pennsylvania Press for helpful comments and references.

1. Sylvia Huot, *From Song to Book: The Poetics of Writing in Old French Lyric and Lyrical Narrative Poetry* (Ithaca, N.Y.: Cornell University Press, 1987), 109.

2. Jean Renart, *The Romance of the Rose or of Guillaume de Dole (Roman de la Rose ou de Guillaume de Dole)*, ed. and trans. Regina Psaki (New York: Garland, 1995), 15–17 (lines 290–332).

3. *Guillaume de Dole*, 25–27 (lines 511–50).

4. Hendrik Van der Werf, "Jean Renart and Medieval Song," in *Jean Renart and the Art of Romance: Essays on Guillaume de Dole*, ed. Nancy Vine Durling (Gainesville: University Press of Florida, 1997), 172–73.

5. Marcia Citron, *Gender and the Musical Canon* (Cambridge: Cambridge University Press, 1993), 44–119.

6. John Plummer, "Introduction," in *VF*, 5–6.

7. Maria Coldwell, "*Jougleresses* and *Trobairitz*: Secular Musicians in Medieval France," in *Women Making Music: The Western Art Tradition, 1150–1950*, ed. Jane Bowers and Judith Tick (Urbana: University of Illinois Press, 1986), 43–44; Sami Hanna, "Al-Jawārī al-Mughanniyāt: The Singing Arab Maids," *Southern Folklore Quarterly* 34 (1970): 325–30.

8. For references to several of these songstresses, see Henry George Farmer, *A History of Arabian Music to the XIIIth Century* (London: Luzac, 1929), 54–55, 132–36, 212–13.

9. Amnon Shiloah, *Music in the World of Islam: A Socio-Cultural Study* (Detroit: Wayne State University Press, 1995), 29–30.

10. On *jāriyah* and female *nadīms* see George Dimitri Sawa, *Music Performance Practice in the Early 'Abbāsid Era, 132–320 AH/750–932 AD* (Toronto: Pontifical Institute of Mediaeval Studies, 1989), 119–20; on *mawālī*, see Shiloah, *Music in the World of Islam*, 12.

11. Sawa, *Music Performance Practice*, 116–17, 123. According to Shiloah, *Music in the World of Islam*, 27, both male and female musicians often sang behind a curtain.

12. Sawa, *Music Performance Practice*, 129, 190.

13. For some examples of songs by *jāriyah* and princesses, see Sawa, *Music Performance Practice*, 130. On a *qayna* who composed her own book of songs, see Shiloah, *Music in the World of Islam*, 30.

14. Sawa, *Music Performance Practice*, 183–84.

15. Shiloah, *Music in the World of Islam*, 75.

16. María Rosa Menocal, *The Arabic Role in Medieval Literary History: A Forgotten Heritage* (Philadelphia: University of Pennsylvania Press, 1987), 27.

17. For a historical introduction and translations, see Teresa Garulo, *Dīwān de las poetisas de Al-Andalus* (Madrid: Hiperión, 1986).

18. Two recent editions of the *trobairitz* corpus are *SWT* and Angelica Rieger, *Trobairitz: Der Beitrag der Frau in der altokzitanischen höfischen Lyrik; Edition des Gesamtkorpus* (Tübingen: Niemeyer, 1991).

19. See Chantal Phan, "The Comtessa de Dia and the Trobairitz," in *Women Composers: Music Through the Ages*, vol. 1, *Composers Born Before 1599*, ed. Martha Furman Schleifer and Sylvia Glickman (New York: G.K. Hall, 1996), 61–68.

20. Fredric L. Cheyette and Margaret Switten, "Women in Troubadour Song: Of the Comtessa and the Vilana," *Women and Music: A Journal of Gender and Culture* 2 (1998): 37. I am grateful to Margaret Switten for sending me a copy of the article before it went to press.

21. On the *vidas* of the *trobairitz*, see Rieger, *Trobairitz*, 53–54; for the texts with commentary, see Katharina Städtler, *Altprovenzalische Frauendichtung (1150–1250): Historisch-soziologische Untersuchungen und Interpretationen* (Heidelberg: Carl Winter, 1990), 73–75.

22. Billee Bonse, in "*E.l son de n'Alamanda*: Another Melody by a Trobairitz?" (presented at the Annual Meeting of the American Musicological Society, November 1999), argues that the melody of the *tenso* "S'ie.us qier cosseill, bell'ami Alamanda" may have been composed by Alamanda.

23. Cheyette and Switten, "Women in Troubadour Song," 36–37.

24. Ibid., 26–31; here 31.

25. This correspondence is described in A. R. Nykl, *Hispano-Arabic Poetry and Its Relations with the Old Provençal Troubadours* (Baltimore: J.H. Furst, 1946), 107–18.

26. The probable effects of performance of Marcabru's *pastorela* by different performers are discussed by Cheyette and Switten, "Women in Troubadour Song," 45.

27. Ibid., 44.

28. The *tenso* was most recently edited and translated with its *razo* in *Songs of the Troubadours and Trouvères: An Anthology of Poems and Melodies*, ed. Samuel Rosenberg, Margaret Switten, and Gérard Le Vot (New York: Garland, 1998), 151–53.

29. For the most recent discussion of the performance practice of troubadour song, see Elizabeth Aubrey, *The Music of the Troubadours* (Bloomington: Indiana University Press, 1996), 237–62.

30. Rieger, *Trobairitz*, 240.

31. On the depiction of *trobairitz* and *joglaressa* in manuscript illumination, see Angelica Rieger, "'Ins e.l cor port, dona, vostra faisso': Image et imaginaire de la femme à travers l'enluminure dans les chansonniers de troubadours," *CCM* 28 (1985): 385–415. On the mistaken identification of *soldadeira/soudadeira* with *puta*, and evidence for its equivalence with *joglaressa*, see Rieger, "Beruf: *Joglaressa*: Die Spielfrau im okzitanischen Mittelalter," in *Feste und Feiern im Mittelalter*, ed. Detlef Altenburg, Jörg Jarnut, and Hans-Hugo Steinhoff (Sigmaringen: Jan Thorbecke, 1991), 233–35.

32. Yvonne Rokseth, "Les femmes musiciennes du XIIe au XIV siècle," *Romania* 61 (1935): 473–75.

33. Coldwell, "*Jougleresses* and *Trobairitz*," 44–47, 50, 55.

34. Cheyette and Switten, "Woman in Troubadour Song," 37, n. 36; see also Christopher Page, *The Owl and the Nightingale: Musical Life and Ideas in France, 1100–1300* (Berkeley: University of California Press, 1989), 102–3; Alice Hentsch, *De la littérature didactique du moyen âge s'adressant spécialement aux femmes* (Cahors: A. Coueslant, 1903), 89.

35. Maria Coldwell, "*Guillaume de Dole* and Medieval Romances with Musical Interpolations," *MD* 35 (1981): 66.

36. *Guillaume de Dole*, 56–56 (lines 1144–1216).

37. Michel Zink, *Les chansons de toile* (Paris: Champion, 1977), 61–70; Zink, *The Enchantment of the Middle Ages*, trans. Jane Marie Todd (Baltimore: Johns Hopkins University Press, 1998), 94.

38. Emmanuèle Baumgartner, "Les citations lyriques dans le *Roman de la Rose* de Jean Renart," *RP* 35 (1981): 260–266.

39. Sylvia Huot, "Voices and Instruments in Medieval French Secular Music: On the Use of Literary Texts as Evidence for Performance Practice," *MD* 43 (1989): 92.

40. Maureen Boulton, *The Song in the Story: Lyric Insertions in French Narrative Fiction, 1200–1400* (Philadelphia: University of Pennsylvania Press, 1993), 85; Michel Zink, "Suspension and Fall: The Fragmentation and Linkage of Lyric Insertions in *Le roman de la rose (Guillaume de Dole)* and *Le roman de la violette*," in *Jean Renart and the Art of Romance*, ed. Nancy Vine Durling (Gainesville: University Press of Florida, 1997), 116–17.

41. Huot, "Voices and Instruments," 89.

42. The two ladies sing together in lines 4163–69; Bele Doete sings in lines 4566–83.

43. Coldwell, *"Guillaume de Dole"*; Van der Werf, "Jean Renart and Medieval Song."

44. Page, *The Owl and the Nightingale*, 156.

45. Ibid., 86–92, 227; Plummer, "The Woman's Song in Middle English and Its European Backgrounds," in *VF*, 137.

46. Page, *The Owl and the Nightingale*, 110–33, here 117.

47. Translation in Aubrey, "References to Music in Old Occitan Literature," *Acta musicologica* 61 (1989): 139.

48. Boulton, *The Song in the Story*, 128–29.

49. Huot, "Voices and Instruments," 65–68.

50. Ibid., 67.

51. Thomas, *Le Roman de Tristan*, lines 833–46, ed. Félix Lecoy (Paris: Champion, 1992), 44. My translation.

52. Aubrey, "References to Music," 123.

53. Ed. Tatiana Fotitch and Ruth Steiner, *Les lais du roman de Tristan en prose* (Munich: Fink, 1974).

54. Translation from Boulton, *The Song in the Story*, 154.

55. Fotitch and Steiner, *Les lais*, from Vienna, Österreichische Nationalbibliothek 2542, f. 380v–381r. My translation.

56. Boulton, *The Song in the Story*, 132–33.

57. Gottfried von Strassburg, *Tristan*, lines 8058–63, 8072–75, 8139–41, trans. A. T. Hatto (Harmondsworth: Penguin, 1960), 147–49. Ed. Friedrich Ranke (Stuttgart: Reclam, 1980), 1:484, 488. For comments on the repertory, see Louise Gnaedinger, *Musik und Minne im "Tristan" Gotfrids von Strassburg* (Düsseldorf: Pädagogischer Verlag Schwann, 1967), 64–68.

58. *Reggimento e costumi di donna*, ed. Giuseppe Sansone (Rome: Zauli, 1995).

59. Eleonora Beck, *Singing in the Garden: Music and Culture in the Tuscan Trecento* (Innsbruck: Studien/Lucca: LIM, 1998), 142.

60. William Prizer, "Renaissance Women as Patrons of Music: The North-Italian

Courts," in *Rediscovering the Muses: Women's Musical Traditions*, ed. Kimberly Marshall (Boston: Northeastern University Press, 1993), 187.

61. Eleonora Beck, "Women and Trecento Music," in *Women Composers*, 74–75.

62. See particularly Howard Mayer Brown, "Women Singers and Women's Songs in Fifteenth-Century Italy," in *Women Making Music*, 62–89.

63. Timothy McGee, *The Sound of Medieval Song: Ornamentation and Vocal Style According to the Treatises* (Oxford: Clarendon Press, 1998), 89 (Latin text on p. 164: E quibus pars altera, favorosi videlicet sexus feminei, que quanto rarior tanto preciosior, dum in dulcinomi gutturis epigloto tonos librate dividit in semitonia, et semitonia in athomos indivisibles garritat, ineffabili lascivit melodiomate quod magis putares angelicum quam humanum).

64. Paula Higgins, "The 'Other Minervas': Creative Women at the Court of Margaret of Scotland," in *Rediscovering the Muses*, 181.

65. Marshall, "Symbols, Performers, and Sponsors: Female Musical Creators in the Late Middle Ages," 166; Martin Picker, "Margaret of Austria (1480–1530)," in *Women Composers*, 89–91.

66. Paula Higgins, "Parisian Nobles, a Scottish Princess, and the Woman's Voice in Late Medieval Song," *Early Music History* 10 (1991): 145–200; Higgins, "The 'Other Minervas,'" 179.

67. Marshall, "Symbols, Performers, and Sponsors," 160–61.

68. Brown, "Women Singers," 62–63; for a full account of Isabella's patronage in context, see Prizer, "Renaissance Women."

69. Jennifer Post, "Erasing the Boundaries Between Public and Private in Women's Performance Traditions," in *Cecilia Reclaimed: Feminist Perspectives on Gender and Music*, ed. Susan C. Cook and Judy S. Tsou (Urbana: University of Illinois Press, 1994), 35–51; see also Judith Cohen's essay in this volume.

70. Peter Jeffery, *Re-envisioning Past Musical Cultures: Ethnomusicology in the Study of Gregorian Chant* (Chicago: University of Chicago Press, 1992), 71–72.

71. Pierre Bec, "'Trobairitz' et chansons de femme: Contribution à la connaissance du lyrisme féminin au moyen âge," *CCM* 22 (1979): 235–62.

72. Plummer, "The Woman's Song in Middle English," 137.

73. Gale Sigal, *Erotic Dawn-Songs of the Middle Ages: Voicing the Lyric Lady* (Gainesville: University Press of Florida, 1996), 18.

74. Gerbert de Montreuil, *Le Roman de la Violette ou de Gerart de Nevers*, lines 317–32, ed. Douglass Labaree Buffum (Paris: Champion, 1924), 15–16.

75. Boulton, *The Song in the Story*, 36–38.

76. Ibid., 122.

77. Giovanni Boccaccio, *Decameron*, ed. Vittore Branca (Turin: Einaudi, 1980), 783. All translations from the *Decameron* are my own.

78. Eleonora Beck, "Music in the Cornice of Boccaccio's *Decameron*," *Medievalia et Humanistica: Studies in Medieval and Renaissance Culture* 24 (1997): 34; for full discussion of music in the *Decameron*, see Beck, *Singing in the Garden*, 35–50.

79. Beck, *Singing in the Garden*, 106–15.

80. Jeremy Yudkin, "The *Ballate* of the *Decameron* in the Musical Context of the Trecento," *Stanford Italian Review* 2 (1981): 57.

81. After the completion of this article in 1999, several forthcoming studies came

to my attention that must be cited here for their significant contribution to research on the role of women in the creation and performance of the medieval lyric: Marilyn Lawrence, "Women as Writer and Performer of Narrative in the medieval French Romance *Ysaÿe le Triste*," forthcoming in *Performing Medieval Narrative*, ed. Evelyn Birge Vitz and Nancy Freeman Regalado; idem, "The Woman Composer and Performer: The Heroine Marthe in *Ysaÿe le Triste*," forthcoming in *Public Performance/Public Ritual*, ed. Laurie Postlewate; idem, "Minstrel Disguise in French Medieval Narrative: Semiotics of Identity" (dissertation, New York University, 2001); Nancy Freeman Regalado, "Women's Dance Games in the Tournoi de Chauvency: Theatricalizing the Narrative of Chivalry," forthcoming in *Medieval Theatricality*, ed. Hans Ulrich Gumbrecht, Andreas Kablitz, Jan-Dirk Müller, and Stephen J. Nichols (Stanford, Calif.: Stanford University Press). I thank the authors for sharing their work with me before its publication. Also appearing after this book went to press were Walter Salmen, *Spielfrauen im Mittelalter* (Hildesheim: Georg Olms, 2000) and *Songs of the Women Trouvères*, ed. and trans. Eglal Doss-Quinby, Joan Tasker Grimbert, Wendy Pfeffer, and Elizabeth Aubrey (New Haven, Conn.: Yale University Press, 2001).

Part III
Poetry and Music

[7]
POETICS AND MUSIC

Elizabeth Aubrey

The Medieval Arts of Poetry and Prose

The troubadours were engaged in a very pragmatic occupation, that of producing songs for an audience. But while they were not theoreticians, they were learned and familiar with many of the texts of their contemporaries and predecessors, and often with a wider range of literature, including epic narratives and classical Latin works. Even if an individual troubadour did not study poetics systematically, much of the poetry appears to have been shaped at least indirectly by the late medieval arts of poetry and prose, whose roots lay in the classical disciplines of grammar and rhetoric developed during the first centuries B.C. and A.D.

Cicero's *De inventione* (c. 100 B.C.), the anonymous *Rhetorica ad Herennium* (c. 100 B.C.), portions of Quintilian's *Institutio oratoria* (c. A.D. 92), and Horace's brief *Ars poetica* (23–13 B.C.) were widely known and portions of them were translated into various vernaculars during the later Middle Ages.[1] In classical theory, rhetoric involved inventing persuasive public orations within the judicial (forensic) and political (deliberative) spheres especially, and also the epideictic sphere, "praise or censure of a particular individual."[2] Within one of these three broad subjects (the *materia*), a discourse focused on a specific "issue" or question to be argued,[3] and this issue was expressed by means of arguments (*loci* or *topicii*).[4] The classical authors described multifarious *loci* or *topicii*, inventing countless examples to illustrate their points; Boethius (early sixth century) devoted an entire treatise to it, *De differentiis topiciis*. The category of praise and blame eventually was broadened to encompass the subject matter of poetry in the Middle Ages.

An argument was designed mentally before the actual formulation of the speech, during *inventio*, the first of five stages or "parts" of rhetoric. Once the issues and arguments were determined by the orator, he could set about arranging the components of the speech (*dispositio*), fashioning the specific words that he wished to use (*elocutio*), fixing the speech in his memory (*memoria*), and finally executing the oration (*pronuntiatio*):

> Invention is the discovery of valid or seemingly valid arguments to render one's cause plausible. Arrangement is the distribution of arguments thus discovered in the proper order. Expression is the fitting of the proper language to the invented matter. Memory is the firm mental grasp of matter and words. Delivery is the control of voice and body in a manner suitable to the dignity of the subject matter and the style.[5]

The arrangement, expression, and delivery of the speech fell into one of three "styles" according to the type of language used, ranging from the impressive and ornate to the colloquial: grand or high (*gravis* or *grandiloquus*), middle (*mediocris*), and simple or low (*adtenuata* or *humilis*).[6] To express these styles, the orator learned to use figures of thought and of speech (*colores* or *figurae*), and the creative orator could vary styles within a speech.[7]

The mechanics of poetry, in particular metrics and versification, eventually came to be understood as falling within the province of grammar. In classical theory, grammar entailed the correct use of language (*recte loquendi*), which was learned principally by imitating master authors (later "interpreting the poets," *enarratio poetarum*). Horace's *Ars poetica*, which touches on poetic meter, is in this tradition.[8] Donatus' *Ars minor* (c. A.D. 350) deals with the parts of speech, but also appropriates from rhetoric instruction in how to use certain figures and tropes in the service of speaking not only correctly but also effectively. Priscian (fl. c. 510) treats the parts of speech, letters, syllables, diction, sentence construction, etc., in the *Institutiones grammaticae*; and in another treatise he discusses the poetic meters of classical Latin, with Virgil as the supreme model.

The Venerable Bede (673–735), in *De arte metrica*, signaled the existence of a new type of Latin versification, in which verses were ordered not by classical quantitative meters, but by *rithmus*, or syllable-counting, "as in the songs of the vernacular poets."[9] Gradually the art of versification began to include instruction not only in counting syllables, but also in rhyme, stanza construction, and qualitative or accentual meters that eventually supplanted quantitative meters. Even though Latin poetry, including hymns, had departed significantly in style, content, and structure from its classical models, emulation of the masters remained paramount in the training of poets, who studied collections of *exempla* of the poetry of classical authors, imitated them, and drew from them lessons on language, style, structure, and content.[10]

The development of the system of liberal arts gradually provided a place for grammar and rhetoric, along with dialectic, in the *trivium*, the arts of language. But a demarcation between the two—the evident tidiness of the *trivium* notwithstanding—was not always very clear, especially because the figures and tropes were used by both orators and grammarians to arrange and embellish their speech. From a theoretical point of view poetry was still seen as imitation rather than creation, and hence was a grammatical rather than a rhetorical art. But by the late Middle Ages poetry increasingly received specific attention from theorists as an art distinct from both rhetoric and grammar.

Several well-known treatises on the arts of poetry and prose were produced between about 1170 and 1280: John of Salisbury's *Metalogicus* (c. 1159), Matthieu de Vendôme's *Ars versificatoria* (before c. 1175), Geoffroi de Vinsauf's *Poetria nova* (c. 1208–1213) and *Documentum de modo et arte dictandi et versificandi* (after 1213), Gervase de Melkley's *Ars versificaria* (c. 1208–1213?), Jean de Garlande's *Parisiana poetria* (after 1229), Évrard (Eberhard) l'Allemand's *Laborintus* (before 1280), and Brunetto Latini's *Li livre dou tresor* (c. 1260) and *Rettorica* (a translation of Cicero's *De inventione*, c. 1260). Their subject was mainly Latin poetry, although some of them acknowledge in one way or another the existence of vernacular literature.[11]

These authors were indebted to the traditions of both rhetoric and grammar. From grammar they adapted instruction on the correct use of language, the imitation and interpretation of poetry, and versification. Some, like Gervase and Jean, discussed all forms of verse-making, including classical quantitative meters, syllable-counting rhymed verse, and the more recent qualitative (accentual) type of poetry, such as the Aquitanian *versus*, with which many troubadours were probably familiar. From the realm of rhetoric they adopted the Ciceronian framework of the five parts—*inventio, dispositio, elocutio, memoria,* and *pronuntiatio*—devoting space to the subject matter of the composition, to its arrangement and delivery, and especially to the rhetorical *colores*, the tropes and figures taken from both rhetoric and grammar.

The "material" or subject matter of the poem was conceived in the imagination during *inventio*, and it played a part in defining a poem's genre.[12] The high, middle, and plain styles, which in classical *dispositio* and *elocutio* had been distinguished by the style and arrangement of language, now became important factors in *inventio* as well. The personages (nobles, bourgeois, peasants) by whom, about whom, or for whom a poem was composed distinguished a poem's "material style," along with its subject matter, its function, and its speaker.[13] The medieval Latin theorists sometimes categorized the tropes and figures as either *ornata difficultas (gravitas)* or *ornata facilitas (levitas)*, difficult or easy, which found a direct counterpart in the *trobar clus* and *trobar leu* (discussed below in Chapter 5) of some of the early troubadours.[14]

Geoffroi de Vinsauf's *Poetria nova* was glossed heavily and disseminated widely during the Middle Ages.[15] It relies on Horace, Cicero, and the author of the *Rhetorica ad Herennium*, all of whom it generously quotes. Geoffroi colorfully presents the paradigm of imagination in the process of fashioning a poem, urging careful contemplation as the first step, before taking up pen or opening the mouth:

> If a man has a house to build, his impetuous hand does not rush into action. The measuring line of his mind first lays out the work, and he mentally outlines the successive steps in a definite order. The mind's hand shapes the entire house before the body's hand builds it. Its mode of being is archetypal before it is actual. . . . Let the poet's hand not be swift to take up the pen, nor his tongue be impatient to speak; trust neither hand nor tongue to the guidance of fortune. To ensure greater success for the work, let the discriminating mind, as a prelude to action, defer the operation of hand and tongue, and ponder long on the subject matter. Let the mind's interior compass first circle the whole extent of the material. . . . As a prudent workman, construct the whole fabric within the mind's citadel; let it exist in the mind before it is on the lips.[16]

Once the subject matter has been invented and the poem mentally designed, then the steps of arranging the materials and choosing suitable words can take place: "When due order has arranged the material in the hidden chamber of the mind, let poetic art come forward to clothe the matter with words."[17] Subject and audience are both important in the determination of the style of the poem: "Regard not your own capacities, therefore, but rather his with whom you are speaking. Give to your words weight suited to his shoulders, and adapt your speech to the subject. . . . In a common matter, let the style be common; in specialized matters let the style be proper to each. Let the distinctive quality of each subject be respected."[18]

After treating the figures and tropes, Geoffroi makes traditional remarks about proper use of the voice in delivery, including an admonition to keep in mind the subject matter: "Modulate your voice in such a way that it is in harmony with the subject; and take care that voice does not advance along a path different from that which the subject follows. Let the two go together; let the voice be, as it were, a reflection of the subject."[19] In delivering a poem of anger, for instance, the performer is to "imitate genuine fury, but do not be furious." One should use a "caustic voice," "an inflamed countenance," and "turbulent gestures" (lines 2044–2049).

Jean de Garlande, perhaps today the most recognized among late medieval poetic theorists (but not of widest dissemination during the period), is of particular interest to students of Occitanian literature. As pointed out in Chapter 1, he was a *magister* of grammar at the University of Toulouse from 1229 to 1231. Educated at Oxford and Paris, Jean spent most of his professional career in Paris. Although he did not stay in Toulouse long, he took note of at least some musical practices in the city, as we know from a reference he later made to the performance of liturgical organum there in a tract that describes the Albigensian Crusade, *De triumphis ecclesiae* (c. 1252).[20] In his *Parisiana poetria* he demonstrates his familiarity with Boethian *musica speculativa*, at the same time drawing a direct connection between music and poetry, but the context seems to suggest a theoretical rather than a practical connection, the common element being mathematical proportion or counting:

> Rhymed poetry is a branch of the art of music. For music is divided into the cosmic, which embraces the internal harmony of the elements, the humane, which embraces the harmony and concord of the humors, and the instrumental, which embraces the concord evoked by instruments. This includes melody, quantitative verse, and rhymed verse. There is nothing here about the other branches; my present subject is rhymed poetry only.[21]

In his writings about poetry Jean is concerned with Latin literature, but he acknowledges some similarity between Latin versification and the versification of vernacular poetry.[22] He had a personal acquaintance with Bishop Foulque of Toulouse, the former troubadour, having assisted at the siege of Toulouse led by the bishop and Simon de Montfort in 1218.[23]

Jean's treatise on poetry is an ungainly hodge-podge of traditional and original material dealing with letter-writing, grammar, poetry, and rhetoric. *Inventio* has "five species: Where, what, what kind, how, and why."[24] "Where"—perhaps to be understood in the Ciceronian sense of "locus" or argument—concerns the characters treated by the poet, corresponding to three styles:

> Three kinds of characters ought to be considered here, according to the three types of men, which are courtiers, city dwellers, and peasants. Courtiers are those who dwell in or frequent courts, such as the Holy Father, cardinals, legates, archbishops, bishops, and their subordinates, such as archdeacons, deans, officials, masters, scholars; also emperors, kings, marquises, and dukes. City dwellers are count, provost, and the whole range of people who live in the city. Peasants

are those who live in the country, such as hunters, farmers, vine dressers, fowlers.[25]

"What" is the subject matter itself, which might be dependent on the persons involved. "What kind," or the "quality of the subject matter invented,"[26] is divided into honorable or disreputable—again determined by the subject matter and persons. "How" concerns the language used, especially tropes and figures.

The last species of invention, "to what end," has to do with the function of the work. In this respect and others, Jean betrays the influence of Aristotle on his thinking. He concludes his discussion of invention with the following:

> *A Way of Inventing Subject Matter.* Here is a device that is useful in certain kinds of writing; students particularly who aim to amplify and vary their subject matter may observe it. I mean they should not overlook the four principal causes—the efficient cause, and so on—of any subject proposed to them. Thus, suppose one of them is treating of his book. He might praise it or criticize it through the efficient cause, that is, through the writer; through the material cause, that is, through the parchment or the ink; through the formal cause, as through the layout of the book or the size of the letters; or through the final cause, by considering for what purpose the book was made, namely, that in it and through it the ignorant may be made more knowledgeable.[27]

Hence Jean claims as the purpose of invention, or its final cause, "to promote what is both useful and right."[28] The final cause includes the choice of persons and the subject matter:

> With persons there is always a pair of alternatives; as with kings: to rule the kingdom well, or to tear the kingdom to pieces like a tyrant; with prelates: to pursue divine contemplation, or to idle about in secular affairs; with city dwellers: to carry on the business of the city, to strengthen the republic, or to squander it; with peasants, it means sweating over rural duties, or giving up.[29]

To discuss the choice of words, Jean returns to the three styles—high, middle, and low—which he attributes to Virgil.[30] He identifies them respectively with soldiers and governers, farmers, and shepherds, and the styles appropriate for each are expressed in the language: "The level of style itself amplifies the material, when high sentiments are chosen for the high style, middling ones for the middle style, low ones for the low style—provided that in treating a low subject we be not too lackluster and unfigurative, confusing that style with inarticulateness. . . ."[31] Like other writers, Jean allows the poet to use "high" language for a "low" subject, and vice versa, if this serves a rhetorical purpose. "High matter can be lowered, in imitation of Virgil, who calls

Caesar—or himself—Tityrus and Rome a beech; and low matter can be exalted, as when in a treatment of a high subject women's distaffs are called 'the spears of peace'. . . .[32]

Jean provides definitions of words for narrative and poetic genres (*genera narrationum* and *genera carminum*, Chapter V), derived from classical catalogs of quantitative verse types.[33] He defines them according to the subject matter, or sometimes the speaker, and although the names do not usually appear in lists of genres of medieval lyric songs, some of the types he describes are certainly to be found among songs by the trouvères (and perhaps by troubadours) that he undoubtedly knew. The "Epichedion," for example, is "a plain song apart from a burial, that is, one that is composed for someone not yet buried,"[34] which has its parallel in the Occitan *planh*. A few years later Jean added to his treatise a section on *ars ritmica*, including discussion of versification and stanza structure.[35]

Thus in medieval Latin poetics, a conception of the subject matter of a song, which included the speaker, the topic, the function, the audience, and the specific points made about the topic, was the principal business of *inventio*. Arranging the parts, choosing the words, and uttering the song depended on the content determined in the mind at the outset, as did the "style" by which the poet arranged, expressed, and delivered the poem.

The Art de trobar *and the Art of Music*

Several treatises on poetry and language—the *art de trobar*—were written in the *langue d'oc* during the late twelfth through the mid-fourteenth centuries, all modeled to some degree on these classical and medieval texts on Latin grammar, rhetoric, and poetics. Most of them were written by and for Catalan patrons, amateurs, and beginners in the art of poetry, not for native speakers of the *langue d'oc* or for professional poet-composers.[36]

Two of these treatises were produced before the middle of the thirteenth century: Raimon Vidal's *Las Razos de trobar* (Catalonia, c. 1190–1213[37]) and Uc Faidit's *Donatz proensals* (Italy, c. 1225–45[38]). The latter, as its title implies, is mainly a treatise on grammar in the tradition of Donatus. The former is extant in several redactions, reflecting various stages of revision and probably scribal intervention.[39] It is a rather idiosyncratic and superficial prose tract mainly on Occitan grammar, despite its author's claims in the opening sentences that it offers a method for learning to compose poetry.[40]

Raimon follows the tradition in rhetoric and grammar of encouraging the emulation of great poets, quoting from Bernart de Ventadorn, Guiraut de Bornelh, Arnaut de Maruelh, Gaucelm Faidit, Bertran de

Born, Folquet de Marselha, Peire Vidal, Peire Raimon de Tolosa, Peirol, and Guilhem de Saint Didier.[41] He does not mention music, but of twenty poems that Raimon quotes, thirteen ultimately survived with melodies: seven by Bernart de Ventadorn, two by Folquet by Marselha, and one each by Guiraut de Bornelh, Arnaut de Maruelh, and Peirol.[42] Eight of these poems survive with melodies in at least two manuscripts, and four of the songs by Bernart[43] have three extant melodies each, in manuscripts W, R, and G; all are found in manuscript R except for the melody by Peirol.

Thirteen out of twenty citations is far out of proportion to the number of melodies that survive in the repertoire as a whole. Raimon clearly was highlighting songs that were part of a living tradition. All these troubadours probably were still alive when Raimon wrote his treatise, but more important, these particular songs were widely known (as far as Catalonia, anyway) and revered. And they remained part of a living tradition, in that their melodies as well as their texts were ultimately preserved in writing. Marshall postulates that Raimon may have been quoting many of his citations from memory; if so, the melody may have aided in this remembering.[44] Thus music may have played a role in the durability of certain songs, not just within the song tradition itself, but also in the theoretical and the written traditions.

Several decades later, after the "classical" period of the troubadours was past, two more Catalan treatises appeared, one definitely by Jofre de Foixà, the *Regles* [*de trobar*] (c. 1286–91), and the other probably by Jofre, the *Doctrina de compondre dictats*. The *Regles* is extant in two manuscripts, with differences between them significant enough to lead Marshall to postulate some active scribal intervention in both versions.[45] Jofre relied somewhat on Raimon Vidal's treatise in producing an elementary Occitan grammar for his lay Catalan audience.

Although like Raimon, Jofre does not refer to music in the *Regles*, he gives some basic information on versification and quotes from eleven poems, including works by Bernart de Ventadorn, Gaucelm Faidit, Bertran de Born, Folquet de Marselha, and Aimeric de Peguilhan. Five of the eleven songs from which Jofre quotes are extant with music: two by Gaucelm and one each by Bernart, Folquet, and Aimeric.[46] Four of these melodies are found in both manuscripts R and G; one of Gaucelm's two melodies[47] is found only in manuscripts X and G. Here again, the theorist cites many songs whose melodies ultimately survived. Besides possibly quoting from memory, Jofre may have had access to poetic readings that were related to those found in the Languedocian sources C and R.[48]

The *Doctrina de compondre dictats* is a short exposition on the versification and subject matter of the different genres of troubadour poetry; it is the earliest thorough description of these poetic genres and represents a crystallization that was not as strict in the earlier period.[49] The text is found in only one manuscript, and Marshall considers it to be "the concluding section of the *Regles de trobar*" of Jofre, erroneously separated from it by an inattentive scribe.[50] The details of structure given for some of the genres do not square with many earlier Occitanian examples of them, and the discussion of some genres betrays its author's Catalan background.[51] The inclusion of rather dogmatic instructions on the structural features appropriate to each genre may reflect the later thirteenth-century taste for defining types by form as much as (or more than) by subject matter. As will be discussed in Chapter 4, the author of the *Doctrina* alludes to the musical style and structure of the music suited to the various genres,[52] which seem tied to the poem's material or content.

Although these poetic theorists gave little attention to music, their remarks and their treatment of song in general suggest that they were aware on some level of how critical music was to the essence of the songs. They certainly knew that the texts were sung; indeed their own acquaintance with particular songs may have been through the medium of music (as opposed to written texts). As we shall see in the next chapter, they seemed to assume that a "song" was words and music together, and that text and melody were in a certain sense both products of a common purpose.[53] At the very least, the theorists knew that musical and textual structures must match numerically—verse and stanza lengths must coincide. Although they did not have the vocabulary to express it, one senses that these theorists knew that the melodies of the best songs were as much a feature of their essence as were the rhyme schemes and stanza structures, and that in some way the poet-composers conceived the poems and melodies together.

The poetic theorists probably did not have any formal musical training beyond a fundamental, probably Boethian, education in music as an art of the *quadrivium*. Until the late Middle Ages, many authorities considered poetry to fall under the rubric of Musica, from at least as early as the fourth century.[54] That this philosophical tradition survived in the late Middle Ages is evident from the passage in Jean de Garlande's treatise (quoted above): "Rhymed poetry is a branch of the art of music."[55] But by the twelfth and thirteenth centuries, as we have seen, the art of poetry had been taken over largely by rhetoricians and grammarians, and their writings seem to imply a new practical and theoretical relationship between music and text. Poetry now was treated less as a subcategory of music than as an art in its own right, which operated with its own rules, in cooperation with music. Music itself was seen in a much more pragmatic light than in the early Middle Ages. From a song's initial conception, at least, poet and composer were the same person (except for cases of borrowing, as in the *sirventes*). As the twelfth and thirteenth centuries progressed, poets and composers developed, and theorists articulated, rules for poetry and rules for music that resulted in increased separation between the two arts. The poetry and the poetic rules took new directions and became extraordinarily sophisticated. The music and music theory also veered into radical new areas.

Just as a practical theory of poetry and a practical theory of music developed along parallel but largely distinct paths, the songs themselves embraced the autonomy of each art, treating them as equal but separate partners. The music of the troubadours was not dependent on poetry for all of its coherence or meaning; yet it was in its essence "poetic" in the sense that it relied on the poetry for its structure and was wedded to the text in its delivery. A poem, in its turn, was governed by complex processes of invention, arrangement, and style, yet it was "musical" in that it relied on music for its performance.[56]

The art of poetry of the twelfth and thirteenth centuries can be seen as a bridge, both theoretical and practical, between rhetoric in the *trivium* and music in the *quadrivium*. By the end of the period, though, music and poetry began to diverge altogether, and poet and composer need not be the same person. While at the beginning of the fourteenth century Dante could call poetry "rhetorical invention set to music,"[57] he could also presage a type of poetry that was not dependent on music for its delivery, or even conceived with a melody at its outset.

The music treatises that began to appear in the second half of the thirteenth century reflected enormous practical, theoretical, and philosophical changes in music. As in other scholastic disciplines, the position of music began to shift from its neo-Platonic foundations to an Aristotelian framework.[58] Practically, music was emerging from its function as a servant of the liturgy or of the art of poetry. Music theorists increasingly concerned themselves with exciting developments in notation and rhythmic systems, techniques, and genres. *Discantus, organum, conductus*, and especially the motet represented novel ways of organizing music; innovations occurred in the use of music in the liturgy; and in particular new attitudes arose about the place of music in the larger, secular, world.[59] Canon, hocket, voice-exchange, and other contrapuntal devices enriched the harmonic and melodic vocabularies. Musical structures that were dependent less on text and more on repetition schemes and counterpoint began to overshadow the texts that originally generated the music. And theorists began discussing instrumental music—music without text—as a species of "art" music.

Northern France was the center of these scholastic and practical developments. Secular music in the second half of the thirteenth century, like poetry, began to manifest its own signs of a changed aesthetic, especially in the appearance of structural schemes based on repetition that matched the rhyme scheme of the poetry. Where genres earlier had been defined by subject matter, they now began to be defined by musical and poetic structure—*rondeau, ballade, virelai*.[60] Melody began taking on an autonomous identity, less tied to a text or to a theme. While music was becoming less dependent on the text for its nature, poetry was at least in a structural sense becoming more "musical."

The Parisian Johannes de Grocheio in some ways expressed the expansion of music beyond the *quadrivium* and the liturgy better than any other late medieval music theorist, by treating vocal and instrumental secular music on a par with liturgical chant and polyphony. He appears to have been the first theorist to give untexted music serious attention. Grocheio also was the first to discuss vernacular music systematically. He has long been consulted for insight into French monophony of the twelfth and thirteenth centuries, but it has been pointed out recently that Grocheio, writing c. 1300, expressed many of the new aesthetic ideals of the late thirteenth century.[61]

Yet at the same time that Grocheio expounds ideas that are proper to the late thirteenth century, he also articulates some concepts that seem relevant to music and poetry of the earlier period. Despite the fact that the late thirteenth-century music theorists did not devote much attention to the intricacies of poetry and prose, they certainly did not ignore the presence of texts in the music they discussed. Indeed, it is a constant undercurrent in their expositions on music for the liturgy, in discussions of such things as ligatures and their relation to syllables, and in descriptions of styles of music appropriate to particular genres— defined by the content of their texts. Grocheio and other music theorists no doubt were familiar with the same theoretical traditions that served as background for Jean de Garlande, Geoffroi de Vinsauf, Raimon Vidal, Jofre de Foixà, and other grammarians and rhetoricians. The connection between Paris and Toulouse, exemplified by the early thirteenth-century career of Jean de Garlande, implies an intellectual atmosphere common to the south and the north.

The concepts in Grocheio's treatment of vernacular song concerning the interconnection between words and music are very similar to those found in poetic treatises that deal with courtly lyric.[62] Grocheio views text and melody as together constituting a song's substance, and he uses the Aristotelian concepts of *forma* (music) and *materia* (words) to convey this idea.[63] Each element serves its own function, one to express the theme of the song, the other to give it tangible shape, and the composer must consider both in the process of composing. These ideas are found also in the art of rhetoric. The "material" is created by the composer in the first stage of *inventio*, and is then given "form" in the steps of *dispositio* and *elocutio*—all perhaps mentally.[64] To Grocheio, the music is what ultimately gives the song its form; in other words, it is not actuated, or realized, until it is sung aloud, the rhetorical stage of *pronuntiatio*.[65]

Like the poetic theorists, Grocheio asserts that an author must take into account the subject matter of the song he is composing before he can arrange his materials accordingly. Grocheio discusses the differences among types of secular song, which are determined in part by subject matter, style, function, audience, and performance style.[66] He further implies that the music must be appropriate for the text, since together they serve a common function. He suggests that certain guidelines must be followed in devising an appropriate melody for a song. Grocheio's discussion of melodic form, while intricate and in some respects apparently contradictory, nonetheless reflects his view that, as in poetry, the way in which the elements of a melody are arranged is a factor in the song's success. Like the poet, the musician has certain means of moving the audience.

Poetic and music theorists, then, were concerned that poets and composers utilize the tools of their respective arts appropriately and effectively. Theorists of both disciplines insisted that text and music complement each other in theme, structure, style, and performance. According to the art of poetry, an author first had to determine what type of song he wished to compose; that is, he had to determine its theme, expressed by the Occitan word *razo*. A general idea of the character of the poem and of the melody took shape in the composer's mind, even if the exact words and notes had not. The melody is as much bound by the theme, or *razo*, as is the poem.

To what extent can we take these theorists' remarks to explain how troubadours composed? They almost certainly did not learn their craft by studying these pedagogical tracts.[67] They were more likely to have learned by hearing, memorizing, perhaps reading, and imitating poetry—the ancient ones, as well as more recent *exempla*, including Latin hymns and *versus*.[68] It is conceivable that some chansonniers were intended as pedagogical aids, repositories of *exempla* for instruction in the Occitanian *art de trobar*, not only for the patrons and amateurs who would never excel beyond an elementary level of composing but perhaps also for some (late) troubadours.

But did the poet-composers see words and music as equal partners as they imagined or created their songs? Given the common practice of sharing melodies among poems, as well as the presence of phrase repetition within a song and the reuse of the melody for several stanzas, it is obvious that the words of a particular text and the notes of a particular melody were not inextricably and exclusively linked.[69] However, in a larger sense, the troubadours seemed to see their task as forging a song out of words and music—*motz e son*, in a formula commonly found in the poems. For example, Bernart de la Fon uses the phrase in an explanation of his compositional process:

Leu chansonet' ad entendre	An easy little song to understand,
ab leu sonet volgra far,	with an easy little tune, I want to
coindet' e leu per apendre	make, graceful and easy to learn and
e plan' e leu per chantar,	smooth and easy to sing, for the
quar leu m'aven la razo,	subject came to me easily, and the
e leu latz *los motz e.l so*.[70]	words and melody lie easy.

In a song that uses the same rhymes and verse structure as Bernart's poem, Uc de Saint Circ describes the kind of song that pleases him most, one in which words and music fulfill their proper roles in expressing the song's *razo*, or theme:

Chanzos q'es leus per entendre	The song that is easy to listen to and
et avinenz per chantar,	graceful to sing, so that no one can
tal qu'om non puescha reprendre	reprove the words or correct the
los motz ni.l chant esmendar,	singing [or melody], and which has
et a douz e gai lo son	a sweet and happy melody and a
e es de bella *razon*	beautiful theme and is graceful in
ed avinen per condar,	measure, pleases me and I wish to
mi plai e la voil lauzar	praise it to whomever criticizes it,
a qi la blasm'e defendre.[71]	and to defend it.

Both of these texts describe the words and the melody in terms that place them on a par, and also declare that the performance itself—the singing, the learning, and the hearing—is critical to an appreciation of the song. Together the words and the melody convey the song's theme, its *razo*. (Neither of these poems, unfortunately, survives with a melody, although since they share the same versification scheme, they may have been sung to the same tune.[72])

These passages suggest that the troubadours imagined their texts and melodies as cohesive parts of a whole, and that they understood the peculiar capacity of each to convey what they intended. They also imply that the troubadours, whether or not they saw their songs in Aristotelian terms, assumed that the fullest realization of a song could come about only through performance.

The structure, style, and delivery of both text and melody were governed to some degree by the song's subject matter. Several genres were associated with a particular broad subject (*materia*), including the love song (*canso*), dawn song (*alba*), lament (*planh*), moral or political commentary (*sirventes*), debate (*tenso*), and pastoral scene (*pastorela*). But within a genre the topics could vary widely. *Cansos* could be simple expressions of adulation or unmitigated complaints about the beloved's cruelty. A *planh* might celebrate the lamented one's life, or describe the miseries of the abandoned. A *tenso* could be about any question whatever, so long as there were at least two protagonists to argue it. A *sirventes* likewise could draw on an extraordinary range of issues.

During the process by which the words and notes actually took shape and style, the troubadour to some extent had to deal with poem and music separately, since each followed different rules: rhyme scheme, verse and strophe scheme, vocabulary, syntax, etc., for the former; melodic contour, tonal orientation, intervallic and motivic content, incipits and cadences, etc., for the latter. These issues are explored in detail in later chapters. But even though poetic and musical style and structure were devised according to the tools particular to each art, they must have interacted to some degree because the troubadours composed with the delivery of a song very much in mind. The processes involved in conceiving, arranging, and expressing one's ideas through words and music may have been so intertwined at the moment of performance that they occurred almost simultaneously. As suggested in Chapter 2, the stages in composition, performance, and dissemination are difficult to separate diachronically. For the troubadours there was no sharp dividing line separating the mental conceptualization and the oral actualization of a song.

It is difficult to say to what extent the troubadour was conscious of following any particular steps while composing. But what does seem certain is that while melody and poem were separate in following their own rules, the two elements must be understood as equal parts of a whole, and that to understand fully a troubadour's melody we must examine its pitches, its structure, and its style along with the words, structure, and style of its text, and both within the context of the song's performance.

3. Poetics and Music

1. See James J. Murphy, *Rhetoric in the Middle Ages*; Charles S. Baldwin, *Medieval Rhetoric and Poetic (to 1400)*, 127ff.; Douglas Kelly, *The Arts of Poetry and Prose*, 41–49.
2. See H. M. Hubbell, ed. and trans., *Cicero: De inventione, De optimo genero oratorum, Topica*, 12–17; and Harry Caplan, ed. and trans., *[Cicero]: Ad C. Herennium, De ratione dicendi (Rhetorica ad Herennium)*, 4–5, and 172ff..
3. Hubbell, *Cicero*, 20–21.
4. Ibid., 180–181 and 386–387. See also Murphy, *Rhetoric*, 16.
5. Hubbell, *Cicero*, 18–19; and Caplan, *Ad Herennium*, 6–7, 184ff.
6. Caplan, *Ad Herennium*, 252–263.
7. Murphy, *Rhetoric*, 20–21; Caplan, *Ad Herennium*, 266–269 and 275ff.
8. Murphy, *Rhetoric*, 29–31, gives a resumé of Horace's treatise.
9. Quoted, ibid., 78.
10. See Kelly, *Arts*, 60, for description of the sources used by medieval poets for study.
11. Useful studies of the late medieval *ars poeticae* include Edmond Faral, *Les arts poétiques du XIIe et du XIIIe siècle*; Kelly, "The Scope of the Treatment of Composition in the Twelfth- and Thirteenth-Century Arts of Poetry," and "Theory of Composition in Medieval Narrative Poetry and Geoffrey of Vinsauf's *Poetria Nova*." See also Margot E. Fassler, "Accent, Meter, and Rhythm in Medieval Treatises 'De rithmis,'" and "The Role of the Parisian Sequence in the Evolution of Notre-Dame Polyphony"; and especially Kelly, *Arts*.
12. Kelly, *Arts*, 65. See also Kelly's definitive work, particularly as it concerns fourteenth- and fifteenth-century literature, *Medieval Imagination: Rhetoric and the Poetry of Courtly Love*; and Jacques Le Goff, *L'Imaginaire médiéval*.
13. Kelly, *Arts*, 71–77.
14. Ulrich Mölk, *Trobar clus trobar leu: Studien zur Dichtungstheorie der Trobadors*.
15. Kelly, *Arts*, 110.
16. Margaret F. Nims, trans., *Poetria nova of Geoffrey of Vinsauf*, 16. Ernest A. Gallo, *The Poetria Nova and Its Sources in Early Rhetorical Doctrine*, 16: "Si quis habet fundare domum, non currit ad actum/impetuosa manus: intrinseca linea cordis/praemetitur opus, seriemque sub ordine certo/interior praescribit homo, totamque figurat/ante manus cordis quam corporis; et status ejus/est prius archetypus quam sensilis. Ipsa poesis/spectet in hoc speculo quae lex sit danda poetis./Non manus ad calamum praeceps, non lingua sit ardens/ad verbum: neutram manibus committe regendam/fortunae; sed mens discreta praeambula facti,/ut melius fortunet opus, suspendat earum/officium, tractetque diu de themate secum./Circinus interior mentis praecircinet omne/materiae spatium. Certus praelimitet ordo/unde praearripiat cursum stylus, at ubi Gades/figat. Opus totum prudens in pectoris arcem/contrahe, sitque prius in pectore quam sit in ore."
17. Nims, *Poetria nova*, 17. Gallo, *Poetria nova*, 16: "Mentis in arcano cum rem digesserit ordo,/materiam verbis veniat vestire poesis."
18. Nims, *Poetria nova*, 55. Gallo, *Poetria nova*, 72: "Proprias igitur ne respice vires,/immo suas, cum quo loqueris. Da pondera verbis/aequa suis humeris, et pro re verba loquaris.... In re communi communis, in appropriatis/sit sermo proprius. Sic rerum cuique geratur/mos suus."
19. Nims, *Poetria nova*, 90. Gallo, *Poetria nova*, 124: "Voces quas sensus dividit,

illas/divide; quas jungit, conjuge. Domes ita vocem,/ut non disordet a re, nec limite tendat/vox alio, quam res intendat; eant simula ambae;/vox quaedam sit imago rei."

20. See William G. Waite, "Johannes de Garlandia, Poet and Musician," esp. 181. Waite believed that the grammarian Jean was also the music theorist Johannes de Garlandia, author of one of the most important documents describing Parisian polyphony in the twelfth and thirteenth centuries, although some scholars remain skeptical.

21. Traugott Lawler, ed. and trans., *The Parisiana poetria of John of Garland*, 158–161: "Rithmica est species artis musice. Musica enim diuiditur in mundanam, que constat in proporcione qualitatum elementorum, et in humanam, que constat in proportione et concordia humorum, et in instrumentalem, que constat in concordia instrumentali. Hec diuiditur in mellicam, metricam, et rithmicam. De aliis speciebus nihil ad presens; de rithmica uero ad presens dicetur." See Fassler, "Accent."

22. Lawler, *Parisiana poetria*, 174–175.

23. Thomas Wright, ed., *Johannis de Garlandia, De triumphis*, 92–93. See Stronski, *Folquet de Marseille*, 107–108.

24. Lawler, *Parisiana poetria*, 8–9: "Sub inuencione species sunt quinque: vbi, quid, quale, qualiter, ad quid."

25. Ibid., 10–11: "Tria genera personarum hic debent considerari secundum tria genera hominum, que sunt curiales, ciuiles, rurales. Curiales sunt qui curiam tenent ac celebrant, ut Dominus Papa, cardinales, legati, archiepiscopi, episcopi, et eorum suffraganei, sicut archidiaconi, decani, officiales, magistri, scolares. Item, imperatores, reges, marchiones, et duces. Ciuiles persone sunt consul, prepositus, et cetere persone in ciuitate habitantes. Rurales sunt rura colentes, sicut uenatores, agricole, uinitores, aucupes."

26. Ibid., 20–21: "'Quale' ponit qualitatem materie inueniende. . . ."

27. Ibid., 28–31: "De Arte Inueniendi Materiam. Hoc artificio vtendum est in aliis orationibus, quod pueri uolentes ampliare et uariare materiam obseruent, non pretermittentes causas principales quattuor, scilicet causam efficientem, cuiuslibet rei sibi proposite. Ut, si tractet de libro suo, commendet eum uel uituperet per causam efficientem, idest per scriptorem; per causam materialem, idest per pargamenum et incaustum; per causam formalem, ut per libri disposicionem et litterarum protractionem; per causam finalem, considerando ad quid factus est liber, ad hoc uidelicet ut in eo et per eum nescientes scientes reddantur." The examples Jean gives following this passage are all from the *ars dictamini* (letter-writing).

28. Ibid., 20–21: "Qvia dicitur in premissis 'ad quid,' attendendum est quod per hoc denotatur finis inuentoris, scilicet vtilitas et honestas. . . ."

29. Ibid., 10–11: "In personis duo, ut in regibus: bene regnum regere, vel regnum tirannide dilacerare; in prelatis: diuine contemplationi insistere, uel negociis secularibus ociari; in ciuilibus: urbis negocia tractare, rem publicam augere uel dissipare; in ruralibus, contingit circa ruralia desudare uel cessare."

30. See Ibid., 230–231 n.124.

31. Ibid., 78–79: "Item tenor ipsius stili ampliat materiam quando ad grevem stilum graues eliguntur sentencie, ad mediocrem, mediocres, ad humilem, humiles—si tamen ne in humili materia nimis deiecti simus et sine coloribus, ipsius stili elingues. . . ."

32. Ibid., 86–87: "Potest grauis materia humiliari exemplo Virgilii, qui uocat Cesarem Titirum—uel seipsum, Romam fagum; potest et humilis materia exaltari, ut in graui materia coli muliebres uocantur 'inbelles haste'. . . ." See also 237 n.46.

33. Ibid., 254ff., notes.

34. Ibid., 100–101: "nudum sine seputura carmen, scilicet quod fit de insepultis."

35. Kelly, *Arts*, 98; Fassler, "Accent."

36. The fourteenth-century documents include Raimon de Cornet, *Doctrinal de trobar* (Catalonia, 1324); Guilhem Molinier, *Leys d'Amors*, Version A (Toulouse, 1328–46); *Leys d'Amors*, Version B (Catalonia, 1337–43); Joan de Castellnou, *Compendi de la coneixença dels vicis en els dictats del Gay Saber* (Catalonia, 1337–43); Joan de Castellnou, *Glosari al Doctrinal de Ramon de Cornet* (Catalonia, 1341); Guilhem Molinier, *Leys d'Amors*, Version C (Catalonia, 1355–56). They fall within the tradition spawned by the late development of poetic contests in the north, and they provide evidence mainly of the reception of the art of the troubadours in the fourteenth century. See Kelly, *Arts*, 156–157, 168–174; Gérard Gonfroy, "Les genres lyriques occitans et les traités de poétique."

37. J. H. Marshall, ed., *The "Razos de trobar" of Raimon Vidal and Associated Texts*.

38. J. H. Marshall, ed., *The "Donatz Proensals" of Uc Faidit*.

39. See Marshall, *Razos*, xvi–xxviii, for discussion of the manuscript tradition.

40. Ibid., 2: "voill eu far aqest libre per far conoisser et saber qals dels trobadors an mielz trobat et mielz ensenhat, ad aqelz qe.l volran aprenre, con devon segre la dreich maniera de trobar." See Marshall's commentary, lxxx–lxxxi. See Elizabeth W. Poe, *From Poetry to Prose*, 67–79, and "The Problem of the Prologue in Raimon Vidal's *Las Razos de trobar*."

41. See list in Marshall, *Razos*, xxii–xxiii.

42. They are PC 70,1; 70,6; 70,7; 70,12; 70,25; 70,41; 70,43; 155,3; 155,18; 242,45; 30,23; and 366,21.

43. PC 70,1; 70,7; 70,41; and 70,43.

44. Marshall, *Razos*, xxi–xxviii.

45. Ibid., xxxv–xxli.

46. PC 167,56; 167,59; 70,6; 155,14; and 10,25.

47. PC 167,56.

48. Marshall, *Razos*, xli–xliv.

49. See William D. Paden, "The System of Genres in Troubadour Lyric."

50. Marshall, *Razos*, lxxviii. See lxxv–lxxvi on the paleographical peculiarities of the text.

51. Ibid., xciv–xcv.

52. See Aubrey, "Genre."

53. Ibid.

54. Augustine in *De Musica* (completed A.D. 391), after offering the famous definition of music as "scientia bene modulandi," devoted most of the rest of his tract to a discussion of quantitative metrics.

55. Lawler, *Parisiana poetria*, 158–161. See Kelly, *Arts*, 54, 150–151.

56. See Zumthor, *Poésie orale*, 177–206, for a wide-ranging discussion of this idea.

57. Aristide Marigo, ed., *De vulgari eloquentia*, II.iv.2 (p. 188); "fictio rethorica musicaque poita."

58. See Nan Cooke Carpenter, *Music in the Medieval and Renaissance Universities*; and Jeremy Yudkin, "The Influence of Aristotle on French University Music Texts."

59. For documentation of some of these changes, see Craig Wright, *Music and Ceremony*; and Christopher Page, *The Owl and the Nightingale*, and *Discarding Images*.

60. Kelly, *Arts*, 150ff.

61. See Christopher Page, *Voices and Instruments*. Grocheio's confusing classification system has been subjected to several analyses. It is difficult to match up with surviving pieces and is sometimes simply impenetrable. But we should not be surprised that we cannot find neat analytical details that would help us delineate the elements that constitute secular songs. Providing such details interested Grocheio much less than accounting for the existence of secular music and demonstrating that it is of value within the musical world hitherto dominated, among theorists at least, by sacred music. Grocheio is concerned not so much with describing a *cantus* or a *cantilena* as with justifying it. To do so, he invokes an Aristotelian framework, Ciceronian rhetoric, and Boethian philosophy to ground his discussion in *auctoritas*. See Aubrey, "Genre."

62. Aubrey, "Genre"; and a similar analysis of Grocheio in Christopher Page, *Discarding Images*, 75–76.

63. "But the manner of composing these generally is one and the same, in the manner of [their] nature. For first the texts are prepared in the place of matter, but after this, the melody is introduced in the place of form in proportion to whatever text. I speak, however, of 'in proportion to whatever [text]' because *chanson de geste* or *cantus coronatus* or *cantus versiculatus* [each] has a different [type of] melody, as their descriptions differ, in the manner that was said above. So then concerning musical forms that are performed by the human voice, these have been discussed." Ernst Rohloff, ed., *Die Quellenhandschriften zum Musiktraktat des Johannes de Grocheio*, 134: "Modus autem componendi haec generaliter est unus, quemadmodum in natura. Primo enim dictamina loco materiae praeparantur, postea vero cantus unicuique dictamini proportionalis loco formae introducitur. Dico autem *unicuique proportionalis*, quia alium cantum habet cantus gestualis et coronatus et versiculatus, ut eorum descriptiones aliae sunt, quemadmodum superius dicebatur. De formis igitur musicalibus, quae in voce humana exercentur, haec dicta sint." See Aubrey, "Genre." The reader will recall Jean de Garlande's evocation of Aristotelian causality in reference to inventing subject matter.

64. Quintilian, who speaks freely of musicians and artists, used remarkably similar language along with an analogy from the plastic arts, in speaking of how a work of art comes into being: "A very few critics have raised the question as to what may be the instrument of oratory. My definition of an instrument is that without which the material cannot be brought into the shape necessary for the effecting of our object. But it is not the art which requires an instrument, but the artist. Knowledge needs no instruments, for it may be complete although it produces nothing, but the artist must have them. The engraver cannot work without his chisel nor the painter without his brush. I shall therefore defer this question until I come to treat of the orator as distinct from his art." H. E. Butler, ed. and trans., *The Institutio Oratoria of Quintilian*, I:366–367: "Quaesitum a paucissimis et de instrumento est. Instrumentum voco, sine quo formari materia in id quod velimus effici opus non possit. Verum hoc ego non artem credo egere sed artificem. Neque enim scientia desiderat instrumentum, quae potest esse consummata, etiamsi nihil faciat, sed ille artifex, ut caelator caelum et pictor penicilla. Itaque haec in eum locum, quo de oratore dicturi sumus, differamus."

65. See Mathias Bielitz, "*Materia* und *forma* bei Johannes de Grocheo," for a discussion of other ways in which Grocheio uses these Aristotelian concepts. See also Wulf Arlt, "Musica e testo," 306–308; Margherita Beretta Spampinato, "'Mot' e 'so' nella lirica trobadorica"; and Patricia A. M. Dewitt, *A New Perspective on Johannes de Grocheio's Ars musicae*.

NOTES FOR PAGES 77–79

66. "*Cantus coronatus* usually is composed by kings and nobles, and is sung in the court of kings and princes of the land, so that their spirits might be moved to boldness and courage, magnanimity and liberality, which all produce a good government. For this sort of *cantus* concerns delightful and difficult material, like friendship and charity, and is made from all sorts of longs, even perfect [ones]." Rohloff, *Grocheio*, 130: "Cantus coronatus . . . etiam a regibus et nobilibus solet componi et etiam coram regibus et principibus terrae decantari, ut eorum animos ad audiciam et fortitudinem, magnanimitatem et liberalitatem commoveat, quae omnia faciunt ad bonum regimen. Est enim cantus iste de delectabili materia et ardua, sicut de amicitia et caritate, et ex omnibus longis et perfectis efficitur." See Aubrey, "Genre." Recall Jean de Garlande's discussion of classes of persons.

67. See Joan M. Ferrante, "Was Vernacular Poetic Practice a Response to Latin Language Theory?" on the extent to which troubadours were aware of Latin and Occitan grammar; Sarah Spence, *Rhetorics of Reason and Desire*; and Douglas Kelly, "The Poem as Art of Poetry: The Rhetoric of Imitation."

68. Recent studies on reception and intertextuality, such as Jörn Gruber, *Die Dialektik des Trobar* and Maria Luisa Meneghetti, *Il pubblico dei trovatori*, demonstrate the influences that composers had on one another.

69. See Aubrey, "Genre."

70. PC 62,1; Appel, ed., *Bernart von Ventadorn*, 301 (emphasis added). See Aubrey, "References," 112.

71. PC 457,8; Jeanroy and Salverda de Grave, *Uc de Saint-Circ*, #20, verses 1–9.

72. I am grateful to Elizabeth W. Poe for this observation.

[8]
Johannes de Grocheio on secular music: a corrected text and a new translation

CHRISTOPHER PAGE

It has long been recognized that Johannes de Grocheio's *De musica*[1] is an outstanding source of information about Parisian musical practice c. 1300. However, the critical text of the treatise published by Rohloff in 1972 can be improved by returning to the manuscripts,[2] and the pioneering English translation, by Albert Seay, can now be corrected in some important particulars.[3] The purpose of this article is therefore to present a corrected text and a new (annotated) translation of Johannes de Grocheio's remarks about secular music, both monophonic and polyphonic, generally regarded as the most important part of his treatise.[4]

To judge by Grocheio's comments on measured notation, he was writing c. 1300; he mentions Franco (whose *Ars cantus mensurabilis* was probably compiled c. 1280, according to current opinion), and he refers to the division of the tempus 'into two, into three, and in the same way on up to six'.[5] The text deals with Parisian musical practices, and Grocheio's thoroughness in this regard leaves no doubt that he had sampled the musical life of the capital; his passing references to Aristotelian concepts such as *forma et materia*, and to commentaries upon the *De anima* (among other books), suggest that he had studied in Paris, presumably by attending a

---

[1] I adopt this title since it is the one that Grocheio employs himself; see E. Rohloff, ed., *Die Quellenhandschriften zum Musiktraktat des Johannes de Grocheio* (Leipzig, 1972), p. 171.
[2] Some of Rohloff's interpretations and readings are challenged and discussed in P. A. M. DeWitt, *A New Perspective on Johannes de Grocheio's Ars Musicae*, Ph.D dissertation, University of Michigan (1973). After some years of independent work on French music in the thirteenth century I have returned to this dissertation and found many points of agreement. For further material of interest and importance, see T. J. McGee, 'Medieval Dances: Matching the Repertory with Grocheio's Descriptions', *The Journal of Musicology*, 7 (1989), 498–517, and D. Stockmann, '*Musica Vulgaris* bei Johannes de Grocheio', *Beiträge zur Musikwissenschaft*, 25 (1983), 3–56.
[3] A. Seay, trans., *Johannes de Grocheo* [sic]: *Concerning Music*, 2nd edn (Colorado Springs: Colorado College Music Press, 1974).
[4] This article incorporates and develops the results of research presented in C. Page, *Voices and Instruments of the Middle Ages: Instrumental Practice and Songs in France, 1100–1300* (London, 1987), *passim*, but especially pp. 196–201; idem, *The Owl and the Nightingale: Musical Life and Ideas in France 1100–1300* (London, 1989), *passim*; and idem, *Discarding Images: Reflections on Music and Culture in Medieval France* (Oxford, 1993), Chapter 3, *passim*.
[5] For the text see Rohloff, *Die Quellenhandschriften*, p. 138.

course of lectures.[6] There is no proof that he proceeded to take a degree, however (for this was not an automatic step), and it may be wise to keep an open mind about the note in the Darmstadt manuscript of the text where he is given the title 'magister' and named as a resident teacher at Paris ('regens Parisius');[7] the scribe may have been guessing on the basis of what he had read in the treatise. (It is noteworthy that the word 'Parisius' is added in a later hand.) If modern scholars are agreed that the treatise was written in Paris then it is partly because Paris exerts an extraordinary magnetism in most areas of Ars Antiqua studies; one might well argue that it is a quintessentially *provincial* activity to classify and describe the musical forms and fashions of a capital. Viewed in this light, the *De musica* might have been written in any part of France.

Johannes de Grocheio was almost certainly a Norman by birth. It is conceivable that he took his name from the coastal hamlet of Gruchy some 12 km west of Cherbourg, but a much more tempting hypothesis is that he belonged to the distinguished Norman family of de Grouchy. The de Grouchys are first recorded in the eleventh century (as 'de Groci') and were to become a distinguished minor family in the military history of France.[8] They possessed several fiefs between Rouen and Gournay-en-Bray. The family name derives from the region of Gruchy, near Blainville, about 16 km to the south-west of the de Grouchy lordship of Montérolier (see the Map). In view of the Norman fiefdoms of the de Grouchys it is striking that Normandy is the only provincial region of France that Grocheio mentions in his treatise (see the section below on the *ductia*). It may also be significant that Grocheio, by his own account, explored some important aspects of his treatise in a discourse with a certain Clement, who has recently been identified as a monk of the Benedictine Abbey of Lessay in Normandy.[9] It is possible that Grocheio had some link with this important monastic house, a community of more than thirty monks in his lifetime.[10] It is also possible that Grocheio was a priest, but I have been unable to verify the assertion of Mgr Glorieux that he was definitely a priest 'since we possess some sermons by him'.[11] Those sermons – if they ever existed – are not listed in Schneyer's monumental *Repertorium sermonum*.

---

[6] On this aspect of Grocheio's treatise see DeWitt, *A New Perspective*, *passim*, and M. Bielitz, 'Materia und forma bei Johannes de Grocheo', *Die Musikforschung*, 38 (1985), 257–77.

[7] See the facsimile in Rohloff, *Die Quellenhandschriften*, p. 107.

[8] On the de Grouchys during the Middle Ages see Le Vicomte de Grouchy and E. Travers, *Etude sur Nicolas de Grouchy* (Paris and Caen, 1878), pp. 4–9; le Marquis de Grouchy, *Mémoires du Maréchal de Grouchy*, 5 vols. (Paris, 1873-4), pp. iv-vii; *Dictionnaire de la Noblesse*, 3rd edn, 9, sv. 'Grouchy'. For the name 'de Groci' in the eleventh century see *Mémoires de la Société des Antiquaires de Normandie*, 4th series, 6 (1961), p. 374 ('Hugo de Groci').

[9] For the identification of Clement's monastery see Page, *The Owl and the Nightingale*, pp. 171–2, and p. 246 note 3. The evidence in question is obliterated in Rohloff's text by his emendation of Grocheio's 'Exaquiensem monachum' (i.e. 'monk of Lessay') to '[exequiarium] monachum' (*Die Quellenhandschriften*, p. 130).

[10] See the references to the community of Lessay in the celebrated *Register* of Odon Rigaud, conveniently accessible in S. M. Brown, trans., *The Register of Eudes of Rouen* (New York and London, 1964), p. 100 (visitation of 1250, thirty-six monks), p. 277 (visitation of 1256, thirty-four monks) and p. 634 (visitation of 1266, thirty-one monks).

[11] P. Glorieux, *La faculté des arts et ses maîtres au XIIIe siècle*, Etudes de philosophie médiévale, 59 (Paris, 1971), sv. Jean de Grouchy.

Johannes de Grocheio on secular music

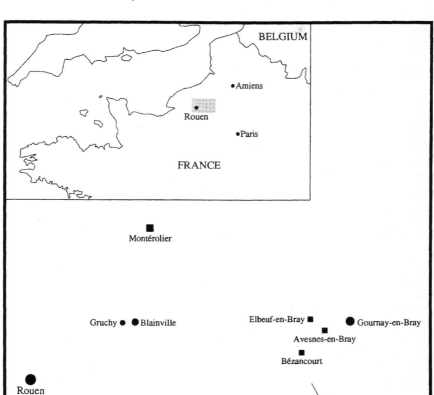

■ de Grouchy fiefs and principal lordships c. 1300
Rouen to Gournay-en-Bray is approximately 30 km

The text given here is derived from the facsimiles of the two manuscript sources of the treatise accompanying Rohloff's edition (a most lavish provision for which the editor and his publishers are to be warmly thanked). Each extract is cued with the appropriate page number in that edition. Rohloff's text has been compared with these manuscripts, producing a significant number of new readings, signalled below. For the sake of consistency, Rohloff's classicizing orthography has been retained. It should be emphasized that what follows is not intended as a comprehensive bibliographical guide to recent research on Grocheio's text and the notes to the translation are therefore generally confined to matters of lexical or interpretative difficulty; the reader is referred to Rohloff's edition for bibliographical material pertaining to the songs and other pieces mentioned by Grocheio.

p. 124 [From the preliminary discussion of how music may be classified.] Alii autem musicam dividunt in planam sive immensurabilem et mensurabilem, per

planam sive immensurabilem intellegentes ecclesiasticam, quae secundum Gregorium pluribus tonis determinatur. Per mensurabilem intellegunt illam quae ex diversis sonis simul mensuratis et sonantibus efficitur, sicut in conductibus et motetis. Sed si per immensurabilem intellegant musicam nullo modo mensuratam, immo totaliter ad libitum dictam deficiunt eo quod quaelibet operatio musicae et cuiuslibet artis debet illius artis regulis mensurari. Si autem per immensurabilem non ita praecise mensuratam intellegant, potest, ut videtur, ista divisio remanere.
...Partes autem musicae plures sunt et diversae secundum diversos usus, diversa idiomata vel diversas linguas in civitatibus vel regionibus diversis. Si tamen eam diviserimus secundum quod homines Parisius[12] ea utuntur, et prout ad usum vel convictum civium est necessaria et eius membra, ut oportet, pertractemus, videbitur sufficienter nostra intentio terminari eo quod diebus nostris principia cuiuslibet artis liberalis diligenter Parisiis inquiruntur et usus earum et fere omnium mechanicarum inveniuntur. Dicamus igitur quod musica qua utuntur homines Parisiis potest, ut videtur, ad tria membra generalia reduci. Unum autem membrum dicimus de simplici musica vel civili, quam vulgarem musicam appellamus; aliud autem de musica composita vel regulari vel canonica quam appellant musicam mensuratam. Sed tertium genus est quod ex istis duobus efficitur et ad quod ista duo tamquam ad melius ordinantur quod ecclesiasticam dicitur et ad laudandum creatorem deputatum est.

Others divide music into 'plain' or 'immeasurable' music and 'measurable', understanding 'plain' or 'immeasurable' music to be that of the Church which, following Gregory, has its boundaries set by various modes. By 'measurable' music they understand the music which is made from diverse pitches simultaneously measured and sounding, as in *conducti* and in motets. But if by the term 'immeasurable' they understand music which is in no way measured, but which is entirely performed in an arbitrary fashion, then they are at fault, because every process of music – and of any art – must be calculated according to the rules of that art. If, however, by the term 'immeasurable' they understand music which is not so precisely measured,[13] then it is evident that this division may be allowed to stand.
...There are many elements of music according to diverse usages, diverse dialects and diverse languages in different cities and regions. But if we divide it according to the usage of the Parisians, and if we treat the elements of music, as is fitting, according to how they are necessary for the entertainment and use of [Parisian] citizens, our intention will be seen to be adequately accomplished because in our days the Parisians diligently enquire into the fundamentals of every liberal art and ascertain the practice of them and of virtually every skill. We declare therefore that the music which is employed by the Parisians can be classified, as may be seen, into

---

[12] So both MSS. Rohloff: *Parisiis*
[13] This passage has been much discussed; see H. Van der Werf, 'The "Not-So-Precisely Measured" Music of the Middle Ages', *Performance Practice Review*, 1 (1988), 42–60, and J. Stevens, *Words and Music in the Middle Ages: Song, Narrative, Dance and Drama 1050–1350* (Cambridge, 1986), p. 433 *et passim*.

three general categories. We call one of these monophonic, 'civil' or the lay public's music, and the other comprises composed, regulated or 'canon'[14] music which they call measured music. But there is a third kind which is made from these two and for which these two are structured as if for the better; it is called ecclesiastical music and has been instituted for the praise of the Creator.

p. 128 [From the discussion of the gamut]...alium modum diversitatis invenerunt dicentes unum lineam et aliud spatium, incipientes a Γ ut usque ad d la sol procedentes. Sic itaque apparet quod ponendo signa vel notas in lineis et spatiis omnes concordantias et omnem cantum sufficienter describere potuerunt. Moderni vero propter descriptionem consonantiarum et stantipedum et ductiarum aliud addiderunt, quod *falsam musicam* vocaverunt, quia illa duo signa, scilicet ♭ et ♮ quae in ♭ fa ♮ mi tonum et semitonum designabant, in omnibus aliis faciunt hoc designare ita quod ubi erat semitonus per ♮ illud[15] ad tonum ampliant ut bona concordantia vel consonantia fiat, et similiter ubi tonus inveniebatur illud[16] per ♭ ad semitonum restringunt.

[the Ancients] devised another means of distinguishing [the notes of the gamut], declaring one to be a line and another a space, beginning on gamma *ut* and proceeding as far as d *la sol*. It is therefore apparent that by putting signs or marks upon lines and spaces they were able to notate all intervals, and every melody, in an adequate manner. The Moderns, moreover, in order to produce a notated record of consonances, of *stantipedes* and of *ductiae*,[17] have added another [means of distinguishing the notes of the gamut] which they have called *musica falsa* because they extend the two signs ♭ and ♮, which they use to indicate a tone and semitone step in ♭ fa ♮ mi, to all other [degrees of the gamut] with the same meaning, so that, where there was a semitone, they make it into a tone with ♮, so that there may be good line and good harmony,[18] and in the same way, where there was tone to be found, they compress it into a semitone by means of ♭.

---

[14] The term 'canon' music (*musica canonica*) balances 'civil' music (*musica civilis*), both terms to be understood as in 'canon' and 'civil' law, i.e. as relating to the clergy and to the laity respectively. It is unfortunate that Seay's translation 'composed or regular music by rule' for Grocheio's *musica composita vel regulari vel canonica* misses this distinction (*Concerning Music*, p. 12).

[15] So both MSS. Rohloff: *illum*

[16] So both MSS. Rohloff: *illum*

[17] The passage might also be rendered 'in order to produce a notated record of the consonances of *stantipedes* and of *ductiae*', which narrows the range of purposes for which *musica ficta* was devised in what is perhaps an unacceptable way, and which also, given the meaning Grocheio attaches to *consonantia*, implies polyphonic *stantipedes* and *ductiae*, which seems out of the question in this discussion of monophonic music. On the meaning of the term 'consonantia' in Grocheio's usage see the following note, and for Grocheio's description of the *stantipes* and *ductia* see below.

[18] 'bona concordantia vel consonantia'. Grocheio distinguishes (p. 144) between *concordantia*, when one musical sound relates in a harmonious way to another (*concordantia* therefore relates to line), and *consonantia*, when two or more notes sound simultaneously (*consonantia* therefore relates to harmony). Compare DeWitt, *A New Perspective*, pp. 76f.

p. 130 Dicamus igitur quod formae musicales vel species contentae sub primo membro, quod vulgare dicebamus, ad hoc ordinantur, ut eis mediantibus mitigentur adversitates hominum innatae, quas magis particulavimus in sermone ad Clementem Exaquiensem[19] monachum, et sunt duobus modis, aut enim in voce humana aut in instrumentis artificialibus exercentur. Quae autem in voce humana fiunt duobus modis sunt, aut enim dicimus cantum aut cantilenam. Cantum autem et cantilenam triplici differentia distinguimus. Aut enim [cantum] gestualem aut coronatum aut versiculatum, et cantilenam [aut] rotundam aut stantipedem aut ductiam appellamus.

We say, therefore, that the musical forms or genres that are subsumed by the first category, which we have called the music of the lay public,[20] are ordained for this purpose: that they may soften the sufferings to which all men are born and which I have detailed further in a discourse to Clement, a monk of Lessay.[21] And [these musical forms] are of two kinds, for they are either performed with the human voice or with musical instruments. Those that are made with the human voice are of two kinds: we call them either 'cantus' or 'cantilena'[22] and distinguish three kinds of each. There is a *cantus gestualis, coronatus* and *versiculatus*; there is a *cantilena rotunda, stantipedes* and *ductia*.

p. 130 Cantum vero gestualem dicimus in quo gesta heroum et antiquorum patrum opera recitantur, sicuti vita et martyria sanctorum et proelia et adversitates quas antiqui viri pro fide et veritati passi sunt, sicuti vita beati Stephani protomartyris et historia regis Karoli. Cantus autem iste debet antiquis et civibus laborantibus et mediocribus ministrari dum requiescunt ab opere consueto, ut auditis miseriis et calamitatibus aliorum suas facilius sustineant et quilibet opus suum alacrius aggrediatur. Et ideo iste cantus valet ad conservationem totius civitatis.

---

[19] So MS H; MS D: *exaquiansem*. Rohloff: [*exequiarium*].

[20] There can be no fully satisfactory translation of Grocheio's *vulgare*, here rendered 'of the lay public'. It appears to denote all the laity, from working people to royalty. Seay's translation 'vulgar music' (*Concerning Music*, p. 12) is somewhat unsatisfactory – if etymologically justifiable – given the modern associations of the word 'vulgar'. Compare DeWitt, *A New Perspective*, pp. 122f (an excellent discussion), Stevens, *Words and Music*, p. 431, and Page, *Discarding Images*, Chapter 3, *passim*.

[21] The words 'quas magis particulavimus in sermone ad Clementem Exaquiensem monachum' are consistent with the view that Grocheio discussed these matters with Clement, but it may rather imply a letter or treatise, now lost. The translation offered here ('which I have detailed further in a discourse to Clement, a monk of Lessay') is designed to accommodate both possibilities which are not, of course, mutually exclusive.

[22] Perhaps modelled upon the Old French terms *chanson* and *chansonette*. Grocheio's classification of musical forms has been much discussed and paraphrased; see, for example, DeWitt, *A New Perspective, passim*; F. A. Gallo, *Music of the Middle Ages II* (Cambridge, 1985), pp. 10–13; C. Page, *Voices and Instruments*, pp. 196–201; Stevens, *Words and Music*, pp. 491–5; Stockmann, 'Musica Vulgaris'; H. Wagenaar-Nolthenius, 'Estampie/Stantipes/Stampita', in *L'Ars Nova Italiana del Trecento: 2nd Congress* (Certaldo, 1969), pp. 399–409. A vital essay for the study of French song in Grocheio's lifetime is now L. Earp, 'Lyrics for Reading and Singing in Late Medieval France: The Development of the Dance Lyric from Adam de la Halle to Guillaume de Machaut', in R. A. Baltzer *et al.*, eds., *The Union of Words and Music in Medieval Poetry* (Austin, 1991), pp. 101–31.

We call that kind of *cantus* a *chanson de geste* in which the deeds of heroes and the works of ancient fathers[23] are recounted, such as the life and martyrdom of saints and the battles and adversities which the men of ancient times suffered for the sake of faith and truth, such as the life of St Stephen, the first martyr, and the story of King Charlemagne. This kind of music should be laid on[24] for the elderly, for working citizens and for those of middle station when they rest from their usual toil, so that, having heard the miseries and calamities of others, they may more easily bear their own and so that anyone may undertake his own labour with more alacrity. Therefore this kind of *cantus* has the power to preserve the whole city.[25]

p. 130 Cantus coronatus ab aliquibus simplex conductus dictus est, qui propter eius bonitatem in dictamine et cantu a magistris et studentibus circa sonos coronatur, sicut gallice *Ausi com l'unicorne* vel *Quant li roussignol*, qui etiam a regibus et nobilibus solet componi et etiam coram regibus et principibus terre decantari, ut eorum animos ad audaciam et fortitudinem, magnanimitatem et liberalitatem commoveat, quae omnia faciunt ad bonum regimen. Est enim cantus iste de delectabili materia et ardua, sicut de amicitia et caritate, et ex omnibus longis et perfectis efficitur.

The *cantus coronatus* has been called a 'monophonic conductus' by some; on account of the inherent virtue[26] of its poetry and music it is crowned by masters and students [of the art of songmaking] among pieces,[27] as in the French *Ausi com l'uni-*

---

[23] The 'ancient fathers' are probably not the Fathers of the Church, despite the ubiquity of *Vitae patrum* collections in the Middle Ages; no *chansons de geste* dealing with the lives of Fathers of the Church have survived. Grocheio probably means the ancient fathers of France – such as Charlemagne – whose wars and struggles brought the realm of France into being. See Page, *The Owl and the Nightingale*, pp. 30–33, and idem, 'Le troisième accord pour vièle de Jérôme de Moravie: Jongleurs et "anciens pères de France"', in C. Meyer, ed., *Jérôme de Moravie: un théoricien de la musique dans le milieu intellectuel parisien du XIII siècle* (Paris, 1992), pp. 83–96.

[24] 'should be laid on' translates *debet ministrari*; Grocheio sometimes chooses verbs which imply the politic provision of music for the mitigation of laymen's vices.

[25] It remains uncertain whether *civitas* should be translated 'city' here or taken in the broader sense 'State'. The former conveys Grocheio's interest in the music of a single city, Paris. However, when Grocheio speaks of the way music instils virtue and obedience his conception of the *civitas* is perhaps more expansive. See D. Luscombe, 'City and Politics Before the Coming of the *Politics*: Some Illustrations', in D. Abulafia, M. Franklin and M. Rubin, eds., *Church and City 1000–1500: Essays in Honour of Christopher Brooke* (Cambridge, 1992), pp. 41–55.

[26] The word *bonitas* demands a translation in excess of mere 'excellence', especially in the context of this imagery of crowning. Grocheio is presumably trying to convey a deeper virtue in the *cantus coronatus*, arising from the lofty subject-matter of the poetry, the excellence of its music and the high status of its composers. Grocheio's description of the *cantus coronatus* has been much discussed; for recent accounts see Stevens, *Words and Music*, p. 431, idem, 'Medieval Song' in D. Hiley and R. Crocker, eds., *The Early Middle Ages to 1300*, New Oxford History of Music II, 2nd edn (Oxford, 1990), p. 392, and Page, *Voices and Instruments*, pp. 196–201.

[27] A difficult passage; the sense of 'circa sonos' is not clear. Seay (*Concerning Music*, p. 16) takes it to refer to instrumental accompaniment, as does Rohloff, *Die Quellenhandschriften*, p. 131, but that seems strained. The matter is amply discussed in DeWitt, *A New Perspective*, pp. 133–4. The interpretation offered here is much the same as that of Stevens (*Words and Music*, p. 431). For a very different interpretation see C. Warren, 'Punctus organi and cantus coronatus in the Music of Dufay', in A. Atlas, ed., *Dufay Quincentenary Conference* (Brooklyn, 1976), pp. 128–43.

corne [see Ex. 1] or *Quant li roussignol*. This kind of song is customarily composed by kings and nobles and sung in the presence of kings and princes of the land[28] so that it may move their minds to boldness and fortitude, magnanimity and liberality, all of which things lead to good government. This kind of *cantus* deals with delightful and lofty subject-matter, such as friendship and love, and it is composed entirely from longs – perfect ones at that.[29]

pp. 131–2 Cantus versualis est qui ab aliquibus cantilena dicitur respectu coronati et ab eius bonitate in dictamine et concordantia deficit, sicut gallice *Chanter m'estuet quar ne m'en puis tenir* vel *Au repairier que je fis de Prouvence*. Cantus autem iste debet iuvenibus exhiberi ne in otio totaliter sint reperti. Qui enim refutat laborem et in otio vult vivere ei labor et adversitas est parata. Unde Seneca: Non est viri timere sudorem. Qualiter igitur modi cantus describuntur, sic apparet.

The *cantus versualis* is a species of *cantus* which is called a *cantilena* by some with respect to the [*cantus*] *coronatus* and which lacks the inherent virtue [of the *cantus coronatus*] in poetry and melody, as in the French *Chanter m'estuet quar ne m'en puis tenir*, or *Au repairier que je fis de Prouvence*.[30] This kind of song should be performed for the young lest they be found ever in idleness. He who refuses labour and wishes to live at ease has only travail and adversity in store. Whence Seneca says that 'It is not for a man to fear sweat'.[31] Thus it is plain how the various kinds of *cantus* are to be described.

p. 132 Cantilena vero quaelibet rotunda vel rotundellus a pluribus dicitur eo quod ad modum circuli in se ipsam reflectitur et incipit et terminatur in eodem. Nos autem solum illam rotundam vel rotundellum dicimus cuius partes non habent diversum cantum a cantu responsorii vel refractus. Et longo tractu cantatur velut cantus coronatus, cuiusmodi est gallice *Toute sole passerai le vert boscage*. Et huius-

---

[28] In this passage Grocheio seems determined to present a traditionalist and (by the later thirteenth century) a somewhat archaic image of trouvère monody in the High Style as an aristocratic art, rather than the increasingly urban, mercantile art that it had become with the expansion of the *puis*. In part, Grocheio's comment reflects the prominence of Thibaut, King of Navarre (d. 1253) in the later thirteenth-century conception of the trouvères' art. *Ausi com l'unicorne*, which Grocheio cites, is one of his chansons. In the *Chansonnier de l'Arsenal* Thibaut's songs are presented first, preceded by an illumination which shows a fiddler performing before a seated king and queen as courtiers stand nearby. This exactly matches Grocheio's remark that such songs should be performed 'in the presence of kings and princes of the land'. The *Chansonnier de l'Arsenal* continues (again, as some other sources do), to present the works of trouvères whose noble or aristocratic status was well known or assumed, such as Gace Brulé.

[29] The idiomatic translation is required to capture the quality of emphasis in the second conjunction: 'et ex omnibus longis *et* perfectis efficitur'. For discussions of this passage see J. Knapp, 'Musical Declamation and Poetic Rhythm in an Early Layer of Notre Dame Conductus', *Journal of the American Musicological Society*, 32 (1979), pp. 406–7, and Stevens, *Words and Music*, pp. 431–2, with bibliography there cited.

[30] On the distinction between the *cantus coronatus* and the *cantus versualis* see Stevens, 'Medieval Song', pp. 412 and 420, and Page, *Voices and Instruments*, pp. 199–200.

[31] *Epistulae Morales*, XXXI.

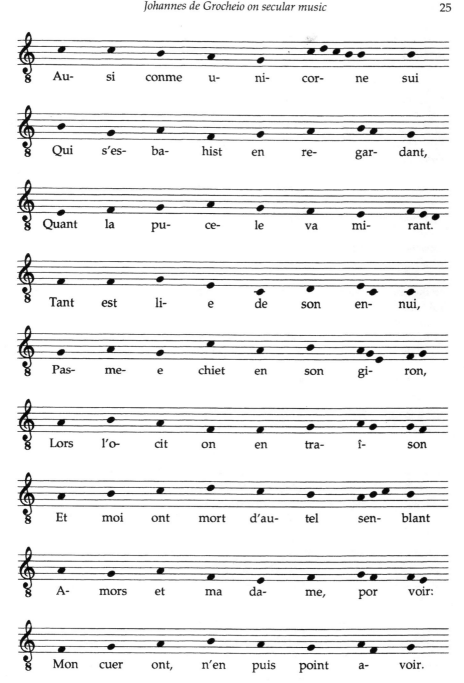

Ex. 1

modi cantilena versus occidentem, puta in Normannia, solet decantari a puellis et iuvenibus in festis et magnis conviviis ad eorum decorationem.

There are indeed many who call any *cantilena* a 'rotunda' or 'rotundellus' because it turns back on itself in the manner of a circle, beginning and ending in the same way [i.e. with a refrain].[32] However, I only call the kind of song a 'rotunda' or 'rotundellus' whose parts have the same music as the music of the response or refrain.[33] When it is sung it is drawn out in an expansive way like the *cantus coronatus*. The French song *Toute sole passerai le vert boscage* is of this kind. This kind of song is customarily sung towards the West – in Normandy, for example – by girls and by young men as an adornment to holiday celebrations and to great banquets.[34]

p. 132 Cantilena quae dicitur *stantipes* est illa in qua est diversitas in partibus et refractu tam in consonantia dictaminis quam in cantu, sicut gallice *A l'entrant d'amors* vel *Certes mie ne cuidoie*. Haec autem facit animos iuvenum et puellarum propter sui difficultatem circa hanc stare et eos a prava cogitatione divertit.

In the kind of *cantilena* which is called 'stantipes' there is a diversity – both in the rhymes of the poem and in the music – that distinguishes the verses from the refrain, as in the French song *A l'entrant d'amors* or *Certes mie ne cuidoie*. On account of its difficulty, this [distinction] makes the minds of young men and of girls dwell upon this [kind of *cantilena*][35] and leads them away from depraved thoughts.

p. 132 Ductia vero est cantilena levis et velox in ascensu et descensu quae in choreis a iuvenibus et puellis decantatur, sicut gallice *Chi encor querez amoretes*. Haec enim ducit corda puellarum et iuvenum et a vanitate removet et contra passionem quae dicitur 'amor hereos'[36] valere dicitur.

The *ductia* is a kind of *cantilena* that is light and rapid in its ascents and descents and which is sung in caroles[37] by young men and girls, like the French song *Chi encor querez amoretes*. This [kind of cantilena] directs the sentiments[38] of girls and

---

[32] As it is a distinguishing feature of *cantilene* that they begin and end with a refrain it would appear that some musicians called them all *rotunda* or *rotundellus*, since this term denoted the rondeau (see next note), beginning and ending with a refrain.

[33] Indicating that Grocheio's *rotunda* or *rotundellus* is a rondeau, no doubt of standard fourteenth-century structure, already cultivated at this date by his Parisian contemporary Jean de l'Escurel.

[34] On this reference to Grocheio's homeland see above.

[35] 'dwell upon this [kind of *cantilena*]' renders Grocheio's idiom *circa hanc stare*, an etymologizing phrase (compare *stare*, present participle *stans*, accusative *stantem*, and *stantipes*). Grocheio employs this idiom again in his later remarks about the *stantipes*.

[36] So both MSS. Rohloff: *amor vel* εροσ

[37] Seay (*Concerning Music*, p. 17) translates 'sung in chorus', but this is an error; the translation 'in caroles' is in accordance with standard usage in thirteenth-century Latin. Grocheio is referring to company dances performed in a ring or in a line. See Stevens, *Words and Music*, pp. 162–71; Page, *Voices and Instruments*, pp. 77–84; idem, *The Owl and the Nightingale*, pp. 110–33.

[38] 'directs the sentiments' (*ducit corda*); once again, Grocheio is etymologizing the name of a genre (*ductia*), or at least assaying a point of Latin style, by establishing the pairing *ductia/ducere*.

young men and draws them away from vain thoughts, and is said to have power against that passion which is called 'erotic love'.[39]

p. 133 Est etiam alius modus cantilenarum, quem *cantum insertum* vel *cantilenam entatam*[40] vocant, qui ad modum cantilenarum incipit et earum fine clauditur vel finitur, sicut gallice *Je m'endormi el sentier*.

There is also another kind of *cantilena* which they [i.e. the Parisians] call 'ornamented song' or 'grafted song'.[41] It begins in the manner of *cantilene* and ends or comes to a close in their fashion, as in the French song *Je m'endormi el sentier*.

p. 132 Sic igitur apparet descriptio istorum tam cantuum quam cantilenarum. Partes autem eorum multipliciter dicuntur, ut versus, refractorium vel responsorium et additamenta. Versus autem in cantu gestuali [est] qui ex pluribus versiculis efficitur et in eadem[42] consonantia dictaminis cadunt; In aliquo tamen cantu clauditur per versiculum [both MSS: versum] ab aliis consonantia discordantem, sicut in gesta quae dicitur de Girardo de Viana. Numerus autem versuum in cantu gestuali non est determinatus sed secundum copiam materiae et voluntatem compositoris ampliatur. Idem etiam cantus debet in omnibus versiculis [both MSS: versibus] reiterari.

---

[39] Unaccountably, Rohloff abolishes the readings of both manuscripts at this point and emends *amor hereos* to *amor vel eros*, breaking into Greek characters for the last word. There is no doubt about the correctness of the MS readings, however, for Grocheio's term *amor (h)ereos* (or simply *(h)ereos*) is found in numerous medical textbooks of the thirteenth and fourteenth centuries. Compare B. Lawn, ed., *The Prose Salernitan Questions*, Auctores Britannici Medii Aevi, V (London, 1979), p. 280: 'in passione que hereos dicitur'. These questions, by an anonymous English author, date from *c*. 1200. The phraseology of the passage quoted is very similar to Grocheio's and may therefore stand close to a source consulted by him. Grocheio had certainly read some material by the celebrated physician Galen, whom he mentions (Rohloff, *Die Quellenhandschriften*, p. 144).

[40] So both MSS. Rohloff: *entratam*

[41] 'Grafted' translates *entatam*, which is clearly the reading of both manuscripts. Rohloff's emendation to *entratam* is not necessary; there is no difficulty in regarding *entatam* as a Latinized form of the Old French past participle *enté* (from *enter*, 'to graft'), a term whose use in musical contexts during the thirteenth century is well established. See Godefroy, *Dictionnaire de l'ancienne langue française*, sv. *enter*; Tobler-Lommatzsch, *Altfranzösisches Wörterbuch*, sv. *enter*. The term has long been used in modern scholarship to denote motet texts that begin and end with quotations of the music and/or the words of pre-existing songs. Grocheio is presumably referring to a kind of song that begins and ends with a quotation, perhaps both musical and poetic, from a pre-existing song, and therefore to one manifestation of the phenomenon known to literary scholars and musicologists as the *refrain*. This is consistent with his statement that the *cantilena entata* begins and ends in the fashion of a *cantilena*, that is to say it begins and ends with a refrain or with something that, in registral terms, could be one. The song cited by Grocheio as an example of this form appears not to have survived. There may be little reason to perpetuate the musicological convention of limiting the thirteenth-century term *motet enté* to denote the texts of motets with refrain insertions split between the beginning and end of a text; as is well known, the meaning of the term *motet* was quite broad in Old French, and in Old French usage a *motet enté* may have been any song, whether monophonic or polyphonic, that contained *refrain* citations.

[42] So both MSS. Rohloff: *ex pluribus versiculis efficitur. [Versiculi] in eadem*.

Thus the description of these things, both of the varieties of *cantus* and of *cantilena*, is plain. Their parts are referred to in many ways, as verse, refrain or response, and the supplements.[43] The verse in a *chanson de geste* is that which is constituted from many versicles[44] which fall together with the same accord of verbal sound;[45] in some *chansons de geste* the verse ends with a versicle which does not accord in verbal sound with the others, as in the *geste* which is called 'Concerning Girard de Vienne'.[46] The number of verses in a *chanson de geste* is not fixed and may be extended according to the abundance of the raw material and the wish of the one whom makes the song. The same melody must be repeated in every versicle.

pp. 132–4 Versus vero in cantu coronato est qui ex pluribus punctis et concordantiis ad se invicem harmoniam facientibus efficitur. Numerus vero versuum in cantu coronato ratione septem concordantiarum determinatus est ad septem. Tot enim versus debent totam sententiam materiae, nec plus nec minus, continere.

The verse in a *cantus coronatus* is composed from numerous verbal constructions[47] and harmonious members producing a mutual accord. By analogy with the seven concords the number of verses in a *cantus coronatus* has been set at seven. This number of verses – no more and no less – must encompass all the subject-matter.

p. 134 Versus vero in cantu versiculari illi de cantu coronato, secundum quod potest, assimilatur. Numerus vero versuum in tali cantu non est determinatus, sed in aliquibus plus, in aliquibus minus, secundum copiam materiae et voluntatem compositoris ampliatur.

The verse in a *cantus versicularis* is made as similar to that of a *cantus coronatus* as is possible. The number of verses in such a *cantus* is not fixed, but is extended more in some, less in others, according to the wealth of the raw material and the wish of the poet.

---

[43] Rendering *additamenta* and denoting all the material of a refrain form which is not the refrain as fully constituted as both its text and music.

[44] Since this passage provides the only surviving description of the way *chansons de geste* were performed it is alarming that both manuscripts agree in transmitting a text that appears to confuse the crucial terms *versus* (laisse) and *versiculus* (line). The confusion has rarely been given its proper weight in discussions of Grocheio's evidence. Compare Stevens, *Words and Music*, pp. 233, 236 and 241; *idem*, 'Medieval Song', pp. 408–10.

[45] Literally 'in the same consonance of poetry'. Many of the surviving *chansons de geste* are constructed from assonating laisses. Some later examples, under the influence of romance, are in monorhymed laisses. Grocheio, writing c. 1300, may be thinking of both.

[46] Seay's translation (*Concerning Music*, p. 18) 'in the chanson de geste which is said to be by Girarde de Viana' is wide of the mark. Grocheio is referring to the *chanson de geste* of *Girard de Vienne*, composed, perhaps between 1205 and 1225, by Bertrand de Bar-sur-Aube. For this identification, with an extract from the text of the epic (which exactly corresponds to Grocheio's description of it), see Page, *The Owl and the Nightingale*, pp. 72–3.

[47] At first sight Grocheio's Latin ('ex pluribus punctis') suggests that he is referring to musical phrases, but throughout this section Grocheio's comments seem to relate exclusively to the poetic forms of the genres described. My translation assumes that he is referring to the pointed (i.e. punctuated) constructions of the sense. If Grocheio is using the term 'versus' to mean stanza here, then seven seems a large number.

p. 134 Responsorium vero est quo omnis cantilena incipit et terminatur. Additamenta vero differunt in rotundello, ductia et stantipede. In rotundello vero consonant et concordant in dictamine cum responsorio. In ductia vero et stantipede differunt quaedam et alia consonant et concordant. In ductia etiam et stantipede responsorium cum additamentis versus appellatur quorum numerus non est determinatus sed secundum voluntatem compositoris et copiam sententiae augmentatur.

The refrain is the part with which every *cantilena* begins and ends. The supplements differ in a *rotundellus*, *ductia* and *stantipes*. In the *rotundellus* [i.e. the rondeau] they rhyme and agree in their metrical form with the refrain. In the *ductia* and *stantipes* some supplements differ [from the refrain] and others rhyme and agree in their metrical form. Also, in the *ductia* and *stantipes* the refrain with the supplements is called the verse and the number of verses is not fixed but may be augmented according to the wish of the poet and the scope of the subject-matter.[48]

p. 134 Haec itaque sunt partes cantus et cantilenae diversae. De modo igitur componendi cantum et cantilenam nunc dicamus. Modus autem componendi haec generaliter est unus, quemadmodum in natura, primo enim dictamina loco materiae praeparantur, postea vero cantus unicuique dictamini proportionalis loco formae introducitur. Dico autem *unicuique proportionalis* quia alium cantum habet cantus gestualis et coronatus et versiculatus ut eorum descriptiones aliae sunt, quemadmodum superius dicebatur.

These are therefore the elements of the various kinds of *cantus* and *cantilena*. Let us therefore now discuss the manner of composing a *cantus* and a *cantilena*. There is generally one way of composing these things, as in nature,[49] for in the first place the poems are prepared beforehand, serving as the raw material, and then a correctly designed melody is introduced into each poem, serving as the form. I say 'correctly designed into each [poem]', because the *cantus gestualis, coronatus* and *versiculatus* all have their own kinds of melody just as their descriptions are different, as has been said above.

pp. 134–6 De formis igitur musicalibus quae in voce humana exercentur haec dicta sint. De instrumentalibus vero nunc prosequamur. Instrumenta vero a quibusdam

---

[48] This is a difficult passage because Grocheio is using musical terms for aspects of poetic form. It would appear that the verb 'consono' (or as a noun, sometimes reinforced as 'consonantia dictaminis') denotes rhyming, while 'concordo' (sometimes reinforced as 'concordant in dictamine') denotes identity of metrical form.

[49] Grocheio's point is that the composition of these song forms is analogous to creation in the natural world. He makes this plain by using the terms *materia* and *forma*, an ultimately Aristotelian distinction. Cf. *De anima*, II:1 'Matter is identical with potentiality, form with actuality'. Grocheio is therefore regarding the poems of these musical forms as *materia* – as matter with the potentiality to become a certain kind of song – while the music is the *forma*, transforming the raw material into a form by creating the set of musical repeats and changes that define the musical form of the genre in question. See M. Bielitz, '*Materia* und *forma* bei Johannes de Grocheo', and DeWitt, *A New Perspective*, pp. 51f.

dividuntur divisione soni artificialis in eis generati, dicunt enim sonum in instrumentis fieri afflatu, puta in tubis, calamis, fistulis et organis, vel percussione puta in chordis, tympanis, cymbalis et campanis. Sed si haec omnia subtiliter considerentur, inveniuntur a percussione fieri cum omnis sonus percutiendo causetur prout in sermonibus de anima comprobatum est. Nos autem hic non intendimus[50] instrumentorum compositionem vel divisionem nisi propter diversitatem formarum musicalium quae in eis generantur. Inter quae instrumenta cum chordis principatum obtinent, cuiusmodi sunt psalterium, cithara, lyra, quitarra sarracenica et viella. In eis enim [est] subtilior et melior soni discretio[51] propter abbreviationem et elongationem chordarum. Et adhuc inter omnia instrumenta chordosa visa a nobis viella videtur praevalere. Quemadmodum enim anima intellectiva alias formas naturales in se virtualiter includit et ut tetragonum trigonum et maior numerus minorem, ita viella in se virtualiter alia continet instrumenta. Licet enim aliqua instrumenta suo sono magis moveant animos hominum – puta in festis, hastiludiis et torneamentis tympanum et tuba – in viella tamen omnes formae musicales subtilius discernuntur et ideo de his tantummodo nunc dicatur.

These things have been said concerning the musical forms which are performed with the human voice. We now turn to consider instrumental forms. Instruments are classified by some according to the different kind of manufactured sound that is generated by them, for they declare that sound is produced in musical instruments by the breath, as in *tube, calami, fistule* and *organa*, or by beating, as in strings, *tympana, cymbala* and *campana*.[52] But if all these things are given careful consideration then all these sounds are found to be made by beating since every sound is produced by striking, as has been proved in the discourses concerning the soul.[53] Here, however, we do not intend to encompass the construction or classification of musical instruments unless it relates to the diversity of the musical forms that are executed with them. Among which instruments the strings hold pride of place; of this kind are the *psalterium*, the *cithara*, the *lyra*, the *quitarra sarracenica* and the *viella*.[54]

---

[50] So both MSS. Rohloff: *intendimus [notificare]*
[51] So MS H (f. 4v). MS D (f. 61v): *soni descriptio*
[52] These instrument-names cannot all be identified with certainty. *Tube* will be trumpets, while *fistula* may denote flutes and/or duct flutes. *Calami* presumably denotes wind instruments with reeds. *Organa* may safely be interpreted as organs. *Tympana* are probably frame drums of various kinds, while *cymbala* may be identified with cymbals or small bells (but perhaps not with rows of chime bells). There seems no reason to doubt that *campana* are large, tower bells or other signalling bells.
[53] The reference is to Aristotle's *De anima*, II:8, or possibly to a commentary upon it, perhaps by Grocheio himself.
[54] *Psalterium* may be safely associated with psalteries, generally of pig-snout shape in Grocheio's time and strung with metallic materials. *Cithara* is generally (but by no means exclusively) associated with forms of the Germanic word *harp(e)* in medieval word lists and translations, generally denoting a pillar harp c. 1300. The *lyra* may possibly be the lute, while the *quitarra sarracenica* is perhaps to be associated with either the gittern or the citole, although this is very uncertain. The *viella* is undoubtedly the fiddle. For the evidence on which these identifications are based see P. Bec., *Vièles ou Violes* (Paris, 1992), *passim*; Page, *Voices and Instruments*, pp. 139–50; L. Wright, 'The Medieval Gittern and Citole: A Case of Mistaken Identity', *Galpin Society Journal*, 30 (1977), 8–42 and C. Young, 'Zur Klassifikation und ikonographischen Interpretation mittelalterlicher Zupfinstrumente', *Basler Jahrbuch für Historische Musikpraxis*, 8 (1984), 67–103.

With these instruments there is a more exact and a better means of distinguishing[55] any melody on account of the shortening and lengthening of the strings. Furthermore, the *viella* evidently prevails over all the musical instruments known to us, for just as the scope of the intellective soul includes other natural forms within itself, and as the square includes the triangle and the greater number includes the lesser, so the scope of the *viella* includes all other instruments within itself.[56] Even if there are some instruments whose sound has greater power to move the souls of men – as the *tympanum* and *tuba* do in feasts, hastiludes[57] and tournaments – on the *viella* all musical forms can be discerned more exactly, and therefore it only remains to speak of those musical forms.[58]

p. 136 Bonus autem artifex in viella omnem cantum et cantilenam et omnem formam musicalem generaliter introducit. Illa tamen quae coram divitibus in festis et ludis fiunt communiter ad tria generaliter reducuntur, puta cantum coronatum, ductiam et stantipedem. Sed de cantu coronato prius dictum est, de ductia igitur et stantipede nunc [est] dicendum. Est autem ductia sonus illiteratus cum decenti percussione mensuratus. Dico autem *illiteratus* quia licet in voce humana fieri possit et per figuras repraesentari non tamen per litteras scribi potest quia littera et dictamine caret. Sed *cum recta percussione* eo quod ictus eam mensurant et motum facientis et excitant animum hominis ad ornate movendum secundum artem quam ballare vocant, et eius motum mensurant in ductiis et choreis.

A good player of the *viella* generally performs every *cantus* and *cantilena*, and all achieved musical design.[59] The genres which are usually performed before mag-

---

[55] Or possibly, following the reading of MS D, 'a better account'.
[56] The concept of an instrument which includes the scope of all others within itself is a familiar one in medieval music theory; compare John 'of Affligem' on the *musa* which, he says, *omnium [instrumentorum] vim atque modum in se continet* (J. Smits van Waesberghe, ed., *Johannis...De Musica*, Corpus Scriptorum de Musica 1 (American Institute of Musicology, 1950), p. 54). Grocheio's comments upon the *viella*, however, reveal a higher level of abstraction than those of Johannes two centuries earlier and reflect Grocheio's reading of Aristotle's *De anima*, II:3 'The types of soul resemble the series of figures. For, both in figures and in things animate, the earlier form exists potentially in the later, as, for instance, the triangle exists potentially in the quadrilateral and the nutritive soul exists potentially in the sensate soul'. The intellective soul is the highest function of the soul, standing above sensate soul (characterized by sense perception, more or less complex depending upon the species of creature at issue), and nutritive soul (characterized by the basic functions of nutrition and reproduction). This analogy between the status of the *viella* and intellective soul therefore implies the highest possible standing for the *viella* as an instrument that can encompass what every other instrument can do but which adds qualities that Grocheio compares to the distinctively human faculties of intellection and abstraction. In the context of thirteenth-century theology – much preoccupied with the nature of the soul – this analogy is less strained than it may now appear.
[57] On the distinction between hastiludes and tournaments, which is often difficult to establish, see J. Vale, *Edward III and Chivalry* (Woodbridge, 1982), pp. 57ff.
[58] Grocheio thus signals his intention to speak only of *viella* repertory. It remains unknown whether other instruments performed the musical forms he now goes on to describe, or whether other instruments were associated with specific repertoire in the same way as the *viella*.
[59] The construction is *bonus artifex in viella...formam introducit*, which might be translated 'a good player creates *forma* upon the *viella*...'. This seems a rather cumbersome and gratuitously cerebral way for Grocheio to express his meaning, but the sense seems clear none the less. The verb *introduco* here has

nates in festivities and sportive gatherings⁶⁰ can generally be reduced to three, that is to say the *cantus coronatus*, the *ductia* and the *stantipes*. However, since we have already given an account of the *cantus coronatus*, we must now therefore speak of the *ductia* and the *stantipes*. The *ductia* is a melody without words, measured with an appropriate beat. I say 'without words' because even though it can be performed by the human voice and expressed in musical notation, it cannot be written down with letters because it lacks a text and a poem. But it has 'a correct beat' because beats measure the *ductia*⁶¹ and the movement of one who dances it, and [these beats] excite people to move in an elaborate fashion according to the art which they call 'dancing', and they measure the movement [of this art] in *ductiae* and in caroles.

p. 136 Stantipes vero est sonus illiteratus habens difficilem concordantiarum discretionem per puncta determinatus. Dico autem *habens difficilem* etc. propter enim eius difficultatem facit animum facientis circa eam stare et etiam animum advertentis et multoties animos divitum a prava cogitatione divertit. Dico etiam *per puncta determinatus* eo quod percussione quae est in ductia caret et solum punctorum distinctione cognoscitur.

The *stantipes* is a textless melody having a difficult structure of agreements and distinguished by its sections.⁶² I say 'having a difficult [structure of agreements]' for, on account of its difficulty, it causes the mind of anyone who performs it – and of anyone who listens – to dwell upon it⁶³ and it often diverts the minds of the powerful from perverse reflection. I say 'distinguished by its sections', because it lacks the beat of the *ductia* and is only recognized by the distinction of its sections.

---

nothing to do with the performance of 'introductory' preludes upon the fiddle; *introduco* + accusative + *in* + ablative is Grocheio's idiom for referring to the creation of *forma* in its Aristotelian sense of actual, accomplished form rather than mere raw material (*materia*). For a parallel passage in Grocheio's treatise compare Rohloff, *Die Quellenhandschriften*, p. 114. Grocheio's point is that with the *viella* a good player can play every *cantus* and *cantilena* and can shape every kind of achieved musical design. For contrasting proposals about the interpretation of Grocheio's evidence see H. M. Brown, 'Instruments', in H. M. Brown and S. Sadie, eds., *Performance Practice*, 2 vols. (London, 1989), 1, pp. 18–23; D. Fallows, 'Secular Polyphony in the Fifteenth Century', *ibid*, p. 206; L. Gushee, 'Two Central Places: Paris and the French Court in the Early Fourteenth Century', in *Bericht über den Internationalen Musikwissenschaftlichen Kongress Berlin 1974*, ed. H. Kuhn and P. Nitsche (Kassel, etc., 1980), p. 143.

⁶⁰ The appropriate translation for 'ludi' is not easy to establish; it may encompass tournaments.

⁶¹ 'correct beat' renders *recta percussione*. The noun *ictus* is not a common one in either the plainchant theory or the polyphonic theory of the Middle Ages, but its appearance in this context can be explained in terms of the choreography of *caroles*. There is abundant evidence that *caroles* were sometimes danced with clapping of the hands and stamping of the feet; Grocheio is here presenting such accentuation as a characteristic feature of melodies designed for the *carole*. See Page, *The Owl and the Nightingale*, p. 115.

⁶² There is no adequate English equivalent of Grocheio's *puncta*, denoting a complex musical phrase capable of forming one unit of an estampie and of bearing an open or closed ending.

⁶³ On the etymologizing explanation *circa eam stare* see above. For commentary upon this passage see L Hibberd, '*Estampie* and *Stantipes*', *Speculum*, 19 (1944), 222–49; K. Vellekoop, 'Die Estampie: ihre Besetzung und Funktion', *Basler Jahrbuch für Historische Musikpraxis*, 8 (1983), 51–65, and H. Wagenaar-Nolthenius, 'Estampie/Stantipes/Stampita', in *L'Ars Nova Italiana del Trecento: 2nd Congress* (Certaldo, 1969), pp. 399–409.

p. 136 Partes autem ductiae et stantipedis puncta communiter dicuntur. Punctus autem est ordinata aggregatio concordantiarum harmoniam facientium ascendendo et descendendo, duas habens partes in principio similes, in fine differentes, quae *clausum* et *apertum* communiter appellantur. Dico autem *duas habens partes* etc. ad similitudinem duarum linearum quarum una sit maior alia. Maior enim minorem claudit et est fine differens a minori. Numerum vero punctorum in ductia ad numerum trium consonantiarum perfectarum attendentes ad tria posuerunt. Sunt tamen aliquae *notae* vocatae quattuor punctorum quae ad ductiam vel stantipedem imperfectam reduci possunt. Sunt etiam aliquae ductiae quattuor habentes puncta puta ductia 'Pierron'. Numerum vero punctorum in stantipede quidam ad sex posuerunt ad rationes vocum inspicientes. Alii tamen de novo inspicientes forte ad numerum septem concordantiarum vel naturali inclinatione ducti, puta Tassinus, numerum ad septem augmentant. Huiusmodi autem stantipedes [sunt] 'res cum septem cordis' vel difficiles 'res Tassini'.

The elements of the *ductia* and *stantipes* are commonly called *puncta*. A *punctus* is a structured collection of agreements producing euphony as they rise and fall, having two parts, similar at the beginning, different at the end, which are commonly called 'open' and 'closed'. I say 'having two parts etc.' by analogy with two lines, one of which is longer than the other. The greater includes the lesser and differs from the lesser at its end. [Musicians] have set the number of *puncta* in a *ductia* at three, giving consideration to the three perfect consonances. There are some [*ductiae*], however, with four *puncta*, called *notae*, which can be assimilated to an imperfect *ductia* or *stantipes*. There are also some *ductiae* having four puncta, such as the *ductia* 'Pierron'.[64] Some [musicians] have set the number of *puncta* in a *stantipes* at six by analogy with the hexachord. Others, however, such as Tassin, considering the matter afresh, have enlarged the number of *puncta* to seven [see Ex. 2] perhaps by analogy with the seven concords or because they were led by natural inclination to do so. *Stantipedes* of this kind are 'the piece with seven strings' or the difficult 'pieces of Tassin'.[65]

pp. 136–8 Componere ductiam et stantipedem est sonum per puncta et rectas percussiones in ductia et stantipede determinare. Quemadmodum enim materia naturalis per formam naturalem determinatur ita sonus determinatus[66] per puncta et per formam artificialem ei ab artifice attributam. Quid igitur sit ductia et stantipes, et quae earum partes et quae earum compositio, sic sit dictum. In quo propositum

---

[64] It remains uncertain whether this is a reference to a *ductia* called Pierron or *by* Pierron. It may be both.
[65] There is a severe textual difficulty in the last sentence of the Latin. The manuscripts are unanimous in their readings for the whole sentence, save that only MS H has the *sunt*, added by a later hand and placed here in square brackets. Rohloff emends the received text in two places, reading 'Huiusmodi autem stantipedes sunt res cum septem *concordantiis, ut* difficiles res Tassini' (my italics). It is not certain that these emendations are required; 'res cum septem cordis' is presumably the title of an estampie (or if *res* is construed as a plural, as a series of estampies), analogous to 'res Tassini'.
[66] So both MSS. Rohloff: *determinatur*

34 Christopher Page

Ex. 2

de simplici seu vulgari musica terminatur. De musica igitur composita et regulari sermonem perquiramus.

To compose a *ductia* and *stantipes* is to shape musical sound into the *puncta* and correct pulses for a *ductia* and *stantipes*. Just as raw material in nature is given identity by natural form, so musical sound [is given identity] through *puncta* and through the man-made design that the composer gives to it. Thus we have given an account of the *ductia* and the *stantipes*, their parts and their composition. This discussion of monophonic or the music of the lay public now comes to a close. Let us turn our discussion to constructed[67] and regulated music.

p. 138 Quidam autem per experientiam attendentes ad consonantias tam perfectas quam imperfectas cantum ex duobus compositum invenerunt, quem *quintum* et *discantum* seu *duplum organum* appellaverunt, et de hoc plures regulas invenerunt, ut apparet eorum tractatus aspicienti. Si tamen aliquis praedictas consonantias sufficienter cognoverit ex modicis regulis poterit talem cantum et eius partes et eius compositionem cognoscere, sunt enim aliqui qui ex industria naturali et per usum talem cantum cognoscunt et componere sciunt. Sed alii, ad tres consonantias perfectas attendentes, cantum ex tribus compositum uniformi mensura regulatum invenerunt, quem *cantum praecise mensuratum* vocaverunt, et isto cantu moderni Parisiis utuntur quem antiqui pluribus modis diviserunt; nos vero secundum usum modernorum in tres generaliter dividimus, puta *motetos*, *organum* et cantum abscisum quem *hoquetos* vocant.

Some musicians, moreover, studying both perfect and imperfect consonances through experience of them, devised a kind of music composed in two parts, which they have called 'quintus' and 'discantus' or 'organum duplum', and they have devised many rules pertaining to this, as will be apparent to anyone who looks into a treatise of theirs.[68] However, if anyone is sufficiently familiar with the aforementioned consonances he will be able to have a thorough knowledge of such music, its component parts and its composition, from a few rules, for there are some who are proficient in this music and who know how to compose it through experience and innate diligence. Others, however, pondering upon the three perfect consonances, devised a form of music composed in a threefold way,[69] regulated according to a uniform measure, which they called 'precisely measured music', and it is this kind of music which the Moderns in Paris employ. The Ancients divided it in numerous ways; we, following the usage of the Moderns, generally distinguish three kinds, that is to say motets, organum and a 'cut' music that they call 'hockets'.

[67] 'constructed' renders Grocheio's *composita*, which cannot mean simply 'composed' because this would not distinguish polyphony from monophonic forms. The key sense here is surely that of 'assembled, put together', having reference to the scrupulous calibration of polyphonic parts in terms of intervals and duration.
[68] On this passage see K.-J. Sachs, 'Die Contrapunctus-Lehre im 14. und 15. Jh.', in *Die Mittelalterliche Lehre von der Mehrstimmigkeit*, ed. H. H. Eggebrecht (Darmstadt, 1984), pp. 161–256, especially pp. 169–70.
[69] 'in a threefold way', rendering *ex tribus*, a reference to the perfection; cf. Rohloff, *Die Quellenhandschriften*, p. 140: 'Est enim perfectio mensura ex tribus temporibus constans. ...Ista autem mensura moderni utuntur et hac totum summ cantum et cantando et figurando mensurant'.

36   *Christopher Page*

[An account of the rhythmic modes follows, Grocheio expressing his preference for the standard division into six. The symbols of mensural notation are discussed and Grocheio emphasizes the variability of their meaning for different singers. He now begins his account of polyphonic genres.]

p. 144 Motetus vero est cantus ex pluribus compositus, habens plura dictamina vel multimodam discretionem syllabarum, utrobique harmonialiter consonans. Dico autem *ex pluribus compositus* eo quod ibi sunt tres cantus vel quattuor, *plura* autem *dictamina* quia quilibet debet habere discretionem syllabarum, tenore excepto qui in aliquibus habet dictamen et in aliquibus non. Sed dico *utrobique harmonialiter consonans* eo quod quilibet debet cum alio consonare secundum aliquam perfectarum cononantiarum, puta secundum diatessaron vel diapente vel diapason de quibus superius diximus cum de principiis tractabamus. Cantus autem iste non debet coram vulgaribus propinari eo quod eius subtilitatem non advertunt[70] nec in eius auditu delectantur sed coram litteratis et illis qui subtilitates artium sunt quaerentes. Et solet in eorum festis decantari ad eorum decorationem, quemadmodum cantilena quae dicitur rotundellus in festis vulgarium laicorum.

The motet is a music assembled from numerous elements, having numerous poetic texts or a multifarious structure of syllables, according together at every point. I say 'assembled from numerous elements' because in a motet there are three or four parts; [I say] having 'numerous poetic texts' because each [part] must have its structure of syllables save the tenor, which in some [motets] has a poetic text and in some does not. I say 'according together at every point' because each [part] must harmonize with the other according to one of the perfect consonances, that is to say a fourth, fifth or octave, which we discussed above when we treated the fundamentals. This kind of music should not be set before a lay public[71] because they are not alert to its refinement nor are they delighted by hearing it, but [it should only be performed] before the clergy[72] and those who look for the refinements of skills. It is the custom for the motet to be sung in their holiday festivities to adorn them, just as the *cantilena* which is called 'rotundellus' [is customarily sung] in the festivities of the lay public.[73]

p. 144 Organum vero, prout hic sumitur, est cantus ex pluribus harmonice com-

---

[70] So both MSS. Rohloff: *animadvertunt*
[71] This passage has given rise to much misunderstanding. Seay's translation 'the vulgar' (*Concerning Music*, p. 26) has been highly influential but is most ill-judged, since Grocheio is contrasting the *laity* with the *clergy* at this point. See the next note and, for a full discussion of this point, Page, *Discarding Images*, Chapter 3, *passim*, and compare Stevens, *Words and Music*, p. 431 and note 50.
[72] Grocheio's term *litterati* has been translated in many ways by modern scholars ('the literati', 'men of letters', 'exclusive social circles'); see, for example, DeWitt, *A New Perspective*, p. 177. Virtually all of these authors seek to convey what they take to have been the elite audience for the motet; there can be little doubt that Grocheio is using the word *litterati* in its traditional sense of 'the clergy'.
[73] Grocheio is alluding to his own phraseology at this point. See his account of the *rotundellus* above.

positus unum tantum habens dictamen vel discretionem syllabarum. Dico autem *tantum habens unum dictamen* eo quod omnes cantus fundantur super unam discretionem syllabarum. Cantus autem iste dupliciter variatur. Est enim quidam qui supra cantum determinatum, puta ecclesiasticum, fundatur, qui ecclesiis[74] vel locis sanctis decantatur ad dei laudem et reverentiam summitatis, et cantus iste appropriato nomine *organum* appellatur. Alius autem fundatur supra cantum cum eo compositum qui solet in conviviis et festis coram litteratis et divitibus decantari, et ex his nomen trahens appropriato nomine *conductus* appellatur. Communiter tamen loquentes totum hoc *organum* dicunt et sic communis est eis descriptio supradicta.

Organum, as it is interpreted here, is a music harmoniously assembled from numerous elements, having only one poem or structure of syllables. I say 'having only one poem' because all the parts are founded upon one structure of syllables. This music is of two kinds. There is one kind which is founded upon a modal melody,[75] that is to say an ecclesiastical one, which is sung in churches or in holy places[76] to the praise of God and for the worship of the Most High, and this is appropriately named *organum*. Another is founded upon a melody composed with it and which is customarily sung at meals and festivities before clergy and magnates, and taking its name from them it is called by the appropriate name *conductus*.[77] All of this is commonly called *organum* and thus the above description relates generally to them all.

pp. 144–6 Hoquetus est cantus abscisus ex duobus vel pluribus compositus. Dico autem *ex pluribus compositus* quia licet abscisio vel truncatio sit sufficiens inter duos, possunt tamen esse plures ut cum truncatione consonantia sit perfecta. Cantus autem iste cholericis et iuvenibus appetibilis est propter sui mobilitatem et velocitatem, simile enim sibi simile quaerit et in suo simili delectatur.[78] Partes autem istorum plures sunt puta *tenor, motetus, triplum, quadruplum* et in hoquetis *primus, secundus* et ultimo eorum *duplum*. Tenor autem est illa pars supra quam omnes aliae fundantur quemadmodum partes domus vel aedificii super suum fundamentum et eas regulat et eis dat quantitatem quemadmodum ossa partibus aliis. Motetus vero est cantus ille qui supra tenorem immediate ordinatur et in diapente ut plurimum incipit et in eadem proportione[79] qua incipit continuatur vel diapa-

---

[74] Rohloff: [in] *ecclesiis*
[75] For the use of *determinare* to indicate definition according to (plainchant) mode see Grocheio's remarks in the first Latin passage given above (Rohloff, *Die Quellenhandschriften*, p. 124).
[76] The phrase 'holy places' is often used in medieval Latin to denote the immediate environs of any ecclesiastical building. Grocheio may be referring to the use of organum in processions.
[77] Grocheio is presumably judging *conductus* to be an appropriate name for a genre performed where the learned and powerful are gathered together because *conductus* can be etymologized as 'brought or drawn together'. See B. Gillingham, 'A New Etiology and Etymology for the Conductus', *Musical Quarterly*, 75 (1991), 59–73, especially pp. 61–2.
[78] Compare Walther, *Sprichwörter*, 7418, 11012, 15304 etc.
[79] Rohloff: *proportione* [in] *qua incipit*

38

son[80] ascendit, et in hoquetis ab aliquibus dicitur *magistrans*, ut in hoqueto qui dicitur *Ego mundus*.[81] Triplum vero est cantus ille qui supra tenorem in diapason proportione incipere debet et in eadem proportione ut plurimum continuari. Dico autem *ut plurimum* quia aliquoties in tenore[82] vel diapente descendit propter euphoniam, quemadmodum motetus aliquando in diapason ascendit. Quadruplum vero est cantus qui aliquibus additur propter consonantiam perficiendam. Dico autem *aliquibus* etc., quia in aliquibus sunt tantum tres et ibi sufficiunt cum perfecta consonantia ex tribus causetur. In aliquibus vero quartus additur ut dum unus trium pausat vel ornate[83] ascendit, vel duo adinvicem se truncant, quartus consonantiam servet.

The hocket is a 'cut' song composed from two or more parts. I say 'composed from more parts' because even though the cutting away or truncation can be adequate between two parts, it is possible for there to be more so that the harmony may be complete with the truncation. This music appeals to the choleric and to the young on account of its motion and speed, for like seeks like and delights in it. The elements of these [genres] are many, including the tenor, motetus, triplum and quadruplum, and in hockets the prime, the second and – the last of them – the duplum.[84] The tenor is the part upon which all the others are founded, as the parts of a house or edifice [rest] upon a foundation, and it regulates them and gives substance, as bones do, to the other parts. The motetus is the part which is placed immediately above the tenor, and as often as possible it begins a fifth above the tenor and continues in the same proportion as it began, or ascends to the octave; in hockets, some call this part the *magistrans*, as in the hocket which is called *Ego mundus*. The triplum is the part which should begin above the tenor in the proportion of an octave and which should be continued in the same proportion as often as possible. I say 'as often as possible', because it sometimes descends into the range of the tenor, or descends a fifth, for the sake of euphony, just as the motetus sometimes ascends to the octave. The quadruplum is the part which is added in some pieces to complete the harmony. I say 'to some' etc., because in some pieces there are only three parts and they suffice, since complete music can be established with three parts. In some pieces, indeed, a fourth voice is added, so that while one of the three voices pauses or ascends in an ornate fashion, or two together have rests, the fourth may preserve the harmony.

p. 146 Primus vero in hoquetis est[85] qui primo truncare incipit, sed secundus qui

---

[80] Rohloff: *vel [in] diapason ascendit*
[81] So both MSS. Rohloff: *Echo montis*
[82] So both MSS. Rohloff: *motetum*
[83] So both MSS. Rohloff: *ordinatim*
[84] Grocheio's phraseology seems designed to exclude the possibility of four-part hockets. For an account of a four-part hocket see P. Jeffery, 'A Four-Part *In seculum* Hocket and a Mensural Sequence in an Unknown Fragment', *Journal of the American Musicological Society*, 37 (1984), 1–48.
[85] So both MSS. Rohloff: *hoquetis est [cantus]*

secundo post primum truncat. Duplum vero est[86] qui cum tenore[87] minutam facit abscisionem et cum eo aliquoties in diapente consonat et aliquando in diapason proportione, ad quod multum iuvat bona discretio decantantis. Volens autem ista componere primo debet tenorem ordinare vel componere et ei modum et mensuram dare. Pars enim principalior debet formari primo, quoniam ea mediante postea formantur aliae, quemadmodum Natura in generatione animalium primo format membra principalia, puta cor, hepar, cerebrum, et illis mediantibus alia post formantur. Dico autem *ordinare,* quoniam in motellis et organo tenor ex cantu antiquo est et prius composito, sed ab artifice per modum et rectam mensuram amplius determinatur. Et dico *componere,* quoniam in conductibus tenor totaliter fit[88] et secundum voluntatem artificis modificatur et durat.

The 'prime' voice in hockets is the one which begins to have rests first, and the second is the one that begins to have rests after it. The duplum is the part which has minute rests with the tenor and which harmonizes with it sometimes at the fifth and sometimes at the octave, an effect which relies greatly upon the good accuracy of the performer. Anyone who wishes to compose these kinds of music should first lay out or compose the tenor and assign it both [rhythmic] mode and measure. The principal part must be formed first for it is with its help that the others are formed, just as Nature, when she forms animals, first makes the principal members such as the heart, the liver, the brain; with the help of these others are formed afterwards. I say 'lay out' because in motets and organum the tenor is derived from an old melody and is pre-composed, but it is given further definition with mode and correct measure by the composer. I say 'compose', because in *conducti* the tenor is created entire; it is modified, and its extent is set, according to the wish of the composer.

pp. 146–8 Tenore autem composito vel ordinato debet supra eum motetum componere vel ordinare qui ut plurimum cum tenore in diapente proportione resonat et propter sui harmoniam aliquoties ascendit vel descendit. Sed ulterius debet istis triplum superaddi quod cum tenore ut plurimum debet in diapason proportione resonare et propter sui harmoniam potest in locis mediis sistere vel usque ad diapente aliquoties descendere. Et quamquam ex istis tribus consonantia perficiatur potest tamen eis aliquoties decenter addi quadruplum quod cum alii cantus descendent vel ascendent ordinate vel abscisionem facient vel pausabunt consonantiam resonabit. In componendo vero organum modorum alternationem quam plurimum faciunt sed in compondendo motellos et alia modorum unitatem magis servant. Et cum in motellis plura sint dictamina, si unum syllabis vel dictionibus aliud excedat potes eum per appositionem brevium et semibrevium alteri coaequare. Volens autem hoquetum ex duobus, puta primo et secundo, componere,

---

[86] So both MSS. Rohloff: *Duplum vero est [cantus]*
[87] So both MSS. Rohloff: *qui [supra] tenorem*
[88] So both MSS. Rohloff: *totaliter [de novo] fit*

debet cantum vel cantilenam supra quod fit hoquetus partiri et unicuique partem distribuere. Et potest aliquantulum rectus cantus exire cum decenti additione nisi quod eius mensuram observet. Sic enim unus iacet super alium ad modum tegularum et cooperturae domus et sic continua abscisio fiet. Volens ultimo duplum componere debet minutam abscisionem supra tenorem facere et aliquoties consonare.

Once the tenor has been composed or laid out, the motetus must be composed or laid out upon it, sounding with the tenor in the interval of a fifth as often as possible; for the sake of euphony it sometimes ascends or descends. The triplum must be further added to these, and it should sound with the tenor as often as possible in the proportion of an octave, and for the sake of euphony it may stand in medial positions or sometimes descend to the fifth. And even though complete harmony can be made from these three parts, a quadruplum may sometimes be fittingly added to them so that, when the other parts descend or ascend in an ordered fashion, or have a momentary rest or pause, [the quadruplum] will produce consonance. In composing organum [duplum, composers] produce as much variation of [rhythmic] mode as possible, but in composing motets and other genres they chiefly preserve unity [of mode]. And since there are several poems in motets, if one exceeds the other in syllables or words you can make it equal the other by the juxtaposition of breves and semibreves. He who wishes to compose a hocket in two parts, that is to say with a *primus* and *secundus*, must divide the *cantus* or *cantilena* upon which the hocket is to be made and distribute it among the two parts. And the true melody may proceed with a degree of appropriate ornamentation, unless it must keep to the measure of the original tune.[89] Thus, one part lies upon the other in the manner of tiles[90] and the covering of a house and thus continuous hocketing may be accomplished. He who wishes to add a duplum to this must make a minute 'cutting' upon the tenor and make it accord somewhat.
[Grocheio now introduces his section on plainchant, from which the following excerpts are taken, the selection being restricted to those that confirm or elucidate matters relating to secular forms.]

p. 160 Cantus autem iste [i.e. antiphona] post psalmos decantatur et aliquoties neupma additur puta post psalmos evangelistas. Est autem neupma quasi cauda vel exitus sequens antiphonam quamadmodum in viella post cantum coronatum vel stantipedem exitus quem *modum* viellatores appellant.

This kind of chant [i.e. an antiphon] is sung after the psalms, and sometimes a

---

[89] This passage, a difficult one, presumably means that when a melody is split up between different voices to make a hocket, it can be ornamented and added to in various ways, unless it is important for some reason that the hocketed version of the melody should last exactly the same amount of time as the original.

[90] Rohloff's emendation of *regularum* (in both MSS) to *tegularum* ('of tiles') can surely be accepted and is accordingly followed here.

neuma is added – as after the evangelistic psalms. A *neuma* is a kind of tail or postlude following the antiphon, comparable to the postlude which is performed on the *viella* after the *cantus coronatus*, or *stantipes*, which fiddlers call a *modus*.

p. 162 Isti autem cantus [i.e. *Gloria in excelsis deo* et *Kyrie eleison*] cantantur tractim et ex longis et perfectis ad modum cantus coronati ut corda audientium ad devote orandum promoveantur et ad devote audiendum orationem quam immediate dicit sacerdos vel ad hoc ordinatus.

These chants [i.e. *Gloria in excelsis deo* and *Kyrie eleison*] are sung slowly and from perfect longs in the manner of a *cantus coronatus*, so that the hearts of those who listen may be moved to devout prayer and to devoutly hear the prayer which the priest, or the one deputed to the task, says immediately afterwards.

p. 164 Responsorium autem et alleluia decantantur ad modum stantipedis vel cantus coronati, ut devotionem et humilitatem in cordibus auditorum imponant. Sed sequentia cantatur ad modum ductiae. ...Offertorium...cantatur ad modum ductiae vel cantus coronati ut corda fidelium excitet ad devote offerendum.

The responsory and alleluia are sung in the manner of a *stantipes* or of a *cantus coronatus* so that they may bring devotion and humility to the hearts of those who hear them. The sequence, however, is sung in the manner of a *ductia*. ...The offertory...is sung in the manner of a *ductia* or of a *cantus coronatus* so that it may inspire the hearts of the faithful to make their offerings devoutly.

[9]

Genre as a Determinant of Melody in the Songs of the Troubadours and the Trouvères

ELIZABETH AUBREY

As musicologists are fond of pointing out, the songs of the troubadours and the trouvères are not merely poems but must be accompanied by their melodies. One of the most often cited "proofs" of this is found in a *cobla* by Bertran Carbonel:

> Cobla ses so es enaissi
> co·l molis que aigua non a;
> per que fai mal qui cobla fa
> si son non li don' atressi;
> c'om non a gaug pas del moli,
> mas per la moutura que·n tra.[1]

> A *cobla* without a melody
> is like a mill that has no water;
> therefore, he who composes a *cobla* does badly
> if he doesn't give it a melody too;
> for one has no pleasure from the mill itself,
> but from the meal that one gets out of it.

The image evoked here implies that a poem is set in operation and driven by its melody—that both its meaning and its delivery are energized by the music. Because music is an aural phenomenon, the act of singing was central to the realization of the lyric songs. But we might wonder whether the poet-composers themselves consciously strove for what scholars sometimes refer to as a "wedding" between poem and melody, and if so, in what way.

Scholars have sought answers to this question in a variety of places, including the relation between the structures of poems and melodies, the possible connection of musical rhythm to text scansion, and overt melodic depiction of the meaning of words.

As for the last, it must be pointed out that a quest for musical text-painting in its more obvious form is difficult and perhaps unwise, because particular notes and particular words were not necessarily inseparable. The manuscript sources evince this, in that most melodies are transmitted with pitch variants of anywhere from one or two notes to entire phrases; this means that whatever composers might have intended, by the time songs were written down the notes easily could have shifted. Furthermore, in a strophic song the same series of pitches was used over and over for several different strophes, matching new words up with the notes each time. And the practice of borrowing a melody for different poems—creating what we call musical contrafacta—is attested both by surviving examples and by the sanction of contemporary theorists; in addition, sometimes a single poem was given more than one musical setting.

But if pitches and words are not necessarily inextricably linked in a song, surely the formal structures are interrelated. At least the number of syllables in the poem must be matched by an equal number of notes or note groups in each verse (although some manuscripts are not as careful about this as others). But beyond the syllable count, as musicologists have long been aware, structural correspondence between poem and melody does not always include an accord between the poetic rhymes and the musical cadences, nor do musical or textual repetition necessarily mirror one another.[2] Except for certain nonstrophic types, melodic structure in vernacular lyric does not become fixed until the late thirteenth century, with the rise of such genres as the rondeau and the virelai, in which the genre itself is defined by the interconnection of poetic and musical form. For the troubadours and the trouvères, however, poetic form and musical form were not necessarily intimately linked.

Some poetic and musical theorists of the twelfth and thirteenth centuries commented on the relationship between poem and melody, and their discussions suggest that composers conceived this relationship within the scholastic tradition of grammar and rhetoric. Specifically, the form, material, and oral delivery of both text and tune are interrelated with the song's genre, which itself is defined by its subject matter. Poetic theorists discussed not only the themes of various types of poems but also their structural building blocks, including rhyme, verse, syllable count, and strophic interrelationships.[3] They also sometimes alluded to how songs were delivered

GENRE AS A DETERMINANT OF MELODY

by singers. Music theorists, on the other hand, rarely discussed the musical structure, style, or performance of courtly lyric.[4] In fact, the only medieval treatise on music that included an extensive discussion of secular monophony at all was produced by a late thirteenth-century Parisian, Johannes de Grocheio.[5] One section of Grocheio's tract, quite familiar to musicologists, presents a complex and confusing classification system for secular monophony (*musica vulgaris*), including both vocal and instrumental pieces. Grocheio deals with poetic elements like verse and strophe structure, and discusses musical repetition schemes, cadences, and other formal ingredients. Numerous scholars have studied this passage in detail; let it suffice here to say that his descriptions of the various forms of secular music are neither altogether lucid in themselves nor easily accommodated to the structures of surviving pieces.[6]

But verse, rhyme, and strophe structure, and their musical counterparts, which by Grocheio's day were well on their way to becoming central elements in defining secular song, were not necessarily Grocheio's only—or even chief—concern. Music theorists of the thirteenth century barely acknowledged even the existence of secular music, devoting their attention rather to plainchant and to the polyphony that grew out of it. Grocheio was the first to include vernacular song in his typology, and in so doing he evidently felt it necessary to demonstrate its value and justify its existence. His descriptions of secular songs, as might be expected, call on concepts from the arts of poetry and prose, but they are cast in the language of Aristotelian thought; the resulting passages constitute a subtle and sophisticated synthesis between the specific art of rhetoric and the philosophy that underlay all scholastic thought. How a work is composed, according to the arts of poetry and prose, is determined by subject matter, speaker, audience, purpose, and mode of delivery.[7] Grocheio asserts that different types of French songs, which he calls *cantus* and *cantilena* (structurally distinguished, he says, mainly by the presence of a refrain in the latter), are set apart by differences in these rhetorical characteristics.[8] For instance, in his description of the *cantus coronatus*, the noblest lyric song in his typology, Grocheio invokes the rhetorical ideas of invention, style, structure, and performance. But the conceptual framework of his argument is Aristotelian:

> Cantus coronatus ab aliquibus simplex conductus dictus est, qui propter eius bonitatem in dictamine et cantu a magistris et studentibus circa sonos coronatur..., qui etiam a regibus et nobilibus solet componi et etiam coram regibus et principibus terre decantari, ut eorum animos ad audaciam et fortitudinem, magnanimitatem et liberalitatem commoveat, quae omnia faciunt ad bonum regimen. Est enim cantus iste de delectabili

materia et ardua, sicut de amicitia et caritate, et ex omnibus longis et perfectis efficitur.[9]

Cantus coronatus has been called by some a simple conductus, which on account of the goodness of its words and music is celebrated [wreathed] for its sounds [notes?] by masters and students . . . , which usually is composed by kings and nobles, and is sung in the court of kings and princes of the land, in order to move their spirits to boldness and courage, magnanimity and liberality, which all make for a good government. For this sort of *cantus* concerns delightful and difficult material, like friendship and charity, and is made from all sorts of longs, even perfect [ones].

These words explain a *cantus coronatus* as a product of the art of rhetoric, in which a song is judged by the social status of audience and speaker ("sung in the courts of kings and princes"), elegance of language and subject matter ("delightful and difficult matter"), and formal coherence ("made from all sorts of longs"). But Grocheio establishes the authority of his treatment of such vernacular songs by suggesting the four causes: *cantus coronatus* "concerns delightful and difficult matter" (material cause), "is made from all sorts of longs" (formal cause), and "is composed by kings and nobility" (efficient cause), "in order to move their spirits to boldness" and so forth (final cause).[10]

Further on, Grocheio insists that the rhetorical properties in the poem are determinants of an appropriate melody, and that a melody that works for one type of text is not suitable for another. In a well-known passage, he refers to how the text and melody of any *cantus* or *cantilena* are composed:

Modus autem componendi haec generaliter est unus, quemadmodum in natura. Primo enim dictamina loco materiae praeparantur, postea vero cantus unicuique dictamini proportionalis loco formae introducitur. Dico autem *unicuique proportionalis,* quia alium cantum habet cantus gestualis et coronatus et versiculatus, ut eorum descriptiones aliae sunt, quemadmodum superius dicebatur. De formis igitur musicalibus, quae in voce humana exercentur, haec dicta sint.[11]

But the manner of composing these generally is one and the same, in the manner of (their) nature. For first the texts are prepared in the place of matter, but after this, the melody is introduced in the place of form in proportion to whatever text. But I say "in proportion to whatever (text)" because chanson de geste, or *cantus coronatus,* or *cantus versiculatus* (each) has a different (type of) melody, as their descriptions differ, in the manner that was said above. So then let these things be said concerning musical forms that are performed by the human voice.

This passage clearly says that the composer prepares the poem first, and then the tune. But its Aristotelian language does not suggest that the mu-

GENRE AS A DETERMINANT OF MELODY

sic is invented merely to serve as a vehicle for the poem,[12] rather something more fundamental. "Form" and "material" together comprise a song's substance, or its "being." Grocheio is saying that the particular thing called a *cantus* or a *cantilena* consists of a complex of text and melody—*dictamen* and *cantus*. The text occupies the place called matter, and the music, the place called form. In Aristotelian thinking, form (here the music) has no existence apart from matter (here the text); and matter (the text) is given shape by form (the music). Matter represents the potentiality of a thing, form its actuality, so a poem is potentially a song, while a sung text is actually the song. Aristotle's matter is indeterminate and limitless, requiring form to limit and define it.[13] In other words, music and text in a secular song together constitute its substance, and neither element alone constitutes a song, just as neither body nor soul alone, but both together, comprise a living being.

The concepts of "material" and "form," synchronic in an Aristotelian explanation of substance, play a crucial role also in the medieval art of rhetoric, where they have a diachronic meaning. The first step in the creation of a literary work is *inventio,* in which the material, or the idea or theme, is created. The material is given order (arrangement) in the next step, *dispositio,* and then the actual words are put together—given form and expression—in the process of *elocutio,* or style.[14] Working within the context of the Aristotelian intellectual system, Grocheio calls on the art of rhetoric to account for the various traits of secular songs.

The art of rhetoric is concerned with communication: the intent of the rhetor is to persuade the audience. In a secular song, two essential elements, the text and the music, together are the vehicle for this communication. Both text and melody appeal to the emotions: the text through verbal language, the melody through sung notes. When Grocheio speaks of a song's *dictamen,* he assumes that the theme or content (*materia*) of the song already exists as a *locus,*[15] and that the words expressing this material need but be prepared. When he speaks of the song's melody (*cantus*), he speaks of something that already exists in the *locus* of shape (*forma*), which then is introduced into the song. What gives a song form, according to Grocheio, is its audible delivery (*pronuntiatio,* as the art of rhetoric would put it) or its actuality (in Aristotelian terms), and this occurs only through music.

In short, Grocheio seems to be saying that a text and its melody are inseparable in that they arise from the same process of conception, and that the song itself does not exist except as a combination of both text and melody. A melody of a *cantus* or a *cantilena,* without its text, has no meaning; and a text, without music, has no form.[16] Furthermore, Grocheio indicates that the same rhetorical demands that dictate the composer's decisions about a poem's structure, language, and function also guide his or her musical choices, and that these decisions are circumscribed by what type of song it is. In other words, the melody, like the text, is dependent upon the song's genre.

Grocheio was a northern music theorist writing at the end of the thirteenth century. Trained in Aristotelian logic, he appears to have been familiar also with teachings on medieval grammar and rhetoric.[17] Many passages in his treatise resonate with certain passages in the grammatical and rhetorical treatises on Occitan language and literature of the late twelfth through the mid-fourteenth centuries, which mention music in a variety of contexts.[18] One of the earliest of these treatises, Raimon Vidal's *Razos de trobar*,[19] written around the turn of the thirteenth century, begins with some observations about the social classes occupied by audiences and performers of troubadour songs, the topics addressed, and circumstances of their performance; while the account is a bit hyperbolic, its language is similar to that found in Grocheio's discussion of secular music:

> Totas genz cristianas, iusieuas et sarazinas, emperador, princeps, rei, duc, conte, vesconte, contor, valvasor, clergue, borgues, vilans, paucs et granz, meton totz iorns lor entendiment en trobar et en chantar, o q'en volon trobar o q'en volon entendre o q'en volon dire o q'en volon auzir; qe greu seres en loc negun tan privat ni tant sol, pos gens i a paucas o moutas, qe ades non auias cantar un o autre o tot ensems, qe neis li pastor de la montagna lo maior sollatz qe ill aiant an de chantar.[20]

> All people, Christian, Jewish and Saracen, emperors, princes, kings, dukes, counts, viscounts, lesser nobles, vavasors, clerics, bourgeois, and peasants, small and great, daily give their minds to verse-making and singing, whether they want to invent or listen, speak or hear; for you can scarcely be in a place so isolated or solitary, as long as there are a few people or many, that you will not hear one person sing, or another, or all together; even the shepherds in the mountains know of no greater joy than song.

Raimon later enjoins the poet to choose his theme carefully, and he implies that a song is defined—or constrained—by its theme or subject matter. This appears to be one of the earliest attempts to systematize a taxonomy of songs that relies mainly on subject matter.[21] Raimon offers a typical observation about the composition of a poem in accordance with an appropriate and unified theme (*razo*, Latin *ratio*) throughout:

GENRE AS A DETERMINANT OF MELODY

> Per aqi mezeis deu gardar, si vol far un cantar o un romans, qe diga rasons et paraulas continuadas et proprias et avinenz, et qe sos cantars o sos romans non sion de paraulas biaisas ni de doas parladuras ni de razons mal continuadas ni mal seguidas.[22]

> In the same way he should take care, if he wants to make a song or a narrative [*roman*], to say themes and words [that are] sustained and proper and pleasing, and that his song or narrative not be of unsuitable words or of two [different] languages or of themes [that are] poorly sustained or poorly followed up.

While Raimon does not make a connection between a theme and a specific genre, later authors do. The Catalan theorist Jofre de Foixà, writing his *Regles de trobar* about 1290, echoes Raimon and asserts that the "rayso" is important in the concept of genre:

> Rayso deu hom guardar per ço cor la mellor causa que ha mester totz cantars es que la rasos sia bona e que hom la vage continuan, ço es a entendre que de aquella rayso que començara son cantar, perfassa lo mig e la fi. Car si tu comences a far un sirventesch de fayt de guerra o de reprendimen o de lausors, no·s conve que·y mescles raho d'amor; o si faç cançoo dança d'amor, no·s tayn que·y mescles fayt d'armes ne maldit de gens, si donchs per semblances no o podiets aportar a raho.[23]

> One should take care with the theme, for the most important thing that all songs require is that the theme be good and that one continue with it, so it is understood that one will complete the middle and the end with the same theme that begins the song. For if you begin making a *sirventes* about deeds of war or about reproof or about praise, it is not appropriate to mix in a theme of love; or if you make a *canso* or a *dansa* about love, it is not appropriate to mix in deeds of arms or slander of people, if you cannot bring it back suitably to the theme.

As Occitan treatises on poetry began to address the differences among genres, they also began to include music in their discussions, characterizing the type of melody that is appropriate to each genre. Among the detailed descriptions of poetic genres in the anonymous *Doctrina de compondre dictats*,[24] written in the late thirteenth century, are found what appear to be the first prescriptions by a poetic theorist concerning the melodies of troubadour songs. The author suggests that certain standards of propriety attend different genres, especially whether or not it is acceptable to use a preexisting tune for a particular type of song. His statements imply that the character of a song's melody is in some way connected with the poem's genre, which is defined by its theme or subject matter.

The melody of a *canso*, reflecting the love theme that eschews anything evil, should be "as beautiful" as possible, and both *canso* and *vers* should have newly composed melodies:

> E primerament deus saber que canço deu parlar d'amor plazenment, e potz metre en ton parlar eximpli d'altra rayso, e ses mal dir e ses lauzor de re sino d'amor. Encara mes, deus saber que canço ha obs e deu haver cinch cobles; eyxamen n'i potz far, per abeylimen e per complimen de raho, .vj. o .vij. o .viij. o .ix., d'aquell compte que mes te placia. E potz hi far una tornada o dues, qual te vulles. E garda be que, en axi com començaras la raho en amor, que en aquella manera matexa la fins be e la seguesques. E dona li so noveyl co pus bell poras.
>
> Si vols far vers, deus parlar de veritatz, de exemples e de proverbis o de lauzor, no pas en semblant d'amor; e que en axi com començaras, ho prosseguesques e·u fins, ab so novell tota vegada. E aquesta es la differencia que es entre canço e vers, que la una rayso no es semblant de l'altra. E cert aytantes cobles se cove de far al vers com a la canço, e aytantes tornades.[25]

And first you should know that a *canso* must speak pleasingly of love, and you can put in your poem examples of other themes, but without slander or praise of anything but love. Furthermore you should know that a *canso* needs and must have five stanzas; but all the same you can make six or seven or eight or nine, to adorn and perfect the theme, whatever number pleases you best. And you can give it one or two tornadas, whichever you wish. And take care that you continue and finish with the same theme with which you begin. And give it a new melody, as beautiful as you can.

If you want to make a *vers*, you must speak of truth, of examples and proverbs, or of praise, but not in the guise of love; and just as you begin, you should proceed to the end, to a new melody every time. And this is the difference between a *canso* and a *vers*, that the theme of one is not like the theme of the other. And certainly one must give as many stanzas to a *vers* as to a *canso*, and as many tornadas.

This suggests that just as the poet manipulates his language, syntax, rhyme patterns, and so forth, to achieve the most eloquent expression of the song's theme of love, the composer should manipulate musical features of style, perhaps including motives, intervallic structure, melodic texture, and so forth, to produce an effective expression of the same theme. These musical ingredients, which rhetoricians did not explain with the analytical precision that we might desire, are described here and in other places as being beautiful or pleasing. Such qualities could take many guises, judging from the broad range of style found in the extant melodies.[26] But this is not inconsistent with the astonishing variety that poets used to express the theme of love in words.

GENRE AS A DETERMINANT OF MELODY

Some passages of the *Doctrina,* however, hint broadly at certain elements of musical style or structure. For instance, the author says that the melody of the *lay* could be newly composed, in which case it should be pleasing, or it could be borrowed from a church piece or "another type":

> Si vols fer lays, deus parlar de Deu e de segle, o de eximpli o de proverbis, de lausors ses feyment d'amor, que sia axi plazent a Deu co al segle; e deus saber que·s deu far e dir ab contriccio tota via, e ab so novell e plazen, o de esgleya o d'autra manera. E sapies que·y ha mester aytantes cobles com en la canço, e aytantes tornades; e segueix la raho e la manera axi com eu t'ay dit.[27]

> If you wish to make a *lay,* you must speak of God or of the world, or of examples or proverbs, of praise without pretence of love, which thus would be as pleasing to God as to the world; and you should know that it must be done with contrition always, and with a new and pleasing melody, or one of the church or another type. And know that it needs as many stanzas as in the *canso,* and as many tornadas; and it follows the theme and manner as I have told you.

The suggestion that there is some affinity between the courtly *lay* and a certain type of church music is intriguing, because the double-cursus versicle form of the melodies of many vernacular *lais* is similar to that of the ecclesiastical sequence. A few Old French *lais,* in fact, actually borrow the melodies of sequences. In such songs, there is a closer structural interdependence between text and music than in strophic types, in that a new melody is required for each stanza since the stanzas do not share the same poetic structure. Two Occitan songs, the anonymous "Lai Markiol" and "Lai Non-par," have irregular repetition structures that are similar to those of late sequences; they also foreshadow the fourteenth-century French *lai* as it was standardized by Guillaume de Machaut, in that the poetic structure and the melody of the first stanza are repeated, with some variation, for the last stanza.[28] The subject matter of the four surviving Old Occitan *lays,* three of which survive with music,[29] is not didactic or religious, as this definition requires, but the themes of many Old French *lais* are.[30]

Many extant *descorts* also have a double-cursus poetic form, although the author of the *Doctrina* again does not specify that its stanzas should be so structured. There are two extant Occitan *descorts* that have been transmitted with melodies, one of which, "Qui la ve en ditz" by the late twelfth-century troubadour Aimeric de Peguilhan, survives in two manuscripts with two different melodies. One of these melodies does have a double-cursus musical form that is quite closely allied with its poetic structure, as does another Occitan *descort,* "Ses alegratge," by Guillem Augier Novella.[31]

The *Doctrina* includes a provocative statement about the style of a *descort* melody:

> Si vols far discort, deus parlar d'amor com a hom qui n'es desemparat e com a hom qui no pot haver plaser de sa dona e viu turmentatz. E que en lo cantar, lla hon lo so deuria muntar, que·l baxes; e fe lo contrari de tot l'altre cantar. E deu haver tres cobles e una o dues tornades e responedor. E potz metre un o dos motz mes en una cobla que en altra, per ço que mils sia discordant.[32]

> If you wish to make a *descort*, you must speak of love like a man who is distressed by it or a man who cannot have pleasure from his lady and lives in torment. And when this is sung, wherever the tune ought to rise, let it be low; and it does the opposite of all other songs. And it must have three stanzas and one or two tornadas and a refrain. And you can put one or two more words in one stanza than in another, to make it more discordant.

The text of a *descort* is supposed to speak of love's torment, reflecting the "disharmony" suggested by the genre's name.[33] This might explain the *Doctrina*'s instructions that "when this is sung, wherever the tune ought to rise, let it be low," implying that the contour of the melody, like its text, should develop in an unexpected or displeasing way. Whatever it means, the remark at least suggests that the *razo* of a *descort*, as well as its structure, produces a particular style of melody.[34]

In the *sirventes*, as is well known, structural imitation was a common practice. The theorist says that the troubadour could borrow the stanza and rhyme structure as well as the melody of another song, usually a *canso*, but that rare cases of newly composed melodies might occur:

> Si vols far sirventez, deus parlar de fayt d'armes, e senyalladament o de lausor de senyor o de maldit o de qualsque feyts qui novellament se tracten. E començaras ton cantar segons que usaran aquells dels quals ton serventez començaras; e per proverbis e per exemples poretz hi portar les naturaleses que fan, o ço de que fan a rependre o a lausar aquells dels quals ton serventez començaras. E sapies que·l potz fer d'aytantes cobles co la un d'aquestz cantars que·t he mostratz. E pot[z] lo far en qualque so te vulles; e specialment se fa en so novell, e maiorment en ço de cançó. E deus lo far d'aytantes cobles com sera lo cantar de que pendras lo so; e potz seguir las rimas contrasemblantz del cantar de que pendras lo so, o atressi lo potz far en altres rimes.[35]

> If you wish to make a *sirventes*, you must speak of feats of arms, and in particular either of praise of a lord or of calumny or of some deeds that have been talked about recently. And you will begin your song following the custom of those with whom your *sirventes* began [i.e., using customary titles]; and by proverbs and examples you can bring in the allegiances

GENRE AS A DETERMINANT OF MELODY 283

> they swore, or what they deserve to be reproved for or praised for, those about whom you will begin your *sirventes*. And know that you can give it as many stanzas as one of the other songs I discussed. And you can make it to whatever tune you wish, exceptionally a new melody, but usually that of a *canso*. And you must give it as many stanzas as there are in the song from which you take the melody; and you can follow the rhymes corresponding to the song from which you take the melody, or you can make it on other rhymes.

The theorist describes the appropriate *razo* of a *sirventes*, then says that the melody can be whatever the composer wishes, and that the number of stanzas must be, and the rhymes may be, those of the song from which the tune is borrowed. Here and a little later the author seems to place some weight on the integrity of the melody, whose essence remains intact along with the rhyme scheme:

> Serventetz es dit per ço serventetz per ço com se serveix e es sotsmes a aquell cantar de qui pren lo so e les rimes, e per ço cor deu parlar de senyors o de vassalls, blasman o castigan o lauzan o mostran, o de faytz d'armes o de guerra o de Deu o de ordenances o de novelletatz.[36]

> A *sirventes* is so called because it serves and is subordinated to the song from which it takes the melody and rhymes, and because it must speak of lords or of vassals, blaming or chastising or praising or accusing them, or of feats of arms or of war or of God or of laws or of recent events.

The structure of the new poem can be determined only after the model song—with its melody—is chosen, and evidently the structure of the melody retains its shape even after it is separated from the original poem and joined with a new one.[37] The *Doctrina*'s remarks about the *tenso* suggest the same thing: "Si vols far tenso, deus l'apondre en algun so qui haia bella nota, e potz seguir les rimes del cantar o no. E potz fer .iiije. o .vj. cobles o .viij., si·t vols" (If you want to make a *tenso*, you must join it to some melody that has beautiful notes, and you can follow the rhymes of the song, or not. And you can make four or six stanzas, or eight, if you wish).[38]

In one extant pair of *sirventes,* we can see how one troubadour devised a new poem for a borrowed melody, modifying the music's structure but retaining its essential elements. The Monge de Montaudon used the melody of a *sirventes* by Bertran de Born, "Rassa, tan creis e mont' e puoia" (P-C 80,37), for his own *sirventes* text, "Fort m'enoja, so auzes dire" (P-C 305,10). Both songs survive in BN fr. 22543, Bertran's on folio 6v, and the monk's on folio 40r with the rubric "el so de la Rassa." The stanzas of Bertran's song have eleven verses, but the monk omitted verses 5–6, to create a nine-verse stanza.[39] The melody thus must be truncated:

284

Bertran:	a	a	a	a	a	a	b	b	b	b	b	rhyme
	8'	8'	8'	8'	8'	8'	8	8	8	8	8	syllables
	A	B	C	D	C'	D'	B'	C"	E	F	E'	melody
Monk:	a	a	a	a			b	b	b	b	b	rhyme
	8'	8'	8'	8'			8	8	8	8	8	syllables
	A	B	C	D			B'	C'	E	F	E'	melody

The musical phrases of these verses in Bertran's melody are simply varied repeats of the music for verses 3–4.[40] The essential material of the melody thus remains intact in the monk's adaptation. The truncation makes perfect sense if we assume that the monk adopted the tune first, choosing to eliminate the two repeated musical phrases (C' and D'), and then abbreviated his stanza form accordingly. He used the rhyme scheme of Bertran's poem but not the same rhymes, merely dropping the a rhymes of verses 5–6. In this case, the borrowing appears to have been as carefully planned as the author of the *Doctrina* urges, and the new song is as coherent a marriage of poem and tune, at least structurally, as is the model. Of course, because BN fr. 22543 is the only musical source for either song, it cannot be ruled out that it was the scribe who was responsible for the melodic adaptation as it appears in that manuscript.

The *alba* and the *retroncha*, says the theorist, must have newly composed melodies:

> Si vols far alba, parla d'amor plazentment; e atressi [deus] lauzar la dona on vas o de que la faras. E bendi l'alba si acabes lo plazier per lo qual anaves a ta dona; e si no·l acabes, fes l'alba blasman la dona e l'alba on anaves. E potz hi fer aytantes cobles com te vulles, e deus hi fer so novell.[41]

> If you wish to make an *alba*, speak pleasantly of love; and also you must praise the lady to whom you go or about whom you compose it. And praise the dawn if you have won the pleasure for which you went to your lady; and if you did not win it, make the *alba* censuring the lady and the dawn when you went. And you can make it to as many stanzas as you wish, and you must give it a new melody.

> Si vols far retronxa, sapies que deus parlar d'amor, segons l'estament en que·n seras, sia plazen o cossiros; e no·y deus mesclar altra raho. E deus saber que deu haver quatre cobles, e so novell tota vegada. E deus saber que per ço ha nom retronxa car lo refray de cada una de les cobles deu esser totz us.[42]

> If you wish to make a *retroncha*, know that you must speak of love, according to the state in which you will be, whether pleasant or thoughtful; and you must not mix in another theme. And you should know that it must have four stanzas, and a new melody every time. And you should know

GENRE AS A DETERMINANT OF MELODY 285

that it is called *retroncha* because the refrain at the end of one of the stanzas must be used for all of them.

There are only three *retronchas* that survive with melodies, all by the late thirteenth-century poet Guiraut Riquier.[43] The extant examples have textual refrains consisting of the last two verses of each stanza, as required by the theorist's definition. The *Doctrina* does not require a musical refrain, nor do these three songs or the few extant French *rotrouenges* have one.[44]

The theorist remarks that a *pastora* melody can be new or borrowed:

> Si vols far pastora, deus parlar d'amor en aytal semblan com eu te ensenyaray, ço es a saber: si·t acostes a pastora e la vols saludar o enquerer o manar o corteiar, o de qual razo demanar o dar o parlar li vulles. E potz li metre altre nom de pastora, segons lo bestiar que guardara; e aquesta manera es clara assatz d'entendre. E potz li fer .vj. o .viij. cobles, e so novell o so estrayn ia passat.[45]

> If you wish to make a *pastora*, you must speak of love in the way I teach you, that is to say: if you meet a shepherdess and wish to greet her or woo or pursue or court her, or to ask or give or speak however you wish. And you can give it another name besides *pastora*, according to the animal that she keeps; and this genre is understood clearly enough. And you can give it six or eight stanzas, and a new melody or a borrowed melody that is no longer current.

The subject matter of a *pastorela*, vividly described here, obviously concerns the peasant class. But the song is still a courtly genre, and these songs entertained the upper classes as much as a *canso* did. If my translation of the phrase "ia passat" in the last sentence is correct, it might imply using a popular or folk melody that used to be widely sung. Using such a tune might have been heard as a conceit that added a flavor of the low class, even while staying within the courtly idiom.[46]

The *dansa*, on the other hand, according to the author of the *Doctrina*, requires a newly composed melody:

> Si vols far dança, deus parlar d'amor be e plasentment, en qualque estament ne sies. E deus li fer dedents .iij. cobles e no pus, e respost, una o dues tornades, qual te vulles; totes vegades so novell. E potz fer, si·t vols, totes les fins de les cobles en refrayn semblan. E aquella raho de que la començaras deu[s] continuar e be servar al començament, al mig, e a la fi.[47]

> If you wish to make a *dansa*, you must speak of love well and pleasantly, in whatever state you may be. And you must make it in three stanzas and no more, and a refrain and one or two tornadas, as you wish; every time [it has] a new melody. And you can, if you wish, make all the ends of the

stanzas on a similar refrain. And whatever theme with which you begin, you must continue and make serve well for the beginning, the middle, and the end.

But the melody of a *planh* may be borrowed:

> Si vols fer plant, d'amor o de tristor deus la raho continuar; e pot[z] lo fer en qual so te vulles, salvant de dança. E atressi potz lo fer d'aytantes cobles con la [un] dels damunt dits cantars, e en contrasembles o en dessemblants. E no·y deus mesclar altra raho sino plahien, si per comp[ar]acio no·y ho podies portar.[48]

> If you wish to make a *planh*, you must sustain the theme on love or on sorrow; and you can make it to any tune you wish, except that of a *dansa*. And likewise you can make it with as many stanzas as one of the other songs discussed above, corresponding or not [i.e., with the same or different rhymes]. And you must not mix in another theme besides mourning, unless you can introduce it through a comparison.

The author draws attention to the marked thematic difference between the two types by saying that a *planh* can use a melody borrowed from any kind of song except a *dansa*.[49] The mournful sentiment of the text of a *planh*, this suggests, would be ill served by a *dansa* melody. Only two Occitan *planhs* survive with music; both are somewhat melismatic, and both use a scale based on D, with its characteristic minor third.[50] The more famous of these, the lament by Gaucelm Faidit on the death of Richard Cœur de Lion, survives in four Occitan versions. The fact that its melody was borrowed for an Old French *plaint* text, "E, serventois, arriere t'en revas,"[51] might mean that the French poem's ascribed author, Alart de Chans, heard something in Gaucelm's music that struck him as being appropriate for his own lament.

The *dansa* consists of three stanzas plus a refrain, and one or two tornadas.[52] Any mandatory structural relationship between poem and music is not evident from this passage, nor do the four extant Occitan *dansa* melodies survive in a state that unequivocally elucidates their form.[53] Three of them survive with only one stanza, so whether or not there is a textual refrain cannot be determined. Their melodies, though, have a ternary structure, the first and last verses or pairs of verses being identical (giving an overall musical form of ABA); this feature has prompted some to regard them as early virelai types.[54] Moreover, in the stanzas of the songs that survive, the poetic rhyme schemes and the musical structures are closely parallel, just as they are in double-cursus *descorts* and *lais*. The *estampida* is similar to the *dansa* in that neither should have a borrowed melody, suggesting that their characters are quite distinct from those of the graver types—*canso, vers, retroncha, alba, tenso:* "Si vols far estampida, potz parlar de qualque fayt vulles, blasman o lauzan o merceyan, qui·t vulles; e deu haver .iiije. cobles e responedor e una o dues tornades, e so novell" (If you wish to make an *estampida,* you can speak of whatever matter you wish, blaming or praising or supplicating; and it must have four stanzas and a refrain and one or two tornadas, and a new melody).[55]

The *dansa* and the *estampida* are courtly types in theme, style, and structure, but their composition seems to have depended to some degree also on how they were to be performed, which according to the author of the *Doctrina* was as important to their identity as a punctiliously arranged structure and a coherent *razo*. He makes it clear, for example, that musical instruments played some role in the performance of a *dansa:* "Dansa es dita per ço com naturalment la ditz hom danca[n] o bayllan, cor deu [haver] so plazent; e la ditz hom ab esturmens, e plau a cascus que la diga e la escout" (A *dansa* is so called, naturally, because one performs it while dancing or leaping, so that it must [have] a pleasant melody; and one performs it with instruments, and it delights everyone who performs and hears it).[56] He also sets apart the *estampida* by its manner of performance: "Stampida es dita per ço stampida cor pren vigoria en contan o en xantan pus que null autra cantar" (An *estampida* is so called because it takes vigor in singing,[57] more than any other song).[58] The single surviving Occitan *estampida* with music, "Kalenda maia," by the late twelfth-century troubadour Raimbaut de Vaqueiras (P-C 392,9), was created about a hundred years before the *Doctrina*'s definition appeared. If we can believe an early fourteenth-century anecdote about the origins of "Kalenda maia," its melody preceded its Occitan poem. According to this famous *razo,* Raimbaut heard two French fiddlers playing the tune, to which the troubadour afterwards provided a text.[59]

Other twelfth-, thirteenth-, and early fourteenth-century texts, from north and south, associate the *estampie* with instruments.[60] Both the fourteenth-century *Leys d'amors* and Johannes de Grocheio refer to two types of *estampies,* one a vocal *cantilena* and the other an instrumental type.[61] Grocheio's description of the instrumental *stantipes* refers to the double-cursus structure, and indeed all of the surviving thirteenth-century untexted French *estampies* and the later fourteenth-century untexted Italian *istanpitte* have this paired form.[62] But no theorist to my knowledge explicitly says that the vocal *estampie* has this same structure. Grocheio and the *Doctrina,* in fact, both say rather that the poem has a refrain, and the latter says it should have four stanzas.[63] "Kalenda maia," however, has neither a textual nor a musical refrain; moreover, its text and melody do have the double-cursus structure that Grocheio calls for in the instrumental type.[64] In fact, very few vocal *estampies* in any language survive (nineteen in French and seven in Occitan), none of which has a verse refrain, although some have a word refrain. Five of the seven Occitan *estampidas,* including "Kalenda maia," have a double-cursus poetic structure, achieved by pairing groups of from two to six verses. The remaining two Occitan *estampidas* begin with paired groups of verses but conclude with several unpaired verses. The French vocal *estampies* tend not to have a regular double-cursus structure.

The instrumental *estampie* may have migrated from the north to the south during the late twelfth century.[65] The audibly repetitive musical form engaged the fancy of some meridional composers who apparently devised poems to match the music's structure. The anecdote about "Kalenda maia" is in this sense quite believable. The author of the *Doctrina* (and probably later Guilhem Molinier, compiler of the *Leys d'amors*), aware of the existence of the *estampie,* quite possibly had never actually seen or heard one, but he dutifully included the type among his courtly genres, ascribing to it a courtly theme. He even offered instructions on its form, similar to his instructions for the other types. A clear relationship between the vocal *estampie* and the instrumental type remains elusive.[66]

These passages offer insight into how some theorists regarded the relationship between text and music in the songs of the troubadours and the trouvères, particularly as both were to be created within the context of the art of rhetoric. What is clear is that the interdependence between poem and tune is not so superficial as simply a relationship between rhyme scheme and musical phrase or between words and pitches, nor is it a monolithic concept that applies across all genres. The kinship between poem and melody is one of style, structure, sentiment, and delivery, as defined in the art of rhetoric. The melodies of the troubadours and the trouvères, by these accounts, served the same rhetorical purpose of expressing the song's theme—and hence its genre—that the poems did.

This hypothesis helps explain how a strophic poem that is essentially "through-composed" can be well served by a melody that is repeated five or six times in the delivery of the several stanzas. The words of a poem serve the larger rhetorical purpose of its author; each strophe, in fact, addresses the overall theme in some way, and the fact that different sources often disagree on the number of stanzas and their order suggests that there was not necessarily a diachronic constraint, but that each strophe has a certain thematic autonomy.[67] If the melody also serves the same rhetorical purpose, then its reiteration reinforces the theme. The poem's structure and theme remain the same in all stanzas, but its words change as they develop and unfold the subject matter to the listener. The melody's notes remain the same, but their impact on the listener changes as they carry forward each strophe's expression and shading of the theme.

A poem's effectiveness depends on an elegant arrangement of its matter; the cleverest rhyme scheme is mere pedantry without potent words artfully arranged to express the poem's theme. The music has its own expressive elements, such as rhythm and repetition patterns, motivic development, intervallic content, and texture. The song takes on audible form in its performance, bringing to fruition the rhetorical goal of moving the audience. Grocheio evidently believed this; for him a song was not an abstraction but came to life only when it was sung. In this sense, the songs of the troubadours and the trouvères embody the principles of the medieval art of rhetoric, and the music no less than the poem was an essential component in their realization.

NOTES

1. I am grateful to Elizabeth W. Poe for bringing this *cobla* to my attention and for this translation. The *cobla* is identified in Alfred Pillet and Henry Carstens, *Bibliographie der Troubadours* (Halle: Niemeyer, 1933; reprint, New York: Burt Franklin, 1968 [hereafter cited as P-C]), as item 82,33; for a recent edition see Martín de Riquer, ed., *Los trovadores: historia literaria y textos* (Barcelona: Planeta, 1975), vol. 3, no. 289. Gustave Reese quotes the first two verses of Bertran's *cobla* but attributes them mistakenly to Folquet de Marselha, in *Music in the Middle Ages* (New York: Norton, 1940), 205. See also Elizabeth Aubrey, "References to Music in Old Occitan Literature," *Acta Musicologica* 61 (1989): 112, n. 6.

2. See Theodore Karp, "Interrelationships between Poetic and Musical Form in Trouvère Song," in *A Musical Offering: Essays in Honor of Martin Bernstein*, ed. Edward H. Clinkscale and Claire Brook (New York: Pendragon, 1977), 137–61.

3. Important studies of the late medieval arts of poetry and prose, as disseminated by the theorists Matthieu de Vendôme, Jean de Garlande, Geoffroi de Vinsauf, Gervais de Melkley, Evrard l'Allemand, and others, include Douglas Kelly, *The Arts of Poetry and Prose* (Turnhout: Brepols, 1991); Edmond Faral, *Les arts poétiques du XIIe et du XIIIe siècle; recherches et documents sur la technique littéraire du Moyen Age* (Paris: Champion, 1924); Douglas Kelly, "The Scope of the Treatment of Composition in the Twelfth- and Thirteenth-Century Arts of Poetry," *Speculum* 41 (1966): 261–78; Kelly, "Theory of Composition in Medieval Narrative Poetry and Geoffrey of Vinsauf's *Poetria Nova*," *Mediaeval Studies* 31 (1969): 117–48; Kelly, *Medieval Imagination: Rhetoric and the Poetry of Courtly Love* (Madison: University of Wisconsin Press, 1978); and Linda M. Paterson, *Troubadours and Eloquence* (Oxford: Clarendon Press, 1975). See also John Stevens, *Words and Music in the Middle Ages: Song, Narrative, Dance and*

Drama, 1050–1350 (Cambridge: Cambridge University Press, 1986), and Jörn Gruber, *Die Dialektik des Trobar; Untersuchungen zur Struktur und Entwicklung des occitanischen und französischen Minnesangs des 12. Jahrhunderts* (Tübingen: Niemeyer, 1983).

4. The formal elements of a poem that limited musical borrowing, namely rhyme, verse, and strophe structure, are well known, thanks to the work of several scholars, especially Frank M. Chambers, "Imitation of Form in the Old Provençal Lyric," *Romance Philology* 6 (1952–53): 104–20; Friedrich Gennrich, "Internationale mittelalterliche Melodien," *Zeitschrift für Musikwissenschaft* 11 (1928–29): 259–96 and 321–48; Gennrich, *Der musikalische Nachlass der Troubadours,* Summa Musicae Medii Aevi, vols. 3, 4, 15 (Darmstadt: Friedrich Gennrich, 1958–65); Gennrich, *Die Kontrafaktur im Liedschaffen des Mittelalters,* Summa Musicae Medii Aevi, vol. 12 (Langen bei Frankfurt: Friedrich Gennrich, 1965); Hans Spanke, "Zur Formenkunst des ältesten Troubadours," *Studi medievali* n.s. 7 (1934): 72–84; and Spanke, *Untersuchungen über die Ursprünge des romanischen Minnesangs,* part 2: *Marcabrustudien,* Abhandlungen der Gesellschaft der Wissenschaften zu Göttingen, Philologische-historische Klasse, 3d series, no. 24 (Göttingen: Vandenhoek & Ruprecht, 1940).

5. Ernst Rohloff, ed., *Die Quellenhandschriften zum Musiktraktat des Johannes de Grocheio, im Faksimile herausgegeben nebst Übertragung des Textes und Übersetzung ins Deutsche, dazu Bericht, Literaturschau, Tabellen und Indices* (Leipzig: Deutscher Verlag für Musik, 1972 [hereafter cited as Rohloff, *Grocheio*]).

6. See the attempt by Timothy J. McGee to reconcile Grocheio with extant works, "Medieval Dances: Matching the Repertory with Grocheio's Descriptions," *Journal of Musicology* 7 (1989): 498–517. See also a new edition and translation of these passages by Christopher Page, "Johannes de Grocheio on Secular Music: A Corrected Text and a New Translation," *Plainsong and Medieval Music* 2 (1993): 17–41.

7. These elements are most fully described in Jean de Garlande's treatise of around 1220, ed. and trans. Traugott Lawler, *The Parisiana Poetria of Jean of Garland* (New Haven: Yale University Press, 1974). See especially the first chapter, entitled "De Inventione." Two articles by Margot E. Fassler show how Garlande's discussion relates to the development of the late medieval sequence: "The Role of the Parisian Sequence in the Evolution of Notre-Dame Polyphony," *Speculum* 62 (1987): 345–74, and "Accent, Meter, and Rhythm in Medieval Treatises 'De rithmis,'" *Journal of Musicology* 5 (1987): 164–90. On the possible identity of the grammarian Jean de Garlande with the famous music theorist known as Johannes de Garlandia, see William G. Waite, "Johannes de Garlandia, Poet and Musician," *Speculum* 35 (1960): 179–95.

8. See Rohloff, *Grocheio,* 130–31, paragraphs 107–21.

9. Ibid., 130, paragraphs 112–13. The phrase "circa sonos coronatur" has excited extensive commentary among musicologists. My interpretation takes the words at face value, which I believe makes this sentence most consistent with the thrust of the surrounding text. Page translates the last clause "and it is composed entirely from longs—perfect ones at that" (Page, "Grocheio," 24; see also his n. 29). The interpretation hinges in large part on the meaning of "et"—whether it means literally "and," implies an antithetical delimitation (as in Page's translation), or provides emphasis (as in my interpretation).

10. Compare Jean de Garlande's suggestion of how students ought to invent their subject matter (Lawler, *Garland,* 28–32, lines 515–20): "They should not overlook

the four principal causes—the efficient cause, and so on—of any subject proposed to them. Thus, suppose one of them is treating of his book. He might praise it or criticize it through the efficient cause, that is, through the writer; through the material cause, that is, through the parchment or the ink; through the formal cause, as through the layout of the book or the size of the letters; or through the final cause, by considering for what purpose the book was made, namely, that in it and through it the ignorant may be made more knowledgeable" (non pretermittentes causes principales quattuor, scilicet causam efficientem, cuiuslibet rei sibi proposite. Ut, si tractet de libro suo, commendet eum uel uituperet per causam efficientem, idest per scriptorem; per causam materialem, idest per pargamenum et incaustum; per causam formalem, ut per libri disposicionem et litterarum protractionem; per causam finalem, considerando ad quid factus est liber, ad hoc uidelicet ut in eo et per eum nescientes scientes reddantur). See also Rohloff, *Grocheio,* 132–34, paragraph 127b: "Now the verse in a *cantus coronatus* is what is effected out of many phrases and concordances that produce harmony with one another. But the number of verses in a *cantus coronatus* has been set at seven, because of the seven concords. Indeed this number of verses must contain all of the sense of the material, no more and no less" (Versus vero in cantu coronato est, qui ex pluribus punctis et concordantiis ad se invicem harmoniam facientibus efficitur. Numerus vero versuum in cantu coronato ratione septem concordantiarum determinatus est ad septem. Tot enim versus debent totam sententiam materiae, nec plus nec minus, continere).

11. Rohloff, *Grocheio,* 134, paragraphs 130–32.

12. Albert Seay's translation, for example, implies this interpretation: "First, the words are prepared on the level of the raw material, afterwards a melody on the level of the formed material is adapted to the text in an appropriate way" (Albert Seay, trans., *Johannes de Grocheo, Concerning Music (De Musica),* 2d ed. [Colorado Springs: Colorado College Music Press, 1973]: 18–19). See also Patricia Alice Mitchell DeWitt, "A New Perspective on Johannes de Grocheio's 'Ars Musicae'" (Ph.D. diss., University of Michigan, 1973), 43–54. Page has come to a similar conclusion about the Aristotelian framework in this passage ("Grocheio," 29, n. 49), although his less literal translation deemphasizes this framework. I am grateful to Professors Katherine Tachau in the Department of History of the University of Iowa and Scott MacDonald in the Department of Philosophy of Cornell University for their help in translating and interpreting these critical passages in Grocheio.

13. Compare a later passage on the form of instrumental pieces where Grocheio says, "Just as in a certain way the material of a natural thing is bound by the form of a natural thing, so sound [i.e., the natural material of music] is bound by phrases, that is by the artificial form given it by the craftsman" (Quemadmodum enim materia naturalis per formam naturalem determinatur, ita sonus determinatur per puncta et per formam artificialem ei ab artifice attributam) (Rohloff, *Grocheio,* 138, paragraph 147).

14. See James J. Murphy, *Rhetoric in the Middle Ages: A History of Rhetorical Theory from St. Augustine to the Renaissance* (Berkeley: University of California Press, 1974), for a thorough treatment of Ciceronian rhetoric as it was understood in the Middle Ages.

15. A *locus* in Ciceronian rhetoric is defined as "the region of an argument." See ibid., 16.

16. Grocheio devotes some attention to untexted melodies, saying that every good fiddle player can perform any type of music, including *cantus* and *cantilena* (Rohloff, *Grocheio*, 136, paragraphs 139–47). The "materia" of such pieces is defined, evidently, by the purpose (dancing) and the performance (with marked beats). He also asserts in this section that the human voice can perform an untexted piece.

17. See ibid., 124, paragraphs 81–82. Although it seems unlikely that rhetoric was a central part of the university curriculum in the thirteenth and early fourteenth centuries (see Murphy, *Rhetoric*, 89–132), Cicero's *De inventione* and the *Rhetorica ad Herennium* were widely known.

18. It cannot be demonstrated that Grocheio or the authors of the Old Occitan grammatical treatises knew one another's work. Grocheio, in fact, says he is describing music "according to how the men of Paris use it" (qua utuntur homines Parisiis) (Rohloff, *Grocheio*, 124, paragraphs 77–79), deliberately avoiding the claim that his discussion pertains to music in other "regions," "languages," or "idioms." This has cautioned scholars against applying his comments about musical types or structures to the melodies of Occitania, certainly a prudent course. However, the philosophical attitude in his treatise is neither controversial nor parochial, and the rhetoricians of the Midi no doubt were as well versed as he in Aristotelian philosophy.

19. J. H. Marshall, ed., *The "Razos de trobar" of Raimon Vidal and Associated Texts* (London: Oxford University Press, 1972 [hereafter cited as Marshall, *Raimon Vidal*]).

20. Ibid., 2, lines 20–27. I am grateful to William D. Paden for his expert help and advice in my translations from Old Occitan.

21. Important studies of lyric genres and their themes include Hans Robert Jauss, "Littérature médiévale et théorie des genres," *Poétique* 1 (1970): 79–101; Paul Zumthor, *Essai de poétique médiévale* (Paris: Seuil, 1972); and Pierre Bec, *La lyrique française au Moyen-Age (XIIe-XIIIe siècles); contribution à une typologie des genres poétiques médiévaux* (Paris: Picard, 1977–78). See also Frank M. Chambers, *An Introduction to Old Provençal Versification* (Philadelphia: American Philosophical Society, 1985), 191–279; and Elizabeth Aubrey, *The Music of the Troubadours* (Bloomington: Indiana University Press, 1996), 84–85.

22. Marshall, *Raimon Vidal*, 22, lines 451–54.

23. Ibid., 56–57, lines 30–37. That this *razo* is the same as rhetoric's *materia* is confirmed in an anonymous treatise of the mid-fourteenth-century, now in Barcelona, the so-called Ripoll treatise, which consistently uses the word *materia* to refer to the subject matter of the poem, e.g.: "La materia de les cancons es de amor o de lahor de dones" (The subject of the *canso* is love or the praise of ladies) (ibid., 101).

24. Marshall argues convincingly on stylistic grounds that this treatise might have been written by the same Jofre de Foixà who produced the *Regles de trobar;* see ibid., lxxv–lxxviii.

25. Ibid., 95, lines 7–21. See Stephen G. Nichols, Jr., "Toward an Aesthetic of the Provençal Canso," in *The Disciplines of Criticism*, ed. Peter Demetz and others (New Haven: Yale University Press, 1968): 349–74, on the poetic content of the *canso*.

26. For examples from the troubadour repertoire, see Aubrey, *Music*, 86–95.

27. Marshall, *Raimon Vidal*, 95, lines 22–27. See Richard Baum, "Les troubadours et les *lais*," *Zeitschrift für romanische Philologie* 85 (1969): 1–44, and Jean Maillard, *Evolution et esthétique du lai lyrique des origines à la fin du XIVe siècle* (Paris: Centre de Documentation Universitaire, 1963).

GENRE AS A DETERMINANT OF MELODY

28. Pierre Bec has argued that both of these melodies probably had northern origins (*Lyrique française*, 1:204–6).

29. They are listed in the index of P-C as 461,37; 461,122; and 461,124. See Elizabeth Aubrey, "Issues in the Musical Analysis of the Troubadour *Descorts* and *Lays*," in *The Cultural Milieu of the Troubadours and Trouvères*, ed. Nancy van Deusen (Ottawa, Canada: Institute of Medieval Music, 1994), 67–98; and Aubrey, *Music*, 106–9.

30. See Bec, *Lyrique française*, 1:197, 201.

31. The other tune for Aimeric's poem is through-composed. The two Occitan *descort* texts are listed in P-C as 10,45 and 205,5. There is some disagreement about what to call "Qui la ve en ditz." Unlike other *descorts*, it has three stanzas with the same rhyme scheme (albeit not the same rhymes), and the double-cursus version is, in fact, strophic. István Frank considered the song to be a *canso* (*Répertoire métrique de la poésie des troubadours* [Paris: Champion, 1953–57], item 528:1), while both P-C and Gennrich (*Der musikalische Nachlass*) label it a *descort*. Following Frank, Richard H. Hoppin omitted it from his count of *descorts* and *lais* (*Medieval Music* [New York: Norton, 1978], 276). I regard it here as a *descort* because of its poetic structure and because double-cursus structure does appear in one version of its melody. See Ismael Fernández de la Cuesta and Robert Lafont, eds., *Las cançons dels trobadors* ([Toulouse: Institut d'Estudis Occitans, 1979], 402 and 531) for transcriptions of the three *descort* melodies. See also Jean Maillard, "Structures mélodiques complexes au Moyen Age," in *Mélanges de langue et de littérature médiévales offerts à Pierre le Gentil*, ed. Jean Dufournet and Daniel Poirion (Paris: S.E.D.E.S., 1973): 523–39, on "Ses alegratge"; and Aubrey, *Music*, 105–8, on "Qui la ve en ditz."

32. Marshall, *Raimon Vidal*, 97, lines 81–86. The structural similarity between *descort* and *lai* has prompted many scholars to reason that there is no substantive difference between the two courtly genres. See Bec, who argues in *Lyrique française* that the term *descort* was peculiar mainly to the south and *lai* to the north, while the only real difference between them was a closer association in the south of the genre with the courtly *canso:* "La seule différence entre les deux genres—qui n'est pas structurale—est peut-être la plus grande indépendance typologique du lai français par rapport à la *canso;* alors que le *descort* occitan, pourtant conçu au départ comme une sorte de repoussoir formel de la *canso*, ne parvient pas à s'en émanciper" (1:199–206, quotation on 202).

33. Compare the *Donatz Proensals* of Uc Faidit (c. 1240), which includes the word in its rhyme lists with the Latin translation "discordia, vel cantilena habens sonos diversos" (J. H. Marshall, ed., *The "Donatz Proensals" of Uc Faidit* [Oxford: Oxford University Press, 1969], 230, line 2861). Richard Baum, in "Le *descort* ou l'anti-chanson," labels the *descort* the "anti-canso" (in *Mélanges de philologie romane dédiés à la mémoire de Jean Boutière*, ed. Irénée-Marcel Cluzel and François Pirot [Liège: Soledi, 1971], 75–98). Christopher Page argues on the strength of this that the *descort* "lies on the edge of the troubadour art" and "subverts the High Style manner as represented above all by the *canso*" (*Voices and Instruments of the Middle Ages: Instrumental Practice and Songs in France, 1100–1300* [Berkeley, University of California Press, 1986], 23). Pierre Bec, however, points out that only in its structure, but not in its theme, is the *descort* different from the courtly *canso:* "Sa thématique en effet, quoi qu'on en ait dit, est la même que celle de la *canso*, c'est-à-dire courtoise et amoureuse dans sa grande majorité.... C'est par sa discordance formelle avant tout que ce type

de poème se caractérise et qu'il représente à ce titre une *anti-canso*. Genre très élaboré et aristocratisant, il pourrait être avec quelque raison intégré au registre du 'grand chant courtois'" (*Lyrique française*, 1:196). See further Erich Köhler, "Deliberations on a Theory of the Genre of the Old Provençal *Descort*," in *Italian Literature: Roots and Branches, Essays in Honor of Thomas Goddard Bergin*, ed. Giose Rimanelli and Kenneth J. Atchity (New Haven: Yale University Press, 1976), 1–13.

34. Marshall (*Raimon Vidal*, 139–40, nn. 81–86) points out that no *descorts* were being composed by the late thirteenth century, which could account for the inexactitude of the theorists' descriptions. Jean Maillard, "Problèmes musicaux et littéraires du *descort*," should be consulted for a thorough discussion of the music and structures of Occitan and French *descorts* (in *Mélanges de linguistique et de littérature romanes à la mémoire d'István Frank* [(Saarbrücken): Universität des Saarlandes, 1957]: 388–409).

35. Marshall, *Raimon Vidal*, 95–96, lines 28–39. In fact, there are a number of extant *sirventes* melodies that lack surviving models, notably thirteen by the late thirteenth-century troubadour Guiraut Riquier.

36. Ibid., 97, lines 104–8.

37. See Aubrey, *Music*, 111–12.

38. Marshall, *Raimon Vidal*, lines 90–92.

39. The number of stanzas is not the same, at least in manuscript BN fr. 22543.

40. The music of both songs is given in Aubrey, *Music*, 112–17.

41. Marshall, *Raimon Vidal*, 96, lines 62–66. An example of an Occitan *alba* with its melody is found in Aubrey, *Music*, 102–5.

42. Marshall, *Raimon Vidal*, lines 40–44.

43. P-C 248,57; 248,65; and 248,78; see Aubrey, *Music*, 127–29. Pierre Bec contends that the Occitan *retroncha* was imported from the north, where it was known as the *rotrouenge* (*Lyrique française*, 1:48 and 185). He points out that it does not appear in the south before c. 1220.

44. See Marshall, *Raimon Vidal*, 137, nn. 40–44. Despite the absence of musical repetition in the extant examples, Gennrich argued that it was musical structure that distinguished a *rotrouenge* from other lyric types (*Die altfranzösische Rotrouenge: Literarhistorisch-musikwissenschaftliche Studien*, vol. 2 [Halle: Niemeyer, 1925], 1–14).

45. Marshall, *Raimon Vidal*, 96, lines 45–50.

46. The only extant Occitan *pastorela* melody, by Marcabru, is given in Aubrey, *Music*, 96–99.

47. Marshall, *Raimon Vidal*, 96, lines 51–56.

48. Ibid., lines 57–61.

49. Marshall (ibid., 138, nn. 58–60) refers to two cases of melodic borrowing, but he apparently means poetic modeling; the poems he mentions do not survive with melodies, so musical borrowing cannot be substantiated.

50. P-C 167,22 and 248,63. See Aubrey, *Music*, 96–102.

51. Listed as item 381 in Hans Spanke, ed., *G. Raynauds Bibliographie des altfranzösischen Liedes, erster Teil*, reprinted with discography and alphabetical index of songs by A. Bahat (Leiden: Brill, 1980).

52. An internal refrain consisting of the last verses of each stanza is optional. See Marshall, *Raimon Vidal*, 138, nn. 52–56.

GENRE AS A DETERMINANT OF MELODY

53. The songs are P-C 244,1a; 461,92; 461,196; and 461,230. See Page, *Voices and Instruments*, 24, 247, n. 22, and 43, example 8; and Aubrey, *Music*, 123–26.

54. Paul Meyer suggested that the Occitan *dansa* was the prototype of the northern virelai ("Des rapports de la poésie des trouvères avec celle des troubadours," *Romania* 19 [1890]: 21). Bec points out that the poetic structure of the *dansa* is more complex than that of the virelai. Its courtly theme and sophisticated structure cause Bec to place it, along with the *balada*, which has similar characteristics, in the "aristocratic register": "Il en est donc de même sans doute de la *dansa* que de la *balada*, genres qui se sont désolidarisés de leur possible origine popularisante et chorégraphique pour s'intégrer finalement (mais non sans quelque interférences) au registre du grand chant courtois" (*Lyrique française*, 1:239).

55. Marshall, *Raimon Vidal*, 97, lines 72–74.

56. Ibid., 98, lines 115–17.

57. See ibid., 141, nn. 124–25.

58. Ibid., lines 124–25.

59. See this *razo* in Jean Boutière and A. H. Schutz, eds., *Biographies des troubadours*, 2d ed., rev. Jean Boutière and Irénée-Marcel Cluzel (Paris: Nizet, 1964), 465–66.

60. See Bec, *Lyrique française*, 1:241–46.

61. Adolphe-F. Gatien-Arnoult, ed., *Las flors del gay saber, estiers dichas "Las leys d'amors,"* Monumens de la littérature romane, vols. 1–3 (Toulouse: J.-B. Paya, 1841–43), 1:350. Rohloff, *Grocheio*, 132, paragraph 120, and 136, paragraph 141.

62. See the edition of these pieces by Timothy J. McGee, *Medieval Instrumental Dances* (Bloomington: Indiana University Press, 1989).

63. In "Medieval Dances," Timothy J. McGee argues that the *Doctrina*'s "cobla" might be translated "couplet" instead of "stanza," which would make the description consistent with the paired-verse structure associated with the instrumental *estampie* (502–6). There are problems with this interpretation, however. In the first place, the author of the *Doctrina* uses the word "cobla" consistently throughout the entire passage on genres to mean "stanza," and nowhere else can it be taken instead to mean "couplet." Secondly, a *tornada* is usually at least two verses long, with the same structure as the final verses of the poem's stanzas. If the "coblas" in the *Doctrina*'s *estampida* are couplets and not stanzas, then the word *tornada* in the passage is meaningless.

64. Marshall suggests that the "responedor" mentioned in the *Doctrina* refers to some kind of musical rhyme at the ends of verses, as in the *descort* (*Raimon Vidal*, 139, nn. 72–74). But while most of the French and Italian instrumental pieces do have refrains concluding each musical section, the music for "Kalenda maia" only hints at musical rhyme. McGee attempts to explain the prescription for a refrain by suggesting "that there must have been a convention for selecting certain lines of each *estampie* to serve in that capacity," and that these lines would have been repeated in performance ("Medieval Dances," 503). Admitting that this is speculative, McGee goes on to demonstrate how it might have been done with "Kalenda maia." See also Lloyd Hibberd, "Estampie and Stantipes," *Speculum* 19 (1944): 222–49.

65. See Bec, *Lyrique française*, 1:243–44.

66. For further exploration of the differences between northern and southern

estampies, and between vocal and instrumental versions of the genre, see Elizabeth Aubrey, "The Dialectic between Occitania and France in the Thirteenth Century," *Early Music History* 16 (1997): 40–52.

67. Pierre Bec, among others, has pointed out that a lyric poem is more topical than narrative, so each strophe can express some aspect of the poem's theme (ibid., 1:21–2).

[10]

'La Grande Chanson Courtoise':
The Chansons of Adam de la Halle

JOHN STEVENS

FAR more attention has been given over the last century to the polyphonic compositions of Adam de la Halle and his plays than to his courtly chansons. Yet, if the number of surviving manuscripts is a guide, it was as a trouvère in the high courtly style, a courtly 'maker' in the tradition of *la grande chanson courtoise*, that his contemporaries chiefly valued him. His courtly chansons survive in eight main manuscripts and several lesser ones.[1] In the manuscript (Paris, Bibliothèque Nationale, fr 25566) containing his Collected Works, as it were, the chansons have pride of place and are notated in a different style from the polyphonic rondeaux and motets and from the monophonic *refrains* of the same manuscript. Their notation is the square, non-mensural notation analogous to that of contemporary Gregorian chant and traditional for vernacular monophonic song.[2]

My chief concern in this paper is a stylistic one. I shall not discuss notational problems at all but shall enquire into what may, broadly, be termed the aesthetic of Adam de la Halle's chansons. The rhythmic problem is indeed central and has proved peculiarly intractable. But a great deal can be said, and needs to be said, about the courtly chanson, whilst leaving the rhythmic problem open.[3] The musical analyses offered in the second section of this paper are not dependent on any one style of rhythmic interpretation. Nevertheless, one cannot present written evidence, let alone live performances, in a completely neutral style. The hypothesis, therefore, which I have adopted is the one normally called 'isosyllabic'.[4] That is to say, each syllable of the text and each note, or group of notes, corresponding to it is thought of as having an approximately equal value. I have chosen this isosyllabic, equal-unit style, not merely because I find it personally more satisfying and musical for the

---

[1] They are conveniently listed in J. H. Marshall's literary edition (*The Chansons of Adam de la Halle*, Manchester, 1971), using the familiar *sigla* of G. Raynaud, *Bibliographie des altfranzösischen Liedes*, rev. Hans Spanke, Leiden, 1955. I use Marshall's numbering of the chansons and Raynaud's *sigla*. The only modern musical editor of Adam's chansons, Nigel Wilkins (*The Lyric Works of Adam de la Hale* (Corpus mensurabilis musicae, xliv), American Institute of Musicology, 1967), uses an individual set of *sigla* and the numbering of *Oeuvres complètes du trouvère Adam de la Halle*, ed. E. de Coussemaker, Paris, 1872 (reprinted Farnborough, 1966). The texts quoted in this paper follow Marshall's edition, by kind permission.

[2] I discuss the diverse manifestations of this notation in a forthcoming article, 'The Manuscript Presentation and Notation of Adam de la Halle's Courtly Chansons', *Source Materials and the Interpretation of Music: a Memorial Volume to Thurston Dart*, ed. Ian Bent and Michael Tilmouth (in the press).

[3] W. Apel (*Gregorian Chant*, Bloomington, Indiana, 1958) adopts a similar policy without invalidating his analyses.

[4] The isosyllabic or 'isochronous' style of transcription is advocated for example in R. Monterosso, *Musica e ritmica dei trovatori*, Milan, 1956.

12 'LA GRANDE CHANSON COURTOISE': THE CHANSONS OF ADAM DE LA HALLE

'high courtly' style of song, but because it conforms more nearly, in my opinion, than any other to what we may call the historical aesthetic of the chanson as it can be reconstructed from a close consideration of the nature of the poems, from an analysis of the melodies in their agreed, not controversial, aspects, and from the remarks of the earliest vernacular theorists on the nature of courtly poetic metre.

What I am attempting to do, then, in brief is to see whether the artistic traditions and conventions which recent literary scholarship has so clearly brought to light can give us insight into the nature of the melodies, the way they were composed, and the intentions of poet and composer in relation to one another.

THE POEMS

'The poet has an over-riding concern with beauty. He is a maker of beautiful objects.' The quotation, from K. Foster's and P. Boyde's penetrating introduction to their edition of Dante's lyric poetry, perfectly introduces what needs to be said about the courtly poems of Adam de la Halle.[5] Whatever our interpretation of Adam's revue-like *Jeu de la feuillée* or his courtly-pastoral *Robin et Marion*, of his *Congé* (or 'farewell') or his unfinished epic, *Roi de Sezile*, the courtly chansons show Adam the craftsman, the maker of beautiful objects. To a casual reader the 36 poems seem for the most part extraordinarily the same. They all belong to the imagined, idealized world of *fine amours*, are spoken by a lover to his perennially inaccessible lady, and refer to his experiences at inordinate length. (Their place in the real world, incidentally, as *envois* to some of them show, was in the part-bourgeois, part-aristocratic society of Arras; and their natural habitat was the *puy*, or literary forum, of the town, presided over by the prince of the *puy*, in which chansons were performed, judged and sometimes 'crowned'.) The combination of the real and imagined worlds give us a clue, in fact, to the kind of objects they are. They are artefacts of an extraordinary, self-concious elegance and formal ingenuity whose professed subject is the courtly experience which sustained the aristocratic social code.[6]

It will be best to work from an example. 'Au repairier en la douce contrée' (No. 14)[7] must have been widely known and appreciated since it survives in nine versions, eight of them with music, and was twice imitated in form.[8]

---

[5] *Dante's Lyric Poetry*, Oxford, 1966, i, p. xvii.
[6] J. Huizinga, *The Waning of the Middle Ages*, London, 1924 (reprinted 1950), ch. 8: 'Love Formalized'.
[7] For the numbering system here adopted, see footnote 1.
[8] See Marshall, *The Chansons of Adam de la Halle*, p. 118n., and Raynaud-Spanke, *Bibliographie*, Nos. 514, 537. Italics indicate a conjectural stress-scheme. For a more detailed stress analysis see below, p. 17.

'LA GRANDE CHANSON COURTOISE': THE CHANSONS OF ADAM DE LA HALLE 13

I *Au* repair*ier* en la *douce* con*trée*
   U *jou* lais*sai* men *cuer* au *de*par*tir*
   Est ma *douce* do*l*ors renouve*l*ée
   Ki ne me *laist* de can*ter* plus te*nir.*
     Puis ke d'un *seul* souvenir
     *J*olis *es*tre ail*lors* so*l*oie,
     Por k*oy chi* ne *le* seroie
     Quant jou *senc* et *voi* ce*li*
       Ki moy *tient* joli?

II On *dist* ke *point* n'ai mani*ere* mu*ée*
   Pour le *re*v*iel* ki me *plaist* a si*ev*ir;
   Selonc sen *mal* et *selonc* sa pen*sée*
   Se doit amans deduire et *maintenir.*
     *Co*nment porr*oit cuers* sentir
     Si douc *mal* sans *es*tre en *joie?*
     Car du *pis* c'*A*mors en*voie*
     C'est c'on de*sire* mer*chi,*
       Et il *m'est* en*si.*

III Mais tant me *plaist* ceste *paine* et a*grée*
    Que *jou* le *prenc* a sa*veur* de goïr:
    On *prent* en *gre* le *cose* pres*en*t*ée*
    Selonc le *lieu* dont on le *voit* venir,
      Si *doi* en *gre* recuel*lir*
      Mon *mal,* car *miex* m'i en*ploie*
      Ke se *d'*autre a*més* es*toie,*
      N'onkes mais *nus* ne sen*ti*
        Mal si *c*ongoï*i.*

IV *Dame* gen*tix,* de *tout* le *mont* a*mée*
    Pour la bon*té* ki ne *puet* amenrir,
    Douce amour*euse* y*mage* desir*ée,*
    Wel*lié*-me en *vo service retenir.*
      Jou ne *quier autre* merir
      Ne deman*der* n'oseroie,
      K'encore a*v*is m'est que *soie*
      Trop *pau* sof*fissans* d'*es*tre i,
        S'*A*mors n'est pour *mi,*

V Et *vos gens cors,* u fran*cise* est mos*trée*
  A *v*o res*gart* riant a *l'*entrov[r]*ir*
  Sean*t* en une *face* desir*ée,*
  Dont je ne *puis* *ieux* ne *cuer* espanir.
    Ains vous *voi* de tel desir
    Et si m'en*tente* i em*ploie*
    C'a*v*is m'est ke je ne *v*o*ie*
    Adont *ciel* ne *terre, si*
      M'en *senc* jou ra*v*i.

[I] On returning to the delightful country where I left my heart when I went away, my sweet sorrow is renewed, my sorrow which does not allow me to hold back from singing. When I was accustomed elsewhere to be happy with a single memory, why should I not be so here, when I hear and see her who gives me happiness? [II] They say that I have not

14 'LA GRANDE CHANSON COURTOISE': THE CHANSONS OF ADAM DE LA HALLE

changed my outward behaviour in regard to the revelry which I like to engage in; a lover ought to enjoy and to conduct himself with due regard to his sickness and his state of mind. How could heart feel such a sweet sickness without being joyful? For the worst that Love sends is a longing for love's reward, and so it is with me. [III] But so pleasant and agreeable to me is this suffering that I accept it as if it had the savour of joy: one willingly accepts a gift which is offered having regard to the source whence it comes; and I ought willingly to embrace my suffering, for I do better to engage myself here than if I were loved by someone else; nor did ever anyone feel a woe so welcome. [IV] Gracious lady, loved by all the world, for your goodness that can never lessen, sweet, lovely countenance, object of my desire, will you keep me in your service? I do not look for other recompense nor would I dare to ask for one; for as it is I think I am unworthy to be here, if Love is not on my side, [V] and your fine person also, where generosity is shown in your smiling face, with eyes half open—generosity seated in a desired countenance from which I cannot tear my eyes or my heart. Rather, I look at you with such longing, and give my attention there so intently, that I think I do not then see heaven or earth, so do I feel myself carried away.

There is nothing strikingly new about the sentiments or the phraseology of this poem. We may take as an example the central oxymoron—the bittersweetness of love. Turning to the preceding poem, 'On me demande mout souvent k'est Amors' (No. 13), we find 'les douces dolors' in the very third line, and No. 12 opens 'Merchi, Amors, de la douce dolor'. Another ever-recurrent thought is of the connection between love and song—the lover's 'douce dolor' compels him to sing. In No. 9, he will be 'jolis et cantans'; in No. 10, he says, 'doi je bien estre chantans'; in No. 15 he sings because it delights him to be in the power of love, 'en amoreus dangier'. J. H. Marshall, the most recent editor of the poems, has succinctly described their nature:

> These are songs about love, rather than love songs in any Romantic sense. More than celebrations of the physical and moral qualities of a shadowy beloved, they are celebrations of the idea and nature of love itself.

The lover's imagined personal situation

> is less the subject of the *chanson* than its pretext, the framework within which the poet chooses to express thoughts and aspirations dictated by the convention of the genre itself rather than by any purely personal compulsion.[9]

The conventional 'thoughts and aspirations' of 'Au repairier' are: the paradoxical experience of absence and presence (st. 1); the sustaining power of *joie* (st. 2); the lover's unique good fortune (st. 3); his desire to serve the lady without reward, and his unworthiness (st. 4); the state of being totally possessed by love (st. 5).

To say that a poem is 'conventional' is by some standards to damn it. But we shall never understand medieval artistic creation in any medium unless we can accept the overriding importance of convention, the accepted and agreed way of saying or doing a thing. One medieval master of the art of rhetoric, that body of rules, conventions and advice which governed verbal communication in the Middle Ages, describes its purpose as 'to clothe the bare subject [i.e. the commonplace, the *topos*] with the garment of new form'.[10]

[9] Op. cit., p. 3.
[10] 'Ut rude thema novae formae sibi sumat amictum' (Geoffroi de Vinsauf).

'LA GRANDE CHANSON COURTOISE': THE CHANSONS OF ADAM DE LA HALLE   15

The courtly chansons of Adam de la Halle are fine examples of the art of courtly rhetoric. The conventions affect every aspect of the chanson—choice of theme, choice of style (in this case the 'noble' or 'tragic' style), choice of vocabulary (the range is limited and lofty—Adam does not use dialect words in these poems), choice of figures (metaphors from feudal service, from religion &c.) and so on. The rhetoric of the trouvère chanson has been exhaustively studied by Roger Dragonetti,[11] and our perspective has been further deepened by the close linguistic analyses of Paul Zumthor.[12] Dragonetti concludes his long book by asking whether the courtly chanson can reach us, can touch us, today, and says:

> Mais à supposer qu'elle ait perdu tout pouvoir sur notre sensibilité, elle garderait encore la valeur d'un haut enseignement par l'idée qu'elle nous propose du jeu poétique, et la severité de conditions qu'elle impose à sa reussité.[13]

It is the craftsman side of trouvère lyrics, the sense of technical difficulty grappled with and overcome, the sense of unresting inventiveness within prescribed bounds—this is what we are most likely to carry away from studying them, and it is this which will best help us to understand the musician's art.

The craftsmanship of 'Au repairier' is characteristic not only of Adam's chansons but of trouvère songs in the high style generally. It has the expected five stanzas, and the optional *envoi*, four lines long. Each stanza has the same rhyme-scheme and the same line-lengths: *a* 10* / *b* 10 / *a* 10* / *b* 10 / *b* 7 / *c* 7* / *c* 7* / *d* 7 / *d* 5 (* indicates a weak or 'feminine' ending). This metrical pattern is preserved intact, so that each stanza has 73 syllables (77 including the unstressed final syllables). What is more, the rhyme-sounds remain the same through the poem. This procedure represents a norm between the 'easy', and therefore uncommon, procedure of allowing the rhyme to change from stanza to stanza, and the 'hard', indeed virtuoso, achievement of, say, Arnaut Daniel in his *sestina*, which retains not simply the same rhyme-sounds but the very same rhyme-words in every stanza.

It is not easy for us to grasp the significance of the extraordinary emphasis twelfth- and thirteenth-century poets laid on the precise numbering of syllables and on the proper handling of rhyme. The significance lies in the concept of 'harmoniousness'—not mere euphony, but a positive balanced structural accord in sound. Paul Zumthor sums up the courtly poet's ideal when he observes that the only aesthetic philosophy the Middle Ages could understand was that of *Musica*.[14] Rhymes and syllable-counting—these are what the theorists agree on and insist on. The number of theorists is not great, and the earliest treatments of vernacular poetry come from the south of

---

[11] *La Technique poétique des trouvères dans la chanson courtoise*, Bruges, 1960.
[12] *Langues et techniques poétiques à l'époque romane* (Bibliothèque française et romane, C 4), Paris, 1963. Among Zumthor's other studies, see especially 'Entre deux esthétiques: Adam de la Halle', *Mélanges Frappier*, Geneva, 1970, ii. 155–71.
[13] Op. cit., p. 580.
[14] *Langues et techniques*, p. 221.

16 'LA GRANDE CHANSON COURTOISE': THE CHANSONS OF ADAM DE LA HALLE

Europe in the thirteenth and early fourteenth century. Most of them are late codifications. But the song tradition they codify was not dead: this was indeed the period in which the big chansonniers were being compiled. Brunetto Latini, Dante, Antonio da Tempo, and the authors of the huge *Las Leys d'Amors*, belong to this time. And the unanimity of their testimony is impressive. We read in *Las Leys*: 'The task is to make a new poem [*dictat*], measured in syllables, rhymed, sometimes in several stanzas, sometimes in one'.[15] There is some discussion in the treatises of verbal stress and its relation to the caesura and to the close of a line. But what never seems to be discussed is what we should call the metre (a supposed underlying pattern of, for instance, iambs or trochees) or the overall rhythm (the pattern of actual stressed and unstressed syllables, heavy and light syllables, in the words that form a given line).

This is not the place to examine in detail the problem of whether French verse of the thirteenth century has metre of the kind familiar to us in most varieties of English verse—i.e. a regular predictable pattern of stressed and unstressed syllables. It seems most likely that Adam de la Halle's chansons are not in a regular metre. But they are rhythmical: the syllables fall into natural groups of two or three. These rhythms do not necessarily recur at the same places in each stanza; Jean Beck claimed to have examined more than 10,000 trouvère chansons without finding a single one with perfect strophic construction.[16] An analysis of the verbal stresses in 'Au repairier en la douce contrée' will, I hope, clinch the point, even if some of the details remain controversial (Fig. I).[17]

The combination of total silence from the theorists on the question of 'poetic rhythm' with a fair consensus of modern scholarly opinion inclines one strongly to believe that the trouvère sought in his delicate word-rhythms that balance of 'unity and diversity' which distinguishes his art and defines our pleasure in it. Concepts of iambic, trochaic, dactylic metres are never mentioned and seem totally irrelevant.[18]

Two quotations sum up what we need to understand about the poetic art of the trouvères. The first is from Dragonetti:[19]

> Le cliché, source d'emotions et de pensées, résume et stylise des siècles de vie spirituelle; il est abstraction en ce sens qu'il retient virtuellement la part durable d'une culture, et c'est par quoi il est *appel*, relai et source des valeurs d'une tradition.

---

[15] *Leys d'Amors*, ed. A. F. Gatien-Arnoult (Monuments de la littérature romane, i–iii), Toulouse, 1841-3, i. 8-9.
[16] *Le Chansonnier Cangé*, ed. Jean Beck (Corpus cantilenarum medii aevi, i/1), Paris, 1927, ii. [43]–[44].
[17] I am grateful to Dr. Leslie Topsfield for allowing me to consult him about this problem.
[18] Beck (*Die Melodien des Troubadors*, Strasbourg, 1908, p. 104) quotes an anonymous theorist who describes the iambic decasyllable, authentic, 'est ab antiquo tempore' (i.e. used by Statius), which rather suggests its absence as an 'authentic' metre from the contemporary scene.
[19] *La Technique*, pp. 543-4.

'LA GRANDE CHANSON COURTOISE': THE CHANSONS OF ADAM DE LA HALLE 17

Fig. I

```
           I                                  II
.  (1)  .  .  4  .  .  7  .  .  10+    .   2   .  4  .  .  7  .  .  10+
.  .  (2)  .  4  .  6  .  (8)  .  10   (1)  .  .  4  .  .  7  .  .  10
.  (1)  .  3  .  .  6  .  (8)  .  10+  .  (2)  .  4  .  .  (7) .  .  10+
.  (1)  .  .  4  .  .  7  .  .  10     .  (2)  .  4  .  6  .  (8) .  10
            1  .  .  4  .  .  7                  1  .  .  4 (5)  .  7
            1  .  3  .  (5)  .  7+               .  .  3  .  5  .  7+
            .  (2) 3  .  (5)  .  7+              .  .  3  .  5  .  7+
            1  .  3  .  5  .  7              (1) .  .  4  .  .  7
              (1)  .  3  .  5                    .  .  3  .  5

           III                                IV
.  .  4  .  .  7  .  .  10+         1  .  .  4  . (6)  .  8  .  10+
2  .  4  .  .  7  .  .  10         (1)  .  .  4  .  .  7  .  .  10
2  .  4  .  6  .  .  .  10+         1  .  .  4  .  6  .  .  .  10+
?  .  4  .  .  .  8  .  10          .  2  .  4  .  6  .  8  .  10
.  2  .  4  .  .  7                 .  .  3  4  .  .  7
.  2  .  4  .  .  7+                .  .  .  4  .  .  7+
.  .  3  .  5  .  7+                .  (2)  .  4  .  .  7+
.  .  .  4  .  .  7                 .  2  .  .  5  .  7
    1  .  (3)  .  5                 .  2  .  .  5

                        V
            .  (2) (3)  4  .  .  7  .  .  10+
            .  (2)  .  4  .  .  .  (8)  .  10
            .  2  .  (4)  .  6  .  .  .  10+
            .  .  .  4  5  .  7  .  .  10
                1  .  3  .  (5)  .  7
                .  .  .  4  .  .  7+
                .  2  .  .  .  .  7+
                .  .  3  .  5  .  7
                .  2  .  .  5
```

The second is from the encyclopedist, Brunetto Latini;[20] it is short and to the point:

Ki bien voudra rimoier, il li covient a conter toutes les sillabes de ses dis.

The poetry is, one might say, 'a harmony of commonplaces'.

---

[20] *Li Livres dou Tresor*, ed. F. J. Carmody, Berkely and Los Angeles, 1948, p. 327.

18 'LA GRANDE CHANSON COURTOISE': THE CHANSONS OF ADAM DE LA HALLE

THE MELODIES

If 'unity in diversity' serves as a description for the courtly chanson in its literary aspect, it is equally apt to describe the music. Henrik van der Werf, who has published the only substantial account in English of troubadour and trouvère song, complains of their paying 'little attention to the form of the melody' and of their 'lack of interest in small details of the melody' as well as 'in correspondence between form and melody'. He writes:[21]

> Considering the care with which the troubadours and trouvères designed the form of their poems and considering the agreement among the manuscripts regarding rhyme and stanzaic form, one would expect the authors, composers and scribes to pay equal attention to detail regarding the musical form. But the manuscripts make it clear that the form of the poem must have been of far greater interest to everybody involved than the form of the melody. Convention and lack of sophistication in the form of the melody are typical, while originality and attention for detail are exceptional.

The ground of van der Werf's dissatisfaction evidently lies partly in the relationship of the melody to the poem. For the present, however, I wish to take issue only with his depreciation of the music *per se*. Are the charges he brings against the melodies meaningful? The foregoing literary analysis has suggested that the cliché (perhaps we should say 'commonplace') is the starting-point for the artist, and a pre-established meeting-point of understanding between the poet and his audience. What in the light of this can we say about the music of *la grande chanson courtoise*?

The first thing to observe is that Adam's 36 chansons are in a high style, with the exception of one, 'Amours m'ont si doucement' (No. 31); in this, the light-courtly style of a *chanson de femme* (the high-style courtly songs always have a man speaking) is mirrored in a lighter melody and in one manuscript a different notational style.[22] It is a reminder of the existence of a more 'popular' courtly style and a foil, in its simple structure, simple pattern and simple balance to the more complicated objects we are going to consider.[a]

The 'noble style', the *stylus grandiloquus*, is musically speaking one of considerable complexity; it has rarely, to my knowledge, been analysed in its own terms—that is, purely musically, and without reference to the words—and never so far as Adam de la Halle is concerned. And there is a great deal to be said about it simply as melody. But first we must note that there are one or two verbal aspects, verbal controls, which are undisputed and are reflected in every trouvère song: (i) the musical phrase is the line-length; (ii) the lines with weak endings (i.e. unstressed additional syllables) must have weak cadences; (iii) the number of notes or groups of notes must precisely correspond to the number of syllables in the poetic line— deviations from this rule are very rare indeed.

A representative example of Adam de la Halle's melody is the song 'Tant me plaist vivre en amoureus dangier' (No. 15) (Ex. 1).[b] There is the same

---

[21] *The Chansons of the Troubadours and Trouvères*, Utrecht, 1972, pp. 63–64.
[22] See Marshall, *Chansons*, p. 126, for the sense and structure of this piece, 'misunderstood by earlier editors'; see Stevens, 'Manuscript Presentation', for comments on the notation.

'LA GRANDE CHANSON COURTOISE': THE CHANSONS OF ADAM DE LA HALLE 19

Ex. 1

kind of 'unity-with-diversity', sameness-with-variety, in the music as in the poem. The unchanging features of the style are as follows.

(i) The musical structure of the chanson almost invariably follows the form A A B: that is to say, the two *pedes* (A A) of the first section, metrically identical, are also melodically identical—phrases 3 and 4 echo phrases 1 and 2. The *cauda* (B) uses, for the most part, new material.

(ii) The musical units (corresponding in fact to syllables of the text) are composed of between one and four notes, plicas (represented here by small notes) included. Adam rarely uses groups of more than four. (There is seldom any ambiguity about groupings: grouped notes are always bound in ligature.) And groups do not follow consecutively more than three or four in a row, even if notes with plicas are included. The stability of the style seems to require the balancing of groups with single notes. The most melismatic line in 'Tant me plaist vivre' is the fifth—but 'melismatic' is hardly the word for such a restrained usage. Characteristically, the groups consist of either ornamental or passing notes. Line 5 has ornaments only—the movement would be conjunct without them. Line 6, on the other hand, has passing notes, filling in the descending thirds.

(iii) The movement of the melody is essentially by step. In our example there are several instances of a third; only two phrases are perfectly conjunct, the sixth and the tenth. Line 8 contains a rather unusual use of thirds which is not part of the common idiom.[23] Interesting in our example is the extension of this principle to the joining of phrases. Breaks are only used to mark the main structure. The strong expectation of movement by step, with its atmosphere of deliberate restraint and deliberate limitation of choice is analogous to the poet's adoption of, say, a limited vocabulary, a courtly 'register' of expressive terms. The 'serene ceremoniousness' of the chanson owes much to its economy of melodic means.

(iv) Another recurrent feature of the style is the use of motifs and of formulae, 'motif' referring for present purposes to an internal feature of any one particular song, 'formula' to something out of the common stock of melodic vocabulary. They are not mutually exclusive: a common formula, such as the conjunct ascent through the interval of a fourth (f–g–$b\flat$), can be used in a single chanson, 'Tant me plaist vivre' for example, with unifying effect, i.e. as a motif. In this particular case it forms part of an extended musical rhyme linking the *pedes* with the end of the *cauda*. Many, probably most, motifs turn out to be formulae, the clichés, the commonplaces, of the musical style. But most chansons will embody isolated formulae from the repertory without necessarily using them as motifs. Such a formula in 'Tant me plaist' is the snake-wise descent of line 7. Compare[24]

Other constantly recurring formulae include:

(a) single-note rising scales of from three to six notes. Song 23 even opens with such a scale (Ex. 3a),[25] but makes no further use of it. Songs 8 and 10

---

[23] The three manuscripts differ at this point (line 8, notes 1–4): MS *R* reads b–a–c'–a; MS *T* reads a–c'–a–c'; MS *W* as given above (for an explanation of the *sigla*, see footnote 1).

[24] (a) No. 20 (MS *a*), 6.1; (b) No. 1 (MS *W*), 7.4; (c) No. 23 (MS *W*), 8.3; (d) No. 20 (MS *a*), 8.2.

[25] No. 23 (MS *W*), 1.1.

'LA GRANDE CHANSON COURTOISE': THE CHANSONS OF ADAM DE LA HALLE

introduce a climb of six in line 5, i.e. at the beginning of the *cauda*. This is more characteristic. The 'climb' renews the melodic energy at a needed moment. In the case of Song 8 (Ex. 3b)[26] the formula picks up a three-note rising motif in lines 1 and 3 (*a–b–c'*), adding at the bottom another three-note motif from line 2 (*e–f–g*).

(b) what one may call recitation figures, borrowing a term from plainsong, i.e. phrases of movement so limited as to be virtually static (Exx. 4a and 4b).[27] Close to recitation, but perhaps *merely* static, is Ex. 4c[28] (from a religious chanson).

(c) finally, an example of a rhythmic formula (the two previous ones were defined solely by pitch relations). A very great number of seven-syllable lines (whether with strong or weak endings) fall into the pattern of alternating single notes (occasionally plicated) and groups (Ex. 5).[29]

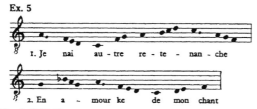

[26] No. 8 (MS *P*), 5.1.
[27] No. 1 (MS *W*), 5.1; No. 12 (MS *P*), 7.1.
[28] No. 36 (MS *W*), 9.1.
[29] No. 3 (MS *W*), 1.2.

It may be that the pattern implied or at least created a recurrent rhythmic pattern in the music—the single (or plicated) notes being strong, the melismas weak. But there is no necessary rhythmic musical meaning in melismas; and melismas are not related to verbal stress in any way whatsoever. Adam's chanson 'Glorieuse virge Marie' (No. 36) has three separate melodies to the same text, and the disposition of melismas is completely different in each.[30]

I have tried to convey some idea of the constant features which unify the 'noble' style of Adam's chansons—the basic parallelism between the melody and the verse-structure, extending from the whole down to each individually numbered syllable or note; the economical and predictable contrast of single note and small melisma; the restrained, step-wise melodic movement; the repetition of easily identifiable formulae from song to song; and their development as unifying motifs within the song.

But Adam's chansons are as noteworthy for their diversity as for their unity. The effects are deployed with extraordinary variety. Trouvère poetry has been described as 'un jeu de la poésie du lieu commun'—a playing, a game, of poetry of the common-place.[31] This was said not in sorrow, but in admiration, and the emphasis should fall at least as strongly on 'play' as on 'common-place'. Moreover, it applies as strongly to the music as to the poetry. There are all kinds of things that a good author or composer can do with a cliché besides displaying it in all its banality. And one is to exercise a fine invention on it.

In writing their melodies within the strict conventions of form and style which I have outlined, the trouvères indeed exercised a fine invention. The accepted derivation of their name from *trover*, 'to find', is rhetorically appropriate. *Inventio materiae,* not invention in the modern sense of finding something totally fresh and new but the searching out of appropriate material with which to 'clothe' the chosen theme, this *inventio* is the quality which these composer-poets most show.

It may seem paradoxical to insist that such 'convention-happy' composers wished at all costs to avoid the obvious. But this is the case. We may take their treatment of phrase-endings as an example. Adam de la Halle's cadences (phrase 'terminations') appear at first sight so stereotyped as to be quickly reducible to a few formulae. Close investigation proves the opposite. Taking the last two units of each phrase as constituting the 'cadence' I found in the first twelve melodies about 60 different melodic formations (plicas were treated as full-notes, and transpositions were excluded; but weak and strong cadences were taken separately). Considering that formal convention more or less required the precise repetition of phrases 1 and 2 (A B) as phrases 3 and 4 (A B), the count shows a quite extraordinary inventiveness. No doubt an

---

[31] R. Guiette, 'D'une poésie formelle en France au moyen âge', *Revue des sciences humaines,* liv (1949), 67; quoted in Dragonetti, *La Technique,* p. 541.
[30] *The Lyric Works,* ed. Wilkins, No. 28, gives the melody of *W* only.

'LA GRANDE CHANSON COURTOISE': THE CHANSONS OF ADAM DE LA HALLE

analysis of all 36 songs would show a gradual reduction in novelty. But No. 14, 'Au repairier en la douce contrée' (Ex. 6), has five new items to add to the repertory; its cadence figures are as follows, from MS *Wx*: lines 1 and 3 first appearance in this 'phrygian' form; 2 and 4 first appearance of a single monotone cadence note (with or without plica); 5 appears in No. 12, line 8 up a fifth; 6 first appearance as semitone plus tone; 7(=1, first appearance in 'phrygian' form); 8 first appearance with b♮ (if ♮ is intended); 9 first appearance (leading-note effects are conspicuous by their absence, as in Gregorian chant). It is worth remarking that the composer does not go for the extreme of variety, for 'diversity' regardless of 'unity'. His unifying produces the musical rhyme of phrase 7 with phrases 1 and 3, all phrygian; and the final cadence is, as it were, an inverted phrygian—and this is possibly the sense in which we are to hear it?[c]

Ex.6

'Au repairier' tells us more about Adam's melodic art than simply that he had an inventive ear for a cadence. It shows, for instance, the way in which he, like others, played the musical shape off against the verbal structure. The one instance of musical rhyme between *frons* and *cauda* (phrase 7) does not correspond with a verbal rhyme. On the other hand the melodic shape,

24 'LA GRANDE CHANSON COURTOISE': THE CHANSONS OF ADAM DE LA HALLE

as it seems to me, does in this usual instance correspond rather closely with the stanzaic sound-pattern, constant throughout the poem and constituted by the rhymes (not, be it observed, by the syntax of each stanza). The open-endedness of phrase 6, with its rising figure, moves conjunctly towards phrase 7 and the apex of the whole melody. They are surely a pair. And they are answered by phrases 8 and 9. The end of 8 is lower than 6 and only lightly questioning, but it moves, conjunctly again, into the last line. It is worth noting that 6 and 7 are amplified seven-unit lines as befits a climax: they have the extra syllable of the weak ending ('sŏlóiĕ', 'sĕróiĕ'). Line 8 has only seven units, and the melody finally comes to rest on the shortest line of the whole song, with five units.

Some more observations about poetic structure and musical shape will need to be made later. (The contrast in terms is deliberate—between 'structure', implying something predetermined and rigidly fixed, and 'shape', implying the more dynamic rise and fall, thrust and withdrawal, of the melodic line.) But while we are considering 'Au repairier', some questions about its tonality. They are, indeed, questions rather than answers. Rhythm apart, no aspect of these melodies is more puzzling than what in the broadest sense may be called their 'tonality'. The very common (though by no means invariable) repeat of phrases 1 and 2 as 3 and 4 establishes, often, certain tonal expectations—i.e. that the melody will continue to embody certain progressions and intervals and will reach points of rest and climax which stand in an identifiable relation to them. If our example is any indication, the 'final' does not in itself establish a tonality, even in the last phrase of the song. The end of 'Au repairer' has the first termination on F in this nine-phrase song. On the other hand the presence of B flats in two manuscripts does something to destroy the authentic phrygian feeling of the melody.

The tonal 'meaning' of 'Au repairier' seems to lie in a tension between E and F; it is reflected in the two 'members' of the first (and third) phrase—the fourth unit (before the customary caesura) is f, and then the melody turns upwards and away, arching back down to e; it is reflected again at the melodic climax in phrase 7—e'–f'–e' (an octave higher). Much of the time E predominates. Phrase 5 is a terse summary, as it were, insisting on the statement made by 1 and 3. But there is usually an F waiting to re-assert itself (6.1 and 8.1) and the tension is hardly resolved by what seems to me at least an ambiguous end. If modal terminology is to be used, then this song might possibly be described as being in the phrygian mode. However, it may be that another kind of analysis, based on what are sometimes called 'melody-types' (melodic formulae, stereotyped figures, tonal progressions, ornamentations and so on) will turn out in the end to be more fruitful.[32]

One thing at least can be said with certainty: to judge by cadences alone, the trouvère composer markedly exercises here as elsewhere his fine inventiveness and playful freedom within the conventions. The first 24 melodies of Adam de la Halle show that it is quite common for a chanson to have five or

[32] See, for example, Gustave Reese, *Music in the Middle Ages*, New York, 1940, p. 217.

six different terminations and that seven or eight are acceptable. Moreover, in only just over half the analysed songs does the end of the *cauda* 'agree' with the end of the *frons* (phrase 4) (*f* is the favourite final in both positions, then *c* and *g* and *d* almost equally). Within the frame nothing is predictable.

The same can be said of the musical organization of the song as a whole and especially of the *cauda*. The opening of the song, the *frons*, with its normal A B—A B repetition, is settled and predictable; but there seem to be no absolute rules governing the shape of the *cauda*. Since the length of Adam's chansons varies between eight and eleven lines, of which four are used in the *frons*, the *cauda* varies between 4 and 7 lines (= musical phrases). Precise formal relationships are rare in the high style, though, for example, in 'Tant me plaist vivre' (No. 15) the last phrase does more than rhyme musically with the *frons*—it takes units 4 to 10 of the earlier phrase (phrase 2), almost unmodified, to form its whole seven-unit phrase (see Ex. 1 above). But, if precise formal relationships are rare, organic ones are not. The real musical life of these melodies is, as with Gregorian chant, in the delicately balanced arches of melody. In 'Tant me plaist vivre', the melodic climax is reached early. Phrase 5 picks up the insistent c' of the opening (phrases 1 and 3) and takes it up to f', only sinking back a little (cadence on c'). Phrase 6 shoots straight up again to f' but then falls back and quickly down to g; phrase 7 droops a bit, hesitates, revives, and then leads into 8. In this rather unusual oscillating figure (a–c'–c'–a–c'), an ambiguity of intention (up or down?) is finally resolved in the unexpected close b–a–g–f–e (related to, repeating in fact, the descent of phrase 1. 4–7). Finally, phrases 9 and 10 are two balanced but descending arches: the first, of ten units, overlaps the line unit, pivoting at 10.3, while the second is lower and shorter (six units); the first embodies a motif (it is also a stock formula) from the climax in phrase 5 (c'–d'–f' is now g–a–c'), and the second, as already remarked, is an extended musical rhyme with the *frons* (2 and 4, 5–10).

Detailed analysis of this kind, though laborious, is strictly necessary if generalizations about the inexhaustible inventiveness and sophistication of the 'noble style' in music are to have any substance. Even without the words, the melody of 'Tant me plaist vivre' has a refinement and coherence of its own.[d] If the poems of these trouvère chansons are sophisticated creations in carefully designed forms, so indeed are the melodies. They are artefacts, delightful artefacts, every bit as rewarding to study and hear as the poems themselves. I do not claim in this respect to have made a novel discovery. But, as van der Werf's book shows, there has been as yet an inadequate appreciation both of the nature of our pleasure in their musical art and of its implications. One may well ask why, when liturgical chant has been so deeply studied and, within limits, properly appreciated, the huge repertory of vernacular melody lags behind. The reason, I believe, is this. If any single aspect of the songs has hindered an appreciation of their remarkable melodic inventiveness, it is what seem to me entirely false assumptions about the relationship of the poem to the music.

26 'LA GRANDE CHANSON COURTOISE': THE CHANSONS OF ADAM DE LA HALLE

WORDS AND NOTES

The historical study of words and music is bound to show, if nothing else, how manifold the possible relationships are between the two. Each age has its own characteristic notions of how they should be joined in song; and it requires a genuine effort of the historical imagination to shake off the assumptions of our own, or another age, and to engage with the object as it really is. It was Dante's *De vulgari eloquentia* that first brought home to me the strangeness of some medieval attitudes to aesthetic problems, including the problem of words and music. The three techniques which have to be studied in the composition of a courtly *canzone* are, as Dante states them: (i) *cantus divisionem,* the formal melodic structure of the stanza, divided into *frons* (= *pedes*), *diesis, sirma (*or *versus) sub certo cantu* (i.e. 'so as to establish a unique melody'); (ii) *partium habitudinem,* the harmonious putting-together, or proportioning, of lines and rhymes; (iii) *numerum carminum et sillabarum,* the 'harmony' of lines and syllables.[33]

Dante never mentions, and I am sure did not have in mind, either a conceptual relationship between the poem and the melody (the musician is not concerned with intellectual ideas as Renaissance composers so intensely were) or an emotional one (the musician is not concerned with real or imagined feelings). What is left? There is, obviously, the sound of individual words and the sound of words in phrases. The difficulty of doing justice to individual word-sounds in strophic song at any time is notorious. But in any case where is the evidence in these songs of Adam de la Halle that he cared at all? The evidence is almost solely in the rhyme-word. Brunetto Latini says 'the rhyme is not correct if the word-accent does not fit it' ('certe la risme n'ert ja droite se l'accent se descorde'). His advice about the rest of the line has already been quoted; it amounts to this: 'If you want to write good poetry, you must count all the syllables in your poems'.[34]

If practical demonstration is required, the first stanza of 'Au repairier' (see Ex. 6) should suffice. This at least is where we would expect the musician-poet to be on his mettle. If musical phrase A gives us a sensitive representation of the stress (let alone the intonation) of line 1, it cannot serve equally for a representation, an imitation in sound, of line 3, and vice versa. The same applies to lines 2 and 4 (phrase B). The point need not be laboured. It is a difficulty that all exponents of modal rhythm have had to contend with. On the other hand, it must be said that the music of these songs never goes so far as to do violence to the word-accent. A great deal of later medieval music seems positively hostile to the natural sounds of words. The trouvère style could be described as at least neutral and possibly even accommodating. The melody is a soft mould rather than a Procrustean bed.

To talk in these terms, however, perhaps implies a dominance of poem over melody, which has not been established. The normal accepted way of talking about these songs assumes that the words were written first and were

---

[33] *De vulgari eloquentia*, II. ix. 4.
[34] See above, p. 17, and footnote 20.

then set to music. There are some reasons for thinking that the opposite may have sometimes been true. One reason is the testimony of the poets themselves. The troubadour Bernart de Ventadorn, for instance, says in one poem: 'tan sui entratz en cossire/com pogues bos motz assire/en cest son, c'ai apedit' ('I have been so worried as to how I might best 'seat' words [i.e. set them] in this melody which I have [?] constructed in *pedes*').[35] The other and main reason for believing that the melody often came first is the widespread practice of *contrafactum* composition. The facts have long been known and studied and speak for themselves.[36]

This, however, is not the end of the enquiry. The implications of a theory of words and music which allows even for the possibility of the music preceding the words it is supposed to set are worth pursuing. In a short article a few years ago I argued that we could be sure from the whole tenor of Dante's discussion in the *Convivio* and in the *De vulgari eloquentia* that

> the relationship between the words and music of a poem was in essence a *physical* matter, a question of pure sounds ... dependent ... on 'numbers' (*numeri* are the special province of the musician); on *armonia;* on the realization, in the comparatively formal terms of music, of the 'musical potential' *of the poem*.[37]

I now think that these conclusions are questionable; they did not go far enough. In brief, the relationship between words and music in these courtly songs is better called metaphysical than physical—it goes beyond the 'musical potential of the poem' into the realm of the Ideal. In plain language, the musician did not set the words of the poem to music; he set its pattern. It was this pattern, a purely numerical structure of stanzas, lines and syllables, which preceded both the melody and the poem. The pattern had to be realized in two media—the medium of words and the medium of notes— and it did not matter in the least which was realized first.

I have spoken in temporal terms. But it might be better to say that the *numeri*, the rhythmic proportions and relations, took precedence over the melody and the poem rather than that they necessarily preceded them both in time. As a matter of common sense and ordinary experience, when one man, like Adam de la Halle, was in charge of the whole process, the pattern, the *numeri*, may have emerged gradually as he played with the actual words and notes. But this does not affect the fundamental point at issue, which is that the *armonia* of the song (Dante is always stressing this concept) exists in ideal form, as a numerical reality waiting to be incarnated, as it were, either as music or as poetry (verbal music) or both. To talk, therefore, about a direct relationship between music and poetry is misleading. The notes and the words are not so much related to one another as related both to a single numerical Idea.

[35] *The Songs of Bernart de Ventadorn*, ed. S. G. Nichols and J. A. Galm, Chapel Hill, 1962, Nos. 27, lines 4–6 (the reading 'apedit' is doubtful).
[36] E.g. by F. Gennrich in 'Internationale mittelalterliche Melodien', *Zeitschrift für Musikwissenschaft*, ii (1928–9), 259, and many others.
[37] 'Dante and Music', *Italian Studies*, xxiii (1968), 16.

28 'LA GRANDE CHANSON COURTOISE': THE CHANSONS OF ADAM DE LA HALLE

This hypothesis is not put forward merely as a possible *philosophical* basis for the aesthetic of courtly song. It is intended as a practical suggestion about the way trouvère songs in the high style came into being and about the way we should both study and hear them. One practical result, if the hypothesis is true, could be that we should cease to be so preoccupied as we have been about a rational relationship directly between the words and the notes and begin to study the implications of having two parallel, synchronous shapes. In this case the traditional rhythmic problem does not, alas, disappear; but it is reducible to purely musical terms: It is no longer relevant to take into account the real or imagined metre of the poem when considering the rhythm of the music. As a musical problem, it has two aspects—a notational (which I treat of elsewhere) and a stylistic (which I opened to some extent in the second part of this paper).

The realization in purely musical terms of the ideal pattern does indeed raise the problem of rhythmic style. In Adam's chanson 'Il ne muet pas' (No. 4) the difficulties are immediately apparent. It is unusual in being written entirely in decasyllables, i.e. ten- or eleven-unit lines (according as to whether the endings are strong or weak). Otherwise it is a typical chanson in the noble style. There seems to be no more justification for imposing a regular metre on the music than there is on the words. The words tend to group themselves into rhythmic groups of three syllables, or two, or four (with a subsidiary stress):

> Il ne *muet* pas de *sens* che*lui* ki *plaint*
> *Paine* et tra*vail*, ki a*quert* avan*tage*;
> Pour *chou* ne *puis* ve*oir* ke *cil* bien *aint*
> *Ki*, pour go*ir* d'a*mors*, souf*france gage*.

The music does the same to my ear, though the groups do not coincide with the verbal ones (Ex. 7). What guides the ear is surely, as so often in Gregorian chant, the combination of various factors: the number of notes (units to be more precise) in the phrase; the placing of plicas and grouped notes; the melodic shape of the whole and of each member; the placing of disjunct progressions; and one's sense of the tonality.

Clearly, the grouped notes as such do not indicate either strong or weak beats, stress or its absence. The final phrases of the chansons tend to accumulate melismas (e.g. 'Li maus d'amors', last line); they cannot all have equal weight. But, on balance, a light (usually therefore weak) treatment of the melisma seems stylistically more in keeping with the smooth harmoniousness, the *dolcezza*, the stateliness, which were admired and sought after. The *plica*, on the other hand, with its light, ornamental passing or returning note sung, it is thought, in a different style, seems to attract stress to its main note.[38]

The notion of the two realizations of a single Idea obviously raises practical

---

[38] For further information on Adam de la Halle's use of the plica, see Stevens, 'Manuscript Presentation'.

'LA GRANDE CHANSON COURTOISE': THE CHANSONS OF ADAM DE LA HALLE 29

Ex. 7

problems in performance. Whatever the speculative *musicus* (the man who thinks about music) may propose, it is the down-to-earth *cantor* who disposes. The problem, in brief, is how to reconcile the two patterns when actually singing them; that is, to find a way of singing that does not give too much prominence to the words and yet respects them; that does not, either, allow the music to tyrannize and yet respects that too. It seems to me indisputable that the melodies of Adam's chansons have a life and shape of their own, *qua* music, and that this life is essentially unrelated to the autonomous life of the words themselves. It may be a long time before agreement is reached, if ever, on the precise way each melody is organized. But the general approach might commend itself as it is formulated by Willi Apel in regard to that other and greater corpus of Western melodic music, the plainchant of the Church. He writes:[39]

> I cannot help feeling that the importance of the rhythmic problem has been somewhat exaggerated. The numerous efforts made in this direction appear to me like so many answers to a question that was never raised. This does not mean to say that Gregorian chant had no rhythm. Music without rhythm is obviously a contradiction in itself. However, rhythm is not the same as a fixed rhythmic system.

We should I suggest be prepared to think about what I have called the two parallel synchronous shapes. The author of *Las Leys d'Amors* may have the last word on this. A 'melodious song' arises, he observes, from the poem when every word is properly pronounced as it should be; but, he goes on, this is different from the musical melody which usually does not observe accent 'as we can see from the respond "Benedicta et venerabilis" '.[40]

The easy reference to Gregorian chant in a treatise about courtly song is striking and revealing. Besides its practical implications, there are other point of analogy. That other and greater corpus of Western melodic music contributed, surely, not only musical material, notational techniques, and, perhaps, a way of looking at the relationship (it is better called a non-relationship) between music and poetry, but more importantly a musical ethos. The music of *la grande chanson courtoise* is music in the 'high style', restrained, traditional, and devoid of personal idiosyncrasy. It is, one might say, the music of a courtly liturgy.

The following songs by Adam de la Halle were sung by Judith Nelson during the course of the lecture:
a 'Amours m'ont si doucement'.
b 'Tant me plaist vivre en amoureus dangier'.
c 'Au repairier en la douce contrée'.
d 'Tant me plaist vivre' (melody only, without the words).

---

[39] *Gregorian Chant*, p. 126.
[40] Éd. Gatien-Arnoult, i.59.

[11]

Interrelationships between Poetic and Musical Form in Trouvère Song

THEODORE KARP

The troubadour, Folquet de Marseilles, wrote that "a verse without music is a mill without water." While this remark may be one of the more picturesque expressions of the closeness of the union between poetry and music during the Middle Ages, it is by no means the only or the most telling testimony pointing in this direction. Much weightier evidence can be found elsewhere, especially in Dante's treatist *De vulgari eloquentia*. Were one to consider the central importance of our topic to the study of medieval lyric forms together with the fact that it is now more than a century and a quarter since the work of Ferdinand Wolf and nearly a century since the work of scholars such as Raynaud, Schwan, and Bartsch, one might easily imagine that a large quantity of information has already been amassed with regard to the relationship between Folquet's "mill" and its propellant power. This, however, is not the case. Various systems for the classification of lyric forms have been proposed and vigorously discussed. Indeed, a viable classification of forms is an indispensable prerequisite and foundation for the investigation of the interrelationship between poetic and musical form. But while earlier scholars have done much to prepare this foundation, it remains for those working now and in the future to complete it and to erect thereon a sound superstructure.

The essential historiography of our topic can be sketched very briefly. Well past the turn of the present century, little attention was paid to the interaction of music and poetry in producing an aesthetically satisfying, complex form. (I use complex not in the sense of complicated or intricate, but in the sense of being compounded of two parts.) Musicologists were occupied primarily with the thorny problem of the rhythmic interpretation of a notation that is rarely indicative of rhythm, and philologists were occupied chiefly with cataloguing, establishing manuscript filiations, and editing the literary texts. The importance of music in the medieval aesthetic was recognized by several scholars, but this recognition did not generate more than a few specific observations. More frequently, philologists ignored the *trouvère* melodies entirely.

The next stage of our historiographic outline is represented by the work of Friedrich Gennrich, culminating in his *Grundriss einer Formenlehre des mittelalterlichen Liedes*, published in 1932. This work is essentially a protest against previous neglect of musical values. In effect, Gennrich claims that of the two elements, poetry and music, it is the latter that is pre-eminent in establishing and identifying form. A full classification of lyric forms is based on this premise. Gennrich's work was necessary and valuable for its time, and it has continued to influence musicologists. Its corrective value was of importance, but many now consider that in his zeal Gennrich pushed his theories further than was wise. At any rate, there soon followed a sharp swing of the pendulum in the opposite direction, a trend represented by Hans Spanke's *Beziehungen zwischen romanischer und mittellateinischer Lyrik*, published in 1936, and Roger Dragonetti's *La Technique poétique des trouvères dans la chanson courtoise*, published in 1960. Spanke's position is the more extreme of the two. The eminent German scholar declares that: (1) the melody constitutes a characteristic not of form, but of content; (2) that a song in chanson form may display a variety of musical repetition schemes without altering its formal identity; and (3) that even in those instances in which the musical form may predetermine the poetic form, as in works of the sequence type, information regarding the number of syllables and the rhyme order will normally provide a full account of the lyric form.[1] Dragonetti contents himself with the more limited and correct observation that—as Spanke himself had demonstrated—the musical form of a chanson is not necessarily identical with the poetic form.[2] After documenting this statement, Dragonetti proceeds to consider various constituents of poetic form.

---

[1] Hans Spanke, *Beziehungen zwischen romanischer und mittellateinischer Lyrik* (*Abhandlungen der Gesellschaft der Wissenschaften zu Göttingen, Philologisch-Historische Klasse, Dritte Folge*, No. 18) (Berlin, 1936), pp. 3f.
[2] Roger Dragonetti, *La Technique poétique des trouvères dans la chanson courtoise* (*Rijksuniversiteit te Gent, Werken uitgegeven door de Faculteit van de Letteren en Wijsbegeerte*, No. 127) (Bruges, 1960), pp. 384ff.

Interrelationships in *Trouvère* Song

While the very substantial contributions of these scholars command recognition and respect, they offer little of positive value in the area that is of concern to this study. Granted that the musical form of a work may not be identical with its poetic form, is there not anything further that one can say concerning the relationship between the two? To what extent may one normally expect the two formal elements to reinforce one another? In what areas may one encounter independence, and perhaps even conflict?

To begin to respond to questions such as these, it will be profitable to review the criteria on which classifications may be based and to examine various possible systems of classification. The traditional criteria used in the classification of poetic forms have been: (1) the number of lines per strophe; (2) the number of syllables per line; (3) the order of rhymes; and (4) the presence or absence of refrains. While one ought to acknowledge that there are other elements that enter into the constitution of poetic form, such as the presence or absence of caesurae or enjambments and the placement of these when present, such elements do not appear to be of an order that requires consideration in establishing a classification of the nature that we are considering. Furthermore, one may remark that classification emphasizing numbers of lines per strophe has been largely discarded over the past several decades. The traditional criterion for the discussion of musical form has been repetition pattern. Essentially we have sought to distinguish between those phrases that are identical or nearly identical, those that embody both basic similarities and important divergencies, and those that are largely or entirely unrelated in content. The musical phrase has been assumed to be equivalent in length with the poetic line and comparisons between the two formal elements are made on this basis. Many other elements enter into the constitution of musical form, but these need not necessarily be taken into account for present purposes. More ought to be said regarding this aspect of our topic, but this will be reserved for a later point in the discussion.

Those familiar with the great formal variety present in *trouvère* song—and the still greater variety if other medieval lyric repertoires are included—may concede that the subject matter is so diverse that no one system of classification is likely to prove suitable for all purposes. Different systems of classification can be proposed to suit specific needs. For the present study we might, for example, employ a classification that would adhere as closely as possible to medieval thought by expanding on the one suggested by Dante in his treatise *De vulgari eloquentia*. There the poet distinguishes between the generic meaning of *cantio*, in the sense of "all words of whatever kind written for music,"[3] and a specific meaning, that of a song which adheres to certain stylistic char-

---

[3] *Le Opere di Dante Alighieri*, ed. Edward Moore and Paget Toynbee, 4th ed. (Oxford, 1924); see Book II, Chapter VIII (p. 396).

acteristics. He then limits his discussion to an examination of the specific meaning, promising to take up other varieties of vernacular song in later books. (These, however, either were not written or were not preserved.) Dante classifies the possible stanzaic structures of the *cantio*—for which term I shall substitute chanson—first and foremost with reference to the form of the melodies. Four types of melodic structure are recognized. One category consists of melodies that are constructed without any repetition of phrases and are thus without a *diesis*, i.e., a point of transition. Melodies with repetition of phrases are then subdivided into three categories, depending upon whether the repetition occurs before the *diesis*, after it, or both before and after. This system of classification could be expanded, and, in a sense, the Gennrich classification might be regarded as such an expansion. However, while it is important that we understand and appreciate Dante's thought, it is likely that for present purposes a systematic classification on the basis of musical structure will group together works that we would prefer to keep separate, while separating works that we would regard as belonging together.

The alternative of a classification according to poetic structure seems much more practical. Such a classification might proceed in various ways. Spanke, for example, achieves a classification that has the merit of reflecting to some extent the likely historical derivation of the several types. Nevertheless, it would seem that the most practical system of classification would be one modeled after that proposed by Dragonetti, who adopts Dante's general outlook while transferring Dante's terminology from the musical to the poetic structure. Some form of expansion is necessary, since Dragonetti does not discuss all forms of *trouvère* song. A division suitable for our purposes may be made as follows. We may begin by separating those works, including *lais*, that do not need to observe a constant strophic structure from those that do. Within the latter group, we would make provision for the separation of works that avoid internal rhyme—in other words, those which observe the same rhymes only between corresponding lines of successive stanzas—from those with internal rhyme. Works belonging to the former category are of extreme rarity in the *trouvère* repertoire, one example being the anonymous *Nouvele amour dont grant paine m'est nee* (R. 531);[4] they are, of course, present in modest frequency in the troubadour repertoire. Strophes with internal rhyme—by far the most important group—would be subjected to a fourfold subdivision:

1) those structures in which the length and rhyme of the initial line is duplicated immediately, as in the pattern, **a a b B**, but not as part of a larger group such as *aab aab w x y z*;[5]

---

[4]The works to be mentioned in this essay will be identified according to their number in Hans Spanke's revision of the Raynaud bibliography (*G. Raynauds Bibliographie des altfranzösischen Liedes*, 1955).

[5]In this essay, lower-case letters will be used to symbolize rhyme patterns, while upper

2) those structures in which the lengths and rhymes of the initial group of lines—normally two, but sometimes three or even four—are repeated without change of order, as in **ab ab w x y z**;

3) those structures in which the lengths and rhymes of the initial group of lines are repeated in reverse order: **ab ba w x y z** or **abc cba y z**; and

4) those structures with other combinations of line lengths and rhyme patterns.

Specific examples of the last category would include Jehan Erart's *Pastorel* (R. 585): **3a 4a 4b 5c' 5c' 5b 5d 3d 7c'**; the anonymous *Ma douce souffrance* (R. 250): **5a' 7b 5a' 5b 7c 10c**; and the anonymous *J'ai maintes fois chanté de cuer marri* (R. 1054a): **10a 10b 5b 5c' 7c' 5a 7c'**.

Within each of the four groups still further subdivisions are possible, depending upon the depth of the study envisaged. One basic subdivision appropriate to each group would segregate structures with refrains from those without; one might also distinguish structures with variable refrains from those with fixed refrains. However, for purposes of the present study, it is not necessary to go beyond the division outlined above and given in Table 1.

A word of caution may be appropriate at this point. The recommendation that primacy be accorded to poetic structure in the classification of lyric forms is not equivalent to a recommendation that poetic structure be studied isolated from musical structure. To be sure, under most circumstances textual information regarding the number, length, and grouping of lines is both sufficiently accurate and sufficiently unequivocal that we are not obliged to look for confirmation of such information within the musical structure. But there are occasions, admittedly rare, when a study of the melody will either reveal an error in the textual transmission or clarify larger structural aspects of a poem that may be analyzed logically in more than one way. The importance of these points may be demonstrated through the discussion of an example of each situation.

Jehan Erart's chanson, *En Pascour un jour erroie* (R. 1718), survives in five sources, four of which preserve the music. The poetic form, according to Spanke,[6] is **7a' 7b 7b 7a['] 7c 7c 7b 7b 7d' 10E 10D'**. When we examine the various manuscript readings, we find that the textual refrain, which makes heavy use of a nonsense syllable, is not the same

---

case letters will be used to designate text refrains and also musical repetition patterns. The letter **v** will indicate a variable line of verse that precedes and rhymes with a variable refrain (**R**) that follows. The letters **w**, **x**, **y**, and **z**, are used when the specific rhyme pattern and number of lines are immaterial to the point under consideration. A prime appearing after a letter indicates a feminine rhyme. The virgule is used in order to indicate the place of the *diesis*. The spellings of the first lines follow the forms employed by Raynaud and Spanke (see footnote 4), and the information about poetic form has been adapted from the latter. (Spanke, however, does not concern himself with the place of the diesis.) Since the idiosyncracies of specific text readings in the manuscripts are often reflected in the music, the full texts follow the manuscript cited for the particular example, being changed only through the addition of punctuation.

[6]G. Raynauds *Bibliographie des altfranzösichen Liedes (Erster Teil)* (Leiden, 1955), p. 237.

TABLE 1. Proposed Classification of *Trouvère* Forms

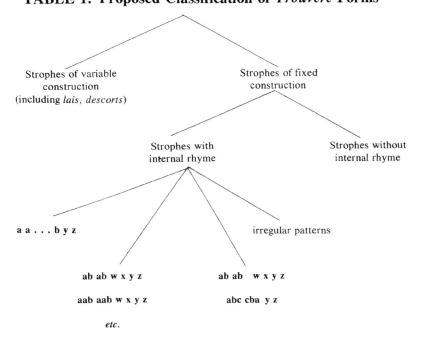

in all the sources. Nor is there any consensus that would make it obvious which of the textual readings is to be preferred. It would appear that Spanke's poetic analysis is based on the reading of the Rome manuscript,[7] and that a typographical error is involved, the refrain apparently consisting not of 10 but of 12 syllables per line. But when we examine the music for the Rome reading of the refrain, we notice a curious fact. The melody seems to be built of a varied sequence plus a coda, so that the melodic division is not bipartite, 12–12, but tripartite, 9–9–6.

Example 1. Jehan Erart, *En Pascour un jour erroie*, refrain. Vatican, Bibl. Ap. Vat., Reg. lat. MS 1490.

Et dont do do do do do do [do] do do do
Et dont do do do do do (et) de la lupinele

[7]Vatican, Biblioteca Apostolica, Regina latina MS 1490.

When we then re-examine the textual and musical readings of the remaining sources, we find that despite the differences among them, they do agree on one basic essential: the refrain has three lines, not two. In the Chansonnier de Noailles,[8] both text and melody are divided 9–9–6, in agreement with the melody of the Rome chansonnier, while in the two remaining sources, members of the closely knit Arsenal family, the division is 6–6–8. At the very least, the study of the Rome melody should convince us that the text in this source is defective and that a summary of the poetic form should not be based on this reading.

Our second example is taken from the Chapelain de Laon's *chanson avec des refrains, Un petit devant le jour* (R. 1995). The poetic structure is as follows: **7a5b 7a5b 7a5b 7a5b 7a6b 7a6b 7a 9a v Refrain**. On the lowest level of organization the chanson text poses no problems. But it is not quite so simple to determine whether the couplets constituting the majority of the strophe submit to any higher organization. To put the question in Dante's terms, does the section before the *diesis* consist of four lines, or is it larger? A hasty answer would pounce on the fact that the *pedes* normally consist of two lines each, and that the number of *pedes* is almost always two. But a more cautious approach, including consultation of the melody, would show that the original composer—possibly (but not necessarily) the poet himself—looked upon the poem as being constructed of three groups of four lines each, concluded by an irregular group with the variable refrain, and that the *diesis* occurs after the eighth line.[9]

Example 2. Chapelain de Laon, *Un petit devant le joun*. Paris, Bibl. nat., f. fr. MS 20050.

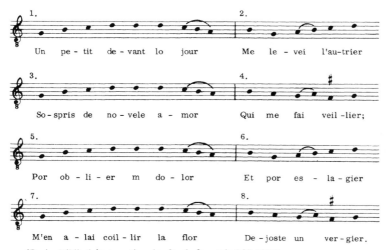

[8]Paris, Bibliothèque nationale, fonds français MS 12615.
[9]See also Gennrich, *Formenlehre*, p. 22ff.

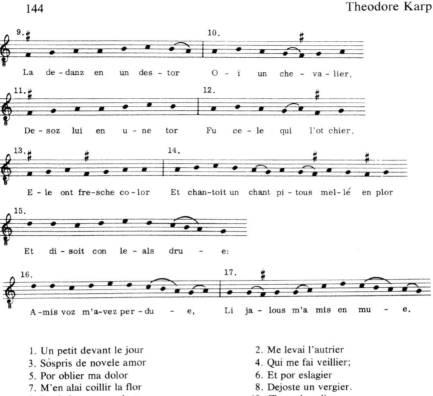

1. Un petit devant le jour
2. Me levai l'autrier
3. Sospris de novele amor
4. Qui me fai veillier;
5. Por oblier ma dolor
6. Et por eslagier
7. M'en alai coillir la flor
8. Dejoste un vergier.
9. La dedanz en un destor
10. Oï un chevalier,
11. Desoz lui en une tor
12. Fu cele qui l'ot chier.
13. Ele ont fresche color
14. Et chantoit un chant pitous mellé en plor
15. Et disoit con leals drue:
16. Amis voz m'avez perdue,
17. Li jalous m'a mis en mue.

Having covered most of the preliminaries, we may now turn our attention to questions of the *trouvère* musicians' response to poetic texts, beginning at the most elementary levels possible. This response was not entirely uniform. From the musical standpoint the repertoire is heterogeneous. Many texts are set two, three, and even four times, and there is even an instance of a text set polyphonically in the middle of the fourteenth century in a musical style quite removed from those of the previous centuries.[10] Normally there is a fairly clear differentiation, both in terms of manuscript tradition and in terms of style, between the earliest settings and the later replacements; we may thus speak of a central as well as a peripheral musical repertoire.

On the broadest level, composers were accustomed to provide strophic texts with one melody to be repeated for all strophes. In the

[10]See this author's article, "The Textual Origin of a Piece of Trecento Polyphony," in the *Journal of the American Musicological Society*, XX (1967), pp. 469–73.

case of *chansons avec des refrains* some manuscripts provide music for each or at least most of the refrains, but others do not provide any space for music at all. Exceptions to the strophic musical setting exist, but these appear to be very rare. Three examples, all peripheral, all late additions, occur in the *Manuscrit du Roi*.[11] These were written out by persons familiar with the advanced features of notation made famous in the treatise of Franco of Cologne and undoubtedly belong to the last quarter of the thirteenth century. The musical traits that pertain to our present concerns are as follows. First, within each work the structures of the different musical strophes are equivalent. In the setting of *Quant je plus voi felon rire* (R. 1503), by Guiot de Dijon, each stanza is provided with an individual setting consisting of two repeated segments (*pedes*) and a nonrepetitive conclusion (*cauda*). In the remaining two works, all strophes are set to individual, nonrepetitive melodies. Second, in each work all strophes conclude on the same tone, so that one cannot speak of larger formal structure in terms of change of tonality. However, there does seem to be some awareness of larger aspects of structure in terms of the impression of musical climax that may be generated through local control of pitch range. Third, the rhythmic response to lines containing equivalent numbers of syllables does not remain fixed. Furthermore, the rhythmic changes indicated in this unequivocal notation seem to have been generated by musical needs, rather than by a desire to adjust the music to shifts in textual accentuation or changes in the pace of the poetic thought.

In order to make the next level of comparison, that dealing with the internal structures of the strophes, as meaningful as possible, it would be helpful to reflect first on the nature of the comparisons that we make. It is my impression that a clearer understanding of the differences between the natures of the formal controls governing poetry and those governing music may afford a sounder orientation towards our subject and may result in a different view of the same factual material. Within the *trouvère* repertoire, at least, the primary formal poetic control is exercised by rhyme. The periodic return of one of a small group of sounds serves to divide the strophe into discrete segments and to mark the boundaries of the larger rhythmic groups. The depth of division, which affects the nuances of poetic rhythm, results from the interaction between rhyme and the divisions of sense that also serve to shape the verbal structure. Clearly, when the rhyme coincides with the end of a thought, the division produces a much sharper effect than when the rhyme occurs at the end of a subsidiary phrase or within a word group that would otherwise be uninterrupted.

The factors that shape musical form are more diverse, and we often tend to pass over the subtler means of control in order to focus on the grosser ones. A melody without readily perceptible repetitive elements

---

[11] Paris, Bibliothèque nationale, fonds français MS 844.

is by no means formless. It may be shaped through the control of pitch range, through the ways in which the various successions of tones are made to relate to one or more primary tonal centers, through the rhythmic progressions of the individual lines, or through an overall rhythmic progression that may be definable only in retrospect, after the entire melody has been heard. The melody, like the poem, will be cut into discrete segments by means of cadences, and cadential control is one of the elements that affect musical form. The parallelism between the functions of rhyme and of cadence is sufficient that when in a lyric form we find the return of a given melodic cadence we speak of musical rhyme. The technique of musical rhyme does play a part in *trouvère* musical forms, but only a relatively modest part. The device is used particularly to permit the listener to associate the endings of major subdivisions of the melody, specifically furnishing a link between the end of the *pedes* and the end of the *cauda*.

However, the major determinant in *trouvère* musical forms is the repetition or lack of repetition of entire phrases. It is this feature that we catalogue by means of alphabet symbols and it is this feature that has served as the focus of almost all past discussions of medieval song forms. Comparisons between poetic and musical forms have, therefore, been comparisons of rhyme schemes versus repetition schemes. The point that must be stressed is that in taking such action we are comparing elements that are vastly different in scope and effect. Whereas the rhyming syllables serve as a form of punctuation and account for only a very small portion of the total sound content of the poem, a musical repetition pattern will normally encompass a substantial segment of the tonal fabric. Even the briefest reflection immediately indicates that in an eight-phrase setting having the usual form of two *pedes* and a *cauda* each *pes* (that is, each repeated segment) will account for 25% of the total musical content. Whereas it is possible for a skillful poet to produce an eight-phrase strophe of stirring beauty while employing only two rhymes, an eight-phrase melody constructed through the repetition of two relatively simple and syllabic phrases will be at best a rude affair, regardless of the repetition pattern chosen.[12] There would be no room in such a work for musical development, for any subtlety of shape or other ingenuity, or for any sense of climax. If we remember Dante's emphasis on the nobility of the chanson, his concept of worthiness or suitability, and his desire that all elements, from the rhythm of line on down to the nature of the individual word, should contribute to this nobility, and if we remember Johannes de Grocheo's somewhat similar concept of the

---

[12]There are occasional examples in which there is complete or nearly complete correspondence between rhyme scheme and repetition pattern. The setting of the Manuscrit du Roi of Conon de Bethune's *L'autrier avint en cel autre päis* (R. 1574) and the same trouvère's *Tant ai amé c'or me convient häir* (R. 1420) are two such works. However, the members of this small group are not among the more interesting of the *trouvère* musical creations. Of course, the early polyphonic *rondeaux* are founded on the repetition of two simple phrases; but despite the rude charm that these works possess, the form itself does not acquire major artistic significance until there is poetic and musical expansion.

cantus coronatus, we will realize at once that we ought not expect a one-to-one correspondence between rhyme and musical repetition pattern. This does not mean that our comparisons are, therefore, invalid and meaningless, but that they ought to be employed in a somewhat different way. If, instead of proceeding line by line, we compare the larger formal articulations, we can arrive at much more meaningful results. A last-ditch protest based on the contention that it would have been possible for the *trouvère* musician to have constructed a viable form founded primarily on cadential control dwindles into insignificance in view of the fact that no lyric repertoire has ever been so designed.

Our overview of the relationship between poetic and musical form on the strophic level will begin with a consideration of practices observed in the setting of poetic forms in which the structure of the opening group of lines is repeated immediately. That is, we shall treat of works cast in the form of *pedes* plus *cauda* or *pedes* plus *volta*.[13] Of the various groups within the classification system that we have proposed, this is by far the largest and best represented in the manuscripts. In the vast majority of instances the poems in this group are set by melodies that are also built on the *pedes* principle. Furthermore, the exceptions to this rule seem to fall mainly into two groups, both of which are comprised of nonrepetitive melodies;[14] the larger of these is formed by late, peripheral melodies. In other words, when we reach the fringe of the *trouvère* musical tradition, the normal relationships between peotic and musical structure are no longer observed systematically. The second of the two groups is comprised of settings of poems in which the *cauda* consists of only two—or sometimes three—lines.

The aesthetic reasons that were responsible for the formation of the latter group are not entirely clear, but at least one plausible explanation can be envisaged. It would appear that both poets and composers felt that in this class of strophe the *diesis*, the point of transition, marked the dividing line between the strict portion of the structure and the free. [The free section offered the poet the widest opportunities for structural individuality and offered the musician the opportunity for expansion, or a free fantasy that might draw on elements presented earlier but that more often would be largely independent.] Evidence that would support such an interpretation may be obtained by studying the transmission of various melodies. While the variants in the different readings of the *pedes* are proportionately fewer and normally affect only matters of detail, those involving the *cauda* are more far-reaching. Changes of form and insertion of new material may be involved; indeed, there are examples in which either the entire original *cauda* or a major portion thereof is replaced by new material. If the musicians did in fact regard the form

---

[13] If we transfer Dante's musical definition of *volta* to poetic usage, this writer would suggest that the term be used to indicate the concluding section of a poem, beginning immediately after the *diesis*, and constructed by the duplication of the structure of a group of lines, without inversion, alteration, or addition.

[14] Melodies employing unusual repetition patterns may be found, but they are comparatively rare.

in the manner suggested, it is quite possible that they felt that a two-line *cauda*—or even one with three lines—would not offer enough scope for musical expansion and would not possess enough weight to balance the repetition of the *pes*. This would account for the abandonment of the normal symmetrical form under such circumstances and for the employment of one based on the continuous exposition of new musical ideas.

There is, however, a difficulty to this explanation that is encountered when we turn to the class of strophe based on the immediate repetition of the structure of the opening line. Poems belonging to this class seldom occur in more than two or three sources, and the group is not a very large one. (Viewed from these twin standpoints, the group would not be considered as part of the core of *trouvère* practice even though some individual works belong to the earliest stratum of the repertoire.) Strophes of this class, normally consisting of less than eight lines, are associated with two main types of musical settings. One employs immediate repetition of the opening phrase, while the other is based on the repetition of the opening pair of phrases. The equivalent of *pedes* plus *cauda* construction is thus present in the latter group despite the brevity of the *cauda*; apparently no lack of balance among the musical sections was felt here. However, this potential contradiction to our hypothesis may perhaps not be as real as it first seems. The poetic and musical content of the strophic class opening with a group of **a a** rhymes—this class including the *pastourelles* and *rotrouenges*— is lighter than that of the strophic class opening **ab ab**. This distinction may have bearing on formal structure. It is quite possible that the formal requirements of the first of these groups were considered to be less demanding, that the concluding sections were not regarded as the main vehicle for structural elaboration, and, therefore, no need for a substantial free fantasy was felt.

Before passing on to a consideration of other strophic types, some further remarks concerning the musical construction of the *pedes* may be appropriate. Whereas by definition the two poetic *pedes* of a chanson are identical in structure, their musical counterparts need not be so, although more often than not, they are. The variants found in this portion of the structure usually belong to one of two main types. Some are of either decorative or distributive nature and, therefore, of little structural consequence. Others, however, involve the concluding cadence and sometimes even the entire concluding phrase of each *pes*. In many instances, the cadence of the fourth phrase will be altered so that this phrase will provide a greater sense of tonal stability at its close than is provided by the second phrase. It would appear to me that the very differentiation between the *ouvert* and *clos* halves has the effect of binding the *pedes* closely together while sharpening the point of transition to the *cauda*. However, the opposite treatment is also to be found, namely, that the fourth phrase is apparently changed in order to lead more smoothly into the *cauda*.

Interrelationships in *Trouvère* Song

On infrequent occasions strong differences may be observed between the first and third phrases of the music. One of the most unusual treatments of the *pedes* occurs in the setting of *Mout me merveil de ma dame et de moi* (R. 1668) by Guiot de Provins. In this melody, preserved only in the Chansonnier de Saint Germain,[15] the relationships between lines 1 and 3 and between lines 2 and 4 are established solely by means of extensive musical rhymes. The materials setting the first five syllables of lines 1 and 3 and those setting the first six syllables of lines 2 and 4 are individual. Only the materials underlying the last five and four syllables, respectively, of these pairs are the same. We might note that in compensation for this freedom the composer brings back the opening half of the second *pes* as the setting for the penultimate text phrase and the closing half of the first *pes* as the setting for the final text phrase. On the level of primary structural subdivisions the correspondence between textual and musical structure is again a matter of similar general principles rather than of identical details.

Whereas we have observed a substantial correspondence between the larger divisions of strophes built on the *pedes* principle and their musical settings, we find an entirely different situation with regard to strophes that repeat the structure of their opening lines in reverse order. Here a correspondence between poetic and musical form is clearly possible without violating norms of musical construction. Indeed, sixteenth-century French composers frequently set quatrains with an **a b b a** structure by a musical form based on the return of the opening material at the end. However, this kind of structure seems to have been extremely rare within the formal vocabulary of the *trouvère* musicians.[16] Sometimes these composers will treat a poem belonging to this class as if the opening structural elements were *not* reversed and provide a musical setting consisting of *pedes* plus *cauda*. More frequently, however, such a poem provides the basis for a nonrepetitive, continually evolving setting. To state the same fact from a different point of view, we find that within the central musical repertoire the vast majority of through-composed settings accompanies either texts of this class or the class consisting of unusual structural combinations.

To sum up our previous findings concerning the interrelationships between *trouvère* poetic and musical structures on the strophic level, we may note that in the vast majority of cases, the musical form will either match the large outlines of the poetic form or at least be neutral. In the latter category one may place the two main kinds of settings for strophes opening **a b b a** as well as the **A B A B** musical openings for strophes that begin with one or more repetitions of the opening a rhyme. Perfect accord in the realm of detail is rare, but the reason for this lies in the differences between the two forms of artistic expression.

There are, however, exceptional examples in which the musical con-

---

[15] Paris, Bibliothèque nationale, fonds français MS 20050.
[16] See, for example, *Joliement doi chanter* (R. 803), attributed to Gillebert de Berneville and Robert de la Pierre, which begins with the pattern **A B B A'**.

structions are in actual conflict with the poetic forms on either of two levels, and these works offer fascinating insights into the possible complexities of our subject. The broader of the two levels concerns the large groupings of poetic and musical lines within the strophe. In the works considered up to this point the *pedes* in the poetry are matched by *pedes* of equivalent size in the music. Even in those instances in which an **a b b a** rhyme pattern is set by an **A B A B** musical pattern, the *diesis* occurs at the same point in the two components of the lyric form. But there are rare examples in which the *diesis* in the poetry and that in the music occur at different points, creating a mismatch that is of an entirely different order from the kind discussed by Spanke and Dragonetti.

Consider, for example, the setting of Richart de Fournival's *Talent avoie d'amer* (R. 760) in the Arras chansonnier.[17] The form of the poem is **7a5b′5c 7a5b′5c / 4c 6a**;the *pedes* consist of three lines each and the *diesis* occurs between the sixth and seventh lines. The music, however, follows the pattern **ABC AB / DEF**. From the mere indication of the repetition pattern one might think that lines 4, 5, and 6 constitute a single group and that the second *pes* is merely a variant of the first with a changed ending. However, by examining the melody itself we find (1) that the potential flow between lines 5 and 6 is broken by the seldom used leap of a sixth, and (2) that line 6 begins the exploration of a higher tessitura not previously employed in the melody. The two devices combine to indicate a dividing point in the musical construction that occurs a line previous to the dividing point in the poetic construction.

Example 3. Richart de Fournival, *Talent avoie d'amer*. Arras, Bibl., mun., MS 657.

[17]Arras, Bibliothèque municipale, MS 657.

Interrelationships in *Trouvère* Song

K'il l'ont main-te-nu Sai per-chu K'il n'en pue-ent tor-ner.

1. Talent avoie d'amer;
2. Mai pauour m'est prise, 3. Ki le m'a tolu.
4. Kar j'oi cieus d'Amours blasmer
5. Et de son serviche
6. K'il l'ont maintenu 7. Sai perchu 8. K'il n'en pueent torner.

Examples in which the dividing point in the musical construction occurs later than the dividing point in the poetic construction—though still quite rare—are more numerous, and we shall briefly describe a handful of these. Devices similar to those observed in our previous example occur also in the peripheral setting of Conon de Bethune's *Chançon legiere a entendre* (R. 629) in MS f. fr. 1591 of the Paris Bibliothèque nationale. The poetic strophe consists of seven heptasyllabic lines in the pattern **a′b a′b / b c′ c′**. The musical repetition pattern, however, may be expressed by the letters **ABC AB′ / D E**. The fifth line is separated from the sixth both by the leap of a sixth and by the exploration of a new and higher tessitura. Two other examples occur in the same manuscript. In the peripheral setting of Thibaut de Champagne's *Tout autresi con l'ente fait venir* (R. 1479) on folio 73^v, the musical pattern **AA′B AA′ / C D E E′ F** accompanies a poetic structure that opens with six decasyllabic lines, followed by four heptasyllabic lines, in the pattern **ab ab / b a c c c c**. In this example, the musical *diesis* occurs one line later than the poetic, but the shift may even take in two lines, as in the setting of Thibaut's *Li dous penser et li dous souvenir* (R. 1469) on folio 29^v. The decasyllabic strophe, rhyming **a b b a / c′ c′ a a**, with a *diesis* between lines 4 and 5, is accompanied by a melody whose form may be represented **ABC AB′C′ / D E**.

A similar shift may be observed in Gautier d'Espinal's *Ne puet laissier fins cuers c'adès se plaigne* (R. 119) in the Chansonnier de Saint Germain. The decasyllabic strophe, rhyming **a′ b b a′ / b c′ c′**, is set by the musical pattern **ABC A′B′C′ / D** despite the fact that this form conflicts not only with the rhyme organization but also with the alternation of masculine and feminine rhymes, causing an unusual dislocation of cadence.

Example 4. Roi de Navarre, *Li dous penser et li dous souvenir*. Paris, Bibl. nat., f. fr. MS 1591.

Mi dous pen-ser et mi dous sou-ve-nir

152   Theodore Karp

Mi dous penser et mi dous souvenir
Me font mon cuer eprendre de chanter,
Et fine Amour qui ne un lait douter,
Qui fait les siens de joie maintenir

Et met es cuers la doutance ramembrance
Pour ce est Amours de trop haute puissance
Car en sa esmai sait homme resjoir
Ne pour doulour ne laist de lui partir.

Our final example represents a kind of middle ground. The setting of Gillebert de Berneville's *D'Amours me vient li sens dont j'ai chanté* (R. 410) in the Chansonnier de Noailles seems at first to match the poetic construction quite well. The strophe displays the pattern **10a6b 10a6b / 3c 5c 3d 7d 7e 4E**. And the musical setting begins quite suitably **A B A B**; the continuation proceeds **C D E**, and then, despite the difference in line lengths between the opening of the strophe and the close, ends **A′ B′ C′**. After one has reached the end it becomes clear that **A B** and **C** form one unit—the C acting as a reinforcement of the B cadence—and that the musical grouping is actually **AB ABC / D E A'B'C'**. (One will note that the **D** and **E** phrases are set apart in terms of tessitura and that in order to compensate for the brevity of lines 8 the first three musical units of the **A** phrase are omitted.)

Example 5. Gillebert de Berneville, *D'Amours me vient li sens dont j'ai chanté*. Paris, Bibl. nat, f. fr. MS 12615.

1. D'Amors me vient li sens dont j'ai chanté
2. Et dont je chanterai
3. Se je n'amaisse vie n'euse amé
4. Tot certainement sai   5. Cuns chaitis
6. Fuisse mal apris   · 7. Amors rent
8. Riche guerredonement
9. Ceaus ki le sevent servir   10. Sans li trair

The second level of conflict between poetic and musical structure in the *trouvère* repertoire carries weightier implications for our knowledge of medieval musical practice. Up to this point in our discussion and in all previously published studies, there has been a tacit assumption that poetic lines and musical phrases coincide in length. To be sure, it is questionable whether one ought to describe a brief musical section setting of two to four syllables as a phrase, but such sections often do constitute coherent subsections of musical thoughts. Thus there has been no real hindrance to the consistent description of *trouvère* musical form in terms of segments delineated by poetic lines. While this procedure is sound in almost all instances, there are a handful of examples that demonstrate that past procedures ought not be followed blindly. We have already touched on one such example, although in that instance the conflict between verbal and musical phrasing is probably attributable to textual corruption. However, the hypothesis of corruption in the textual or musical reading will not suffice to explain the examples that we shall discuss now.

The clearest and most extensive illustration of the independence of musical and poetic forms is furnished by the setting of Gautier de Dargies' *Chançon ferai mout marris* (R. 1565) in the Arras chansonnier. The poetic structure is quite irregular: **7a 7b 7b 4a 8a 8b 10b**. At first glance it might seem that the short line of verse—which has three syllables, not four, in the Arras reading—is set by a brief declamatory musical gesture that introduces a section of new material. But a reflective examination will reveal first that this brief segment is almost identical with the opening of the chanson. Pursuing this observation further, we find that the first four musical units of the following line correspond to the last four units setting the first line of poetry, while the last four units of this line correspond to the first four units setting the second line of poetry. This out-of-phase repetition scheme is continued still further. The first three musical units of line 6 correspond with the last three setting line 2, while the following section—concluding with the third unit of the final line—constitutes a free variation of the third musical phrase. The concluding, independent musical phrase corresponds to the last seven syllables of the decasyllabic line. The musical repetition pattern, in short, is **ABC ABC' / D**.

Example 6. Gautier de Dargies, *Chançon ferai mout maris*. Arras, Bibl. mun., MS 657.

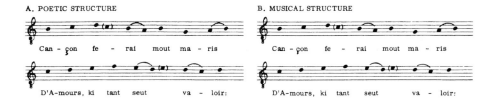

Interrelationships in *Trouvère* Song

A. Poetic Structure

Cançon ferai mout maris
D'Amours, ki tant seut valoir:
Faus l'ont laissié dekaoir;
S'en est pris
Li mons et vaincus et faillis;
Drois est puis k'Amours n'a pooir;
Ke li siecles ne puist mais riens valoir.

B. Musical Structure

Cançon ferai mout maris
D'Amours, ki tant seut valoir:
Faus l'ont laissié dekaoir;
S'en est pris li mons et vaincus et faillis:
Drois est puis k'Amours n'a pooir; Ke li
siecles ne puist mai riens valoir.

Similar complexity of form occurs also in the Arras setting of *Maintes fois m'a on demandé* (R. 419), again by Gautier de Dargies. As above, the poetic form is irregular: **8a 8b 8a 2b / 10a 4a 8b 4a 4b 4b 8a 10a**. The rhyme scheme, again based on two vowels, is one that might be employed in a poem built of two *pedes* and a *cauda*. And it is this form that is employed by the composer, regardless of the conflict produced in the middle section. Instead of a construction that is grouped 8, 8, 8, 2, 10, 4, etc., we find a construction that begins with the groups 8, 8, 8, 9, 7. In other words, the fourth line, which consists of only two syllables, begins the second half of the musical repeat, and this repeat is continued through the first seven syllables of the following decasyllabic line. Following the conclusion of the fifth line, accord between poetic and musical structures seems to prevail again.

Example 7. Gautier de Dargies. *Maintes fois m'a on demandé*. Arras, Bibl. mun., MS 657.

A. Poetic Structure

Maintes fois m'a on demandé
Si s'en mervilloient la gent
Si j'ai d'amourours cuer kanté

Souvent;
Mais sacent bien j'en dirai verité
De mon pensé
Et de cou k'Amours me consent
Ki n'a painné
De son tourment,
Qu'il sent souvent;
Mais de tant m'a Diex houneré
K'encor n'ai pas sans tres fin cuer kanté.

B. Musical Structure

Mainte fois m'a en demandé
Si s'en mervilloient la gent
Se j'ai d'amourours cuer kanté

Souvent; Mais sacent bien j'en dirai verité,
De mon pensé
Et de cou k'Amour me consent
Ki n'a painné De son tourment,

Qu'il sent souvent;
Mais de tant m'a Diex houneré
K'encor n'ai pas sans tres fin cuer kanté

Interrelationships in *Trouvère* Song

Conflicts between musical and poetic forms are not restricted to settings of texts of irregular structure. The *jeu-parti* entitled *Adan, mout fu Aristotes sachans* (R. 277), by Adam de la Halle is very regular in its structure. The isometric, eight-line strophe is constructed of decasyllabic lines rhyming **ab ab / c' c' d d**. If one were to compare musical segments in terms of the poetic structure, one might conclude that the setting is through-composed. But it is to be hoped that such an analysis would be averted upon noticing the strong resemblance between the music of the opening of line 4 and that of line 2. With this observation as an initial premise, pursuing an investigation to determine the closeness and extent of this relationship, one would find that in the melody starting with line 3, syllable 10 and ending at line 5, syllable 6 is identical with an earlier portion of the melody that begins with line 2, syllable 1 and ends at line 3, syllable 9. The division of this material into musical phrases is problematic, as is the division of most other portions. More than one reasonable account of the material may be offered. It would seem that the most likely point of division would occur at the final unit of line 2, which corresponds with the sixth unit of line 4.

Example 8. Adam de la Halle, *Adan, mout fu Aristotes sachans.* Arras, Bibl. mun., MS 657.

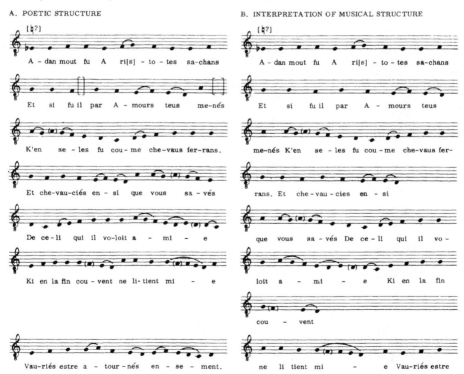

A. Poetic Structure

Adan mout fu Ari[s]totes sachans
Et si fu il par Amours teus menés
K'en seles fu coume chevaus ferrans.
Et chevauciés ensi que vous savés
De celi qui il voloit amie
Ki en la fin couvent ne li tient mie

Vauriés estre atournés ensement

De vo Dame si vous tenist couvent.

B. Interpretation of musical structure

Adan mout fu Ari[s]totes sachans
Et si fu il par Amours teus menés K'en
seles fu coume chevaus ferrans. Et
chevauciés ensi que vous savés De celi qui
il voloit amie Ki en la fin couvent ne li
tient mie Vauriés estre atournés ensement
De vo Dame si vous tenist couvent.

Except for the final musical phrase the musical material following the two identical sections may perhaps best be understood as a series of free elaborations based on the repeated material. We may view this highly original form as consisting of a frame of independent members enclosing a main core, the material of which is presented first in strict form and then in free variation.

The previous three examples serve to illustrate conflicts between poetic and musical structure that affect reasonably broad areas of the individual works. However, not all conflicts of this nature are of similar scope. For example, in the Arsenal reading of *Douce Dame, tout autre pensement* (R. 714) by Thibaut de Champagne, Roi de Navarre, the setting of the *pedes* and the opening of the *cauda* display the normal correlation between the lengths of the text phrases and those of the musical phrases. But this correlation appears to be broken in line 6 and 7 of the nine-line strophe. The musical segment from line 6, syllable 7, through the end of the short seventh line corresponds quite closely with the opening phrase of the melody. Instances of brief conflict between poetic and musical structure appear to be slightly more numerous than those involving broad areas, but further discussion of individual examples does not seem to be warranted here.

In evaluating the import of the evidence presented above, one must beware the blandishments of two opposite, simplistic extremes. On the one hand, those who are fascinated by the new vistas of formal complexity need not exaggerate the importance of these examples. They represent nothing more than a rare, fringe practice. On the other hand, it is equally dangerous to dismiss the examples out of hand because of their rarity. There is no easy explanation for these works. One might perhaps suspect that the melodies were created for other texts and were merely adapted to present usage through some arbitrary and illconsidered decision. But no evidence is available to document such suspicions. The musical structures discussed above do not correspond in length of phrases to any *trouvère* poem presently known to this writer. Moreover, the ramifications of these examples go far deeper than might be implied by their small number. We are prodded to re-examine and revise some of our past assumptions and thus to study *trouvère* song more closely. Most important, we are impelled to seek new means for recognizing and defining *trouvère* musical phrases. In later music, phrases may be defined—quite apart from their relationship to a text—by virtue of harmony, tonal relationships, and rhythmic shape. In dealing with the music of the *trouvères*, however, the harmonic factor is nonexistent and we know little concerning tonal practice. Furthermore, rhythmic shape, which can be the most telling factor, is usually unknown. If we can no longer rely blindly on the assumption that the musical phrase is *always* identical in length to the poetic phrase, then we must seek to increase our sensitivity to purely melodic structures.

To explore briefly a bit further, we may consider the readings of the central melody for *Autres que je ne suel fas* (R. 376) by Gautier de Dargies in the Manuscrit du Roi (M) and the Chansonnier de Noailles (T). Both begin on F and ascend steadily until reaching the upper seventh, at which point the melody turns briefly downward. In the M reading, the melody promptly rebounds and reaches the stable octave at the cadence. In T, however, there is a prolongation of the brief downward turn by means of a repetition, and the melody returns only to the sixth degree at the end of the text phrase. The tone of the octave is reached at the beginning of the second text phrase, and all subsequent musical material is shifted one syllable later in comparison with the reading in M. A superfluous syllable is present in the T reading of the second text phrase and this absorbs the additional musical material. It is not likely, however, that the musical shift was caused by the textual corruption since the musical shift occurs at a prior point. That the shift is not the result of a careless error is shown by the fact that it occurs again in conjunction with the second *pes*; this time there is no added text syllable, so that eight musical units are provided for the seven syllables of line 4.

Example 9. Gautier de Dargies, *Autres que je ne suel fas*. Comparison between the readings of the Manuscrit du Roi (M) and the Chansonnier de Noailles (T).

160   Theodore Karp

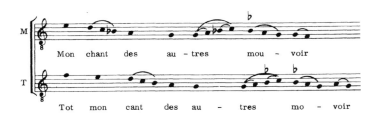

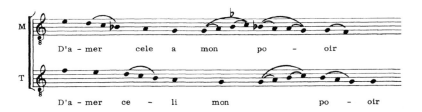

Autres que je ne sueill fas
Autres ke jou ne suel fas

Mon chant des autres mouvoir
Tot mon cant des autres movoir

Quar ainc ne sui un jour las
Car ainc ne sui un jor las

D'amer cele a mon pooir.
D'amer celi mon pooir.

The musical logic of the M reading is based on the consonant function of the octave. And inasmuch as this reading is corroborated through the readings of the Arsenal family of manuscripts, it is undoubtedly the one to be preferred. But note that the T reading possesses a logic of its own. After reaching the point of comparative tension represented by the major seventh, there is a downward stepwise resolution that dips to the stable interval of a fifth before returning to the sixth at the end of the text phrase. In the process, the sixth itself has acquired greater than normal stability by virtue of numerous repetitions. Has there been a recasting of the phrase itself, or is this still another instance of conflict between musical and poetic structures? What kind of tonal direction (or lack thereof) is implied within the phrase should we opt for the former alternative?

Problems of phrase length and tonal direction are by no means unique to *Autres que je ne suel fas*. Similar problems occur with respect to the Arras setting of *Bien [=Or] cuidai vivre sans amour* (R. 1965) by the Chastelain de Couci. This melody, however, is an *unicum* and the cadential displacement comes to light upon comparison of the differences between the two *pedes*. In other examples, such as Gautier d'Espinal's *Ne puet laissier fins cuers c'adès ne plaigne* (R. 119), discussed previously, displacement occurs when a phrase employed originally in conjunction with a line having a masculine ending is re-used without adjustment for the same length line with feminine ending—or vice-versa.

As we begin to study musical phrase structure more closely, we begin to investigate the internal structure of these phrases. And this in turn leads to comparisons with the internal structures of poetic phrases when these are divided by caesurae. We find that several musical phrases are comprised of two similar halves. In our brief final example, from the peripheral setting in the Arras chansonnier of *Mout m'est bele la douce començance* (R. 209) by the Chastelain de Couci, we find that the seventh musical phrase is comprised of two equal halves of five units each, even though the poetic phrase suggests a division of 4–6.

Example 10. Chastelain de Couci, *Mout m'est bele la douce començance*, line 7. Arras, Bibl. mun., MS 657.

Ne sai lequel, se n'ai joie et pauour.

Step by step we shall be drawn deeper into the subject. But the present study has reached its terminal point. On the one hand, this writer has sought to establish an approach to the study of the interrelationship between musical and poetic structure in *trouvère* song that will lead to positive rather than negative results. And certain broad correlations have been set forth. On the other hand, by demonstrating hitherto unsuspected complexities to the subject, the author has tried to provide the impetus for still further work in the field.

[12]
Andalusian Music and the *Cantigas de Santa Maria*

Manuel Pedro Ferreira

When the question of the relationship between the *Cantigas de Santa Maria* and medieval Hispano-Arabic music is raised, the shadow of Julián Ribera's partial musical edition of the *Cantigas*, published in 1922, cannot be avoided.[1] In Ribera's edition, the Alfonsine songs are presented as derivatives of classical Arab music, and transcribed according to what Ribera thought was typically Arab; as a consequence, their original notation was often disregarded. Ribera's approach came under heavy criticism from professional musicologists, amongst them Higinio Anglés, who in his monumental work of 1943–58 buried—seemingly for good—scholarly pretensions to read Arab music into the *Cantigas*.[2] In the past half-century (1943–93), the pro-Arab stance has therefore been confined to the performing domain as a kind of colouristic exoticism, of doubtful historical seriousness, which is sometimes made vaguely respectable through mention of the Islamic instruments depicted in one of the manuscript sources of the *Cantigas* (MS E). This tendency to value instrumental colour can be explained not only on the basis of Ribera's claim that the repertory has an 'orchestral' character,[3] but also in relation to the history of the modern 'early music' movement; in actual practice, instrumental colour has been served as a kind of dressing added to Anglés's transcriptions, which have been generally accepted by performers.

A lot has none the less changed after Ribera's edition in our knowledge of medieval Arab music; and our understanding of the original notation of the *Cantigas* has progressed in the past few years. The time has come to re-evaluate the Arab question from a scholarly point of view.

8   Manuel Pedro Ferreira

The first thing to do is to rephrase the question, substituting 'Andalusian' for 'Arab'. Moorish-Andalusian (or Ibero-Arab) music is not just, or even mainly, Arab music *per se*. It is a hybrid Western tradition which evolved independently from oriental trends from the ninth century onwards and reached its highest level of integration of Western and oriental elements in the twelfth century.[4] The originality of Andalusian music, when compared with other Western medieval traditions, is to be sought primarily in the aspects of form and rhythm. Form represents the Peninsular indigenous element; rhythm the Arab one.

The question of musical form in medieval Andalusian song has generally been ignored; recently, Vicente Beltrán and, most importantly, David Wulstan have faced the problem and attempted to give it a solution.[5] Both take as their starting point the formal structure of the poems, to which they remain anchored as their only secure evidence; naturally, since the textual data gives minimal musical information, their conclusions cannot be firmly founded from a musical point of view. I have therefore taken the opposite approach: to start with the surviving music from Moorish Andalusia.

My work was made possible by the recent publication, by James Monroe and Benjamin Liu, of nine surviving *azjal* and *muwashshahat* composed in Al-Andalus between *c.*1100 and the mid-fourteenth century.[6] As complementary data, I have used the analysis of a representative sample both of today's North African music of Andalusian origin[7] and of the *muwashshah* oral tradition in general.[8] The results of this undertaking, which I will summarize here, will be published in detail elsewhere.[9] The main conclusion is that the *muwashshah* and the symmetrical *zajal* seem originally to have had mainly two kinds of formal scheme, corresponding to the *virelai* (AA ‖ BBB AA, AB ‖ CCC AB) or to a special kind of *rondeau* (AB ‖ BBB AB, [...] AAA BA). The *zajal* proper, textually asymmetrical, must have had related schemes, for the *zajal* and the *muwashshah* are two faces of the same tradition.[10]

At this juncture, the example of the *Cantigas de Santa Maria* has to be taken into account. Poetically speaking, most of them have the *zajal* form. Musically, they tend to present the *virelai* form, which as we have seen is also characteristic of the *muwashshah*. In itself, this fact is not conclusive, for the French *virelai* could be taken as both the poetical and musical model for the *Cantigas*; the only problem with this hypothesis is that the *virelai* hardly existed in France before *c.*1300, while the *Cantigas* were composed before 1284; this fact led Willi Apel to propose a Spanish origin for the *virelai*.[11] Moreover, in the *Cantigas* the influence of the French *rondeau* is slight when compared with the important presence of the reverse kind of *rondeau* (AB || BB AB), also characteristic, *mutatis mutandis*, of the *muwashshah*; this is found in more than seventy *cantigas*.[12] Since this last form is virtually unknown elsewhere in medieval Europe,[13] it is probably indigenous; and since the *Cantigas* were mostly composed in a cultural environment where the Ibero-Arab presence was strongly felt, it probably derives from the *zajal* or its mozarabic counterpart. The *Cantigas de Santa Maria* appear therefore, from a formal point of view, to encapsulate typical features of medieval Andalusian music: the *virelai* form and what I propose to call the *Andalusian rondeau*.

Let us now turn our attention to rhythm. Rhythm is intrinsically linked with the musical notation of the manuscripts. The notation has been variously described by different authors, depending on the interpretative model used to approach it. Hendrik van der Werf, for instance, compared the notation with the late-thirteenth-century Franconian system, and inevitably concluded that the Alfonsine notation is not Franconian,[14] which is hardly surprising since this system was formulated in writing only around 1280, when most of the *Cantigas* were in the process of being copied.[15] It does not follow, though, that the Alfonsine notation lacks a mensural character, for there were mensural systems in existence before Franco of Cologne. On the contrary, I think that it can be proved that the mensural dimension is an important one, regardless of how we choose to interpret it.[16]

Interpretation is about ways to make the data historically intelligible. Anglés was right when he accepted the notation as it stands without trying to force it into preconceived moulds, as Ribera did; he also realized that the rhythms written down by the copyists were often equivalent to the contemporary French patterns known as 'rhythmic modes', but that this was not always true. Unable to accept Ribera's hypothesis of an Arab derivation, he championed the theory of a folkloric origin for the cases of non-modal rhythm; needless to say, the 'folk music' label could embrace everything, and because of this generality could be neither proven nor challenged; it was an easy way out of the problem. In my own work, I have expanded the framework of possible pre-existing models—French developments of modal rhythm, troubadouresque isosyllabism and the rhapsodic rhythm found in the *cantigas d'amigo*; since even this large range of possibilities does not exhaust the rhythmic variety found in the repertory, I had eventually to confront the long-discredited hypothesis of an Andalusian connection.

According to one of the leading specialists in Arab music, Baron Rodolphe d'Erlanger, 'le rythme est, en musique arabe, l'élément principal et prépondérant de toute composition vocale ou instrumentale'. He also remarks that the rhythmic system used by Arab musicians today is substantially the same as it was during the first centuries of Islam.[17] This system is based on the principle of periodicity: the repetition of a rhythmic period defined by the number and quality of the attacks and the time elapsing between them. This time is strictly measured, meaning that it is counted in units of time. Among the ancient music theorists, Al-Farabi (d. 950) is the only one who tries to describe actual musical practice, instead of following Greek music theory;[18] he eschews the Greek definition of the basic time-unit as the shortest perceptible time value, choosing instead as time-unit a compound time, as Arab musicians do today.[19] According to Al-Farabi, a rhythmic period is typically composed of two identical rhythmic cycles. A cycle is a repeated rhythmic pattern superimposed on a given metre. From an abstract point of view each cycle has a basic form in which all the attacks are separated by equal time-intervals, and the last attack is followed by a silence of the same length (the disjunction). In actual practice, this basic scheme gives way to more complex rhythmic patterns which have the status of standard metric fillings. These metric fillings can be varied over a wide range, and two different variants can be joined together in a period. Al-Farabi himself lists a large number of rhythmic periods derived from each of the seven basic metres, and describes the conventional variation procedures which lead to them; his list is not exhaustive, as he simply wants to show how these variation procedures work in practice.[20]

In the following examples, the spacing between two apostrophes (' ') illustrates the minimum time-unit; if an audible attack marks the beginning of a time-unit, it will be represented (| '); time signatures will be used for convenience, the minimum time-unit being equivalent to a quaver.

When the chosen metre is the 'First Thaqil' (or 'First-Heavy')

(a)   (4/2) | ' ' ' | ' ' ' | ' ' ' ' ' '

doubling of the attacks will produce the following pattern:

Andalusian Music and the Cantigas 11

(b) (4/2) | ' | ' | ' | ' | ' | ' ' ' '

Adding a loud attack to allow a proportional disjunction will change it into:

(c) (4/2) | ' | ' | ' | ' | ' | ' | ' ' '

If we reproduce this cycle twice in a row, we have one of the forms of the 'First-Heavy' rhythmic period listed by Al-Farabi.

Another example is the 'Heavy-Ramal' metre:

(a) (3/2) | ' ' ' | ' ' ' ' ' '

With another attack added for continuity, this changes into:

(b) (3/2) | ' ' ' | ' ' ' | ' ' '

and with doubling of the second attack, it becomes

(c) (3/2) | ' ' ' | ' | ' | ' ' '

which corresponds to another form of the cycle mentioned by Al-Farabi.

Variation can also produce syncopation: if we take the continuous pattern, double all attacks and then drop out the fifth, the result is

(d) (3/2) | ' | ' | ' | ' | ' ' ' | '

This is one of several syncopated cycles in Al-Farabi's list. If it is repeated once, we have a homogeneous rhythmic period; if it is combined, for instance, with the continuous double-attack cycle, we have an heterogeneous variant also listed in Al-Farabi; if combined with the basic 'Ramal' cycle, we have the *al-ḥafīf* rhythm, used in a thirteenth-century Andalusian composition which survives in today's oral tradition.[21]

It is important not to forget that the musical tradition that Al-Farabi describes travelled West from Baghdad to Al-Andalus, where it found fertile ground. Furthermore, Arab rhythmic periodicity has a number of features which distinguish it from the medieval Western European rhythmic tradition: the larger scale of some cycles and rhythmic periods, the use of syncopation and the importance of quadruple metre may be mentioned. Accordingly, when a medieval repertory composed in Spain, written for the most part probably in Toledo or Seville, next door to a Moorish-Andalusian environment, uses large-scale cycles or periods, with syncopated patterns or in a quadruple metre, this is likely to reflect the influence of Arab music.

The *Cantigas de Santa Maria* are such a repertory. In the 'Heavy-Ramal' metre, the combination of variants (c) and (d) listed above produces the rhythmic period found in *CSM* 92 (Ex. 1). If we take the above-mentioned form (c) of the 'First-Heavy' cycle and double the second attack, we encounter a variant found in *CSM* 424.[22] If, in the second presentation of the rhythmic variant, we add a final attack for support, as recommended by Al-Farabi, we will have a long rhythmic period identical to that found in *CSM* 25 (Ex. 2).[23] The long rhythmical period which begins *CSM* 100 has two versions which differ in the second half (Ex. 3); the initial version survives in the *al-Bṭāyḥī* rhythm of the Andalusian tradition (Ex. 4);[24] both versions can be described as heterogeneous periods made up of two of the 'First-Heavy' cycles listed in Al-Farabi.[25] In this same song, there is another heterogeneous rhythmic period which shares its second half with the second version of the first period (Ex. 5). The first half presents a cycle that is another variation on the 'First-Heavy' metre,[26] and is found in the *al-qā'im wa-niṣf* rhythm of the Andalusian tradition (Ex. 6).[27] *CSM* 353 uses exclusively this same cycle. *CSM* 116 uses a related rhythmic period, made up of this same cycle followed by the basic form of the 'First-Heavy' metre (Ex. 7). This period is strikingly similar to that found in two sister-compositions by Juan del Encina, 'Señora de hermosura' and 'Una sañosa porfía', which share the same melodic openings;[28] and it is reproduced almost exactly in the first version of 'Norabuena vengas' in the *Cancionero de Palacio*.[29] *CSM* 109 exhibits a more complex period based on the same cycle, produced by repeating part of it in the middle of the period—a variation procedure also mentioned by Al-Farabi (Ex. 8).

Medieval French rhythmical theory and the alternative models mentioned above are unable to explain these seemingly anomalous facts, whereas they make complete sense in the light of Arabian rhythmic theory and its influence on Andalusian song. Given the historical context, one cannot but reach the conclusion that at least the above-mentioned *cantigas* were influenced by Ibero-Arab music.

That being so, perhaps there are other traces of this influence. Again, the first thing to do is to look more closely at what seems to be a rhythmic anomaly from a French-centred perspective: dotted rhythm, which is impossible to write within the normal usage of thirteenth-century French notational systems. It can be observed in seventeen of the *Cantigas*;[30] in two of them it is used to the exclusion of any other rhythmic pattern.[31] The way the Toledo and Escorial

Andalusian Music and the *Cantigas* 13

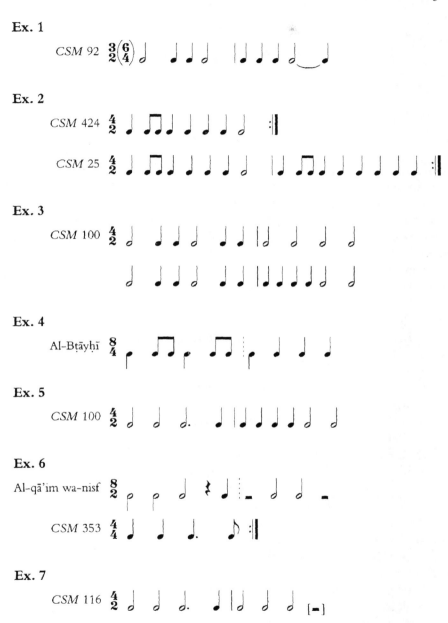

Ex. 9

*To
*E/T

Ex. 10

*E
E/T

manuscripts solve the notational problem is similar: they add a brevis to the long, and then write an isolated brevis; or they use short vertical lines after the long to signal its *ultra mensuram* quality, and then write an isolated brevis (Ex. 9).[32] The rhythmical meaning of these procedures is clear from the different ways the scribes chose to write down the same musical idea, whether in the same manuscript, when a phrase is rewritten several times, or in different manuscripts which have the same song; comparative work shows that a long with a brevis attached to it is rhythmically equivalent to a long followed by a short double bar; it also shows that this augmented long is equivalent to a long followed by a ligature *cum opposita proprietate*, or a binary oblique ligature followed by a brevis or a double bar.[33] Sometimes the Escorial MSS substitute what seems to be a semibrevis for the brevis,[34] but this can easily be explained as a case of notational inertia—forms of the Toledo notation which are reproduced without translation in the Escorial notation (Ex. 10).

The important presence in this repertory of dotted rhythm, ignored in the surviving Galician-Portuguese troubadour songs and in all the remaining written European music, can be explained through the influence of the Andalusian tradition. We have seen that one of the Andalusian rhythmic cycles uses dotted rhythm; in the Middle East, it is also found in the *Sufiyan* rhythm;[35] both derive from classical Arab rhythmic practice. In some of the surviving medieval Andalusian songs,[36] dotted rhythm is pervasive: it tends to be associated with the successive occurrence of a long and a short syllable (Ex. 11). This probably means that dotted rhythm was a standard declamation procedure in Ibero-Arab song, and that it may have influenced the composers of the *Cantigas*.

Another feature of the Andalusian tradition is the use of a five-beat metric pattern already listed in Al-Farabi. Among the seven basic musical metres acknowledged by this theorist, three have five beats per cycle; each of them has a variant which is similar to the French third

Andalusian Music and the Cantigas   15

Ex. 11

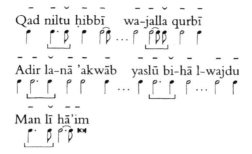

Ex. 12

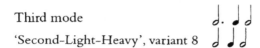

rhythmic mode, except that the first long has only two units of time instead of three (Ex. 12). This rhythmic pattern surfaces in a Hispano-Arab song which has been identified as a *muwashshah* and was partly transcribed, in the sixteenth century, by Francisco Salinas (Ex. 13a);[37] the influence of this pattern on folk music is attested to by several traditional songs which have come down to us in polyphonic settings by Encina, Anchieta and others: its survival may be illustrated here by the song 'Tan buen ganadico' as transcribed by Juan del Encina (Ex. 13b).[38] It can also be found in *CSM* 223—alternative interpretations of the notation leading, in my view, to unsatisfactory results (Ex. 13c).

Ex. 13

Ex. 14

CSM 339 — Ca a-cor-re en coit' e en pe-sar

This last case may not be the only one. It happens, on the one hand, that some melodies (Prologue, *CSM* 10 and 105) or isolated phrases (cf. *CSM* 38, 41) in the *Cantigas de Santa Maria* are notated in such a way that both the five-beat and the six-beat transcriptions are possible. On the other hand, *CSM* 339 has a phrase which is clearly reminiscent, from both a melic and a rhythmic point of view, of the Ibero-Arab song quoted by Salinas (Ex. 14); its notation indicates the third rhythmic mode, which implies a six-beat metre instead of a five-beat one; this suggests that the use of the third rhythmic mode could, in some cases, be seen as a rhythmic variant based on the 'Light-Ramal' metre, or indicate a notational adaptation of an original five-beat pattern.

Although the presence of the five-beat metre in the *Cantigas* cannot be proven with absolute certainty due to its notational ambiguity, the important presence in this repertory of Andalusian forms and Arabic rhythmic features makes it historically plausible, and helps to explain the relatively generous use of the third rhythmic mode by Alfonso's collaborators. From this point of view, the preponderance of the second rhythmic mode over the first in the *Cantigas*, especially in the Toledo MS, could also derive from the coincidence between, on the one hand the French second mode, and on the other the fundamental form of the Arab 'Light-Ramal' metre.

In short, although Anglés rightly identified a strong French flavour in the Marian *Cantigas*, Ribera was also justified in pointing out its debt towards Al-Andalus. To these important influences one could add those of liturgical music, the troubadours and the Galician-Portuguese love song. We have to conclude that this extraordinary Marian collection juxtaposes and combines a number of musical styles which we are just beginning to identify.

Notes to Chapter 2

1. Julián Ribera, *La música de las Cantigas: estudio sobre su origen y naturaleza, con reproducciones fotográficas del texto y transcripción moderna* (Madrid: Real Academia

Andalusian Music and the Cantigas 17

Española, 1922), meant as a companion volume to *Cantigas de Santa María de Don Alfonso el Sabio*, ed. Leopoldo del Cueto, Marqués de Valmar (Madrid: Real Academia Española, 1889), iii.

2. Higinio Anglés, *La música de las Cantigas de Santa María del Rey Alfonso el Sabio*, 3 vols. (Barcelona: Biblioteca Central, 1964, 1943, 1958). The last-published volume is a facsimile edition of MS E.
3. Ribera, p. 117: 'siendo todas las melodías de las Cantigas destinadas a ejecución por varias voces y por orquestra numerosa'.
4. For a historical summary, see Manuel Pedro Ferreira, '*Rondeau* and *Virelai*: Notes on the Music of Al-Andalus', *Plainsong and Medieval Music*, forthcoming.
5. Vicente Beltrán, 'De zéjeles y *dansas*: orígenes y formación de la estrofa con vuelta', *Revista de Filología Española* 64 (1984), 239–66; David Wulstan, 'The Muwashshah and Zagal Revisited', *Journal of the American Oriental Society* 102 (1982), 247–64.
6. Benjamin M. Liu and James T. Monroe, *Ten Hispano-Arabic Strophic Songs in the Modern Oral Tradition: Music and Texts* (Berkeley: University of California Press, 1989).
7. Leo J. Plenckers, 'Les Rapports entre le muwashshah algérien et le virelai du moyen âge', *The Challenge of the Middle East: Middle Eastern Studies at the University of Amsterdam*, ed. I. A. El-Sheikh, C. A. Van de Koppel and R. Peters (Amsterdam: University of Amsterdam, 1982), 91–111; Jozef M. Pacholczyk, 'The Relationship between the Nawba of Morocco and the Music of the Troubadours and Trouvères', *The World of Music* 25 (1983), 5–16; id., 'Rapporti fra le forme musicali della *nawba* andalusa dell'Africa settentrionale e le forme codificate della musica medievale europea', *Culture musicali: quaderni di etnomusicologia* 3.5–6 (1984), 19–42. To the data presented in these articles some more analytical information was added, based on Moroccan sources.
8. Lois Ibsen al Faruqi, 'Muwashshah: a Vocal Form in Islamic Culture', *Ethnomusicology* 19 (1975), 1–29.
9. Ferreira, '*Rondeau* and *Virelai*'.
10. According to the traditional view, the former derives from the latter, but the reverse seems now to be more likely: Wulstan, 'The Muwashshah'; Samuel C. Armistead and James T. Monroe, 'Beached Whales and Roaring Mice: Additional Remarks on Hispano-Arabic Strophic Poetry', *La Corónica* 13 (1985), 206–42.
11. Willi Apel, 'Rondeaux, Virelais, and Ballades in French 13th-Century Song', *Journal of the American Musicological Society* 7 (1954), 121–30.
12. This calculation is based on the tables published by Anglés, *La música*, iii/1ª Parte, pp. 397–400.
13. Friedrich Gennrich, *Grundriss einer Formenlehre des mittelalterlichen Liedes als Grundlage einer musikalischen Formenlehre des Liedes* (Halle: Max Niemeyer, 1932), 67–8.
14. Hendrik van der Werf, 'Accentuation and Duration in the Music of the *Cantigas de Santa Maria*', *Studies on the 'Cantigas de Santa Maria': Art, Music, and Poetry*, ed. Israel J. Katz and John E. Keller (Madison: The Hispanic Seminary of Medieval Studies, 1987), 223–34.
15. Most of the originals which underlay the final compilation of the *Cantigas* (i.e. between 250 and 300 pieces) were written before 1280. The collection is

presumed to have been completed or nearly so by the time Alfonso died (1284). On the dating of the manuscripts, see Manuel Pedro Ferreira, 'The Stemma of the Marian *Cantigas*: Philological and Musical Evidence', *Bulletin of the Cantigueiros de Santa Maria* 6 (1994), 58–98.

16. I have dealt with this problem elsewhere: Manuel Pedro Ferreira, *O som de Martin Codax: sobre a dimensão musical da lírica galego-portuguesa (séculos XII–XIV) / The Sound of Martin Codax: On the Musical Dimension of the Galician-Portuguese Lyric (XII–XIV Centuries)* (Lisbon: Imprensa Nacional–Casa da Moeda, 1986); id., 'Bases for Transcription: Gregorian Chant and the Notation of the Cantigas de Santa Maria', *Los instrumentos del Pórtico de la Gloria: su reconstrucción y la música de su tiempo*, coord. José Lopez-Calo (La Coruña: Fundación Pedro Barrié de la Maza, 1993), ii. 573–621.
17. Baron Rodolphe d'Erlanger, *La Musique arabe* (Paris: Paul Geuthner, 1959), vi. 1, 4.
18. George Dimitri Sawa, *Music Performance Practice in the Early Abbasid Era, 132–320 AH / 750–932 AD* (Toronto: Pontifical Institute of Mediaeval Studies, 1989), 16.
19. D'Erlanger, 7.
20. Sawa, 46, 54.
21. Liu and Monroe, 82.
22. In Anglés's edition, this song is the second in the second Appendix [*FJC* 2]; its form belongs to the 'Andalusian rondeau' type.
23. This is true of the version recorded in the Escorial codices E and T, not of the version in To.
24. D'Erlanger, 148.
25. Sawa, 'First-Heavy' cycles nos 11+3 and 11+9.
26. This variant is arrived at by adding an attack for continuity, doubling this attack, and dropping out the first articulation.
27. Liu and Monroe, 82.
28. Juan del Encina, *Poesía Lírica y Cancionero Musical*, ed. R. O. Jones and Carolyn R. Lee (Madrid: Castalia, 1972).
29. The *Cancionero de Palacio* shows a few striking continuities with the *CSM*: for instance, the rhythmic pattern minim-crotchet, minim-crotchet, crotchet-minim, minim-crotchet (or dotted minim), which ofter recurs in this repertory, can already be found in at least ten *CSM* (34, 46, 104, 199, 232, 295=388, 300, 328, 345 and 398).
30. *CSM* 1, 26, 37, 47, 51, 61, 88, 89, 101, 109, 112, 116, 118, 158, 193, 353 and 393. See also *CSM* 100, 315 and 352.
31. *CSM* 118 and 393.
32. The double vertical line may also be used at the end of a musical phrase or piece, with no apparent rhythmical consequences (see *CSM* 123, 159, 160, 341, 386 and 394). The *Cantigas* 88 and 116 use a long with a double vertical bar to mean either long plus brevis, when followed by a brevis, or double long, when followed by a long (in *CSM* 88, the Toledo MS makes it clear that in the latter case the augmentation applies to a three-tempora long).
33. See *CSM* 1, 47, 51, 89, 116 and 393.
34. *CSM* 37, 47, 193 and 353.
35. D'Erlanger, 53.
36. Liu and Monroe, songs I, III, V (occasionally in other compositions).

37. Francisco Salinas, *De musica libri septem* (Salamanca, 1577). It is the song *Calvi vi calvi / Calvi aravi* ('My heart is in [another] heart / [because] my heart is arabic'), quoted by Gil Vicente in both the *Comédia de Rubena* and the *Tragicomedia de Don Duardos*; see Emílio García Gómez, 'La canción famosa Calvi vi calvi / Calvi aravi', *Al-Andalus* 21 (1956), 1–18, 215–16, and Juan José Rey, *Danzas cantadas en el Renacimiento español* (Madrid: Sociedad Española de Musicologia, 1978), 25–6. Salinas's musical quotation was wrongly transcribed (in 6/8) by Anglés, *La música*, iii/2ª Parte, p. 440.

38. Juan del Encina, *Poesía Lírica*, pp. 45, 294, 354; see also the commentary by Manuel Pedro Ferreira, in *Cancioneiro da Biblioteca Hortênsia de Elvas* (Lisbon: Instituto Português do Património Cultural, 1989), pp. ix–x. On quintuple-time Spanish songs from the Renaissance, see Marius Schneider, 'Studien zur Rhythmik im *Cancionero de Palacio*', *Miscelánea en homenaje a Monseñor Higinio Anglés* (Barcelona: CSIC, 1958–61), ii. 833–41, and Rey, *Danzas cantadas*, 30–3.

[13]
Rondeau and virelai: the music of *Andalus and the* Cantigas de Santa Maria

MANUEL PEDRO FERREIRA

ABSTRACT. *Between the eighth and the thirteenth centuries the southern part of the Iberian Peninsula was dominated by its Arab and Berber conquerors and their direct political heirs. In this large and rich territory, called Andalus, an original mixture of Eastern and Western cultural elements gradually emerged. The southward expansion of the northern Christian kingdoms, beginning in the eleventh century, eventually displaced, circumscribed and debilitated Andalusian culture, which finally found in northwestern Africa its only stable refuge. Although the literary and artistic achievements of Andalus have long attracted attention, the place of music in medieval Andalusian culture has not lately been subject to close scrutiny. The present study, based largely on the analysis of Andalusian survivals in contemporary North African musical traditions, will attempt to identify what could have been the most typical musical forms of Andalusian song and evaluate their possible influence on the thirteenth-century* Cantigas de Santa Maria *and French secular song.*[1]

The character of Andalusian music

The invasion of the Iberian Peninsula in 711 by Moslem armies from North Africa and the consequent military occupation and migratory movement do not seem to have had initially any major effects on the musical traditions of the Peninsula nor on its cultural traditions taken as a whole. Indeed, the invading warriors (mostly Berbers) lived at first in relative isolation. The Arab ruling class, few in number, had limited cultural impact, and the immigrants from Africa and the Near East likewise constituted a small minority. We may thus assume that until the ninth century the overwhelming majority of the population continued to adhere to its cultural and religious traditions. By establishing permanent communication with the Mediterranean South, however, the Moslem conquest stimulated the circulation of people, information and

E-mail: mpf@netcabo.pt

[1] This article was originally written in 1993/1994 in Portuguese as an Appendix to *Cantus coronatus*, a book on the notated *cantigas d'amor* of Dom Dinis (forthcoming); translated by Dr David Cranmer with the support of the Fundação Luso-Americana para o Desenvolvimento, it was later revised for independent publication. It should be read in conjunction with my chapter 'Andalusian Music and the *Cantigas de Santa Maria*' (note 31 below). I would like to express here my gratitude to Dr Adel Sidarus (University of Evora) for his advice on the sections of this article relating to Ibero-Islamic culture; this enabled me to make significant improvements to their contents and presentation. Any defects contained in these sections remain, however, entirely the author's responsibility.

musical instruments between the Peninsula and the Islamic world, which in due course would have important consequences.

The arrival in 755 of 'Abd al-Rahman, the only survivor of the Ummayad dynasty, whose caliphate, based in Damascus, had been overthrown, and the consequent foundation of the independent Emirate of Cordoba brought about the beginning of a period of stability and progress favourable to letters and the arts. With the arrival in 822 of the famous singer and lutenist Ziryab, a noted pupil of either Ibrahim or Ishaq al-Mawsili (and therefore an authentic representative of the classical school of Baghdad), oriental music came to occupy a more prominent place in Andalusian high society.[2]

The influence of Ziryab and his followers is reported to have had a marked effect on the history of Andalusian music, but it was certainly less widespread than is generally supposed. Given the intimate relationship between Arab music and poetry, as well as the dependence of music on patronage, it is probable that adherence to the oriental style of singing would have been restricted to the principal Islamicized urban circles, especially those of a higher social condition and dependent on central power. These constituted just a tiny minority of the population. For this reason courtly and popular musical environments must be considered separately.

The musical style imported by Ziryab from Baghdad was essentially a synthesis of traditions of Byzantine, Persian and Near Eastern traditions, adapted to the language, metre and spirit of Arabic poetry. According to George Sawa, the repertory consisted of songs which kept an individual identity, linked to style and authorship. They were sung by just one voice or by several in unison. The song melody followed a traditional rhythmic pattern, on the basis of which it was classified within a musical genre. Ornamental modifications governed by conventions were permitted during performance.

The song could be preceded by a vocal or instrumental prelude. Since instrumental music was considered inferior to vocal music, it was limited to the playing of preludes,

---

[2] A reliable historical biography of Ziryab is still lacking; the exact dates and circumstances of his career are reported differently by modern authors. The most detailed, accessible account is still, to my knowledge, Julián Ribera, *Historia de la música árabe medieval y su influencia en la española* (Madrid, 1927; repr. New York, 1975), 168–81; re-edited as *La música árabe y su influencia en la española*, (Madrid, 1985), 99–110. The real historical contribution of Ziryab appears nowadays to have been more modest than was initially supposed: see Jozef Pacholczyk, 'Early Arab Suite in Spain: An Investigation of the Past through the Contemporary Living Traditions'; Christian Poché, 'Un nouveau regard sur la musique d'al-Andalus: le manuscrit d'al-Tifashi', *Revista de Musicología*, 16 (1993), 358–66 and 367–79; idem, *La musique arabo-andalouse* (Paris, 1995), 35–7, esp. 42. Ziryab's success as a musician gave him a value as a teacher too. According to some commentators, he founded a conservatoire; see, for example, E. Lévi-Provençal, *España Musulmana*, Tomo IV of the *História de España* ed. Ramón Menéndez Pidal (Madrid, 1950), 173; followed by Adalberto Alves, *O Meu Coração é Árabe* (Lisbon, 1987), 25; and *Arabesco* (Lisbon, 1989), 30. Ziryab's private teaching activity may be described as a 'school' in the generic sense, but this has nothing to do with a conservatoire in the modern sense of the term – an autonomous, public, officially regulated, non-profit-making institution for specialized artistic training. Teaching them could be a very lucrative profession, given that the powerful would pay as much as a slave-girl's weight in gold if she were well trained as a singer and knowledgeable of a wide repertory. Naturally, Ziryab exploited this business to the full, teaching music at home not only to his own sons and daughters and to selected pupils, but to slave-girls whom he could afterwards sell.

Rondeau and virelai: the music of Andalus and the Cantigas de Santa Maria 129

interludes and postludes, in addition to its accompanimental role. (Instrumentalists sometimes performed versions of vocal pieces but such a practice was exceptional.) Instrumental accompaniment consisted of duplicating the melodic line in an ornamented form, generally at the unison or octave, thus giving a heterophonic effect. Wind or plucked stringed instruments could be used to accompany the singer, but never bowed stringed instruments. Generally the singer demanded just one accompanist, who typically played a plucked instrument. On certain occasions the accompaniment was reinforced (e.g., two lutes or one lute and a wind instrument). The number of lutes could be multiplied in the event of a group of singers accompanying themselves, but the resulting ensemble never included percussion. By contrast, a singer when singing alone could accompany him or herself with percussion instruments, such as the *duff* or castanets.[3]

Alongside the courtly oriental style and Berber or Bedouin-Arab folksong, there was also a strong current of indigenous vocal music, sung in Ibero-Romance dialects.[4] This indigenous current has been used to explain the emergence of the poetic-musical genres which are typically Andalusian, the *zajal* and the *muwashshah*, and the success they obtained.

The poetic-musical genre known as the *muwashshah*, said to have been invented around 900 by a blind man from Cabra, is a strophic song composed in a learned language (literary Arabic, or Hebrew), generally characterized by the presence of a

---

[3] George Dimitri Sawa, *Music Performance Practice in the Early Abbasid Era 132–320 AH/750–932 AD* (Toronto, 1989), 145–54 and 202–5. The *duff* (square-shaped, double-sided tambourine) and the castanets seem to have originated at the eastern end of the Mediterranean, but they may have been introduced to the Iberian Peninsula prior to the Moorish period through Jewish or Byzantine connections: see Ernesto Veiga de Oliveira, *Instrumentos Musicais Populares Portugueses*, 2nd ed. (Lisbon, 1982), 403 and 446. The lute, on the other hand, is one of the many oriental instruments which owes its spread in Europe to Arab dominance in the Peninsula. Habib Hassan Touma, in his article 'Indications of Arabian Musical Influence on the Iberian Peninsula from the 8th to the 13th Century', *Revista de Musicología*, 10 (1987), 137–50, esp. 143–4 and 147, cites specifically not only the lute but also the *nafir* (a straight trumpet), the *shabbaba* (a small recorder), the *rabab* (a bowed chordophone), the *tabl* (a drum) and the *nakarat* (a pair of drums). One could add the *darbukka* (a waisted drum), the *mandora* (a plucked chordophone) and the *al-buq* (a wind instrument). We should bear in mind that it is not always easy to specify the instrument corresponding to the nomenclature used in medieval Arab sources, nor does the reference to an instrument in Andalusian sources imply that it was unknown in Western Europe prior to the Moslem invasion of the Peninsula. On the other hand, there are instruments of oriental origin which may have made their way into Europe via Byzantium or the Mediterranean. We should also remember that the adoption of an instrument does not always imply the adoption of the functions associated with it, the appropriation of its repertory or the imitation of its original playing techniques, which is why the musical implications of such adoption often remain obscure.

[4] We ought not to forget that Andalusian urban society seems to have continued to be bilingual until the end of the eleventh century, when the Moslem population of the south of the Peninsula reached roughly 80 per cent of the total. Indeed it was only in the tenth century that Arabic overthrew Latin as the language of culture among Mozarabs, and only in the second half of the century that the Moslem population overtook the Christian in numerical terms: cf. Thomas F. Glick, *Cristianos y musulmanes en la España medieval (711–1250)* (Madrid, 1991), 43–7. The progress of religious conversion during the tenth and eleventh centuries does not, however, imply a relegation of traditional Hispanic music in the face of Arab music, since, from the point of view of the prevailing opinion in rigorously orthodox Islam, all music, irrespective of its kind, is morally suspect or open to condemnation as a matter of principle.

prelude (or opening refrain?)⁵ sometimes omitted, followed by several verses divided into two parts: one with rhymes that vary from verse to verse, the other with invariable rhymes, the same as those of the prelude, as in the following example:

```
... A ... B
... A ... B

... c ... d
... c ... d
... c ... d
... a ... b
... a ... b

[... A ... B
... A ... B]?

... e ... f
... e ... f
... e ... f
... a ... b
... a ... b
```

These are long lines with internal rhyme (which was optional). Taking only end-rhyme into account, the scheme may be simplified as: AA bbbaa [AA] cccaa, etc. In the last verse, the second part was made up of a *kharja* (exit) or *markaz* (stirrup), normally distinguished by its use of a vernacular language (vulgar Hebrew, colloquial Arabic, Romance dialect or a mixture of Arabic and Romance dialects). It is on the rhyme, the metre and the music of the *kharja*, itself a quotation of a pre-existing composition, that the whole song is based.⁶

The typical *zajal* has a similar poetic structure but is distinguished from the *muwashshah* by its use of colloquial language and a tendency towards a more narrative content, by not making use of a pre-existing composition quoted in the *kharja*, by not repeating all the lines of the prelude or refrain in the second part of the verse but rather half of them (AA bbba [AA] ccca, etc.) and by often displaying a less complex metrical structure (short lines or long lines broken into hemistichs but without internal rhyme).⁷ There is, however, a *muwashshah*-like *zajal* variety, whose

---

⁵ Scholars do not agree on the status of the introductory distich. Those who defend a folk, Romance derivation of the genre, tend to consider it a refrain, while those who claim an Arab origin for the *muwashshah* see it as a prelude. The character of the introductory lines could however depend not on the roots of the genre, but rather on the performance context. Taking into account that the composition could either be sung or read aloud, the introductory distich could assume both the function of a refrain, when sung, and that of a prelude, when recited.

⁶ The key concept is that all the relevant properties of the *kharja* are built into the main body of the *muwashshah*, so that it is prefigured long before it appears. For more information, see the synthesis by Pilar Lorenzo, 'Muwaxaha', in *Dicionário da Literatura Medieval Galega e Portuguesa*, ed. G. Lanciani and G. Tavani (Lisbon, 1993), 470–2 (with bibliography).

⁷ Emilio García Gómez, ed., *El mejor Ben Quzmán en 40 zéjeles* (Madrid, 1981); Samuel G. Armistead and James T. Monroe, 'Beached Whales and Roaring Mice: Additional Remarks on Hispano-Arabic Strophic Poetry', *La Corónica*, 13 (1985), 206–42.

only distinguishing feature is the use of colloquial language instead of a learned one. A *zajal* where only part of the introductory distich is reinstated is called asymmetrical, the muwashshah-like alternative, symmetrical. The Arabic *zajal* is explicitly documented from the first half of the twelfth century. However, the Hebrew *zajal*, which is dependent upon it, appears a century earlier,[8] and recent research provides firm support for the idea that the history of the genre may go back as far as the tenth or even the ninth century,[9] as Baron d'Erlanger proposed as long ago as 1959.[10]

The *muwashshah* seems generally to have been sung by a single voice, possibly accompanied by a stringed instrument or alternating with a wind instrument, played by the singer him or herself.[11] This form of performance does not stray very far from the classical Arab tradition, which is coherent with the fact that the *muwashshah* was written in classical Arabic. The *zajal*, written in colloquial Arabic and closer to romance metrical models, may have been performed differently, and its initial lines may have been used more often as a refrain. The popularity and peculiarity of the peninsular musical traditions (among which the *zajal*) are attested to by an oriental traveller on a visit to Malaga in 1015. He complained of the din of the voices and instruments produced during the night throughout the city, contrasting it with the gentleness of the musical style imported from Baghdad which he heard in the house of a highly placed Andalusian dignitary.[12]

Andalusian music in this phase, then, was built upon three separate traditions: Arab-oriental, indigenous and Hispano-Arabic. The political evolution of Andalus, however, was to alter this panorama. The disintegration and consequent fall of the Emirate of Cordoba in 1013–31 led to a fragmentation of power. New Andalusian kingdoms were set up as regional powers, often entrusted to local families of long standing. This situation brought about an increase in opportunities for professional musicians, but it may just as well have contributed to a dilution of the influence of the classically rooted tradition in the face of indigenous currents. The religious intransigence of the new Murabit power, which established itself definitively from

---

[8] Ezra Fleischer, *Shirat ha-qodesh ha-ʿivrit biymei ha-benayim* (Jerusalem, 1975), as cited by Amnon Shiloah, 'The Jews of Spain and the Quest for Cultural Identity', *Revista de Musicología*, 16 (1993), 380–4, esp. 383; David Wulstan, 'The Muwashshah and Zagal Revisited', *Journal of the American Oriental Society*, 102 (1982), 247–64.

[9] James T. Monroe, 'Which Came First, the *Zajal* or the *Muwashshaha*? Some Evidence for the Oral Origins of Hispano-Arabic Strophic Poetry', *Oral Tradition*, 4/1–2 (1989), 38–64. The author tackles the question from a theoretical stance, quotes both direct and indirect literary references to the *zajal* or its composition, dating back to the ninth and tenth centuries, and concludes that 'both the Arab and the Romance zajalesque forms descend from a native Romance prototype and are therefore sisters. In contrast, the *muwashshah* is a learned development of the popular *zajal* in Arabic and Romance, and is therefore its Arab daughter' (p. 60). This interpretation was challenged by Federico Corriente, who proposed the existence, around 900, of a non-strophic, proto-*zajal*; see Federico Corriente, *Poesía dialectal árabe y romance en alAndalús* (Madrid, 1998), 70–97.

[10] Baron Rodolphe d'Erlanger, *La Musique Arabe*, vol. 6 (Paris, 1959), 635.

[11] Consuelo López-Morillas, 'Was the *Muwashshah* Really Accompanied by the Organ?', *La Corónica*, 14 (1985–86), 40–54. The author answers the question posed by the title in the negative.

[12] Benjamin M. Liu and James T. Monroe, *Ten Hispano-Arabic Strophic Songs in the Modern Oral Tradition: Music and Texts* (Berkeley, 1989), 27–8.

1091, had among its consequences, at least in the first instance, the condemnation of the practice of music and the halting of musical relations with the East.

The strength of the local traditions and the weakening of oriental influence at the beginning of the twelfth century, may have led the philosopher Ibn Bajja (known in the West as Avempace) to combine, in the words of the encyclopaedist Ahmad al-Tifashi (first half of the thirteenth century), 'the songs of the Christians with those of the East, thus inventing a specifically Andalusian style corresponding to the temperament of its people; the latter came to reject any other styles'.[13] This comment probably refers to a systematization rather than a radical change. It does, however, document the full acceptance of Ibero-Islamic musical taste, as opposed to the oriental, classically rooted tradition. The Hispano-Arabic component thus absorbed the oriental component at the same time as it definitively superseded the indigenous component, which, however, can be presumed to have remained alive amongst the Mozarab minority, especially in rural areas.

The testimony given above seems to imply that the evolution from the classical modal system, which was basically diatonic,[14] to the *maqam* system, which prevails in the Mediterranean to this day – an evolution that was achieved in the East only in the thirteenth century – did not have a decisive effect on the musical evolution of Andalus. Zyriab was connected with the conservative school of Ibrahim and Ishaq al-Mawsili, who rejected the first non-diatonic additions to the classical system. This allows us to suppose that he did not use the Persian notes and the zalzalian intervals introduced by some of his contemporaries. Even if the new oriental fashion eventually arrived in Andalus, as it probably did, it is unlikely that these innovations survived local musical habits and Ibn Bajja's reform. The diatonicism of late medieval Andalusian music is further confirmed through both historical and analytical indications.[15]

The hybrid style invented there, as epitomized in Al-Tifashi's description, was slower in tempo and melodically more 'spun-out' than the oriental style. From the second half of the twelfth century the professional singers delighted in the free insertion of additions and repetitions which could lengthen songs almost indefinitely[16] (a practice that left a characteristic residue in the present-day *muwashshah* and in the North African repertory of Andalusian origin).[17] It is unreasonable, therefore,

---

[13] Liu and Monroe, *Ten Hispano-Arabic Strophic Songs*, 42. See also Poché, 'Un nouveau regard'.

[14] Owen Wright, ' 'Ibn al-Munajjim and the Early Arabian Modes' *The Galpin Society Journal*, 19 (1966), 27–48; Sawa, *Music Performance Practice*, 72ff.

[15] The observation of Al-Tifashi according to which the Andalusians cultivated the ancient Arab musical style and the classical tuning of the lute (translation and commentary in Liu and Monroe, *Ten Hispano-Arabic Strophic Songs*, 30–1 and 35–44); the lute method *Ma'rifat al-naghamat al-thaman*, quoted by Owen Wright, *The Modal System of Arab and Persian Music A.D.1250–1300* (Oxford, 1978), 7; and the overtly diatonic system cultivated by the Moroccan Andalusian tradition, a system which is probably also the historical core of the Algerian and Tunisian traditions; cf. Philip D. Schuyler, 'Moroccan Andalusian Music', *The World of Music*, 20 (1978), 33–46, esp. 36; C. Poché, *La musique arabo-andalouse*, 77–84.

[16] Liu and Monroe, *Ten Hispano-Arabic Strophic Songs*, 37.

[17] Lois Ibsen al Faruqi, 'Muwashshah: A Vocal Form in Islamic Culture', *Ethnomusicology*, 19 (1975), 1–29, esp. 7; Schuyler, 'Moroccan Andalusian Music', 37.

to suppose that thirteenth-century Andalusian music should display the same characteristics as Eastern Mediterranean music of the same period.[18]

To sum up, the musical tradition of the Hispano-Arabs in the thirteenth century displayed varying degrees of hybridism. At the top of the social scale, oriental Arab music of the classical school gave way to a cross between classical and indigenous Iberian elements; the lower the position on the social scale, the greater importance given to the European element. The popularization of the hybrid Ibero-Arabic tradition must, however, have made its entry possible at all levels of the social fabric. If Andalusian popular music seems to have been permeable to oriental influence only to a limited degree, actual Arab ethnic influence must have been very minimal, bearing in mind the very few traces present in popular Spanish song that can be shown to be of Bedouin-Arab origin.[19] Medieval Andalusian music should be regarded, therefore, as a hybrid tradition of local origin developed locally and not Arab music *tout court*.

The musical form of Andalusian song

The musical form of the medieval *zajal* and of the *muwashshah* has been the object of various suppositions made without sufficient foundation. Pierre Le Gentil suggested that early *zajal* settings would have reflected the asymmetry of its text, whether it was put into the form of a French rondeau or a form related to that of the virelai. Vicente Beltrán, taking up the latter suggestion and combining it with some of the parallels drawn by Anglès between the form of the *zajal* and certain musical forms to be found in the *Cantigas de Santa Maria* and in the *Cancionero musical de Palacio*, proposed that the *muwashshah* would have been characterized musically by a structure of the type AB /CCC AB, while the *zajal* would have followed the structure AB /CCCB.[20] David Wulstan, on the other hand, made a detailed analysis of the contrafaction of poems of the *zajal* and *muwashshah* type, seeking to draw out hints as to the musical form underlying them. By combining this analysis with more general observations on the poetic metre of Andalusian poetry, he suggested that the *muwashshah* and symmetrical *zajal* would probably have assumed musical forms involving repetition patterns like those of the simplest virelai (AA /BBB AA) or rondeau (AB /AAA AB or

---

[18] In the fourteenth century, Eastern Mediterranean music had a spasmodic influence on European instrumental music: Timothy J. McGee, 'Eastern Influences in Mediaeval European Dances', in *Cross-Cultural Perspectives on Music*, ed. Robert Falck and Timothy Rice (Toronto, 1982), 79–100; Shai Burstyn, 'The "Arabian Influence" Thesis Revisited', *Current Musicology*, 45–47 [Festschrift for Ernest H. Sanders] (1990), 119–46.

[19] Marius Schneider, 'A propósito del influjo árabe – ensayo de etnografia musical de la España medieval', *Anuario Musical*, 1 (1946), 31–141, esp. 47–9 and 53–6; Josep Crivillé i Bargalló, *Historia de la música española, VII: El folklore musical* (Madrid, 1983), 267–84.

[20] Pierre Le Gentil, *Le virelai et le villancico. Le problème des origines arabes* (Paris, 1954), 235; Higinio Anglès, *La música de las Cantigas de Santa María del rey Alfonso el Sabio*, vol. III/1ª parte: *Estudio crítico* (Barcelona, 1958), 394; Vicente Beltrán, 'De zéjeles y *dansas*: orígenes y formación de la estrofa con vuelta', *Revista de Filología Española*, 64 (1984), 239–66, esp. 245.

AB /BBB AB) types.[21] The *zajal* with an asymmetrical structure is considered, by extension, as musically asymmetrical.[22]

Both Beltrán's and Wulstan's proposals are based on the presupposition that a parallel can be drawn between the poetic and musical forms, a presumed parallel that historical evidence shows to be far from universally applicable. If it is true that in a given song certain metrical conditions demand certain compatible musical features, it is also true that the fact that the words display an asymmetry as regards their rhyme scheme does not prevent the music from being symmetrical in form (like the virelai). It is also important to bear in mind a fundamental methodological difficulty, namely that a comparison of metrical forms may tell us about the presence or absence of musical contrasts, but it does not entirely resolve the problem of whether two lines have the same melody or not. The same kind of contrast may be obtained by opposing A to B or B to C. To give an example: both the structure AB /AAA B and the structure AB /CCC B (and not solely the first of these) are compatible with the metrical contrast between the refrain and the first three lines of the verse, as observed by Wulstan in a *zajal* by Ibn Quzman:[23]

ʿaynayk bi-hal al-guyush   hin tahush
wa-lak ʿidar fi-l-wara
lays billah mitlu yura
ma kannu illa tira –   zi-l-nuqush

In the present author's view, the only way to test the hypotheses put forward hitherto and to reach a tentative, though not merely speculative, conclusion about the problem of musical form in Hispano-Arabic poetry is through evidence from the Andalusian oral tradition. This can be facilitated by the analysis of the few authenticated medieval examples which have been transmitted from generation to generation by both ordinary folk and the professional musicians who inherited the Iberian repertory.[24]

Although it can reasonably be doubted how faithful this transmission may be when considered in abstraction, it must be borne in mind that oral tradition, in its most

---

[21] The form of the rondeau is exemplified musically in Wulstan's article 'The Muwashshah' through a *muwashshah* by Ibn Sahl (*Hal dara*) as preserved by oral tradition.

[22] From David Wulstan's observations we may conclude that, in his view, the *zajal* assumed the forms AA /BBBA, AB /AAAA, AB /BBBB, aaB /AAAaB or aaB /BBBaB (cf. pp. 254–6). He makes an explicit contrast between the formal symmetry of the virelai and the supposed musical asymmetry of the *zajal* in a more recent article: 'Boys, Women and Drunkards: Hispano-Mauresque Influences on European Song?' in *The Arab Influence in Medieval Europe*, ed. Dionisius A. Agius and Richard Hitchcock (Reading, 1994), 136–67, esp. 140.

[23] Wulstan, 'The Muwashshah', 255.

[24] A step in this direction was taken by Leo J. Plenckers, who recently proposed that the musical form ($\alpha\beta$ $\alpha\beta$ $\alpha\beta$ $\gamma\gamma$ $\alpha\beta$) of the 'bald' Algerian *sanʿa*, an offshoot of the *muwashshah*, reflects that of its Andalusian predecessor. Plenckers's article, 'The Cantigas de Santa Maria and the Moorish Muwashshah: Another Way of Comparing Their Musical Structures', *Revista de Musicología*, 16 (1993), 354–7, came to my attention after the original version of this paper had been written.

Rondeau and virelai: the music of Andalus and the Cantigas de Santa Maria 135

conservative guise, has enabled complete melodies to cross hundreds of years without substantial alteration.[25] Generally speaking, the faithfulness of oral transmission is dependent upon chosen musical constraints and general cultural stability.[26] In the Islamic tradition the musical kernel of the compositions may be considered to include at least three fundamental aspects: the rhythmical mode (not only because of its mnemonic value, but also because it constitutes a culturally privileged parameter of composition and transmission), the overall melodic shape, and the order of the phrases (psychologically stable aspects which, together with the rhythmical mode, confer an identity on the composition).

It may be assumed that the cultural environment in the west of North Africa (in the area now shared by Morocco, Algeria and Tunisia) experienced no major upheavals until the twentieth century. Now, the fact that songs composed between about 1100 and the middle of the fourteenth century, written in an idiom which subsequently fell into disuse, have continued to be sung up to the present is in itself evidence of the enormous conservatism of the Andalusian musical tradition, sustained both by the artistic prestige and political symbolism of the repertory and by the nostalgic memory of its origins.[27] It should be added that even before the migratory movements which occurred during the Christian reconquest, the tradition from the west of North Africa imbibed its repertory from the Iberian Peninsula and was known as early as the thirteenth century for its conservative character.[28] The tendency towards a fossilization of this professional repertory has been constantly reinforced. According to current scholarship, from the sixteenth century onwards new pieces apparently ceased to be composed in the traditional Andalusian style; every effort centred on memorizing the classical repertory. While this goal does not exclude some degree of transformation and the introduction of new texts, it points to the preservation of generic musical identities.[29] Thus it is reasonable to accept that, at least in general terms, the most fundamental aspects of Andalusian composition have undergone only unimportant changes, while its most flexible aspects (small-scale behaviour,

---

[25] The great antiquity of certain melodies is the focus, for example, of Schneider's essay (see n. 19) and the following studies: Constantin Brailoiu, 'Concerning a Russian Melody', in *Problems of Ethnomusicology*, ed. Constantin Brailoiu (Cambridge, 1984), 239–89; Paul Collaer, 'Notes concernant certains chants espagnols, hongrois, bulgares et géorgiens', *Anuario Musical*, 9 (1954), 153–60; 10 (1955), 109; Judith Etzion and Susana Weich-Shahak, 'The Music of the Judeo-Spanish Romancero: Stylistic Features', *Anuario Musical*, 43 (1988), 221–55; Judith R. Cohen, 'A Reluctant Woman Pilgrim and a Green Bird: A Possible Cantiga Melody Survival in a Sephardic Ballad', *Cantigueiros*, 7 (1995), 85–8.

[26] Mantle Hood, 'The Reliability of Oral Tradition', *Journal of the American Musicological Society*, 12 (1959), 201–9.

[27] In Morocco, Andalusian music, as an ancient form of court music, maintained its association with monarchy and symbolizes the legitimacy of the dynasty: see Jozef M. Pacholczyk, 'The Relationship Between the Nawba of Morocco and the Music of the Troubadours and Trouvères', *The World of Music*, 25 (1983), 5–16, esp. 10.

[28] According to Al-Tifashi, as quoted in Liu and Monroe, *Ten Hispano-Arabic Strophic Songs*, 32.

[29] P. Schuyler, 'Moroccan Andalusian Music', 41; Pacholczyk, 'The Relationship', 8–10. The only suite known to have been composed in modern times (eighteenth century) departs from traditional Andalusian modality.

time length, performance practice, and possibly also melodic mode)[30] have probably undergone progressive modifications which, through a process of accumulation, may ultimately have had a significant effect on the content of the songs.

For our present purposes, given a representative musical sample, the tendency to preserve the formal characteristics (identity and order of phrases) is sufficient to lend retrospective validity to the analysis of the available musical examples. Modality, melodic particulars, overall size of the song and performance practice will not be considered here; rhythm deserves separate treatment.[31]

I begin with a formal analysis of eight of the ten compositions identified as being of Andalusian origin and published in 1989 by Benjamin M. Liu and James T. Monroe (excluding one of doubtful authenticity and another because it exists in too fragmentary a state).[32] Half of these eight songs (two *muwashshaha*s and two *zajal*s with incorporated refrain) have the musical structure AB /BBB AB,[33] to which may be added another *zajal* in *muwashshah* form without refrain, which originally probably had a similar structure (AAA BA).[34] Of the remaining three compositions, a *muwashshaha* and a *zajal* in *muwashshah* form display a virelai-type structure (AA' /BBB' AA',[35] AB /CCC AB), while the remaining *muwashshaha* has the structure AB / AB AB B'.[36] It should be noted that the form AB /BBB AB corresponds to the definition of a rondeau (*rotundellus*) as given around 1300 by Johannes de Grocheio. This is a song

---

[30] Modal structure is easily changed in oral transmission. The centrality of modal classification in the transmission of Arabic song seems to be a circumscribed and relatively late phenomenon in the Middle Ages, and is compatible with changes in the meaning of modal names. The fact that the actual modes associated with Andalusian repertory are not exactly the same in Tunisia or Morocco suggests some resilience in its modal tradition.

[31] Manuel Pedro Ferreira, 'Andalusian Music and the *Cantigas de Santa Maria*', in *Cobras e Son: Papers on the Text, Music and Manuscripts of the Cantigas de Santa Maria*, ed. Stephen Parkinson (Oxford, 2000), 7–19.

[32] The compositions are: *Qad niltu hibbi*, a *zajal* (with an incorporated refrain) by al-Shushtari (ca.1212–69), transcribed in Ra'is et al., *La Musique andalouse marocaine: nawbat 'gribt l-hsin'* (Casablanca, 1985); *Umzuj al-akwas*, a *zajal* (with an incorporated refrain) by Ibn al-Khatib (1313–75), in Ra'is; *Adir la-na akwab*, a *muwashshaha* by Al-A'mà (d. 1126) or Ibn Baqi (d. 1145/50), in Ra'is; *Ila mata*, a *muwashshah* by Al-A'ma, ibid.; *Man li ha'im*, a *zajal* with the form of a *muwashshah*, attributed by oral tradition to Ibn Zuhr (1113–98), in Ra'is; *Hal tusta 'adu*, a *muwashshaha* by Ibn Zuhr, excluded as too fragmentary; *Hal dara zabyu l-hima*, a *muwashshaha* by Ibn Sahl (d. 1251), in Rodolphe d'Erlanger, *La musique arabe*, vol. 6; *Man habbak*, an anonymous *zajal* excluded as being of doubtful Andalusian origin; *Wa-husnak qad ishtahar*, an anonymous *zajal* probably of Andalusian origin, gathered in the Middle East by Salim al-Hilw, *Al-Muwashshahat al-Andalusiyya*: Beirut, 1965; and *Ayyuha s-saqi ilay-ka l-mushtakà*, a *muwashshaha* by Ibn Zuhr, sung by Palestinian informants and transcribed in J. Monroe and D. Swiatlo, 'Ninety-Three Arabic Kharjas in Hebrew Muwashshahs', *Journal of the American Oriental Society*, 97/2 (1977), 141–63.

[33] *Qad niltu hibbi*: AB AB' /CB" AB" AB" ||: CB" AB" AB' : CB" AB" AB /AB AB' /CB" AB" AB'. *Umzuj al-akwas*: AB BBB AB. *Adir la-na akwab*: AA BA /BA BA BA / AA BA. *Hal dara zabyu l-hima*: AB B[B]B' AB.

[34] This concerns the composition *Wa-husnak*, which comes down to us with a very corrupt text to which the corresponding musical form is ||: A A' B B' B" C :||: D :|| D' [A A' B B' B" C]; the medieval text suggests the structure ABC ABC ABC DD ABC.

[35] *Ila mata*: ||: ABA' :|| B' |: C D :|| (||: E :|| E) C' [ABA ABA B]. The B' section is merely a melodic extension without structural significance. A spurious poetic-musical addition, indicated here in rounded brackets, is omitted in the simplified structure.

[36] *Ayyuha s-saqi*; in Appendix III of Liu and Monroe, the final section has been inadvertently identified as containing new material, but in the transcription it has been correctly identified as being a variant of B. David Wulstan, 'The Muwashshah', 261, doubts that the form of this piece represents its original state and proposes two hypothetical reconstructions corresponding to the formal types rondeau and virelai.

Rondeau and virelai: the music of Andalus and the Cantigas de Santa Maria   137

which begins and ends with a refrain and whose internal parts have the same music as the refrain.[37] It differs, however, from the musical form of the French rondeau in that it repeats the second rather than the first melodic phrase of the refrain in the first lines of the verse. This particular feature and the fact that it is linked to a specific region, as will be seen below, justifies our christening it the 'Andalusian rondeau'.[38]

The results obtained through the analysis of the medieval examples are confirmed and complemented by Andalusian oral tradition at large. According to Jozef Pacholczyk, the sections with *Bsit* rhythm in the *nawba Oshshaq* of the professional Moroccan repertory are typically in the forms AAA BA (for poems of five lines) and AB BBB AB (for poems of seven lines).[39] The same author subsequently demonstrated that these forms are also known in the Tunisian repertory.[40] Leo Plenckers drew attention to the use of the form AAA BA in the Algerian Andalusian tradition, not only today but in a transcription published in the eighteenth century.[41] The virelai and Andalusian rondeau structures, ‖: A :‖: B :‖ B' A and ‖: AB :‖: B :‖ B' AB respectively, are well represented in Younes Chami's transcriptions of the Moroccan *nawba* of Rasd ed Dhil.[42]

Further East, the more mixed the situation becomes. In the Mediterranean *muwashshah* studied by al-Faruqi, a variety of typical forms co-exists but it is not difficult to separate out two principal types: one, which al-Faruqi calls the 'modified rondo' (because instead of the rondo form AbAcAx . . . A, we have aBcBx . . . B), may be interpreted as a late transformation of the Andalusian rondeau form. The other type, which forms the majority, corresponds to the AABA global form, in which each section consists of two or more phrases. The latter structure may be realized as a form

---

[37] Christopher Page, 'Johannes de Grocheio on Secular Music: A Corrected Text and a New Translation', *Plainsong and Medieval Music*, 2 (1993), 17–41, esp. 24–6.

[38] Wulstan draws a technical distinction between the two types of rondeau on the basis of the vertical layout of their formal schemes: the French rondeau is 'left-handed' since it repeats phrase A, while the Andalusian is 'right-handed' since it repeats phrase B.

[39] Jozef M. Pacholczyk, 'The Relationship'. Corpus studied: eighteen songs drawn from the *Corpus de Musique Marocaine (Fasc.1)*, ed. Alexis Chottin (Paris, 1931).

[40] Jozef M. Pacholczyk, 'Rapporti fra le forme musicali della *nawba* andalusa dell'Africa settentrionale e le forme codificate della musica medievale europea', *Culture musicali: quaderni di etnomusicologia*, 3/5–6 (1984), 19–42.

[41] Leo J. Plenckers, 'Les rapports entre le muwashshah algérien et le virelai du moyen âge', in *The Challenge of the Middle East: Middle Eastern Studies at the University of Amsterdam*, ed. Ibrahim A. El-Sheikh, C. Aart van de Koppel and Rudolph Peters (Amsterdam, 1982), 91–111.

[42] *Les nawbas de la musique andalouse marocaine, II: La nawba de Rasd ed Dhil*. [Notation musicale de Younes Chami; interprétation du Maître A. Iabzour Tazi; préface de M. Iarbi Temsamani] (n.p., 1980). For our purposes fifty-one vocal pieces were analyzed (pp. 75–130), of which ten are in Andalusian rondeau form and ten more in virelai form. The structures given correspond to the musical form as represented in the notation. In practice, according to the description found in the preface [p. 26], the form ‖: A :‖: B : B' A is interpreted for a five-line poem as A(A)A(A)AB(B)B'A, in which A corresponds to the melody of a line, (A) to the instrumental repetition of the A melody, B or B' to the melody of a hemistich, and (B) to the instrumental repetition of the B melody. Four-line poems are interpreted as A(A)A B (B) B' A. Those of nine lines are symmetrical between the initial and final sections (the A melody is applied to both the first and last three lines). The form ‖: AB :‖: B :‖ B' AB always appears in association with five-line poems – in four cases it is interpreted as AB (AB) AB (AB) AB B(B)B' AB and in six cases the B melody is presented three times in a row instead of two. I am grateful to Salwa Castelo-Branco for the help she gave me in enabling me to refine the analysis of the forms in question.

of virelai, but it is found mostly in an intermediate form between the virelai and the Andalusian rondeau, which may be regarded as and called a 'cyclical virelai' (‖: *AA*′ :‖ BA′ AA′, or ‖: *AB* :‖ CB AB, in which the A and C sections may be subdivided and longer than B, and ‖: AB :‖ may be repeated).[43]

Thus it is probable that the musical form of the medieval *muwashshah* and the symmetrical *zajal* would have been mainly of the type AB /BBB AB (Andalusian rondeau), though sometimes acephalous (AAA BA), but the virelai types AA /BBB AA and AB /CCC AB and possibly the intermediate types AA /B[B]A AA and AB /C[C]B AB (cyclical virelai, hypothetically expanded) would also be represented.

The *zajal* and the *Cantigas de Santa Maria*

The musical form of the Andalusian *zajal* with asymmetrical strophes must certainly have been similar to that of the *muwashshah*, given that the *zajal* and *muwashshah* are the popular and erudite realizations of the same poetic-musical phenomenon; in the absence of direct evidence of the *zajal*'s musical form, we shall have to investigate how it was realized through indirect evidence. The Galician-Portuguese *Cantigas de Santa Maria* compiled by Alfonso X of Castile and León (1221–84) are relevant here not only on account of the known geographical and cultural connections of Alfonso's court with Andalus, but especially because they present an overwhelming predominance of *zajal* poetic structure, associated with musical forms of the virelai or Andalusian rondeau types.

The Andalusian rondeau appears in this Marian collection as AB /BB AB, a compressed version of AB /BBB AB. This form, which is virtually unknown elsewhere in the medieval Christian repertory, is to be seen in a large number of *cantigas* and is much more important in this collection than the form of the French rondeau.[44] It is unlikely that two varieties of Andalusian rondeau, a Moorish and a Christian one, should have arisen independently of each other in the same geographical area. It is more logical that Alfonso X's team should have imbibed Ibero-Arab culture, especially the more popular varieties.

---

[43] L. al Faruqi, 'Muwashshah', 3–4, 16–17. The corpus studied: 246 examples, of which 92 were published by d'Erlanger, *La musique arabe*, and 115 by al-Helou (=al-Hilw, *Al-Muwashshahat al-Andalusiyya*), the remaining 39 having been collected and transcribed by the author.

[44] Cf. Friedrich Gennrich, *Grundriss einer Formenlehre des mittelalterlichen Liedes als Grundlage einer musikalischen Formenlehre des Liedes* (Halle, 1932), 67–8, where the only example given of the AB BBBA form is taken from the *Cantigas de Santa Maria*. Taking as the corpus the compositions with strophes of four and eight lines and using as a working basis the scheme published by H. Anglès, we see that in 354 *cantigas* 71 (that is one-fifth), represented by the structures 12, 65, 73, 86, 88, 95 and 103, have the form of the Andalusian rondeau while only twelve, represented by the structures 7, 69 and 70, fit into the tradition of the French rondeau. The article by Jozef M. Pacholczyk, 'Rapporti', reached the author's hands only after completion of the first version of this paper. There for the first time the form of the Andalusian rondeau has been linked to the *Cantigas de Santa Maria*. Based on the schemes set out by Anglès, structures 12, 39, 103 and 104, the author gives 55 *cantigas* with this form. It should be noted that structure 39 (just as structures 37 and 40, which are related to it) corresponds to compositions with strophes of six lines and that structure 104 is open to a variety of interpretations.

Rondeau and virelai: the music of Andalus and the Cantigas de Santa Maria 139

A large majority of *cantigas* respond to the virelai formal type. These virelai structures are mostly symmetrical (AA /BB AA , AB /CC AB), but some songs have a shortened recapitulation, a variety which can be described as an asymmetrical virelai, rarely found in its simplest version (AA /BBB A , AB /CCC B). We must also consider the presence of the cyclical virelai (AB /CB AB), in which the anticipated recapitulation may betray the influence of the Andalusian rondeau.[45]

The favour given in the *Cantigas* to the virelai musical form, at a time when it was virtually ignored in France, suggests a connection of the virelai with Iberian traditions. A Catalan precedent, the conductus *Cedit frigus hiemale*, dates from the first half of the thirteenth century. The virelai appears northeast of the Pyrenees around 1260, in the wake of the Aragonese and Castilian conquests in Andalus, but is clearly marginal in France until the end of the thirteenth century.[46] On the other hand, it dominates the *Cantigas de Santa Maria*, compiled for the most part in recently-conquered Seville. The most plausible explanation for these facts is that it was Andalusian song, in its Romance, Ibero-Arab or Hebrew manifestations, which gave rise, directly or indirectly, to the virelai.[47]

Thus, the two most important musical forms found in the *Cantigas de Santa Maria*, a collection largely compiled in the Andalus, cannot be shown to depend on foreign models, and find, on the contrary, close parallels in the orally transmitted *muwashshah* and *muwashshah*-like *zajal*. The *Cantigas* have an asymmetrical *zajal* literary structure, which is extremely rare and late in the Galician-Portuguese and other troubadour traditions. This leaves Andalusian song as the most plausible model for both poetical and musical structures. Since it is unlikely that a *zajal*-structured song would turn to the *muwashshah* for its music, this model is to be identified with the *zajal*. The Andalusian rondeau form seems to have been predominant in the *muwashshah*; the larger role of the virelai in the *Cantigas* may in fact be due to their proximity to the *zajal*.

We can therefore propose not only that the typical *zajal* had musical forms similar to those of the *muwashshah*, but also that in the mid-thirteenth-century *zajal* the virelai reigned over the Andalusian rondeau, as suggested by the *Cantigas*. Its asymmetrical strophic structure would not always have been reflected in the music; a symmetrical musical form would have been privileged.

---

[45] I find only four *Cantigas de Santa Maria* which clearly have the simple asymmetrical virelai form (that is, where in the verse the same melody or melodies are repeated until the recapitulation of the last phrase of the refrain): nos. 59, 88, 294 and 320; to these may be added, though less certainly, nos. 81 and 195. By contrast, taking as a provisional basis the scheme of musical forms published by H. Anglès, *La Música de las Cantigas*, vol. 3/1, 397–400, I count twelve pieces as being embellished asymmetrical virelais (i.e., in which the partial recapitulation is preceded by a new melody): structures 13, 20, 23, 41, 108, 126, 130. The cyclical virelai form is represented by seven *cantigas*, following structures 16, 98 and 129b.

[46] Higini Anglès, *La música a Catalunya fins al segle XIII* (Barcelona, 1935; repr. Barcelona, 1988), 256–7; Willi Apel, 'Rondeaux, Virelais, and Ballades in French 13th-Century Song', *Journal of the American Musicological Society*, 7 (1954), 121–30.

[47] Since we know virtually nothing about the hypothetical Romance predecessors of the *zajal* in southern France and Italy, an alternative scenario would make greater demands on the imagination. The reader may prefer to identify this Andalusian song with its central, Ibero-Arab *zajal* variety, but other interpretations are admissible.

In the face of this data, it would be wrong to insist that the musical form of the virelai is proper to the French tradition. On the contrary, it was probably encountered in Andalusian sung poetry at some distant date. We may also conclude that the rondeau, as defined by Grocheio, existed in two principal forms – the French and the Andalusian – the latter being at least as ancient as the former. These forms met in the thirteenth century at the court of Alfonso the Learned under the invocation of Mary. In succeeding centuries, however, their divergent fate came to mirror in some respect the deep divide in the West between the Christian and the Islamic worlds.

Part IV
Transmission

[14]

The Trouvère MS Tradition

by Theodore Karp

For many decades, scholars dealing with medieval secular monophony have been both vexed and fascinated by the presence of large numbers of variants among different readings of many trouvère chansons. In the first place, we wish to know how to account for these differences. And, secondly, the variants themselves often pose problems in transcription unlike those encountered in later polyphonic repertoires. These problems have been dealt with in different fashions by various scholars. Some have presented transcriptions based on a single reading, ignoring the variants in remaining sources. Others have given conflations based on several sources, but without indicating specific variants. Still others have presented conflations and cited variants by one means or another. Significant steps in the investigation of the trouvère MS tradition have been taken by Gennrich,[1] Aarburg,[2] and Bittinger,[3] but there is still much that remains to be done. This article will be concerned primarily with an inquiry into the nature of the trouvère MS tradition, prefaced by a review of general problems confronting the editor of trouvère chansons. However, the bearing of our material on transcription practice will also be considered. The conclusions to be presented are based on a study of the works of the Châtelain de Coucy, Conon de Béthune, Hugues de Berzé, Pierre de Molins, and the Vidame de Chartres, together with a miscellaneous handful of works by other trouvères. The segment of the repertoire involved consists of about 60 pieces. Obviously, any conclusion based on such a small sampling may require modification when further detailed information becomes available.

In preparing an edition of the music associated with a given poem, the scholar must frequently begin by deciding which of several unrelated settings is the original. For example, the collation of the known versions of chansons attributable[4] to the

Châtelain de Coucy reveals that, among a group of 22 poems, 18 survive with more than one melody. Twelve of these are set twice, four are set three times each, while two others have four settings apiece. All of the eight chansons attributable to the Vidame de Chartres and all of the four attributable to Pierre de Molins survive with more than one melody, as do three of the five works attributable to Hugues de Berzé and three of the ten attributable to Conon de Béthune. Fortunately, there is seldom any difficulty in recognizing the late settings. In the first place, these pieces--termed <u>contraposita</u> by Bittinger and <u>peripheral melodies</u> by the present author--occur in only one source each. Secondly, one can single out certain MSS whose contents consist primarily of contraposita as well as certain others with a fairly high percentage of contraposita.

Among the 17 poems attributable to the Châtelain de Coucy that survive in MS V (Paris, Bibl. nat. f.fr. 24406),[5] twelve are accompanied by melodies unrelated to their counterparts elsewhere. A cursory examination of the entire MS indicates that the melodies entered on the first two gatherings (works attributable to Thibaut de Champagne, Roi de Navarre) belong to the central repertoire, while approximately 75-80 percent of the remainder--excluding unica--belong to the peripheral repertoire. Occasionally, close study will reveal that a melody first regarded as a contrapositum is actually a corrupt version of the original melody. However, instances of this sort are rare and a major departure from the estimate given above is not expected.

MS R (Paris, Bibl. nat. f.fr. 1591) is another chansonnier containing a high percentage of peripheral melodies. Although a complete survey of the MS is not yet available, I would estimate, on the basis of limited personal observation, that the percentage of peripheral melodies in this source is at least as high as, if not higher than, that in V. MS R consists of three parts (R_1, R_2, R_3), and one should not draw general conclusions regarding the source until the nature of the relationship among these parts is more clearly established. Among the various melodies in R that I have studied in depth, only one--A vous, amant plus qu'a nule autre gent (R. 679) by the Châtelain de Coucy--belongs to the central repertoire. This piece is found in the third section of the MS.

In the event that a melody in either V or R is unrelated to a melody setting the same poem in a more reliable source, one may be quite certain that it is the latter which is the earlier of the two. For example, Chançon legiere a entendre (R. 629) by Conon de Béthune survives with music in only two sources, MS R and MS T (Paris, Bibl. nat. f.fr. 12615--the MS de Noailles). The melodies are unrelated. The quantitative equivalence of the conflicting evidence might ordinarily render it difficult, if not impossible, to decide which of the two melodies is the original. However, the qualitative difference in the evidence--MS T containing few, if any, peripheral melodies--is so great that there is little question but that the R setting of Chançon legiere is a late substitution. On occasion, there may be reason to question the authenticity of musical unica in V and R. As indicated by Spanke,[6] the poetic form of the anonymous chanson, Nus ne porroit de mauvaise raison (R. 1887), is based on that of Je chantasse volentiers liement (R. 700) by the Châtelain de Coucy. The two works coincide in line lengths and rhyme schemes, and both are examples of the vers capcauda. (In a poem exhibiting this technique, the first rhyme of each new strophe is drawn from the last rhyme of the preceding strophe.) Although the melody accompanying Nus ne porroit in V is unrelated to the one normally accompanying the Châtelain's poem, data presented regarding V indicate that it is likely that the former melody is merely a contrapositum. The resemblance in form between the two poems is so strong that it is quite probable that Nus ne porroit was conceived as an ordinary contrafactum.

Although the peripheral settings in MSS V and R exhibit a range of styles, it is possible to indicate certain general traits that distinguish these melodies from their counterparts in the central repertoire. As a rule, the former are much more restricted in motion, using smaller ranges and fewer skips. They tend to be more syllabic than the central melodies, have less clearly established tonal centers, and use less literal repetition.

The Arras and Rome chansonniers (MSS A and a, resp.) apparently represent a midpoint between the peripheral and central sources. A cursory check of the majority of melodies in the former indicates that approximately forty percent of the Arras readings belong to the peripheral repertoire. The percentage of contraposita in the Rome MS appears to be much lower, but no estimate, however sketchy, is yet available. <u>Bien cuidai vivre sans amour</u> (R. 1965) by the Châtelain de Coucy is preserved with music only in these two MSS. The readings are unrelated. Because of stylistic differences between each of these two settings and authenticated melodies attributable to the Châtelain, I am of the opinion that both are to be classified as peripheral.

Contraposita are to be found also in normally reliable central sources. The main scribe of MS M (Paris, Bibl. nat. f.fr. 844--the MS du Roi) left blank the staves accompanying several dozen poems. According to Beck, the number of such works presently stands at 78;[7] folios now missing may have contained still other poems without music. Melodies in a markedly different script were provided for 28 of the 78 poems, presumably after the MS was completed. Apparently all are contraposita. In general, the peripheral melodies in the Arras and Rome chansonniers and in the MS du Roi have little stylistic resemblance to those in MSS V and R. I have elsewhere pointed out an unusual contrapositum in Egerton MS 274.[8]

In his article "Die Lieder des Jacques de Cysoing,"[9] Zitzmann fails to make any distinction between variants within the central tradition and readings of contraposita. Both are given together, by means of alphabet letters, following the conclusion of the various transcriptions. Bittinger has criticized this practice as unsound,[10] and I am in full agreement with his criticism. A peripheral melody should either be presented independently of its central counterpart, or, preferably, be transcribed on separate staves together with the central melody, so that the two may easily be compared.

Variants occurring between readings deriving from the central tradition itself may be of different sorts. One may encounter phrases in one MS that are entirely unrelated to their counterparts in other sources. Corrupt readings are fairly frequent, and small variants of different degrees of importance are usually numerous.

A lack of relationship between corresponding phrases of different readings may be caused either by the introduction of new material of late origin or by the use of an abnormal repetition pattern. For example, the Rome reading of S'onques nus hom por dure departie (R. 1126) by Hugues de Berzé repeats the opening phrase in conjunction with the third line of poetry, while no other source does so. MSS K, P, and X immediately repeat the fourth phrase of Je chantasse volentiers liement by the Châtelain de Coucy, whereas all other sources use new material for the setting of line 5. MSS K, N, P, and X use the second phrase of Quant foillissent li boscage (R. 14), attributed variously to Pierre de Molins and the Vidame de Chartres, to set the fourth text-line, while MSS O (Paris, Bibl. nat. f.fr. 846--the Chansonnier Cangé) and T use fresh material.[11] The use of an abnormal repetition pattern may affect any part of the chanson. The introduction of newly composed material--the most frequent cause of melodic disparity between readings--seems to occur only in the cauda. Any number of lines may be affected, and sometimes the entire cauda consists of new material. For example, the reading in MS V of Quant li rossignols jolis (R. 1559), attributable to the Châtelain de Coucy and to Raoul de Ferrières, employs new material for the last six lines of the ten-line strophe. (See Example 1.) I have coined the term "deviated phrase" to designate any phrase unrelated to the hypothetical original.

288 Poets and Singers

Comparison of the K and V readings of Quant li rossignols.

Example 1

There are occasions when it is not entirely clear whether one is dealing with newly composed material or with a corrupt version of the original. Before illustrating this point, I shall first cite an example of a simple corruption and consider its bearing on transcription procedures.

When working on the third staff of <u>Quant li rossignols jolis</u>, the main scribe of MS T was apparently distracted, with the result that he wrote a passage a line too low. One's attention is drawn to this section because of the presence of a flat appearing before a note ostensibly to be read as <u>g</u>. Comparison with other readings reveals not only that the entire penultimate phrase was intended a third higher than written but also that the fifth phrase was intended a fifth lower than written. Nothing more than a pair of errors in clef reading is involved here; unquestionably a transcription based on this source should correct these errors while providing a proper annotation concerning their existence.[13]

Sometimes, however, a transposition--such as proposed for the T reading of <u>Quant li rossignols</u>--or other manipulation[14] will reduce the degree of dissimilarity between variant readings but yet fail to produce a resemblance strong enough to remove possible doubts concerning the origin of the reading judged inferior. The Cangé and V readings of Hugues de Berzé's <u>Nus hon ne set d'ami qui puet valoir</u> (R. 1821), line 6, vary considerably from those of other sources. If one assumes that the portion of these readings from the second musical unit on was written a third higher than intended and compensates for this hypothetical error by means of a downward transposition of the affected passage, a loose resemblance will be observed between the emended reading and the readings of other sources. (See Example 2.) The seventh phrase in O is clearly related to its counterparts in other sources, and the fact that the first two notes in this passage are respectively a fourth and a third higher than the notes in MSS A, D, and T lends some measure of support to the suggestion that the variants in the preceding phrase arose through

Comparison of the A and O readings of <u>Nus hom</u>, line 6.

[musical notation: staff A, staff O, staff O with "Possible emendation."]

Example 2

carelessness in clef reading. Nevertheless, the number of variants existing between the proposed emendation and more accurate readings is too high to permit one to reach a definitive conclusion regarding the soundness of the suggested hypothesis. In instances such as this, it is safest to transcribe the questioned reading as it stands in the MS and to point out the possible emendation by means of a footnote.

Variants of small extent are so numerous that they cannot be discussed in any detail without straying from our main objectives. Suffice it to say that some consist of melodic embellishments of various sorts, while others involve minor errors, deliberate alterations of isolated notes, and redivisions of the melodic line into different ligatures.

It has been suggested from time to time that the presence of numerous variants among different readings of trouvère melodies may reflect the influence of an oral tradition. At first glance, this hypothesis has a certain strength and simplicity. However, it does not accord with philological findings concerning the origins of trouvere sources: namely, that surviving chansonniers were copied from still older anthologies, now lost. The philologists' reasoning rests on a twofold foundation. There are certain groups of MSS whose members agree in terms of general contents and also present large numbers of chansons in identical order. Furthermore, the MSS within each group normally agree in their readings of the poetic texts, while often conflicting with readings in MSS outside the group. As we shall presently show, musicological evidence supports the findings of the philologists in general, though not always with regard to particulars.

In 1880, Brakelmann treated the topic of MS genealogy in an article entitled "Die dreiundzwanzig altfranzösischen Chansonniers in Bibliotheken Frankreichs, Englands, Italiens und der Schweiz";[15] he pursued his investigation only far enough to arrive at a loose grouping of MSS. Three years later, Fath arrived at a similar grouping and, in addition, suggested a specific filiation for the MSS he consulted.[16] (See Figure 1.) In 1886, Schwan published a study of the interrelationships between

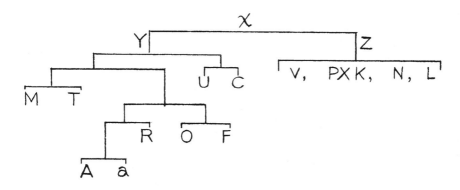

Figure 1

trouvère MSS that provided the basis for most subsequent work in this area. His filiation is basically similar to that proposed by Fath, though more comprehensive and detailed.[17] (See Figure 2.)

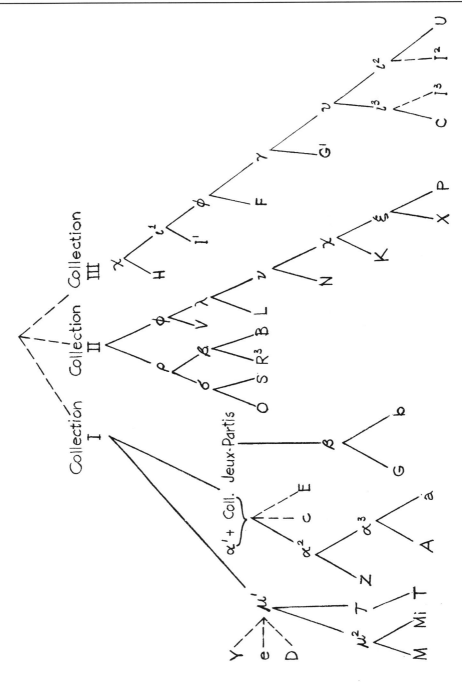

Figure 2

Graphic representation of MS filiations has, however, certain inherent weaknesses. For example, it is difficult to represent the filiation of MSS derived from a variety of sources. Consequently, since the turn of this century, it has been the practice either to graph genealogies for individual chansons rather than for entire MSS[18] or to rely on purely verbal descriptions of MS interrelationships.

These filiations show that the musicologist is concerned primarily with two MS families. MSS C, F, G, H, I, and U constitute a third family, but among these, only F and U survive with music. While their musical contents are important, they are not extensive. In the following discussion, we shall first treat MSS K, N, P, X, and L; then MSS M, T, a, A, and D; and finally MSS O, V, and R.

A small sampling of the philological data demonstrating the very close relationship among MSS K, N, P, and X was given in my article "A Lost Medieval Chansonnier."[19] Among the few dozen trouvère chansonniers, these MSS are the only ones to exhibit a high degree of unanimity in their musical readings. Among the chansons attributable to the Châtelain de Coucy, one seldom finds during the course of an entire chanson more than three or four variants within this family. Most of these involve only a single note or ligature; extensive variants occupying a large portion of a phrase are very rare indeed. It is ironic to observe that the care exercised in the preparation of MSS K, N, P, and X apparently exceeded that employed in the preparation of the anthology from which they drew. This source evidently contained several major errors as well as deviated readings.[20] The fact that MSS K, N, and P share several peculiarities in musical script further points up the close relationship between these sources. It is possible that these MSS were the product of the same atelier. MS L is closely linked to this group, but its melodies--like its texts--were apparently copied hastily, if one is to judge by the number of errors found therein.

The close agreement among the musical readings of MSS K, N, P, X, and L is so consistent that one may safely conclude that the melodies in these five sources derive, directly or indirectly, from a single, written archetype. Oral tradition may conceivably have influenced the archetype itself, but there can be no question of its direct effect on any of the five surviving chansonniers. The genealogy proposed for these MSS by Schwan was later rejected by Spanke,[21] who pointed to certain gaps in Schwan's data and to weak points in his method. Musicological evidence now at hand merely corroborates philological findings regarding the closeness of the relationship between these sources but does not suggest any particular line of filiation.

Quite another situation obtains with regard to the music in the MS family that includes MSS M, T, a, and A. Substantial agreement among the musical readings within this family is infrequent. There are instances in which two MSS present identical or nearly identical readings for individual phrases, but close similarity between readings rarely extends throughout an entire piece. The proof that these MSS too are part of a written tradition rests on an analysis of the variants themselves. This analysis, in turn, demonstrates a need for the modification of previous conclusions based on philological evidence alone.

Philologists have subdivided the M-T-a-A family into two branches, MSS M and T forming one branch and MSS a and A the other. We can discuss only a tiny sampling of the evidence supporting this hypothesis. MSS M and T, for example, attribute to the Châtelain de Coucy an identical series of 12 chansons. The series of eight pieces attributed to Conon de Béthune in M is identical with the first eight of nine pieces attributed to that trouvère in T. The series of five pieces attributed to Hugues de Berzé in T is identical with the first five of six pieces attributed to Hugues in M. A series of five pieces is attributed to the Vidame de Chartres in M, and this series is duplicated in T, where, however, the last piece is attributed to Thibaut de Blason. Several long successions of pieces attributable to Gace Brulé,

Guillaume li Viniers, Blondel de Nesles, Audefroi li Bastars, and Moniot d'Arras are to be found in identical order in both MSS, although one must take into consideration the fact that M often has a larger selection of pieces attributable to a given trouvère than does T.

Similar evidence demonstrates the close relationship between the Arras and Rome chansonniers. The latter MS, for example, originally contained nine chansons attributable to the Châtelain de Coucy; the first of these is now lost. The series of eight chansons attributed to the Châtelain in the Arras MS is identical with the first eight of the original series in Rome. Other comparisons between the two MSS are made more difficult because only a fraction of the original contents of the Arras MS survives. Sometimes a series of works in the a-A subgroup is identical or nearly identical with its counterpart in the M-T subgroup; the respective series attributed to the Châtelain, however, differ considerably.

There is some musical evidence to support the philologists' filiation. For example, the M and T readings of <u>Encor ferai une chançon</u> (R. 2071) by Hugues de Berzé are closely related; the respective readings of line 7 are identical, those of lines 2-4, nearly so. M and T give identical readings for lines 2 and 4 of <u>A vous, amant, plus qu'a nule autre gent</u> (R. 679) by the Châtelain de Coucy. <u>Li nouviaus tens et mais et violete</u> (R. 985), by the Châtelain, provides a third instance of a close relationship between musical texts in M and T. However, a far greater bulk of musical evidence shows that M and T are by no means as closely related as has been previously postulated.

If, for example, one compares the readings of <u>Je chantasse volentiers liement</u> by the Châtelain de Coucy in MSS M, T, a, and A, one will find that the range of the M version lies a fifth lower than that of the other three. Furthermore, the pitch relationship between the M reading and the T, a, A readings does not remain constant. (For purposes of present convenience, we shall assume an upward transposition of a fifth for the M reading.) Variants within the MS family in the first five lines are not noteworthy. The first four musical units of line 6, however, are a third lower in T, a, and A than in M. Because the M version is corroborated by the readings of MSS K, P, O, and U, and because the T, a, A readings lack any corroboration outside of the family, one may safely conclude that the M version is historically authentic and that the T, a, A readings are corrupt. The passage in question recurs in a related--though not identical--form at the middle of line 8; the situation with regard to the musical readings is the same as before. In line 9, the T, a, and A readings lie a fourth lower than the one in M; again the latter is corroborated by sources outside the family, while the former lacks such support. Obviously, MSS M and T did not draw upon the same source for the music of Je chantasse.

The musical texts given in T and a for the Châtelain's Coment que longue demeure (R. 1010) also contrast markedly with the reading in M. Although the three readings begin on the same note and end on the same note, line 7 in a and T is a third lower than in M. The latter version is corroborated by MSS U, K, N, and X, while the former is not supported by any outside source. With regard to the music setting line 1, syllable 2; line 2, syllable 6; line 5, syllables 2, 4, and 5; line 8, syllables 1 and 2; and the first syllable of the refrain, MSS a and T share variants that conflict with the M reading.[22]

A similar situation exists with regard to the readings of Merci clamant de mon fol errement (R. 671) and Mout m'est bele la douce commençance (R. 209), both by the Châtelain. The range of the M reading of Merci clamant lies a fifth lower than that of the readings in T and a;[23] a downward transposition of the latter two is assumed for present purposes. In line 8, the T and a readings are a third higher than that of M. The fact that the M reading is supported by the O reading and by the K, N, X, and O readings of a contrafactum shows clearly that the M reading is authentic and that the T and a readings are corrupt. The T and a readings of lines 9 and 10 of Mout m'est bele are badly garbled.[24] After compensating for overall differences of pitch level, one will find that the first six musical units of line 9 are a third too high in these sources, while the cadence of line 9 and the first five musical units of line 10 are a third too low. (See Example 3.)

Example 3

Evidence of similar nature is to be found also through the comparison of readings of works by trouvères other than the Châtelain. A study of Ausi con cil qui cuevre sa pesance (R. 238) by Hugues de Berzé shows that the last four musical units of line 5 and the first nine musical units of line 6 are a second higher in T and A than in M, the latter version being corroborated by the readings in D and O.

Further similar examples might be cited,[25] but these should suffice for the present. Several conclusions may be drawn from the above data. In the first place, it is obvious that MSS M and T are not related in the manner envisaged by the philologists; their actual relationship is more distant and more complex than has heretofore been contemplated. In the second place, musical evidence shows that MS T is more closely related to MSS a and A than was previously realized. Lastly, several of the corrupt variants cited above strongly indicate the presence of a written rather than an oral tradition. I refer to those that may safely be attributed to mechanical errors in copying. To postulate that the corruptions in Example 3, let us say, are of improvisational nature and represent the laxness of an oral tradition strains credibility; they are lacking in the most elementary musical logic. Undoubtedly these variants arose through careless clef-reading committed in the preparation of a source used by the scribes of both T and a. One may reasonably assume the existence of a written tradition not only when faced with a lack of variants but also when faced with striking variants shared by a small group of sources.

In this fashion it is possible also to link MS M to a written tradition. For the moment, I shall merely call attention to the very close relationship between the musical texts of <u>Ausi con cil qui cuevre sa pesance</u> in MSS M and D. Undoubtedly the two were derived from the same source. Unfortunately, D is only a tiny fragment; the other melodies it contains were originally in M, but the M versions have been lost through the terrible mutilation of that MS. Philologists have postulated a close relationship between M and D, and we may conjecture that the music in the two MSS was derived from a single archetype. Nevertheless, a definitive conclusion cannot be reached on the basis of such scant evidence. Further evidence regarding the musical texts in M will be considered shortly.

In the meantime I wish to discuss an abortive attempt to reach a genealogy of the M-T-a-A family that would account for the divergences between musicological and philological evidence. Because, in the examples discussed to this point, the readings of MS M have consistently been corroborated by other sources, while the readings of MSS T, a, and A have lacked such corroboration, one may conclude that the former are not only of higher authenticity but also stand in closer relationship to the hypothetical original, symbolized in our chart by the letter alpha. (See Figure 3.) One might conjecture that the musical variants common to MSS T, a, and A

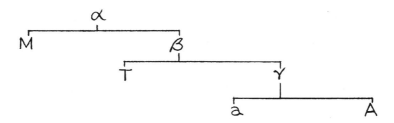

Figure 3

originated in a lost source beta, while the reorganization of contents that, together with certain variants in poetic readings, marks MSS a and A, occurred in the lost source gamma. Unfortunately, this hypothesis will not account for a wider range of data.

If one examines the various readings of Combien que j'aie demouré (R. 421) by the Vidame de Chartres, one will again find important differences between the readings of MSS M and T. Here, however, M is corroborated only within the family-- i.e. by the reading of MS a--while T is generally supported by MSS outside of the family. The M and a readings lie a fourth higher than those of other sources (T, U

K, N, and P). The U and K-N-P readings use literal repetition of the first two phrases in setting the third and fourth textlines. There are variants between the two halves of the <u>pedes</u> in the T reading, but these are primarily the result of an error in clef reading committed at the beginning of line 4. MSS M and a, however, exhibit a variety of variants between the two halves of the <u>pedes</u> and the correlation between the two MSS is especially striking. (See Example 4.) This correlation continues to the end of the fifth line. The correspondence between the two readings up to that point is so close that the lack of correspondence during the last three lines does not shake the conviction that the two versions derived directly or indirectly from the same source.

The first two lines of <u>Tant con je fusse fors de ma contree</u> (R. 502), also by the Vidame de Chartres, lie a fifth higher in the readings of MSS M and a than in the readings of MSS T, U, K, N, P, and X. With the opening of line 3, however, all readings are at the same pitch level. The M reading is preserved only as far as the first two musical units of line 3; the remainder of the piece was torn out. There is a major variant between the M and a readings at the cadence of line 2. Nevertheless, the agreement between the two versions with regard to the sudden shift of pitch level is so significant, in my opinion, that I conclude that the two derive in some manner from a common source.

In these chansons one observes a filiation quite different from that suggested by our previous examples. Here the readings of T, rather than those of M, are closer to the hypothetical originals. Before analyzing the further significance of this new evidence, which leads into another area, I propose to discuss certain random data linking MSS O, V, and R to a written musical tradition.

According to present interpretation of philological evidence, MS O (the chansonnier Cangé) is derived from several sources, the principal source being related to the Arsenal family archetype. MS V is also related to the Arsenal family according to philological evidence. Numerous long series of chansons in V follow exactly the same order as their counterparts in K, N, P, and X.[27] However, the study of poetic variants indicates that the relationship between V and K, N, P, and X is by no means as close as that which exists among the four MSS themselves.

Example 4

Earlier in this article, I commented on the difficulty of analyzing variants common to O and V in line 6 of Hugues de Berzé's Nus hom ne set, without, however, drawing attention to the very close relationship between the two readings throughout the chanson. Almost all of line 5 in O and V is a second higher than in MSS A, D, N, and T. Moreover, the last four musical units in O and V are quite distinctive--they present an exact end rhyme to the cadence of lines 2 and 4. There is little doubt that the two readings were derived in some fashion from a common source. While the tiny repertoire constituting the basis for this study does not yield further evidence of this strength, it does provide some corroboration of an O-V relationship. There are two instances in which O and V form part of a larger MS group sharing an important variant in common. La douce vois du rossignol salvage (R. 40) by the Châtelain de Coucy survives with two divergent readings of line 8: one in MSS A, a, O, and V, the other in MSS M, K, P, and X. The opening of the former resembles the opening of phrases 2 and 4; that of the latter does not. Quant li rossignols jolis survives with two basic versions of phrase 4. The reading in V is related to the readings in O (fol. 117r) and T, rather than to the readings in M, K, P, X, and O (fol. 110v). It is possible that a comprehensive study of MSS O and V will permit a more precise appraisal of the relationship between the two sources.[28]

Philological evidence also links MS V with the third section of MS R, and there is one significant bit of musicological evidence corroborating this relationship. As previously noted, only one of the pieces studied in R belongs to the central repertoire, that one being A vous, amant, plus qu'a nule autre gent, by the Châtelain de Coucy. Although the V and R versions of this piece are not identical, the resemblance between them is exceptionally striking. Lines 6 and 8 of the chanson lie, for the most part, a second lower than in other sources, while the first three notes of line 7 lie a second too high. Moreover, the treatment of details is quite consistent in the two readings: cf. the use of ternariae for the last syllable of lines 1 and 3, the penultimate syllable of line 5, and syllable 7 of line 7. Undoubtedly these readings derive, directly or indirectly, from a common source.

The above evidence shows that there is sound reason to conclude that the majority of trouvère MSS depended upon a written rather than an oral tradition for their musical texts. The ramifications of this conclusion are far reaching.

When discussing deviated readings, I pointed out that MSS K, N, P, and X employ the second phrase of Quant foillissent li boscage as a setting for the fourth line of text, while MSS O and T employ new material, shared by both. If each of the six readings had been arrived at independently of the others, one would conclude that the version existing in four MSS was more likely to be authentic than the one existing in only two. Since, however, MSS K, N, P, and X derive from a single source, their combined testimony is not to be valued much more highly than the testimony of any one of them. Because T and O are not closely interrelated, their mutual corroboration is significant. It is their version that is most likely authentic. In other words, mere numerical superiority favoring one of a set of conflicting readings may be deceptive. Our best criterion lies in the distribution of the readings: the more distantly linked the corroborating versions, the greater the significance of the corroboration. There are, of course, instances in which readings in one MS family conflict with readings in another, neither being supported by any outside source. As a general rule, present practice accords greater weight to the readings of the M-T-A-a family than to those of the K-N-P-X family. This accords with philological findings, which credit the former group with greater accuracy than the latter.

From our repertoire of some 60 chansons it is possible to cull evidence concerning details of the written musical tradition of the trouvères other than those pertaining to MS filiation. I refer not to the identity of the scribes, but to their methods, the sources they used, their knowledge of the music, and their prerogatives. Data at hand are too scanty to permit definitive conclusions, but a preliminary outline may nevertheless be useful.

In the X reading of Je chantasse volentiers liement by the Châtelain de Coucy, both the text and music of a section involving lines 3, 4, and 5 are repeated bodily. In the L version of Bele dame me prie de chanter (R. 790), also by the Châtelain, lines 5 and 6 are omitted from the text. The music seems to present the first three notes of line 5 and then skips to the fourth note of line 7. The two examples suggest that in these sources--and perhaps also in other sources of the K-N-P-X family-- the text and music were copied concurrently by a single scribe. One would assume that if the texts of these chansons had been copied first and the music later, the oversights in the texts would have been noticed as the music was being notated and that an effort would have been made towards their correction. The fact that all of the musical readings of the K-N-P-X family examined during this study are closely related suggests further that each of the scribes worked primarily from one large anthology--perhaps, in several cases, the same one. Had the scribes drawn on heterogeneous assortments of small collections, it is likely that instances of marked intrafamily variants would crop up more often.

Turning to the M-T-a-A family, one may find evidence suggesting exactly an opposite pair of conclusions. One finds, for example, that the text scribe of MS T left out the word "acomplis," when he moved from the third staff of Quant li rossignols jolis to the fourth. Later, two lines of the third staff were extended into the margin and the missing word, together with the accompanying music, was inserted in a different hand. The same hand is apparently responsible for remedying a textual omission occurring in Conon de Béthune's L'autrier un jor après la saint Denise (R. 1623). In MS M, line 4 of Hue de la Ferté's contrafactum Je chantasse volentiers liement (R. 699) is garbled; a few syllables of text are missing. Although this oversight was not remedied as in the examples cited from T, the musical symbols at this point are suddenly squeezed into a small space. Had the scribe been copying alternately a few syllables and then a few notes, one would assume that the textual gap would be mirrored by a gap in the music. One cannot be certain whether text and music were written by the same scribe or not, but it does seem probable that the text had been copied out before the music, that the omission was noted even though not corrected, and the spacing of the music was altered in order to match text and music as nearly as possible. Other occasional bits of evidence seem to support the theory that the text and music of these two sources were copied separately rather than concurrently.

Evidence that we have cited thus far with regard to the filiation of the M-T-a-A family suggests also that each of these sources was prepared from a number of small collections rather than from one large anthology. Two groups of readings from this family have been discussed. In the first, by far the larger, it was noted that the readings of MS M stand closer to the hypothetical original than do those of MSS T, a, and A. This conclusion was reached by virtue of the fact that the M readings are corroborated by sources belonging to other MS families, while the T-a-A readings are not. With regard to the second group of chansons, the positions of M and T are reversed. Here the readings of MS T are of greater historical authenticity. This reversal is strange indeed, and I see no way of accounting for it within a uniform genealogy for the entire family. Philologists have postulated that individual trouvères ordered small collections made of their works and that these collections provided the basis for the early dissemination of the repertoire. A hypothesis to the effect that the scribes of MSS M, T, a, and A drew on a group of collections a few generations removed from the earliest ones would permit one to account both for the philological data regarding the interrelationships between these MSS and also for the shifting musical relationships within the family and between individual members and other sources.

This hypothesis has distinct bearing on transcription procedures. Because MSS K, N, P, and X are of homogeneous nature, one may draw valid conclusions concerning their general reliability. Evidence obtained in the study of one portion of the contents of these MSS may be employed in evaluating the authenticity of variants found in other portions. With regard to MSS M, T, a, and A, such a procedure is not possible. MS M, for example, is one of the most trustworthy sources for the works of the Châtelain de Coucy, but is among the less reliable sources for the works of the Vidame de Chartres. MS T, on the other hand, exhibits a high incidence of error among pieces attributable to the Châtelain and yet is much more reliable in its readings of pieces attributable to the Vidame. When evaluating the merits of conflicting variants within the M-T-a-A family, each case must be judged afresh.

I have from time to time commented on the probable existence of errors in clef reading in sources constituting the basis for surviving chansonniers. The frequency of such errors argues forcefully that the scribes of surviving sources often lacked first-hand knowledge of the music they were copying. Otherwise they surely would not have scrupulously reproduced so many garbled passages that had never been intended to sound as written.

This situation notwithstanding, it appears that the scribes would occasionally alter deliberately certain details of the music. A possible example of this practice may be observed in the P reading of the line 4 of <u>A vous, amant, plus qu'a nule autre gent</u> by the Châtelain de Coucy. The extended recitation tone that opens the line in other MSS is replaced in P by a more varied melodic contour. (See Example 5.) Mechanical errors in copying may take several forms: repetitions, omissions, faulty clef-reading, and so forth. But none of these seem to be involved in the example. The most logical explanation is that these variants are the result of a deliberate alteration.

It is quite possible that certain large-scale variants affecting repetition patterns are also the result of deliberate changes brought about by individual scribes. The Rome version of line 3 of <u>S'onques nus hom</u> and the K-N-P-X version of line 4 of <u>Quant foillissent li boscage</u>--both discussed previously--may have originated in such fashion.

The belief that the deliberate alteration of a trouvère melody during the course of transmission was accepted medieval practice affects fundamental concepts of transcription technique. As one becomes willing to recognize the validity of more

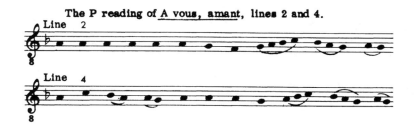

Example 5

than one version of a given phrase, less emphasis is accorded the search for a hypothetical original. The conflation, preferred by many scholars, assumes a far lesser importance. While acknowledging the many merits of Ursula Aarburg's advocacy of transcription by means of conflation, I remain of another opinion. Obviously, errors of a mechanical nature should be weeded out in the transcription process. But I suggest that by creating an amalgamation based on many readings we are often in danger of creating a new hybrid that may fail to represent accurately any medieval presentation of the piece in question. For my part, I feel that an ideal edition of a trouvère melody would present in score arrangement all surviving readings of that melody, including those appearing as contrafacta. I would place the most reliable reading on top and arrange the others below in such fashion that readings belonging to the same family appear on successive staves. Pertinent remarks concerning noteworthy variants may be entered either together with the music or separately.

A conflation placed at the bottom of each system would constitute a useful study guide. I advocate for performance purposes a version based on the best available reading, shorn of mechanical errors.

Footnotes

1. E.g., "Grundsätzliches zu den Troubadour- und Trouvère- Weisen," <u>Zeitschrift für romanische Philologie</u>, LVII (1937), 31-56; "Die Repertoire-Theorie," <u>Zeitschrift für französischer Sprache und literatur</u>, LXVI (1956), pp. 81-108.

2. E.g., "Muster für die Edition mittelalterlichen Liedmelodien," <u>Die Musikforschung</u>, X (1957), pp. 209-217.

3. E.g., <u>Studien zur musikalischen Textkritik des Mittelalterlichen Liedes</u>, 1953.

4. The word, "attributable," is used in this article to denote both genuine works and <u>opera dubia</u>. The four works to be mentioned in the main text in connection with Pierre de Molins include one with a conflicting attribution to the Chatelain de Coucy (and also Gace Brulé) and one with a conflicting attribution to the Vidame de Chartres. Thus there are two instances of duplication in our list.

5. The symbols used in this article are those of Schwan. MS A: Arras, Bibl. munic. 657; B: Berne, Stadtbibl. 231; C: Berne, Stadtbibl. 389; D: Frankfurt am Main, Stadtbibl. <u>olim</u> 29; F: London, Brit. Mus. Egerton 274; H: Modena, Bibl. Estense, R 4,4; I: Oxford, Bodleiana, Douce 308; K: Paris, Bibl. de l'Arsenal 5198; L: Paris, Bibl. nat. f.fr. 765; M: Paris, Bibl. nat. f.fr. 844; N: Paris, Bibl. nat. f.fr. 845; O: Paris, Bibl. nat. f.fr. 846; P: Paris, Bibl. nat. f.fr. 847; R: Paris, Bibl. nat. f.fr. 1591; T: Paris, Bibl. nat. f.fr. 12615; U: Paris, Bibl. nat. f.fr. 20050; V: Paris, Bibl. nat. f.fr. 24406; X: Paris, Bibl. nat. n.a.fr. 1050; Z: Siena, Bibl. com. H.X. 36; a: Rome, Bibl. vat. Reg. 1490.

6. "Das öftere Auftreten von Strophenformen und Melodien in der altfranzösischen Lyrik," <u>Zeitschrift für französischer Sprache und Literatur</u>, LI (1928), p. 96.

7. <u>Le Manuscrit du Roi</u> (<u>Corpus cantilenarum medii aevi, no. 2</u>), II, 1938, p. 157.

8. "Borrowed Material in Trouvère Music," <u>Acta Musicologica</u>, XXXIV (1962), pp. 100f.

9. <u>Zeitschrift für romanische Philologie</u>, LXV (1949), pp. 1-27.

10. <u>Studien zur musikalischen Textkritik</u>, p. 26.

11. This example will be re-examined later with regard to the relative merits of the conflicting variants.

12. Notes in parentheses in our examples are represented by plicas in the sources. The V reading is transposed down an octave to facilitate comparison.

13. An example similar to the above is cited in "Borrowed Material...," pp. 91f.

14. E.g., altering the text-underlay given by the MS; <u>cf. ibid.</u>, p. 89.

15. <u>Herrigs Archiv</u>, XLII, pp. 43-72.

16. <u>Die Lieder des Castellans von Coucy</u>, p. 24.

17. Die altfranzösischen Liederhandschriften, pp. 72, 171, 222.

18. See, for example the editions of Wiese (Blondel de Nesle) and Steffens (Perrin d'Angicourt).

19. The Musical Quarterly, XLVIII (1962), pp. 58f.

20. Particulars are cited in my doctoral dissertation, The Chansons of the Châtelain de Coucy, I, pp. 130-50.

21. Eine altfranzösische Liedersammlung, 1925, pp. 263-80.

22. To be sure, the a and T readings do not agree in all respects. There is a pitch error in lines 1 and 2 in T that is not present in a. Moreover, the variants in MS a at the cadence of line 4 are not reflected in T. The notes in the former source for the last two musical units of that line are apparently a third higher than intended, judging by comparison with other readings.

23. MS A contains a peripheral setting of this work.

24. MS A contains a peripheral setting of this work.

25. An additional example is cited in "Borrowed Material...," pp. 92f.

26. Lines 3 and 4 of the M and a readings are transposed down an octave to facilitate comparison.

27. Cf. "A Lost Medieval Chansonnier," p. 60.

28. Evidence relating MS O to MS M is discussed in "Borrowed Material...," p. 93.

[15]
THE TROUVÈRE CHANSONS AS CREATIONS OF A NOTATIONLESS MUSICAL CULTURE

Hendrik Van der Werf

THE TROUVÈRES occupy a curious and bifarious position in the cultural history of the Middle Ages. According to tradition they were both poets and composers, which leads us to ask whether they were poets first and musicians second, whether their poems existed by grace of the melodies, or whether they attained the apogee of lyrical art: complete unity of poem and melody. Whichever is the case, the trouvères stand apart from their fellow poets, and especially from their fellow composers, in their predilection for monodic chansons which are often esoteric in content. Some medieval authors such as Chrétien de Troyes, Richard de Fournival and Jean Bodel, who are primarily known for literary works, also wrote chansons, but the famous trouvères, except for Adam de la Halle, produced chansons exclusively. Adam seems to have been exceptionally venturesome in his choice of literary and musical genres. As far as we know, no other trouvère composed polyphonic music, and he and Guillaume d'Amiens were the only trouvères to write chansons in fixed forms.

Hundreds of trouvère chansons have been preserved.[1] They evoke colorful images and arouse great curiosity about the personalities of the trouvères and the circumstances in which the chansons were created and performed. The scarcity of information has stimulated rather than dampened this curiosity, making it difficult sometimes to distinguish fact from fancy. In the last analysis, knowledge of the conditions surrounding the chansons remains quite incomplete.

It is often pointed out that there were many noblemen among the troubadours, the earliest authors of vernacular lyric poetry; the ranks of the trouvères, on the other hand, included

---

[1] For a list of the trouvère chansons with complete information about their sources, see Spanke 1955.

HENDRIK VAN DER WERF graduated Ph.D. in Musicology at Columbia in 1964 and is presently teaching at the Eastman School of Music, Rochester.

burghers as well. We may further assume that the trouvères, whatever their social status, were in general not professional authors or musicians. It is widely accepted that the trouvères left the performance of their chansons to professional performers, the so-called jongleurs. Everything considered, it is easier to establish the characteristics of a trouvère chanson than of a trouvère or a jongleur.

A trouvère chanson is often preserved in more than one manuscript, but the melody of the chanson is seldom identical in all sources. In some cases the versions differ only slightly, whereas in others there does not seem to be any relationship between them, even though the text demonstrates that we deal with the same chanson. Nevertheless, there is usually no doubt about the common parentage of the preserved melodies even if the discrepancies are considerable. Thus editors of trouvère melodies are confronted with the problem of establishing the original melody, while wondering how so many significant changes could occur.

Nearly all editors of trouvère melodies appear to have been guided by the principle that most of the discrepancies in the sources are deteriorations caused by scribal inaccuracy or by inadequacies of the oral tradition. Friedrich Gennrich, the acknowledged authority in the field of secular medieval monody, formulated the following simple and seemingly undebatable principle for deriving the critical version of a medieval song from its various versions: correct the recognized errors and record the variants (1937:33). He explicitly rejects the opinion of those, notably Pierre Aubry (1909:XXVII), who warn that attempts to reconstruct the original melody of the trouvère chanson may well result in the creation of a new composition. Instead, Gennrich claims that "at present we are able to establish a critical version of the melody with equal if not greater certainty than the text" (1955:XIV). At first sight Gennrich's principles seem quite acceptable even though he seldom mentions the corrections he makes in his own editions. But a closer examination reveals a number of aspects that are questionable to say the least. Gennrich's method of editing medieval monody is extensively explained by Werner Bittinger (1953), who gives the careful reader the impression that this method consists of a set of directions for distilling the best possible melody from a number of different versions of a chanson, and for proving that the versions we find in the chansonniers are scribal deformations of this best version. Aubry's observation—certainly startling for its time—that the discrepancies were legitimate variants rather than errors goes unheeded. He regarded the indistinct melodies and the imprecise notation as the chief causes of the variants (1909:XXIV).

Philologists who publish the poems of the trouvères encounter problems similar to those of the musicologists who edit the melodies. Since very few of the melodies but nearly all of the poems have been published, it is worthwhile examining the philologists' approach. We find that the 19th- and early 20th-century editions of poems were based upon the principle that somewhere under a blanket of scribal errors and other deteriorations lay the original poem in all its charm and beauty. Accordingly, the editors set out to correct all errors and emend all changes made by later hands. However, they gradually concluded that their basic principle implied some questionable assumptions, such as, that the scribes were extremely inaccurate and made scores of mistakes, and that the chansons could only deteriorate during the process of being performed and copied. According to these assumptions, each chanson was sent into the world as a good chanson which the performers and scribes corrupted and forgot parts of, offering a poor substitute for the original poem. Realizing these implications, some editors came to the conclusion that efforts to reconstruct the original had produced only a new version.

A hallmark of the old editorial policy can be seen in the following announcement on the title page of a collection of chansons by the Chastelain de Coucy: *Die Lieder des Castellans von Coucy nach sämtlichen Handschriften kritisch bearbeitet* (Fritz Fath, ed. 1883). In a later edition by Arthur Langfors we see the emergence of a new approach. He remarks that "by making a small number of corrections [in a certain version] one obtains an excellent text; we shall indicate only the principal variants in the other manuscripts" (1917:65). The new editorial method invited discussion among scholars concerning the nature of the small corrections one should make, but in general there were no more attempts to reconstruct the original.

The philologists came to the conclusion that for a long time studies of medieval literature were influenced by "prejudices and prepossessions which years of association with printed matter have made habitual . . . If a fair judgment is to be passed upon literary works belonging to the centuries before printing was invented, some effort must be made to realize the extent of the prejudices with which we have grown up, and to resist the involuntary demand that medieval literature must conform to our standards of taste" (Chaytor 1945:1). In the study by H. J. Chaytor just quoted we find revealing information about medieval reading and writing habits, about oral tradition, and about the methods of copying texts, and we are made aware of the enormous change in attitude towards language in general, and the written or printed word in particular. This change has come about mainly since the invention of printing.

If the findings of the philologists are applied to the study of the melodies, the discrepancies in the manuscripts become sources of abundant information about the compositional technique of the trouvères, the performance habits of the jongleurs, and the scribal methods of copyists.

Our first and probably most important conclusion is that, in general, the different versions of a chanson present that chanson as it was performed by different jongleurs who had learned the chanson by rote either directly or indirectly from the trouvère himself. In other words, the chansons were in the first place disseminated by oral tradition and not by copies made from the trouvère's autograph. Only towards the end of the trouvère era did the chansons become "collectors' items," and only then was the chanson written down as it was performed at the time. It follows that we should not judge the melodies from their appearance in notation, but rather we should sing them while thinking of an audience; instead of basing the analysis of a chanson upon one melody reconstructed from several sources, we should analyze all the melodies as they appear in the sources. Then, when comparing these different versions we should realize that it was not compulsory for a performer always to sing a chanson with exactly the same melody. For him a chanson was not an untouchable entity with a sacred "original form" to be respected and preserved. It was normal for a jongleur to perform in the way he thought that particular chanson ought to be performed and we should not pass judgment on a jongleur who invented part of a melody or even an entire one. Thus the differences in the versions are not necessarily infractions of the rules for performing someone else's composition, as present-day audiences would be inclined to think;

64

neither should they be considered as conscious improvisations upon a given theme in the modern sense of the word. On the contrary, according to the jongleur's concept, he was singing the trouvère's melody even though, according to our concept, he was varying it. The difference between these concepts reflects the fact that our attitude towards printed music differs considerably from the jongleur's attitude towards the poetry and melody of a chanson learned by rote.

As a second conclusion from the work of the philologists, we must stress the important effect of oral tradition on scribal copying methods. There may be insufficient documentary evidence for the oral tradition of the melodies,[2] but without dissemination of this kind the discrepancies among the versions of a given chanson would have been different, unless it is assumed that the scribes either did not know anything about music or that they continually did their best to change the original as much as possible without writing a new chanson. A chanson may have been notated on different occasions after performances by one or several different jongleurs; each such notation may have been copied several times, and the version which we find in a manuscript may be a first notation or a remote copy of it. We may safely assume that the scribes (those who first notated it and those who made copies) did make changes but that only an infinitesimal number of these changes are caused by real scribal inaccuracy; instead, they are the consequence of the attitude towards a chanson transmitted by oral tradition and of the medieval methods of copying. I do not wish to imply that medieval methods of copying were primitive, only that in several respects circumstances were different from those of today. There was no one prescribed way of performing a certain chanson, nor was there the uniformity in musical notation that we now know. Monody was much less uniformly notated than the measured polyphony of the period, though they were perhaps notated by the same scribes. Furthermore, we may conclude that the scribes did not copy at sight symbol for symbol. Instead, certain manuscripts show clearly that a scribe must have sung to himself

---

[2] We are not trying to establish the extent to which oral tradition affected the dissemination of the text. Since there are empty staffs above the words of so many chansons we may conclude that it was more difficult to obtain the music than the words, and that there may well have been more copying of the poems than of the melodies.

a section from the manuscript in front of him—not necessarily the melody of exactly one entire line—and then copied from memory what he had *heard* rather than what he had *seen*. Consequently he put himself in the position of a jongleur notating his own performance. In this process he could make deliberate changes and corrections, but he may also have unconsciously varied the melody more or less extensively by changing the distribution of the melody over the text, by ornamenting the melody, or by simplifying it.

Furthermore, it may be assumed that many of the notators and copyists had respectable educations and knew more about the theory of music and the rules of rhetoric than many a trouvère or any jongleur did. Consequently, we have to take into account a tendency on the part of notator and copyist to correct the trouvère and jongleur. Thus in some cases the changes made by the scribe are in accordance with performance practices, but in other cases the scribe's objective was to make the chanson conform to the theories. In some chansons he may even have transformed free rhythm into modal.[3]

Of course, it is conceivable that among the many jongleurs who knew a given chanson there was one who performed it in its original form; subsequently, this chanson may have been written down exactly as the trouvère had created it. Thus we may possess the original melody for some chansons, but we cannot be sure of our ability to distinguish the original from among the recorded versions. We cannot simply assume that the version we think is best is the original, for it is quite possible that the jongleurs, who were experienced singers, were better musicians than many trouvères and improved upon the latter's creation. More important, even if we could determine the original version, we should not discard the others, because in most cases the chansonniers present us with various fully acceptable melodies in the best manner of the period.

---

[3] In light of this knowledge we observe that most of the chansons in the manuscripts K, L, N, P and X were copied directly or indirectly from one common source. On the other hand, many of the chansons in the manuscripts M and T are related in a different fashion: they were probably not copied from one common source but notated from different renditions, which, however, may have come from the same performer. Furthermore, we may conclude that the scribe of the Chansonnier Cangé was thoroughly familiar with motets, chansons in fixed form, and the like, and that this strongly influenced his opinion of the notation and the performance of the true trouvère chansons. (The manuscript sigla are those used in Spanke 1955.)

Rather than accepting the above observations as premises for further examination of the trouvère repertoire, we should regard them as two aspects of one complex theory. Other aspects of this theory concern rhythm, tonal structure, melodic form, and the position of the trouvères in medieval culture, aspects which I shall discuss fully in future articles. Here I will briefly mention their major features:

1. Careful examination of the variants discloses that only a very small number of the chansons were meant to be performed in a strict, a modified, or a mixed modal rhythm. If all the chansons had been performed in modal rhythm, as is generally assumed, the variants would have been quite different. In fact, the variants are such that they could originate only in declamatory performances of which the rhythm is free in two ways: first, accented and unaccented tones and syllables may come at irregular intervals, and second, there is not necessarily a simple ratio between the duration of one tone or syllable and that of another.

2. It also becomes obvious that there is no reason to assume that the trouvères were guided by the system of the so-called church modes in composing their melodies, or that they wrote in major or minor scales with tonics, dominants, and leading tones, as has sometimes been suggested. Nor is there always the close interdependence between versification and melodic form which Gennrich describes. Instead, the melodies give the impression of being "remembered improvisations" with little design and a rather loose organization.

3. The chansons in fixed form, the French motets, and the Spanish cantigas stem from the world of *learned* musicians, whereas the chansons of the trouvères originated and circulated in a *notationless* musical culture in which notation and theory exercised little or no influence, but in which the rules of rhetoric were well-known and faithfully observed. Instances of border-crossing are only occasional; therefore, a trouvère chanson resembling a monophonic motet is a rare exception. But it is just these exceptions that mislead so many musicologists who approach the chansons as intricate musical settings of a text. Instead, a trouvère chanson is a poem to be declaimed to an unobtrusive melody which leaves the performer ample freedom for a dramatic rendition of the text and sometimes for showing off his beautiful voice.

REFERENCES

AUBRY, PIERRE, ed.
 1909 Joseph Bédier, Chansons de Croisade . . . avec leurs mélodies. Paris

BITTINGER, WERNER
 1953 Studien zur Musikalischen Textkritik des Mittelalterlichen Liedes. Friedrich Gennrich (Ed). Literarhistorisch-Musikwissenschaftliche Abhandlungen, Würzburg. Vol. 9.

CHAYTOR, H. J.
 1945 From Script to Print: an Introduction to Medieval Literature. Cambridge.

GENNRICH, FRIEDRICH
 1937 Grundsätzliches zu den Troubadour- und Trouvère-Weisen. Zeitschrift für Romanische Philologie 57.
 1955 Altfranzösische Lieder, Vol. 1. Tübingen. Sammlung Romanischer Übungstexte, Vol. 36.

LANGFORS, ARTHUR
 1917 Les Chansons attribuées aux seigneurs de Craon. Helsinki.

SPANKE, HANS, ed.
 1955 Gaston Raynauds Bibliographie des altfranzösischen Liedes, neu bearbeitet und ergänzt. Leiden.

[16]

PROBLEME UM DIE MELODIEN DES MINNESANGS

VON URSULA AARBURG

I. Singen oder sagen[1]

Als die Liebhaber einer verklungenen Kunst um die 13. Jahrhundertwende begannen, das verstreute Gut der mittelhochdeutschen klassischen Lyrik in repräsentativen Codices zu sammeln, – es sei an die Große Heidelberger Liederhandschrift, die sogenannte Manessische, erinnert, – verzichteten sie auf die Melodien. Daraus hat die Forschung mitunter die Schlüsse gezogen, die notationslos niedergeschriebene Lyrik sei in dieser Spätzeit nur noch für den Sprechvortrag bestimmt gewesen, ja, sie sei überhaupt niemals gesungen worden.

Diesem Schluß widersprechen jene (zwar wenigen) Niederschriften aus demselben Zeitraum, die mit Noten versehen sind: das bis 1910 als Aktenumschlag verwendete Münsterer Fragment mit Melodien Walthers von der Vogelweide, die Neidhart von Reuentalhandschriften, die Jenaer Sangspruch- und die Wiener Leichhandschrift, die deutschen neumierten Carmina burana-Strophen und überdies einige andere, gut bezeugte, aber bisher unauffindbar gebliebene Musikaufzeichnungen zur mittelhochdeutschen Lyrik. Dem widerspricht auch der Usus in den zeitgenössischen romanischen Chansonniers, die besonders im nordfranzösischen Raum verschwenderisch mit Noten ausgestattet worden sind. Auch die höfischen und bürgerlichen Lyriker selbst erwähnen in ihren Liedern den 'Sang', den musikalischen Vortrag, und Walther von der Vogelweide bekennt in seinem Abschiedslied, dem sogenannten Alterston: *wol vierzec jâr hab ich gesungen ... / von minnen* (W. 66,27 f.), – ähnlich Ulrich von Lichtenstein, als er im Jahre 1255 seine Minnebiographie, den 'Frauendienst' abschloß: *zwei minner sehzic doene ich hân / gesungen* (L. 592,11 f.). Den sanglichen Vortrag bezeugt auch die Familienchronik der Steinacher (1491), die berichtet, daß anläßlich eines von Kaiser Heinrich VI. veranstalteten Festgelages alle Teilnehmer: Fürsten, Grafen, Herren, Ritter, darunter auch der als Minnesänger bekannte und im Gefolge Heinrichs VI. nachweisbare Bligger von Steinach, ein Lied vorsingen mußten. Und ein Jahrhundert später, um 1304/08, definiert Dante Alighieri die höfische volkssprachige Lyrik in seiner Abhandlung über die lyrischen Formen Italiens und Frankreichs als *fictio rhetorica musicaque*

---

[1] Die bibliographischen Hinweise zu den einzelnen Abschnitten stehen am Ende des Beitrags.

composita (De vulgari eloquentia. Teil II. Kap. 4); einige Kapitel weiter analysiert er die Elemente der Canzone, der edelsten lyrischen Gattung (Kap. 3), und beschreibt als erstes ihre Melodie und deren Formung (Kap. 9–11). Wie eng das Singen – nun zum inneren Singen gewandelt – in die lyrische Mitteilung eingeschlossen ist, bewahrt noch Hölderlins wehmütige Frage, die er 1797/98 an sich selbst richtete:

> Warum bist du so kurz! liebst du, wie vormals, denn
> nun nicht mehr den Gesang? fandst du, als Jüngling, doch
>   in den Tagen der Hoffnung,
>   wenn du sangest, das Ende nie?
> Wie mein Glück ist mein Lied ...

Aber – so wird man fragen – warum verzichteten die Sammler bei der Fixierung einer so eminent musikgebundenen Kunst auf das ihr wesentliche Element, auf die Melodien? Es könnte, so möchte man annehmen, an Mitteln für Pergament und fachlich vorgebildeten Schreibern gefehlt haben. Dies trifft wahrscheinlich für eine altfranzösische Handschrift zu, die ausnahmsweise und ähnlich der 'Manessischen' oder der Weingartner Sammlung als reine Texthandschrift angelegt ist, obwohl sie u. a. ausgeprägt sangliche Lyrik enthält: Tanzlieder (Rondeaux, Balletes, Estampien) und Motetten, die sonst mehrstimmig überliefert sind (Oxford, Bodleian Library, Douce 308). An Mitteln kann es aber beispielsweise dem Auftraggeber der großzügig und kostbar ausgestatteten 'Manessischen' Handschrift kaum gefehlt haben. Auch der Einwand, die alten Melodien seien ein Jahrhundert später als unmodern empfunden und daher fallen gelassen worden, verfängt nicht, da man sie hätte umarbeiten können, wie ja auch die Texte modernisiert oder dort, wo sie unverständlich waren, redigiert worden sind. Auch die Meistersänger änderten Melodien und Textformen nach ihrem Geschmack, und der Notator des altfranzösischen Chansonnier Cangé (Paris, Bibl. Nat., f. fr. 846) 'bessert' stellenweise die Melodien, indem er Strophenschlüsse meistersängerisch den Aufgesangsschlüssen angleicht.

Man könnte nun annehmen, daß die Melodien, mündlich tradiert (vergleichbar der alten Hoflyrik Indiens, Chinas, Griechenlands, Arabiens, um nur die wichtigsten Kulturkreise zu nennen) und leichter einprägsam als mehrstrophige Texte, allenthalben noch gut bekannt waren, so daß die Notierung sich erübrigte. Aus diesem Grunde blieben ja Meistersanghandschriften, Volks- und Kirchenlieddrucke häufig notationslos: ein Hinweis auf den 'Ton' (die Melodie also) genügte, um die Texte musikalisch zu realisieren.

Aber diese Liederbücher waren für den praktischen Gebrauch bestimmt; unsere großen mittelhochdeutschen Sammelhandschriften stehen dagegen schon am Ende der klassischen Tradition und stellen eher Gesamtausgaben des noch erreichbaren Liedguts dar. Daß dabei auch dynastische Repräsentationszwecke mit verfolgt wurden, ist kürzlich für die 'Manessische' Sammlung und ihre (verschollene) Hauptquelle wahrscheinlich gemacht worden: dieses ursprünglich spätstaufische Liederbuch mit dem Bild Kaiser Heinrichs VI. am Anfang könnte um 1260/70 schon als Konkurrenzunternehmen zu den großen Liederhandschriften des französischen und spanischen Königs angelegt worden sein. Ähnlich ist die Jenaer Liederhandschrift, nach romanischem Muster mit Quadratnotation ausgestattet, als Repräsentationsbuch der Wettiner aufzufassen.

Da nun aber die Notation im Gegensatz zu den ausländischen Sammlungen in den meisten Fällen fehlt, ist eher anzunehmen, daß der flüchtigere Stoff der Melodien im Umkreis der Sammler längst vergessen war. Vielleicht waren einige Vorlagen mit linienlosen Neumen versehen, – einer Art Kurzschrift für melodische Details als Gedächtnisstütze des Sängers, der freilich Tonart und Gesamtanlage im Kopfe haben mußte, um die Melodie dann mit Hilfe der Neumen präzise in ihren Einzelheiten nachvollziehen zu können. Die um 1250 geschriebene Carmina burana-Sammlung überliefert solche Neumen, und auch der Anfang von Walthers Preislied *Si wunderwol gemachet wîp* (W. 53,25), das ein Kleriker am Ende eines Psalteriums nachgetragen hat, ist mit derartigen Zeichen versehen, die unentzifferbar bleiben werden, solange sich keine eindeutig lesbare Parallelüberlieferung findet.

Daß Melodien untergehen konnten, berichtet uns Adam Puschman, ein später Zeuge mündlicher Melodieüberlieferung. Dieser Meistersänger, der bis Ende 1587, wie er angibt, 350 Melodien auswendig konnte, darunter auch solche von Walther von der Vogelweide, hatte 1584 begonnen, ein 'Singebuch' anzulegen, damit, wie er im Kommentar vom 1. 1. 1588 bemerkt, *nicht auch ein zimliche Anzal der töne, sonderlich der Alten, mit mir absterben teten, wie zu voren mit ettlichen verstorbenen Singern geschehen* (fol. 101). Daß die Melodien des älteren Minnesangs für den Auftraggeber der 'Manessischen' Sammlung also nicht mehr greifbar gewesen sind, ist anzunehmen. Aus Gründen der Konsequenz wird er daher auch auf die Mitteilung der jüngeren, sicher noch erreichbaren Melodien Frauenlobs, Regenbogens, Hadlaubs, Ottos zum Turne, des Kirchherrn von Sarnen u. a. verzichtet haben, um wenigstens das Substantiellere dieser Lyrik, die Texte zu bewahren.

Sind die Texte dieser Spätsammlungen nun aber gesprochen aus den Handschriften vorgetragen worden, wie man vermutet hat? Für die großformatigen, kostbar mit Bildern geschmückten und meist angeketteten Codices, die eher Prunkstücke einer Hofbibliothek gewesen zu sein scheinen, ist dies unwahrscheinlich; für die anderen Sammlungen wissen wir es nicht. Wenn auch der endgültige Übergang von der gesungenen zur gesprochenen Lyrik irgendwann angesetzt werden muß, so ist doch zu bedenken, daß die Tradition des gesungenen Gedichts noch jahrhundertelang weiterlebte, – nicht nur im einstimmigen Spruch- und Meistersang, im Volkslied, Kirchenlied und religiösen Drama, sondern auch im Ritterlied Wizlavs von Rügen (1265/8–1325), Hugos von Montfort (1357–1423) und Oswalds von Wolkenstein (1377–1445) und überdies im mehrstimmigen Lied seit seiner frühen Blüte in der französischen Conductus- und Motettenkunst des 12. bis 14. Jahrhunderts über die Madrigal- und Ballatenkompositionen der italienischen Ars nova (14. Jh.) bis zur niederländischen Chanson- und der gleichzeitig aufblühenden Hofweisenkunst des deutschen Liederjahrhunderts (um 1450 – um 1550).

Der Übergang von der obligat gesungenen Lyrik zur reinen Sprechlyrik wird jedoch nicht abrupt vonstatten gegangen sein. Beide Vortragsarten müssen noch lange nebeneinanderher gelebt haben, denn der vielseitige Berufssänger und spätere Schultheiß Michael Beheim (1416–74) bemerkt zum Vortrag seines strophisch abgefaßten Chronikwerks über den Wiener Bürgeraufstand von 1462–65, *das man es lesen mag als ainen spruch oder singen als ain liet*. Die Melodie für die rund 2000 sechszeiligen Strophen nennt er *angstweis*, da er *in grossen angsten* gewesen sei, während die Wiener die Hofburg belagerten. Auch für die Vita Friedrichs des Siegreichen, die er 1469 im selben Strophenmaß dichtete, gibt er eine Melodie, die Osterweise, an.

Ein solcher *ad libitum*-Vortrag wäre *cum grano salis* auch für den Minnesang denkbar. Ulrich von Lichtenstein bringt in seiner oben erwähnten Minnechronik anschauliche Beispiele für die Vortragspraxis seiner Zeit, die, das zweite Viertel des 13. Jahrhunderts umfassend, ihrer retrospektiven Haltung wegen stellvertretend auch für die Zeit des klassischen Minnesangs gelten mag. Ulrich läßt seine ersten Lieder der Herrin, um deren Gunst er wirbt, durch Boten übermitteln. Zunächst fungiert eine Verwandte, seine *niftel*, als Botin, die der Herrin, deren Vertrauen sie genießt, das erste, im Winter 1222/3 komponierte und schriftlich fixierte Lied *vorliest;* sie singt es also nicht. Vielleicht war sie nicht sangeskundig, vielleicht auch schickte es sich nicht für sie, einer anderen Frau das kecke Werbelied eines Mannes vorzusingen. Die nächsten drei Lieder übersendet Ulrich gleichfalls geschrieben (und als Brief getarnt) durch einen Boten, den ihm die *niftel* zur Verfügung stellt, an die Herrin: diese nimmt sie *lesend* zur Kenntnis. Als Antwort erhält Ulrich eine von der Herrin verfaßte Strophe, die ihm, der nicht lesen kann, von seinem Schreiber *vorgelesen* wird; zum Singen war diese Strophe, eine Art Reimbrief, wahrscheinlich aber nicht bestimmt. Da ihm dann weitere Sendungen untersagt werden, bleiben die Lieder 5 bis 7 ungehört. Die Melodie von Lied 7 freilich, – jener bekannte Beleg für die Kontrafakturpraxis, das Neutextieren einer fremden, hier wohl provenzalisch-italienischen oder französischen Weise, – wird Ulrich im Sommer 1225 von dem

Boten einer anderen, liederkundigen Dame *vorgesungen, in* der er, wie er sich ausdrückt, sogleich einen allgemeinen Frauenpreis in deutscher Sprache dichtet; er wird schriftlich fixiert und an die Auftraggeberin zurückgesandt. Ulrich muß sich also, wie dieser Auftrag bekundet, ein gewisses Ansehen als Liederkomponist erworben haben, seit sein 4. Lied *In dem walde süeze doene / singent kleiniu vogelîn,* das noch die Romantiker entzückte und seither in keiner Minnesangsanthologie fehlt, im Mai 1224 auf dem Friesacher Fürstentreffen vor einem Ritterpublikum *für komen,* also 'uraufgeführt' worden ist und Beifall geerntet hat. Für die Überbringung des 8. Liedes findet Ulrich dann einen redegewandten und sangeskundigen Boten, der die schriftliche Ausfertigung überreicht und der Herrin gleichzeitig das Lied *singend* zu Gehör bringt. Auch das 10. Lied wird ihr vorgetragen, während sie Lied 11 und 12 nur in schriftlicher Form erhält. Von Lied 11 waren *wîs unde wort ... mit guoter schrift ... geschriben* (L. 321,22 + 24) worden, ehe sie an die Empfängerin gesandt wurden, – wir haben bei Ulrich also insgesamt neun Belege für die alte Liederblatt-Theorie Beneckes (auf germanistischer Seite) und Gröbers (auf romanistischer Seite), die von Gennrich unlängst angefochten wurde. Seit seinem 13. Liede bedurfte Ulrich keines Boten mehr (dessen Entsendung ihm gerade wieder untersagt worden war): seine Lieder gingen als begehrte Novitäten offenbar schnell von Mund zu Mund, denn er bekundet mehrfach: *diu liet vernam mîn vrowe wol* (s. Nr. 13; 14; 20; 22; 23) und überdies an vielen Stellen, daß seine Lieder Publikumserfolg hatten (s. Nr. 16; 18; 30; 33; 47; 54) und viel *gesungen* wurden (s. Nr. 22; 38; 39; 52; 53); in zwei Fällen gibt er an, *diu wîse wart getanzet vil* (Ld. 19) bzw. *diu liet ... wurden oft getanzet vil* (Ld. 52). In dem einen Fall könnte *diu wîse* nur instrumental ausgeführt worden sein, im anderen Falle ist aber der Text aller Strophen *(diu liet)* eindeutig zum Tanze *gesungen* worden. Das erinnert an Dantes Definition der Ballata: sie bedürfe, um realisiert zu werden, der singenden Tänzer (s. die oben erwähnte Abhandlung, Kap. 3). Die instrumentale Ausführung (oder Begleitung?) bezeugt Ulrich schließlich für seinen Minneleich (Nr. 25).

Der gesungene Vortrag stellt – zumal im festlichen oder geselligen Rahmen – offenkundig den Regelfall, der gesprochene Vortrag eines lyrischen Gedichts den durch besondere Umstände bedingten Ausnahmefall dar. Und auch hier wird der Vortrag eher einem halbsanglichen Rezitieren als einer schlichten Rede entsprochen haben. Aus früheren Kulturen und ihren in Randgebieten bewahrten Relikten wissen wir, daß jede feierliche oder gebundene Rede rezitiert wurde. Noch zu Beginn des 19. Jahrhunderts trugen japanische Gesandte ihre Botschaften rezitierend an den europäischen Höfen vor. Die Erzählungen des Eskimos werden gesungen, ihre Gerichtsverhandlungen in dialogisierender Liedform ausgetragen.

Dante betrachtete die gesungene Canzone als höchste Kunstform. Ihre Strophenform sei, so führt er im 10. Kapitel seiner schon erwähnten Abhandlung aus, auf eine *Melodie* eingestimmt. Diese könne eine *oda continua* sein (eine der Hymnenform ähnliche Melodie ohne innere Wiederholungen). Ihrer habe sich der Trobador Arnaut Daniel (fl. 1180–1200) vorwiegend bedient (tatsächlich sind die beiden erhaltenen Melodien *odae continuae*) und er, Dante, sei ihm gefolgt, als er das Lied *Al poco giorno ed al gran cerchio d'ombra* (aus den *Rime*) gedichtet habe. Keine der zwanzig überlieferten Canzonen Dantes ist mit Melodie erhalten, und doch wissen wir von einer Vertonung, die Dante selbst erwähnt: im Purgatorium habe ihm der Musiker Pietro Casella da Pistoia seine Canzone *Amor che nella mente mi ragiona* vorgesungen und ihn dadurch aufs höchste entzückt (*Divina comedia: Purgatorio* II, 110 ff.). Ein Dichter, der die „höchsten Dinge besingen will", solle die Form der Canzone wählen, sagt Dante an anderer Stelle seiner Abhandlung, „zuvor vom Helikon trinken, die Saiten stimmen, fest das Plektrum ergreifen und zu schlagen beginnen" (Kap. 4), – ein Bild, das die zur Lyra gesungene altgriechische 'Lyrik' beschwört. Daß aber das Mittelalter seine lyrischen Verse zu einer musikalischen Vorlage schuf, zeigt schon das Dichten in Strophen und darüber hinaus die weitverbreitete Kontrafakturpraxis. Umgekehrt ist freilich auch erst das Gedicht und dann die Weise geschaffen worden, wie wir von Hugo von Montfort wissen, der seine Lieder von Burk Mangolt vertonen ließ, – doch ist das umgekehrte Verfahren die Regel.

Aber so eindringlich Dante die lyrische Text-Melodie-Einheit begründet (und daher als Zeuge der mittelalterlichen Grundkonzeption für uns bedeutsam ist), so zeigt sich doch leise schon der Übergang zu einer musikfreien Lyrik, wenn er in dem wichtigen 8. Kapitel seiner Abhandlung einschränkt, daß die Worte der Kanzone zwar für eine Melodie in Einklang gebracht worden seien, daß die Kanzone aber auch für sich, d. h. nur *in chartulis* (Liederblatt!) geschrieben und ohne Realisierung durch einen Vortragenden, existent sei. Schon die *actio completa*, der kompositorische Vollzug also, sei eine Kanzone. Im 3. Kapitel betont Dante, daß die Kanzone durch sich selbst zu wirken vermöge, während, wie schon oben erwähnt, die mindere Gattung der Ballata der Tänzer und des gesungenen Vortrags bedürfe, um zu existieren.

Dieser frühe Ansatz einer l'art pour l'art-Auffassung, die sich von der mittelalterlichen Konzeption einer Zwecklyrik zu lösen beginnt, ist auch für jene Sammelcodices faßbar, die das lyrische Erbe nur noch um seiner selbst willen, nicht mehr für Vortragszwecke bewahren. Sie führt dann folgerichtig zur gesprochenen oder nur noch lesend aufgenommenen Lyrik. Aber Dante läßt ausdrücklich beide Vortragsarten gelten, die musikgebundene und die musikfreie (Kap. 8), die gesungene ist ihm noch die vollkommenere, die ideale Form.

Einen Abglanz von der Wirkung und Macht des Liedersingens bewahren einige aus dem sangesfrohen Frankreich des Mittelalters stammende Redewendungen wie *voilà une autre chanson* (das hört sich schon anders an) oder *chanter pouilles à quelqu'un* (jemanden beschimpfen) oder *chansons que tout cela* (das alles ist nicht wahr), und auch wir können heute noch *ein Lied von etwas singen*, wenn wir – wie unsere mittelalterlichen Vorfahren – ein intensives Erlebnis oder eine einschneidende Erfahrung zu schildern uns anschicken.

II. Rekonstruktionsprobleme

Überlieferungskritische Forschung möchte den Urtext zurückgewinnen. Daß die mittelalterlichen Melodien überwiegend mündlich in Raum und Zeit weitergetragen wurden und meist erst in einem Spätstadium zu Pergament oder Papier kamen, erschwert nicht allein die Rekonstruktionsbemühungen der Musikwissenschaft; die Aufzeichnungen selbst sind so hölzern, so primitiv und unzureichend, daß sie kein lebendiges Bild der ihnen zugrundeliegenden Melodien geben können. Fast immer fehlt die Rhythmusangabe. Unlesbar sind die linienlos notierten Melodien (Carmina burana), schwierig zu rekonstruieren die schlüssellos und oft auch textlos (Berliner Neidhart-Handschrift) notierten Weisen. Viele Melodien sind nur teilweise erhalten, sei es, daß nur noch ihr Anfang bekannt war, sei es, daß eine fragmentarische Handschrift inmitten der Notenaufzeichnung abbricht (Münsterer Fragment). Auch mit Fälschungen müssen wir rechnen, zumindest sind sie in romanischen Handschriften, angefertigt für musikunkundige Auftraggeber, denen der Notator nicht beschaffbare Weisen vortäuschen konnte, nachweisbar. Schließlich ist das Problem der Schreibfehler zu lösen und von dem der Varianten zu trennen. Oft fehlen Akzidentien (b- oder Kreuzvorzeichnungen), die zu ergänzen sind. Oft ist zu fragen, ob eine schlichte Fassung nur den Melodiekern geben will und für die Aufführung der Weise mit auszierender Improvisation gerechnet werden muß, wie es die substantiell ähnlichen, in der Melismatik aber unterschiedlichen Aufzeichnungen von Neidharts Lied *Sinc an, guldîn huon, ich gibe dir weize* (N. 40,1) nahelegen.

Wir besitzen eine verschwindend geringe Anzahl von Autographen (vom Schreiber der Kolmarer Handschrift f. 492 z. B.) oder autorisierten Niederschriften bzw. deren Abschriften (die Liederhandschriften Oswalds von Wolkenstein oder König Alfons' des Weisen z. B.). Überwiegend werden die Melodien aus dem Gedächtnis niedergeschrieben und diese Notierungen dann wieder für Abschriften benutzt worden sein. Adam Puschman, der schon erwähnte Meistersänger, schildert dieses Verfahren anschaulich: er habe alle Töne zunächst aus dem Gedächtnis skizziert und diese Skizzen dann von einem musikverständigen

Cantor, der *kein* Meistersänger gewesen sei, nachsingen lassen. So habe er feststellen können, an welchen Stellen seine Notierung nicht mit den im Gedächtnis bewahrten Melodien übereinstimme, um dann mit dem Cantor gemeinsam die Fehler zu bessern und diese korrigierten Fassungen in sein 'Singebuch' zu übertragen (ds. fol. 101). Hier ist also alle wünschenswerte Sorgfalt angewandt worden, um ein authentisches Manuskript herzustellen. Aber auch sie vermag – auf eine bloße Gedächtnisleistung gestützt – keine Urtexte, sondern nur die in Puschmans Umkreis lebendigen Fassungen zu reproduzieren, wie etwa ein Vergleich mit den abweichenden Melodie-Autographen des Hans Sachs zeigt. Kaum anzunehmen ist, daß die sorgsame Methode Puschmans Regel gewesen ist. Im Gegenteil müssen wir mit unzähligen Fehler- und Variantenquellen rechnen, die nicht nur beim Schreiben, sondern auch schon beim Singen und 'Zersingen' auftreten konnten.

Unsere Bilanz sieht also kläglich genug aus. Und doch lohnt die forschende Mühe, wenn es gelingt, das mittelalterliche 'Gesamtkunstwerk' wieder zum Leben zu erwecken, eine ausdrucksvolle Melodie wie die Liebesklage Wizlavs von Rügen *Nâch der senenden klage môt ik singen* oder die eigentümlich reizvolle, rhythmisch überlieferte Weise zu Neidharts Sommerlied *Blôzen wir den anger ligen sâhen* (N. 26,23) oder schließlich jenes Wunder an melodischer Schönheit, das Walther von der Vogelweide uns in seinem Palästinalied hinterlassen hat, zurückzugewinnen.

Die musikwissenschaftliche Forschung hat sich freilich oft, begünstigt durch diese unzureichende Überlieferung und benachteiligt durch mangelhafte Kenntnisse des mittelalterlichen Melodiestils, einen weiten Spielraum für eigenmächtige Manipulationen angemaßt und hat gern – was noch bedenklicher ist – gegenüber dem Nichtfachmann auf eine Begründung des von ihr angebotenen Melodietextes verzichtet. Hierher gehört besonders das unrühmlich von Lehrmeinungen belastete Kapitel der Rhythmusrekonstruktion, das wir unten noch kurz streifen müssen. Eine Revision der bisher meist üblichen Editionspraxis ist dringlich, wenn das längst erschütterte Vertrauen in die musikologischen Melodieausgaben zurückgewonnen werden soll. Eine Mindestforderung ist die unmittelbar aus dem Notentext ersichtliche Angabe, ob die Melodierhythmisierung aus der Handschrift stammt oder Zutat des Herausgebers ist. Um eine größtmögliche Transparenz der formalen Anlage zu erreichen, ist – genau wie beim Abdruck der Textstrophen – die Melodiestrophe zeilenweise abzusetzen; Wiederholungen sollten nicht ausgeschrieben werden. Ideal wäre die Unterlegung sämtlicher Textstrophen unter die zugehörige Melodie. Selbstverständlich sollte sein, daß man dem musikalischen Laien keinen Tenor- oder Baßschlüssel zumutet, ebenso, daß man moderne Notenformen verwendet, die im übrigen dieselbe Behelfslösung bieten wie eine mittelalterliche mensurierte Notation: die

Fülle vortragspraktischer Freiheiten vermögen auch sie ohne genaueste Vortragszeichen nicht auszudrücken. Empfehlenswert ist bei transponierten Melodien die Rücktransposition in den Grundmodus, da jede mittelalterliche Tonart ihre eigene Melodiesprache, ihre eigene melodische 'Syntax' (s. u.) hat, die für den modernen, an andere tonale Gesetzmäßigkeiten gewöhnten Betrachter optisch am deutlichsten wird, wenn sie untransponiert ist. Natürlich muß die Transposition über dem Notentext angegeben werden. Daß mittelhochdeutsche lyrische Texte taktisch gegliedert sind, sollte auch in den Melodieausgaben zum Ausdruck kommen, – wer freilich mit Recht moderne Taktstriche scheut, kann andere Lösungen verwenden, um die Taktgliederung eines Verses transparent zu machen. Über die Innengliederung dieser Takte – Tripeltakt, Dupeltakt, Melismatik – wird unten noch kurz zu sprechen sein. Für eine kritische *Text*edition ist selbstverständlich, daß die abweichenden Lesarten synoptisch mitgeteilt werden. Wenn kritische *Melodie*ausgaben überhaupt Abweichungen mitteilen, verbannen sie diese in einen Anhang, da eine synoptische Anordnung schwierig und aufwendig ist. Und doch wäre sie anzustreben, ja, es wäre wünschenswert, wenn einer Melodiebearbeitung ein Faksimile oder doch ein diplomatischer Melodieabdruck beigegeben würde, damit die kritische Entscheidung des Herausgebers unmittelbar nachgeprüft werden kann. Freilich wird ein derart idealer Editionsmodus schwierig zu verwirklichen sein.

In den letzten Jahren erschienen drei größere Auswahleditionen mit Melodien zur mhd. Lyrik, die leicht zugänglich sind und daher für die folgenden Beispiele herangezogen werden sollen: zunächst der Beispielband in der Reihe ‚Das Musikwerk' von F. Gennrich: Troubadours, Trouvères, Minne- und Meistergesang. Köln 1951. ²1960, der 32 Melodien von Hausen bis Hans Sachs bietet; sodann die umfänglichste und interessanteste Sammlung von E. Jammers: Ausgewählte Melodien des Minnesangs. Tübingen 1963 (ATB, Ergänzungsreihe Bd. 1), mit rund 120 deutschen und weiteren zehn außerdeutschen Beispielen nach Gattungen geordnet; schließlich die handliche und instruktive Ausgabe in der Sammlung Metzler von R. J. Taylor: Die Melodien der weltlichen Lieder des Mittelalters (2 Teile, Stuttgart 1964) mit 24 Beispielen von Ratpert bis Wolkenstein. Keine dieser Editionen vermag alle Wünsche zu erfüllen, doch als informatorische Quelle und Materialsammlung hat jede auf ihre Weise Bedeutung.

Um nun die editorischen Schwierigkeiten zu demonstrieren, seien hier einige der bekanntesten deutschen Melodien des Mittelalters herangezogen. Die Weise von Walthers PALÄSTINALIED (Gennrich S. 51, Jammers S. 205, Taylor S. 20), auf die wir im III. Teil noch zurückkommen werden, ist offenkundig relativ korrekt überliefert, da sie mit den beiden Melodien ihres lateinischen bzw. niederdeutschen Kontrafakts, die erst 1475 aufgezeichnet wurden, bis auf geringe

Spuren des Zersingens übereinstimmt. Das mag unser Vertrauen in die Überlieferungstreue des Münsterer Fragments stärken. Aber die beiden anderen (fragmentarischen) Melodien dieser Handschrift zeigen Störungen. Im 2. PHILIPPSTON (W. 18,15; s. Taylor S. 21, Jammers S. 153, Gennrich S. 52, hier mit neu hinzukomponiertem Abgesang), fällt die unmelodische Wiederholung derselben Ternaria am Schluß des 2. Verses auf. Zwischen beiden Ternariae wechselt der Schreiber die Linie (Lw): an diesen Punkten des Übergangs, die häufig auch mit Schlüsselwechseln verbunden sind (Sw), entstehen vorwiegend entweder Fehler, oder schon vorhandene Schreibversehen werden hier wieder einreguliert.

Notenbeispiel 1

Offenkundig hat der Schreiber vor dem Linienwechsel eine Note vergessen (a) oder zwei Einzelnoten versehentlich gebunden (b) und daher die Schlußternaria eine Silbe zu früh notiert, um sie dann, aufmerksam geworden durch den Linien- und Schlüsselwechsel, über der zugehörigen Reimsilbe zu wiederholen. Warum er seinen Fehler nicht korrigierte, bleibt unklar. Aus den großen französischen Prachthandschriften wissen wir, daß die Schreiber ihre Fehler häufig unverbessert ließen und versuchten, die gestörte Notenfolge so unauffällig wie möglich wieder einzurenken, um ihrem Auftraggeber eine äußerlich makellose Arbeit zu liefern. Die Kolmarer Liederhandschrift hingegen weist zahlreiche Korrekturen des Notenschreibers auf, auch die Jenaer Handschrift.

Das Melodiefragment zum KÖNIG FRIEDRICHSTON (W. 26,3; Jammers S. 154 f.) scheint noch stärker gestört zu sein. Die Melodie ist nur zum Finalstollen des nach dem Schema A BB A einer Retrogradenstrophe gebauten Tons

108   Aarburg, Probleme um die Melodien des Minnesangs

überliefert. Daß sie – trotz geringfügiger metrischer Abweichung der Kadenz – in gleicher Form zum Initialstollen erklungen ist, sollte nicht bezweifelt werden, da ja die Kolmarer Handschrift diesen für meistersängerische Formvorstellungen ungewöhnlichen Bau ausdrücklich als *gespalten wys* bezeichnet (f. 732, leider ohne Noteneintragung überliefert). Auffällig ist nun die Notenzusammenballung einer Quaternaria über dem Auftakt der 2. Zeile und ebenso auffällig ist die unmelodische Wiederholung zweier Takte (*) im Innern dieses Verses, wie wir dies auch in den neuen Ausgaben dieser Melodie reproduziert finden. Hier irrten beide: der Schreiber des 14. Jahrhunderts und der Bearbeiter des 20. Jahrhunderts. Der Schreiber übersah den Auftakt und war überdies durch einen Fehler des Textators irritiert worden; die modernen Bearbeiter haben dagegen den Fehler gemacht, der gestörten handschriftlichen Melodiefassung den kriti-

Notenbeispiel 2

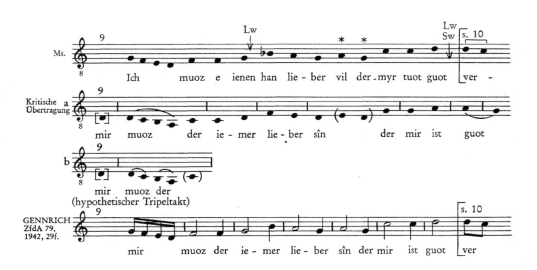

schen Text Lachmanns zu unterlegen. Die Behelfslösungen und Irrtümer des Notators sind ganz durchsichtig: zunächst faßte er diese Zeile genau wie die entsprechende zweite des Initialstollens nicht auftaktig, so daß sich die Notenreihe zu weit nach links verschob. Diesen Fehler glich er jedoch kurz darauf dadurch aus, daß er eine Silbe des Textators *(ie-)* ohne Note beließ. Nach dem Linienwechsel (Lw) notierte er ordnungsgemäß weiter, merkte aber zu spät, daß der Textator wegen einer irrigen Wortumstellung *(hân lieber* statt *l. h.)*, die den Taktrhythmus des Textes störte, eine überzählige Silbe *(vil)* einfügte. Völlig konsterniert muß er nun statt einer Zusatznote deren zwei eingefügt haben, denn jetzt rückt die Notenreihe zu weit nach rechts, was er aber erst nach dem nächsten Linienwechsel bemerkte: er half sich hier, indem er die Silbe *myr* mit zwei Einzelnoten versah.

Unser textkritisches Eingreifen besteht also in nichts anderem als dem Hinzufügen der fehlenden Auftaktnote und dem Streichen der doppelt notierten Einzelnoten über *vil der* (**). Jetzt gewinnt diese sonst merkwürdig zerrissene

Melodielinie, die eine musikwissenschaftliche Hermeneutik 1911 als „Ausbruch einer vergebens zurückgedrängten, mit elementarer Wucht sich geltendmachenden Leidenschaft" deuten zu müssen glaubte, an Ausgeglichenheit und innerer melodischer Logik (s. dazu Teil III). Der Melodieschluß scheint dann einwandfrei zu sein.

Absichtlich gaben wir unsere Beispiele zwar taktweise gegliedert, aber ohne feste rhythmische Innenwerte. Einen Vorschlag für die Rhythmisierung im Tripeltakt mögen die beigefügten Lesarten F. Gennrichs darstellen. Die Melodien lassen sich, zwar weniger gefällig, auch im Dupeltakt singen. Es muß zu denken geben, daß das Mittelalter eine um 1200 in Frankreich entwickelte, relativ präzise Rhythmusschrift kannte, daß es aber für die Aufzeichnung einstimmiger Melodien jahrhundertelang rhythmuslose Zeichen verwendet hat, – auch noch weit nach 1300, als die abendländische Rhythmusnotation, die sogenannte Mensuralnotation immer vollkommener ausgebildet wurde. Mit retrospektiven Tendenzen ist dieses Verfahren nicht allein zu klären. Man muß sich vergegenwärtigen, daß die Rhythmusnotation für eine kunstvolle Mehrstimmigkeit entwickelt wurde, für das Zusammenwirken von mehreren Sängern und Instrumentalisten, das eine straffe rhythmische Übereinkunft und entsprechend eine präzise Rhythmusschrift erforderte. Anders verhält es sich beim Vortrag eines Sololieds. Hier sind dem Sänger alle agogischen Freiheiten erlaubt, die seinen Vortrag so effektvoll wie möglich wirken lassen. So heißt es auch in der mittelalterlichen Musiktheorie, daß die volkssprachige Liedmusik im Gegensatz zur Mehrstimmigkeit „nicht so genau mensuriert" sei. Da die Texte der mhd. Lyrik aber taktisch streng gegliedert sind, werden sie den *latenten* festen Rahmen für den Vortrag abgegeben haben. Die Tendenz jedoch, diesen Rahmen zu sprengen – sei es durch Auftaktdehnungen, durch Kadenzmelismatik, durch Binnenmelismen – ist in der Geschichte des Liedes ebenso stark ausgeprägt wie die gegenläufige Tendenz, meistersingerisch streng und silbenzählend Takt- und Versrahmen zu wahren.

Die strittige Frage, ob die Innenwerte eines Taktes zwei- oder dreizeitig zu nehmen seien, läßt sich nicht lösen. Wir haben für *beide* Taktarten mensurierte Beispiele. Der mittelalterliche Daktylus ist überdies ein Dupeltakt, dessen Innenwerte tripeltaktig untergliedert sind, eine ähnlich reizvolle Taktart also wie der Walzer, der im Grunde ein tripeltaktig unterteilter Marschrhythmus ist: *1 2 3 / 2 2 3*. Der Dupeltakt ist eher ein Abbild natürlicher rhythmischer Vorgänge (Puls, Atem, Schritt), während der Tripeltakt eine kunstmäßig stilisierte, mehr von der *ratio* geprägte rhythmische Formung darstellt. So werden tripeltaktige Lieder im Volksmund bekanntlich schnell dupeltaktig umgesungen.

Mittelalterliche Tanzlieder sind gewiß streng taktisch gegliedert vorgetragen worden, während das merkwürdige, stark melismierte anonyme Lied *Ich sezte mînen fuoz* (das angeblich noch ins 13. Jahrhundert gehören soll) trotz metrisch festen Rahmens unmöglich taktisch, eher frei rhapsodisch vorgetragen worden zu sein scheint (Jammers S. 228 ff.). Der gregorianische Choral des Mittelalters kennt ähnlich divergierende Vortragsarten. Rhythmus, künstlerisch gestaltet, bedeutet Ordnung von Materie und Kraft innerhalb der Zeit; je abstrakter diese Materie (wie etwa die von der Sprache losgelöste Musik, das ausgedehnte Melisma beispielsweise) bzw. die Kraft (wie etwa das vom Tanz oder Marsch losgelöste Wechselspiel der Akzente) ist, desto abstrakter, stilisierter, lebensferner wird sich Rhythmus manifestieren. Und jede Epoche der abendländischen Musikgeschichte hat, wie wir beobachten können, im reizvollen Widerspiel von Natur und Abstraktion, Kraft und Vergeistigung, die ihr ästhetisch zusagenden Rhythmusformen gesucht und entwickelt. Zweifellos stellen die dürren Aussagen der mittelalterlichen Theoretiker zur Modalrhythmik nur einen kleinen Ausschnitt aller rhythmischen Lebensformen des Mittelalters dar. Die Forschung ist hier noch lange nicht am Ende.

III. Melodiesyntax

Die fein ziselierte Linienkunst der mittelalterlichen Melodiesprache, deren Formmittel sich – um mit Arnold Schönberg zu reden – in den „letzten Dezimalstellen" verwirklichen, können wir uns nur erschließen, wenn wir den mächtigen Ballast einer achthundertjährigen polyphonen Musikgeschichte abzuwerfen und wieder auf zarteste Nuancen zu hören bereit sind. Die mittelalterlichen Theoretiker definierten das Wesen der Melodie folgerichtig mit den Termini der Sprachlehre, da für sie der Gesang aus der Sprache entwickelt ist. Die Töne entsprechen den Buchstaben, die Formeln den Silben und Wörtern, die Verse Satzgliedern oder in größerem Verband ganzen Sätzen. Die Melodie ist also auf ihre Weise eine Sprache, und so ist es nicht abwegig, die Lehre von ihren inneren Gesetzmäßigkeiten als Melodiesyntax zu bezeichnen (vgl. W. Mohr: In DU 5 (1953), 2, S. 72).

Da hier der Raum zu beschränkt ist, um dieses weite und bisher noch völlig unübersichtliche Feld ganz abzuschreiten, wählen wir als Ausgangspunkt drei kurze Melodien, deren Formel- und Modulationstechnik typisch für ihre jeweilige Tonart ist. Die Beispielmelodien vertreten je eine der beliebtesten mittelalterlichen Tonarten: den G-, C- und D-Modus. Leider sind die Möglichkeiten, alle Ausführungen durch Notenbeispiele zu erläutern, beschränkt, so daß der Leser die Unbequemlichkeit einer gelegentlichen 'Buchstabennotation' in Kauf nehmen muß.

Als Beispiel des G-Modus (auch als Tetrardus oder Mixo- bzw. Hypomixolydicus bezeichnet) möge ein Fastenhymnus, der im 11. Jahrhundert in Buchstabennotation aufgezeichnet wurde, dienen. Er ist vierzeilig; die Verse sind metrisch gebaut (katalektische anapästische Dimeter). Diese Melodie ist, so schlicht sie zunächst wirken mag, überaus kunstvoll angelegt. Je zwei Zeilen sind

Notenbeispiel 3

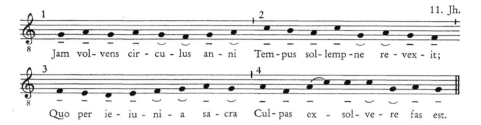

melodisch zu einer Langzeile verbunden, beide Langzeilen sind jedoch, wie wir noch sehen werden, der entwickelteren melodischen Hymnentechnik entsprechend nicht streng voneinander abgesetzt. Die Melodie beginnt nicht sogleich wie unzählige des g-modalen Typs mit der charakteristischen Initialformel ga-c': hier wird zunächst der Initialton g umkreist und damit eine Art Spannungsstau geschaffen. Der typische Aufschwung erfolgt dann erst, über das Ende des Verses hinausgreifend, mit dem Beginn des nächsten Verses, wird durch die melodische Rückbewegung aber sogleich wieder aufgehoben. Die abwärtsführende Form jener ga-c'-Initialformel gehört nun, mehr oder weniger breit – oft über ganze Verse – ausgesponnen, zu den beliebtesten Kadenz- oder besser Finalformeln des Mittelalters. Auch Melodien, die vorwiegend den Quintrahmen benutzen (im G-Modus also den Raum g-h-d'), verwenden in der Regel für die Kadenzierung jene offenbar uralte Quartformel, – analog dem Verfahren auch anderer musikalischer Stilepochen, das Kadenzgeschehen in vertrauten, traditionellen Formeln und Modulationen ablaufen zu lassen. Hier freilich wird der g-modale Finalton, das *clausum*, nicht erreicht. Die Melodie der ersten Langzeile schließt mit einem *apertum*, hier mit der g-modalen Untersekunde f. Ein anderer apertum-Schluß war die Obersekunde a des ersten Verses, die aber gleichzeitig als Bestandteil der hinausgeschobenen Initialformel fungierte. Interessant ist nun an der bisher erklungenen Melodie, daß ihre tonale Zugehörigkeit noch nicht absolut feststeht: ihre Weiterführung könnte deutlich werden lassen, daß hier ein F-Modus (Tritus oder Lydicus bzw. Hypolydicus) gemeint ist: seine charakteristischen Töne f-a-c' erklingen an markanten Stellen der Melodie. Dieses Verschleiern der Haupttonart ist ein Kunstgriff jeden entwickelten Musikstils; erinnert sei an die e-moll-Variation in Max Regers Mozart-

Variationen op. 134. Die Trobadors und Trouvères sind Meister im Verschleiern der modalen Zugehörigkeit; auch bei Walthers oben zitierten Melodien ist anfangs durchaus nicht deutlich, ob sie dem D- oder F-Modus (1. Philippston) bzw. dem C- oder E-Modus (König Friedrichston) angehören.

Die zweite Langzeile befestigt nun den f-modalen Charakter, ja bringt einen Anklang an den D-Modus durch den Nachdruck, der scheinbar auf der d-modalen Grundstruktur d-f-a liegt. Der Hörer weiß jetzt nicht, wie er die Finalis g zu werten hat: ob als apertum eines F- oder D-Modus oder doch als Vorkadenz des G-Modus (nicht als endgültige Kadenz, denn die aufsteigende Quartformel d-g, die gleichfalls zum G-Modus gehört, besitzt keine ausreichende Schlußkraft, – man vergleiche den analog gebildeten Stollenschluß von Walthers 1. Philippston). Erst der Schlußvers bringt die tonartliche Bestätigung, er wiederholt sogar die dreitönige Schlußformel des vorangegangenen Verses, der dadurch eine andere, endgültige Beleuchtung erhält.

Die Melodie steckt noch voller innerer Anklänge und Beziehungen. Von schöner Wirkung sind die gegenläufig korrespondierenden Schlüsse des 1. und 3. Verses und im 4. Vers die in konzentrierter Gegenbewegung geführte Wiederaufnahme der Schlußbewegungen von Vers 2 und 3 am Ende des Hymnus. Überdies nimmt der Schlußvers die Melodielinie des vorangegangenen Verses in transponierter Engführung wieder auf.

Bestimmend für das melodische Geschehen in dieser g-modalen Weise sind zwei Grundstrukturen: die schon erwähnte, im Quartrahmen g-c' ausgespannte Initial- bzw. Finalformel und die Unterquartstruktur d-g. Strukturell wichtig ist also die Septime d-c' mit ihrem Mittel- und Grundton g. Der Musikhistoriker spricht hier von einer Quartenschichtung, die überaus beliebt im keltischfranzösischen Raume gewesen zu sein scheint. Der Septimenrahmen d-c' kann aber auch die Terzenschichtung: d-f-a-c' aufnehmen, die vor allem für d-modale Weisen (s. das letzte Beispiel) charakteristisch und offenbar besonders in Deutschland beliebt gewesen ist. Durch den Wechsel beider Strukturen, den wir in diesem knappen Melodiegebilde wahrnehmen konnten, entsteht ein reizvolles Fluoreszieren, eine eigenartige Mehrdeutigkeit der Töne und Formeln, in die wir uns freilich erst hineinhören können, wenn wir ihre melodiesyntaktischen Funktionen kennen. Falsch wäre es, diesen tonartlich merkwürdigen Modus, zu dessen Charakteristikum der Tritonus f-h gehört (man vergleiche den schönen Pfingsthymnus *Veni creator spiritus!*), durch Fis-Vorzeichnungen gefügig zu machen, wie es noch in jüngsten Publikationen geschieht. (Beispiele dieses Typs s. bei Taylor Nr. 13 und 17, dgl. passim bei Jammers und Gennrich.)

Eine bekannte, schlichte Melodie möge nun den C-Modus (Jonicus bzw. Hypojonicus), der sehr häufig auch in F-Lage vorkommt und offenbar schon früh den echten F-Modus (mit h statt b) verdrängt hat, demonstrieren. Luther hat sich eines überaus volksläufigen Melodiemodells für sein Weihnachtslied *Vom Himmel hoch* bedient. Als Kanonlied ist es bekannt und bei den Meistersängern beliebt, Walther wandelte es in seiner Hofweise ab, dem Spervogelton der Jenaer Liederhandschrift liegt es zugrunde und auch in Trobadorweisen ist es nachweisbar. Die tonartliche Struktur steht unserem Dur so nahe (c-e-g-c'), daß wir hier nicht näher auf sie einzugehen brauchen. Interessant freilich ist die Formelverwendung. Vers 1 und auch die erste Hälfte des folgenden Verses werden ganz aus der schon bekannten Quartformel g-c' bestritten. Die übliche Aufwärts-Abwärtsbewegung (vgl. die Psalmformeln) wird hier umgedreht und so derselbe Effekt erreicht, wie wir ihn bei der Fastenhymne beobachteten: die Spannung wird erhöht und das apertum der 1. Zeile verlangt nach Weiterführung, die konsequent in Zeile 2 erfolgt. Aber die sprunghaft gebrachte Schlußformel hat noch keine befriedigende Schlußkraft, genau wie in der Hymnenmelodie. Auch hier sind die beiden Kadenzen gegenläufig korrespondierend

Notenbeispiel 4

angelegt. Die folgende Langzeile beginnt mit einem erneuten Aufschwung, der wieder mit jener g-modalen Finalformel endet, die hier freilich – inmitten der 2. Langzeile und ohne genügende tonale Befestigung – noch keine Schlußwirkung erreicht. Diese wird erst durch ihre um eine Quint nach unten transponierte Wiederholung erzielt (vgl. auch die ähnliche Kadenzdoppelung im Fastenhymnus). Hingewiesen sei wieder auf die Quartstruktur dieser Kadenz, die wirkungsvoll zur dominierenden c-e-g-c'-Struktur des Schlußverses kontrastiert. Die hier eingesetzte uralte Finalformel e-f-d-c trägt keimhaft bereits die klassische T-S-D-T-Kadenz in sich. Weitere Beispiele dieser Tonart bringen die oben genannten Anthologien.

Die konstituierenden Formeln beider Modi, des G- und des C-Modus, begegnen vorwiegend in einer melodisch meist komplizierten und im mittelalterlichen Deutschland überaus beliebten Tonart, dem E-Modus (Deuterus oder Phrygicus bzw. Hypophrygicus). Walthers schöne Melodie zum König Friedrichston (s. o.) steht im E-Modus. Zu den schon bekannten Quartformeln d-g (s. V. 2 und 3) und g-c' (s. V. 3) des G-Modus und c-f (s. V. 2) des C-Modus benutzt Walther noch eine weitere g-modale Formel, die in Liedern mit dem Ambitus g-f' gern verwendet wird; den oberen Quartrahmen c'-f' (V. 3). Zu diesen Formeln, die Walthers Melodie eine reiche modulatorische Färbung geben, kommen noch die eigentlichen e-modalen Quartstrukturen, die Formeln e-a (V. 1 und 3) und a-d' (V. 2, hier eine Oktave tiefer, und V. 3, hier aber eng verhakt mit den Quartenfolgen f'-c'-g, so daß die Schlußzeile überaus wirkungsvoll nochmals alle bisher verwendeten Strukturen steigernd zusammenfaßt: f'-c', d'-a, c'-g, a-e, g-d). Genauso wie G- und C-Modus neben der Quartenschichtung auch eine Terzenschichtung kennen, also g-h-d' bzw. c-e-g, ist die Terzenkette e-g-h für e-modale Melodien charakteristisch. Auffallend ist, daß Walther diesen Ton vorwiegend aus Quartstrukturen aufbaut; das Ergebnis ist freilich eine ungewöhnlich eindringliche Melodie. Ihre Kadenzen auf einen Takt zusammenpressen bedeutet einen Stilbruch begehen: die Melodie ist weiträumig und großzügig angelegt, sie strebt mit jeder Zeile auf die textlich-melodischen Kadenzen zu, die einen wichtigen Schwerpunkt und Ruhepunkt darstellen und dem Sänger die Möglichkeit geben, Atem zu holen. Die metrisch-syntaktische Fugung geht dadurch keinesfalls verloren, und die Freunde geradzahliger Taktsummen mag überzeugen, daß $7 + 7 + 8$ auch eine gerade Zahl ergeben. Weitere e-modale Melodien bringen Taylor (Nr. 10 und 14), Jammers und Gennrich passim.

Die im gesamten Abendland beliebteste Tonart war der D-Modus (Protus oder Doricus bzw. Hypodoricus). Als Beispiel wählen wir aus Gründen, die gleich zu nennen sein werden, eine hymnenartig gebaute Marienantiphon, die zusammen mit einem zweizeiligen Vorspann heute noch in liturgischem Gebrauch ist. Sie erscheint zuerst als zweistimmige Komposition im Schlettstädter St.-Fides-Codex, der der Heiligengrabkirche dortselbst, einer staufischen Stiftung, entstammt. Ob sie dort entstanden ist, ist nicht sicher, aber denkbar. Sie wurde wohl Anfang des 13. Jahrhunderts in dem genannten Codex nachgetragen.

Notenbeispiel 5

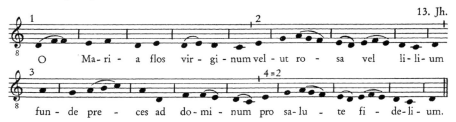

Die Melodie setzt wiederum mit dem Umspielen des Grundtons ein und endet zunächst im 1. Vers auf der charakteristischen d-modalen Untersekunde c, die stets als apertum fungiert und Ausgangston für zweierlei unterschiedliche Strukturen ist: für die Quartstruktur c-d-f, der eigentlich charakteristischen d-modalen Grundstruktur, und der Quintstruktur c-e-g, einer Art Gegenmodus zur primär d-modalen Struktur d-f-a, der einen starken modulatorischen Kontrast bewirkt (ähnlich wie die Struktur f-a-c' im G-Modus, vgl. den Schluß des Fastenhymnus). In dieser Melodie wird die d-modale Untersekunde durch die Folge e-g in Vers 2 sogleich als Grundton des Gegenmodus umgedeutet, der sich weiterhin mit den melismatisch umspielten Tönen g und e behauptet, dann aber der typischen d-modalen Schlußformel d-c-d weichen muß. Die bisher erklungene melodische Langzeile ist also ein in sich geschlossenes Gebilde, ähnlich dem Stollen einer in Barform angelegten Melodie. Auch die Fortsetzung erinnert an diese Liedform: sie transponiert den soeben verklungenen Schluß eine Quinte nach oben und erreicht dadurch einen formal wirkungsvollen Kontrast. Die Fortführung folgt sodann, zuerst leicht abgewandelt, dann genau dem 'Stollen'. Das Ganze hinterläßt den Eindruck einer wohlgefügten und abgerundeten Melodiegestalt.

Der Kenner des deutschen Minnesangs wird inzwischen längst festgestellt haben, daß diese Antiphon Walthers Palästinamelodie *in nuce* enthält. Die charakteristischen Züge dieser Melodie: der Wechsel in den Gegenmodus inmitten des Stollens, der kontrastierende Aufschwung in die Quintlage (und dort die Wiederholung des Stollenschlusses) sowie endlich die Rückkehr zur Stollenmelodie inmitten der vorletzten Zeile sind auch der Marienantiphon eigen. Im Gegensatz zu Walthers Schöpfung fehlt ihr jedoch die Stollenwiederholung und eine Zeile des Abgesangs, die bei Walther melodisch freilich nichts Neues bringt.

Hat Walther diese Melodie im Gefolge der Staufer in Schlettstadt gehört, hat *er* sie komponiert (zweistimmig!) und später für sein Palästinalied durch einfachste Mittel erweitert? Das alles muß Hypothese bleiben. Als Faktum bleibt uns nur, daß die typische, in Hunderten von Liedern gebrauchte d-modale Melodiesprache hier eine ihrer eindrucksvollsten Gestaltungen erfahren hat.

Die Gesetzmäßigkeiten der mittelalterlichen Melodiesprache, die hier nur andeutend vorgeführt werden konnten, ihr Formelvorrat (ihre Topoi quasi) und dessen vielfältige Anwendung, Verflechtung und melodiebildende Funktion, sind gerade für das weltliche Lied noch wenig analysiert worden. Sie zu kennen wird nicht nur das Verständnis dieser Melodien erleichtern, sondern auch der melodischen Textkritik zugutekommen und das Ineinander von Wort-Tonbeziehungen aufhellen können.

Bibliographische Hinweise

Allgemeines: Die Lieder WALTHERS VON DER VOGELWEIDE werden nach der 13. Ausgabe von K. Lachmann–C. v. Kraus (1965 mit einer neuen Einleitung von H. Kuhn hrsg.) zitiert; die Melodienüberlieferung der einzelnen Walthertöne stellte C. Petzsch ds. S. XXXVI ff. mit erschöpfenden Literaturangaben zusammen. Die Lieder NEIDHARTS VON REUENTAL werden nach der leicht zugänglichen Ausgabe E. Wießners (rev. von Hanns Fischer, Tübingen ²1963 [= ATB 44]) zitiert. Zu den verschiedenen musikwissenschaftlichen Termini, den Liederautoren und -handschriften etc. sind zweckmäßig die Schlagworte der Enzyklopädie: Die Musik in Geschichte und Gegenwart (Abk.: MGG). Kassel 1949 ff., z. Zt. 13 Bde. von A–Volk, mit ihrer jeweils weiterführenden Literatur, heranzuziehen.

Zu I: Die hier mehrfach erwähnten Autoren wurden nach folgenden Ausgaben zitiert:
ULRICH VON LICHTENSTEIN. Hrsg. von K. Lachmann. Berlin 1841;
DANTE ALIGHIERI: Opere VI. Firenze. ³1957. Ders.: Über das Dichten in der Muttersprache. Übers. v. Fr. Dornseiff u. J. Balogh. Darmstadt 1925 u. 1966;
ADAM PUSCHMAN: Singebuch. Hrsg. v. G. Münzer. Leipzig 1906;
M. BEHEIM: s. MGG 1, Sp. 1570 ff.
Sprechvortrag vermuten R. J. Taylor (s. o. S. 106), Darstellungsbd. S. 24 u. 60; U. Pretzel in: Deutsche Philologie im Aufriß III. ¹1957. Sp 428 f.; ²1962.
Zu den deutschen *Musikhandschriften:* s. Linker, Robert White: Music of the Minnesinger and Early Meistersinger. Chapel Hill. 1962, S. XI ff., ferner zuletzt R. J. Taylor: o. c., S. 23 ff., ferner MGG passim; zu den romanischen Musikhandschriften F. Gennrich: Der Nachlaß der Troubadous. Kommentar. Darmstadt 1960. S. 1 ff. und ders.: Altfranzösische Lieder I. Halle ¹1953 und Tübingen ²1955. S. XXVIII ff.; zu den spanischen Musikhandschriften: den Art. Cantigas in MGG 2. Neue Studien zur 'Manessischen' Hs. und ihrer Entstehung s. bei E. Jammers: Das Königliche Liederbuch des deutschen Minnesangs. Heidelberg 1965; ds. S. 23 f. Näheres zur *Steinacher Familienchronik.* Der Versuch, ältere Töne formal zu glätten, ist z. B. in der meistersängerischen Überlieferung zweier offenbar authentischer Walthertöne (Hofweise und Feiner Ton. Lit. s. Petzsch) zu beobachten; zu den *Modernisierungstendenzen* des Chansonnier Cangé s. U. Aarburg in: Arch. f. Musikwiss. 15 (1958), S. 27. Zur *Liederblatt-Theorie* s. zuletzt U. Mölk in: ZfromPh. 80 (1964), S. 176 ff.

Zu II: Zu den *Fälschungen* mittelalterlicher Notenschreiber s. Schubert, J.: Die Trouvèrehandschrift R. Diss. Frankfurt/M. 1963. S. 50 ff., 81 ff., 92 ff. et passim. Zu den S. 106 genannten *Auswahleditionen* kommen in Bälde noch hinzu: Moser, H. und Müller-Blattau, J.: Lieder, Leiche, Sprüche des deutschen Mittelalters. Stuttgart 1967; Taylor, R. J.: The art of the Minnesinger. 2 Bde. University of Wales and Oxford Presses 1967. Zu den *typischen Fehlern* der Notatoren s. U. Aarburg in: Die Musikforschung 10. 1957. 214 ff. Über die *Rhythmusprobleme* unterrichten einführend die MGG-Artikel Modus und Rhythmus; dort weitere Literatur. Zur *Hermeneutik* des König Friedrich-Tons s. Molitor, R.: Sammelbände der JMG 12 (1911), S. 497.

Zu III: Zu den allgemeinen Fragen s. die MGG-Artikel Modus, Tonalität, Melodie, Kadenz/Klausel. Zur musiktheoretischen Auffassung des Mittelalters s. Abert, H.: Die Musikanschauung des Mittelalters und ihre Grundlagen. Halle 1905 u. Tutzing 1964. Hrsg. v. H. Hüschen, bes. S. 255 ff. Wichtig zum gesamten Problemkreis ist der Beitrag von Stäblein, B.: Zur Stilistik der Troubadour-Melodien. In: Acta musicologica 36 (1966), 27 ff. *G-modale* Melodietypen behandelt zusammenfassend Aarburg, U.: Die Laissenmelodie zu ‚Aucassin et Nicolette'. In: Die Musikforschung 11 (1958), 138 ff. und dies.: Melodiesprache im G-Modus. In: Fs. H. Osthoff 1966. S. 40–64 (noch ungedruckt). Über *c-modale* Melodietypen s. dies.: Zu den Lutherliedern im jonischen Oktavraum. In: Jb. f. Liturgik u. Hymnologie 5 (1960). 125 ff., dort weitere Literatur. Zur Melodiesprache *d-modaler* Melodien s. dies.: Arch f. Musikwissenschaft 15 (1958), 27 ff. Die heute noch gesungene *Antiphona* in honorem B. Mariae virginis ‚Ave Regina caelorum' mit der Fortsetzung ‚O Maria flos virginum' findet sich im Liber usualis (1956), S. 1864. Zu ihrer Überlieferung hoffe ich noch Einiges in der ZdfA nachzutragen.

Part V
Performance

[17]
The twelfth century in the South

Christopher Page

> e auziratz, si com yeu fi,
> als trobadors dir e comtar
> si com vivion per anar
> e per sercar terras e locx.
>
> Raimon Vidal, *Abril issia*

I

Any attempt to place instrumental accompaniment within the genre system of troubadour and trouvère poetry must take its bearings from the genre which dominates the surviving corpus of lyrics: the elaborate love-song which Dragonetti has termed the *grand chant courtois*. I shall also refer to it as the High Style song. Throughout the later twelfth and thirteenth centuries this kind of song, which the trouvères inherited from their predecessors in Occitania, was the 'classic' form of the courtly songwriter's art. As an example of the prevailing poetic and musical manner of the High Style, here is the first stanza of a song by Arnaut de Maroill:[1]

> Las grans beutatz e.ls fis ensenhamens
> e.ls verais pretz e las bonas lauzors
> e.ls autres ditz e la fresca colors
> que vos avetz, bona dona valen,
> me donan genh de chantar e sciensa,
> mas gran paor m'o tol e gran temensa,
> qu'ieu non aus dir, dona, qu'ieu chant de vos,
> e re no sai si m'es o dans o pros.

> The great beauty, the fine discrimination, the true
> worth, the fine praise, and other things and
> the fresh colour that is yours, good and perfect
> lady, give me skill and ability to sing – but my

great fear and fright take them away from me for
I do not dare mention, my lady, that I sing of you
and I do not know whether I will come to harm or good.

Example 2

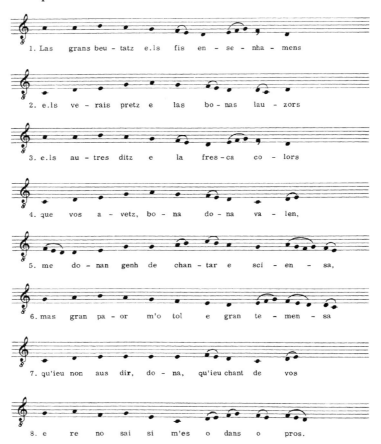

1. Las grans beu-tatz e.ls fis en - se - nha - mens
2. e.ls ve - rais pretz e las bo - nas lau - zors
3. e.ls au - tres ditz e la fres - ca co - lors
4. que vos a - vetz, bo - na do - na va - len,
5. me do - nan genh de chan - tar e sci - en - sa,
6. mas gran pa - or m'o tol e gran te - men - sa
7. qu'ieu non aus dir, do - na, qu'ieu chant de vos
8. e re no sai si m'es o dans o pros.

Like many other melodies for High Style songs this one is essentially rhapsodic in character. Lines 1 and 2 are set to the 'same' music as lines 3 and 4, but this is a conventional patterning in this repertory and in this instance (as often) it is far from strict; line 2 has a 'closed' ending but 4 has an 'open' one. There are other relationships, but the essence of the rhapsodic musical style of the *grand chant courtois* is that they are disguised. Thus there are significant resemblances between the settings of lines 1/3, 2 and 6:

Songs and instruments

Example 3

while the music for lines 2 and 4 is closely related to the melody for line 7:

Example 4

These relationships do not necessarily strike us when we hear the first stanza; they gradually materialise as we hear the full song. As the performance proceeds, our sense of coherence and focus in the rhapsodic flow of the music becomes more pronounced. This is part of what is *grand* about the *grand chant courtois*: these songs reject the conspicuous and short-range patterns that give an easy and instant tunefulness to dance-songs such as the *rondet de carole* (see Music example 5).[2]

In contrast to dance-songs such as this, the essence of a High Style song like Arnaut's *canso* is that it makes us aware of the voice which is singing to us. In a performance of a dance-song like *C'est la gieus en mi les préz* the voice of the singer dissolves into the voices of the dancers (who sing the refrains) and thence into the dance; but the high seriousness of Arnaut's song forbids us to sing or to do anything which will remove the song and the singer from the centre of our attention.

Example 5

Whence the characteristic manner of the High Style song: neither gregarious in impulse nor indulgent towards its listeners, it usually lacks any choric refrains which might invite us across the space that separates us from the singer and draw us into the song. Arnaut de Maroill maintains the distance between singer and hearer by a great show of decorum achieved by an accumulation of potent courtly words (*verais, valen*) and by strewing his poem with connectives that give it the appearance of discursiveness and debate (*quand...car...perque...*). Presented in this way the *grand chant courtois* becomes a form of oration and the antithesis of a 'performerless' dancing song. Indeed the idea of the song as the composition of a self-conscious artist is constantly kept in the listener's mind and is a crucial element of the *grand chant* manner:[3]

> The expressive technique of the Provençal love-song...the exploration in the first person of an emotional state which the poet alleges to be his own, evidently supposes that, by convention if not in literal fact, the poet is presenting himself. To this extent, then, the poet is self-conscious. But, in Provençal practice, he is not self-conscious merely as (according to the convention) a happy or dejected lover, but as a poet. The *canso* does not only present an emotional state: it often presents the poet in the act of presenting

Songs and instruments

that emotional state or in the act of reflecting upon the artistic means of presenting it. The troubadour is not only self-consciously a practitioner of the art of poetic composition, he says, even boasts, that he is so, sometimes at considerable length.

The contrasts which we have drawn between Arnaut de Maroill's *canso* in Old Provençal and an Old French *rondet* can be gathered into a rudimentary typology of twelfth- and thirteenth-century songs:

HIGH STYLE	LOWER STYLES
POETRY	
Tendency towards stanzas of isometric lines	Tendency towards stanzas of polymetric lines, especially brief lines multiplying short-range and conspicuous effects of rhyme and metre
No refrain or refrain rare	Refrains common
Exclusively lyric	Lyrico-choreographic Lyrico-narrative
Beloved not named (except in enigmatic terms)	Beloved may be named, or protagonist(s) named
MUSIC	
Rhapsodic	Conspicuous short-range repetitions and effects to create an instant 'tunefulness'
No strict metre (Figure 2)	Strict metre in many forms (especially those connected in some way with dance) (Figure 2)

Figure 2 *An anonymous* dansa *beginning* Tant es gay es [*sic*] avinentz *and a High Style* canso *by the troubadour Blacasset, beginning* Ben volgra que.m vengues mer[c]es *(commencing on the third stave on the right hand side). The* dansa, *whose form reduces to ABBa[A], is in mensural notation, whereas Blacasset's through-composed* canso *is in unmeasured notation. Both songs are additions of the early fourteenth century to the Manuscrit du Roi. Paris, Bibliothèque Nationale, MS fr. 844, f.78v. Photographed under ultraviolet light. Reproduced by permission. See further Chapter 4.*

Songs and instruments

II

Where did instrumental accompaniment belong in this system of contrasts? The search for an answer begins with an aristocratic musician whom we encountered in Chapter 1. He is the Catalan nobleman, Guiraut de Cabreira, 'dashing in warfare ... gracious in manners ... [and] highly skilled on musical instruments'.

It may have been as early as 1150 that Guiraut addressed a mocking *sirventes* to a certain minstrel named Cabra (?Guiraut himself), playfully rebuking him for the accomplishments he had not mastered. Guiraut's own mastery of the fiddle—remembered long after his death by those who had heard him play—sharpens the edge of what is already a pointed *sirventes*.[4] 'Whoever taught you to bow and finger the fiddle made a bad job of it', he proclaims to the unfortunate minstrel in the hearing of all; 'you fiddle badly and sing worse, from start to finish':[5]

> Mal saps viular e pietz chantar
> del cap tro en la fenizon.
> ......
> Mal t'ensegnet cel qe.t mostret
> los detz a menar ni l'arson.

At one point Guiraut rebukes Cabra for not being familiar with a variety of lyric genres, including the *sirventesc, estribotz, retroencha, contenson* and *balaresc*—a useful but rather featureless list which does not mention particular works or name individual troubadours. Yet, in the lines which follow, Guiraut finds a more specific charge to level against Cabra: he cannot sing songs by the famous troubadours of the last and the present generation: Jaufre Rudel, Marcabrun, Ebles II de Ventadorn, a certain Anfos, and 'en Egun' (perhaps a mocking pun on *negun*, 'nobody'):[6]

> Ja vers novel   bon d'en Rudel
> non cug que.t pas sotz lo guingnon;
> De Markabrun   ni d'en Egun
> ni d'en Anfos ni d'en Eblon.

This suggests that some minstrels who fiddled and sang for a living included songs by celebrated troubadours in their repertory. As we might expect from one who was probably a younger contemporary of both Marcabrun and Jaufre Rudel, Guiraut de Cabreira refers to their songs in the correct way; by referring to their *vers novel* he is following the usage of both Marcabrun:[7]

> dist Macabruns lou vers del son

and Jaufre Rudel:[8]

The twelfth century in the South

> No sap cantar qui.l so no.m ditz
> ni.l vers trobar qui.ls motz no fay

So there is no doubt about Guiraut's meaning; but what do his words imply about performance practice? Here I have to confess that I have been as mischievous in beginning with Guiraut's *sirventes* as Guiraut was mischievous in writing it. For while the poem deserves pride of place in this chapter on chronological grounds, it also illustrates the principal difficulty that besets any attempt to answer questions about medieval performance practice with the aid of literary texts. This is that many literary sources are suggestive in a way that supports conventional wisdom (which is how that wisdom arose), yet prove, in the final analysis, to be vague and inexact. Guiraut de Cabreira's *sirventes* is a particularly vexing example. There is no doubt that Cabra's talents (if that is the right word to use in his case) include singing and playing the fiddle (*viular e chantar*), and it is implied that *vers novel* by Marcabrun and Jaufre Rudel are songs which a minstrel of Cabra's stamp would normally be expected to know. So it seems that some *joglars* in twelfth-century Occitania played the fiddle and had songs by noted troubadours in their repertory. What we cannot so readily conclude is that these minstrels used their instruments to accompany the *vers novel* which they performed.

At first sight this may seem a precious or perverse objection. Medieval courtly monody has been regarded as an art of instrumentally accompanied song for many years; an effort is needed to recognise that there is no *prima facie* case in favour of that view. Much of the literary evidence bearing upon the question of accompaniment suffers from what might be called the 'discontinuity problem': it mentions *this* (singing, perhaps), then mentions *that* (string-playing, let us imagine) but rarely allows us to establish whether this and that happen at the same time, whether they happen in the same place, or even whether they are associated with one another.

Then there is the problem of unwritten and lost repertory. Guiraut's *sirventes* offers an excellent illustration. In his determination to embarrass Cabra, Guiraut spends six lines on troubadour lyric, but he lavishes one hundred and fifteen lines (almost twenty times as many) on the epic stories which Cabra does not know. As Guiraut gets into his stride, names (some famous and some obscure) come tumbling out pell-mell: Charlemagne, Ganelon, Aiol, Erec, Amic, Berart, Aimar, Merlin, Alexander, and so on until Cabra must have despaired of ever finding employment again. This litany of heroes from Antiquity, the Bible and medieval epic tradition leaves us in no doubt that southern minstrels, like their northern counterparts, passed a great deal of their professional lives telling stories, and if a wealth of northern evidence may be believed, these narratives were often sung to instrumental accompaniment.[9] None of these songs has survived with music, yet this kind of material may lie behind many of the literary references to vocal and instrumental music which scholars have associated with the surviving troubadour and trouvère repertories.

19

Songs and instruments

III

After Guiraut de Cabreira's harangue against the unfortunate minstrel Cabra (whose bad luck must have begun when he took on the professional name 'Goat'), it is a relief to turn to the roughly contemporary epic of *Daurel et Beton* and two passages which may bring us a little closer to the kind of information which we seek.[10]

The story of this epic tells how Daurel, a minstrel, sacrifices his own son to save his boy-lord, Beton, from being massacred by a French duke named Guy. To guarantee Beton's safety Daurel sets off with the boy in a boat, and this stage of the narrative brings the first musical reference. When the child cries during their hazardous and uncertain voyage, Daurel takes his fiddle (*viola*) and[11]

> ... fai .i. lais d'amor.

A second reference to vocal and instrumental music involves Beton, now matured into an expert instrumentalist and so courteous that nobody at the court of the Emir of Babylon can believe that he is the son of a minstrel. To test the point they arrange for Beton to play in the chamber of the princess while other courtiers hide; the trick being that if Beton refuses to accept the money offered to him after the performance then he cannot be a minstrel's son. Needless to say, Beton does refuse it; but what interests us most is not the outcome of the story but its incidentals. At first, Beton is requested to play some *laices* upon his fiddle for the princess, but Beton's name for what he has to offer is *bels verses*, and the poet follows Beton's usage: 'he sang his *verses* and was courteously attended to':[12]

> 'De bels verses sai, dona, vueilh que n'aujatz.'
> E dit sos verses e fon ben escoltatz;
> Lo rei l'auzi que s'era amagatz
> Entorn la cambra e.il reïna delatz,
> Et ab lor so .c. cavaliers prezatz.
> Que tuh escolto cossi s'es deportatz.
> Una gran pessa s'es laïns deportatz,
> Canta e vihola, es se fort alegratz.

> 'I know beautiful *verses*, lady, I wish you to hear
> some of them.' He sang his *verses* and was courteously
> attended to; the king, who had hidden himself within
> the chamber, heard him, and the beautiful queen, and
> with them are one hundred excellent knights who all
> listened to how [Beton] rejoiced in himself. [Beton]
> lingered within [the chamber] a good while.
> He sings and fiddles, and enjoys himself
> a great deal.

In the first extract the term *lais* is a suggestive one whose meanings in Old Provençal are many and various, often amounting to little more than 'a song', 'a tune (whether vocal or instrumental)'.[13] The context shows that Daurel's *lais* is played upon the fiddle, and that it is a love-song, .i. *lais d'amor*, which he is presumably either singing to his own accompaniment or

Example 6

Songs and instruments

playing as instrumental music to soothe the troubled child. The likelihood that Daurel's *lais* is a lyric lai—a polymorphous lyric where each subdivision of the text has its own metrical form and musical setting—seems remote at this date (possibly as early as c1150). However, *lais* could also be applied to lyrics in the High Style, including the *canso*. Folquet de Marseilla (d.1231) calls his song *S'al cor plagues be fora huei may sazos* a *lais*, even though its subject matter and musico-poetic form mark it as a *canso* in the High Style tradition (see Music example 6).[14]

The *lais d'amor* played by Daurel to comfort the young Beton may be a High Style troubadour *canso* sung to the fiddle, although it seems to have been an unusual practice for a troubadour to refer to his words, his music, or both together as a *lais*.

In the second extract Beton's pieces are called *vers*, the prevailing term for a troubadour lyric until the later twelfth century when *canso* began to make an appearance.[15] Unfortunately it is not clear whether Beton is fiddling and singing at the same time, or whether the *verses* in his repertory are to be identified with troubadour songs such as those by Jaufre Rudel, since *vers* seems to have been used by the early troubadours for any kind of poem.[16] On balance *Daurel et Beton* only seems to offer hints in whispers.

A brief passage from *Jaufre* (c1170) speaks in bolder tones. In this romance, the only Arthurian verse narrative in Old Provençal, there is a description of a court celebration where[17]

> ...joglars que sun el palais
> Víulon descortz et suns et lais
> E dansas e cansonz de gesta.
> Jamais nun veira hom tal festa.

> ...minstrels who are in the palace play
> *descortz* and *suns* and *lais* and *dansas* and
> *cansonz de gesta* on the *viula*. No-one will
> ever see such a celebration again.

The *suns* are probably instrumental melodies, for *so* (<Latin *sonus*) in the sense 'a tune, a melody' is attested in numerous troubadour lyrics (where the *so*, or melody, of a lyric composition may be contrasted with the words, the *vers* or *motz*).[18] Perhaps the same meaning may be assigned to *lais*, given the frequency with which this word carries the sense 'melody, whether vocal or instrumental' in Old Provençal.

As for *descortz* and *dansas*, there is another twelfth-century source which joins these two terms to the minstrel's fiddle: a *partimen* with stanzas by the troubadours Raimbaut de Vaqueiras, Perdigo, and the nobleman Adémar II of Poitiers, Count of Valentinois and Diois, 1188–1230. The first *tornada* of this poem opens:[19]

The twelfth century in the South

> Senher n'Aymar, vos etz vencuts primiers;
> e.n Perdigos viule descortz o dansa....
>
> Lord Adémar, you are the first to lose; and let
> sir Perdigo play a *descort* or *dansa* on his fiddle....

This double confirmation of a link between the fiddle and the genres of *descort* and *dansa* is striking and surely significant. Both of these lyric forms may be said to occupy a very minor position in the corpus of troubadour lyrics with music. Only a handful of *descort* settings have come down to us with music[20] and only a few *dansas*, all of which are written in various forms of Franco-Occitan and preserved as additions of the early fourteenth century to the Manuscrit du Roi (Figure 2). In terms of survival, therefore, this association between the fiddle and the genres of *descort* and *dansa* carries instruments to the very periphery of the troubadour corpus.

Patterns of survival can be the result of accident or caprice, but there is another sense in which both the *descort* and the *dansa* lie on the edge of the troubadour art. Each one, in its own way, subverts the High Style manner as represented above all by the *canso*. The *descort* was a polymorphous lyric in which each subdivision of the text had its own metrical form and musical setting. Its form therefore subverted the dignity of the *canso* in which each stanza has the same form and the same melodic setting. As Baum has argued, the *descort* is not simply unlike the *canso*; it is the anti-*canso*:[21]

> The study of different writings concerning the
> *descort* and a preliminary examination of the Old
> Provençal *descorts* suggests the following hypothesis:
> for the troubadours of the classic period, the *descort*
> was the anti-chanson. Beside the regular *canso* which
> followed the principle of regularity, they conceived
> the irregular *canso* which followed the principle of
> irregularity... the opposition of the categories regular/
> irregular is the generating principle of the *descort*.
> This opposition may manifest itself on one level or
> on several levels at once; on that of form, on that
> of music, or on that of content.

This interpretation sets us wondering about the relationship which seems to have existed between the *descort* and the fiddle; was this relationship also designed to counter the High Style manner, this time in the realm of performance? Was instrumental accompaniment therefore inimical to the High Style manner in music and poetry?

This brings us to the *dansa*, associated with the fiddle in both the romance of *Jaufre* and the *partimen* between Raimbaut, Perdigo and Adémar. The

Songs and instruments

dansas of the twelfth century have passed into eternal silence, for not one survives—neither words nor music—but their poetic form is probably preserved in the *dansas* which began to be written down in the next century (none of which are much older than c1250). Here is the outline of that form:

A   called the *respos*

b   the stanza, using different rhymes and a different metrical form to the *respos*

a   the closing section of the stanza, using the same rhymes and the same metrical form as the *respos* (but not necessarily reproducing its whole form).

If the *respos* were repeated at the end, then the result could be identical to the French virelai:[22]

A bb a A

A glance at the list of High Style and Lower Style characteristics on p.16 is enough to show that the *dansa* belongs in the region of the Lower Styles. The *dansa*, as its name implies, was a lyrico-choreographic form which must often have been performed for dancing; on those occasions, at least, it will have been performed in some kind of strict metre. When the *respos* was repeated at the end of the stanza the *dansa* had a refrain (in the strict sense: a combined musical and textual reprise); at all times the *dansa* had a conspicuous musical reprise (A b a). In all these respects it is a Lower Style form.

But what of the texts? Here we may be able to pursue the link between instruments and unwritten repertory a little further. For the most part the surviving *dansa* poems are courtly in the sense that they are love lyrics which exploit the conventions of literary love whose natural home is the *canso*. Yet no twelfth-century *dansas* seem to have survived, and there are no *dansas* surviving among the works of the major thirteenth-century troubadours.[23]

One explanation for this state of affairs is that the *dansa* began life as a trivial, ephemeral and perhaps even popular form: one which lay too low for the troubadours to cultivate. This would not stop *dansas* from being played and enjoyed at court, but it would prevent them from becoming the vehicle of a High Style lyric genre.

There are traces here and there of what these unrecorded *dansas* may have been like. A song by the Catalan troubadour Guillem de Berguedà (d.1192/6) claims to take its melody from a song sung 'by the young men of Pau', and the verses end with a (slightly variable) refrain which may well incorporate material from a dance-song:[24]

Puis van xantan liridunvau,
balan, notan gent e suau.

The twelfth century in the South

> . . . . . .
> Puys van xantan liridunvar,
> balan, notan autet e clar.
>
> Then they go singing (?playing) 'liridunvau', dancing, singing
> sweetly and pleasingly.
>
> At once they go singing 'liridunvar', dancing, singing
> loudly and clearly.

The nonsense words 'liridunvau' and 'liridunvar' carry us some considerable distance from the High Style manner, as do these closing lines from a disembodied verse:[25]

> Varalalito
> varalalito
> deu!
> varalatitondeÿna.

If this is an accurate picture of the prehistory of the *dansa* then we can shed some fresh light on the association between the fiddle and the *dansa* which we have met in two sources of the period 1170–1200. We have already seen that the musical style of the thirteenth-century *dansas* lies in the region of the Lower Styles; it now appears that the texts and general ethos of *dansas* in the twelfth century may have been foreign to the High Style.

Our most explicit twelfth-century sources therefore suggest that fiddle-accompaniment was associated with one form which subverts the musico-poetic decorum of the High Style (the *descort*), and another which, at the time we hear of it in relation to the fiddle, may well have been an ephemeral genre which the troubadours ignored, the *dansa*. Thus we have a provisional answer to the question of where instrumental accompaniment belonged in the system of contrasts presented on p.16. As far as the twelfth century in the South is concerned, the evidence—admittedly very meagre—suggests that instrumental accompaniment did not have a High Style ethos.

It may be that these two references to accompanied *descorts* and *dansas* are misleading, but I believe the next chapter will show that we have reason to trust them. Let us leave the twelfth century with a text of c1210 which offers a remarkable portrait of a minstrel with High Style troubadour songs in his repertory: *Abril issia* by the Catalan poet and poetic theorist of the early thirteenth century, Raimon Vidal.

IV

In this poem the narrator tells how he walked out one morning when 'April was leaving and May entering'. Low in spirits, he enters the town square of

Songs and instruments

Besalú (in Catalonia) and is pleased to see a minstrel approaching him, 'dressed and shod after the fashion of the time in which valour and worth were both found in the barons'.[26] The two characters fall into conversation and it becomes clear that in some measure the minstrel is an archetypal figure found throughout medieval literature: the professional entertainer nostalgic for a vanished age of generous and discriminating patrons when inferior entertainers, 'bad men who have come to work their vile and ill desires', did not displace men of true talent.[27] Raimon Vidal's poem therefore gives an idealised and archaising picture of minstrelsy, but this increases its value as a testament to the high seriousness and sense of professional pride which the minstrel craft could encompass in the twelfth and thirteenth centuries.

The minstrel introduces himself by listing his skills:[28]

> Senher, yeu soy us hom aclis
> a joglaria de cantar,
> e say romans dir e contar,
> e novas motas e salutz,
> e autres comtes espandutz
> vas totas partz azautz e bos,
> e d'en Guiraut vers e chansos
> e d'en Arnaut de Maruelh mays,
> e d'autres vers e d'autres lays...

> Sir, I am a man inclined to the profession of minstrelsy of
> singing, and I know how to tell and narrate romances and
> many tales and love-greetings, and other charming and
> good stories known everywhere, and *vers* and *chansos* of
> sir Guiraut [de Bornelh] and more by sir Arnaut de Maroill,
> and other *vers* and other *lays*...

Although he specialises in *joglaria de cantar*, 'the profession of minstrelsy of singing', this minstrel seems to have no wish to advertise any instrumental skills that he may possess.

As the story unfolds it emerges that this *joglar* has a high opinion of his own craft. In his view minstrels have a responsibility to promote the highest values of courtly society by conversation, songs and tales. The minstrel craft therefore deserves to be regarded as a kind of learning (*saber*) which can only be acquired by men of great personal gifts; they must be both charming (*avinens*) and wise (*savis*).[29] Accordingly, the best minstrel travels to courts where he may seek out 'select' people (*chauzitz*) and 'increase wisdom and excellence amongst them' (*a lur pujar sens e valors*), for his professional satisfaction comes from inspiring noble people to magnanimous actions and virtuous thoughts—to courtesy in the fullest sense of the term.[30]

As for troubadour songs, Raimon Vidal presents them as an effective means of moral instruction through pleasure, *solatz*. His taste in troubadour lyric is an elevated one, for it centres upon Guiraut de Bornelh (*honratz per los valenz homes*, according to the Vidas),[31] and Arnaut de Maroill (*onratz hom de cort*).[32] Since a minstrel lives entirely by his voice, and since his art, in all its manifestations, is an art of eloquence—of 'how one should speak' (*si co hom ditz*)—the narrator takes a lofty view of lyric genres, disdaining performers whose only concern is to learn love-debates in verse, or *jocx partitz*, together with 'every wisecrack that one says to fools'.[33] In contrast, he regards the *canso* as an art of eloquence in the service of moral instruction. Thus a poem of Arnaut de Maroill 'instructs undiscriminating people', while Guiraut de Bornelh is pictured as a teacher of 'refined people in order to strengthen their good behaviour'; viewed in this light the troubadour's chief gift is his wisdom, or *sen*, and his task is to instil it into others, whence, to *ensenhar*, or to 'teach' those who hear his works.[34]

To anyone familiar with the idiosyncratic works of the first troubadours, whose sexual morality is sometimes less than exemplary, this earnest view of a lyric repertory which is often concerned with erotic love may seem somewhat ingenuous,[35] and it is certainly difficult to believe that a theorist of poetic art like Raimon Vidal, who acknowledges the primacy of didactic aims in poetry with such candour, can capture more than a fraction of what was truly enjoyed by those who cared for troubadour poetry. Yet it is doubtful whether Raimon Vidal's contemporaries would have considered his faith in the moral seriousness of troubadour song to be misplaced, nor need we assume that the troubadours and their listeners would have turned to some other defence of their art than the moralistic one which Vidal offers. The articulate mind of the Middle Ages was never dissatisfied with the view of good poetry as something *utilis* as well as *dulcis*.

In accordance with his elevated view of the High Style song the minstrel in Raimon Vidal's *Abril issia* is accustomed to be listened to. When he asks the narrator to listen to his account of himself 'as attentively (*puramen*) as if it were a message of love', he may be alluding to High Style love-songs of the troubadour tradition, and the adverb *puramen*, whose meaning in this context may amount to something like '[listen] in a pure fashion, unsullied by any base thought or distraction', suggests that a minstrel with High Style songs in his repertory held high expectations of his listeners.[36]

Needless to say, these songs could not be sung to any audience at any time; they needed to be prepared for, and one of the most fascinating sections in Raimon Vidal's poem is the passage where the narrator explains how a minstrel should bring his audience to the point where they are ready for them.[37] It seems that a skilled minstrel began by working his way into the flow of conversation; then, *petit à petit*, he manoeuvred himself into a dominant position within the party by exploiting his learning, his *saber*. On the simplest level this *saber* consisted of traveller's gossip, for in any courtly circle a minstrel enjoyed a conversational advantage by virtue of his travels that enabled him to report items of news he had learned as he moved from

Songs and instruments

place to place. In the opinion of Raimon Vidal this was one way that an entertainer could help to maintain and stimulate aristocratic courtesy, for courtesy was the common culture of a network of *cortz* and it was the privilege of minstrels, who travelled regularly between these courts, to report which lords of the region were the most courteous, and which ladies the most virtuous, as an example to all. Conversation such as this was the minstrel's first deployment of his *saber*. Next, if he saw that the company was with him and eager for more, he turned to *novas*, or stories in verse which retained the themes of courtesy and noble deeds but which represented a move away from conversation as the company (which the minstrel had by now turned into an audience) fell silent to listen to his material in rhyme.

Once the *novas* were over, the minstrel reached the most sensitive point in the management of his audience. His next and final stage was to offer to sing, but it was only worth proceeding to *chantars* if the audience had shown itself *adreitz, prims* and *entendens*—to be clever, of fine sensibility and discriminating. This, it seems, was the kind of audience, moulded and tested at each stage by a skilful performer, which proud *joglars* sought for the performance of songs by troubadours such as Guiraut de Bornelh and Arnaut de Maroill. Raimon Vidal seems to regard all his skills as facets of the same gift—the gift of eloquence. Whether it be the improvised eloquence of conversation, or the prepared eloquence of tales and troubadour songs, a good minstrel sees himself as one who, in all the manifestations of his art, shows how one should speak to the pleasure and moral profit of others. He does not emerge as a manually skilled or dexterous individual, whether the skills be those of the knife-thrower, the juggler or the instrumentalist.

The evidence assembled in this chapter might suggest that the High Style troubadour *canso* was not generally accompanied in the twelfth century. However, we have found no positive evidence for that view, for none of the texts that we have so far encountered mentions the High Style *canso* in clear and unmistakable terms (although a passage from Daurel et Beton may do so; see above). All that can be said is that as early as the second half of the twelfth century there are signs of an association between instruments and certain song-forms (the *descort* and the *dansa*) which, in their own way, stand well apart from the High Style *canso*.

Notes

1 Text and music from Van der Werf, *Extant Troubadour Melodies*, p.17*.

2 Gennrich, *Rondeaux, Virelais und Balladen*, 1, p.10. On this and associated genres see for example Bec, *La Lyrique Française*, pp.220ff; Delbouille, *Bele Aëlis*; Doss-Quinby, *Les Refrains*, and Le Gentil, *Guillaume de Dole*.

3 Marshall, *Linguistic and Literary Theory*, 2, pp.66–7.

Notes

4   Text in Bartholomaeis, *Insegnamenti pe' giullari*, pp.3ff.

5   *Ibid.*

6   *Ibid.*

7   For the text and music see Van der Werf, *Extant Troubadour Melodies*, p.227*.

8   *Ibid.*, p.220*.

9   For some of the evidence see, for example, Faral, *Les Jongleurs*, Appendix 3, item 91, and the testimonies of Albertus Magnus (Borgnet, *Beati Alberti Magni Opera Omnia*, 8, p.748), Thomas de Chobham (Broomfield, *Summa Confessorum*, p.292), Gerbert de Montreuil (Buffum, *Roman de la Violette*, lines 1400–29; see Appendix 3:33 of this book), and an anonymous thirteenth-century preacher quoted in Techener, *Description Raisonnée*, 1, p.273.

10 I am assuming here that the text dates from the middle decades of the twelfth century, as argued by Kimmel (*Daurel et Beton*), pp.34ff, although it may date from significantly later (c1200, perhaps?). For further material from this epic see Appendix 3:1.

11 Kimmel, *Daurel et Beton*, line 1173ff.

12 *Ibid.*, lines 1498–1505.

13 The meanings of *lais* in Old Provençal are discussed, with lavish documentation, in Baum, 'Troubadours et les lais'.

14 Text and music from Van der Werf, *Extant Troubadour Melodies*, pp.96*–7* (MS *R*).

15 For the relative chronology of these terms see Marshall, *Linguistic and Literary Theory*, pp.864ff.

16 *Ibid.*, p.889.

17 Text from Lavaud and Nelli, *Les Troubadours*, 1, lines 9811–14.

18 See, for example, the usage of Marcabrun in his famous *Pax in nomine Domini* (text and music in Van der Werf, *Extant Troubadour Melodies*, p.227* (line 2)). See also Marshall, *Linguistic and Literary Theory*, pp.669ff.

Notes

19 Text from Linskill, *Raimbaut de Vaqueiras*, p.140, lines 49–50.

20 For the surviving *descort* tunes see De la Cuesta, *Cançons dels Trobadors*, pp.402ff (*Qui la vi en ditz*, by Aimeric de Peguillan), and pp.531ff (*Ses alegratge*, by Guillem Augier Novella). There is some doubt about the structure of *Qui la vi en ditz*; Maillard ('*Lai lyrique*', p.125, n.28a) interprets it as two poems, the second beginning *Cilh qu'es caps e guids*. De la Cuesta, *op. cit.*, interprets it (correctly, in my view), as one poem.

21 Baum, 'Descort', p.97. On an important sub-division of the descort repertory see Marshall, 'Isostrophic *Descort*'.

22 There is some dispute as to whether the final *A* in this scheme represents the traditional form of the *dansa*. As pointed out above, the five surviving *dansas* with music (all anonymous) are preserved in a French chansonnier, the Manuscrit du Roi, and are thus both late and peripheral witnesses to the Occitan *dansa* tradition which reaches back to at least the mid-twelfth century. In one instance (here Music example 8) there can be no doubt that the final *A* is certainly intended, since the scribe has signalled it (the hint is not properly taken up by De la Cuesta (*Cançons dels Trobadors*, p.741). Perhaps the final *A* was a Gallicism. De la Cuesta lists all these *dansas* as virelais (save *Ben vòlgra, s'èsser pogués*, which he inventories as 'Dança, virelai'). For text and music of these pieces see his edition, pp.726–7 (*Amors, m'ard com fuoc amb flama*); pp.738–9 (*Ben vòlgra, s'èsser pogués*); pp.741–2 (*Dòmna, pos vos ai chausida*; here Music example 8); pp.805–6 (*Pos qu'ieu vei la fuèlha*), and pp.810–11 (*Tant es gaia et avinents*). For a meticulous handling of the descriptions of the *dansa* given by the poetic theorists see Marshall, *Razos de Trobar*, pp.138 and 141–2; idem, *Linguistic and Literary Theory*, 2, pp.904ff; Lewent, '*Dansa*', p.517.

23 The only significant troubadour who has left an important body of *dansas* (none of them surviving with music) is the Catalan Cerveri de Girona. Cerveri's work also includes some *estampidas* and is notable for the high proportion of late and traditionally minor forms which it includes.

24 For an edition of the full text see Riquer, *Guillem de Berguedà*, 2, pp.64ff. For further material on refrains in troubadour poetry (including refrains of this type) see Gorton, 'Arabic Words and Refrains', and Newcombe, 'The Refrain in Troubadour Lyric Poetry'.

25 Text from Suchier, 'Provenzalische Verse', p.513.

26 Field, *Raimon Vidal*, lines 1ff. and p.61. In what follows I paraphrase or

Notes

quote the text and translation in this edition.

27 *Ibid.*, lines 48ff and p.61.

28 *Ibid.*, lines 38–46, and p.61.

29 *Ibid.*, lines 52–3.

30 *Ibid.*, line 1245 and p.80.

31 Boutière and Schutz, *Biographies des Troubadours*, p.39.

32 *Ibid.*, p.33.

33 Field, *Raimon Vidal*, lines 1580ff and p.85.

34 *Ibid.*, lines 1020ff and p.76.

35 Whilst it would be impossible to deny the pervasive eroticism of much troubadour poetry, the distinctive excellence of this love-poetry at its best is that erotic desire and moral ardour coalesce in one passion which can only be felt by the refined heart. The tendency of the poetry to centre on words denoting moral prestige (*valors, pretz, onors,* and even the seemingly evanescent *joi* and *jovens*) gives many troubadour *cansos* a high moral tone which is partly responsible for the altitude of the 'High' Style.

36 Field, *Raimon Vidal*, line 108 and p.62.

37 *Ibid.*, lines 1580ff and pp.85–6.

[18]

VOICES AND INSTRUMENTS IN MEDIEVAL FRENCH SECULAR MUSIC: ON THE USE OF LITERARY TEXTS AS EVIDENCE FOR PERFORMANCE PRACTICE

Sylvia Huot

One of the most important questions facing historians and performers of medieval music today is the respective roles of voices and instruments. We do not know exactly which instruments were used for a given repertoire, or in what combinations; and we do not know for sure under what conditions, if any, these instruments (whatever they were) would be combined with the voice.[1] Although considerable literary, archival, and iconographic evidence for medieval performance practice exists, scholars and musicians attempting to codify this material face a task of monumental proportions. The sheer quantity of the material is in itself daunting, and much of it remains unexamined. Moreover, even once a body of material has been assembled, the task of interpreting its lessons is far from easy. Documents are rarely as explicit as we would like them to be; literary and artistic representations of performance often cannot be identified securely with a

---

[*] Preliminary work for this study was supported by a grant from the Exxon Education Foundation for research at the Newberry Library, Chicago. Subsequent work was supported in part by a faculty summer research stipend from the Graduate School, Northern Illinois University. I am extremely grateful for this support. I would also like to thank Mary Springfels of the Newberry Library, Howard Mayer Brown of the University of Chicago, Peter Lefferts of the University of Chicago, and Lawrence Earp of the University of Wisconsin, Madison, for many helpful suggestions during the preparation of this study.

[1] Some studies that address questions of instrumentation and performance practice include the general survey by E. Faral, *Les Jongleurs en France au moyen âge* (Paris, 1910); I.F. Finlay's "Musical Instruments in Gotfrid von Strassburg's "Tristan und Isolde"‹ *Galpin Society Journal* 5 (March 1952), pp. 39-43; E.A. Bowles, "Instruments at the Court of Burgundy (1363-1467)", *Galpin Society Journal* 6 (July 1953), pp. 41-45; H.M. Brown, "Instruments and Voices in the Fifteenth-Century Chanson", in J.W. Grubbs, et al, eds., *Current Thought in Musicology* (Austin and London, 1976), pp. 89-137; C. Page, "The Performance of Songs in Late Medieval France: A New Source", *Early Music* 10 (1982), pp. 441-50. For a general survey of descriptions of musical performance in Old French literature, see C. Page, "Music and Chivalric Fiction in France, 1150-1300", *Proceedings of the Royal Musical Association* 111/112 (1984-85), pp. 1-27; and Page's *Voices and Instruments of the Middle Ages: Instrumental Practice and Songs in France 1100-1300* (Berkeley and Los Angeles, 1986).

specific repertoire, present ambiguities, and may in any case contain at least as much fancy as fact.

In the present study I have concentrated on descriptions of musical performance in Old and Middle French literature, ranging from the late twelfth to the turn of the fifteenth century: that is, from the time of the trouvères through the first generation of post-Machaut composers. I have not attempted to gather together all descriptions of performance from this period, for that would be a nearly impossible task. My purpose is not to present a history of performance descriptions in medieval French literature, but rather to address the methodological issues that these texts raise. A host of textual, linguistic, and literary problems must be confronted before we can even begin to weigh the evidence of these descriptions. By examining a manageable number of exemplary passages, I hope to establish guidelines for the analysis of literary texts as evidence for performance practice. My approach is twofold. The first part of the study is concerned with philological considerations: the establishment of the text and the resolution of lexical and syntactic problems. The second part examines the content of performance descriptions: the treatment of different repertoires and the literary conventions that influence this treatment. Finally, the examination of the passages included in this study will allow for some preliminary conclusions about the performance of secular music in France during the thirteenth and fourteenth centuries. Owing to the relative scarcity of explicit references to polyphonic performance, these conclusions will be largely about monophony; but certain issues in the performance of polyphony will be addressed as well.

Reading Performance Descriptions, I: Philological Considerations

Before any medieval text can be studied, it must be established. And if a text exists in multiple versions, it is necessary to examine the variant readings before analysis can even begin. The modern critical edition can be misleading: the text it prints does not necessarily correspond to most, or even to any, of the medieval sources. Since my purpose here is not to provide a comprehensive analysis of medieval performance practice as revealed in literary texts, but only to establish the guidelines for such study,

I will limit myself to two examples of manuscript variants in performance description. The first passage is taken from Chrétien de Troyes' *Chevalier au Lyon (Yvain)*, composed in the late twelfth century; it appears in seven manuscripts ranging from the early thirteenth century to the turn of the fourteenth century.[2] The subject is Arthur's ceremonial entry into Yvain's newly won castle. All versions agree that Arthur was honored with loud flourishes on horns and buisines and entertained by male acrobats, and all refer as well to an assortment of wind and percussion instruments and to the presence of maidens. The principal variants occur in the three lines that identify these latter instruments and specify the activity of the maidens. Here are the lines as printed in Foerster's edition:

> Contre lui dancent les puceles,
> Sonent flaütes et freteles,
> Timbre, tabletes et tabor.

> The maidens dance towards him; flutes and freteles, tambourines, cymbals and tabors play.
> *(Yvain,* vv. 2351-53)

This reading, however, does not actually appear in any manuscript. The variants include the instrumentation, the activity of the maidens, and the relationship of the instrumental music to whatever the maidens are doing. MS *V* is the closest to Foerster's text, differing only in the instrumentation: it reads "trompes" instead of "timbre" in v. 2353. In MSS *G* and *S*, where the instrumentation agrees with Foerster's text, the girls do not dance but simply go out to meet the king, as do, evidently, the musicians:

> Contre lui ivent les puceles, [MS *G*: Encontre 1. vont l.p.]
> Les flahutes et les fresteles,
> Timbres, tabletes et tabors. [MS *G*: et tables]

> Towards him went [go] the maidens, the flutes and the

---

[2] I use the sigla adopted by Foerster for the edition of *Yvain:* A = Chantilly, Musée Condé, MS 472; F = Paris, Bibliothèque Nationale fr. 1450; G = B.N. fr. 12560; H = B.N. fr. 794; P = B.N. fr. 1433; S = B.N. fr. 12603; V = Vatican Library Reg. 1725. I am grateful to David Hult of The Johns Hopkins University for his assistance in checking manuscript variants.

freteles, tambourines, [and cymbals] and tabors.
(MS *G*, fol. 15r-15v MS *S*, fol. 95r)

In MS *A*, the girls themselves are the musicians – a possibility perfectly compatible with the reading of MSS *GS* – and the instrumentation is slightly different:

> Contre lui sonnent les puceles
> Et lor timbres et lor vïeles,
> Flahutes, tabletes et tabors.

> The maidens play their timbres, their fiddles,
> flutes, cymbals and tabors towards him [i.e., as a musical welcome].
> (fol. 181v)

The passage in MSS *GSV* conjures up the image of maidens dancing or processing towards the king; in addition, there is ongoing music from wind and percussion, which might or might not be the music to which the girls dance. MS *A*, however, describes a group of female musicians playing for the king. MSS *F* and *H* in turn make it clear that the flute and percussion is the accompaniment for the maidens' procession or dance, without specifying that this takes place as a movement towards (or even anywhere near) the king:

> Et la ou dansent les puceles,
> Sonent flaütes et freiteles,
> Timbres, tabletes et tabor.

> And there where the maidens dance, flutes and freteles,
> tambourines, cymbals and tabors play.
> (MS *F*, fol. 214r)

> La ou descendent les puceles,
> Sonent flaütes et vïeles,
> Tympre, freteles et tabor.

> There where the maidens come down, flutes and fiddles,
> tambourines, freteles and tabors play.
> (MS *H*, fol. 88r)

Finally, MS *P* portrays the flutes and percussion as accompaniment not for dance or movement of any kind, but for song:

> Et la ou chantent les pucheles,
> Sonnent fleütes et freteles,
> Timbres, tabletes et tabours.

> And there where the maidens sing, flutes and freteles,
> tambourines, cymbals and tabors play.
> (fol. 81v)

A single descriptive passage is thus in reality seven descriptions, no two of them quite alike. In the present context, I am not concerned with the issue of what may have been the "original" text or how – and if – we may arrive at it. Rather, I believe that in our search for evidence of medieval performance practice, we must attend to all surviving medieval texts, whether they are the product of a poet or a scribe. Assuming that the scribe in each case was attentive enough not to write anything that did not make sense, how do we account for these discrepancies? There is nothing difficult about the passage, nothing to suggest that scribes were forced to reconstruct, each in his own way, an obscure or corrupt source.[3] Perhaps the answer to this question is that a medieval reader would not have felt that there were any real discrepancies among these seven versions. With the possible exception of "trompes", which could be simply a misreading for "timbres" (sometimes spelled "timpres"), the variations in instrumentation are not enormous: in all cases we have flutes and percussion, and there is nothing odd about finding fiddles in such a context. As for the question of whether the maidens are singing, dancing, or playing instruments, scribes may have been inattentive to this distinction because it would be assumed that maidens would be doing all of these things.

---

[3] The philological problems involved in the study of variant readings for specific passages in the works of Chrétien de Troyes are explored in detail by A. Foulet and K.D. Uitti, "Chrétien's "Laudine": *Yvain*, vv. 2148-55", *Romance Philology* 37 (1983-84), pp. 293-302; K.D. Uitti, "Autant en emporte *li funs:* remarques sur le prologue du *Chevalier de la charrette* de Chrétien de Troyes", *Romania* 105 (1984), pp. 270-91; D.F. Hult, "Lancelot's Two Steps: A Problem in Textual Criticism", *Speculum* 61 (1986), pp. 836-58. For more general discussions of textual criticism and stemmatology, see C. Kleinhenz, ed., *Medieval Manuscripts and Textual Criticism,* Studies in the Romance Languages and Literatures, Symposia 4 (Chapel Hill, 1975).

Certainly it was not uncommon for medieval women to dance to their own singing, often for the pleasure of male spectators.[4] We also know that female musicians could play musical instruments. And as we will see, terms used for performance are not exclusive of other terms: "sonner", for example, does not necessarily exclude singing.

Collectively, the seven versions of the festivities in *Yvain* add up to a scene very much like that of the carol in the first part of the *Roman de la rose* (ca. 1230). The carolers dance to the singing of Lady Happiness *(Rose,* vv. 727-28); flute players and unidentified minstrels are present (vv. 745-46); there are ladies playing cymbals and tambourines who toss their instruments on high and balance them on their finger tips, possibly while executing some sort of dance steps (vv. 751-56); and two maidens do a special dance together for the entertainment of the others (vv. 757-69). Dancing, singing, and playing percussion, in close proximity with flute players and other musicians, are the three interrelated activities engaged in collectively by the ladies in the Garden of Delight. In *Yvain,* the scene that Guillaume de Lorris took nearly fifty lines to describe is evoked in a mere three lines. If each version is slightly different, it is because for a medieval reader the presence of maidens, with a certain type of instrumentation and in a certain context, is sufficient to conjure up a complete picture; the choice of details to be presented is up to the individual scribe.

A note of caution must also be sounded, however: manuscript variants do not invariably provide accurate insights. Sometimes a variant really is an error. The twelfth-century *Roman de Brut,* for example, includes a description of festivities that begins with references to lais being performed on several kinds of instruments, and then continues with a typical catalogue of numerous other instruments, of which I cite here only the first line:

> Lais de vïeles, lais de rotes,
> Lais de harpes, lais de frestels,
> Lires, tympes e chalemels ...

> Lais on fiddles, lais on rotes, lais on harps, lais on
> fretels; lyres, tympes and shawms.
> *(Brut,* vv. 10548-50)

---

[4] See J. Bédier, "Les Plus Anciennes Danses françaises", *Revue des Deux Mondes* 31 (1906), pp. 398-424.

Most of the manuscripts agree with this reading. In MS Bibliothèque Nationale fr. 1416 (dated 1292), however, we find the variant provided by Arnold in his edition:

> Lais de harpes, lais de rotes,
> Lais de corons, lais de frestels,
> Lais de tympes, de chalemels.

> Lais on harps, lais on rotes, lais on horns, lais on fretels, lais on tympes, on shawms.

Were lais really performed on horns and on tympes? Perhaps so. But in this particular case, I think it is likely that the scribe, having grown accustomed to the repetitive use of "lais" at the beginning of every line and half-line, simply misread "lires" for "lais" in v. 10550, an easy enough mistake to make. A similar inattentiveness might account for the appearance of "corons" in the preceding line; in fact, all manuscripts agree on the reappearance of "coruns" three lines later. Lengthy catalogues of instruments are conventional in medieval narrative poetry, and generally communicate an atmosphere of festive abundance rather than a mimetic account of specific performing ensembles. The scribe might be forgiven for feeling that the precise order in which the instruments were mentioned was not essential, just as a scribe transcribing *Yvain* might not be concerned with the choice of the terms "chanter" or "danser" to describe a group of maidens that he assumed were doing both at once.

Manuscript variants must thus be interpreted with care. We must be alert to outright misreadings, as well as to possible explanations for scribal emendation or inattentiveness to detail. But given the impressionistic nature of most descriptions of musical performance found in medieval literature, the modern scholar needs as much help as possible in reconstructing a complete picture. The judicious comparison of multiple versions is an essential part of the reading of medieval texts, and can help considerably to clarify difficult passages.

Even once we are sure that we have an authentic medieval text, it is not always easy to be sure just what it says. A variety of verbs are used to signify the activity of musical performance, of which the most important are "dire", "chanter", "noter", "sonner", "jouer", and the various terms for playing specific instruments, such as "vïeler" or "harper".[5] In addition, the term "accorder" is commonly used to describe the relationship between the voices and/or instruments in a group performance. Interpreting these terms in a given passage can be difficult for several reasons. Each term can have a range of meanings; usage can be imprecise, as when a musician is said to "play" a song even though he is clearly also singing it; and it can sometimes be difficult, when both singing and playing are described, to determine whether the actions are meant to be simultaneous or sequential.

Precise meaning is most difficult for the first four terms listed above, whose range of meanings in the context of musical performance includes "to speak", "to discourse upon", "to sing", or "to play an instrument". Usually, however, "dire" and "chanter" both imply voice, while "noter" and "sonner" are used for instrumental music. While "chanter" can be used for instrumental music when the instrument is the subject of the verb, this is a figurative use that does not really change the association of "chanter" with voice: the instrument "sings".

Conversely, "sonner" can be used for speech in the phrase "sonner un mot"; but this usage parallels the construction "sonner un instrument", with "sonner" in both cases meaning "to sound".

The distinction between "dire" and "chanter" rests on the association of the former with the spoken word, and the association of the latter with music. The noun forms "dit" and "chant" in particular reflect this distinction: "dit" refers either to a poem without music or to the words of a song, while "chant" refers to music in general, to a song, or even to the tune, as opposed to the words, of a song. I will return below to particular uses of the terms "dit" and "chant". The verbs "dire" and "chanter" are sometimes used in opposition in order to express a distinction between musical and non-musical discourse, as in the mid-thirteenth century *Bestiaire d'amour,* where the narrator refers to the movement from song to prose declamation as that from "canter" to "dire" (p. 10). Often, however, "dire" is used interchangeably with "chanter" to indicate singing. In Jean Renart's early thirteenth-century *Guillaume de Dole,* for example, is the following exchange:

---

[5] Two other lexical studies useful in reading performance descriptions are R. Morgan, "Old French *jogleor* and Kindred Terms", *Romance Philology* 7 (1953-54), pp. 279-325; W. Ulland, *Jouer d'un instrument und die altfranzösischen Bezeichnungen des Instrumentenspiels,* Romanistische Versuche und Vorarbeiten 35 (Bonn, 1970).

VOICES AND INSTRUMENTS ... 71

> – Dame, fet il, une *chançon*
> car nos *dites*, si ferez bien.
> Ele *chantoit* sor tote rien ...
>
> "Lady", he says, "do sing us a song, you will do well". She habitually sang about anything at all.
> (vv. 1144-46, emphasis mine)

> – Ha, ma tres douce dame, voire,
> *dites* nos en. ...
> Quant el ot sa chançon *chantee* ...
>
> "Oh, my very sweet lady, truly, sing us some" ... When she had sung her song ...
> (vv. 1152-53, 1167, emphasis mine)

Ambiguity arises when "dire" and "chanter" are used in conjunction with musical instruments, in phrases of the form "dire"/"chanter" + preposition + instrument. Are we to understand combined vocal and instrumental or solely instrumental music? In some cases the full context makes it clear that we are meant to understand an activity consisting of singing or chanting the words of a song or tale to instrumental accompaniment:

> Cest vers de bele Marguerite
> ...
> li fet chanter en la vïele:
>   Cele d'Oisseri
>   ne met en oubli ...
>
> This poem about beautiful Margaret ... he has him sing on the fiddle: She of Oisseri does not forget ...
> (*Guillaume de Dole*, vv. 3415, 3418-20)

The citation of the words of the song, as well as the use of the term "vers", which commonly refers to a non-musical poem or to the words of a song, support the interpretation of "chanter en la vïele" as song accompanied by fiddle. A similar case is this reference to the performance of *chanson de geste* in the late twelfth-century *Moniage Guillaume:*

> Hui mais orés canchon de fiere geste,
> Chil jougleour en cantent en vïele.

> Now you will hear a song of bold deeds; these jongleurs sing of it on the fiddle.
> *(Moniage Guillaume,* vv. 2071-72)

"Canter en vïele" here can only imply recitation or chanting with instrumental accompaniment, as one could hardly imagine a purely instrumental rendition of a *chanson de geste.*

The same logic could be applied to Marie de France's statement in *Guigemar* about the Breton lai of Guigemar. The full passage *(Guigemar,* vv. 883-86) appears in two manuscripts:

> De cest cunte k'oï avez
> Fu Guigemar li lais trovez
> Que hum fait en harpe e en rote;
> Bone en est a oïr la note.

> From this tale that you have heard, Guigemar the lai was composed, which people do on harp and on rote; the tune [note] is nice to hear.
> (British Library, Harley 978, mid 13th c.)

The passage is the same in Paris, Bibliothèque Nationale fr. 2168 (Picard, second half of the 13th century), except that v. 885 reads "que hum dist en harpe e en rote". The verb "faire" can mean "to do", "to make", "to compose a poem or a tune", or "to say"; "dire" in Bibl. Nat. fr. 2168 presumably means "to sing" or "to recite". "Note" could mean either the tune to which the tale is sung or, quite possibly, the genre of poetico-musical composition in which the medieval audience would encounter the tale of Guigemar. Although Marie stresses in particular the musical quality of the lai, it is unlikely that she imagines a purely instrumental rendition. In the context of her work, as in Old French literature in general, the Breton lai is important precisely as a sung text recording a particular adventure. In the Prologue appearing in the Harley manuscript, she states that the Breton lais were made "pur remambrance ... des aventures" (in remembrance of the adventures) *(Prologue,* vv. 35-36) and that "Plusurs en ai oï conter" (I have heard many of them recounted) (v. 39). Given the importance of the lai text, both in general and for Marie's project in particular, it would be strange if the reference to the performance of the lai on which her narrative is based was phrased in such a way as to exclude the text. In this case, at least, "faire en harpe/rote" and "dire en harpe/rote" must refer to a process of singing coupled with playing.[6]

In light of these relatively straightforward examples, it is likely that this more ambiguous passage in the prologue of the *Comte d'Anjou* (1316) refers to a combined vocal and instrumental rendition of a variety of pieces:

> Li autre dient en vielles
> Chançons royaus et estempies,
> Dances, noctes, et baleriez,
> En leüst, en psalterion,
> Chascun selonc s'entencion,
> Lais d'amours, descors et balades.

> Others sing on the fiddle chanson royaus and estampies,
> dance tunes, notes and baleries, on the lute, on the psaltery,
> each according to his taste, lais of love, descorts and ballades.
> *(Comte d'Anjou*, vv. 12-17)

The list of pieces included as suitable for rendition on fiddle, lute, or psaltery includes not only various types of dance music, which might be purely instrumental, but also the lai, descort and ballade, poetic forms; and even the chanson royal, a poetic form of which only one musical example – Guillaume de Machaut's *Joie, plaisence et douce nourriture* – is even known today. It may be that the verb "dire" is used in a loose sense that can include either purely instrumental or combined vocal and instrumental rendition. The point of the passage, indeed, is the variety of pieces and of performance techniques: each performer arranges his rendition as he sees fit.

We arrive at a more problematic ambiguity when the instruments linked with "dire" or "chanter" are wind instruments, which one could not possibly play *while* singing. Three possibilities present themselves: (1) a musician plays on his instrument a tune whose words are so well known that they are implied by the mere sound of the melody; (2) a single musician alter-

---

[6] P. Ménard concludes that "les anciens lais bretons étaient à la fois instrumentaux et vocaux", in *Les Lais de Marie de France: Contes d'amour et d'aventure du Moyen Age* (Paris, 1979), p. 55. On the lai more generally, see J. Maillard, *Evolution et esthétique du lai lyrique des origines à la fin du XIVe siècle* (Paris, 1963); and Maillard's "Coutumes musicales au moyen âge d'après le *Tristan* en prose", *Cahiers de Civilisation Médiévale* 2 (1959), pp. 341-53.

nately sings and plays; or (3) a performer sings to the accompaniment of an instrumentalist. It is possible to find less ambiguously worded examples of each of these possibilities.

(1) The purely instrumental rendition of a piece that presumably does have words is implied in certain instances where the verb used is not "dire" or "chanter" but "noter", as in this example from the first half of the thirteenth century:

> En sa main a pris un flagueil
> Molt doucement en flajola
> Et par dedens le flaguel a
> Noté le Lai del Chievrefueil
> Et puis a mis jus le flagueil.

> In his hand he took a flute; he played the flute very sweetly, and by means of the flute he played the Lai of the Honeysuckle, and then he set down the flute.
> *(Tristan ménestrel,* vv. 758-62)

Tristan here wishes to give a secret message to Iseut by playing the lai that she and he composed together and have never made public. The purely instrumental rendition is entirely appropriate to such a situation, since he does not wish to tell the story expressed by the lai, but only to reveal his identity to Iseut and to remind her of the sentiments it expresses. Since the text specifies that Tristan does not put down the flute until after he has done the lai, it is unlikely that any singing is involved.[7]

(2) The thirteenth-century pastourelle tradition provides several examples in which it is fairly clear that a shepherd or shepherdess alternately sings and plays on flute or pipes:

> Si avoit

---

[7] On the *Lai de Chevrefeuille*, see J. Maillard, "Le "Lai" et la "Note" du Chèvrefeuille", *Musica Disciplina* 13 (1959), pp. 3-13. I would like to add that since the history of musical instruments and their terminology is not central to this essay, and since the translation of medieval terms of musical instruments is often problematic, I have decided to use the general English term "flute" to translate three different Old French words, no doubt designating different types of instruments: "flageol[et]", "fl[ah]ute", and "estives". The reader desiring more specific designation is referred to the Old French passages, none of which are translated without being cited in the original.

VOICES AND INSTRUMENTS ...

> flaiol pipe et baston:
> en haut dist et si notoit
> un novel son,
> en sa pipe refraignoit
> le ver d'une chanson
> puis a dit "amor, amor ..."

> Thus she had flute, pipe and [drum?]stick: aloud she sang and also played a new song: she played on her pipe the verse of a song and then she sang, "Love, love ..."
> (Bartsch, III, no. 51, vv. 3-9)

> S'amie apele au calemel,
> si chante et note "dorenlot!
> eo eo ae ae! oo dorenlot!
> d'amors me doint dex joie."

> He calls his girl friend with the shawm; thus he sings and plays, "Dorenlot! eo eo ae ae! oo dorenlot! God grant me joy in love."
> (Bartsch, III, no. 20, vv. 6-9)

The second example above refers to a performance like that in the preceding example: "Dorenlot! eo eo ..." is an onomatopoeic allusion to instrumental music, which is followed by a sung refrain. A similar performance is evidently intended in the description of the song of Polyphemus in the early fourteenth-century *Ovide moralisé*. The cyclops plays a set of pipes, but he also clearly sings:

> En sa main tint une fleüste
> De cent rosiaus, dont il fleüste.
> ...
> Le chant dou jaiant escoutai
> Et ses paroles bien notai.

> In his hand he held a flute of a hundred reeds, which he played.
> ... I listened to the giant's song, and I paid close attention to his words.
> (Book 13, vv. 3823-24, 3831-32)

(3) The pastourelle also provides an example in which a singer is accompanied by a bagpipe player:

> Helos nu fu pas muele,
> ains cantoit si a devis
> k'a son cant s'acordoit Guis
> qi leur muse et chalemele
> en la muse au grant bourdon.

> Helos wasn't lax, for he sang so perfectly that Gui,
> who played for them on the bagpipe with the big
> drone, played along with his singing.
> (Bartsch, III, no. 27, vv. 38-42)

A similar kind of performance may be intended in Machaut's description of his patron's singing in the *Fonteinne amoureuse* (ca. 1360):

> Il disoit des dis et des chans
> De lais, de dances et de notes,
> Faites a cornes et a rotes.
>
> He sang the words and tunes of lais, of dance songs
> and of melodies rendered on horns and rotes.
> (vv. 2800-02)

This latter example of singing is not a formal performance, of course; most likely, Machaut's young nobleman – probably meant to represent Jean, duc de Berry – is simply amusing himself and giving free rein to his exuberant spirits by singing along with what would otherwise have been a purely instrumental rendition.

Given that all three types of rendition are possible, then, how are we to interpret statements like the following one in a late twelfth-century epic:

> .i. harpere de l'Trase est de l'roi aprociés.
> De lais dire a flahute estoit bien ensigniés.
> ...
> Devant le tref le roi est li harpere asis
> et commença .i. lai dont il ot mult apris,
> de la harpe à flahute dont il estoit apris.
>
> A harpist from Thrace approached the king. He was very accomplished at performing lais on the flute ... The harpist sat at the king's feet and began a lai, of which he had learned many, on harp and flute [OR: began a lai, of which he had learned many on the harp, on the flute, which he had learned how to do].
> (*Alexandre*, p. 73, vv. 9-10, 15-17)

This passage actually raises several questions: exactly which instrument or instruments are being played, and by how many different performers; how, by whom, and indeed whether the text of the lai is being sung. It seems unlikely that the same person would play both harp and flute at the same time. Yet there are no references to other musicians, and the harpist's performance is motivated by his desire to attract Alexander's attention so that he can plead a case with the emperor; this would suggest a solo performance. Enjambement is rare in verse of this type; one would expect the phrase "de la harpe à flahute" to constitute a syntactic unit. The phrase in fact parallels the language used to refer to the playing of pipe and tabor by a single performer in a pastourelle:

> Gui dou tabor au flahutel
> Leur fait ceste estampie.
>
> Gui played this estampie for them on pipe and tabor.
> (Bartsch, III, no. 21, vv. 49-50)

Perhaps, then, the performance in question – an exceptional one, since it gained the musician an audience with the emperor – does involve a combination of flute and harp, with the harp perhaps used to accompany the voice and the flute providing an instrumental prelude or interludes between strophes.

There is, in fact, evidence that some musicians performed lais by alternating vocal and instrumental renditions of each strophe. In a famous passage in the late thirteenth century Anglo-Norman *Horn*,[8] a Breton performs a lai with what is evidently a rather elaborate instrumental prelude:

> Lors prent la harpe a sei. qu'il la ueut atemprer.
> Deus ki dunc lesgardast. cum la sout manier.
> Cum ces cordes tuchoit. cum les fesoit trembler.
> As quantes feiz chanter. as quantes organer.[9]
>
> ...
>
> Quant ses notes ot fait. si la prent a munter.
> E tut par autres tuns. les cordes fait soner.
> Mut se merveillent tuit. quil la sout sibailler.
> E quant il out issi fait. si cummence a noter.
> Le lai dunt orains dis. de Batolf haut e cler.

---

[8] This passage is the main focus of J. Levy, "Musikinstrumente beim Gesang im mittelalterlichen Frankreich, auf Grund altfranzösischer Texte (bis zum 14. Jahrhundert)", *Zeitschrift für Romanische Philologie* 35 (1911), pp. 492-94. It has been discussed in numerous other places as well. Page comments upon the passage and provides references to other discussions of it in *Voices and Instruments*, pp. 4-5 and 92-107.

[9] T. Gérold cites these lines, suggesting that "chanter" means to play the melody of the lai on the harp, while "organer" refers to the addition of "une sorte de contrepoint", in *La Musique au moyen âge*, Classiques Français du Moyen Age (Paris, 1932), p. 375.

> Si cum sunt cil bretun. ditiel fait costumier.

> Then he takes up the harp, for he wants to tune it. God! Whoever then watched him [seeing] how he knew how to handle it, how he touched the strings, how he made them vibrate, sometimes he made them sing, other times play a counterpoint ... When he had done his tune, then he takes it up. And he makes the strings sound with all different tones. Everyone marvels that he knows how to manage it like that. And when he had done so, he begins to play the lai that Orains composed about Batolf, loudly and clearly, just as those Bretons are accustomed to doing it.
> (vv. 2830-33, 2836-41)

Although this is evidently an exceptionally skilled performer, the last line makes it clear that he does not actually depart from standard practice. First the musician plays an instrumental prelude; then he does the lai itself. And here, it seems that he first sings words, then repeats the melody on the harp:

> Apres en lestrument. fet les cordes suner.
> Tut issi cum en uoiz. laveit dit tut premier.
>
> Afterwards he made the strings sound in the instrument,
> just as he had first sung it with his voice.
> *(Horn, vv. 2842-43)*

As we will see in subsequent examples, lais were often described as being performed with simultaneous voice and instrument. But it may be that the musician would still sing a strophe with an instrumental accompaniment, then play that tune again at the end of the strophe. In fact, even a description of a lai being sung without any instruments still calls for antiphonal performance. The *Perceforest* (second quarter of the 14th century) describes an *a capella* performance of the *Lay des jeunes filles* by forty maidens in a pagan temple.[10] The singers are divided into two groups that perform alternate half strophes:[11]

> A ce s'acorderent les pucelles qui estoient en nombre quarante, dont les vingt se mirent en rencg en l'un des lez et les autres vingt a l'autre rencg. Sy commencerent celles du dextre lez a chanter la clause prumiere moult devotement et les autres l'autre clause du lay. Et ainsi le chanterent en la maniere qui s'ensieut tant doulcement que c'estoit droite melodie de les ouÿr.

> The maidens, who were forty in number, agreed to this; twenty of them lined up along one side and the other twenty on the other side. And those on the right side began to sing the first half strophe very devoutly and the others the next half strophe of the lay. And thus they sang it, in the manner that follows, so sweetly that it was a real treat to hear them. [The words of the lay follow.]
> (Bibl. Nat. fr. 109, fol. 288v)

Given this association of the lai with a pattern of alternating vocal and/or instrumental rendition, then there is no reason why a lai could not be sung with wind as well as with string instruments.

Just as the terms "dire" and "chanter" can be used for singing that is actually accompanied by playing, so terms like "sonner" and "jouer" can be used for playing that accompanies song. For this reason, descriptions of instrumental renditions should never be used as evidence for lack of vocal accompaniment unless it is completely clear that such is the case. In the *Perceforest*, for example, the author sometimes states explicitly that a performance includes both voice and instrument, as for example, "Quant

---

[10] The *Perceforest* is largely unedited, and my study of it is based on manuscript consultation. See J. Lods, *Le "Roman de Perceforest": Origines, composition, caractères, valeur et influence*, Société de Publications Romanes et Françaises 32 (Geneva and Lille, 1951); J.H.M. Taylor, ed., *Le Roman de Perceforest: première partie*, Textes Littéraires Français (Geneva, 1979). The lais have been published by J. Lods, ed., *Les Pièces lyriques du "Roman de Perceforest"*, Publications Romanes et Françaises 36 (Geneva and Lille, 1953). I discuss an account from the *Perceforest* of the composition and performance of two lais in my *From Song To Book: The Poetics of Writing in Old French Lyric and Lyrical Narrative Poetry* (Ithaca, N.Y., 1987), pp. 297-98; the passage in question is printed as Appendix C, pp. 347-50.

[11] Godefroy defines "clause" as "fin de vers, rime, puis groupe de rimes" (end of a poetic line, rhyme, then group of rhymes). The meaning of "demistrophe" is further borne out by Froissart, who describes the complainte of the *Espinette* as containing "cent clauses desparelles" (v. 2340) (one hundred different *clauses*). The poem contains neither a hundred lines (it has 800) nor a hundred stanzas (it has 500). But it does contain a hundred different rhymes, and each stanza is of the form aaabaaab/bbbabbba. "Clause" most likely refers to a rhyme unit, that is, to the half-stanza unit of the form xxxyxxxy.

la damoiselle eut son lay tres bien joué en la harpe et bien chanté de la bouche" (When the maiden had played her lai very well on the harp and sung it well with her mouth) (Bibl. Nat. fr. 346, fol. 372v). Quite often, however, the author avoids such wordiness – his purpose, after all, is not to provide a manual on performance practice – and simply uses the term "harper" or "jouer" to refer to a performance that must, to judge from the context, include voice as well. In the following passage, for example, the only verb used is "harper", yet the conversation that ensues between minstrel and audience after the performance focuses exclusively on the story told by the lai:

> Lors s'assist ... et prist sa harpe, et commença a harper le dit si hault et si bien que c'estoit une pitié a oÿr. Mais quant il l'eut harpé ... dist l'une des damoiselles au menestrel, "Dy moy, par amours, qui fist ce lay et qui te l'apprist?" – "Dame, dist il, il le m'aprist celluy qui le fist. Et celluy qui le fist est le chevalier a qui le fait est advenu que le lay devise."

> Then he sat down ... and took his harp, and began to play the poem on the harp so loudly and so well that it was a pity to hear. But when he had played it on the harp ... one of the maidens said to the minstrel, "Tell me, for love, who made that lai and who taught it to you?" – "Lady", he said, "he who made it taught it to me. And he who made it is the knight to whom the event described in the lai happened."
> (Bibl. Nat. fr. 346, fol. 236r)

In a subsequent reference back to this passage, the author states that "les pucelles l'avoient trouvé jouant son lay" (the girls had found him playing his lai) (Bibl. Nat. fr. 346, fol. 242v). Yet clearly the minstrel had been singing as well as playing, or the girls could not have known what "the event described in the lai" was.

One can easily gather other examples of passages in which the only form of performance explicitly mentioned is instrumental, yet in which voice is strongly implied. How, for example, could the jongleur in the twelfth-century *Amis et Amile* play a song "about love and friendship" unless he was singing as well as playing:

> Devant li vait un jouglers de Poitiers
> Qui le vielle d'ammors et d'ammistié.

VOICES AND INSTRUMENTS ... 81

> Before him went a jongleur from Poitiers, who played for
> him on the fiddle about love and friendship.
> (vv. 2325-26)

Similarly, the Breton fiddler in the early thirteenth-century *Anseïs de Carthage* tells a story:

> Mais il faisoit un Breton vïeler
> Le lai Guron, coment il dut finer;
> Par fine amor le covint devier.

> But he had a Breton play the lai of Guron on the fiddle, how
> he had to die; he had to die from perfect love.
> (vv. 6145-47)

Such examples show that we must not assume too quickly that instrumental performances by minstrels do not include voice.[12] Adenet le Roi, for example, describes a string trio in *Berte aus grans piés* (ca. 1272-74):

> Li uns fu vieleres, on l'apeloit Gautier,
> Et l'autres fu ha[r]peres, s'ot non maistre Garnier;
> L'autres fu leüteres, molt s'en sot bien aidier.

> One was a fiddler, he was called Gautier, and the other was a harpist, and his name was Garnier; the third was a lutenist, and he knew how to do well for himself.
> (vv. 294-96)

Might such a band have included singers? The suggestion of vocal accompaniment to a minstrels' band is especially strong, if tantalizingly short of conclusive, in the following passage from Froissart's Chronicles (1350):

---

[12] Page, "Performance of Songs", argues that the dance music provided by minstrels in the fifteenth-century romance *Cleriadus et Meliadice* is purely instrumental and that the "chansons" to which people dance after the minstrels stop playing are purely vocal; he makes a similar assertion with regard to the carol in *Voices and Instruments*, p. 83. While this may be true, it does not mean that minstrels could not have sung chansons with instrumental accompaniment in a different context. The distinction between "danser aux menestrex" and "danser aux chansons" entails two different styles of dance: that appropriate to the ceremonial music provided by professional minstrels and that conducted to the dancers' own singing. It is indeed unlikely that dancers would play instruments, or that loud wind bands would include singers. But these are not the only two kinds of possible performance situations.

> Et faisoit ses menestrelz corner devant lui une danse d'Alemagne, que messire Jehan Chandos, qui là estoit, avoit nouvellement raporté. Et encores par esbatement il faisoit ledit chevalier chanter avoech ses menestrelz, et y prendoit grant plaisance.
>
> And [the King of England] had his minstrels play for him on loud winds a German dance, which Sir John Chandos, who was there, had recently brought back. And then for entertainment he had the said knight sing with his minstrels, and he took great pleasure in it.
> *(Chronicles, IV, p. 91)*

Were the minstrels still playing instruments – perhaps a selection of softer winds – when the knight sang with them? The possibility cannot be ruled out.

This last example raises a second interpretive difficulty often encountered in descriptions of musical performance: when a passage includes references to both singing and playing, are these activities simultaneous or sequential? This problem arises in the ubiquitous phrases of the type "And then the minstrels sang and played their instruments". Ambiguity is often no less present even in more elaborately spelled out descriptions, as in this passage from the early thirteenth-century romance *Blancandin*:

> Semonez moi les jugleors
> Et si mandez les harpeors;
> Les harpes ovuec les vïeles
> Orra on bien et les queroles.
> Ne vueil mais qu'il soient en pes,
> Et me diront sonez et les.
>
> Summon me the jongleurs, and also call the harpists; we will well hear the harps with the fiddles, and the carols. I don't want them ever to be still, and they will sing me songs and lais.
> (vv. 4263-68)

Evidently the king plans to listen to harp and fiddle ensembles; will the singing of "sonez" and lais take place along with the instrumental music or separately? The contemporary *Bueve de Hantone* tells us that a lai certainly could be sung to the accompaniment of harp and fiddle:

> Lors commencha Josïenne a chanter,
> Notes et lais moult bien a vïeler,
> Li vius Soybaus comencha a harper,
> Bien se commenchent lor son a acorder.

> Then Josienne began to sing, to play notes and lais on the fiddle; old Soybaus began to play the harp; their melodies began to harmonize well.
> (vv. 12087-90)

Thanks to the clarifying statement in v. 12090, we can be reasonably sure that the chain of verbs, chanter – vïeler – harper, represents simultaneous activity. We also know from another contemporary poem, *Gilles de Chyn*, that a "son" could be sung by two minstrels accompanying themselves on fiddles:

> Li vïeleur .i. son d'amour
> A haute vois mout cler cantoient,
> O les vïelez s'acordoient.
>
> The fiddlers sang a love song aloud and very clearly; they sang in tune with the fiddles.
> (vv. 460-62)

Finally, the *Roman de Silence* (second half of the 13th century) provides one unequivocal reference to the use of harp and fiddle to accompany the voice:

> Dont prent sa harpe et sa viiele,
> Si note avoec a sa vois biele.
>
> Then she takes her harp and her fiddle, and she plays on them to [the accompaniment of] her beautiful voice.
> *(Silence,* vv. 3521-22)

Such supporting examples do not, of course, prove that the performance in *Blancandin* is also one involving mixed vocal and instrumental music. But they do show that such performances took place, and there is no reason why the less precise descriptions could not have referred to such practices.

We encounter a similar problem in the prose romance *Paris et Vienne* (ca. 1400). The anonymous author gives us a description of Paris and his friend Edardo serenading Vienne that seems at first glance to be extremely precise, yet upon closer analysis eludes complete resolution.[13] The two young men appear under Vienne's window,

---

[13] On *Paris et Vienne* see Brown, "Instruments and Voices", pp. 102 ff.; Page, "Performance of Songs", p. 445-46.

> faisant oubades de leurs chanssons, quar ilz chantoient souveraynement bien, et puys jouoyent de leur instrumens chanssons mellodyoses, come ceulx qui de celluy mestier estoient les maistres.
>
> serenading her with their songs, for they sang supremely well, and then played on their instruments melodious songs, like those who are masters at this profession.
>
> *(Paris et Vienne, p. 77)*

At first glance one might easily believe that this passage draws a clear distinction between vocal and instrumental music: Paris and his companion first sang and then played. Such is Christopher Page's reading of the passage: "There is more than a hint of such a separation of vocal and instrumental music in *Paris et Vienne* where the hero and his companion, Edardo, sing and *then* play beneath Vienne's window."[14]

But it must be remembered that the very term "jouer" can be a shorthand way of referring to a performance that does, in fact, include voice as well. Perhaps the passage could be summarized like this: "they serenaded her with chansons, for they were excellent singers; and then they went on to other pieces involving instrumental accompaniment, for they could play beautifully too, like real masters."

In any case, vocal and instrumental music in *Paris et Vienne* are somehow linked. Performance is consistently referred to as "chanter et jouer" or "chanter et sonner". The account begins to sound suspiciously as though the singing and the playing really are two inseparable parts of one and the same activity: "ilz commensserent a chanter et a sonner ... et quant ilz eurent chanté et soné tout a leur plaisir ..." (they began to sing and to play ... and when they had sung and played all they wanted ...) (p. 79). In one source, the terms are reversed, showing at least that the order of singing and playing seemingly specified in the first passage cited above was not inviolable: "ilz commensserent a sonner de leurs instruments et a chanter" (they began to play their instruments and to sing) (cited by Kaltenbacher). The construction "chanter et sonner" closely resembles the wording found elsewhere in texts where the performance surely does involve voice with instrumental accompaniment. In the *Lai de l'Epine* (first half 13th century), for example, we are told:

---

[14] "Performance of Songs", p. 445, emphasis his.

> Le lai escouterent d'Aelis
> Que uns Ireis sone en sa rote,
> Molt doucement le *chante et note.*

> They listened to the Lai of Aelis, which an Irishman plays on his rote; very sweetly *he sings and plays* it.
> (*Epine*, vv. 176-78, emphasis mine)

In light of the foregoing, it seems quite plausible to interpret the text as saying that Paris and Edardo began with vocal music and then proceeded to accompany their singing on instruments. This possibility is supported by analogy with other texts in which vocal and instrumental portions of a performance are distinguished. We have seen that the anonymous author of the *Perceforest* sometimes uses the construction "harper + chanter de bouche" (play on the harp + sing with the mouth) to describe the performance of lais. In a similar vein the author of the *Tristan en prose* commonly employs the construction "dit + chant" in reference to the performance of lais, as: "Quant le harpeur a tout son lay finé et de dit et de chant" (when the harpist had finished his whole lay, both words and melody) (Bibl. Nat. fr. 336, fol. 2*r*).[15] Since it would be very odd to distinguish in this way between the words and the tune to which the voice sings them, I feel that the construction "dit + chant" most likely refers to the coupling of vocal and instrumental music. Voice and instrument are, after all, distinct components of a performance, even if they are simultaneous during most or even all of it. As we have seen, there is some evidence that the performer of a lai would begin with an instrumental prelude. Such a practice is very explicitly described in one instance in the *Tristan en prose:*

> Lors comence le lay en tele maniere, mes avant fist l'entree,
> puis le commença issi: *Aprés ce que je vi victoire.*

---

[15] One version of the *Tristan en prose* has now been edited in its entirety by R. L. Curtis, *Le Roman de Tristan en prose,* I (Munich, 1963); II (Leiden, 1976); III (Woodbridge, Suffolk, and Dover, N.H., 1985). The text exists in other versions, however, and I have based my study on manuscript consultation. See also E. Baumgartner, *"Le Tristan en prose": Essai d'interprétation d'un roman médiéval* (Geneva, 1975); E. Löseth, *Le Roman en prose de Tristan, le roman de Palamède et la compilation de Rusticien de Pise, analyse critique d'après les manuscrits de Paris* (Paris, 1890). On the lais, see J. Lods, "Les parties lyriques du Tristan en prose", *Bulletin Bibliographique de la Société Internationale Arthurienne* 1955, pp. 73-78; J. Maillard, "Lais avec notation dans le Tristan en prose", *Mélanges Rita Lejeune* (Gembloux, 1969), pp. 1347-64. The lais have been published by T. Fotitch and R. Stein, eds., *Les Lais du roman de Tristan en prose,* Münchener Romanistische Arbeiten 38 (Munich, 1974).

> Then she began the lai in such a manner, but first she did the prelude, then she began it thus: *After I saw victory.*
> (Bibl. Nat. fr. 772, fol. 285v)

At another point, though, the narrator stresses (perhaps because it is atypical?) that the harpist begins to sing along with the harp without any instrumental prelude: "Et li harperers comence maintenant le chant et le dit, tot ensemble" (And the harpist now begins the tune and the words, all together) (Bibl. Nat. fr. 12599, fol. 194r). In MS Bibl. Nat. fr. 335, the text reads "le chant et le dit avec" (the tune and the words along with it) (fol. 415v). Still another lai performance is described in terms parallel to those of the *Paris et Vienne* passage: "Et quant il a bien atrempee, il commence son chant et puis son dit" (When he has tuned [the harp] well, he begins his tune and then his words) (Bibl. Nat. fr. 335, 217v). Surely what is at issue here is not an instrumental version of the entire lai followed by a separate vocal rendition, but simply an instrumental opening followed by a rendition with voice and harp. The performance is made up of two kinds of sound, vocal *(dit)* and instrumental *(chant)*; but these are essentially simultaneous and closely linked elements. The unity of vocal and instrumental components is stressed in the narrator's closing reference to the performance: "Quant il a parfiné ses vers et harpés au mieulx qu'il scet" (when he has finished his verses and played them on the harp the best he knows how) (Bibl. Nat. fr. 335, fol. 218r). Similarly, the maiden who played the "entree" is said afterwards to have "son lay si bien chanté et noté si doucement" (so well sung and so sweetly played her lai) (Bibl. Nat. fr. 772, fol. 285v). These closing comments cannot be descriptions of a temporal sequence of singing, then playing, for the narrative account of the performance made it quite explicit that the performer first played and then sang.

Again, these supporting examples do not tell us definitely what the author of *Paris et Vienne* intended. But we have seen that the term "jouer" need not exclude voice; that the term "puis" could be used to distinguish not two entirely separate pieces, but simply two moments within one and the same piece; and that a seeming distinction of voice and instrument could be a way of articulating two interacting components of the performance. If this analysis does not arrive at a complete resolution of ambiguous passages, it has at least shown the care with which such passages must be read.

VOICES AND INSTRUMENTS ... 87

Reading Performance Descriptions, II: Social and Literary Analysis

Once we have decided what a given passage literally says, it remains to analyze the description as a record of performance practice. A number of factors must be taken into account. We need to know not merely whether a given performer was singing, playing, or both, but more precisely what kinds of performers (aristocratic amateurs or minstrels) would be most likely to engage in these activities; what kinds of performances (private or public, spontaneous or formal) a given practice appears in; what kinds of pieces (narrative songs, trouvère songs, dance music, etc.) are associated with a given practice and with a given type of performer; and so on. Finally, it is necessary to consider the narrative function of the performance passage within the frame text, and the extent to which literary conventions, rather than contemporary performance practice, might determine the particular details given by the author.

The categorization of performance descriptions according to the social class of the performer reveals one striking fact: most accounts of instrumental music involve not aristocrats but minstrels, aristocrats disguised as minstrels, and shepherds. Although the various wind and percussion instruments that figure in the pastourelle may correspond somewhat to instruments used in the medieval countryside, the musicians who populate the pastourelle surely reflect aristocratic stereotypes of the amorous, flute-playing rustic rather than actual realities of medieval peasant life. With certain exceptions, however, the behavior of aristocratic protagonists and their minstrels is probably closer to the truth; at the very least, these figures embody the ideals that aristocrats held about themselves and the musicians they employed. It is with these two classes of performer that the following discussion will be concerned.

The aristocratic heroes and heroines of medieval literature sing very frequently, and occasionally play instruments; but they almost never do both at once. The primary exception is the aristocratic penchant for playing lais on the harp. Thomas d'Angleterre, for example, described Iseut's rendition of the lai of Guiron:

> La dame chante dulcement,
> La voiz acorde a l'estrument.

> The queen sings sweetly, the voice accords with the instrument.
> *(Tristan,* vv. 843-44)

However, these aristocratic harpers of lais are nearly always set in a distant, Breton past. The most famous aristocratic harpists are Tristan and Iseut, but there are others; one encounters similar figures, for example, in *Horn* and *Galeran de Bretagne*. The narrator of *Horn* even comments on the skill of the Breton lords and ladies for singing and playing lais on the harp, implying that this practice may no longer be current:

> A cel tens sorent tuit. harpe bien manier.
> Cum plus fu gentilz hom. e plus sout del mester.
>
> At that time everyone knew well how to handle a harp. The more noble a man was, the more he knew of this art.
> *(Horn,* vv. 2824-25)

Whether or not real thirteenth- and fourteenth-century lords and ladies actually learned to accompany themselves on the harp, lords and ladies in thirteenth- and fourteenth-century French literature generally did not unless they belonged to this slightly exotic past. Indeed, there is some evidence that the practice of accompanying one's own singing on an instrument was perceived specifically as an art cultivated by minstrels. In *Aucassin et Nicolette* (ca. 1175-1225), it is not entirely clear whether Nicolette is secretly learning a minstrel's art when she learns to play the fiddle, or taking up an accepted aristocratic pastime. We are told only that "Ele quist une viele, s'aprist a vieler" (she sought out a fiddle, and learned to play it) (38: vv. 13-14) in preparation for her plan to seek Aucassin, disguised as a minstrel. In any case, it is as a minstrel that she sings the tale of Aucassin and Nicolette to the accompaniment of her fiddle. In the slightly later *Roman de la violette* (early 13th century), it is suggested more explicitly that the act of singing and playing simultaneously is proper to the minstrel and not to the aristocrat. The knight Gerart sings love songs on numerous occasions. But when disguised as a minstrel, he must perform a *chanson de geste*. On this occasion he reflects,

> Faire m'estuet, quant l'ai empris,
> Chou dont je ne sui mie apris:
> Chanter et vïeler ensemble.

VOICES AND INSTRUMENTS ...   89

> Since I have undertaken it, I must do that which I never learned to do: sing and play the fiddle at the same time.
> *(Violette*, vv. 1401-3)

As Christopher Page points out, a slight change in punctuation – easily justified, since the medieval text is not punctuated at all – would change the meaning of the text, suggesting that it was formal public performance rather than instrumental accompaniment to song that Gerart had never learned.[16] The *chanson de geste* itself belongs to the repertoire of the minstrel and not to that of the aristocratic amateur. Still, this is the only one of Gerart's many songs to have instrumental accompaniment. However we punctuate the text, there remains a strong association of simultaneous singing and playing with the profession and repertoire of the minstrel. Aristocrats do sometimes play instruments in contemporary settings, but then there is usually no mention of singing. In the late thirteenth-century *Tournois de Chauvency*, for example, an aristocratic lady plays a fiddle as accompaniment for a masquerade dance staged by two other maidens (*Tournois*, vv. 2547 ff.). Since the author gives the words to so many refrains sung both formally and informally during the festivities, it is probable that the omission of any reference to singing in this instance really does mean that the music was purely instrumental.

Does this mean that aristocrats really never, or hardly ever, did sing and play at the same time? Certainly we would expect an aristocratic amateur to perform in a less virtuosic or professional manner than a trained minstrel or chapel singer; perhaps the combination of voice and instrument was a hallmark of the professional. But what would this mean: that aristocrats performed a repertoire wholly different from that of the minstrels or that they performed a shared or partially shared repertoire without combining voices and instruments? These questions must be answered with extreme caution. I will begin here with a survey of the repertoire associated with aristocratic and professional performers respectively. My remarks, as always, are based entirely on literary sources.

With the exception of the *chansons de toile* sung by ladies and maidens in their chambers, and the lais sung by Breton aristocrats, narrative songs belong to a minstrel/jongleur repertoire. Minstrels also performed lais, as well as *chansons de geste* and unspecified *contes*. And narrative songs seem

---

[16] Page, *Voices and Instruments*, pp. 188-90.

always to be sung or recited to the accompaniment of instruments.[17] The lai in particular could be performed with a wide variety of instrumentation. We have already seen numerous examples of lais played on harps, as well as on fiddles or rotes, and even on flutes. The variety of possible instrumentation is summed up in Wace's *Roman de Brut:*

> Lais de vïeles, lais de rotes,
> Lais de harpes, lais de fresteles.
>
> Lais on fiddles, lais on rotes, lais
> on harps, lais on freteles.
> *(Brut,* vv. 10548-49)

There was evidently considerable flexibility in the instrumentation that could be used for the ubiquitous lai. To what extent, if any, the different instruments might team up to perform lais as small ensembles is unfortunately impossible to determine from this passage, as is the way that the text of a lai would be handled (if at all) by someone playing it on a wind instrument. But this passage and others like it are nonetheless important reminders of the fluidity of medieval performance practices: we must be careful not to assume that a given text prescribes *the* way that a particular piece would be performed. Even the same lai could be performed with different instrumentation. Gerbert de Montreuil's continuation of *Perceval* (ca. 1230) refers to the performance of a "lai Goron" on *estives* (see *Tristan ménestrel,* p. 526); the early thirteenth-century *Anseïs de Carthage* mentions the performance of a "lai Guron" on fiddle (vv. 6145-46, cited above); and the *Roman de Silence* (ca. 1250) refers to a performance of a series of lais, including a rendition of "Gueron" on harp *(Silence,* v. 2762). Iseut, in the passage cited above, sings the lai of "Guirun" to a harp. These are almost certainly all versions of the same lai.[18] As Maillart states in the Prologue to the *Comte d'Anjou,* cited above, each performer builds up his repertoire and chooses his instrumentation, "chascun selonc s'entencion."

---

[17] Page concludes from his study of *Guillaume de Dole* that instrumental accompaniment is limited to songs of the "Lower Style" and has a "strong link with dance, with narrative and with refrain-form" *(Voices and Instruments,* p. 38).

[18] On the *Lai de Guiron,* see G.E. Brereton, "A Thirteenth-Century List of French Lays and Other Narrative Poems", *Modern Language Review* 45 (1950), pp. 40-45, entry no. 15; and J. Bédier, ed., *Le Roman de Tristan* by Thomas, I, Société des Anciens Textes Français (Paris, 1902), pp. 51, 52-53.

Chansons de geste are usually sung to the fiddle, as in the passages cited above from *Moniage Guillaume* and the *Violette;* one can find other similar examples. But they could also be sung to the hurdy-gurdy:

> On appelle en France cymphonie ung instrument dont les aveugles jouent en chantant les chansons de geste.
>
> In France "cifonie" [hurdy-gurdy] is the term for an instrument that blind people play in singing *chansons de geste.*
> (J. Corbechon, "Propriétés des choses" (dated 1372); cited in Godefroy, s.v. "cifonie")

Obviously, the blind people in question sing for their living, and so can be included in the class of jongleurs. Various stringed instruments are also associated with the performance of other sorts of narratives. In *Claris et Laris* (ca. 1268), for example, an unspecified narrative includes refrains played on the fiddle:[19]

> La escoutoient bonement
> .l. conteor, qui lor contoit
> Une chançon et si notoit
> Ses refrez en un viele.
>
> There they were listening well to a story-teller, who told [narrated] them a song and also played its refrains on a fiddle.
> (vv. 9940-43)

And in a fourteenth-century translation of *Pamphile et Galatée,* the old lady tells the tale of Aristotle's seduction, adding, "Or n'i a villain qui n'en rote" (Now there isn't a peasant who does not play on the rote about it) *(Pamphile,* v. 1783). Again "villain" probably refers to lower-class jongleurs; in any case it certainly excludes aristocrats.

---

[19] It is hard to say exactly what this narrative song with refrains was. Perhaps the "refrains" are simply instrumental interludes between the *laisses* of a *chanson de geste* or the stanzas of a lai. Assuming that they are actual refrains with words, the song could have been a *chanson de toile.* Or it may have been some other sort of sung or chanted narrative with regularly recurring refrains that could be played on a fiddle. There is a hint of such a practice in the *Chastelaine de Saint Gille,* a stanzaic fabliau with a different refrain at the end of each stanza. One of these is introduced: "S'en doi bien dire par réson / Les vers que j'ai tant violé: / J'ai trové le ni de pie ..." (Thus I should well and rightly sing the verses that I have fiddled so often: I found the magpie's nest) (vv. 271-73). Page suggests that the piece in question may have been a rondeau *(Voices and Instruments,* p. 84); but to my mind the verb "conter" implies a narrative song.

The fact that these narrative songs are nearly always specified as being sung to instrumental accompaniment poses no contradiction, then, to our earlier impression that a combined vocal and instrumental performance was the domain of the minstrel. Indeed, this impression is supported in *Guillaume de Dole,* where *chansons de toile* are performed in different situations. When Lïenor and her mother sing the songs of Aude and Doon, Bele Aye, and Bele Doe for the entertainment of the emperor's envoy, there is no instrumental accompaniment. At a later point, however, the song of Bele Aiglentine is sung by a man:

> Uns bachelers de Normendie
> chevauchoit la grande chaucie,
> commença cesti a chanter,
> si la fist Jouglet vïeler.
>
> A young man from Normandy was riding along the great path; he began to sing this, and he had Jouglet play it on the fiddle.
> *(Guillaume de Dole,* vv. 2231-34)

The Norman may be an aristocrat, but he is only the singer; the instrumental accompaniment is provided by Jouglet, the emperor's minstrel. All *chanson de toile* performances described in the text are informal; what distinguishes them is the presence of the minstrel in the latter. The passage is a very suggestive indication of the different ways that the *chanson de toile* could be rendered by different types of performers.

Monophonic love songs, such as trouvère and troubadour songs, rondeaux and virelais, and refrains, seem at first glance to belong to an aristocratic repertoire. When such songs appear as lyric insertions in romances, they are virtually always either placed in the mouth of an amorous aristocrat, or sung at the aristocrat's request by his resident minstrel, in celebration of the aristocrat's love affair. They are never accompanied by instruments in any of these instances. But does this mean that such songs really were performed only in spontaneous, purely vocal renditions? Might not the "son d'amour" sung to instrumental accompaniment by the two fiddlers in *Gilles de Chyn* be of the trouvère repertoire?[20] The early thirteenth-century monk Gautier de Coinci, whose songs are closely modelled on trouvère songs in

---

[20] Page cites *Gille de Chyn* and points out that there is no way to tell whether the "son d'amour" is of the High Style or the Lower Style *(Voices and Instruments,* p. 33).

form, language, imagery, and in the incorporation of secular refrains, introduces these songs with references to fiddle and lyre:[21]

> Or veil atant traire ma lire
> Et atemprer veil ma vïele
> Se chanterai de la pucele.

> Now I want to get out my lyre and I want to tune my fiddle, thus I will sing of the virgin.
> *(Miracles,* I, Book 1, Second Prologue, vv. 56-58)

> Ma vïele
> Vïeler vieut un biau son.

> My fiddle wants to play a pretty song.
> *(Miracles,* III, Book 2, Ch. 8, vv. 1-2)

Perhaps the "rule" of vocal performance by aristocrats or by their minstrels, in private spontaneous performances, of trouvère songs, is not in fact universal, though it may indeed have been the most common practice. I will return to this point below, in the discussion of literary conventions.

It is extremely difficult to find clear references of any kind to the performance of polyphonic music. One of the few unmistakable references to polyphonic performance is a humorous passage in Gace de la Buigne's *Roman des deduis* (composed 1359-77), in which the baying of a pack of hunting dogs is described as polyphony:

> Les uns vont chantans le motet,
> Les autres font double hoquet.
> Les plus grans chantent la teneur,

---

[21] Page argues that the references to musical instruments in Gautier de Coinci's songs do not reflect possible instrumental accompaniment of such pieces, but are rather imitations of the references to bards in Latin poetry; he also cites the symbolism of musical instruments in Biblical exegesis and in much medieval religious writing *(Voices and Instruments,* pp. 191-93). Yet Page also cites Gautier's version of the Roc-Amadour miracle, in which a minstrel honors the Virgin by singing and accompanying himself on the fiddle *(Ibid.,* pp. 193-94). While Gautier's allusions to fiddle and lyre may indeed carry literary and theological reverberations, and while there is no reason to assume that Gautier himself played either of these instruments, I see no reason why these texts could not be taken as evidence that trouvère songs and their religious imitations and contrafacta were sometimes sung to instrumental accompaniment.

> Les autres la contreteneur.
> Ceulx qui ont la plus clere gueule
> Chantent le tresble sans demeure,
> Et les plus petis le quadouble
> En faisant la quinte sur double.
> Les uns font semithon mineur,
> Les autres semithon majeur,
> Diapenthé, diapazon,
> Les autres dyathesseron.
>
> Some go singing the motet, the others do a double hoquet. The largest sing the tenor, the others the contratenor. Those who have the clearest voice sing the treble without hesitation, and the smallest the fourth part, doing the fifth above the duplum. Some do a minor semitone, the others a major semitone, diapente, diapason, the others diatessaron.
> *(Deduis,* vv. 8081-92)

As the argument is expanded, the dogs are credited with "singing" not only motets and double hoquets, but also rondeaux. Their music is said to be even more beautiful than the *respons* or *alleluye* of the royal chapel.

Though obviously playful, the passage does shed a certain light on the performance of court polyphony. First of all, the plethora of technical terms, together with the comparison to royal chapel musicians, support an identification of polyphony as proper to highly trained, specialized musicians. Secondly, the description refers pretty clearly to a purely vocal rendition of motets or other polyphonic compositions. Not only does the author find no difficulty in conceiving of the mixture of dogs' "voices" as polyphony; but also the definition of polyphony offered in support of the claims being made for dogs' musical abilities stipulates vocal performance:

> Et est verité que motés,
> Balades ne doubles hoqués
> Ne sont rien, bien en sui recors,
> Que des chans de divers accors,
> Mesurés par proporcions
> Pour faire plus gracieux sons,
> De pluseurs chantés par mestrie
> De doulce et plaisant melodie.
>
> And it is true that motets, balades and double hoquets are nothing, of this I'm sure, other than melodies of different harmonies, measured by proportions so as to make more graceful songs, sung by several through mastery of sweet and pleasant melody.
> *(Deduis,* vv. 10603-10)

VOICES AND INSTRUMENTS ...

It is because "chiens ont vois si flexible" (dogs have such flexible voices) (v. 10632) that they are capable of song. Evidently, the a capella rendition of polyphonic balades, rondeaux, hoquets and motets was sufficiently well established that the author could take it for granted in building his fanciful case for dogs.

Most other allusions to polyphony are much less explicit than the foregoing. One can find references to things that might be polyphonic; the problem is that it is frequently impossible to determine whether the passage refers to a monophonic group performance or to polyphony. Contrasting with the emphasis on the voice in the *Roman des deduis,* for example, are the many descriptions of minstrels playing in ensembles, some of which probably refer to instrumental polyphony. We have seen the trio of fiddle, harp and lute mentioned in *Berte aus grans piés* (vv. 294-96). In the *Roman d'Eledus et Serene* (first half of the 14th century), minstrels play in ensembles, although instruments are not specified:

> Et menestriers de maintes manieres
> Qui de leurs istrumens jouoient,
> Et tous ensemble si s'acordoient.

> And minstrels of all kinds who played their instruments, and thus they harmonized all together.
> *(Eledus et Serene,* vv. 4398-4400)

Finally, there are a few passages – some more explicit than others – that suggest the combination of voices and instruments in polyphony. In the citation above from the *Fonteinne amoureuse,* for example, the duke could be singing to a polyphonic accompaniment of horns and rotes, though we cannot be certain. Similarly, the songs alluded to in *Renart le contrefait* (1319) might be polyphonic pieces with instrumental settings:

> Plus ameroit quatre garchons
> De nuit chanter quatre chanssons
> Avec la trompe et la guisterne.

> He [the average minstrel] would prefer four boys to sing four songs, with trumpet and gittern, at night.
> *(Renart,* vv. 36135-37)

The early thirteenth-century *Durmart le Galois* contains a passage that may be a humorous parody of polyphony. A malevolent knight arrives at court, accompanied by five dwarves:

> Li doi nain vienent flajolant,
> Et li troi vienent tot chantant
> A grosses vois sens point tenir.
> ...
> Les vois ont grosses et bruians,
> Et si n'apointent riens lor chans.
>
> Two of the dwarves came playing flutes, and three came singing in raucous voices without harmonizing at all ... They had raucous and noisy voices, and their respective tunes didn't correspond at all.
> (vv. 10033-35, 10053-54)

This cacophonous "performance" is clearly a violation of good musical taste. Since the narrator stresses that the problem lay in the harshness of the voices and the lack of harmony among parts, we can infer that an ensemble of three singers and two flute players would not be unusual in itself, and that they could be expected to sing or play melodic lines which did harmonize. Still, we do not know whether such a performance would involve actual polyphony or merely a group rendition of a monophonic piece.

The mid-fourteenth century *Voie d'Enfer et de Paradis* includes several descriptions of both angelic and lascivious music. While these tend to be vague, there is one that suggests the rendition by voice and instruments of a polyphonic rondeau: we are told that the angels were

> Jüans de flagols, de fretel,
> D'orghes, harpes, et vïeloient,
> Si glorïeusement cantoient
> Li un, li autre respondoient
> De la Vierge un trés douch rondel.
>
> Playing flutes and fretels, organs, harps, and they were playing the fiddle; thus some were singing gloriously, the others were responding, a very sweet rondeau about the Virgin.
> (*Voie d'Enfer*, vv. 3605-09)

The profusion of voices and instruments, and the sumptuous nature of the performance, raise the very distinct possibility of polyphony.

VOICES AND INSTRUMENTS ...

In a more clearly worded passage in the *Roman de la rose* (1270s), Pygmalion sings motets while accompanying himself on the portative organ:

> Orgues i ra bien maniables,
> a une seule main portables,
> ou il meïsme soufle et touche,
> et chante avec a pleine bouche
> motet ou treble ou teneüre.
>
> There are organs easily handled, which can be held in a single hand, which he himself pumps and plays, and sings along with a full voice, motet or triplum or tenor.
> *(Rose,* vv. 21007-11)

As the text stands here, it is possible to read it as a monophonic rendition, doubled in voice and organ, of one part of a motet: the motetus part, or the triplum, or the tenor. In fact, the term "motet" is used for monophonic refrains in the contemporary *Renart le nouvel*. However, Langlois in his edition gives the variant reading "motet a treble ou teneüre" [motet with triplum or tenor], which implies that Pygmalion was singing one part of a polyphonic motet and playing the rest on the organ.

In the *Dit de la panthère d'amours* (ca. 1300), voices and instruments combine in the rendition of chansons, motets and conductus. Describing the God of Love's entourage, the narrator lists numerous string, wind, and percussion instruments, and adds:

> Instrumens de toutes manieres
> Y avoit, et a vois plenieres
> Chantoient cil qui les menoient,
> Et qui bien faire le savoient,
> Chançonetes moult cointement,
> Et moult très envoisieement
> Chantoient motès et conduis.
>
> There was every kind of instrument, and those who were playing them and who knew how to do it well were singing little songs most prettily with full voices, and very very skillfully they were singing motets and conductus.
> *(Panthère,* vv. 165-171)

The profusion of voices and instruments would certainly lend themselves to polyphony, and the repeated emphasis on the skill of the musicians indicates that this is no run-of-the-mill performance.

None of these passages, with the possible exception of that from the *Fonteinne amoureuse*, involve the performance of polyphony by aristocratic amateur musicians. Even in the *Fonteinne*, the aristocrat is of extremely high standing, he is not playing instruments, and the performance is informal. In the other cases, we find "boys", associated with the minstrel class; minstrels; dwarves, parodic figures for the minstrels employed by aristocrats; angels; Pygmalion, a mythological figure of unsurpassed artistic skills who is about to experience a miracle; and the followers of the God of Love, in an allegorical dream vision. Naturally this alone does not prove that aristocratic amateurs never performed polyphony, but it does certainly suggest that, in the thirteenth and fourteenth centuries, polyphony was in a special class. The same can be said for the ability to sing and play an instrument at the same time. If indeed the young men of *Paris et Vienne* were accompanying themselves instrumentally, and especially if they were performing polyphony, this could explain the extreme wonder and admiration expressed by those who heard them "chanter et sonner".

Literary texts, then, make a relatively consistent distinction between narrative songs (performed by professional musicians, with instruments); the Breton lai (performed by past Breton aristocrats and by professionals of all kinds, usually to instrumental accompaniment); monophonic refrains, trouvère or troubadour songs, and *formes fixes* (usually performed by aristocratic amateurs without instruments); and polyphonic motets and *formes fixes* (performed either with or without instruments by minstrels, clerics, and other exceptional or other-worldly figures). How can we determine the extent to which this division corresponds to historical reality? Since my concern here is with literary texts, I will approach the question from the perspective of literary criticism: what role do narrative strategy and literary convention play in determining descriptions of performance? We have already touched on one example of the influence of literary conventions in descriptions of performance in the case of the Breton lai. In fact, when the *Perceforest* describes wandering minstrels who perform quasi-narrative lais on the harp and supplement their song with a narrative account of the adventure that gave rise to the lai, this does not necessarily mean that such was the predominant musical reality in fourteenth-century France. The text is deliberately archaizing, looking back to a sort of pre-history before the Christianization of Britain and imitating the *Tristan en prose*, a text that also looks to the past and, moreover, pre-dates the

Perceforest by about a century. Such texts are no doubt an accurate reflection of the status of the medieval minstrel as source of both news and entertainment. Other details, such as the minstrel's interactions with the aristocratic audience and his or her ability to combine vocal and instrumental performance, may well also reflect fourteenth-century practices; and these texts are in any case invaluable aids in mastering the vocabulary and syntax of Old French performance descriptions. In terms of information about specific poetic and musical genres, however, these accounts undoubtedly tell us less about the performance of lais in fourteenth-century France than about fourteenth-century notions of old-fashioned Breton musical practices.[22]

We must exercise a similar caution in interpreting other literary examples. I have stated, for example, that trouvère and troubadour songs never seem to be sung in formal, public performances. They are usually sung by lovestruck aristocrats, in moments of private meditation on the joys or the sorrows of love. Sometimes, as in a few instances in *Guillaume de Dole*, they are sung by minstrels in a private setting, for the sole benefit of the minstrel's aristocratic patron. Yet we cannot assume that love songs of this type were never performed in formal public presentations. After all, many troubadours and trouvères were minstrels themselves or even tradesmen, who must have encountered the songs in performance situations unlike those recorded in the romances. And one can find allusions to the performance of such songs by minstrels. I have already mentioned the love songs performed by the fiddlers in *Gilles de Chyn,* which may have belonged to the trouvère repertoire. Less ambiguous is the *Castelain de Couci* (late 13th century), where there are occasional references to the Châtelain's songs being performed far and wide, and one explicit statement that his songs were performed by a local minstrel. But these are offhand statements. The songs themselves are inserted into the text in non-performing contexts: the Châtelain composes a song while riding home from a tournament, or on

---

[22] Page similarly concludes that descriptions of harp-playing Bretons probably owe more to literary convention than to contemporary social practices, but also suggests that such conventions may have been powerful enough to influence performance practice at times *(Voices and Instruments,* pp. 102-7). Page's discussion of these texts is most useful, but one of his assertions – that these Breton harpers of lais are always courtly amateurs *(Ibid,* p. 97) – must be modified: both the *Tristan en prose* and the *Perceforest,* to name just two examples, contain numerous descriptions, often quite detailed, of professional minstrels singing lais to the accompaniment of the harp.

his way to or from a meeting with his lady. No medieval writer states that minstrels did not perform love songs or that these songs were not played on instruments. But when these songs are explicitly identified, through lyric insertions, they appear without instruments and usually in the mouth of an aristocrat. When minstrels "sing and play instruments", their repertoire is either the traditional minstrel repertoire of narrative lais and *chansons de geste,* a vague repertoire of "sons", "vers" and "chansonettes" which could include almost anything, or entirely unidentified.

The treatment of trouvère songs, as well as rondeaux, ballades, and other courtly love songs, is as much a function of narrative strategy as of performance practice. These songs are introduced into the narrative for particular reasons, among the most important of which is the desire for greater subjectivity in the development of the amorous hero or heroine. In the later thirteenth and fourteenth centuries, the lyric insertion often fulfills the role of the internal monologue of twelfth-century romance. When love songs are sung in public settings, as is often the case with dance refrains, rondeaux and virelais, lyric insertions may enable a pair of lovers to exchange secret messages in public by singing songs that carry a special meaning for the two of them (and, of course, for the reader). At other times, the refrains allow for general flirtation, as men and ladies alternately sing refrains in a sort of communal dialogue. Sometimes the songs motivate the plot, as when a character hears a song sung by another character, realizes the latter's amorous intentions, and reacts to further or to thwart these intentions. All of these narrative functions of lyric insertions require that the song be sung by the aristocratic protagonist or, at the very least, by a minstrel who speaks for his patron. There is little reason why a medieval romance author would want to focus on the amorous sentiments of a minstrel, and it would serve no narrative purpose to give all the texts of songs performed by minstrels at court festivities. For this reason the professional performances are glossed over fairly rapidly, in sketchy descriptions that evoke a general atmosphere of courtly celebration. And considerable attention is paid to songs, and in particular to the words of songs, that in some cases are hardly even performances at all, any more than the elaborate songs sung by lovers in a Broadway musical can be considered performances – much less reflections of daily life in twentieth-century America – within the context of the play. It is scarcely surprising that musical instruments are not mentioned in these informal "performances". While aristocrats undoubtedly did sing the current popular songs in both public and private, the overwhelming emphasis on this particular type of performance in literary texts should not lead us to believe that it is the only way that these songs were performed.

A similar point can be made with regard to dance music. There can be little doubt that medieval knights and ladies did dance to the accompaniment of their own singing, for there are many accounts of this practice. And at times the author even specifies that this singing is without instrumental accompaniment. In the *Perceforest,* for example, in a scene that probably is based on contemporary practices (there is nothing about it that reflects medieval views of the early Bretons), the assembled company dances for a time to the music of the minstrels. Then, however, the king interrupts the minstrels:

> Car le roy ala dire, "Seigneurs, laissiers ester, car il n'est instrument que de bouche de pucelle." Atant cesserent les menestrelz et le roy dist, "Pucelles doivent commenchier a chanter, car la feste est leur."
>
> For the king said, "Lords, stop, for there is no instrument but the lips of a maiden." At once the minstrels stopped and the king said, "Maidens should begin to sing, for the festivities are theirs."
> (Paris, Bibl. Arsenal 3494, fol. 277r)

In accordance with the king's instructions, two maidens and two knights each sing a "chansonette". Each sings of his or her part in a rather lengthy love debate that the four have been involved in for some time, during which the ladies have never met the men in person. It is in this way that the adventure is revealed to the court and its participants finally allowed to meet face to face.

In the *Prison amoureuse,* Froissart describes a feast at the court of Savoy in 1368, at which the ladies sang to provide music for the carol after the minstrels stopped playing:

> Et quant li menestrel cessoient,
> Les dames pas ne se lassoient,
> Ains caroloient main a main
> Tout le soir jusqu'a l'endemain.
> Et quant chanté li une avoit
> Un virelay, on ne savoit
> Encores s'il avoit fin pris,
> Quant uns aultres estoit repris
> Ou de dame ou de damoiselle.

> And when the minstrels stopped, the ladies didn't grow weary, but they caroled hand in hand all evening until the next day. And when one had sung a virelai, you didn't even know whether or not it was finished yet when another had already been begun by a lady or a maiden.
> *(Prison,* vv. 401-9)

This feast in turn is compared to another, similar carol that Froissart portrays himself as witnessing in the *Prison,* at which ladies again sing virelais after the minstrels cease playing. Froissart is pleased that one of his virelais is sung and well received. But he is shocked when the lady that he loves chooses to sing a virelai in which she rejects the affections of an unwanted admirer, and the following episode is concerned with his meditations on this event, his successful rationalization of her song (it must have been meant for someone other than himself), and the composition of a new song in honor of the occasion.

There is no reason to doubt that dance scenes of this type occured commonly. And in fact the spontaneous, perhaps at times even simultaneous singing of different songs, fragments of songs and refrains by the various dancers could not easily be accompanied by instrumentalists. In the *Perceforest,* indeed, the knights and maidens sing songs that they have composed themselves and which have never been sung before, therefore presumably could not even be known by the minstrels. But should we assume that this was the only way that virelais and other dance tunes could be performed? It is important to remember that the texts cited here are far more specific about the lack of instrumental accompaniment for the songs of the carolers, than about any lack of vocal accompaniment to the instrumental music of the minstrels. In both the *Prison* and the *Perceforest,* there is a clear narrative reason to highlight the songs sung by the participants in the carol, and no reason at all to highlight the songs performed by the nameless musicians. What we see here is not necessarily *the* way, but only one of the ways that dance music could be performed; in particular, it is the way that most lends itself to the use of lyric insertions for narrative development. It may well be for this reason, and not because it was the only method of performance, that it is so commonly featured in romances and *dits*.

Verification of the lack of instrumental accompaniment for caroling ladies can be found in a somewhat unexpected source, the *Contes moralisés* of the fourteenth-century English cleric Nicole Bozon. Bozon, in a passage warning of the dangers of associating with women, draws an analogy between the carol and the hunt. Just as hares flee the sounds of baying hounds and hunting horns, he says, so men should flee the seductive but equally dangerous sounds of caroling maidens:

> quant oyent les chienz questeyer, ce sont les domoiseles qe vont caroler, e lui veneour qe va cornant, e ceo est le tabour qe lour somont a lur peril ...
>
> When they hear the dogs bark, those are the maidens that go caroling; and the hunter who goes sounding his horn, and that is the drum that draws them to their peril.
>
> *(Contes moralisés,* pp. 27-28)

Bozon has no need to highlight in any special way the songs of the maidens; he simply wants to set up his analogy between a typical carol and a hunt. It is relatively straightforward – and in keeping with what we saw in the *Roman des deduis* – that the "voices" of dogs would be compared to those of the carolers; the hunting horns are the instrumental accompaniment. That the horns should be compared to accompaniment by percussive rather than wind or other melodic instruments strongly suggests that maidens dancing to their own singing really would not be accompanied by anything other than a simple drumbeat. The clerical text confirms the evidence offered by courtly literature as to the activity of aristocratic women; but as to the activity of professional instrumental ensembles, we are still largely in the dark.

The tendency to highlight spontaneous and often informal performances by aristocratic amateurs, and the overriding importance of the words rather than the musical aspects of most songs used in narrative texts, may also help to explain the lack of references to polyphony. Of all the romances and *dits* with lyric insertions, only *Fauvel*, which is atypical in more ways than one, contains polyphonic motets.[23] Although Machaut sometimes uses polyphonic chansons as lyric insertions, only the text is performed within the narrative, and there is never any reference to either vocal or instrumental rendition of the other parts. If the purpose of lyric insertions is to allow

---

[23] On lyric insertions in narrative and dramatic works, see M.V. Coldwell, *"Guillaume de Dole* and Musical Romances with Musical Interpolations", *Musica Disciplina* 35 (1981), pp. 55-86. Coldwell gives Tables of Romances with Musical Interpolations, pp. 71-86. Polyphonic motets appear in the dramatic *Ludus super Anticlaudianus*, the *Fauvel*, and the *Miracles Nostre Dame*. None of these are romances describing the performance at court of secular motets.

the protagonist to assume center stage and express his sentiments, then there really is little reason why an author would insert a two- or three-voiced motet into a narrative, or describe the technical details of a polyphonic performance given by professional musicians.

Conclusions

The foregoing discussion allows for preliminary conclusions, to be augmented or modified in future studies. In terms of methodology, I have outlined textual, semantic, and syntactic considerations that must inform the study of literary sources. The scholar using modern printed editions must ascertain that the text corresponds to a medieval version, and should also check to see if variant readings turn up any new evidence. Individual words must be interpreted with caution; in particular, the statement that a performer plays an instrument need not mean that he or she is not also singing, and vice versa. And the separation of vocal and instrumental music in phrases like "chanter et sonner" or "dit et chant" must likewise be interpreted with care, in order to determine whether the distinction implies a temporal sequence or a logical articulation of simultaneous or interlaced activities. While such decisions can be extremely difficult, careful reading can often make the task easier. Sometimes variant readings may support one or another interpretation, as when Paris and Edardo are said to "chanter et sonner" in one source and to "sonner et chanter" in another: if the order of the activities is unimportant, it could be because they are simultaneous. In other cases, the complete passage may contain more than one account of the same performance, as when the performers of lais in the *Tristan en prose* are first said to play and then to sing, while in the completion of the performance they are said to have sung and then to have played: again, the apparent contradiction is easily resolved if simultaneous vocal and instrumental music is assumed. In still other cases, the context of the performance may clarify its nature, as when a minstrel "plays" a piece and then discusses its words with his audience. Finally, the analysis of a given author's linguistic and stylistic habits can help to determine the precise meaning of difficult passages. For example, the repeated use of the phrase "jouer en la harpe et chanter de la bouche" (play on the harp and sing with the mouth) in the *Perceforest* need not be seen as expressive of a temporal sequence of musical activities, but as a variation on the author's tendency to employ dual modifiers in descriptions: "belle et bonne" (beautiful and good), "chanter si bien et si doucement" (sing so well and so sweetly), "si courroucée et a tel meschief" (so irritated and so upset).

The analysis of literary conventions and narrative strategy helps us to realize that although the performance descriptions that we have probably do not contradict contemporary practices, they should by no means be taken as the total picture. Instead, they afford us a glimpse of medieval performances, with an emphasis on certain kinds of music used in certain contexts that lend themselves to narrative development and characterization. Even within this select set of descriptions, we find considerable variety: monophonic love songs are sung either with or without instrumental accompaniment; lais are played on harp, rote, fiddle, flute; a lai is preceded by an instrumental prelude or it is begun at once in a combined vocal and instrumental rendition; motets are rendered by voice and organ, by an unspecified combination of voices and instruments, or by voices alone; popular songs and dance tunes are performed on fiddle, lute, or psaltery, as the individual performer sees fit. And we see that even a single performance event by a solo musician might include a whole variety of elements. The performance of a Breton lai, for example, can begin with a narrative explanation of the origin of the lai and the story to which it refers, perhaps with dialogue between performer and audience; move on to an elaborate process of tuning the harp; then feature an instrumental prelude to the piece; continue with the rendition in voice and instrument of the lai itself; and end with an instrumental echo of the melody just sung. This lai may in turn remind the minstrel or his audience of another lai featuring the same characters or the same geographic location, which is then duly performed in similar fashion. On the other hand, a lai may be sung quite simply to instrumental accompaniment with no narrative account and no prelude. While certain details of these descriptions of the glorified Breton past may be fanciful, it is likely that the overall flavor of the performance situations they present is a reflection of medieval court life. Not only could practices vary, but even the boundaries of the performance are not strictly defined: verbal or instrumental introduction and song, performer and audience are in a constant and fluid dialogue. No given description, no single source, tells the full story of musical performance in the Middle Ages.

In its broad outlines, the total combined evidence of literary sources is undoubtedly an accurate reflection of medieval musical practices. It is no surprise that long narrative songs, like the *chanson de geste,* belong to the minstrel repertoire: it is logical that it would take a professional to master these long pieces. Similarly, it comes as no surprise that the performance of polyphony is limited to particularly talented and well trained musicians. Nonetheless, it must be remembered that the silences of the literary sources are indeed silences, and not assertions. If minstrels are not described as singing dance tunes, for example, this does not mean that they did not ever do it. The occasional references to combined vocal and instrumental performances, the hints of instrumental ensembles being joined by singers, should be taken seriously and given more weight than their relative infrequency might at first glance imply. As I have shown, this can be explained on purely literary grounds. That such descriptions can be found at all argues that the practice was accepted; it could be alluded to in an offhand manner with no need for elaboration.

It is true that it is very difficult to be sure of the repertoire being performed in a given literary description. Perhaps our various descriptions of vocal and instrumental music refer to purely oral, now lost repertoires. But why posit entire bodies of music for which there is no real evidence? Or perhaps all descriptions of combined vocal and instrumental music refer to monody. Still, if a monophonic ballade or other chanson can be sung to fiddle or psaltery, must we assume that the combination of vocal and instrumental music would necessarily be dropped for a polyphonic piece of the same genre? I do not wish to argue that polyphony was never, or hardly ever, performed in either all vocal or all instrumental renditions; there is certainly evidence for this practice, and such may even have been the most common means of polyphonic performance. But the existence of purely vocal and purely instrumental ensembles still does not rule out other possibilities.

Of course, literary texts are not the only sources for medieval performance practices, and when these literary descriptions are systematically coordinated with iconographic or archival evidence it will be much easier to arrive at an accurate picture of medieval music in general. For example, we have seen that the minstrels in *Gilles de Chyn* sing a love song to the accompaniment of the fiddle, and that the Poitevin jongleur in *Amis et Amile* plays a song on the fiddle about love and friendship. When this evidence is considered in light of the miniatures in chansonniers representing trouvères and troubadours playing the fiddle, and the references in various vidas to a given troubadour's talents as fiddle player, the association of the fiddle with the trouvère and troubadour repertoire is virtually inescapable.[24] And the representation of the trouvère Perrin d'Angecourt holding a portative organ in the early fourteenth-century chansonnier *a* takes on an interesting light in view of Pygmalion's rendition of a love song – in this case a motet – to the accompaniment of a portative organ. A trouvère chanson and a motet belong to two distinct repertoires, of course, and would not necessarily be performed in similar fashion. Nor does the presence of a portative organ in a chansonnier miniature prove that trouvère songs were played on this instrument. Nonetheless, the comparison is intriguing, suggesting at least the possibility that the same combination of voice and instrument might be appropriate in both monophonic and polyphonic repertoires.

Such speculations can only be verified or disproved through the accumulation and accurate interpretation of more evidence than is currently available in print. Clearly the project requires the collaboration of

---

[24] H. van der Werf questions the likelihood of trouvère and troubadour songs being performed instrumentally in *The Chansons of the Troubadours and the Trouvères* (Utrecht, 1972), p. 19. Van der Werf argues that the illustrations in chansonniers do not necessarily illustrate the performance of the songs, pointing out that the miniatures used for aristocratic trouvères – a knight on horseback – surely do not tell us that the aristocratic trouvère typically composed or performed his songs on horseback or to the rhythm of his horse's footsteps. Van der Werf's point is well taken; one must always be careful in the interpretation of iconographic evidence, and the trouvère chanson in any case does not lend itself to elaborate (and certainly not to polyphonic) accompaniment. However, the images of knights on horseback do tell us that the songs were associated with members of the knightly class; the images of musicians similarly tell us that these songs are associated with members of a minstrel class. If the illustrators of the chansonniers felt that images of instrumentalists were appropriate identifiers for the composers and performers of trouvère songs, does this not mean that it was at least possible to associate the trouvère repertoire with instrumental music? In trouvère chansonnier *a* (Vatican Library, Lat. Reg. 1490), for example, considerable care has been taken with the miniatures, to judge from those that have survived. Aristocratic trouvères are pictured with the correct coat-of-arms. Williames d'Amiens li paignnierres (William of Amiens the painter) is duly represented as a painter, holding a palette and painting a heraldic *blason*. Why, then, should we disregard as mere fancy or meaningless convention the miniatures in the same manuscript that represent Perrin d'Angecourt with a portative organ and Martin le Beguin de Cambrai with bagpipes? While these particular trouvères may never have played these particular instruments, the illuminator of the manuscript evidently felt that these instruments were logical choices for this type of song. Indeed, he may have had some knowledge of the trouvères in question, since he chose the rustic bagpipes for Martin le Beguin, who appears to have been a transient jongleur, and the more prestigious organ for Perrin, who was associated with the high aristocracy, including Charles d'Anjou and Count Gui of Flanders.

specialists in a variety of fields: musicology, literature, linguistics, art history, social history. The material offered here is a contribution to this larger project, and will, I hope, facilitate the discovery of medieval performance practices and aesthetics, and ultimately the re-creation, on the modern stage, of medieval music as it was performed in the Middle Ages.

VOICES AND INSTRUMENTS ... 109

Primary Sources

Alexandre. Lambert li Tors and Alexandre de Bernay, *Romans d'Alexandre.* Ed. H. Michelant. Bibliothek des Literarischen Vereins, 13. Stuttgart, 1846.

Amis et Amile. Ed. P. Dembowski. Classiques Français du Moyen Age. Paris, 1969.

Anseïs de Carthage. Anseïs von Karthago, ed. J. Alton. Bibliothek des Literarischen Vereins, 194. Tübingen, 1892.

Aucassin et Nicolette. Ed. J. Dufournet. Paris, 1973.

Bartsch, K., ed. *Altfranzösische Romanzen und Pastourellen.* Leipzig, 1870.

Berte aus grans piés. Adenet le Roi, *Berte aus grans piés.* Ed. U.T. Holmes, Jr. University of North Carolina Studies in the Romance Languages and Literatures, 6. Chapel Hill, 1946.

Bestiaire d'amours. Richard de Fournival, *Li Bestiaires d'amours di Maistre Richart de Fornival e Li Response du Bestiaire.* Ed. C. Segre. Milan, 1957.

Blancandin. Blancandin et l'Orgueilleuse d'amour. Ed. F.P. Sweetser. Textes Littéraires Français. Geneva and Paris, 1964.

Brut. Wace, *Roman de Brut.* Ed. I. Arnold. Société des Anciens Textes Français. 2 volumes. Paris, 1938-40.

Bueve de Hantone. Der festländische Bueve de Hantone, Fassung III. Ed. A. Stimming. Gesellschaft für Romanische Literatur, 39 and 42. 2 volumes. Dresden, 1914-20.

Castelain de Couci. Jakemes, *Roman du castelain de Couci et de la dame de Fayel.* Ed. M. Delbouille. Société des Anciens Textes Français. Paris, 1936.

Chastelaine de Saint Gille. Recueil général des fabliaux, I. Ed. A. de Montaiglon. Paris, 1872. No. 11.

Chronicles. Jean Froissart, *Chroniques (1346-56),* IV. Ed. S. Luce. Paris, 1873.

Claris et Laris. Li Romans de Claris et Laris. Ed. J. Alton. Bibliothek des Literarischen Vereins, 169. Tübingen, 1884.

Comte d'Anjou. Jean Maillart, *Le Roman du Comte d'Anjou.* Ed. M. Roques. Classiques Français du Moyen Age. Paris, 1931.

Contes moralisés. Nicole Bozon, *Contes moralisés.* Ed L.T. Smith and P. Meyer. Société des Anciens Textes Français. Paris, 1889.

Deduis. Gace de la Buigne, *Roman des deduis.* Ed Å. Blomqvist. Studia Romanica Holmiensia, 3. Stockholm and Paris, 1951.

Durmart le Galois. Ed. E. Stengel. Bibliothek des Literarischen Vereins, 96. Tübingen, 1873.

Eledus et Serene. Roman d'Eledus et Serene. Ed. J.R. Reinhard. Austin, 1923.

Epine. "Der Lai de l'Epine." Ed. R. Zenker. *Zeitschrift für Romanische Philologie* 17 (1893), pp. 233-55.

Espinette. Jean Froissart, *L'Espinette amoureuse.* Ed. A. Fourrier. Bibliothèque Française et Romane, sér. B.: Editions Critiques de Textes, 2. Paris, 1972.

Fonteinne amoureuse. Guillaume de Machaut, *Oeuvres,* III. Ed. E. Hoepffner. Société des Anciens Textes Français. Paris, 1921.

VOICES AND INSTRUMENTS ... 111

Galeran de Bretagne. Jean Renart, *Galeran de Bretagne.* Ed. L. Foulet. Classiques Français du Moyen Age. Paris, 1925.

Gilles de Chyn. Gautier de Tournay, *L'Histoire de Gilles de Chyn.* Ed. E.B. Place. Northwestern University Studies in the Humanities, 7. Evanston and Chicago, 1941.

Godefroy, F. *Dictionnaire de l'ancienne langue française et de tous ses dialectes du IXe au XVe siècle.* 10 volumes. Paris, 1880-1902.

Guigemar. Marie de France, *Lais.* Ed. J. Rychner. Classiques Français du Moyen Age. Paris, 1973.

Guillaume de Dole. Jean Renart, *Le Roman de la rose ou de Guillaume de Dole.* Ed. F. Lecoy. Classiques Francais du Moyen Age. Paris, 1970.

Horn. Das anglonormannische Lied vom Wackern Ritter Horn. Ed. R. Brede und E. Stengel. Ausgaben und Abhandlungen aus dem Gebiete der Romanischen Philologie, 8. Marburg, 1883.

Miracles. Gautier de Coinci, *Miracles de Nostre Dame.* Ed. V.F. Koenig. 4 volumes. Geneva and Lille, 1955-70.

Moniage Guillaume. Ed. W. Cloetta. Société des Anciens Textes Français. 2 volumes. Paris, 1906-11.

Ovide moralisé. Ovide moralisé, poème du commencement du quatorzième siècle. Ed. C. de Boer. Verhandelingen der Koninklijke Akademie van Wetenschappen te Amsterdam, Afdeeling Leterkunde, n.s. 15, 21, 30, 37, 43 (Amsterdam, 1915-38).

Pamphile. Jehan Bras-de-Fer de Dammartin-en-Goële, *Pamphile et Galatée.* Ed. J. de Morawski. Paris, 1917.

Panthère. Nicole de Margival, *Le Dit de la panthère d'amours.* Ed. H.A. Todd. Société des Anciens Textes Français. Paris, 1883.

Paris et Vienne. *Der altfranzösische Roman Paris et Vienne*. Ed. R. Kaltenbacher. Erlangen, 1904.

Perceforest. *Le Roman de Perceforest*. Consulted in the following manuscripts: Paris, Bibliothèque Nationale fr. 346; Paris, Bibl. Nat. fr. 109; Paris, Bibl. de l'Arsenal 3494.

Prison. Jean Froissart, *La Prison amoureuse*. Ed. A. Fourrier. Bibliothèque Française et Romane, sér. B: Editions Critiques de Textes, 13. Paris, 1974.

Prologue. Marie de France, *Lais*. Ed. J. Rychner. Classiques Français du Moyen Age. Paris, 1973.

Renart. *Le Roman de Renart le contrefait*. Ed. G. Raynaud and H. Lemaître. 2 volumes. Paris, 1914.

Rose. Guillaume de Lorris and Jean de Meun, *Le Roman de la rose*. Ed. F. Lecoy. 3 volumes. Classiques Français du Moyen Age. Paris, 1973-75.

Silence. Heldris de Cornuälle, *Le Roman de Silence*. Ed. L. Thorpe. Cambridge, 1972.

Tournois. Jacques Bretel, *Les Tournois de Chauvency*. Ed. M. Delbouille. Bibliothèque de la Faculté de Philosophie et Lettres de l'Université de Liège, 99. Liège and Paris, 1932.

Tristan. Thomas, *Le Roman de Tristan*. Ed. J. Bédier. Société des Anciens Textes Français. Paris, 1902-5.

Tristan en prose. Consulted in the following manuscripts: Paris, Bibliothèque Nationale fr. 335; Bibl. Nat. fr. 336; Bibl. Nat. fr. 772; Bibl. Nat. fr. 12599.

Tristan ménestrel. Gerbert de Montreuil. "Tristan Ménestrel: Extrait de la continuation de *Perceval* par Gerbert." Ed. J. Bédier and J.W. Weston. *Romania* 35 (1906), pp. 497-530.

Violette. Gerbert de Montreuil, *Roman de la violette ou de Gerart de Nevers.* Ed. D.L. Buffum. Société des Anciens Textes Français. Paris, 1928.

Voie d'Enfer. Jehan de la Mote, *La Voie d'Enfer et de Paradis.* Ed. Sister M. A. Pety. Washington, D.C.: 1940.

Yvain. Christian von Troyes, *Sämtliche Werke,* II: *Der Löwenritter.* Ed. W. Foerster. Halle, 1887.

Northern Illinois University

[19]

References to Music in Old Occitan Literature

ELIZABETH AUBREY (IOWA CITY)

Authors of literature choose words that serve the purposes of literature and not the purposes of historical accuracy. For those who would use poetic or narrative texts to gain historical understanding, then, the necessity of a certain amount of skepticism towards their language is paramount, more so than for music treatises.[1] This is true not only because these works are fictional, but also because their language is conditioned by factors such as theme, use of rhetorical tropes and figures, voice, audience, formal constraints, and genre. A metaphor, for instance, while on occasion used in a musical treatise to illustrate a point, might be the very heart of a poem, and as such may well be the point itself, and not a statement of historical accuracy. Such figurative language, along with structural elements like rhyme schemes, repetition patterns, parallelisms, and so forth, are hallmarks of fiction, so that references to music or to musical events must be not only measured against other sources of information, but also carefully considered within their literary contexts.

Many medieval Occitanian texts contain words of apparent musical meaning, but citing them without assessing the value of the words as they appear in their many guises and contexts can lead to misinterpretation. The intention of the author of the mid-thirteenth-century narrative poem *Flamenca* is to tell a story of love, jealousy, and chivalry, clearly quite different from the aims of Guilhem Molinier, the apparent author of the fourteenth-century poetic treatise *Las Leys d'Amors*. The one stands against a background of courtly narrative and follows compositional principles dictated by the conventions of the twelfth- and thirteenth-century *ars poeticae*,[2] while the other draws upon the medieval rhetorical and grammatical traditions. The romance is entertaining verse, the grammar is didactic prose. While both of these

---

[1] Numerous studies of the semiotics of medieval vernacular literatures have appeared in recent years, and the lexicological difficulties in many medieval music theory texts are becoming increasingly well-documented. Recent studies by E. H. ROESNER (*Johannes de Garlandia on "Organum in Speciali"*, in: Early Music History 2 [1982], p. 129–160) and J. YUDKIN (*The "Copula" According to Johannes de Garlandia*, in: Mus. Disc. 34 [1980], p. 67–84) are among many that focus on specific problems of interpretation. The scholastic background of the important treatise by Johannes de Grocheio, with its unique discussion of secular monophony, is the object of a valuable study by P. DeWITT, *A New Perspective on Johannes de Grocheio's Ars Musicae* (unpublished Ph. D. dissertation, University of Michigan, 1973). Recent collections of essays written by U. ECO are useful surveys of the problems and tasks of semiotics: *The Role of the Reader: Explorations in the Semiotics of Texts* (Bloomington 1979) and *Semiotics and the Philosophy of Language* (London 1984). A forthcoming article by S. HUOT, *Voices and Instruments in Medieval French Secular Music: On the Use of Literary Texts as Evidence for Performance Practice*, which contains a topical analysis of a number of Old French texts, confirms many of the observations made here, and offers a sound methodological approach to literary and lexicological studies. I am very grateful to Dr. Huot for providing me with a copy of this essay before its publication.

[2] Found in the treatises of Matthieu de Vendôme, Geoffroi de Vinsauf, Gervaise of Melkley, Jean de Garlande, and Everardus Alemannus. See studies by E. FARAL, *Les arts poétiques du XIIe et du XIIIe siècle: recherches et documents sur la technique littéraire du Moyen Âge* (Paris 1924); R. DRAGONETTI, *La technique poétique des trouvères dans la chanson courtoise: contribution à l'étude de la rhétorique médiévale* (Bruges 1960); D. KELLY, *The Scope of the Treatment of Composition in the Twelfth- and Thirteenth-Century Arts of Poetry*, in: Speculum 41 (1966), p. 261–278; J. J. MURPHY, *Rhetoric in the Middle Ages: A History of Rhetorical Theory from St. Augustine to the Renaissance* (Berkeley 1974); and M. E. FASSLER, *Accent, Meter and Rhythm in Medieval Treatises 'De rithmis'*, in: The Journal of Musicology (Spring 1987), p. 164–190.

works provide meaty quotations having to do with music, their value with respect to an illumination of medieval musical practices is at least partially determined by the tradition within which each is found.

For this study I examined musical references in the lyric poems, the *vidas* and *razos*, various non-lyric works such as narrative poems and prose, epics, hagiographic, dramatic, and historical compositions, and some didactic works. While the interpretations offered here depend to some extent upon the principles described in Occitanian grammatical and rhetorical treatises of the thirteenth and fourteenth centuries, I have not included musical references in those works here, partly to keep the length of the present essay manageable and partly because those works require a different critical method than the others.[3]

Many of the texts quoted here are already well known to modern scholars.[4] I offer here not so much the fruits of discovery, but rather an examination of the problems of interpretation from the point of view of poetics and rhetoric. It has been my intention to organize the materials by genre and topic, with a view to clarifying some, at least, of the evidence pertaining to Occitanian musical practices, which sometimes seems to be self-contradictory. Many more texts than are quoted in the following pages have musical connotations, but those included illustrate the dangers as well as the rewards of using such passages to expand our knowledge of musical practices in the Midi.

Lyric poems

In some ways the lyric texts of the troubadours, both those that survive with music and those that do not, might be considered least likely to convey dependable information about music. This is because their complexity consists largely of various rhetorical figures, even in the accessible *trobar leu* style, and also because poetic construction and imagery usually take precedence over verity. References to singing, melody, or melodiousness often do not mean music in the physical sense at all. There are, however, various terms, formulas, and motifs in the poems that do quite often have a musical connotation. The citations given here illustrate the most common musical references in the poems.

The word *so* (*son*) has been taken by modern scholars to mean "melody." It literally means "sound," but this rarely creates ambiguity in the lyric works.[5] It is found both in singular and plural forms, coupled with the plural *motz*, or "words":

---

[3] I have treated these works separately, in a forthcoming article entitled *Rhetoric of Song: "los motz e.l son" in Medieval Occitanian Treatises*. E. W. POE, in: *From Poetry to Prose in Old Provençal: The Emergence of the "Vidas," the "Razos," and the "Razos de Trobar"* (Birmingham, Al. 1984), points out some of the differences among lyric poetry, biographies, stories, and poetic treatises in Old Occitan.

[4] Recent essays citing some of these passages include A. RONCAGLIA, *Sul "divorzio tra Musica e Poesia" nel Duecento italiano*, in: *L'Ars nova italiana del Trecento* 4, ed. A Ziino (Certaldo 1978), p. 365–397; and C. PAGE, *Voices and Instruments of the Middle Ages: Instrumental Practice and Songs in France 1100–1300* (Berkeley 1986).

[5] Old Occitan does not use a cognate of the Old French noun *mélodie* to mean melody. The word *melodia* occurs occasionally in some texts, and notably in the rhetoric section of *Las Leys d'Amors*, where it means "euphonious" in the sense of proper delivery in oratory. The author of this treatise declares that he is not using the word in a musical sense. See A.-F. GATIEN-ARNOULT, ed., *Las flors del gay saber, estiers dichas "Las leys d'Amors"* = Monuments de la Littérature Romane 1–3 (Toulouse 1841–43), p. 53–57.

"los motz e.l so," meaning simply "the text and the melody." The phrase has a formulaic flavor by virtue of its frequent use. The singular form is perhaps more common than the plural, but this does not suggest a relationship between a single word and a single pitch; many contexts make it clear that the "sound" is the entire tune rather than an individual note. For example, at the end of the first stanza of the late twelfth-century troubadour Folquet de Marselha's "Chantars mi torn' ad afan," it is clear that the song required of the troubadour must consist of original words and melody:

Mas quex demanda chanso	But everyone demands a song,
e no.lh cal de la razo:	and without concern for the subject:
qu'atressi m'es ops la fassa	so that I need to make it
de nou, quom los motz e.l so.[6]	new, the words as well as the tune.

In a more complex configuration that uses both *so* and its derivative *sonet*, Bernart de la Fon (about whom little is known except that he lived in the second quarter of the thirteenth century) describes a melody as smooth and easy to sing. The connection with the text is clear, for here he boasts of his skill in the *trobar leu*, evidently including the tune (which does not survive), as opposed to the difficult *trobar clus* style:

Leu chansonet' ad entendre	An easy little song to understand,
ab leu sonet volgra far,	with an easy little tune, I want to make,
coindet' e leu per apendre	graceful and easy to learn
e plan' e leu per chantar,	and smooth and easy to sing,
quar leu m'aven la razo,	for the subject came to me easily,
e leu latz los motz e.l so.[7]	and the words and melody lie easy.

Similarly, Raimbaut d'Aurenga (c. 1150–1173), another proponent of the *trobar leu*, casts his words and melody in the "easy" style:

A mon vers dirai chansso	I shall call my chanson my vers
ab leus motz ez ab leu so	with simple words and simple tune
ez en rima vil' e plana.[8]	and in ordinary and common rhyme.

And the Italian Sordello (c. 1225–1260) declares his intention to do the same, characterising his tune as appropriately "gay" and easy both to sing and to listen to:

---

[6] Listed as number 155,7 in A. PILLET and H. CARSTENS, *Bibliographie der Troubadours* (Halle 1933, repr. New York 1968), henceforth PC. Ed. by S. STRONSKI, *Le troubadour Folquet de Marseille, édition critique* (Kraków 1910), p. 78, lines 5–8. Translations are mine unless otherwise indicated. (I am grateful to Professor Samuel N. Rosenberg for reading my translations and offering suggestions. Any infelicities or errors are, of course, my responsibility.) The late Gustave Reese attributed to Folquet a phrase that illustrates the close marriage of poem to melody in the troubadour art: "A text without music is a mill without water" (*Music in the Middle Ages* [New York 1940], p. 205). Reese did not cite a source for this quotation, and I have unsuccessfully searched the works of Folquet for it, as well as the secondary literature that Reese evidently relied upon. The apocryphal verse is credible enough to have been cited frequently, always without reference to a medieval source.

[7] PC 62,1; C. APPEL, ed., *Bernart von Ventadorn, seine Lieder, mit Einleitung und Glossar* (Halle 1915), p. 301.

[8] PC 389,7; W. T. PATTISON, ed. and trans., *The Life and Works of the Troubadour Raimbaut d'Orange* (Minneapolis 1952), p. 171–173.

Bel m'es ab motz leugiers a far	It pleases me to compose, with light words,
chanson plazen et ab guay so,	an agreeable song and with a gay melody,
que.l melher que hom pot triar,	for the best lady that one could choose,
a cuy m'autrey e.m ren e.m do,	to whom I promise and yield and give myself,
no vol ni.l plai chantar de maestria;	does not wish for learned singing,
e mas no.lh plai, farai hueymais mon chan	nor does this please her; henceforth I shall make my song
leu a chantar e d'auzir agradan,	easy to sing and agreeable to hear,
clar d'entendre a prim, qui prim lo tria.[9]	clear to understand and exquisite to one who judges it with exquisite discernment.

The same language is used to refer to the apparently common practice of giving a new set of words to a tune composed by someone else. In the following example Bertran de Born (c. 1181–1194) borrows a melody, he says, by the *trobairitz* Alamanda:

Conseill vuoill dar el son de n'Alamanda	I want to give advice, to the tune of Lady Alamanda,
lai a.n Richart, si tot no lo.m demanda.[10]	to Richard there, although he has not asked me for it.

The form *sonet* is not infrequently used, and the context does not necessarily imply a diminutive meaning, but simply serves as a synonym for *so*, as in this *vers* by Guilhem de Poitiers (1071–1127):

Que.l mot son fag tug per egau comunalmens,	For the words are all built on the same meter,
e.l sonetz, ieu mezeis m'en lau,	and the tune – I myself am pleased with it –
bos e valens.[11]	is good and fine.

Guiraut de Bornelh (c. 1168–1211) also uses the word, again evoking a close relationship between text and tune:

Trop volgra mais donar	I should much prefer to offer
mos gais sonetz joios	my gay, joyous melodies,
ab bels dichs et enters,	with fine, complete expressions,
entendables e plas,	comprehensible and smooth,
que trop escurs ni sobrestorias.[12]	than with ones which are too dark or over-embellished.

---

[9] PC 437,7; M. BONI, ed., *Sordello: Le poesie. Nuova edizione critica con studio introduttivo, traduzioni, note, e glossario* = Biblioteca degli "Studi mediolatini e volgari" 1 (Bologna 1954), p. 22; trans. L. M. PATERSON, *Troubadours and Eloquence* (Oxford 1975), p. 137.

[10] "D'un sirventes no.m cal far loignor ganda," PC 80,13, lines 25–26; W. D. PADEN, Jr., T. SANKOVITCH and P. H. STÄBLEIN, eds., *The Poems of the Troubadour Bertran de Born* (Berkeley 1986), p. 189. Note here the unequivocal evidence that women composed music as well as poetry. See the recent essay on female musicians in medieval France by M. V. COLDWELL, "*Jougleresses*" and "*Trobairitz*": Secular Musicians in Medieval France, in: *Women Making Music: The Western Art Tradition, 1150–1950*, ed. J. BOWERS and J. TICK (Urbana and Chicago 1986), p. 39–61.

[11] "Pus vezem de novel florir," PC 183,11, stanza 7; F. JENSEN, ed. and trans., *Provençal Philology and the Poetry of Guillaume of Poitiers* = Études romanes de l'Université d'Odense 13 (Odense 1983), p. 225–226.

[12] "Dels bels eigz menutz frais," PC 242, 32, lines 9–13; A. KOLSEN, ed., *Sämtliche Lieder des Trobadors Guiraut de Bornelh, mit Übersetzung, Kommentar und Glossar* (Halle 1910), I, p. 430; trans. PATERSON, *Troubadours and Eloquence*, p. 108.

In some contexts, especially where *so* or *sonet* appears alone, it may simply mean "song," just as the word *canso* refers to a poetic type more than a musical genre. For instance, in this poem by Peirol, the author is motivated by his grief to produce a *sonet*, evidently meaning a poem rather than a tune, for his own comfort:

D'un sonet vau pensan	I am minded to compose a song
per solatz e per rire,	for solace and laughter,
e non chanter' ogan	otherwise I would not sing this year
estiers per mon cossire,	on account of my grief,
don mi conort chantan.[13]	for which I find comfort in singing.

The word *chantar*, which in Old Occitan often appears unpalatalized as *cantar*, is fickle. It does not always point directly to musical performance, and frequently seems to mean simply oral recitation of poems. Other than those instances when it is used figuratively (as in "singing a lady's praises"), *cantar* certainly suggests audible performance, whether musical or not. Raimon de Miraval (c. 1185–1213), for instance, speaks of singing as a social activity as well as a personal one, but nothing in the context here refers clearly to music:

Cel que no vol auzir chanssos	He who does not wish to hear songs,
de nostra compaignia.is gar,	let him avoid our company,
qu'eu chan per mon cors alegrar	for I sing for my own delight
e per solatz dels compaignos,	and for the distraction of my companions,
e plus per so q'endevengues	and even more so that it may occur that
en chansson c'a midonz plagues.[14]	in singing I might please my lady.

The same poet voices the perennial complaint of the neglected lover, bemoaning the futility of his singing, but he then finds a poetic image in the situation when he compares the beloved herself to a capricious singer who must be begged for a song. Here, although again music is not explicitly mentioned, the whole passage seems to imply musical performance because of the simile with the *joglar* at the end:

Si.m fos de mon chantar parven	If my singing seemed to me
c'a ma dona.n prezes cura,	to capture the attention of my lady,
ja no.i gardera mezura	I would surely not observe any moderation,
mas al pus que pogra soven;	but would do it as often as I could.
mas car no.m denha escotar,	But since she does not deign to listen to me,
m'a fag de tot solatz giquir.	she has made me abandon all pleasure.
Per qu'ieu sai qu'es vers so c'aug dir	Hence I know that it is true, what I hear,
q'enueia.s om de bel chantar...	that people are bored with fine singing...

---

[13] PC 366,14; S. C. ASTON, ed. and trans., *Peirol, Troubadour of Auvergne* (Cambridge 1953), p. 65. The forthcoming article mentioned in note 3 above deals in greater depth with the concept of a rhetorical "armonia" or union between music and text. The recent book by J. STEVENS, *Words and Music in the Middle Ages: Song, Narrative, Dance and Drama, 1050–1350* (Cambridge, England 1986), presents a sweeping portrait of the structural relationships between texts and melodies in medieval monophony. Structural, rhetorical, and other stylistic traits of the troubadour songs will be dealt with thoroughly in my forthcoming book on their music.

[14] PC 406,20; M. L. SWITTEN, ed. and trans., *The "Cansos" of Raimon de Miraval: A Study of Poems and Melodies* (Cambridge, Ma. 1985), p. 182–183.

> D'aitan fai semblan de joglar
> que canta tro que.s fai grazir,
>
> e cant hom plus lo vol auzir,
>
> el s'en giet'e fay s'en preyar.[15]

> Thus she acts like the joglar
> who sings until he captivates his audience,
> and when they want to hear him some more,
> he backs away and wants to be coaxed.

The word *cantar* and its derivatives are used with a dizzying variety of meanings – ornithological, musical, poetical, and metaphorical – in this *canso* by the early fourteenth-century Peire de Ladils:

> Al mes de junh que chanta la tortera,
>
> e.l rossinhol e.l tort e.l merle calan,
>
> e li pastor non cantan ges ni balan,
> vuelh yeu cantar e far canso mot vera,
>
> car de midons puesc cantar ab tristor.[16]

> In the month of June, when the turtle-dove sings,
> and the nightingale and the thrush and the blackbird keep silent,
> and the shepherds do not sing or dance,
> I wish to sing and make a very sincere song,
> for I can sing of my lady with sorrow.

Here, the singing and dancing of the shepherds and the singing of the birds obviously imply musical notes; but the poet's "singing" and "song" consist of words and not necessarily music.

The troubadours used both *cantar* and *sonar* to mean "to play" instruments, although they rarely referred to instruments in their poems; such language is more common in the narrative works, as will be seen below. *Sonar*, like *cantar*, is used in several ways; just as the noun *so* might sometimes mean simply "sound" or "noise," *sonar* might refer to making musical sounds, to speaking or yelling, or simply to producing anything audible, as in this *canso* by Peire de Ladils:

> Amors, vos me fatz dishendre,
> e midons tan aut montar
> que sol nom vol mot sonar.[17]

> Love, you have pushed me down,
> and raised my lady so high
> that I can hardly speak a word.

To make matters worse, the distinction between *sonar*, *cantar*, and *dire* ("to say") is often quite obscure, and never more so than in this poem of Jaufre Rudel (c. 1130–1170):

> No sap chantar qui so non di,
> ni vers trobar qui motz no fa.[18]

> He cannot sing who says no tune,
> and he cannot compose poems who makes no words.

A like juxtaposition of *chantar* and *dire* is seen in these verses of Raimon de Miraval:

> A penas sai don m'apreing
> so q'en chantan m'auzetz dir.[19]

> I scarcely know where I learn
> what you hear me say in singing.

---

[15] PC 406,39; ibid., p. 214 (my translation).
[16] Not cited in PC. J.-B. NOULET and C. CHABANEAU, eds., *Deux manuscrits provençaux du XIVe siècle, contenant des poésies de Raimon de Cornet, de Peire de Ladils, et d'autres poètes de l'école toulousaine* (Montpellier 1888, repr. Geneva 1973), p. 88, lines 1–5.
[17] Ibid., p. 87, lines 33–35.
[18] PC 262,3; G. WOLF and R. ROSENSTEIN, eds. and trans., *The Poetry of Cercamon and Jaufre Rudel* = Garland Library of Medieval Literature, Series A, 5 (New York 1983), p. 134–135 (with minor changes). Jaufre expresses in these verses the sentiment suggested by the spurious aphorism alluded to in note 3 above.
[19] PC 406,7; SWITTEN, ed. and trans., *Raimon de Miraval*, p. 148–149.

These passages are typical of the nagging ambiguity of all three words, and it is rarely possible to be sure that actual singing is meant. They all evidently refer to performance, and sometimes to composition, of a poem. There is ample evidence that the lyric songs were for immediate consumption and therefore the preferred mode of transmission was oral (although for the sake of preservation some troubadours were happy to see their poems written down). Guiraut de Bornelh, in the following stanzas, suggests that a poem is imperfect unless it is sung aloud, even badly:

A penas sai comensar	I hardly know how to begin
un vers que volh far leuger	a *vers* which I want to make light,
e si n'ai pensat des er	and indeed I have been thinking since yesterday
que.l fezes de tal razo	about how I might compose it on such a theme
que l'entenda tota gens	that all people may understand it,
e qu'el fassa leu chantar;	and how I might make it easy to sing;
qu'eu.l fatz per pla deportar.	for I compose it purely to entertain.
Be.l saupra plus cobert far;	I should certainly know how to make it more veiled;
mas non a chans pretz enter,	but a song has an incomplete reputation
can tuch no.n son parsoner.	when all are not able to share it.
Qui que.s n'azir, me sap bo,	Whoever else may be angry about this, I am pleased
can auch dire per contens	when I hear people vying with each other
mo sonet rauquet e clar	in repeating my melody hoarsely and clearly,
e l'auch a la fon portar.[20]	and when I hear it carried to the well.

As in this song, in another one Guiraut appears to have been so concerned that his songs be heard that he was willing to tolerate poor execution – in fact acknowledging that his tune deserved little more, anyway:

Mos so levatz,	My lofty tune
c'us enraumatz	by a hoarse-voiced singer
lo.m deissazec e.l diga mal,	should be mangled and delivered badly,
que no.l deing ad home sesal.[21]	for it is not fitting for a propertied man.

The *joglar* of the troubadours' poems is almost always addressed as a menial servant, and often in very pejorative terms. These references frequently transmit very blunt accounts of performing practices, both good and poor. Bertran de Born (c. 1181–1194) seems to have had particularly bad luck with one *joglar*, as he complains in this song:

---

[20] PC 242,11; KOLSEN, *Guiraut de Bornelh*, I, p. 14; trans. PATERSON, *Troubadours and Eloquence*, p. 102–103.
[21] "Ara.m platz, Guiraut de Bornelh," PC 389,10a, strophe 6, lines 39–42; KOLSEN, *Guiraut de Bornelh*, I, p. 374; trans. PATERSON, *Troubadours and Eloquence*, p. 111.

Mailolin, joglars malastruc,	Mailolin, you miserable minstrel,
pos acomdat m'a hom de vos	since people have told me about you
e mi venes qerre chansos,	and you come to me looking for songs,
en talent ai q'ie.us en vailha.	I've got a mind to give you one.
Qar iest avols e semblas bos	You may look good, but you're rotten inside;
mieills fora foses campios	you should be a killer for hire,
qe viure d'autrui corailha.	instead of living off other people's guts.
Raimon de Planell qar es pros,	I want Raimon de Planell to hear the
vueilh q'auia.l sirventes de vos;	sirventes from you because he is brave.
e.l sons iesca.n ab trebailha,	Let the melody come out painfully,
car sordei chantatz qe paos	because you sing worse than a peacock,
e gavainhatz los motz e.ls sos;	and you spoil the words and the notes;
per qe.s folls qi los vos bailha![22]	whoever gives them to you is crazy!

Bertran presents an even more unsavory description of a *joglar* in this poem:

La raucha vos, don cridaz en chanta,	What with the raucous voice with which you yell when you sing,
e.l niegre cors don semblas Sarrazi,	and the black body that makes you look like a Saracen,
e.l paupre mot que dizes en contan,	and the poor words you use when you tell jokes,
e qar flairaz sap, e gema, e pi	and because you stink of spruce and pitch and pine
con avols gens de Savoia,	like the dirty people from Savoy,
e qar es lag garnitz e malestan,	and because you are ill equipped and unsavory,
ab qe.us n'anes, farai vostre coman.[23]	if only you'll go away I'll do what you want.

One famous poem by Peire d'Alvernhe (c. 1150–1170) consists of a commentary on the skills of various troubadours, including the author himself. Peire reveals no humility in his assessment of his own abilities, while Guiraut de Bornelh and Guillem de Ribas (known only by reference) in particular earn his utmost disdain. The stanza about Guiraut de Bornelh quite obviously borrows some of the imagery that Guiraut himself used in his poems, as can be seen by comparison with those just cited:

Chantarai d'aquest trobadors	I will sing of those troubadours
que chantan de manhtas colors,	who sing in many manners
e.l pieier cuyda dir mout gen;	and the worst thinks he speaks nobly;
mas a chantar lor er alhors,	but they should sing elsewhere,
qu'entremetre n'aug .c. pastors,	for among them I hear a hundred shepherds,
q.us no sap que.s monta o.s dissen.	who don't know whether [the melody] rises or falls...

---

[22] PC 80,24, stanza 1 and the two tornadas; PADEN, *et al.*, eds. and trans., *Bertran de Born*, p. 312–313 and 316–317.
[23] "Fuilhetas, vos mi preiatz qe ieu chan," PC 80,17, stanza 2; ibid., p. 410–411.

E.l segonz: Guirautz de Bornelh,	The second [troubadour] is Guiraut de Bornelh,
que sembl' odre sec al solelh	who is like a dry goat-skin dried in the sun
ab son cantar magr'e dolen,	with his thin, pitiful singing,
qu'es cans de vielha porta-selh;	which is like the song of an old woman water-carrier,
e si.s vezia en espelh,	and if he saw himself in a mirror,
no.s prezaria un aguilen.	he'd esteem himself less than a needle...
En Guillems de Ribas lo quins,	Lord Guillem de Ribas is the fifth,
qu'es malvatz defors e dedins,	who is wicked outside and in
e ditz totz sos vers raucamen,	and recites all his poems harshly,
per que es avols sos retins,	for his noises are terrible,
c'atrestan se.n faria us chins;	like those made by a dog;
e l'huelh semblan de vout d'argen.	and his eyes look like those of a silver statue.
Peire d'Alverne a tal votz	Peire d'Alvernhe has such a voice
que canta de sobre' e de sotz,	that he sings high and low [lit. above and below],
e siei son son douz e plasen;	and his tunes are sweet and pleasing;
e pois es maistre de totz,	therefore he is master of all,
ab q'un pauc esclarsis sos motz,	although his words are not very clear,
qu'a penas nuillz hom los enten.	so hardly anyone understands them.
Lo vers fo faitz als enflabotz	This verse was made to the bagpige
a Puoich-vert tot iogan rizen.[24]	at Puivert with everyone playing and laughing.

This burst of self-approbation was not altogether well-received by Peire's contemporaries, as might be expected. Some later readings of this poem, in fact, contain a revision of the final stanza – whether by scribes or other poets is unknown – which divulges what at least one person thought of his singing:

Peire d'Alvernhe a tal votz	Peire d'Alvernhe has such a voice
que canta cum granolh' em potz,	that he sings like a frog in a pond,
e lauza.s mout a tota gen.	and he praises himself above all people.

The reference to a bagpige in the *tornada* of this poem is one among not a few indications in Old Occitan literature that instruments were used to accompany *cansos*. A wind instrument like the bagpige obviously would have been played by a performer other than the singer. *Joglars* were occasionally described in the lyrics as having diverse skills, among them instrumental prowess, as well as the ability to learn and deliver songs of various types, as in this late description by the Toulousain Raimon de Cornet (c. 1320s):

---

[24] PC 323,11, stanzas 1, 3, and 6; C. APPEL, ed., *Provenzalische Chrestomathie, mit Abriss der Formenlehre und Glossar* (Leizpig 1902), p. 117–119. The sixth stanza is found in the *razo*, given in J. BOUTIÈRE and A. H. SCHUTZ, *Biographies des troubadours, textes provençaux des XIIIe et XIVe siècles*, 2nd ed. with I. M. CLUZEL (Paris 1964), p. 263–264.

Jotglars an tost apres	A joglar would rapidly learn
coblas e may versetz,	stanzas and many little verses,
cansos e bassas dansas.²⁵	cansos and basses danses.

The reference to "bassas dansas" is striking. There seems to be no earlier, or even contemporary, use of the term, and what sort of musical piece Raimon had in mind is impossible to say. None of the fourteenth-century treatises on poetic types mentions it, and the earliest pieces designated "basse danse" do not appear until over 100 years after this. The dance itself, as this reference testifies, was obviously known in southern Europe very early, and it remained popular there for several hundred years.[26] The author of these verses, who probably had little musical training, most likely was merely stringing together a group of words that he associated with *joglars*, and there is no doubt that improvising dance tunes was a skill possessed by such entertainers. Whether or not there is any relationship between this fourteenth-century genre and the fifteenth-century practice of extemporisation over a fixed bass is unknown.

Troubadours often exhorted singers to learn their songs, many times grumbling that they did not do it very well. Some composers, like Raimon de Miraval, tackled the problem by crafting their melodies carefully, which they thought ought to help singers learn them:

E.ill sonet son dols e bas,	And the melodies are sweet and low,
coind'e leugier e cortes,	charming and light and courtly;
per qe de grat son apres.²⁷	therefore they are learned with pleasure.

A "low" melody is not likely to have anything to do with pitch, since each singer probably chose a range that was easy for him or her. Nor does it mean soft in volume, since that too is done by the performer, and Raimon here is describing the tune itself, not its execution. A "sweet and low" melody is probably Raimon's way of describing something he thought was simple, smooth, and accessible. This tune, extant in one late thirteenth-century manuscript, is not one of Raimon's simpler compositions, however. It is neumatic in texture, not entirely conjunct in motion, covers over an octave in range, and has an irregular overall structure.[28]

Some of the examples cited above suggest that the troubadours saw a direct correlation between the composition of their poems and of their melodies. This is further suggested in this passage by Peire Vidal:

---

[25] "Quar mot ome fan vers" (not cited in PC), lines 235–237. NOULET and CHABANEAU, eds., *Deux manuscrits*, p. 8.
[26] The dance treatise by the provençal Antonius de Arena, *Ad suos compagnones studiantes qui sunt de persona friantes bassas dansas de novo bragarditer*, was first published in 1529, and it reflected its author's experiences in Avignon and Italy.
[27] "Si tot s'es ma domn'esquiva," PC 406,40, stanza 2; SWITTEN, ed. and trans., *Raimon de Miraval*, p. 218–219 (her translation, with minor changes).
[28] The significant implications of a medieval aesthetic of "charm" and "lightness" in a melody that has a complex structure are explored in my forthcoming book on the troubadours' music.

Ajostar e lassar	I know how to couple and lace
sai tan gent motz e so,	words and music together so gracefully
que del car ric trobar	that no one can compete with me
no.m ven hom al talo,	in the precious, rich style,
quant n'ai bona razo.[29]	when I have a good theme for it.

Something of the social position of the *joglars* and a brief account of what could have been a common scene in the Midi is offered by Bertran de Born:

Gent acuillir e donar ses cor vaire	Noble hospitality and giving without fickle heart,
e bel respos e "Ben sias vengut!"	and fair conversation and warm welcome,
e gran hostal pagat e gen tengut,	and a great court, well paid and well kept up,
dons e garnirs et estar ses tort faire,	presents and gifts of arms and living without doing wrong,
manjar ab mazan	eating to the noise
de viol' e de chan	of fiddle and song,
e maint compaingnon	with many a companion
ardit e poissan	bold and mighty
de totz los meillors –	among all the best –
tot voill c'om o teingna.[30]	I want men to stop it all.

A battle scene is portrayed by Bertran de Born, who lists some instruments that had a military association:

Qan vei pels vergiers despleiar	When I see unfurled among the orchards
los cendatz grocs, indis e blaus,	banners yellow, violet, and blue,
m'adoussa la votz dels cavaus	the neighing of the horses soothes me,
e.il sonet que fant li joglar	and the songs the minstrels sing
que viulon de trap en tenda,	as they go fiddling from tent to tent,
trombas e corn e graile clar;	and the trumpets and horns and clarions clear;
adoncs vuoill un sirventes far,	then I want to compose a sirventes
tal qe.l coms Richartz l'entenda.[31]	for Count Richard to hear.

While many lyric poems mention a number of instruments used by the musicians of their day, most of them, like the above, contain no descriptions. The *tromba*, *corn*, and *graile* occur often in narrative works, as will be seen below. Nor do many of the poems clarify how the instruments were used. There can be little doubt that the troubadours were well acquainted with them, however, and expert playing was valued. The Monk of Montaudon (c. 1180–1215) grouses in one poem (which is a complaint about nearly everything) about poor fiddling and also about protracted tuning:

---

[29] PC 364,2; D'A. S. AVALLE, ed., *Peire Vidal: Poesie* = Documenti di filologia 4 (Milan and Naples 1960), I, p. 37; trans. PATERSON, *Troubadours and Eloquence*, p. 96–97, n. 4.

[30] "Mon chan fenis ab dol et ab maltraire," PC 80,26, stanza 3; PADEN, et al., eds. and trans., *Bertran de Born*, p. 220–221 (their translation, with minor changes). The *viol'* (contracted from *viola*) of the sixth verse is comparable to Old French *vielle* or fiddle, and of course is not a viol, as given in Paden's otherwise felicitous translation.

[31] PC 80,35; PADEN, et al., eds. and trans., *Bertran de Born*, p. 276–277 (their translation, with minor changes).

Enoia.m longa tempradura,	I'm annoyed by extended tuning,
e carns quant es mal coita e dura.	and by meat when it is badly cooked and tough.
Et eneuia.m per Saint Salvaire,	And I'm irritated, by St. Salvat,
en bona cort avols violaire.[32]	by a bad fiddler in a good court.

The lyric repertoire is vast, and a search will turn up hundreds more examples of the use of musical terms than there is room to present here. Clearly in Old Occitan words served several purposes, and even more so in poetic contexts. The resultant ambiguities are frustrating only if one hopes to rely on the poems for precise information, an unrealistic purpose that the authors themselves rarely had. Fortunately, the poems of the troubadours are not the only surviving literature from that time and region.

Vidas and razos

The Old Occitan *vidas* and *razos* are without parallel in medieval vernacular literature.[33] While they are fascinating recitals of the lives of a great many poets, composers, and performers, they are somewhat formulaic in structure, and their contents in some cases are known to be apocryphal. The earliest sources are from the middle of the thirteenth century, and some do not appear before the fourteenth. Their authorship is uncertain.

While some of the historical details in these biographies and anecdotes have long been known to be doubtful or erroneous, it is likely that their allusions to social and cultural matters contain some truth. One of the more interesting issues has to do with the distinction between a *trobador* and a *joglar*. In contrast to the lyric poems, which generally place minstrels on a decidedly lower social plane than that occupied by the poets, the biographies confuse the two supposedly separate professions. The *trobador* is just as likely to be poor and destitute as the *joglar* is to be gainfully employed and well off. More important than the social commingling is an evident joint participation in the activities of composing and performing; a well-known poet-composer can take up the mantle of a *joglar*, while a *joglar* might be praised as one who composed good poetry.[34] The *joglars* Cercamon (middle of the twelfth century), Guiraut de Salignac (beginning of the thirteenth century), and Guilhem de la Tor (c. 1215–1240), for example, were also poets:

Cercamons si fo uns joglars de Gascoingna, e trobet vers e pastoretas a la usanza antiga.	Cercamon was a joglar of Gascony, and he invented vers and pastorelas in the old manner.

---

[32] "Fort m'enoia, s'o auzes dire," PC 305,10, lines 28–29 and 46–47; APPEL, ed., *Provenzalische Chrestomathie*, p. 84.
[33] All citations are from BOUTIÈRE and SCHUTZ, *Biographies des troubadours* (henceforth BS). Translations are mine. See also G. FAVATI, *Le biografie trovadoriche, testi provenzali dei secoli XIII e XIV, edizione critica* = Biblioteca degli "Studi mediolatini e volgari" 3 (Bologna 1961); S. STRONSKI, *La poésie et la réalité aux temps des troubadours* (Oxford 1943); and E. W. POE, *From Poetry to Prose in Old Provençal*.
[34] See below (p. 148) for Guiraut Riquier's passionate plea that the professions be more accurately delineated.

| Girautz de Salaingnac si fo de Caersin... Joglars fo; ben adregz hom fo e ben cortes, e trobet ben e gen cansons e descortz e sirventes. | Guiraut de Salignac was from Quercy... He was a joglar; he was a skilled man and very courtly, and he invented good and noble cansos and descorts and sirventes. |

| Guillems de la Tor si fon joglars e fo de Peiregorc... E sabia cansos assatz e s'entendia e chantava e ben e gen, e trobava.[35] | Guilhem de la Tor was a joglar and was from Périgord... And he knew and understood plenty of songs, and he sang and invented nobly and well. |

Trobar means "to compose" or "to invent," and it is usually applied to the poetry, although melodies also are "invented." In contrast to the ambiguity often found in the poems, in the *vidas* and *razos* a clear distinction is drawn between the activities of composing or inventing (*troban*) and singing (*cantan*), meaning perhaps that composing did not necessarily take place in the course of singing. But singing was not the exclusive domain of the *joglar*, nor composing of the *trobador*. The troubadours Guilhem Figueira (c. 1215–1245) and Guilhem de Poitiers (1090–1127), for instance, were known as singers, and Peire Vidal (c. 1180–1206) was said to outshine them all (the opinion of Peire d'Alvernhe, cited above, notwithstanding):

| Lo coms de Peitieus... saup ben trobar e cantar. | The count of Poitiers... knew well how to invent and sing. |

| Guilhems Figuera... saup ben trobar e cantar; e fez se joglars entre los ciutadis. | Guilhem Figuera... knew how to compose and sing well; and he became a joglar among the citizens. |

| Peire Vidals... cantava meilz c'ome del mon.[36] | Peire Vidal... sang better than any man in the world. |

The *joglar* Perdigon (c. 1195–1220) was both a fiddler and a poet:

| Perdigons si fo joglars e saup trop ben violar e trobar.[37] | Perdigo was a joglar and he knew very well how to fiddle and to invent. |

The noun form *trobador*, most familiar to us, only rarely appears in the *vidas*; the more common form is *trobaire*, although this word too is not found often. One of its few occurrences is in the *vida* of Peire de la Mula (c. 1230–1240), a relatively obscure poet, who is called both a *joglar* and a *trobaire*:

| Peire de la Mula si fo uns joglars... E fo trobaire de coblas e de sirventes.[38] | Peire de la Mula was a joglar... And he was an inventor of coblas and of sirventes. |

The well-known description of Guiraut de Bornelh as chief among his peers uses both *trobaire* and *trobador*. He was one of only a few poet-composers who were said to employ their own singers:

---

[35] BS, p. 9, 198 and 236.
[36] BS, p. 7, 434 and 351.
[37] BS, p. 408.
[38] BS, p. 560.

| Girautz de Borneill... fo hom de bas afar, mas savis hom fo de letras e de sen natural. E fo meiller trobaire que negus d'aquels qu'eron estat denan ni foron apres lui; per que fo apellatz maestre dels trobadors... E la soa vida si era aitals que tot l'invern estava en escola et aprendia letras; e tota l'estat anava per cortz e menava ab se dos cantadors que cantavon las soas chansos.[39] | Guiraut de Bornelh... was a man of low condition, but he was a man learned in letters and in natural intelligence. And he was the best inventor among all those who came before or after him; for this reason he was called the master of the troubadours... And his life was such that all winter he was in school and learned letters; and all summer he travelled about the courts and took with him two singers who sang his songs. |

Perhaps because the skills expected of the *joglar* were diverse, there is not a single verb form for *joglar* that designates singing. Whenever a troubadour took up the life of a performer, he was said to "make himself a joglar" (*fetz se joglar*) or "become a joglar" (*venc se joglar*); or he took up the joglar's life (*s'ajoglaria*). This life is never described in the *vidas* and *razos* as being associated with anything other than the courtly occupation of poet-composer-performer. There is no mention of juggling, knife-throwing, acrobatics, animal training, or even dancing; the *joglars* described in the *vidas* seem, in fact, to occupy a somewhat higher social class than the nameless stuntmen who were the minstrels of medieval Europe. Even clerics and knights became *joglars*, like Aimeric de Belenoi (c. 1210–1242), Peirol (c. 1180–1225), and Elias de Barjols (end of the twelfth century), and sometimes this turned out to be a financially sound move:

| N'Aimerics de Belenoi... clercs fo, e fez se joglars, e trobet bonas cansos e bellas e avinenz. | Lord Aimeric de Belenoi... was a cleric and became a joglar, and he invented good songs which were beautiful and charming. |

| Peirols no se poc mantener per cavallier e venc joglars, et anet per cortz e receup dels barons e draps e deniers e cavals. | Peirol was unable to maintain himself in knighthood and became a joglar, and he travelled among the courts, and he received from the barons clothing and money and horses. |

| N'Elias de Barjols... cantet miels de negun home que fos en aquella sason; e fetz se joglars et acompaingnet se com un autre joglar que avia nom Oliver[s], et aneron lonc temps ensems per cortz.[40] | Lord Elias de Barjols... sang better than any other man of his time; and he became a joglar and was accompanied by another joglar named Oliver, and they travelled for a long time together about the courts. |

The verb *trobar* is not the only one used to convey composing. *Far*, literally "to make," also means "to compose," and, since it is often used to describe the activities of the *joglars*, perhaps also connotes "to perform":

| Guillems Magretz si fo uns joglars de Vianes, jogaire e taverniers. E fez bonas cansos e bons sirventes e bonas coblas.[41] | Guilhem Magret [c. 1200–1215] was a joglar from Vienne, a gambler and an innkeeper. And he made good songs and good sirventes and good coblas. |

[39] BS, p. 39.
[40] BS, p. 255, 303 and 215.
[41] BS, p. 493.

Several *vidas* declare that certain troubadours were particularly adept at composing melodies, and both *far* and *trobar* are used:

Peire de Maensac... fez avinenz cansos de sons e de motz.	Peire de Maensac [early 13th century?]... made charming songs of melodies and words.
Peire d'Alverne... savis hom fo e ben letratz... E trobet ben e cantet ben, e fo lo premiers bons trobaire que fon outra mon et aquel que fez los meillors sons de vers que anc fosson faichs.[42]	Peire d'Alvernhe... was a wise man and well educated... And he invented well and sang well, and was the first good inventor who went beyond the mountains, and who made the best tunes for verses that had ever been made.

One troubadour was said to be a poor speaker but a good singer, which suggests that a performance could encompass both speech (of a *vida* or *razo*) and music:

Richartz de Berbesieu... saup mielz trobar qu'entendre ni que dire. Mout fo pauros disenz entre las genz... Mas ben cantava e disia sons, e trobava avinenmen motz e sons.[43]	Richard de Berbezilh [c. 1140–1163]... knew better how to compose than to understand or to recite. He was a poor speaker in front of people... But he sang well and delivered melodies, and he composed words and tunes aptly.

Some troubadours gained praise more for their melodies than for their poems:

Jaufres Rudels... fez de leis mains vers ab bons sons, ab paubres motz.	Jaufre Rudel... made many verses about her [the countess of Tripoli] with good melodies, but poor words.
Et Albertez si fez assatz de cansos, que aguen bons sons e motz de pauca valensa. Ben fo grazitz pres e loing per los bons sons qu'el fasia, e ben fo bons joglars en cort e plasentiers de solatz entre la gen.[44]	And Albertet composed plenty of songs that had good tunes but words of little value. He was esteemed near and far for the good melodies that he made, and he was indeed a good joglar at court and an agreeable companion among the people.

Gaucelm Faidit (c. 1180–1202), although disparaged as a poor singer, nonetheless became a *joglar* for pecuniary reasons, at the same time maintaining his reputation as a poet and composer:

Gauselms Faiditz... cantava peiz d'ome del mon; e fetz molt bos sos e bos motz. E fetz se joglars per ocaison qu'el perdet a joc de datz tot son aver.[45]	Gaucelm Faidit... sang worse than any man in the world; and he made many good melodies and good words. And he became a joglar because he lost all he had in a game of dice.

---

[42] BS, p. 301 and 263.
[43] BS, p. 149.
[44] BS, p. 16–17 and 508.
[45] BS, p. 167.

The author of Uc Brunet's *vida* (end of the twelfth century) claims that he did not compose melodies; if one believes this, then the single surving tune that is ascribed (with its text) to him must have been supplied by someone else.[46] This sentence also suggests that *trobar* did not always imply composing music:

N'Uc Brunecs... fo clerges et enparet ben letras, e de trobar fo fort suptils, e de sen natural; e fez se joglars e trobet cansos bonas, mas non fetz sons.[47]	Lord Uc Brunet... was a clergyman and learned letters well, and knew how to compose with great subtlety, and was of natural intelligence; and he became a joglar and invented good cansos, but he did not compose melodies.

The noun *chantaire* denotes a singer, which again is distinct from *trobaire*. The more common transformation of poet to singer is reversed in Pistoleta's *vida* (c. 1195–1230):

Pistoleta si fo cantaire de N'Arnaut de Marvoill e fo de Proenssa. E pois venc trobaire e fez cansos com avinens sons.[48]	Pistoleta was a singer of Arnaut de Marvuelh's, and he was from Provence. And then he became an inventor and he made songs with pleasing melodies.

Sordello was described as both a *chantaire* and a *trobaire*:

Sordels... fo bons chantaire e bons trobaire, e grans amaires.[49]	Sordello... was a good singer and a good inventor, and a great lover.

The matter of the training and skills of the *trobadors* and *joglars* is mentioned often by the authors of the *vidas* and *razos*. Some were known as good performers, both vocal and instrumental, some as bad:

Ponz de Capduoill... sabia ben trobar e violar e cantar.	Pons de Capduelh [beg. 13th cent.]... knew well how to compose and fiddle and sing.
N'Aimerics de Peguillan... apres cansos e sirventes, mas molt mal cantava.[50]	Aimeric de Peguilhan [c. 1195–1225]... learned songs and sirventes, but he sang very badly.

Some *trobadors* and *joglars* were said to be educated and able to read:

Aquel N'Arnautz [de Marvuelh]... cantava ben e lesia romans.	This Lord Arnaut [c. 1171–1195]... sang well and read the vernacular.
Guirautz de Calanson si fo uns joglars de Gascoingna. Ben saup letras, e suptils fo de trobar.	Guiraut de Calanso [beg. 13th cent.] was a joglar from Gascony. He knew letters well, and was subtle in inventing.
E cant [Peire Cardenal] era petitz, sos paires lo mes per quanorgue en la quanorguia major del Puei; et apres letras, e saup ben lezer e chantar.	And when [Peire Cardenal (c. 1200–1278)] was little, his father had him placed as a canon in the great canonry at Puy; and he learned letters, and knew how to read well and to sing.

---

[46] "Coindas razos e novelas plazens," PC 450,3. The music is found in the late thirteenth-century Occitanian source Paris, Bibliothèque nationale, f.fr. 22543, fol. 66.
[47] BS, p. 199.
[48] BS, p. 491.
[49] BS, p. 562.
[50] BS, p. 311 and 425.

Deude de Pradas... savis hom fo molt de letras e de sen natural e de trobar.[51]	Daude de Pradas [c. 1214–1282]... was a very learned man in letters and in natural intelligence and in composing.

One famous troubadour, Arnaut Daniel (c. 1180–1210), was said to have thrown aside his formal learning when he became a *joglar*, but his education must have stood him in good stead in his fashioning of complex poetry (*trobar clus*):

Arnautz Daniels... fo gentils hom, et amparet ben letras e delectet se en trobar. Et abandonet las letras, et fetz se joglars, e pres una maniera de trobar en caras rimas, per que soas cansons no son leus ad entendre ni ad aprendre.[52]	Arnaut Daniel... was a gentleman, and he learned well letters and took delight in composing. And he abandoned letters and became a joglar, and took up a sort of composing in difficult rhymes, so that his songs were not easy to understand or learn.

Arnaut, highly revered by Dante, had a prodigious memory, probably not unlike that of many of his contemporaries. He, along with many others, functioned comfortably in a vital aural environment. While pleasing as an anecdote whether true or not, the account of poetic larceny given in the following oft-cited *razo* offers tantalizing clues to the evidently equal status of *joglar* and *trobador* as composers, as well as to the compositional process and transmission of a song:

E fon aventura qu'el fon en la cort del rey Richart d'Englaterra, et estant en la cort, us autres joglars escomes lo com el trobava en pus caras rimas que el. Arnautz tenc s'o ad esquern; e feron messios, cascu[s] de son palafre, que no fera en poder del rey. E.l rey[s] enclaus cascu en una cambra. E N'Arnautz, de fasti que n'ac, non ac poder que lasses un mot ab autre. Lo joglar[s] fes son cantar leu e tost; e[t] els non avian mas detz jorns d'espazi, et devia.s jutgar per lo rey a cap de cinc jorns. Lo joglar[s] demandet a.N Arnaut si avia fag, e.N Arnautz respos que oc, passat a tres jorns; e no.n avia pessat. E.l joglar[s] cantava tota nueg sa canso, per so que be la saubes. E.N Arnautz pesset co.l traysses isquern; tan que venc una nueg, e.l joglar[s] la cantava, e N'Arnautz la va tota arretener, e.l so. E can foro denan lo rey, N'Arnautz dis que volia retraire sa chanso, e comenset mot be la chanso que.l joglar[s] avia facha. E.l joglar[s], can l'auzic, gardet lo en la cara, e dis qu'el l'avia facha. E.l reys dis	And by chance he [Arnaut Daniel] was at the court of King Richard of England; and while he was at the court, another joglar challenged him, saying that he composed more difficult rhymes than Arnaut did. Arnaut took it in jest; and they made bets, each his horse, which they put in the power of the king. And the king shut them each up in a room; and Lord Arnaut, being put out, was unable to put one word with another. The joglar composed his song easily and quickly; and they had but ten days of space, then five before they had to submit to the king's judgment. The joglar asked Lord Arnaut whether he had done his; and Lord Arnaut answered yes, three days ago; but he hadn't yet thought of it. And the joglar sang his song all night long, in order to know it better; and Lord Arnaut thought he would play a joke: so there came a night when the joglar was singing it, and Lord Arnaut memorized the entire song and its tune. And when they came before the king, Lord Arnaut

---

[51] BS, p. 32, 217, 335 and 233.
[52] BS, p. 59.

co.s podia far; e.l joglar[s] preguet al rey qu'el ne saubes lo ver; e.l rey[s] demandec a.N Arnaut com era estat. E.N Arnautz comtet li tot com era estat, e.l rey[s] ac ne gran gaug e tenc so tot a gran esquern; e foro aquitiat li gatge, et a cascu fes donar bels dos. E fo donatz lo cantar a.N Arnaut Daniel, que di: "Anc yeu non l'ac, mas ela m'a."[53]	said that he wanted to recount his song, and he began very well the song that the joglar had made. And the joglar, when he heard it, looked him in the face and said that he himself had made it. And the king said how could this be; and the joglar implored the king that he didn't know the truth; and the king asked Lord Arnaut how it came about. And Lord Arnaut told the story, and the king was greatly amused, and he took it all as a big joke; and he cancelled the bet, and gave nice gifts to each of them. And he gave the song to Lord Arnaut Daniel, which says "While I do not have her, yet she has me."

Writing (*escriven*) was apparently among the skills of some. Ferrari de Ferrara was an Italian scribe living in the early fourteenth century who evidently was responsible for the production of some books of troubadour poems:

Maistre Ferrari de Ferrara... sap molt be letras, e scrivet meil ch'om del mond e feis de molt bos libres e de beill[s].[54]	Master Ferrari de Ferrara... knew letters very well, and he wrote better than any man in the world, and he made many good and beautiful books.

Elias Cairel, who lived in the first quarter of the thirteenth century, was not particularly esteemed for his skills as a musician or poet, but he was perhaps the earliest music scribe of the south of France known to us:

Elias Carelz fo de Peiregorc, e saup be letras e fo molt sotils en trobar et en tot qant el volc far ni dire... E fetz se joglars e anet gran temps per lo mon. Mal cantava e mal trobava e mal violava e peichs parlava, e ben escrivia motz e sons.[55]	Elias Cairel was from Périgord, and he knew letters well and was very subtle in composing and in all that he wanted to do and say... And he became a joglar and travelled for a long time around the world. He sang badly and composed badly and fiddled badly and spoke still more badly, but he wrote words and melodies well.

Although there is not enough evidence to assert that troubadours actually used manuscript copies of poems and tunes in performance, the language of the *vidas* and *razos* often suggests a connection between what was written down, what was composed, and what was performed. The scribes of the *razos* developed a formula for the transition from the anecdote to the song itself, a phrase implying that whoever is reading the words from the manuscript will at the same time also "hear" the songs; whether this is in actual performance or in the mind's ear, as it were, is

---

[53] Razo of PC 29,2; BS, p. 62–63.
[54] BS, p. 581.
[55] BS, p. 252 and 254 (conflation of versions).

not clear. The earlier sources place each *razo* immediately before the poem it introduces. In the later manuscripts the stories are found in a section apart from the lyric poems, and each *razo* usually is accompanied by just an incipit of the song. The formula that juxtaposes the words for composing, writing, reading, and hearing is retained in these later versions. The sentence found at the end of a *razo* for two of Raimon Jordan's poems is typical:

Maintas bonas chansos fetz, de las cals son asi escriptas altras, si com vos auziretz.[56]	He made many good cansos, of which others are here written, as you will hear.

Bernart de Ventadorn's *vida*, after many superlatives about his skill as a poet, musician and gentleman, alludes to the role of the learned Uc de Saint Circ in preserving his memory:

Et aveia sotilessa et art de trobar bos motz e gais sons... Et ieu, N'Ucs de Saint Circ, de lui so qu'ieu ai escrit si me contet lo vescoms N'Ebles de Ventadorn... E fetz aquestas chansos que vos auziretz aissi de sotz escriptas.[57]	And he possessed subtlety and the art of composing good words and gay melodies... And I, Lord Uc de Saint Circ, have written about him what the viscount Lord Ebles of Ventadorn told me... And he made these songs which you will hear as they are written below.

Uc had received a clerical education, but he forsook the scholar's life to become a composer and performer:

Cansos fez de fort bonas e de bos sons e de bonas coblas.[58]	He made extremely good cansos and good melodies and good coblas.

One final *razo* is worth mentioning, that of Raimbaut de Vaqueiras (c. 1175–1207) which describes the composition and performance of the famous "Kalenda maia." After a performance of the tune by two visiting fiddlers, Raimbaut is urged by the lady of the court to perform as well, despite his heavy heart. He does so, borrowing the fiddlers' melody, and the word used here for melody is not *so*, but the rarer and more particular *notas*:

Dont Rambaut[z], per aqesta raison qe vos avez ausit, fet[z] la stampida, et dis aisi: "Kalenda maia..." Aqesta stampida fu facta a las notas de la stampida qe.l jo[g]lars fasion en las violas.[59]	The Raimbaut, for this reason that you have heard, made the stampida, which says, "Kalenda maia..." This stampida was made on the notes of the stampida that the joglars had made on their fiddles.

As will be seen below, *nota* appears to be used specifically when music without words is meant, although such usage is not exclusive.

---

[56] *Razo* of PC 404,9 and 12; BS, p. 163.
[57] BS, p. 20–21 and 26 (conflation of versions).
[58] BS, p. 239–240.
[59] *Razo* of PC 393,9; BS, p. 466.

Epic, narrative, hagiographic, dramatic, and historical works

From narrative, epic, and historical works we receive the names of virtually every musical instrument that could have been used in the Midi during the Middle Ages. The variety of instruments that are mentioned is staggering, and the authors often seem to have been aware enough of the nature of the instruments to have grouped them loosely by families or types. The exact meanings of these words, however, is not by any means clear.[60] Consider, for example, this well-known list of instruments found in the mid-thirteenth-century romance *Flamenca*:

Apres si levon li juglar:	Afterwards the joglars got up:
cascus se volc faire auzir.	each wanted to be heard.
Adonc auziras retentir	Then you could hear resound
cordas de manta tempradura.	strings of many temperaments.
Qui saup novella violadura,	Whoever knew new fiddle tunes,
ni canzo ni descort ni lais,	or cansos, descorts, or lais,
al plus que poc avan si trais.	as best he could gave it a try.
L'uns viola[l] lais de Cabrefoil,	One fiddles the lai of the Honeysuckle,
e l'autre cel de Tintagoil;	another that of Tintagel;
l'us cantet cel dels Fins Amanz,	one sang that of the True Lovers,
e l'autre cel que fes Ivans.	and the other the one composed by Ivan.
L'us menet arpa, l'autra viula;	One played a harp, another a fiddle;
l'us flautella, l'autra siula;	one a flute, the other a whistle;
l'us mena giga, l'autra rota;	one played a giga, another the rote;
l'us diz los motz e l'autre nota;	one said the words and another the notes;
l'us estiva, l'autre flestella;	one [played] a pipe, another the pan-pipe;
l'us musa, l'autre caramella;	one the bagpipe, the other a shawm;

---

[60] The rhyme lists given in Uc Faidit's *Donatz Proensals* (ed. J. H. MARSHALL, *The "Donatz Proensals" of Uc Faidit* [London 1969]) include Latin translations, which may be of some help in clarifying exactly what instruments are represented by what words:

viular	viellare	to fiddle
arpar	arpam sonare	to sound the harp
citolar	citariçare	to play the citole
manduirar	mandiuram sonare	to sound the mandora
organar	horganiçare	to play the organ, or make organum?
cornar	tubam sonare	to sound the horn
trumbar	tubis ereis sonare	to sound the brass trumpet
caramelar	[fi]stullis cantare	to sing the whistle
balar	saltare ad vielam vel ad aliquid	to play a dance on a fiddle or some other instrument
cantar	cantare	to sing
sonar	sonare	to sound
tamboreçar	timpanizare	to play the tambourine
tauleiar	tabulas parvas sonare	to sound little sticks (castanets)
sonalhz	parvum ti[n]tinabulum	little bells
descans	cantus contra cantum	song against song
joglars	ioculator vel mimus	jongleur or mime
cantarelz	qui cantat frequenter	someone who sings often
anafils	parva tuba cum voce alta	little trumpet with a high voice
corns	cornu	horn
corns	tuba vel bucina	trumpet or curved? long? trumpet
corns	buccines	long? curved? trumpet

l'us mandura e l'autr'acorda	one the mandora and the other struck
lo sauteri ab manicorda;	the psaltery with one string [i.e., monochord];
l'us fai lo juec dels bavastelz;	one presented a play with puppets;
l'autre jugava de coutelz;	the other juggled knives;
l'us vai per sol e l'autre tomba,	one flew in the air, the other tumbled,
l'autre balet ab sa retomba,	one danced with his glass goblet [?],
l'us passet cercle, l'autre sail;	one jumped through hoops, another leaped;
neguns a son mestier no fail.	none failed in his skill.
Qui volc ausir diverses comtes	Whoever wanted to hear various tales
de reis, de marques et de comtes,	of kings, marquis, and counts,
auzir ne poc tan can si volc.[61]	could hear as many as he wished.

The precision of the translation above is deceiving – it is almost arbitrary in some cases, particularly where words are likely to be synonymous, as "flautella," "siula," "flestella," and "estiva," all of which indicate some sort of pipe or whistle. Not only are the words uncertain in meaning, but the context in which they appear in this and other works of fiction does not by any means afford a reliable picture of performance practices. The scene presented here of a cacophonous celebration accompanied by numerous instruments sounding at once is difficult to reconcile both with other accounts and visual representations of performances as well as with our own musical instincts of order and propriety. Proof of poetic license in this passage is found in its structure. The parallelism in the reiteration of the phrases that follow the pattern " l'us ... instrument, l'autra ... instrument" is reflected in the parallelism of the instruments cited: harp and fiddle, flute and pipe, giga and rote, etc. The author is clearly guided by the needs of his text, by rhyme scheme, by some concern with order, and by the exaggeration common to the genre; one must assume that exact reporting of a potentially real situation was at best only a secondary concern. On the other hand, we cannot say for certain that such a fête might never have occurred, especially in some of the more affluent courts of southern France before the Albigensian Crusade. It seems unlikely, however, that it was more than an occasional event.

By the account of the author of *Flamenca*, 1500 *joglars* entertained at this feast:

Le palais fo e granz e latz:	The palace was large and spacious:
.x. milleir la pogran caber	10,000 knights could find place there
de cavalliers, e larc sezer,	and be seated easily,
part las donas e las donzellas	along with ladies and girls
e l'autre gen ques era ab ellas,	and the others who accompanied them,
part los donzels els servidors	besides the young men and their servants

---

[61] M. J. HUBERT and M. E. PORTER, eds., "The Romance of Flamenca": A Provençal Poem of the Thirteenth Century (Princeton 1962), lines 593–620 (my translation, here and *infra*). Verb tenses are inconsistent in Occitanian narrative works, with past and present freely intermixed. I have translated most of these as past tense. See POE, *From Poetry to Prose*, p. 18ff. and D. R. SUTHERLAND, *Flexions and Categories in Old Provençal*, in: Transactions of the Philological Society (1959), p. 25–70.

que degron servir los seinors,	who had to serve the lords,
e part los juglars eissamen,	and with the joglars too,
qu'eran plus de mil e .v.c.[62]	of whom there were more than 1500.

And some 200 of those, at least, were good fiddlers; they were "in tune" with each other, and apparently they played in pairs while the courtiers danced:

.cc. juglar, bon viulador,	Two hundred joglars, good fiddlers,
s'i son acordat antre lor	got in tune with each other,
que, dui e dui, de luein esteron	two by two they sat scattered about
pels bancs, e la danza violeron,	on the benches, and fiddled the dance,
ques anc de point non i failliron.[63]	not missing a note.

Flamenca also provides evidence of the interchangeability and perhaps collaboration of voices and instruments in the performance not only of epics, *cansos de gesta*, and other narrative works, but also of lyric songs. Verses 597–9 (above) refer to the "fiddling" of the *canso* and the *descort*, which are lyric verse types, defined by their text content and structure.[64] In verse 607 (above) some *joglars* sing while some play "the notes," and a similar construction is found earlier in the work:

Li juglar comensan lur faula,	The joglars began their tale,
son estrumen mena e toca	one took his instrument and played it
l'us e l'autres canta de boca.[65]	and the other sang with his mouth.

Near the end of a long list of histories and epics that the *joglars* performed comes mention of the verses of the twelfth-century troubadour Marcabru, author of over thirty *sirventes* and *cansos*. Taken altogether, these verses strongly suggest that instrumentalists and singers participated freely in the performance of all kinds of lyric and narrative works:

---

[62] Ibid., lines 497–505.
[63] Ibid., lines 728–732.
[64] Johannes de Grocheio (c. 1300) asserts that good performers could play any kind of song – including lyric types – on fiddle: "Bonus autem artifex in viella omnem cantum et cantilenam et omnem formam musicalem generaliter introducit." See E. ROHLOFF, *Die Quellenhandschriften zum Musiktraktat des Johannes de Grocheio, im Faksimile herausgegeben nebst Übertragung des Textes und Übersetzung ins Deutsche, dazu Bericht, Literaturschau, Tabellen und Indices* (Leipzig 1972), p. 136. C. PAGE recently has suggested (*Voices and Instruments*) that during the twelfth and first half of the thirteenth centuries *cansos* and other songs that he classifies as being in the "High Style" were not accompanied by instruments, while those in the "Low Style" could have been. Only after secular music began to be subject to a widespread written tradition, he asserts, and hence became seen from the point of view of a new aesthetic, were instruments associated with courtly lyric. While this is not the place to advance a systematic examination of this hypothesis, I would offer two brief observations. One is that several early Old Occitan texts (including some cited here) do seem to tie performance of all kinds of courtly lyric to instrumental usage, especially in those passages that, like the one in *Flamenca* here cited, freely intermix terms for genres that Page has separated into "Low" and "High" styles (such as *descort* and *canso* respectively). As P. ZUMTHOR, *Essai de poétique médiévale* (Paris 1972), p. 189, points out, the notion of "genre" is inexact in the twelfth and thirteenth centuries, and medieval authors were not very precise in their use of terms. P. BEC, in: *La lyrique française au moyen âge (XIIe–XIIIe siècles): Contribution à une typologie des genres poétiques médiévaux*, 2 vols. (Paris 1977), I, p. 23–39, argues that the distinction between aristocratic and popular lyrics is mainly a product of northern France in the thirteenth century. He suggests that the difference between such "registers" of lyric poetry is less significant than that between lyric and non-lyric (e.g. narrative) genres. Secondly, where so many literary pieces seem almost deliberately to omit reference to instruments when speaking of the performance of a courtly love song, this may be not the expression of a historical reality, but simply a rhetorical device that seeks to place such works within the aesthetic of "fin' amors" and exalted above more popular types. In any case, Page's argument against instrumental accompaniment is *e silentio*, which makes it impossible to prove; by not often mentioning such a practice, medieval authors might have been pointing to its ubiquity rather than its absence.
[65] HUBERT and PORTER, eds., *Flamenca*, lines 317–319.

L'us diz lo vers de Marcabru,	One recited the poem of Marcabru,
l'autre comtet con Dedalus	another recounted how well Daedalus
saup ben volar, e d'Icarus	could fly, and how Icarus
co[n] neguet per sa leujaria.	drowned because of his rashness.
Cascus dis lo mieil[z] que sabia.	Each recited as well as he knew how.
Per la rumor dels viuladors	Because of the sound of the fiddlers
e pel brug d'aitans comtadors,	and the noise of so many story-tellers,
hac gran murmuri per la sala.[66]	there was a great babbling in the room.

A very similar situation is described in the following passage from the late twelfth-century romance *Jaufre*; here again it is clear that the *joglars* might just as easily play the songs on their instruments as sing them. Some familiar names for lyric genres are here, but they are evidently performed on fiddles without the texts. These lines are also interesting for the contrast that they provide to the noisy situation described in *Flamenca*. The musicians not only do not have to fight one another to be heard, but they are actually treated to the undivided attention of their audience:

E.ls joglars que sun el palais	The joglars who are in the palace
viulon descortz et suns et lais	fiddle descorts and tunes and lais
e dansas e cansonz de gesta.	and dances and chansons de geste.
Jamais nun veira hom tal festa.	No one would ever see such festivies again.
E tuit escoutavon joglars	And everyone was listening to the joglars
per la sala, si que.ls manjars	in the hall, so that
n'an laissatz per els ausir.[67]	you stopped in order to hear them.

The authors of narrative works seem to have used the terms for lyric poems relatively indiscriminatingly, often in the same sort of way that they listed instruments. Occasionally the word *so* is thrown in amongst these terms, as one sees in these verses from *Flamenca*:

Per tot Alverg[n]' en fan cansos	All through Auvergne songs are made,
e serventes, coblas e sos,	and sirventes, stanzas, and tunes,
o estribot o retroencha	and estrambots and retroenchas
de N'Archimbaut con ten Flamencha.[68]	about Flamenca and Lord Archambaud.

The word *sonu* is found in the Latin rubrics in the play of *Sancta Aines* (mid-fourteenth century), where it is used in the same way that the word for melody is used in Old Occitan. In this hagiographic work the rubrics often call for the use of an existing melody for new lyrics introduced within the play, and the Latin word for melody in these cases is *sonu*. For example, Guiraut de Bornelh's *alba* tune is to serve the text of a lament:

---

[66] Ibid., lines 703–710.
[67] R. LAVAUD and R. NELLI, eds., *Les troubadours: Jaufre, Flamenca, Barlaam et Josaphat* (Bruges 1960), lines 9811–9817.
[68] HUBERT and PORTER, eds., *Flamenca*, lines 1174–1177.

| Modo veniunt ribaldi et circumdant eam in postribulo, et postea mater facit planctum in sonu albe "Rei glorios verai lums e clardat."[69] | Here come the prostitutes and they surround her in the brothel, and then [her] mother makes a lament to the tune of the alba "Rei glorios, verai lums e clardat." |

Some tunes are used more than once, and the borrowed tune is not always from an Old Occitan song. The tune of the Pentecost hymn "Veni Creator Spiritus," for instance, is called for in verse 769. The melody of the conductus "Quisquis cordis et oculi," corrupted to "Si qis cordis et oculi," is invoked for one text (verse 475), although the probable earlier version of that tune is on the text "Can vei la lauzeta mover" by Bernart de Ventadorn.[70] In one place the rubrics call for the use of the antiphons "Veni, sponsa Christi" and "Hec est virgo sapiens," which are to be "said" or "sung":

| Et postea veniunt quinque angeli, et quando sunt juxta corpus virginis, dicunt istam antiphonam: "Veni, sponsa Christi, accipe coronam quam tibi Deus preparavit in eternum." Et postea flectit se unus ex angelis et accipit animam et defert ipsam ante Deum, cantando istam antiphonam: "Hec est virgo sapiens et una de numero prudencium."[71] | And then five angels come, and when they are near the body of the virgin, they say this antiphon: "Veni, sponsa Christi, accipe coronam quam tibi Deus preparavit in eternum." And afterwards one goes from among the angels and accepts her soul and carries it before God, singing this antiphon: "Hec est virgo sapiens et una de numero prudencium." |

The non-lyric works, like the lyric poems, use the verb *sonar* and its derivatives in various ways, to mean "play," "sound," "sing" and "speak." Both the *joglars* and trumpeters "sound" in *Flamenca*:

| Mant' enseinna e manta crida sonon joglar e cornador.[72] | Many war-cries and many shouts the joglars and trumpeters sound. |

And in the twelfth-century epic *Daurel et Beton*, it is words that might be sounded:

| Tal joia n'ac Daurel que motz non potz sonier.[73] | Daurel had such joy that he could not speak a word. |

A song has a pleasing melody in the history of the battle of Navarre:

---

[69] A. JEANROY, ed., Le *"Jeu de Sainte Agnès," drame provençal du XIVe siècle, avec la transcription des mélodies par Théodore Gérold* = Classiques français du Moyen Âge 68 (Paris 1931), p. 16. The tune given in the fourteenth-century manuscript (Rome, Vatican Libary, Chigi C. V. 151) is closely related to the *alba* melody, although with some structural modifications.

[70] PC 70,43. For concordant readings of this melody, see H. VAN DER WERF, *The Extant Troubadour Melodies* (Rochester, N. Y. 1984), p. 62*–69*.

[71] JEANROY, ed., *Le "Jeu de Sainte Agnès"*, p. 49.

[72] HUBERT and PORTER, eds., *Flamenca*, lines 8037–8038.

[73] A. S. KIMMEL, ed., *The Old Provençal Epic "Daurel et Beton"* = University of North Carolina Studies in the Romance Languages and Literatures 108 (Chapel Hill 1971), line 103.

E fe mainta canço an maint bel son plazent,	And they made many songs with many very pleasing tunes,
e mainta pastorela e maint bel partiment.[74]	and many pastorelas and many beautiful partimens.

More ambiguity attends the use of a rarer term, the verb *notar*. It appears to occur most often either in contexts where purely instrumental music is meant, or else in conjunction with poetic terms that might or might not involve music, as here:

E Betonet pren .i. bel laise a notar,	And Beton began to give notes to a beautiful laisse,
e.l pros Daurel comenset a cantar.[75]	and the valiant Daurel began to sing.

A *laisse* is a stanza of an indeterminate number of poetic verses linked by assonance.[76] Here, perhaps, Beton plays the notes while Daurel sings.

Horns of various kinds are ubiquitous in the epic literature. In one early twelfth-century Occitanian version of the song of Roland, *Ronsasvals*, the words *graile* and *corn* seem to be used interchangeably both for the hero's famous horn as well as for other trumpet-like instruments. In the following passage, Oliver and Roland use both words to refer to the horn, which is both "trumpeted" (*cornatz*) and "sounded" (*sonatz*):

Olivier s'es an Rollan ajustat:	Oliver came up to Roland:
"Rollan, fay cel, un petit m'escoutas:	"Roland," he said, "listen to me a little:
nostre barnage s'es malamens mermatz;	our whole company is badly reduced;
fe que.m deves vostre graylle sonas:	by the truth you owe me, sound your horn:
si o aus Karle ho mans homes honratz,	if Charles or his many brave men hear it,
socorra nos, car grans es son barnatz."	he will rescue us, for his company is large."
"Non plassa a Dieu, sa dis Rollan l'onrat,	"May it not please God," said Roland the honorable;
que per payans sia mos graylles cornatz,	"that, because of pagans, I should blow my horn,
com fay venayre que sobre.l senglar glat."[77]	like a hunter baying after a wild boar."

To this plea Roland later gives the same reply, this time calling himself a "trumpeter":

"No plassa Dieu lo sant glorios payre,	"May it not please God the glorious and holy one,"

---

[74] F. MICHEL, ed., *Histoire de la guerre de Navarre en 1276–77: Collection de documents inédits sur l'histoire de la France* (Paris 1856), lines 284–285.
[75] KIMMEL, ed., *Daurel et Beton*, lines 1942–1943.
[76] Johannes de Grocheio and others use the term *nota* to describe the structure of pieces with paired phrases (see ROHLOFF, ed., *Johannes de Grocheio*, p. 136), but that does not fit the usage here.
[77] M. ROQUES, "*Ronsasvals*," *poème épique provençal*, in: *Romania* 58 (1932), p. 1–28 and 161–189; and 61 (1941), p. 433–450; lines 525–533.

comenset dir lo duc Rollan de bon ayre,	began Duke Roland with a fine air,
que de mon corn yeu en sia cornayre	"that I should be a trumpeter of my horn,
con fay aquel que del porc es venayre,	just like a man who is out hunting boar;
car le cornar non es mas de cassayre."[78]	for blowing it is nothing better than the act of a hunter."

The verb form of *graile* also appears:

E.l payan monta que ha estrieu non si prant,	And the pagan stands up in his stirrups,
e vay sonar e grayllar anb aytant,	and begins to sound and to trumpet then,
e ajustet e poder aut e gran,	and he assembled a noble and great force;
.lx. milia menet d'aquella jant.[79]	he brought together 60,000 of these men.

The words *trompa* and *trompador* are common in narratives and histories as well. They occur often in the long thirteenth-century poem by Guilhem Anelier recounting the history of one of the stages of the Albigensian Crusade:

E ad un jorn bel e clar que'l sols ac resplandor,	And one day beautiful and clear, in the shining sun,
el yssic de Tolosa, y ab lui sei trompador,	he left Toulouse, and with him six trumpeters,
per venir en Navarra.	to come to Navarre.
E 'ls baros s'en aneron ab trompas y ap sonetz	And the barons went there with trumpets and with tunes,
e seynnas desplegadas cornan y ap tamboretz.	and with tambourines, and with standards unfurled, they blew [their horns].
E lo valent N'Estacha yssic primeramens,	And the valiant Lord Eustace went out first,
e 'l trommpados e 'ls grayles e lo corn retindens.	with the trumpets and clarions and horns ringing.
E z al son de las tronpas comencet l'alegrers,	And the rejoicing began at the sound of the trumpet,
e N'Estacha ab sas gentz mes se trastotz prumers.[80]	and Lord Eustace with his men took the very first place.

In some works *graile* and *trompa* are found in the same passage, which suggests two different instruments, as in the following fourteenth-century romance:

| Quant los sarasins foron dels crestians apropriatz, gran gera demeneron, mot fort an graileiat, an trompas, an tombalas menavon lur afar, per so que la gent crestiana pogesan espaventar.[81] | When the Saracens had come near the Christians, a great battle was joined; they made a tumultuous noise with their horns, trumpets, and drums, so that the Christian people would be frightened. |

---

[78] Ibid., lines 909–913.
[79] Ibid., lines 712–715.
[80] MICHEL, ed., *Histoire de la guerre de Navarre*, lines 1452–1454, 2111–2112, 4624–4625, and 4940–4941.
[81] C. CHABANEAU, Le "Roman d'Arles," in: *Revue des langues romanes* 32 (1888), p. 473–542, lines 732–735.

On the other hand, the following parallelism suggests that the two words are synonymous:

Cent trombas ausiras sonar,	A hundred trumpets were heard sounding,
e plus de mil grailes cornar	and more than a thousand horns blowing
lai on Guillems es albergatz.[82]	there where Guillem had his camp.

And occasionally one finds the word *nafil* in the same context as the other words:

Lay pogratz auxir tronpar e campanas sonar,	There you could hear trumpets and bells sound,
e grayles e nafils e tamboretz tocar,	and clarions and horns and tambourines played,
si que anbas las ostz fazian ressidar.[83]	so that they wakened both armies.

In the following verses a "little trumpet" (*graylle menutz*) is mentioned, which along with other metal instruments evidently could emit quite a big sound:

E fon tant grant la noysa e la crida e 'ls brutz	And the uproar and cry and noise were so great
del sonet de las trompas e dels graylle menutz,	of the sound of the trumpets and small clarions,
que retendic la vayll e la puytz qu'er agutz.[84]	that the valley and the steep hills resounded.

A veritable brass and drum corps greets the morning in the following passage from *Flamenca*, which uses the relatively rare word *bozinas* (buisines). It also mentions flutes of a sort that evidently were used for a battle cry (does the author have, rather, a shawm in mind?):

Lo ben mati, quan le soleills,	The next morning, when the sun,
quais vergoinos, parec vermeilz,	as if ashamed, appeared crimson,
apres lo sein de las matinas	after the ringing of matins,
ausiras trombas e bozinas,	you could hear trumpets and buisines,
grailles e corns, cembolz, tabors	horns and bugles, cymbals, tabors
e flautz, non ges de pastors	and flutes, not those of shepherds,
mai [de] cels que la mouta sonon	but those that sound the signal
delz torneis e volontat donon	of tournaments and instill a desire
a cavalliers et a cavals	to knights and to horses
d'anar de galobs e de sals.[85]	to go out galloping and jumping.

The hagiographic work *Barlaam et Josaphat* describes a similarly festive scene:

Corns e bouzinas e cans d'auzels e diversas manieras de jocz li feron annar denant, per so que.l cor de luy s'alegres. D'aytal guiza lo filh del rey fazia sas processions soven.[86]	Horns and buisines and songs of birds and diverse sorts of entertainment they brought before him, to gladden his heart. In this way the son of the king often would make his processions.

---

[82] HUBERT and PORTER, eds., *Flamenca*, lines 7270–7272.
[83] MICHEL, ed., *Histoire de la guerre de Navarre*, lines 4714–4716.
[84] Ibid., lines 4989–4991.
[85] HUBERT and PORTER, eds., *Flamenca*, lines 7690–7699.
[86] LAVAUD and NELLI, eds., *Barlaam et Josaphat*, p. 1084.

A little later, in a passage that intertwines Latin with Old Occitan, the king uses a horn or buisine to convey an ominous message, here foreshadowing an association with death that one finds in music for trombones in the seventeenth and eighteenth centuries. The passage appears to use the words *corn*, *buccina*, and *tuba* to refer to a single instrument:

Acostumada cauza era del rey que cant neguns homs avia deservida mort, el rey trametia sa crida, que cornes a la porta d'aquel. Vespere igitur venienta, misit rex buccinam mortis tubicinare ante ianuam domus fratris sui. E cant hon auzia aquel corn cornar a la mayzon de son frayre, e cant aquel auzi aquel corn, de mort fon segurs e tota nueg et el devezi sas cauzas.[87]	The king was accustomed, whenever any man deserved death, to send a herald to sound the horn before his door. When Vespers had come, the king sent the buisines of death to trumpet in front of the door of his brother. And when this horn was heard trumpeting at the house of his brother, and when the brother himself heard this horn, he knew that death would follow, and all night he tended to his affairs.

Some of these stories contain allusions to the life of a *joglar*, but none treats the subject more thoroughly than *Daurel et Beton*, a *canso de gesta* composed in the middle of the twelfth century. It is the story of the heroic and sacrificial loyalty of a *joglar* who experiences both the best and the worst of a very volatile age, from comfortable patronage at a ducal court to near slavery and persecution at the hands of the duke's enemies. The story itself is doubtless fictitious, but certain descriptive details have the ring of truth. The *joglar* in this tale is an accomplished instrumentalist on fiddle and harp; he dances, sings the songs of others, and evidently composes as well, and these skills earn him a place at court:

E viueulet agradable e gueiamen e clier,	And he fiddled nicely and merrily and clearly,
e fo paubres d'aver, ma be.is sap deportier.	and he was poor in property, but knew how to carry himself well.
Lo ric duc d'Antona li pres a demandier:	The noble duke of Antona began to ask him:
"Cum as tu nom, amicx? garda no m'o v[e]lhas celier."	"What is your name, friend? mind that you hide nothing from me."
Daurel li respon, que bo sap motz gensier:	Daurel answered him, in courteous words:
"Senher, Daurel ay nom, e say motz gen arpier,	"Lord, my name is Daurel, and I can harp most nobly,
e toca vihola e ricamen trobier;	and play the fiddle and richly compose;
e son, senher, vostre om, d'un riche castelier	and I am, lord, your vassal, from a rich castle
que hom apela Monclier."[88]	that is called Monclar."

---

[87] Ibid., p. 1092.

[88] KIMMEL, ed., *Daurel et Beton*, lines 79–87. There is evidence that the entire *Daurel et Beton* epic was sung. This is implied in the second verse of "Ges si tot m'ai ma volontat felonia" (PC 245,1) where the poet Guiraut de Luc suggests using "the tune of [Duke] Boves d'Antona" for his song (printed in M. DE RIQUER, *Los Trovadores: Historia literaria y textos* [Barcelona 1975], p. 550). There is not room here to discuss the intriguing prospect that the tune of an epic work might be considered suitable for the performance of a lyric poem. The reference also raises interesting questions about the relationship between the music used for singing the epic and the music that might go with its lyric insertions.

As the story progresses, the duke is treacherously murdered, and Daurel eventually takes charge of his lord's infant son Beton, spiriting him away to Babylon to seek the protection of the Emir of Cairo. En route, Daurel sings to the baby about the duke's murder:

Cant l'efas plora a lui non [a] sabor	He had no pleasure when the child wept,
e pren sa viola e fai .i. lais d'amor:	and he took his fiddle and performed a *lai* of love:
"Ai!" so ditz el, "mon pauc gentil senhor,	"Ah!" he said, "my poor noble lord,
cum vos lonhat de vostra gran honor!"[89]	how you have lost your great honor!"

Later, in the Emir's court, Daurel is called upon to entertain. In performing a couple of "laisses notatz," seemingly without a text, the *joglar* appears to be creating a musical work with a structure derived from epic poetry:

Pueis pres l'arpa, a .ii. laisses notatz	Then he took the harp, with two musical laisses
et ab la viola a los gen deportat.[90]	and with his fiddle entertained the people.

Daurel undertakes to educate Beton, teaching him the skills of a *joglar*. An apt pupil, Beton learns "to finger" (*tocar*) the instruments, as well as other creative skills:

Qua[n]t ac .vii. ans Beto sap gen violar,	When Beto was seven he knew how to fiddle nicely,
e tocar citola e ricamen arpar	and play the citole and nobly harp,
e cansos dire, de se mezis trobar.[91]	and sing songs, and compose songs himself.

Daurel had attempted to pass off Beton as his own son, but the deception is discovered in a playful scheme whereby Beton is asked to perform and then offered money. When he refuses payment, the courtiers are convinced of his noble birth. At just nine years old Beton has gained great skill as an entertainer. In the following verses he amuses the court by accompanying himself on the fiddle while he sings:

Et a las taulas servia al mangiers,	And at table he would serve the diners,
denan lo rei estava prezentiers,	before the king he presented himself well,
servi li fort de so que.l fa mestiers;	he served them well, as if it were his duty;
puessas los viola e canta volontiers.[92]	gladly he then fiddles and sings for them.

---

[89] Ibid., lines 1179–1182.
[90] Ibid., lines 1208–1209.
[91] Ibid., lines 1419–1421.
[92] Ibid., lines 1573–1576.

Joglars are described in similar fashion in several other narratives, like *Jaufre*:

E juglars de moutas maneiras	And joglars of all sorts,
qe tot jorn van per las careiras	who every day go about in the streets,
cantan e trepan e burden,	singing and dancing and skipping,
e vant bonas novas disen	and go along telling good news,
e las proesas e las gueras	and the noble deeds and wars
qe sun faitas en autras terras.[93]	that are done in other lands.

In the following scene in *Jaufre*, the ladies of the court dance to the accompaniment of the *joglars'* playing. The music seems to have had the extraordinary effect of inspiring both dancing and careful listening because, the author says, the tunes were unfamiliar:

E can trastuit agron manjat,	And when everyone had eaten,
li joglar sun en pes levat,	the joglars rose to their feet,
e cascun pres sun estrument,	and each took his instrument,
e comenson tan dousament	and they began so gently,
per meg lo palais a dansar.	in the midst of the palace, to dance.
Adonx viratz en pes levar	Then you would have seen rise to their feet
donas, qu'anc neguna tener	the ladies, whom no one,
no s'en poc, per negun saber,	by whatever means, could distract
de dous son que fan li strument,	from the sweet melodies the instruments played,
e cascuna mout s'i entent.[94]	and everyone listened to them intently.

Less formal musical situations are alluded to on occasion, particularly pastoral scenes in which shepherds, shepherdesses, and villagers engage in informal pastimes. The *kalenda maia* or maying-song (another word for which was *devinolas*) was quite popular among the peasants, probably one of the many popular refrain-types that accompanied dancing. The music for "Cella domna ben aia / Que non fai languir son amic" mentioned in the verses below is not, to my knowledge, extant:

Las tosetas agron ja trachas	The maidens had already brought out
las maias quel seras son fachas	may-garlands they had made the night before,
e lur devinolas canteron.	and they sang their may-songs.
Tot dreit davan Guillem passeron	They all passed right in front of Guillem
cantan una kalenda maia	singing a maying-song
que dis: "Cella domna ben aia	that goes: "May the lady be rewarded
que non fai languir son amic."[95]	who does not make her lover languish."

---

[93] LAVAUD and NELLI, eds., *Jaufre*, lines 3077–3082.
[94] Ibid., lines 10787–10796.
[95] HUBERT and PORTER, eds., *Flamenca*, lines 3233–3239. The famous *estampida* "Kalenda maya" composed by Raimbaut de Vaqueiras is a much more sophisticated representative of the maying-song.

Later in the same work reference is made to "Breton fiddling tunes" performed in the town of Nantes, on the Loire between Poitou and Brittany; again the music is heard in a rustic setting:

Dansas e viuladura[s] bretas	Dances and Breton fiddling tunes
pogras auzir sai e lai tantas	you could hear near and far,
qu'esser cujaras inz e Nantas	so that you might have thought you were at Nantes
[on] hom las troba e las diz.[96]	where people make them and sing them.

References to singing the Mass and Office are not uncommon in narrative texts:

Turpin l'evesque ha la messa canteya;	Bishop Turpin sang mass;
le duc Rollan l'a de cor escouteya.[97]	the duke Roland listened to it with his heart.

On more solemn occasions reference might be made to "high mass":

L'evesques de Clarmon chantet	The Bishop of Clermont sang
aquel jorn la messa major.[98]	high mass that day.

Sung Vespers and Matins help mark off hours of the day for some narrative poets:

So dis l'evesque: "Tayzies vos, si vos agreya;	The bishop said: "Be silent, if you please;
nos cantarem vespras e matineyas,	we will sing such Vespers and Matins
tals que seran bonas es honoreyas."[99]	as will be good and honored."

The use of "high" and "low" in the following verse is intriguing:

Vespras cantet hom aut e bas.[100]	Vespers were chanted high and low.

Is the poet suggesting a performance that included high and low voices? Or does he mean a dynamic variation between loud and soft? The context does not answer these questions, but we must assume that the poet was concerned with meeting the demands of his rhyme scheme and syllable count, and that he chose the words *aut* and *bas* partly because the phrase is formulaic, and largely because it fits into his poetic structure. To maintain that he intended to be more than loosely accurate about performance practice would be incautious.

A reference to singing the mass *am nota gran* occurs in the romance *Guilhem de la Barra*, written in 1318. This literally means "with large notes":

Si cos tanh, segon nostra fe,	If it is fitting, according to our faith,
le matremoni vay lassar,	the wedding will be allowed,
e pueys vay la messa cantar	and then the bishop will sing
l'avesques, et am nota gran.[101]	mass, and with large notes.

---

[96] Ibid., lines 7477–7480.
[97] ROQUES, ed., *Ronsasvals*, lines 183–184.
[98] HUBERT and PORTER, eds., *Flamenca*, lines 475–476.
[99] ROQUES, ed., *Ronsasvals*, lines 214–216.
[100] HUBERT and PORTER, eds., *Flamenca*, line 936.
[101] P. MEYER, ed., *Guillaume de la Barre, roman d'aventures par Arnaut Vidal de Castelnaudari, publié pour la première fois d'après le manuscrit unique* (Paris 1895), lines 3854–3857.

Here again, the poet uses the phrase to complete the verse, and since it appears to serve an adverbial function modifying *cantar*, it is unlikely that the poet meant "large notes" inscribed on parchment. Both *nota* and the verb *notar* (see above) are ambiguous in all of their infrequent appearances in Old Occitan literature. The poet probably means no more than an expansive or solemn intonation of the chants of the Mass, if he means even that much. It could very well be simply a reference to plainchant, as opposed to the longs and shorts of mensural music.[102]

In other passages, the Mass is "said," although some translators render this "sung":

Tantost con fon dicha la messa,	As soon as mass was said,
tuit van jugar a taula messa.[103]	all began to make sport at the dinner table.

In *Ronsasvals* reference is made to the singing of Mass for the Dead by 100 monks:

Layns aura .c. moynes generals,	Within will be 100 regular [?] monks,
que cantaran las messas mortuials,	who will sing the Mass for the Dead,
que Dieus perdon als comtes naturals.[104]	that God may pardon the true counts.

Occasionally specific chants and words are mentioned, in these two passages evidently the "Confiteor" or prayer of confession before the Eucharist, and the "Agnus Dei" that precedes the Communion:

Le sieus cantars plac mout a totz,	His singing was very pleasant to all,
car mout avia clara voz	for he had a very clear voice,
e cantet ben e volontiers.	and he sang well and gladly.
Que saupes qu'el fos cavalliers,	Had they known he was a knight,
ben amer' on plus [son] cantar.	they would have liked his song even more.
Le preire fon davan l'autar,	The priest was before the altar,
e dis "confiteor" suau.	and he said "confiteor" sweetly.
Guillems hac vos clara e sana,	Guillem had a voice clear and healthy,
e canta ben apertamen	and he sang quite openly
a l'Agnus Dei, et el pren	the "Agnus Dei," and he took
Pas, en aisi con far devia,	the Peace, as he should do,
et a son oste, que sezia	and to his host, who was seated
el cor, desempre n'a donat.[105]	in the choir, he quickly gave it.

The author of *Flamenca* mentions the number of singers in the choir of a small church or chapel at Mass:

El cor non ac mais .ii. enfans,	In the choir there were but two boys,
Guillem e l'oste, que saupesson	Guillem and the host, who knew how to
cantar ni que s'entramezeson.	sing or who were concerned with it.
Guillems dis ben la soa part.[106]	Guillem recited his part well.

---

[102] Compare, for instance, Grocheio's description of the performance of the Kyrie eleison: "Isti autem cantus cantantur tractim et ex longis et perfectis ad modum cantus coronati..." (ROHLOFF, ed., *Johannes de Grocheio*, p. 162).
[103] HUBERT and PORTER, eds., *Flamenca*, lines 302–303. Hubert's rhymed verse translation, which takes considerable liberties with the text, renders these verses: "The mass once sung, they all were able | To make good sport and feast at table."
[104] ROQUES, ed., *Ronsasvals*, lines 1447–1449.
[105] HUBERT and PORTER, eds., *Flamenca*, lines 2499–2505 and 3914–3919.
[106] Ibid., lines 2508–2511.

While the above passages describe the singing of chant during prescribed worship services, the following refers to the singing of a liturgical piece by a single individual outside of the service, evidently as a spontaneous expression of joy:

E Jozaphas, cant auzi la bona confession que fazia, davant son payre comenset a cantar, auzent totz, hymne esperital: "Veni creator spiritus, mentes tuorum visita," etc. E tot lo pobol respondet que grans era le dieus dels crestians.[107]	And Josaphat, after hearing the good confession made [by his father], began to sing before his father, in the hearing of all, the spiritual hymn "Veni Creator Spiritus, mentes tuorum visita." And all the people responded that the God of the Christians was great.

An interesting description of the educational regimen of one individual is found in the romance *Flamenca*: he is said to have been taught the liberal arts in Paris, to read, and to sing:

D'aita[l] faison, d'aital semblanza fo noiris a Paris e Franza. Lai apres tan de las .vii. artz que pogra ben en totas partz tener escolas, sis volgues.	In such fashion and manner he was raised in Paris, in France. There he so well learned the seven arts that he could easily, anywhere, have directed a school, if he had wanted to.
Legir e cantar, sil plagues, en glies[a] saup mieilz d'autre clergue.[108]	If he wanted to, he could read and sing, in church better than most priests.

Women of the nobility were acquainted with the quadrivium and trivium, as this address by Flamenca to her lady-in-waiting suggests:

Flamenca dis: "Qui t'ensenet, Margarida, ni quit mostret, fe qe.m deus, tan de dialetica? S'augessas legit arismetiga, astronomia e musica, non agras meils dig la fesica del[s] mals qu'eu ai loncs tems suffertz."[109]	Flamenca said: "Who instructed you, Marguerite, and who taught you, by faith you owe me, so much dialectic? If you had read arithmetic, astronomy and music, you could have described no better all the evils that I have suffered for so long."

Some narratives imply that it was not uncommon to read Occitanian literature out loud from some sort of written source. One of the clearest references to this is found, surprisingly, in a very early work, the eleventh-century hagiographic poem *Canso de St. Fides*. The author "heard" the song "read":

Tota Basconn' et Aragons e l'encontrada delz Gascons sabon quals es aqist canczons e ss' es ben vera sta razons. Eu l'audi legir a clerczons et a gramadis, a molt bons... E si vos plaz est nostre sons,	All of Basque and Aragon and the country of the Gascons know what this song is and if its subject is true. I heard it read by young clerics and scholars, very good ones... And if our melody pleases you,

---

[107] LAVAUD and NELLI, eds., *Barlaam et Josaphat*, p. 1200.
[108] HUBERT and PORTER, eds., *Flamenca*, lines 1622–1628.
[109] Ibid., lines 5443–5449.

>   aisi con.l guida.l primers tons,   which is guided by the first tone,
>   eu la vos cantarei en dons.[110]   I will thus sing it to you.

Although nothing here compels us to believe that the melody as well as the text was notated in the book, the appearance of the word *son*, "melody," assures us that musical performance was indicated. This passage also points to some connection between the performance of vernacular epic and the system of ecclesiastical modes, in the allusion to the *"primers tons"* to which the poem is to be sung. This work is neither a true epic nor a romance, which most scholars today believe were performed, when sung, according to some simple, possibly modal, formulaic system. The passage does not imply that such modal formulas were used; on the contrary, it seems to say that there was a definite melody constructed by means of the first mode. One cannot infer from this that the performer composed his tune as he sang, but instead that his memory of the melody was aided by the fact that it was crafted on recognizable structural principles. A little bit later in the poem in the midst of a passage that invokes the imagery of the apple tree, the plural verb implies that more than one person is singing the song:

>   Lur umbra streins aqest planczon   Their shadows embrace this seedling
>   de cui cantam esta canczon...[111]   about which we sing this song...

A choral performance reinforces the theory that the melody was in some measure fixed and known.

Ensenhamens, encyclopedias, and other didactic works

Didactic and moral writings contain some incidental references to music, and since they often are not couched in the restrictive figurative language endemic to poetry, or limited to an entertainment function, in some cases their language might be considered somewhat more precise than that found in the lyric poems. At the same time, however, the authors of these works were not so much concerned with thoroughness or accuracy in musical matters as they were with the advocacy of codes of ethics, morality, chivalry, or the like. In addition, most of them were composed as poetry and as such were subject to the same structural limitations as all poetry. Nonetheless, the few references to music in them are of some interest. Passages like the following, an exhortation to a lady from Garin lo Brun's *Ensenhamen de la Donzela* (first half of the twelfth century), are not unfamiliar to us by now. The word *son* is used in such a way as to cast doubt on a purely musical meaning. In addition, there is an opposition between a *joglar* and a *chantador*: the

---

[110] E. HOEPFFNER and P. ALFARIC, eds., *La "Chanson de Sainte Foy"* = Publications de la Faculté des Lettres de l'Université de Strasbourg 32–33 (Paris 1926), I, lines 23–28 and 31–33.
[111] Ibid., lines 63–64.

contrast may be more apparent than real, however, if it is regarded as an example of parallelism so common in medieval poetry:

Joglars e chantadors,	Joglars and singers,
que paraulan d'amors	who speak of love
e canton sons e lais,	and sing melodies and lais,
per que l'om es plus gais,	which gladden people,
e meton en corage	and who inspire courage
de tot prez vassallage,	to undertake all feats of bravery,
retenez amoros.[112]	you should honor with your affection.

An *ensenhamen* by Raimon Vidal, from the turn of the thirteenth century, seems to indicate that a *joglar*, while a "singing" man, was not always obliged to deliver his works (specifically long epic ones) musically but instead may have recited them. One is reminded, however, that the distinction among these verbs is not at all clear:

"Senher, yeu soy us hom acli	"Sir, I am a man inclined
a joglaria de cantar,	to the life of a singing joglar,
e say romans dir e contar,	and I know how to recount and recite romances
e novas motas e salutz	and lots of news and greetings
e autres comtes espandutz	and other tales known
vas totas partz azautz e bos,	in all parts, charming and good,
e d'En Guiraut vers e chansos	and verses and songs of lord Guiraut
e d'En Arnaut de Maruelh mays,	and more of Arnaut de Marvuelh,
e d'autres vers e d'autres lays	and other verses and other lays
que ben deuri' en cort caber."[113]	which should surely establish me in a court."

The same work voices the complaint familiar from other works about rudeness on the part of audiences – and the minstrels clearly see themselves here as too finely bred to whine:

Vos dic qu'entre.ls valens e pros	I tell you that among the valiant and worthy
n'i a que son ses tot esgart,	are those without any consideration,
e que.us diran a una part	who speak to you in private
e mest autrui que lur cantes;	and ask you to sing in front of the others;
e no.y gardaran nulh vetz	and then they will observe neither propriety
ni nulh temps ni nulha sazo,	nor timing nor the occasion,
e al ters de mot de la canso	but at every third word of whatever song
cal que digatz, ilh groniran	you may be performing, they will grumble
e josta vos cosselharan	and whisper with others during it,
o.s metran novas a comtar.	or begin to tell other news.
Anc Dieus sen non lur volc donar	God never wanted to give them sense
ni fara ja, mon essien.	nor will He, in my opinion.

[112] C. APPEL, *L'Enseignement de Garin lo Brun*, in: *Revue des langues romanes* 33 (1889), p. 404–432, lines 541–547.
[113] W. H. FIELD, ed., *Raimon Vidal, Poetry and Prose* II: *Abrils Issia* = University of North Carolina Studies in the Romance Languages and Literatures 110 (Chapel Hill 1971), lines 38–47.

Aquels si tot no son valen	Even though such people are worthless,
menatz al pus gen que poiretz.[114]	you should treat them as gently as you can.

Three "didactic sirventes" composed by different poets in the middle twelfth, early thirteenth, and late thirteenth centuries, respectively, address the life of the *joglar* specifically, and the tone of the earliest one is sternly reproachful. Addressed by Guiraut de Cabreira to a *joglar* named "Cabra," it disparages the skills and learning of the unfortunate entertainer in very specific terms, at the same time providing a prescription for the skills and knowledge that a respectable *joglar* ought to possess. Note the reference to songs – undoubtedly courtly lyric – by Jaufre Rudel, Marcabru, and two other poets of the nobility, the otherwise unidentified Alfonso and Eble:

Mal saps viular	You know how to fiddle badly
e pietz chantar	and to sing even worse
del cap tro en la fenizon;	from the beginning to the end;
non sabs fenir,	you don't know how to finish,
al mieu albir,	in my opinion,
a tempradura de breton.	in the intonation of a Breton.
Mal t'ensegnet	He taught you badly,
cel que.t mostret	whoever showed you
los detz amenar ni l'arson.	where to put the fingers and bow.
Ja vers novel	Even a new vers,
bon d'En Rudell	a good one of Lord Rudel,
non cug que.t pas sotz lo guingnon,	I do not believe can pass from beneath your moustache,
da Markabrun,	of Marcabru,
ni de negun	nor of anyone,
ni de N'Anfos ni de N'Eblon.	nor of Lord Alfonso or Lord Eble.
Del Saine cut	Of [the song of] Saxons I believe
c'ajas perdut	that you have lost
et oblidat los motz e.l son;	and forgotten the words and the tune;
ren no.n dicetz	you have said nothing of it
ni no.n sabetz,	nor do you know of it,
pero no i ha meillor chanson.[115]	even though there is no better song.

After a great list of legends, epics, and histories expected to be found in the repertoire of a respectable *joglar*, Guiraut finally points out that Cabra does not even know how to perform in church:

Non saps upar	You don't know how to rejoice
ni organar	Nor make organum
en glieiza ni dedinz maizon.[116]	in church or inside a house.

---

[114] Ibid., lines 1445–1458.
[115] F. PIROT, ed., *Recherches sur les connaissances littéraires des troubadours occitans et catalans des XIIe et XIIIe siècles: Les "sirventes-ensenhamens" de Guerau de Cabrera, Guiraut de Calanson, et Bertrand de Paris* = Memorias de la Real Academia de Buenas Letras de Barcelona 14 (Barcelona 1972); Guiraut de Cabreira, "Cabra joglar," lines 7–15, 25–30 and 49–54.
[116] Ibid., lines 211–213.

There are two lexicological problems in these verses. The term *upar* is obscure. The context suggests that it might be a corruption of *arpar*, to play the harp. Raynouard cites this passage in his *Lexique roman* and translates it "to sing."[117] He cites other passages in which the word *upa* or *upupa* refers to a kind of bird (French *huppe*). Other translators and commentators, comparing the word to similar ones in Catalan, have suggested that *upar* connotes some sort of vocal outburst of praise at the end of a chant, perhaps like a *jubilus*.[118]

The other problem with this passage concerns the word *organar*. The editor, François Pirot, has modified the text here from the manuscript reading of *mot guariar* or *ni ot guariar* because the word *guariar* is unknown.[119] Assuming that the scribe was confused by the reading given in his exemplar, Pirot suggests a reconstruction based on the context as well as the poetic and grammatical requirements. If this is accepted as an appropriate reading, it does not answer whether the meaning is "to play the organ" or whether it might refer to the performance of polyphony, and it creates the problem of explaining the occurrence of either polyphony or organ-playing in a domestic setting.

The second *ensenhamen* to a *joglar*, composed by Guiraut de Calanso in the early thirteenth century, was patterned to some extent after the earlier work by Guiraut de Cabreira, but its author's attitude is decidedly more positive. It conveys a detailed picture of the all-round entertainer, who was musician, acrobat, composer, dancer, debater, and *raconteur*. Some instruments and their sounds are described, notably the raucous *symphonie* and the shrill pipe:

Sapchas trobar,	Know how to compose,
e gen tombar,	and nobly tumble,
e ben parlar, e jocs partir;	and speak well, and engage in debates;
taboreiar	to play the tambourine
e tauleiar	and the castanets
e far sinphonia brogir.	and make the symphonie roar.
E citolar	And to play the citole
e mandurar,	and the mandora,
e per catre sercles saillir;	and leap [dance] in four circles;
manicorda	[to play] the monochord
ab una corda	with one string
e sedra c'om vol ben auzir.	and the cittern that everyone likes very much to hear.
Sonetz nota,	Sound the notes,
fai la rota	have the rote
ab detz e ot cordas garnir;	supplied with eighteen strings;
sapchas arpar	know how to harp
e ben temprar	and tune well
la guiga el sos esclarzir.	the giga to make the notes clear.

---

[117] F. J. RAYNOUARD, *Lexique roman, ou dictionnaire de la langue des troubadours*, V (Paris 1843), p. 450.
[118] See PIROT, *Recherches*, p. 561, note 211.
[119] Ibid., p. 561, note 212.

Juglar leri,	Happy joglar,
del salteri	the psaltery
faras detz cordas estampir;	of ten strings you will sound;
nou esturmenz,	nine instruments
si be.ls aprenz,	if you learn them well,
ne potz a totz obs retenir.	you will be able to remember for any work.
Et estivas	And sound the pipe
ab votz pivas	with a high voice
e la lira fai retentir;	and the lyre;
e del temple	and on the tympanum
per eissemple,	for example,
fai totz los cascavels ordir.[120]	ring all the bells.

One of the most interesting musical references in Old Occitan literature occurs in the mid-thirteenth-century *Tezaur* of Peire de Corbian. Educated at the scholastic center of Orléans and a cleric and *maistre*, by his own account, Peire picked up no slight knowledge of music and some of its more technical vocabulary. His encyclopedia relies on numerous other authors, from the Venerable Bede to Jean de Holywood, but he is often creative in his incorporation of the earlier material. The following passage is most notable for its use of the word *contrapointamens*, some eighty or so years before the Latin "contrapunctus" appeared in musical treatises:

Senhors, encar sai ieu molt devinablamenz	Lords, now I know very divinely indeed
chantar en sancta glieiza per ponz e per asenz,	how to sing in holy church by points and by accents,
choris *sanctus* et *agnus* tripar contipotens,[121]	dance the "Sanctus" and "Agnus" and the "Cunctipotens,"
entonar *seculorum* que nol faill us *amens*,	intone "seculorum" followed without fail by "amen,"
e far dous chantz et orgues e contrapointamens.	and make sweet chants and organa and counterpoints.
Ja sai chansons enotas e vers bos e valens,	Indeed I know noted songs and good and worthy verses,
pastorelas apres amorozas, plazens,	I have learned pastorelas, lovely and pleasing,
retroenchas e dansas, ben e cortesamens.	retroenchas and dansas, noble and courtly.
De totas res del segle sai aver grazimens,	Of all things of the world I know how to have the favor
de clercs, de cavaliers, de dompnas avinens,	of clerics, knights, and honorable ladies,

---

[120] Ibid., Guiraut de Calanso, "Fadet joglar," lines 13–18 and 25–48.

[121] Verse 498 is intriguing for its implication of dancing during the Mass. Another manuscript reading of this verse is "chantar *sanctus* et *agnus* tripla contipotenz," "to sing the 'Sanctus' and 'Agnus' [and] the triple 'Cunctipotens,'" which makes a little more sense. I am grateful to Professor F. Alberto Gallo for alerting me to the likelihood that "contipotens," otherwise unknown in Old Occitan, refers to the Kyrie trope.

de borces, de joglars, d'escudiers, de servens.¹²²	of burghers, joglars, students, and servants.

The "ponz" and "asenz" of verse 497 seem likely to be references to the notational symbols used in chant manuscripts.

In 1254 the troubadour Guiraut Riquier addressed a letter to Alfonso X of Castile, asking the king to issue a declaration clarifying the exact station and activities of a *joglar*.¹²³ He did this, he said, because all professions have their names, which are universally understood, and he wished to clear up the confusion that plagued contemporary discourse, a confusion that we have already seen in abundance. In this "Suplicatio que fe Gr. Riquier al rey de Castela per lo nom d[els] joglars," the poet named the various levels of hierarchy within the church, the nobility, government, commerce, the laboring class, and the peasantry, and then complained that the term *joglar* was used generically to cover a wide variety of activities, including singing, playing instruments, telling stories, puppetry, composing (*trobar*), juggling, and acrobatics, and covering social classes from the highest courtly performer to the lowest travelling crooner. He begged the king to assign specific terms to these activities, and especially to distinguish the name (and profession) of *joglar* from that of *trobador*. The king's reply of a year later (undoubtedly composed rather by Guiraut himself), "Declaratio, quel senher rei N'Anfos de Castela fe per la suplicatio, que Gr. Riquier fe per lo nom de joglar," not surprisingly complied with the poet's request. He mentioned the Latin terms *istriones* (performers on "low class" instruments – *esturmens dissendens*), *inventores* (Old Occitan *trobador*), and *ioculatores* (dancer or acrobat, Old Occitan *tumbador*). He invoked the Occitan words *tragitador* (juggler) and *contrafazedor* (mime) as well as the Lombard term *bufos* for the less honorable types of entertainers. Guiraut concluded his long-winded diatribe by asserting that the word *joglar* should be reserved for performers with courtly skills and manners, the word *trobador* for poet-composers:

E silh, c'ab cortezia	And those who with their courtesy
et ab azaut saber	and charming knowledge
se sabon captener	know how to conduct themselves
entre las ricas gens	among noble people
per tocar esturmens	by playing instruments
o per novas comtar	or telling news
d'autrui o per cantar	of others, or by singing
autrus vers e cansos	the verses and songs of others
o per d'autres faitz bos	or by other worthwhile deeds
e plazens per auzir,	that are agreeable to listen to,
podon ben possezir	can well bear
aquel nom de joglar.	the name of joglar.

---

¹²² G. BERTONI and A. JEANROY, eds., Le "Thezaur" de Peire de Corbian, in: Annales du Midi 23 (1911), p. 289–308 and 451–471, lines 496–500 and 503–508. The edition is a conflation of readings in two main families, one from Italian manuscripts of the mid- to late thirteenth century, the other from a Provençal source of the end of the thirteenth century. The reading given here is mainly from the probable earliest source, of 1254 (Modena, Biblioteca Estense, α.R.4,4), which is more compact than the other two versions.

¹²³ C. A. F. MAHN, ed., Die Werke der Troubadours in provenzalischer Sprache (Berlin 1846–1886, repr. Geneva 1977), IV, p. 163–191.

E sels, on es sabers	And those who know
de trobar motz e sos,	how to invent words and melodies,
d'aquels mostra razos,	about them the stories teach
com los deu hom nomnar;	how they should be named;
car qui sap dansas far	for whoever knows how to make dances
e coblas e baladas	and stanzas and ballades
d'azaut maistreiadas,	of masterful charm,
albas e sirventes,	albas and sirventes,
gent e be razos es,	it is proper and reasonable
c'om l'apel trobador.[124]	to call such a man troubadour.

Guiraut's indictment of his contemporaries for their sloppy use of words is well-taken. But it could apply not only to the words with which he concerned himself in this poem, but also, as we have seen, to a myriad of words used by Occitanian authors for musical things. Seen in their literary contexts, these words make it abundantly clear that the poets used their language as a tool not for the purpose of communicating accurate information about their culture to historians of 600 years later, but rather for the same ephemeral reasons that poets have always used language. This literature no more lays down prohibitions than it sets up rules, and any attempt to garner its testimony in support of theories about performance practices, evolution of musical forms, or anything else is dangerous. On the other hand, the wealth of references to music found in these works demonstrates the large part that music played in meridional society, and further study is sure to contribute to our knowledge of the troubadours' music and the world that surrounded it.

---

[124] Ibid., lines 222–233 and 246–255.

[20]

Mensura *and the Rhythm of Medieval Monodic Song*

J. E. Maddrell

At least up to c. 1350, monodic music played a larger and more important part in European life than polyphony. Gregorian chant is still a living force among us, but what of the vast body of non-liturgical song? From time to time one can hear performances of troubadour and trouvère songs, although there is an unfortunate tendency to perform only the same few anthologized pieces, while (for instance) the Italian *laude* and the Spanish *cantigas* remain, as far as modern audiences are concerned, mere names in the history books. A wider selection of monodic song ought to be available, in print and in performance; but any responsible attempt to achieve this end is made more difficult by the fact that the notation of the songs, in most cases, gives no indication of the rhythm.

For anyone whose interest in the songs is purely historical, the problem is quickly dealt with. He has merely to enumerate the various scholarly theories, add some comment, and present the would-be transcriber with a choice between several forms of modal rhythm on one hand, and free rhythm on the other. For him, historical scholarship has gone as far as it can with an insoluble problem, and it is useless to discuss the matter further: are not the histories of music written?

But anyone concerned with the culture of the past as a vital reality in the present will have a more serious, more intelligent, interest in the songs; he will insist on the importance of *experiencing* the songs through performance. He simply cannot accept that two quite different methods of transcribing a given song are equally good, and he may feel unable to commit himself to either. The modal theory has, from the start, been admittedly based on assumptions rather than facts, and it is impossible to apply the methods it recommends without at least some misgivings. For instance: even if it is an appropriate method of transcribing French and Provençal love songs, can it be used for, say, English songs, or religious, but non-liturgical, songs in Latin?

One is therefore very grateful to Dr. Hendrik Vanderwerf, who has recently reopened the question. In two articles, which are best read together (1965 and 1967), he considers the trouvère songs in light of the knowledge that many of them were orally transmitted, and points out that the variants which are found whenever a song is preserved in more than one source are not all to be written off as scribal errors in an attempt to establish a supposed "original version"; they are rather necessary consequences of the culture to which the songs belong, and must be taken into account in deciding what rhythm to adopt in transcription. On this point I am in total agreement with Dr Vanderwerf (and gratefully acknowledge the influence of his view on my own work) but his second major conclusion, that "the rhythm is free in two ways: first, accented and unaccented tones and syllables may come at irregular intervals, and second, there is not necessarily a simple relation between the duration of one tone and that of another" (1965: 67), cannot go unquestioned.

"Free rhythm" is an attractive expedient for the transcriber, who merely has to write a melody in stemless neumes, or to represent single notes as quarter notes and ligatures as groups of eighth notes; but it leaves the performer with an uneasy choice between a plainsong-like rendering and his own invented rhythm – in other words, between two methods which have equally slender chances of approximating what might have been a medieval singer's version. Even assuming that the choice of rhythm was originally left to the performer, it is, surely, an editor's duty to minimize discrepancies between medieval and modern choices, by choosing on behalf of the performer a rhythm likely to have been chosen by his medieval counterpart.

The choice need not, indeed must not, rely on strict principles, applied without variation to every song. Each song must be treated on its merits, considering the internal features of its notation and the external evidence of medieval notation in general. Nevertheless, the paleographic evidence is often inconclusive or contradictory, and the transcriber will need some guidance as to the broad lines on which to work. For this he will turn to Johannes de Grocheo, the only medieval writer to discuss secular monody. I have in preparation an article which deals at length with the paleographic side of the matter; at present I wish to make a semantic point about Grocheo's terminology, which seems to call for a reinterpretation of several previously known facts.

Passages from Grocheo have often been cited in support of the free rhythm theory. In a work which contains much of value on the subject of rhythm, we find the following, part of which is quoted with approval by Dr. Vanderwerf:

> Indeed, when we recur once more to the most important theoretical source of the time, there is not a single allusion to either binary or ternary time in Grocheo's lengthy treatise. What this keen observer states is, on the contrary, that musica mensurata *comprises exclusively polyphonic works like conducts and motets but neither Gregorian chant nor any monophonic secular music,* and that the latter type, a *musica non ita praecise mensurata* is sung *totaliter ad libitum.*
> Does this leave any doubt?
> Monophonic music, far from being subject to the *modi,* had the privilege of free rhythm.
> (Sachs 1953: 176. The italics are not mine).

It is not easy to see how this statement could come from anyone who had read Grocheo attentively. His treatise is by no adult standards lengthy, and if he mentions neither duple nor triple time, it is because he is a post-Franconian and does not aim to discuss notation and rhythm. As for "doubt," it is bound to arise, as soon as one sees that phrase *totaliter ad libitum* in its context. Here is the whole passage, which occurs in Grocheo's account of the various methods of classifying music:

> Alii autem musicam dividunt in planam sive immensurabilem, et mensurabilem, per planam sive immensurabilem intelligentes ecclesiasticam, quae secundum Gregorium pluribus tonis determinatur. Per mensurabilem intellegunt illam quae ex diversis sonis simul mensuratis et sonatibus efficitur, sicut in condictibus et motetis.
> Sed si per immensurabilem intellegunt musicam nullo modo mensuratam, immo totaliter ad libitum dictam, deficiunt, eo quod quaelibet operatio musicae et cuiuslibet artis debet illius artis regulis mensurari. Si autem per immensurabilem non ita praecise mensuratam intellegant, potest, ut videtur, ista divisio remanere.
> (Others divide music into plain, or non-mensural, and mensural. By "plain or non-mensural" they mean plainchant, which is classified, following Gregory, in several modes. By "mensural" they mean music made from different notes measured and sounding at the same time, as they do in conductus and motets. But if by "non-mensural" they mean music that is in no way measured, still less performed completely freely, they are wrong, since any performance of music (or any art) must be measured by the rules of that art. If, however, they mean by "non-mensural," "not thus precisely measured" this division can evidently stand.)
>
> (ed. Rohloff, p. 47)

It is not true that Grocheo lumps plainsong and secular monody together as opposed to polyphony. His tripartite division is more subtle: *musica simplex* (or *civilis*, or *vulgaris*), *musica composita* (*regularis, canonica,* or *mensurata*), and *musica ecclesiastica* (ed. Rohloff, p. 47). The second and third categories, polyphony and plainsong, do not directly concern us here, but it is worth noting that Grocheo implies that the liturgical sequences were performed in a regular meter, in contrast to the main body of the chant (ed. Rohloff, p. 65).

Several of his remarks about the music which falls under his first heading warn us that the phrase *non ita praecise mensuratam* does not mean what it at first appears to mean. The instrumental *ductia,* he says, is measured with appropriate percussion, *cum decenti percussione mensurata* (p. 52), since it is a dance form. Again, he tells us that the *cantus coronatus* was performed with instrumental accompaniment (p. 50). Both these facts are difficult to reconcile with "free rhythm" as it is generally understood, but a third fact turns the difficulty into an impossibility. Grocheo helpfully cites a number of French songs to illustrate what he has to say about monodic song forms (for the most part he comments on the effect various forms are intended to produce in the audience), and four of these songs are extant. Of the four, three are found in the Chansonnier Cangé, written in a notation which, although pre-Franconian as to ligatures, clearly uses longs and breves for single notes: *Ausi com l'unicorne* (Spanke 1955: 2075), *Chanter m'estuet, quar ne m'en puis tenir* (1476), *Quant li rossignol* (1559), are all given as examples of *musica non ita praecise mensurata* (ed. Rohloff, p. 50; for the songs see Beck 1927: I, ff. 1, 22v, 110v and 117, and the transcriptions in Vol. II). The phrase can hardly be taken, therefore, as evidence for "free rhythm."

What, then, does Grocheo mean? Perhaps the best way of finding an answer is to consider the different senses of the word *mensura* as used by other theorists in the tradition to which Grocheo made so notable a contribution.

For Johannes de Garlandia, whose work was known to Grocheo, *musica mensurabilis* was *organum* (polyphony) which is, he says, a generic term for all mensural music:

> Habito de ipsa plana musica, que immensurabilis dicitur, nunc est presens intentio de ipsa mensurabili, que organum dicitur, quantum ad nos prout organum generale dicitur ad omnem mensurabilem musicam.
>
> (Coussemaker 1864: I, 175)

Lambert, author of the pseudo-Aristotelian *Tractatus de Musica,* makes a similar distinction. His three categories of *musica mensurabilis* are all polyphonic forms: discant, hocket, and *organum* (Coussemaker I, 269). The distinction here is between plainsong and polyphony, for in common with all theorists earlier than Grocheo, neither Lambert nor Garlandia take account of secular monody; we cannot therefore conclude *ex silentio* that the rhythm of non-liturgical monodic songs was that of plainsong. Indeed, it is clear that the word *mensura* meant to the theorists something more than it means in modern scholarship. In his discussion of the rhythmic modes (Coussemaker I, 97-104), Garlandia describes the third mode, by its very nature mensural in our sense, as *ultra mensuram*. Nor is he alone in this; the *Discantus positio vulgaris* even states that any note of more than two beats or less than one is *ultra mensuram* (Coussemaker I, 94).

These statements, puzzling at first sight, suggest two conclusions: firstly, *musica mensurabilis*, in the medieval sense, is synonymous with polyphony, and secondly, that *mensura,* when it refers to rhythm, denotes a strict modal pattern; thus the author of the *de Musica Libellus* virtually identifies *mensura* with *modus*:

> Modus in musica est debita mensuratio temporis, scilicet per longas et breves; vel aliter: modus est quidquid currit per debitam mensuram longarum notarum et brevium. Notandum quod quidam modus dicitur rectus; alius dicitur in ultra mensuram, qui scilicet excedit rectum modum sive rectam mensuram.
>
> (Coussemaker I, 378)

The key words here are *rectam* and *debitam* (regular and proper), both of which qualify *mensuram*. It is not difficult to imagine a *mensura* which is not, in this extremely strict sense, regular; consequently rhythmic patterns which to the modern scholar are mensural could be regarded by the medieval theorists as *immensurabilis*. When we take into account the additional fact that mensura does not necessarily refer to rhythm in every case, it will be realized that *mensura* has a strong qualitative, as well as a quantitative, force.

It is with this in mind that we must reconsider the significance of what Grocheo has to tell us. For him, the qualitative force of *mensura* is uppermost, and he uses the term in contexts which have nothing whatever to do with rhythm, as in his statement that the church (melodic) modes do not necessarily govern all music:

> Cantus autem iste per toni regulas forte non vadit, nec per eas mensuratur.
>
> (ed. Rohloff, p. 60)

We recall his statement, already quoted, that "any performance of music (or any art) must be measured by the rules of that art." Grocheo's synonyms for polyphony are, from this vantage point, extremely revealing: *musica regularis, canonica, mensurata*. The association of *mensura* with *regula* – both qualitative terms – is significant; the connotations of both words are propriety, reason, regularity, and order (cf. *rectam* and *debitam*). This important meaning of *mensura* is familiar outside musical scholarship, and we have a vernacular example in Langland's recurrent phrase "measurable hire," which means "proper, reasonable wages." This sense has not entirely been lost in modern English, for one can still hear, occasionally something described as "all right in measure," which is practically synonymous with "within reason." To carry the analogy further, one might reflect that *regula* means both "rule" and "ruler," and that the chief use of a ruler in the Middle Ages was not to measure distances (quantitatively) but to ensure that the line drawn was straight, i.e. qualitatively.

The purpose behind Grocheo's threefold division of music is evident. Polyphony is *mensurata* because it is written in accordance with the rules of composition; it is regular, ordered, and logical. Plainsong, though *immensurabilis*, has its own kind of order, provided by the rules of the melodic modes or *toni*. Secular monody differs from both. Though measured (in the modern sense) as to rhythm, it is not written according to the rules of composition; hence it is neglected by most theorists who are concerned with codifying rules. Its rhythms need not conform to strict modal patterns. It is therefore *non ita praecise mensurata*, the *ita* possibly referring back to the rules of composition. Monodic song answers the description well; its frequent melodic sixths, its flexible structures, and relatively wide vocal compasses, are not characteristic of 13th-century polyphony. Rhythmically, too, the songs in mensural notation – those in the Chansonnier Cangé and the later additions in the MS *du Roi* (facsimile in Beck 1938), in both cases written about the same time as Grocheo's treatise – often depart from exact modal patterns. The evidence of Grocheo suggests that it is to these sources, rather than to modern theories of rhythm, that we should look for guidance in transcribing non-mensurally notated songs.

These observations, offered in the hope of provoking discussion, show that there is no justification for "free rhythm" in Grocheo or any other medieval theorist; but we have no proof that it never existed. We must be content with the best explanation of the facts that can be devised. "Free rhythm" is not such an explanation. How can we accept that "the use of a rhythmically noncommittal notation in times when a metrical script was available indicates a free or optional rhythm" (Sachs 1953: 178), when examples abound of motets and conductus in non-mensural notation? Anonymous IV tells us that such pieces were read "by the understanding alone, by saying, 'I take this note as long, and that one as short'...." and on the evidence available there is no reason to suppose that a similar practice was not applied to monodic songs in non-mensural notation.

REFERENCES

Beck, Jean-Baptiste
    1927   *Chansonnier Cangé,* 2 vols., Philadelphia.
    1938   *Le manuscrit du roi,* 2 vols., Philadelphia.

Coussemaker, Charles Henri Edmond de,
    1864   *Scriptorum de musica....,* 4 vols., Paris.

Grocheo, Johannes de
    1943   *Der Musiktraktat des Johannes de Grocheo,* ed. Ernst Rohloff, (Media Latinitas Musica II), Leipzig.

Sachs, Curt
    1953   *Rhythm and Tempo,* New York.

Spanke, Hans, ed.
    1955   *Gaston Raynauds Bibliographie des altfranzösischen Liedes,* Leiden.

Vanderwerf, Hendrik
    1965   The trouvère chansons as creations of a notationless musical culture. *Current Musicology* (1965) 1: 61-68.
    1967   Deklamatorischer Rhythmus in den Chansons der Trouvères. *Die Musikforschung* (1967) 20: 122-144.

[21]
Concerning the Measurability of Medieval Music

Hendrik Van der Werf

I am very grateful to Neal Zaslaw for his invitation to add some commentary to J. E. Maddrell's article printed above. Understandably I am also very appreciative of Mr. Maddrell's acknowledgment of having been influenced by some of my writings, and I am happy to respond to some of his "observations, offered in the hope of provoking discussion." I welcome this opportunity especially since Mr. Maddrell directs attention to medieval theory, a source of information I have not touched upon in my publications in journals, although I have not at all ignored it in my research.

I am very much intrigued with Maddrell's evaluations of some of the medieval statements in relation to rhythm and meter in medieval music, but

I hope that his article is not a return to evaluation of medieval music as it was prevalent early in this century and before. It was customary in those days to concentrate on treatises for one's information on medieval music, without simultaneous evaluation of the preserved music in all its sources; at that time this approach could be pardoned in part because the treatises were much more accessible than the practical sources. Maddrell turns to actual music only once when prompted by Grocheo's mention of four actual songs, three of which occur in the *Chansonnier Cangé*. I suppose that I have no reason to be disappointed that Maddrell does not refer to my evaluation of the notation in that chansonnier, but I think I am justly disappointed by his own evaluation of it and by the lack of evaluation of the other ten sources in which these same chansons occur. One cannot simply say that the *Chansonnier Cangé* "clearly uses longs and breves for single notes." Interestingly, one of the three chansons under discussion, *Quant li rossignol* (R 1559), occurs twice in the *Chansonnier Cangé* (on fols. 110 and 117) and, if it was the scribe's intention to indicate the meter of this chanson by using longs and breves, he must have changed that meter drastically from the first to the second notation.

I had specific reasons for omitting discussion of medieval theories from my article on declamatory rhythm in the chansons of the trouvères. There was first the practical concern of keeping the article reasonably short in order to make it qualify for inclusion in a journal. I hope to have an opportunity to fill this gap in my forthcoming book on the songs of the troubadours, trouvères, and Minnesinger. But there was a second and more important reason for leaving this part of the discussion for a later publication: I have my doubts about the practical value of Grocheo's writing on this whole subject. But before explaining these doubts I would like to question some specific observations made by Maddrell. I fail to see how Grocheo's remark—whatever it may mean—about the ductia, which have no text, can shed any light on the performance of the chansons, which do have text and which, in the opinion of many medievalists, were poems in the first place. I also wonder about Maddrell's observation that Grocheo "tells us that the *cantus coronatus* was performed with instrumental accompaniment" and that this fact is "difficult to reconcile with 'free rhythm' as it is generally understood." Why are free rhythm and instrumental accompaniment so difficult to reconcile? Furthermore, where does Grocheo say that the *cantus coronatus* is accompanied? There are two very cryptic passages in the treatise (Rohloff, p. 52 and p. 63) in which the words "*viella*" and "*cantus coronatus*" occur within the same sentence. Both passages are so obscure that even ardent advocates of instrumental accompaniment hesitate to rely upon them. In addition, there is a rather questionable translation by Albert Seay of a passage (Rohloff, p. 50) in which the word "*coronatur*" is translated as "is accompanied . . . (i.e., instrumentally)" rather than as "is crowned" (i.e., in a contest). (*Johannes de Grocheo Concerning Music*, translated by Albert Seay, Colorado Springs, 1967, p. 16.)

I would also like to question Maddrell's interpretation of the famous statement by Anonymous IV quoted at the very end of the above article. Why is it so certain that the unknown author is referring to clearly measurable music? Is it not possible that there were long and short notes in free rhythm? I for one would think so, although such longs and shorts would not be in a ratio of 1:2 or 1:3.

When trying to pry information about meter and rhythm in medieval music from statements by theorists we have to keep in mind the peculiar tradition of treatises about *Musica*; above all we have to realize that the word *Musica* as used by the learned writers of the Middle Ages is not necessarily synonymous with our word *music*. Indeed many treatises hardly touch upon the latter; instead they discuss numerical laws, partly inherited from the Greeks, which were supposed to govern all movements and functions of the bodies in the universe, of human beings, and of what we call music, the latter seemingly including poetry. It is obvious that in many instances *music* owes the privilege of being discussed in treatises about *Musica* exclusively to its property of being the only readily measurable element in the entire realm of *Musica*. In such treatises we find discussion about scales, about the ratios of intervals, and about verse feet in classical Latin poetry and certain Ambrosian hymns. This poetry was extremely suitable because it was based upon an alternation of long and short syllables in a ratio of 2:1. The entire discussion of duration in medieval music is given in such a way that it is clear that, even if all medieval music had been performed in free rhythm, it would have been unlikely that there would have been a place for something as unmeasurable as free rhythm in a discussion about *Musica*. There are also instances in which learned authors of the Middle Ages write primarily about actual music, but the concept that *music* is part of *Musica* very often makes the authors prejudiced; they insist upon taking it for granted that *music* has all the properties of *Musica* and that therefore *music* must be measurable in all aspects, regardless of whether the author could discern this measurability or not. Thus free rhythm was something medieval theorists tried to circumvent or at best it was mentioned without giving it the proper name. In the statements from Grocheo quoted by Maddrell the distinction between *music* and *Musica* is so blurred that it is impossible to distinguish clearly and consistently between the two. And perhaps the only safe conclusion one may draw is the observation that not all medieval music was as clearly measurable as Grocheo would have liked it to be; in other words, all music was measurable as long as one did not measure too precisely.

When giving his own division of music Grocheo does not lump plainsong and secular monody together, as Maddrell rightly points out, but neither does he lump secular monody together with measurable music. And he may have had good reasons for his division of music into three groups other than a preference for tripartite divisions. One could perhaps argue that, if all chansons by troubadours and trouvères had been performed in some form of clearly measurable meter, Grocheo or some other theorist of the time would have amply described it. Yet we find no such discussion in treatises about either *Musica* or rhetoric, and treatises on the latter certainly present extensive discussions on the art of writing chansons.

Next I would like to respond to Maddrell's observation that "it is, surely, an editor's duty to minimize discrepancies between medieval and modern choices [of "rhythmization"] by choosing on behalf of the performer a rhythm likely to have been chosen by his medieval counterpart." I realize fully that the terms "free" and "declamatory" by themselves do not solve the problem of how each individual chanson was performed seven or eight centuries ago nor how it should be performed now. But, I trust, my discussion of free rhythm in *Die Musikforschung* has made it sufficiently clear that we have to examine each chanson on its own merits, and that different performers and editors are likely to come to different conclusions regarding the choice of rhythm and tempo. One can certainly advocate that an expert editing medieval songs which are to be performed in a free rhythm should notate these songs in such a way that the non-expert also may know how to perform them. Thus there is some reason to publish such songs in modern notation with notes of different length and perhaps even with barlines. But such an editor should certainly go as far as to work out a "rhythmization" for each stanza because of the differences in meaning and distribution of accents from stanza to stanza. And certainly such "rhythmization" should be accompanied by an emphatic statement that these indications for duration and accentuation should be taken very freely.

Although much may be said in favor of this way of editing, one can also make strong objections. The first requirement for performing these chansons is a clear and perfect understanding of the text; fulfillment of this requirement should make "rhythmizations" by the editor superfluous, perhaps even a hindrance. By presenting a chanson as rigidly as our notational system requires one risks asking too much attention for the melody, and one may well obscure one of the most important characteristics of a chanson: it is a poem performed to a simple and unobtrusive melody in such a way that the text receives the almost undivided attention of performer and listener alike.

I would like to take this opportunity to follow Maddrell's example and present some observations of my own in the hope of provoking discussion. When in the treatises about *Musica* the learned authors turn to measurability in time, they all agree that music is measurable. They are specific and clear when discussing measurability in modal or mensural notation and in Latin poetry based upon classical quantitative verse feet, but they are vague, circuitous, or even incomprehensible when discussing duration in plainchant and other monophonic music, as well as in polyphonic music predating modal and mensural notation. For a long time it was acceptable practice to take it for granted that all or most medieval music, especially polyphony, was clearly measurable in time and that determining the exact meter of a given piece was up to the modern researcher. Perhaps it would be more practical to assume that a given piece of medieval music was conceived in free rhythm unless there is good evidence for the opposite interpretation. Mensural or modal notation in one source of a given piece is not necessarily sufficient evidence that the piece was conceived as such; it only indicates that the scribe of that particular manuscript was of the opinion that the piece concerned should or could be performed in the meter indicated.

I also venture to question the usual theories regarding the origin and development of polyphonic music as based upon discussions by medieval theorists. The order in which the successive theorists introduce polyphonic music does not necessarily represent the order in which it originated and developed, only the order in which it gradually became acceptable for inclusion in discussions of *Musica*. No one writing about *Musica* in the eighth or ninth century would have considered discussing "underdeveloped" polyphony, which was measurable in time, in which the singers were not very much concerned about "staying together," and which showed no clear preference for beautiful ratios in the intervals between the different voices. Simultaneously we have to question the assumptions that polyphony was started by the person who was the first to add consciously a second part to a pre-existing melody, that this was first done in the frame of the liturgical music, and that even these earliest polyphonists were consciously trying to "stay together." Instead it may be more in keeping with the findings of anthropological and ethnomusicological studies to assume that the chaotic cacophony of primeval men gradually developed in two different directions: one development led towards singing in unison, the other towards various forms of primitive polyphony—or heterophony as some may call it—which in turn led to the very sophisticated compositorial techniques developed by Western composers from the late 12th or 13th century on. Even if it were possible to distinguish unequivocally between cacophony and primitive polyphony it would probably be impossible to determine now which one of the developments was the first to come to fruition: the branch leading towards unison singing or the one leading to polyphony. One development is likely to have influenced the other, and both are likely to have been influenced by solo singing. A question for which we may be able to find an answer is: how did polyphonic singing creep into the Christian liturgy, an area in which so much symbolic value seems to have been given to singing in unison?

The above observations are not intended to question the general value of the medieval treatises about *Musica*. Although the value of individual treatises differs widely, as a group they are precious sources of information on medieval philosophy, aesthetics, mathematics, astrology, astronomy, and the like. However, as far as the reconstruction of early Western music is concerned, their practical value has been somewhat overrated, while the study of ethnomusicology—or comparative musicology, as some prefer to call it—has been far underrated.

[22]

Grocheo and The Measurability of Medieval Music:
A Reply to Hendrik Vanderwerf

J. E. Maddrell

The pleasure I had in discovering that Dr. Vanderwerf had found my article on *Mensura* (*Current Musicology* 10:64–68) worth replying to was somewhat diminished by the realization that he had not recognized its purpose. My article clearly reveals that I do not rely on treatises for my information on medieval music. The suggestion I made was that a scholar transcribing monody might need non-paleographic guidance in evaluating the often inconclusive evidence of musical notation. There can be no question of relying on "treatises" (in the plural) since Grocheo's is the only work to discuss secular monody. Excerpts from other treatises were quoted because they had a bearing on my semantic discussion of the term *mensura*, except for my brief citation of Anonymous IV's remarks on the interpretation of non-mensural notation. My conclusion was that, while there is no theoretical evidence for "free rhythm," our methods of transcribing monody should take full account of the *Chansonnier Cangé* and the later additions to the *MS du Roi*—neither of which, I might add, supports a strictly modal method of transcription. The main significance of the article, however, was the proof that *mensura*, for Grocheo and other theorists, did not primarily mean quantitative measurement.

A full discussion of the *Chansonnier Cangé* would, therefore, have been hardly appropriate, even if it could have been contained within the limits of a single article. The fact that the *Cangé* scribe did use longs and breves for single notes, however erratically, is not to be explained away by saying that he was influenced by motet notation; nor does it argue for "free rhythm," although it may imply the use of non-modal fixed rhythms.

As for the practical value of Grocheo's treatise, it is hardly good scholarship to dismiss a source merely because it does not support one's own view. The only evidence Dr. Vanderwerf adduces in support of his extraordinary opinion that Grocheo is of questionable value as an authority is a paragraph of generalization, vague in expression as in thought ("many treatises," "in many instances," "such treatises," "learned authors," but not a single concrete instance), about a distinction between *Musica* and music. If by "treatises about *Musica*" Dr. Vanderwerf means philosophical treatises in the Boethian tradition of *musica speculativa*, treatises that were not concerned with practical music, then one can only marvel at the eccentricity of a view which would associate Grocheo, of all theorists, with the speculative tradition—Grocheo, whose avowed intention was to avoid speculative theory and concentrate on the music of Paris as performed in his own day!

Dr. Vanderwerf questions my interpretation of passages from Grocheo dealing with the instrumental *ductia* and the *cantus coronatus*. I cited the former because it is by nature a form in fixed rhythm, yet Grocheo included it with monodic song as "music not precisely measured"; the conclusion is either that Grocheo was a half-wit or that *mensuratam* has a meaning distinct from the modern sense of quantitative measurement. The passage about the *cantus coronatus* is hardly so obscure as Dr. Vanderwerf claims. The "crowning" can refer only to accompaniment or to ornamentation of the melody; I now think ornamentation by the singer to be more likely. In any case, it cannot mean "crowned in a contest," since it would be the singer, not the song, that was crowned.

I am surprised that Dr. Vanderwerf should believe that Anonymous IV was referring to polyphony in free rhythm in the passage quoted at the end of my article. Anonymous IV in this section of his treatise is preoccupied with methods of reading ligatures and single notes, and it is obvious from the context, to say nothing of his use of such mensural terms as "cum proprietate" and "cum perfectione," that he has regular rhythms in mind. Besides, any system which deduced rhythm from the ligatures must have had fixed rhythms. I am equally surprised that Dr. Vanderwerf should feel that if all the trouvère songs were sung in fixed rhythm, some theorist "would have amply described it." I regard this as an *argumentum ex silentio*, one of the classic errors in logic.

Perhaps Dr. Vanderwerf will publish the evidence on which he bases his view that in an ideal performance of a song the text would have "the undivided attention of performer and listener alike," whereas the melody would be only "simple and unobtrusive." Ideal from what point of view? And is one justified in assuming that medieval taste in the relation of text to music was that of any other period—the 16th century, for example, or the 19th?

Happily, I can welcome at least the spirit of Dr. Vanderwerf's closing remarks on the importance of ethnological evidence, which has thus far not received sufficient attention. The real question, after all, is not which kind of evidence—paleographic, theoretical, ethnological—should carry the most weight, but how one can best use all three kinds together.

[23]

RHYTHM, METER, AND MELODIC ORGANIZATION IN MEDIEVAL SONGS

Hans TISCHLER
(Bloomington, Indiana)

More than two thirds of a century have passed since Hugo Riemann, Pierre Aubry, and Jean Beck began to attack the problem of the rhythmic interpretation of the chansons of the troubadours and trouvères and of the minnelieder — as well as each other over it. Yet the discussion has by no means ended. Similarly much ink has been spilled over the melodic organization of these songs without arriving at a generally accepted decision. Several recent publications have once again opened up the discussion of these problems, including that of the concept of poetic meter in medieval poetry — or is it concepts? — and of poetic structure. Four works in particular will serve as points of reference here, viz. Roger Dragonetti's *La technique poétique des trouvères dans la chanson courtoise* ([1]), Paul Sappler's edition of the so-called *Königstein Songbook* ([2]), Hendrik van der Werf's *The Chansons of the Troubadours and Trouvères* ([3]), and Mölk and Wolfzettel's *Répertoire métrique ...* ([4]).

All these books are significant contributions to the literature on their respective subjects. The first is today accepted as the basic treatise on trouvère meter and rhythm; the second makes available the largest 15th-century German songbook, which, moreover, contains the earliest known musical scores for lute, pushing back our knowledge of lute tablatures by about twenty years to the early 1470's, a date that must be the earliest possible one for such tablatures or very close to it ([5]); the third volume reviews the historical and poetic background of the troubadours and trouvères, incidentally involving an important minnesong, and transcribes the various melodies for fifteen poems from numerous sources, discussing both their musical and poetic styles; and the fourth presents all known trouvère poems and French motet texts up to about 1350 in schematic verse and rhyme outlines, ordered by rhyme-scheme similarity ([6]).

The musico-poetic renditions offered in the second and third of these volumes would baffle the modern performer and give the reader a false or

---

[1] Bruges 1960, Rijksuniversiteit Gent.
[2] *Das Königsteiner Liederbuch* (Berlin Ms. germ qu 719 or Mgq 719). *Münchener Texte und Untersuchungen zur deutschen Literatur des Mittelalters*, vol. 20, 1970.
[3] Oosthoek, Utrecht 1972.
[4] Ulrich Mölk and Friedrich Wolfzettel: *Répertoire métrique de la poésie lyrique française des origines à 1350*. Wilh. Fink, Munich 1972.
[5] *Cf.* Hans Tischler, « The Earliest Lute Tablature? », *Journal of the Amer. Musicological Soc.*, 27, 1974, pp. 100-103.
[6] Only previously published texts are included, of which a few have been overlooked; but this accounts for 99 % of all extant French texts.

unclear impression of the relationship between music and text, because no rhythm is conveyed by the musical notations. This is so in the four melodies contained in the *Königstein Songbook* because their transcriber was perplexed himself by scribal errors and omissions, and in van der Werf's volume, because meter is consciously rejected by the author as a regulating guide to performance of this repertory. The schematic outlines offered by Mölk and Wolfzettel, on the other hand, lack delineation of structure and insight into stress patterns ([7]).

This paper makes the following basic assumptions : (1) An edition of secular medieval poems and their melodies must convey to the modern performer, reader, and student the probable intent of the poets and musicians who created these works during a time when they constituted part of a living repertory. This can be achieved only through a careful, correlated study of both poems and melodies, resulting hopefully in (a) the elucidation of the syntactic forms, stress patterns, and rhyme schemes of the poems; (b) a transcription of the music into modern note symbols, based on this elucidation; (c) a satisfactory adjustment of the music to the poetry and of the poetry to the music so that they are suitable to one another. (2) A schematic presentation of the poetry should make visible the structure of both poetry and music, the rhyme scheme, and, if possible, also the stress pattern and versification. This task will be greatly helped by a clarification of what syllables are assumed to rhyme and which lines represent quotations (refrains).

In other words, it seems to this writer that the modern editor-scholar must assume the responsibility for interpreting the poetry and the music for the potential user and for guiding him, rather than merely presenting him with a modernized transliteration that will perplex him and let him, the presumably less learned performer or reader, come to his own conclusions. The scholar's advantage is, of course, that he can relate a particular work or series of works to the entire background into which it fits.

For example, the tradition of medieval German song indicates that each text syllable was usually sung to a single melody tone or figure. Exceptions occur occasionally, particularly on penultimate and final verse syllables, less often within a line, but ornaments rarely go beyond three or four tones. Although the *Königstein Songbook*, which dates from the 1470's, is a very late source of medieval songs, works which cannot be designated as minnesongs, their rhythmic approach certainly continues that of the preceding centuries; for German music was very conservative during the Middle Ages. Moreover, the anonymous repertory collected in this volume is only a generation younger than the songs of the last minnesinger, Oswald von Wolkenstein.

([7]) Besides, they involve numerous errors, leaving the peruser puzzled, unenlightened, and merely wondering at the authors' industry.

Illustration 1 shows an attempt at a transcription of one of the four tunes from this book, parallel with the one in Sappler's edition, transcribed by Dr. Kurt Dorfmüller of Munich (S-D : Sappler-Dorfmüller transcription, T : Tischler's).

Our transcription follows the original and arrives at a thoroughly syllabic rendition, in keeping with the tradition. It requires only one small emendation, namely the repetition of a two-note group in verse 3, which the scribe of this early lute tablature may well have overlooked. This transcription further includes bar lines to convey the iambic meter of the poem, and in so doing it arrives at a well rounded tune. The barring seems particularly important for giving the song a musical shape that reflects the versification and for enabling the modern performer to approach the work intelligently.

It will be seen that the transcription of the melody in Sappler's volume assumes a repetition of the first section of the tune, which, though musically and poetically possible, is neither given in the manuscript nor necessary. This assumption further leads to the interpretation of long portions of the tune as melismatic ornaments, which are alien to the style. Thirdly, this interpretation and the rhythm-less transcription give no support to the strict meter of the poem, in fact disturb it.

To return to the assumptions listed above, our transcription gives the performer reader a definite though not necessarily a definitive interpretation, one that does justice to both poem and melody and can be easily used for performance. The a-a-b, c-c-b, d-e-e'-d structure of the poem is paralleled by a well structured melody which cadences very logically and satisfactorily and displays an excellent pattern of antecedent-consequent, antecedent-consequent, antecedent-consequent-echo-like consequent within a through-composed stanza. The beat pattern reflects the obvious iambic meter of the poem, and the rhythm of equally long beats is in keeping with the conservative German tradition, though a 6/8 meter could easily replace the 4/4 here assumed. (No rhythm is indicated in this tablature.) All in all this resolution leads to a satisfactory poetic and musical rendition — as suggested, not necessarily the only possible one — which will undoubtedly gain from the usual expressive freedom employed in any good performance.

The second illustration takes us back several centuries to a poem by perhaps the most eminent minnesinger, Walther von der Vogelweide, one of the few of his that have survived with their melodies. It offers an opportunity to compare a troubadour chanson and a minnesong, since this tune is melodically related to one of Jaufre Rudel's tunes. The two songs are given in parallel transliterations as the first of fifteen transcriptions in van der Werf's volume. But before discussing the two poems and their tunes several problems must be clarified.

The discussion of, or rather dispute over, the rhythm of trouvère melodies has gone on for a long time. The approach has mostly been to decide between two all-or-nothing alternatives, viz. a rendition of all such music in either

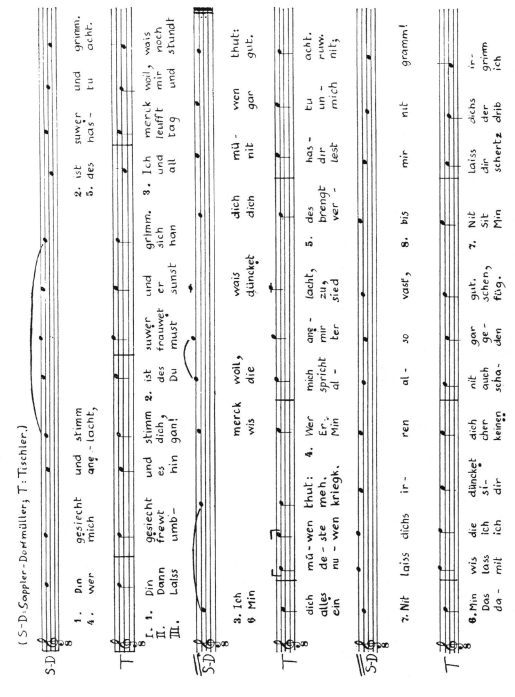

* The MS writes A (⁸)
(⁸) The manuscript has A as the last note of the stanza, though D is the central tone of the song; see below, p. 19f.

« modal » or free rhythm. The advocates of the former apply in their transcriptions, rigidly or with few irregularities, the patterned 6/8 meters of the Parisian clausulae and motets of the late 12th and early 13th centuries. The other editors render the tunes without bar lines, stresses, or relative note values. To be sure, the melodies of a few troubadour chansons and a number of trouvère songs reappear in motets and conductus or employ music from clausulae, and some are extant in mensural notation. Thus it cannot be denied that some later chansons were, at least at times, sung in metric rhythm. It is true, however, that most troubadour songs, from the late 11th century onward, and many trouvère chansons antedate the rise of modal notation and are written in non-mensural note symbols; modal rhythm may therefore not apply to these earlier songs. It should be remembered, however, that most manuscripts containing the music of these repertories were written in the mid-13th century, a period during which also most major motet sources were written in a notation that did not indicate the rhythm of the melodies, although they were doubtless measured and metrically patterned.

Nevertheless many scholars, including van der Werf, have rejected the application of modal rhythm to any or most troubadour and trouvère tunes, because it appears to be historically unsound to assume that it served all of them ([9]). Once this position is taken and only the two above possibilities are admitted, one is therefore left with a free, unmetric and unmeasured interpretation that lacks any practical, stylistic, or historical guide lines for the performer and analyst as well as any relationship to the text. This concept is called, and recommended as, « declamatory » style by van der Werf. It may be observed that this approach seems to be supported by the widely held view that French — as opposed to German, English, or Latin — poetry was based on counting syllables rather than on any quantitative or qualitative stress patterns.

When weighing this approach, it is well to consider the general tendencies of the period that produced these songs — the Gothic, which is characterized in part by its emphasis on arithmetic. This emphasis is manifest in such relations as that of the circle to its inscribed and circumscribed hexagons in the columns of cathedrals, the proportions of length, width, and height in churches, the numerical relationships in literary structures such as Dante's *Commedia*, the introduction of algebra by Leonardo Fibonacci, the invention of rhythmic, measurable music and musical notation, the cultivation of scholastic-mystic numerology, the cabbalah, alchemy, and astrology, as well as the revival of the ancient verse meters and the invention of new ones such as Alexandre de Bernay's Alexandrine. That a period so occupied with numbers would not reflect this tendency in its lyric and epic poetry by metric rhythm is nearly inconceivable. It must be further added that troubadour

---

([9]) Nevertheless van der Werf gives alternate rhythmic readings for two of his fifteen transcriptions and presents three songs exclusively in rhythmic renderings.

poetry was the product of Western Europe's contacts with the Muslim East and with Moorish Spain in particular, where since the 10th century a new vernacular poetry had risen — a poetry based on equally long lines with rhymes and on a strictly observed theory of meters, a poetry always sung to the accompaniment of instruments, most often that of the lute ([10]). Trouvère chanson and minnelied, which sprang in two consecutive steps of direct imitation from troubadour song, must be assumed to share these basic style characteristics, to which belonged rhythmic patterns.

Moreover, the above-mentioned idea that syllable counting precludes the application of metric stress is contrary to the whole context of a culture that stressed architectural rhythm by flying buttresses, produced dance music, hockets, and mensural notation, enjoyed ostinato cantus-firmus patterns, and recited rhymed poetry whose rhyme syllables with very few exceptions demonstrably fall always on metrically strong beats in the music of motets. Indeed, it is a well known fact that the ancient quantitative meters of poetry gave way to qualitative, i. e., stressed meters about the 5th century of our era, and it must be presumed that stress remained fundamental in varying degrees to most Western poetry ever since. If proof of this fact for trouvère lyrics is needed, it is easily found in the feminine verse endings, weak syllables that are not counted by scholars of old French poetry. If it were a matter of mere counting, this procedure would be unthinkable; it can be explained only by assuming that stress was involved; below there will be occasion to refer to anacruses as well. To be sure, the ubiquitous iambs, trochees, and dactyls cannot even be conceived without some kind of agogic, dynamic, or pitch stress or a combination of two or all three of these in languages such as French and English that do not recognize long and short syllables.

As mentioned above, Dragonetti's excellent work has become a standard reference with regard to the versification of trouvère songs. This is what he contributes to the present problem in the key passage in which he analyzes the rhythm and meter of their poetry ([11]) :

> If the rhythm of a line is something different from its meter, the question is to know whether that rhythm is susceptible to analysis. ... In a regular verse the rhythm is organized with the aid of a rational or proportional time value. ... All rhythm, in fact, implies meter, which is not a simple artifice added to it, but coexists with it because it is an essential condition for the perception of rhythm. ... All rhythmic structure introduces a conflict or combination of two temporal orders, namely between rhythm and a homogeneous beat leading to meter; the former cannot be reduced to equal time divisions because it is a unique creation. The rhythmic structure of a regular verse results from the encounter of these two orders; the style differs according to how the metric squareness reinforces or contradicts the rhythm. Meter thus assumes a structural function which emerges clearly from the analysis of courtly verse where the regulatory action of metric schemes plays a particularly important role.

([10]) *Cf.* Robert BRIFFAULT, *The Troubadours* (translated from the French by the author), Indiana University Press, Bloomington, IN, 1965, p. 31ff.
([11]) *Op. cit.*, pp. 500-502; this writer's translation.

True, later in the volume Dragonetti sharply criticizes and rejects the application of modal rhythm to courtly poetry; but his criticism is really directed against the rigid application of modal patterning, practiced by such early scholars as Aubry and Beck, without considering more imaginative possibilities. An interesting argument, illustrated by a dozen examples, is the transcription, by Beck and Aubry respectively, of songs in different modal versions. A dual possibility of interpretation hardly speaks against the application of the rhythmic modes to trouvère poems, of course; indeed, it nicely illustrates a point worth remembering, viz. that the medieval musician might easily perform a piece differently at various times — different in rhythm, in musica ficta (accidentals), in ornamentation, played on an instrument or sung or both, with a different melody to the same poem or with a different text to the same melody. This point is most clearly documented by another song cited by Dragonetti [12] which is actually notated by the medieval scribes of two different manuscripts in two different modes, namely in the third mode in the *Chansonnier Cangé* and in the upbeat first mode in the *Chansonnier du Roi* [13]. And this is a song by Robert de Castel d'Arras who, according to Dragonetti, was active during the third quarter of the 13th century, i.e., during the very time the two manuscripts were copied.

Incidentally, this twofold rhythmic interpretation results, of course, in several metric stresses falling on normally unaccented syllables, a thing that Dragonetti elsewhere calls « massacring the verse. » Apparently, however, the medieval poets felt no great compunction about this crime of giving some naturally weak syllables metric stress and leaving some normally strong ones unstressed; for poetic and prose scanning do not necessarily coincide in any language, whether French, English, or German, not to speak of Latin from which this procedure derives. The ambivalence of stress stands out clearly in 13th-century French motets, all definitely sung in measured rhythm with a strong metric pulse. As is well known, these motets include hundreds of quotations, so-called refrains, from trouvère poetry and *romans*, and all of these confirm not only the appropriate consideration given to feminine endings and anacruses by their metric placement but also the metric treatment of the body of these quoted lines. This source of very pertinent information has been totally neglected hitherto in all discussions of trouvère rhythm.

In general, considering the possibilities of different interpretation and of ambivalent stress or floating accent, it is often difficult to decide which meter was intended. Even the medieval performer had such difficulties, as has just been shown. The problem becomes compounded when the various stanzas of a poem do not exhibit the same stress pattern. In such instances two approaches are helpful for finding the best possible solution: (1) scanning all the stanzas and determining the meter in which the fewest ,,wrong" stresses occur; (2) giving primary evidential weight to the first stanza as the probably most

---

[12] *Op. cit.*, p. 526.
[13] Respectively Paris, Bibl. nat. fr. 846 and 844.

carefully considered one, from which the other stanzas may well deviate here and there.

Once the meter, i.e. musically the barring, has been established, the rhythm is the next problem. To be sure, the problem is complex and must be solved individually for each poem. Certainly a trochee, e. g., can be equally well represented by various rhythms, such as | ♩. ♪|, | ♩ ♪|, | ♪ ♩ |, and each of these rhythms may be varied by using several shorter notes for either of the two note values, e. g., ˙| ♫ ♫ | ˙ ♫ ♫ | ˙ |♫ ♩|

Which of these rhythms may be best applied is a musical question, and it may well be surmised that medieval performers might apply different rhythms to a certain poem at various renderings. Whereas barring, i.e., a basic regularity of stressed and unstressed syllables, seems absolutely necessary for the performer of metric poetry, the choice of rhythm is secondary. It will largely depend on the distribution of the ornaments in the melody, another clue which van der Werf rejects. The reason given is that ornaments do not consistently occur in the same position in various versions of a tune. Here the contemporary motet once more furnishes clear evidence that this circumstance in no way nullifies metric pulse. Indeed, many ornaments were sung on short, unstressed syllables, a fact that van der Werf holds to be contradictory to metric rhythm; and in the multiple versions of many motets the ornaments also freely migrate among strong and weak beats. Yet with the clue to the rhythm furnished in many instances by the patterned tenor (cantus firmus), the overwhelming evidence points to the longer note values of the modal patterns as the carriers of the majority of ornaments. Since this evidence involves many quotations from trouvère songs, its application to the contemporary monophonic repertory in general can be readily accepted.

Although, as has been mentioned, it has hitherto been held that the rhythmic interpretation of trouvère chansons admitted of only two alternatives : either modal rhythm or free declamation, a third possibility does exist. Over twenty years ago Heinrich Husmann showed that at least four trouvère songs share their music with polyphonic conductus [14]. These chansons must therefore be presumed to have been amenable to the same rhythm as the related conductus, and Husmann demonstrated that in both some hexasyllabic verses follow the modified modal rhythm | ♩. ♪♩ | ♪♩ ♩. | . [15]

One of the four chansons is by the late-12th-century trouvère Blondel de Nesle, and all four seem to have antedated the related conductus, as their typical chanson structures are highly unusual for conductus. This observation

---

[14] Cf. «Zur Rhythmik des Trouvèregesanges», Die Musikforschung 5, 1952, pp. 110-113.

[15] Derived from the second mode: |♪♩ ♪♩| ♪♩ ♪ 𝄽 |..

pushes metric interpretation back into the last decades of the 12th century. There seems to be evidence, however, that polyphonic music of the early 12th century, the so-called St. Martial or Aquitanian repertory, was also sung in measured rhythm ([16]). This may have been a rhythm akin to modal rhythm or perhaps one frequently found in early conductus, viz. one in which all or most syllables have an equal duration, as in the Königstein song cited earlier. Latest research would extend rhythmic interpretation even further back. In a recent paper John Boe showed that a trope of the mid-11th century, which thus antedates William of Aquitain's earliest songs, is notated and was sung in what appears to be a 6/8 meter similar to the first rhythmic mode, expressing the rhythm of an *a-b, a-b, a-b, a* stanza as follows ([17]) :

In the light of what has been said above about Moorish-Spanish poetry this is, indeed, quite possible.

To sum up : The basic fact is that courtly poetry does possess metric structure, and metric structure can be reflected in modern musical notation only by means of bar lines and an intelligible note-value system. Otherwise the meter, which, as Dragonetti firmly states, is an essential structural element of this poetry, is lost in the modern edition. The free rhythm proposed by many scholars in fact mistakes poetry for prose. With some flexibility and some musical sense, metric-rhythmic transcriptions that parallel and support the meter and versification of the troubadour, trouvère, and minnesinger poems can and must be produced, if these are to be brought back to life. A single, pervasive modal approach has to be rejected in favor of at least two possible approaches, viz. either modal solutions with frequent so-called «irregularities» and modal mixtures, such as were taught by Franco of Cologne, or transcriptions in which syllables receive equal length except where lengthy melismas occur; but both types must be barred. The initial time signature, however, may well change in the course of a song, a procedure frequently necessary also in motets.

It should be added that the motets of the last decades of the 13th century prove that meter then declined in poetry, and metric stress disappeared, together with regular line length, as an organizing factor. The poetry of these later motets proceeds in free verse, in lines of greatly differing length, held together by rhymes only, but rhymes without pattern. Considerations of stress, let alone regular stress, are completely absent from that poetry, which is contemporary with the demise of troubadour and trouvère poetry.

([16]) *Cf.* Theodore C. KARP's forthcoming book on the music of St. Martial; also, among others, T. C. KARP, « St. Martial and Santiago de Compostela; an Analytical Speculation, » *Acta musicologica* 39, 1967, pp. 144-160; Bruno STÄBLEIN, « *Modale Rhythmen im Saint-Martial-Repertoire?* », *Festschrift Friedrich Blume*, Bärenreiter-Verlag, Kassel 1963, pp. 340-362.

([17]) *Cf.* « Rhythmical Notation in the Beneventan Gloria Trope *Aureas arces*, » *Musica disciplina* 29 (1975), pp. 5-42.

As stated above, Illustration 2 uses one of the transcriptions offered in van der Werf's book. It connects a chanson by Jaufre Rudel with the famous *Palestine Song* by Walther von der Vogelweide, two tunes that are very similar and partially identical, chiefly in the first half of the melody. But if it is true that Walther adapted Jaufre's melody to his poem, as is claimed by van der Werf, Walther made important changes in it.

With respect to the rhythm of these two songs van der Werf writes as follows ([18]) :

> Scholarly opinion on the meter of the songs ... has varied considerably, so much so that (one scholar gave) a synoptic chart of ten different metrizations ... of the melody preserved with Walther's poem ([19]) ... there are no indications ... of fixed meter in Jaufre Rudel's chanson; ... the way in which the melody is distributed over the text suggest(s) a performance in declamatory rhythm ... This conclusion is in no way contradicted by the fact that Jaufre's melody ... was also used for a German poem. Even though the meter of German lyric poetry of the period ... was based upon a predetermined number of stressed (mark: stressed!) syllables per line, there is no evidence that this poetry was ... performed to a melody in fixed meter.

Not only is this statement contradictory, but the fact is that poetry in Provençal was just as metrically conceived as poetry in German or Latin, i. e., it followed several traditional meters. And the change of meter between the Provençal poem by Jaufre and Walther's German one is highly important here. The former clearly runs in iambic dimeters, as follows :

> Lanquan li jorn son lonc en may
>
> m'es belhs dous chans d'auzelhs de lonh,
>
> e quan mi suy partitz de lay
>
> remambra'm d'un' amor de lonh: (etc.)

Walther's poem, on the other hand, proceeds in trochaic dimeters, viz. :

> Nu alerst leb' ich mir werde,
>
> sit min sündich auge siht
>
> hie daz lant undt auch die erde
>
> dem man vil der eren giht. (etc.)

That both poems are completely metric cannot be denied. That such poetry can hardly be considered to have been sung or read without reference to the meter is equally certain. And the music fits this assumption very well.

As the above presentation has tried to show, the mere pitch transcription of the melodies is musically and poetically unsatisfactory. Any line of the Rudel

---

([18]) *Op. cit.*, p. 86.
([19]) *Cf.* Burkhard KIPPENBERG, *Der Rhythmus im Minnesang*. C. H. Beck, Munich 1962, p. 226f.

chanson bears this out. Would it be right, e. g., to give each note approximately the same length? This would render verse 2 much longer than verse 1, although both are octosyllabic. On the other hand, should every syllable receive about the same time value? In order to do so one would have to slow up everything inordinately to accommodate the lengthy ornaments that occur at the ends of lines; moreover, the final syllables of most lines would end breathlessly and without a stop, on the last of three, four, five, or even seven notes. This was hardly the composer's intent; a singer has to breathe at line ends, and a pause there seems essential to a good performance. Should this fact not be conveyed to the modern performer by the editor, as it is, e. g., suggested by the small notes added above the verse endings in Illustration 2? Cadential halts at the ends of lines are needed elsewhere as well, e.g., in hymns and chorales, to keep the rhythm from limping and the singer from getting out of breath. They are something like fermatas which inject some not unwelcome rhythmic irregularities.

Any transcription presents problems, to be sure. But just as in editing a medieval poem emendations and added punctuation are taken for granted to render the text intelligible, the musical transcription must be rendered so as to make musical sense to a performer or reader. In both songs it is probably best to give equal length to all syllables except to some at the ends of lines, but the songs must be barred differently. Immediately both assume pleasing musical forms. As conceived by this writer, the bar lines here carry the same psychological implications as in conventional music; the amount of dynamic and agogic emphasis given by the performer to primary and secondary beats is, of course, a matter of taste and training.

Once more returning to the basic assumptions put forward at the beginning of this paper, our interpretation (a) indicates in both songs the poetic and musical stress patterns through the barring, (b) reflects the poetic structure in the musical phrasing, and (c) gives adequate rhythmic expression to the rhymes.

The rhythmic interpretation of medieval monophonic songs greatly influences the interpretation of their melodic organization as well. With regard to this problem the controversy has been as to whether Gregorian modes apply to these repertories or whether other, non-Gregorian modes may be appealed to. Van der Werf adduces two possible non-Gregorian principles, namely those derived from Curt Sachs's analysis of the folksongs of many cultures and formulated in his last, posthumous work, *The Wellsprings of Music* ([20]). According to these ideas the chansons are divided into those organized around two focal pitches, usually an interval of a second or third apart, and those that unfold along a so-called structural chain of two to four thirds or two thirds and a fourth.

([20]) Jaap KUNST, ed., Martinus Nijhoff, The Hague 1962.

To this writer it seems rather unwarranted to apply an analysis of folk-songs to the sophisticated court art of the troubadours and trouvères. After all, the medieval poet-musicians were principally acquainted with Church music, some of it of recent polyphonic workmanship, and with a long tradition of art song enjoyed by courtiers, Churchmen, and students since the times of Charlemagne and the establishment of the Omayyad caliphate in mid-10th-century Spain. Their social standing as feudal lords or guild artisans would effectively prevent them from mingling with the lower classes and singing their songs. Indeed, one of van der Werf's astute remarks points to a kinship between many first lines of trouvère melodies and psalmodic formulas. As a matter of fact, each of the fifteen transcriptions offered by him is clearly organized in one of the Church modes, whereas structural chains of thirds and two-tone schemes can be adduced only with great difficulties and with many exceptions. The latter methods were similarly applied several years ago to the analysis of the melodies of 13th-century motets by Finn Matthiassen [21] and rejected for that repertory as non-productive by the present writer [22].

It is clear that all melodic analyses that do not consider metric stress run into a great obstacle, viz. how to determine the chief pitches. A most striking example of the inherent difficulties of this approach is provided by Illustration 2 above. These are some of the things van der Werf says about the two songs in the introduction to their transcription [23]:

> In its entirery the melody of Jaufre's chanson has a rather ambiguous structure: most lines have F and one line has high C as the most important structural tones; ... although the low C is not very pronounced as structural tone, it serves ... as ending tone of both pedes and of the entire chanson. Thus ... it is difficult to determine whether this melody is a centric one, moving around F, or a standing one with C or perhaps D as basic tone.
>
> It is interesting to compare this rather loose organization with the strong tertial structure in the melody preserved with Walther's poem. The melody ... is based upon the chain D-F-A-C with perhaps C-E-G as a contrasting or secondary chain ... Especially noteworthy are the differences in ending tones ...

Thus the author is at a loss to find the central tones of these two songs, although he recognizes important differences between them. The fact is that Walther reinterpreted the mode of the melody, and this reinterpretation emerges clearly only when the inherent change in metric stress is observed and notationally carried out. Rudel's melody is organized in a clear sixth Gregorian

---

[21] *Cf. The Style of the Early Motet.* Dan Fog, Copenhagen 1966.
[22] *Cf.* the review of Finn Matthiassen's *The Style of the Early Motet, Journal of the Amer. Musicological Soc.* 20, 1967, pp. 489-492.
[23] *Op. cit.*, p. 85.

mode, based on the central F with the cofinalis C, whereas Walther changed to the first mode with D as both central tone and finalis ([24]).

These facts are evident from the first stressed tone in line 1 to the final cadence. In the seven lines of Jaufre's bar form the cadence tones are D-C, D-C, G-D-C, and in Walther's, C-D, C-D, A-C-D. The respective twenty-eight metric stresses are distributed as follows:

in Rudel's chanson: $10F — 9D — 5C — 2A — 2G$; and

in Walther's song: $9D — 7A — 5F — 4E — 2C — 1G$.

Thus there are 15 F's and C's as against 11 D's and A's in Jaufre's tune and 16 D's and A's as against 7 F's and C's in Walther's. Moreover, only Rudel's song uses the $B_\flat$. Thus these tunes can be easily related to Gregorian modes, whereas their tertial-chain structures are most unclear — in Jaufre's chanson non-existent, in Walther's inconsistent or forced in application.

The analysis of the song given in Illustration 1 has a similarly clear result. Six lines of the poem end on D, two on A, and two on E, and the range of the tune is one octave, a-a^1. The melody therefore employs the second mode, and it is somewhat unexpected to find that the single stanza of music given in the manuscript ends on a^1. The transcription in Sappler's edition changes the A to a D; but when the three stanzas of the poem are scanned, the A appears to be quite appropriate in stanzas 1 and 2, both as reflecting the questions at the ends of these stanzas and as introducing the next stanza. The last stanza, however, does demand a D for its conclusion and perhaps an F natural as the antepenultimate note to reestablish the prevailing mode. Thus the syntactic meaning here seems to lead to a better emendation of the final note.

Just like the musicologist who does not give the poetic clues their due in the interpretation of the tunes and obtains erroneous or at best ambiguous results, so the linguist fails who neglects the study of the tunes and their notation. The recent comprehensive analysis of the trouvère and early motet-text repertories by Mölk and Wolfzettel is a case in point. In trouvère poems the structure is usually quite clear. Nevertheless there are a good many poems in which the intention of the poet becomes evident only when also the music is considered; the phrasing, indicated by rests, bars at the ends of verses, and the repetitions of melodic segments often give well defined information about the line arrangement, without which wrong conclusions may be drawn.

([24]) Here the Gregorian modes are taken in their later meaning, the one particularly applying to the later hymns and sequences which are contemporary with the secular repertories here concerned — viz. as modal scales organized around two pitches. This concept contrasts with the earlier involvement of traditional melodic formulas in each mode, which applies, e. g., to the psalm tones and the Eastern chants.

A simple example is the anonymous « *Quant li dous tens renouvele:* » ([25])

This chanson appears in Mölk's outline as follows :

a b a b b a b a c c;
7' 7 7' 7 7 7' 7 7' 4 12

but the music shows that (a) there is an inaccuracy in the syllable count of the penultimate line and (b), in fact the last two lines are actually three lines, the last one being sung to a melodic variant of lines 2 and 4. Recalling our basic assumptions, the poetic meter here points to that of the music, whereas the pattern of ornaments suggests the changes of rhythm in the tune in lines 5 and 9; the second change seems to imply the presence of a refrain (quotation) at the end, which, as is characteristic of many refrains, includes an unrhymed line.

As was proposed at the beginning of this paper, a schematic outline should convey to the eye all structural details. To this writer the following way of outlining, using the above poem as an illustration, would seem to be best suited to clarify the poetic and musical structures — syntactical, rhyme-wise, metric-rhythmic, and sectional :

$$a(7_4-) + b(7) \qquad b(7) - a(7-)$$
$$1 \qquad 2 \qquad\qquad 1$$
$$a(7-) + b(7) \qquad b(7) - a(7-) + b(3)$$
$$1 \qquad 2 \qquad\qquad 1$$
$$\qquad\qquad\qquad x(7) - b(5)$$
$$\qquad\qquad\qquad 2^1$$

([25]) *Cf.* Hans SPANKE, *G. Raynauds Bibliographie des altfranzösischen Liedes* I, E. J. Brill, Leiden 1955, n° 615. The chanson is extant in Mss. Paris, Bibl. nat. fr. 847, fol. 144-144v, and Paris, Bibl. nat. nouv. acq. fr. 1050, fol. 212v.

Here the letters symbolize the rhymes; the figures in parentheses the numbers of syllables from first to last stress; the subscript figures, the number of stresses (whose pattern is assumed to remain constant unless otherwise indicated, here trochaic); the dashes, feminine endings (or also, ahead of figures, anacruses); the plus sign, the continuous rhythm connecting two lines; the underscoring, a refrain; the figures below letters, recurrent musical phrases (with modifications indicated by subscript or superscript numbers); the lines are arranged in syntactical groups, and a wide space after lines 3-4 or the two-column arrangement of the symbols shows that the poem falls into two stanza-like sections. Whereas (–3) can only mean an iambic dipody, a (4) normally indicates a dactylic line : / ⌣ ⌣ / ; and either line may well conclude with a feminine ending (–3–) or (4–). But (7) may stand for either a trochaic dimeter or a dactylic trimeter : / ⌣ / ⌣ / ⌣ / or / ⌣ ⌣ / ⌣ ⌣ / ; the added subscripts here help to differentiate the two possibilities : (7_4) and (7_3), and unless otherwise indicated, the particular meter will continue in the poem. To be sure, there are many lines that employ irregular stress patterns, such as / ⌣ / ⌣ ⌣ / ⌣ / or / ⌣ / ⌣ / ⌣ ⌣ / (the ancient Glyconic verses), both of which would appear as (8_4); but ⌣ / ⌣ ⌣ / ⌣ ⌣ / would be symbolized by (-7_3).

When it comes to the far more irregularly built texts of motets, the correlated study of music and text becomes even more important ([26]). A short piece may serve as illustration 4 ([27]) :

This is how this poem is presented in Mölk's analysis :

$$a\ b\ a\ b\ a\ a\ a\ a\ a\ c\ a.$$
$$7\ 4\ 7\ 4\ 7\ 7\ 3\ 3\ 9'\ 3$$

The structure and the versification are quite different, however, viz. :

$$\underline{a(7_4) + b(-3)} \qquad\qquad \underline{a(3) - a(3)} + a(3-)$$
$$ \qquad\qquad _1 _2$$

$$a(7) + b(-3) \qquad\qquad \underline{a(3) - a(3)}$$

$$\underline{a(7) + b(-3)} \qquad\qquad \underline{x(5) + a(-7)}$$
$$_{1-2}$$

The division of Mölk's lines 6 and 7, which actually from lines 6-9, is borne out (1) by the structure of the poem, the first section of which thereby gains consistency of formulation; and (2) by the music, which makes no break

---

([26]) In fact, over 40 % of Mölk's motet-text analyses include serious errors, and many more show mistakes in syllable count — because the related melody was not studied — and other minor flaws.

([27]) The example is here given as it appears in the Ms. Montpellier, Fac. de Méd. H 196, as No 121 (cf. the author's new transcription of this manuscript, forthcoming at A-R Editions, Madison, WI.); with the same text this melody also appears in six other manuscripts, and with other texts in six additional ones, as well as once without text in a three-part clausula (cf. the author's forthcoming Complete Edition of the Earliest Motets, forthcoming at Yale University Press, n° 65).

before line 6, but does make one within it. The new division of the last two lines is proved by the fact that (1) this is a refrain whose last line also recurs elsewhere by itself; and (2) this last line parallels the words « benedicamus Domino » in the Latin text that is set to the same music in other manuscripts ([28]). The « x » stands for an unrhymed line, such unrhymed lines being very frequent in refrains. The dashes in front of syllable counts accomplish a task which theorists of old French verse seem never to consider : just as feminine endings do not change the essential character and length of a line, which depends on the number of stresses rather than that of syllables, i. e.,

---

([28]) Among others in Ms. Florence, Bibl. Med. Laur. pl. 29, 1, fol. 409v-410.

on the number of metric, musical units, so the character and essential length of a line is not changed by an anacrusis. As numerous examples in motets prove, both anacruses and feminine endings may be carried by either short or long note values.

To conclude : The basic assumptions proposed at the beginning of this paper aimed at creating transcriptions of medieval songs that are meaningful to performers and schematic outlines that convey all important analytical information. They have led to fundamental considerations of rhythm and meter of both poetry and music, of mode and accidentals in the music, and of the interdependence of poetry and music. This interdependence and the necessity for a correlated approach cannot be stressed enough. The phrasing of the music often clarifies the versification; the meter of the poetry determines that of the music; the distribution of the ornaments is often a guide to the rhythm; the syntactic meaning of the poetry and the repetition of musical phrases both contribute to the overall structuring of a song and therefore to its performance; the phrasing and the cadence points indicate the melodic mode, have implications for the use of accidentals, and suggest pauses or halts. Above all, neither the poetry nor the music of these repertories can be imagined to have been conceived without meter and metric stress guiding the performance.

This paper is an attempt at encouraging a comprehensive fresh look at the entire repertory of the troubadours, trouvères, minnesingers, and other medieval monophonic songs, leading to editions that would aid in the revival of this charming poetry and music — editions combining linguistic and musicological carefulness with a broad sense of humanistic values, on the one hand, and on the other with a musicianly and poetic approach that would shoulder rather than avoid the responsibility of guiding the generally less learned performer and reader in matters of rhythm, meter, mode, form, and actual pitch, perhaps even of general tempo and dynamics. Such editions would yield insights that are historically and structurally more justifiable than vague appeals to chains of thirds and declamatory rhythm, and would finally render the repertory more widely accessible.

[24]

The "Not-so-precisely Measured" Music of the Middle Ages

Hendrik van der Werf

In the area of performance practice few issues have been debated as fervently and as dogmatically as has rhythm and meter in medieval song. For more than a century researchers have tried to reconstruct the original manner in which these songs were performed and, by the middle of the century, almost every conceivable theory had been broached. In a book published in 1962 Burkhard Kippenberg subjected the existing theories to a thorough scrutiny and came to the conclusion that no logical and decisive evidence had been brought forth for any of them.[1] In addition to the objections voiced by Kippenberg one should mention the monolithic approach as a serious weakness of most research in this area: it has been (and sometimes still is) taken for granted that one type of rhythm governed either all songs in a given language or all songs of the entire medieval period.

Several thousand non-liturgical songs have come down to us. For the majority only the texts have been preserved, but we have both text and melody for well over 2,000 of them, the precise figure depending upon one's own definitions of the terms "non-liturgical," "song," and "Middle

---

1. Burkhard Kippenberg, *Der Rhythmus im Minnesang: eine Kritik der literar- und musikhistorischen Forschung mit einer Übersicht über die musikalischen Quellen* (Munich, 1962).

Ages." It may be regretted that so many of the songs with music have a French text, but this accident of history does have a fortunate aspect in that one genre, often called "trouvère song,"[2] or simply "chanson," has been preserved in such abundance that we can learn much about performance practice from the texts and melodies themselves, from the manner in which they were preserved, and especially from the manner in which a given song varies from one manuscript to another. Although we all would prefer a more direct approach, we have little choice but to take the best known genre as a vantage point from which to study the lesser known repertories. With great caution we can try and determine in what respects the trouvère songs differ from, and in what respects they resemble the other ones. For now, we may restrict our attention to monophonic song in French and Occitan.[3] We must bypass plainchant altogether, and leave other "not-so-precisely-measured" genres for a future occasion.[4]

The Texts

Our study of melodic rhythm must begin with the texts. One of the major principles for versification of troubadour and trouvère songs (and of most subsequent poetry in Romance languages) is the "syllable count." A given line, or verse, normally has a fixed number of syllables in each strophe of a given poem, but there is no fixed position for accented syllables in places other than the rhyme and, in a limited number of poems, the caesura. An occasional line may seem trochaic or dactylic,

---

2. For the sake of this study the term "trouvère" has both the advantage and disadvantage of being vague. Some scholars, especially experts on medieval poetry, have used the term sparingly and usually in the meaning to be proposed here. Others, especially authors of textbooks on the history of music, have used it in reference to all French poet-composers of the twelfth and thirteenth centuries. According to their contents the manuscripts allow a conveniently narrow interpretation of the term. The medieval songs in Old-French have been preserved in a dozen large manuscripts (and in many small and fragmentary collections) dating from the middle of the thirteenth through the beginning of the fourteenth century. They contain a rather wide variety of poems and melodies, but one fairly homogeneous group prevails. The poems in this group are strophic in form and content, and most of them deal with *fin' amor*, nowadays often called "courtly love." Only the first strophe of the poem is provided with a melody. I shall restrict the term "trouvère song" to members of this group.
3. The term "troubadour song" will be used for songs in the Provencal, or Occitan, language.
4. Christopher Page, *Voices and Instruments of the Middle Ages: Instrumental Practice and Songs in France 1100-1300*, (London, 1987) comes to largely the same classification, and considers troubadour and trouvère songs to be in a "high style," the others in "lower styles." With more or less the same results, we can also take attribution as a criterion for categorization because most of the songs that are attributed to a specific author belong to the first group; conversely, many of the songs outside of it are anonymous. Fearing that uninitiated readers may see a value judgment in the terms "high" and "low," I prefer not to use them.

but there is no case in which an entire poem or entire strophe has a regular alternation of accented and unaccented syllables. I may recall here that there is such an alternation in many Latin poems of the same time, including many (not all) Latin motet texts and even some French motets. Traditionally, the syllable count is referred to as the "meter" of the poem. In discussions of melodic meter this could lead to confusion, and one might be tempted to reason that, if there is meter in the poem, there must have been meter in the music. This apodictum is flawed because the term "meter" is used in two meanings. A fixed number of syllables in a poem does not necessarily mean that the melody had a fixed alternation of accented and unaccented or long and short units. Except when the context calls for a general term, and in discussions of "modal rhythm," I will avoid the terms "rhythm" and "meter" in preference for less ambiguous ones, such as "syllable count," "accentuation," and "duration."

Medieval Writings Concerning Measurement

Medieval writings about the poetry of the troubadours and trouvères are devoid of information concerning melodic rhythm. Among the treatises dealing with music, only the one by Johannes de Grocheio contains a few remarks that may pertain to trouvère songs. In order to evaluate his remarks, we must keep in mind the development of the discipline called *musica*.[5] St. Augustine is one of several authors who define *musica* as the "art of measuring" or the "art of measuring well." Some of those who were interested in measuring, including St. Augustine, seem to have found great delight in studying the numbers in those Latin poems that have long and short syllables in a ratio of 2:1. In the fifth chapter (the fifth "book" as medieval people called it) Augustine discusses numerical equalities that we can perceive with our intellect, but not with our senses. In the last chapter the real purpose of Augustine's study emerges when he turns to the harmony found in God. Other learned authors were fascinated with the numbers or ratios found among pitches in the scale. Some transferred these numbers to the universe and organized the heavenly bodies as pitches in an octave. In an almost inscrutable development, the meaning of the term *musica* widened and came to include everything that we now call music. For some time this development went hand in hand with a confusing non-sequitur: since

---

5. For two recent and rather different interpretations of *musica* in reference to duration see van der Werf, *The Emergence of Gregorian Chant: A Comparative Study of Roman, Ambrosian, and Gregorian Chant*, vol. I,1 (published by the author, Rochester, N.Y., 1983), 22-30, and John Stevens, *Words and Music in the Middle Ages: Song, Narrative, Dance and Drama, 1050-1350* (Cambridge, 1986), 413-434.

musica concerns itself with precisely measurable phenomena, everything discussed under the heading *musica* was assumed to be precisely measurable. In the second half of the thirteenth century Franco of Cologne and Johannes de Garlandia discuss in detail measurements in motets, while explicitly stating that plainchant was immeasurable. Johannes de Grocheio disagrees with their latter statement. In his opinion calling "music" immeasurable was contrary to the tradition of *musica*. Circumventing the problem in typical medieval fashion, he concedes that plainchant was "not so precisely measured." Although he is not explicit concerning trouvère songs, Grocheio seems to place them among the "not-so-precisely-measured" genres. Even if I am wrong on the last point, we must reckon with the possibility that not all music of the thirteenth century was precisely measured. Above all, we must be very cautious in taking at face value medieval statements about the measurability of any genre of music.

The Musical Notation

Most musical scribes of troubadour and trouvère songs used the square notation which we know from Gregorian chant and which bears no indications of duration aside from double notes. One of the distinctive features of this notation was its use of simple and compound neumes. In the latter one notational symbol comprises several pitches sung to one syllable. Sometime in the thirteenth century the neumes acquired mensural meaning. Not only the presence or absence of a stem, but also the shape of the compound neume, also called a ligature, determined the duration of its individual pitches. We do not know to what extent the scribes of troubadour and trouvère sources were familiar with this innovation, but it is obvious that non-mensural notation was the norm for the chansons. In a manuscript that almost exclusively contains works by Adam de la Hale mensural notation was used for his rondeaux and motets, all of them polyphonic, while non-mensural notation was used for the chansons and jeux-partis, all of them monophonic. The scribe of the manuscript now known as the *Chansonnier Cangé* demonstrated his familiarity with mensural notation by using it for the major part of a motet for two voices, while his notation of most chansons is decidedly non-mensural.[6] Almost as if to confuse us, he gives the impression of having used some half-hearted form of mensural notation in a limited

---

6. For more details on the semi-mensural notation in the *Chansonnier Cangé* see van der Werf, *The Chansons of the Troubadours and Trouvères a Study of the Melodies and Their Relation to the Poems* (Utrecht, 1972), 36-37 and 139-146. See also the photographic reproduction, transcription, and discussion in Jean B. Beck, *Le Chansonnier Cangé*, 2 vols. (Paris, 1927).

number of chansons by clearly distinguishing between stemmed and unstemmed single notes without giving mensural meaning to his ligatures. Furthermore, the alternation of stemmed and unstemmed single notes varies from completely regular in some melodies to absolutely meaningless in others. This leaves us with the problem of distinguishing between real and make-believe mensuration in this particular manuscript. All in all, the scribal habit of giving chansons in non-mensural notation strengthens the idea that duration in chansons was "not so precisely measured."

Multiple Versions

By a stroke of luck the troubadour and trouvère repertories, especially the latter, present us with a source of information that we have just begun to explore. In many instances a given song has been preserved in more than one manuscript; and some songs occur in up to a dozen sources. The multiple versions are rarely identical. For a long time it was assumed that the extant readings were copied, directly or indirectly, from the author's autograph and that copyists were to be blamed for the many discrepancies. Early in this century another explanation emerged, as literary scholars recognized that initially the songs were disseminated by word of mouth, and that only in the mid thirteenth century was dissemination through writing juxtaposed against a continuing oral tradition. Most importantly, the realization arose that, for both performers and scribes, requirements for faithful transmission were much looser than they are in our print-dominated society. In other words, both the persons involved in the oral tradition and those who preserved songs in written form felt free to vary certain aspects of the texts. Consequently, editors of the poems gave up their attempts at reconstructing the original version of a poem. It is now general practice to select one version as basis for an edition and to list variants from other sources in the critical apparatus.

In retrospect, it is difficult to believe that in the early 1960s I was the first to use differences and similarities among multiple versions as a source of information about musical characteristics, especially the rhythm of troubadour and trouvère melodies. Melodic variants are more numerous (and probably more significant) than textual ones. Moreover, oral transmission can be proven much more convincingly for the music than for the poetry, thanks to the many songs in which the music for the first and the second verse are repeated for the third and the fourth verse (i.e. AB AB X). Almost invariably these first four lines differ less in multiple versions than do the subsequent lines. If there had been a written transmission from poet-composer to extant manuscripts, we could have explained this phenomenon only by assuming that musical scribes turned sleepy and sloppy at the beginning of the fifth verse, but returned to fairly accurate copying when they started the next tune. In an oral tradition, however, a person learning a song from listening to it would hear the A and B melodies twice as often as the X section, and thus retain the former better than the latter. Accepting oral transmission as the normal process does not imply that scribes entered the songs directly into the extant sources either from memory or upon hearing. On the contrary, there are ample indications that they (or someone else) made what we might call "a rough copy" that was used as the model, or exemplar, in the production of a collection in book form. Another feature provides valuable information concerning the scribes. Four of the trouvère sources preserve long groups of songs, often by a single author, in the very same order and with few differences. Clearly, these four scribes had access to the same exemplars, and it is encouraging to learn that they could copy very precisely. Obviously, they made some errors, but it is of more importance to note that they also must have made some deliberate changes.

When evaluating similarities and differences among multiple versions, we must choose between two assumptions. Putting things in black and white, we can assume that the transmitters were connoisseurs who left the essential features of a song intact, or that singers and scribes knew virtually nothing about the subtleties of troubadour and trouvère art, and corrupted both text and music. The texts of the chansons help us solve this riddle in that they suggest that troubadour and trouvère poetry is unlikely to have appealed to the masses. Their dissemination is not likely to have been accomplished by footloose and unsophisticated entertainers who eked out a living as jugglers and storytellers in city streets and town squares. Instead, the poems are rather esoteric and are likely to have been appreciated only by afficionados. It may be argued that these connoisseurs, many of them troubadours or trouvères themselves, were responsible for the transmission. At the beginning of the oral tradition stood the poet-composer himself. Regardless of whether he sang in order to teach his creation to someone else or in order to present it to his peers, the author, as a song's first performer, established the manner of presenting it to an audience. If the transmitters were experts and connoisseurs, they are not likely to have altered any characteristics that were essential to either the genre or the individual song, although they may have varied other features within the boundaries of the poetic and musical customs of the time. In this process the author may also have been the first to vary his song from one presentation to another. If this was the case, the similarities and differences among multiple versions afford us a valuable source of information about the manner in which the songs were actually performed.

The "Approximate" Equality of Individual Notes

The differences between multiple versions make it impossible to reconstruct the original melody in all its details, while the similarities assure us that what the scribes left us must have been closely related to what the poet-composer sang at the "world première" of a given chanson. The multiple versions of many songs agree fairly well on the pitches for a given passage, but differ on how the pitches are to be distributed over the text.[7] Taken all together, such differences inescapably lead to a strong but negative conclusion: they could not have come about if all chansons always had been performed in modal rhythm or in any regular alternation of long-short or accented-unaccented units. Fortunately, the study of similarities and differences also allows a positive conclusion, albeit a vague one: the variants could have come about only if essentially all pitches were of more or less equal importance to the flow and the character of the melody. This gives new meaning to Grocheio's remark that pitches in trouvère songs were "not so precisely measured," i.e. that they were of more or less equal duration, with emphasis on, and great uncertainty about the degree of "more or less." In a performance in which pitches do not have a fixed duration and do not come in a fixed sequence of stress and unstress, any text could be sung as the performer desired. The poet-composer as first performer more or less determined the "not so precisely measured" duration of a pitch, a syllable, and a word.

Although this conclusion is vague, it does solve some problems, e.g., why variants in the choice or order of words can bring about variants in the placement of textual accents. In this type of free rhythm, strophes with different distributions of accents can be performed to the same melody, without injustice to either the text or the music. Even better, in this free rhythm both text and melody can receive proper attention and neither is subservient to the other. This gives meaning, too, to the "double note," i.e., the immediate reiteration of a pitch over a syllable. It seems

---

7. Since my conclusions are based upon the overall situation, I would rather not refer to specific examples and instead suggest the study of many songs in multiple versions. For this purpose see van der Werf, *The Extant Troubadour Melodies: Transcriptions and Essays for Performers and Scholars*, Gerald A. Bond, text editor (published by the author, Rochester, N.Y., 1984) and *Trouvères-Melodien*, Monumenta Monodica Medii Aevi, vols. XI and XII, Bruno Stäblein, general editor (Kassel, 1977-1979).

reasonable that a double note represents a pitch that is longer than the one respresented by a single note.[8] And the duration of a given pitch very likely varied from one performer to another and from one strophe to another. Thus, it should be not surprising that two scribes, notating the same melody, might disagree on whether a given pitch was represented by a double or single note. At the present stage of the research, it is risky to draw conclusions from the fact that double notes occur exclusively as part of a compound neume, i.e., over syllables sung to two or more pitches.

Fluctuation in the duration of pitches must have been so pervasive that even as staunch a believer in *musica* as Grocheio was unable to measure them as precisely as he would have liked. On the other hand, something must have enabled scribes to distinguish between pitches of average and longer than average duration, and to consider most of them average. Probably, the duration of pitches was sufficiently close to equal to create a prevailing, although "not precisely measured" unit of time.

Application to a Specific Chanson

Clearly, the above conclusions pertain to troubadour and trouvère songs, in general. In respect to a specific melody, the search for the original rhythm has a disappointing result, for we are unable to reconstruct precisely how it was performed seven or eight centuries ago. However, two aspects of our general conclusions add up to valuable guidance for today's singer of early music. I am optimistic enough to think that we can come reasonably close to an authentic rendition of troubadour and trouvère songs by applying the general conclusion to a specific chanson. Playing the schoolmaster, I may suggest that performers begin by studying the text (not reciting it without the music). In the next step, sing the entire song (not one strophe at a time) making all single notes fairly equal to one another, and making double notes more or less twice as long as single ones. By concentrating on getting the text across to an audience, one is likely to develop small differences in the duration of individual pitches and, especially, almost continuous but subtly executed fluctuations in tempo. A brief elaboration on the two caveats in the above suggestion may be helpful. Beginning the learning process of a song with reciting the text without music may result in a rendition in which the syllables are of equal duration. For basically syllabic songs, this may not be a serious shortcoming but, for more ornate ones, this type of rhythm may fail to do justice to the melody. If one were to learn

---

8. In existing "precisely-measured" transcriptions such lengthening often conflicts with the meter selected by the editor.

50 *Hendrik van der Werf*

a song a strophe at a time, the first strophe might get fixed so strongly in one's mind that its rhythm gets transferred to subsequent strophes. Needless to say, such uniformity will fail to do justice to the differences of meaning and textual flow in individual strophes.

Perhaps, these theories can be elucidated a bit more with the help of a personal note or two. I am not a trained singer and have virtually no experience in reciting poetry to an audience. I do not give recitals but often sing some chansons to illustrate a lecture. I am convinced that one can do justice to both poem and melody. By trial and error, one can learn how to sing several pitches over a seemingly insignificant syllable, and to sing one pitch and one "not so precisely measured" unit of time for the most important syllable of the sentence. In the process one is likely to develop a great appreciation for what at first may appear a duality in medieval songs: one comes to enjoy singing pitches that have primarily melodic meaning at the same time one is "reciting" a poem. Text and melody may not be wedded as they are in songs by Schubert or Fauré, or in an aria of Mozart, yet they go far beyond the point of coexisting or of merely tolerating one another.

The first time I published the above conclusions I used the terms "declaim" and "declamatory" in an unwise attempt to capture a manifold theory in a single word.[9] Paying more attention to the single term than to the entire theory, some fellow medievalists rejected my conclusions as valid only for syllabic passages. Andrew Hughes wrote that my "theory fails to help with melismatic passages."[10] And as the following excerpt (with a quotation from my book) indicates, my choice of terms seems to have misled John Stevens as well:

> My ... task will be to examine some of the deeply held, if not always deeply questioned, beliefs which are current about words-and-music in medieval song. The assumption that it is the words which substantially determine the rhythm of a song is shared not only by convinced adherents of the 'modal' theory but by its strongest opponents, such as Appel, Monterosso and van der Werf. The practical results they come to are very different; but at root they do have certain beliefs in common.... Van der Werf is more ready to subordinate the melodies to the exigencies of the text: 'the rhythm

---

9. Most notably in van der Werf, "Deklamatorischer Rhythmus in den Chansons der Trouvères," in *Die Musikforschung* 20 (1967): 122-44.
10. Andrew Hughes, *Medieval Music: the Sixth Liberal Art* (Toronto, 1974), 160.

in which one might *declaim* the poem without the music' will shape the musical interpretation.[11]

I apologize to those who were led astray by an isolated term but derive solace from those who understood the total theory. More importantly, I hope that this and other recent discussions of rhythm in chansons rectify whatever wrong impressions I may have given on earlier occasions.[12]

Precisely Measured Melodies

Although they do not seem to be very numerous, there are exceptions to the above generalizations. In fact, it has been known for a long time that there are some trouvère songs in which the pitches are precisely measured. Unfortunately, most studies of them, even the most recent ones, are flawed by preconceived notions. Too often, it is taken for granted that, until the middle of the thirteenth century, modal rhythm was the only form of precise measurement for both monophonic and polyphonic music. In addition, the occurrence of modal rhythm in *some* chansons is still taken as evidence that *all* of them are in modal rhythm.[13] In some other cases the researcher seems preoccupied with the "saving" of modal rhythm for the troubadour and trouvère repertories.[14] What we need is an objective study of all songs that show signs of durational measurement. For the sake of the present discussion we may divide such songs into three groups.

Several of the manuscripts saving primarily chansons contain a separate section with motets.[15] This does not prove much more than that

---

11. Stevens, *Words and Music*, 493-494. I cannot understand how Stevens, p. 502, footnote 28, concludes that I speak "of the concept of 'approximate equality' as applying only to syllabic (i.e. single note) progression."
12. See also van der Werf, *The Extant Troubadour Melodies*, 75-83, and my contribution to the forthcoming *Handbook of the Troubadours*, Ron Akehurst and Judith M. Davis, eds.
13. See my review of *Chanter m'estuet: Songs of the Trouvères*, Samuel N. Rosenberg and Hans Tischler, eds. (Bloomington, 1981) in *Journal of the American Musicological Society* 35 (1982): 539-54. See also Tischler's reaction to my review in the same, 36 (1983): 341-44, and my response in 37 (1984): 206-208. In a review of two of my books in *Journal of the Plainsong and Medieval Music Society* 8 (1985): 59, David Hiley called my evaluation of Tischler's theories "one of the best available descriptions (and refutations) of the idea that modal rhythm provides a key to the interpretation of troubadour songs."
14. This seems to be the case with some of Theodore Karp's publications, e.g. "Three Trouvère Chansons in Mensural Notation" in *Gordon Athol Anderson: in Memoriam* (Henryville, Pa., 1984), 474-94.
15. See especially mss. Paris, B.N. f.fr. 12615 (known as "Chansonnier de Noailles") and Paris B.N. f. fr. 844, published as *Le manuscrit du roi*, 2 vols., Jean B. Beck, ed. (Philadelphia, 1938).

collectors who were primarily interested in chansons did not necessarily shun motets, and that modal rhythm was not anathema to the connoisseurs of the "not so precisely measured" chansons. Of more interest is the "split personality" behaviour of those pieces that appear as monophonic songs in chansonniers and as motets for two voices in other collections.[16] In the latter, the relation between tenor and upper voice suggests that they were conceived and normally performed in modal rhythm. It does not seem strange that, at least occasionally, certain motets were performed without tenor, but we can only guess at what happened to their modal rhythm in a monophonic rendition. The type of double occurrence discussed here is not the only form in which an extant chanson is related to an extant motet, and a thorough study of all such cases will teach us quite a bit, not only about the compositions involved but also about the differences and similarities among chansons and motets in general.

Some of the more interesting and more elusive exceptions to be mentioned occur exclusively in the Chansonnier Cangé and are anonymous. As discussed above, the scribe of this manuscript occasionally made use of what some have considered an early form of mensural notation, but which I prefer to call a semi-mensural notation, because only the single notes, not the ligatures, appear to express mensuration.[17] As I have shown before, in most instances the rhythm suggested by the semi-mensural notation is flatly contradicted by differences and similarities among multiple versions of the chansons concerned.[18] But in a few cases good reasons exist for accepting that the chansons combine the modal rhythm of motets with features more typical of chansons,[19] one being that no multiple versions can be found that might argue against these songs having been conceived in modal rhythm. But the strongest reason is that these songs resemble motets in the way the modal rhythm fits the melody. Before we can determine the place of such hybrid songs in the poetry and music of the thirteenth century, we need to know more about this particular manuscript.

---

16. See van der Werf, *The Chansons*, example 12, 134-38.
17. The same type of notation is used in the motet collection Paris, B.N. nouv. acq. fr. 13521, published in photographic reproduction by Friedrich Gennrich, *Ein altfranzösischer Mottetenkodex...La Clayette* (Darmstadt, 1958) and by Luther Dittmer, *Paris 13521 & 11411* (Brooklyn, 1958) and in transcription by Gordon A. Anderson, *Motets of the Manuscript La Clayette* (Rome, 1975).
18. *The Chansons*, 36-40.
19. *The Chansons*, 144-47. Some reservation must be made about my following the standard procedure of maintaining one rhythmic mode throughout a composition. In the case of semi-mensural notation it is impossible to determine how strictly the composer adhered to a given rhythmic mode. As I hope to show in the near future, there are several indications that mixing modes was not uncommon.

Someone involved in its compilation seems to have been interested in making it look like a motet collection, and in making its chansons look like motets. The semi-mensural notation is the most striking consequence of this attempt. The order in which the chansons are entered may be another one. This is the only trouvère chansonnier to present the songs in alphabetical order (exclusively according to the first letter of the text), while at least two motet collectors similarly organized their manuscript.[20]

Finally, some chansons contain internal features atypical of their genre compelling us to consider whether they are more precisely measured than is normal. In a chanson by Blondel de Nesle the uniformity in its multiple versions, including the placement of word accents and distribution of pitches over the text, is unusual for the genre. A close examination of these features made me "conclude that *if* this chanson was meant to be performed in one of the rhythmic modes known to us, it probably was performed" in the third mode.[21] None of the rather diverse commentary upon my transcription has brought us any further to a solution of the problems posed by such atypical chansons.[22] I am still not convinced that it was conceived and normally performed in one of the rhythmic modes known to us, but still consider it likely that its pitches were measured more precisely than was usual for chansons.

Recent Performances and Recordings

Until recently, it was customary to perform all troubadour and trouvère songs in strict modal rhythm, in which syllables were the primary durational units in a ratio of either 1:2 or 1:2:3.[23] For syllabic passages, this resulted in an uninspiringly regular alternation of long and short syllables. Judging by recent recordings, performers of early music have completely abandoned this aspect of modal rhythm. For neumatic and especially for very ornate passages, "modal" performance yielded rhythms

---

20. This is the case for ms. Bamberg, Staatl. Bibl., Lit 115, published in photographic reproduction and transcription by Pierre Aubry, *Cent motets du xiiie siècle*, 3 vols. (Paris, 1980), and published in transcription by Gordon A. Anderson, *Compositions of the Bamberg Manuscript* (Stutgart, 1977). It also is the case for several sections of the ms. known as W2, published in photographic reproduction by Luther Dittmer, *Wolfenbüttel 1099 (1206)* (Brooklyn, 1959).
21. See van der Werf, *The Chansons*, 42 and 100-103. See also my remarks concerning chanson R620 by Blondel de Nesle in *Trouvères-Melodien I*, 559 and 26-32.
22. Stevens in *Words and Music*, 448, Charlotte Roederer in *Schirmer History of Music* (New York, 1982), 72-73, and Theodore Karp, "Three Trouvère Chansons in Mensural Notation," in *Gordon Athol Anderson: in Memoriam* (Henryville, Pa., 1984), 491-94.
23. See footnote 13.

which, depending upon one's point of view, were either "fascinating" or "weird"; they often were contrary to the style of motets. In current practice many singers make the duration of individual pitches quite unequal. In ornate passages this interest in unequal lengths is combined with an apparent desire to make the duration of the syllables close to equal. There seems to be no published defense of this practice, so that one cannot help but wonder whether it arose under the influence of the earlier practice wherein the syllable was the controlling factor, and "fascinating" or "weird" rhythms thereby became associated with the troubadours and trouvères.[24] One may also wonder whether the interest in making individual pitches unequal represents an attempt to make secular songs radically different from Gregorian chant. In two respects this desire is without ground. Firstly, our desire for marked differences between religious and secular music is a relatively modern phenomenon which came about slowly well after the Middle Ages, and seems to have gained its greatest impetus during the nineteenth century. In addition, the often quoted pronouncement of Johannes de Grocheio is not the only indication that, throughout the Middle Ages, duration in plainchant was not precisely measured and may not have resembled the equalistic performance advocated by André Mocquereau and his fellow monks of Solesmes.[25]

Dancing Songs

It was for practical, not for ideological reasons, that my publications on non-liturgical music of the Middle Ages have almost exclusively concerned chansons of the troubadours and trouvères. Going beyond those repertories is difficult, almost risky, because of the low number of extant melodies for the other songs. The troubadour sources contain many poems that clearly fall outside of the genre discussed thus far. Alas, only a very few of them are preserved with a melody, and most of these seem to stem from the late thirteenth or early fourteenth centuries. For songs with French texts fate has been more considerate, but still not generous enough to provide us with multiple versions for many of them. Thus, I may be forgiven for making primarily cautionary remarks in the next few paragraphs.

---

24. Stevens's book, *Words and Music*, advocating "isosyllabic" performance of many genres of medieval song was published long after singers went in this direction. For an evaluation of Stevens's theories see my review of his book in the forthcoming issue of *Journal of Musicological Research*.

25. Concerning accentuation and duration in plainchant see van der Werf, *The Emergence of Gregorian Chant: a Comparative Study of Ambrosian, Roman and Gregorian Chant* (published by the author, Rochester, N.Y., 1983), vol. I, 1, 22-42

At first glance, it would appear that pitches in dancing songs were not only precisely measured but also contained regular alternations of stress and unstress. Unfortunately, we do not know enough about medieval dances to either corroborate or contradict this notion. Probably because modal rhythm is associated with ternary meter, medieval dance songs are traditionally transcribed and performed in some kind of "waltz" rhythm, even though we do not know enough about either the dances or the tunes to exclude binary meter from consideration. To make things worse, we even have difficulty identifying dancing songs. Almost the only undeniable cases occur in narratives in which we are told that (certain) people danced to a song, and here the text may be given but the music usually is lacking. Furthermore, such a dancing song is given various labels, such as some form of the words "rondeau" or "carolle," or something like "chanson de carolle," or simply "chanson."[26] As generic terms were used in the Middle Ages, we should be wary of taking for granted that every text said to be a "rondelet" or "carolle" is a dancing song.

About a dozen poems have been preserved, without music, under the heading "estampie," but there is no indication whatsoever that they are dancing songs, or that they were performed to a clearly measured tune.[27] We also have a number of tunes without text called "estampie" that may be dance tunes, but they stem from the fourteenth century. As far as I know, we have only one case in which both text and music have been preserved for a song called "estampie." Moreover, the melody occurs with both a French and an Occitan text; the former is anonymous, the latter is attributed to Raimbaut de Vacqueiras.[28] Nevertheless, we have no clear indication about duration and accentuation in the melody, per se. A confusing factor in the study of the estampie is that it clearly is related to the Latin *sequence*, the German *Leich*, the French *descort* and lyric *lai*, none of which seem to have had anything to do with dancing. Clearly, we need an extensive study not only of the estampies, but also of the various members of the large sequence family. This research must be without preconceived notions; e.g., it must not start with the premise that the Latin sequence is the ancestor of this group.

There is a theory that the rondeau, the virelai, and the ballade either are, or derive from dancing songs. This usually goes together with the

---

26. See also Christopher Page, *Voices and Instruments*, especially 77-87.
27. See also van der Werf, "Estampie," in *New Grove Dictionary of Music and Musicians*, Stanley Sadie, ed.
28. For a brief discussion and complete transcription of both songs see van der Werf, *The Extant Troubadour Melodies*, 291-93.

assumption that their refrains derive from a practice that dance songs were intoned by a soloist, some of whose verses were repeated by the (other) dancers. It is a thankless task to try to disprove a theory that has never been proven. It may suffice to give the most pertinent facts. It should not surprise anyone to learn from the narratives that medieval people did dance, and (occasionally or often?) did so to a song. From some narratives we may also conclude that an alternation between a soloist and others occasionally occurred in dancing songs. Forms of the word "rondeau" occasionally appear as labels for a dancing song. The noun "ballade" seems to be related to the verb *ballare*, meaning "to dance." Some late entries in *Le Manuscrit du Roi*, which in their form resemble the virelai, have the title *danssa*.[29] Beyond that, there is little or nothing to connect all rondeaux, virelais, and ballades to dancing.

Exploring their origin a bit further, I suggest that if the rondeaux, virelais, and ballades of Guillaume de Machaut were descendants of dancing songs, they are at least as far removed from their origin as Beethoven's scherzos are removed from the courtly minuet. From yet a different point of view, we may recall that playing with recurrent thoughts, words, and sentences is a favorite habit among poets in so-called "primitive" as well as "high" cultures, just as playing with recurrent melodic ideas and phrases is popular among composers in notationless cultures. In the fourteenth century these favorite features became stylized and standardized, and this process seems to have been started before the beginning of that century.[30] It is beyond question that the rondeaux (or the *rondets*, as they are called in their sole source) by Guillaume d'Amiens are different from his chansons and from chansons by other trouvères, but no indication has been found that they have anything to do with dancing.[31] Their melodies may have been measured, but there is no reason to consider ternary meter and modal rhythm axiomatic. Since these are the only extant monophonic rondeaux, and since they occur in only one manuscript, we do not have much material for research on duration in their melodies. Despite all this uncertainty, I urge that some systematic and unprejudiced study be made of all the songs that may have had anything to do with dancing, however remote that connection may have been, even though we may never acquire precise knowledge of rhythm or meter in each individual case.

---

29. For further information see van der Werf, "Estampie."
30. For a discussion of the "balete" preserved (without music) in ms. Oxford, Bodleian Library, Douce 308, see van der Werf, *The Chansons*, 153 and 158-59.
31. For an edition of these *rondets* see Friedrich Gennrich, *Rondeaux, Virelais, und Ballades* (Dresden, 1921), 30-38.

"Not-so-precisely Measured" Music 57

Narrative Songs

Some two hundred French poems can be typified as "narrative songs." This does not include large epics, known as "chansons de geste"; it concerns relatively short, more or less strophic songs, most of which were published a century ago by Karl Bartsch under the general labels "romances" and "pastourelles."[32] Several attempts have been made to subdivide this large group into concise and easily recognizable types. Style and content seem to have been the primary criteria for categorization. To some extant the form of the strophe was also considered, but the style and form of the music played no role. Thus, past research has failed to yield reliable information to those interested in reviving these songs in their original rhythm. My own limited research makes me wonder whether a typological study, taking into account all pertinent aspects of text and music, will yield significantly fewer categories than there are narrative songs.

As a group, the narrative songs combine formal aspects of text and music in a manner that links them with both the trouvère song and *chanson de geste*. The former is strophic in the usual meaning, in the latter the counterpart of the strophe is normally called a *laisse*, the length of which may vary widely. The subdivision of the narrative songs under consideration is usually called a strophe even though the individual strophes of a given song may vary somewhat in their number of lines. Five or six strophes is almost standard for trouvère songs, while the number of *laisses* in a *chanson de geste* is unlimited, and the total epic may have a few thousand lines. In the narrative songs the number of strophes ranges from five to ten in most cases, to twenty or thirty in others. In trouvère songs a ten-syllable line has either ten or eleven syllables, depending on whether the rhyme consists of one or two syllables. This curious form of arithmetic is due to the tradition that in French and Occitan poetry the second (unaccented) syllable of a so-called feminine rhyme is not included in the syllable count. In epic poetry and in many narrative songs a ten-syllable line may have ten, eleven, or twelve syllables. The increase in arithmetical problems is due to the fact that, in addition to an unaccented syllable in the rhyme, there may be an unaccented syllable in the *caesura*, that is in the "break" after the fourth or (less often) the sixth syllable. Beyond the frequently occurring AB AB opening, trouvère songs have relatively little repetition of entire melodic lines. In the narrative songs, however, we often find three- or four-fold repetition of the very first phrase, which may well be

---
32. Karl Bartsch, *Altfranzösische Romanzen und Pastourellen* (Leipzig, 1870).

58 *Hendrik van der Werf*

related to a tradition of singing all the lines of a *laisse*, or of an entire *chanson de geste*, to essentially the same melodic phrase.[33] Differences in choice of rhyme schemes among the three genres are important but not of direct relevance to questions of melodic rhythm and meter.

It seems inconceivable that a *chanson de geste* was performed in modal rhythm or in any other alternation of long and short syllables. If "not so precisely measured" duration was useful in any genre, it must have been in epic poetry. Almost every narrative song turns out to have some formal characteristics of both the *chanson de geste* and of the trouvère chanson. Although this does not give incontrovertible evidence for their rhythm, it does justify the speculation that duration in them was "not so precisely measured."[34] Assuming that duration in all troubadour and trouvère songs, in *chansons de geste*, in all romances and pastourelles, and in all of plain chant was "not so precisely measured" does not necessarily mean that it all sounded alike. On the contrary, this rhythmic freedom allows a wide range of differences in expressiveness and rhythm, however subtle the fluctuations may turn out to be. Let us hope that someone will study the entire group of narrative songs, considering each song on its own merits. The purpose of the research should not be to put each song into a category, to deduce the rhythm for one or two in each category, and to decide that all songs in that category had the same type of rhythm or meter. For the present, however, we are left with no alternative but to consider them all as belonging to one category, and assume that duration in a given narrative was "not so precisely measured," unless evidence to the contrary can be found.

Chromatic Alterations

Finally, we must turn to two "technical" aspects of the performance of medieval songs. *Musica ficta*, or in plain English chromatic alterations, may well form the most elusive problem in the performance of medieval music. Although no all-encompassing study of this phenomenon has been undertaken, many strong opinions have been voiced. The troubadour repertory is small enough that a complete survey can be made of the sharp, natural, and flat signs in the four sources involved; at the same time, it is large enough to give meaningful data.[35] For scholars these data are of great significance, but they fail to offer precise

---

33. In a forthcoming publication I hope to explore the ramifications of the theory that in a *chanson de geste* one line of music was repeated for every textual verse.
34. It is unclear to me why Richard H. Hoppin transcribes narrative songs in modal rhythm in his *Medieval Music* (New York, 1978), 292.
35. For these data, see van der Werf, *The Extant Troubadour Melodies*, 38-61.

prescriptions to performers. To begin with, we have no certainty as to how long a given sign of alteration is valid, although some indication exists that it often pertains only to the pitches on the rest of the staff on which it stands. Beyond that, the variants among multiples versions of troubadour and trouvère songs show that changes were made in the diatonic or chromatic nature of some, but by no means many of the melodies; still they neither reveal who made them nor whether chromatic alterations were added or deleted. Medieval performers do not seem to have been as concerned about note-for-note retention of a melody as are present-day musicians. This attitude appears to have affected chromatic alterations as well as other melodic aspects. Scribes contributed to these differences by adding (or omitting) accidentals in accordance with criteria unknown to us. Since all large chansonniers contain at least some chromatic alterations, we can be fairly sure that troubadours and trouvères themselves did not shun them, but we do not know whether a given composer left us exclusively diatonic melodies, whether he altered a pitch frequently, or whether he seldom did so. Thus, when it comes to determining the diatonic or chromatic state of a melody, it is left to the performer to make decisions where the scholar can only plead ignorance.

Instrumental Accompaniment

Instrumental accompaniment is another thorny issue for scholars and performers alike. For a long time, it was widely accepted that the songs of the troubadours and trouvères were always performed to instrumental accompaniment. As many scholars must have done before me, and as especially Christopher Page did after me, I have searched in vain for information about accompaniment. We know that instruments existed in the time of the troubadours and trouvères, and obviously that they were used. It appears that some troubadours and trouvères could play instruments. We also know that the Middle Ages were not unacquainted with the phenomenon of accompanied song. For example, Tristan often accompanied his own singing.[36] But no evidence is present that troubadour and trouvère chansons were accompanied. It is significant that in troubadour and trouvère poems, as well as in the medieval literature concerning them, we find numerous references to singing, but none to accompanying. The mere fact that, occasionally, a musical instrument is mentioned in a poem is no evidence for instrumental

---

36. The fact that both Tristan and Isolde played instruments is a welcome antidote to the myth that in the Middle Ages playing an instruments was considered a base occupation. Tristan and Isolde were highly admired and the story tellers would not have portrayed them as superb instrumentalists, if playing an instrument would have been in conflict with their noble birth.

accompaniment, and even if we could find evidence for accompaniment of a troubadour or a trouvère song on a certain occasion, we would still have no evidence that they were habitually accompanied. In the only extensive study to date of the medieval use of instruments, Page essentially confirmed what I wrote some twenty-five years ago.[37] He went far beyond the troubadour and trouvère repertories so that we now begin to have some information on what genres actually were accompanied. One thing has not changed: we still do not have any manuscript that actually preserves the accompaniment to any song prior to the fourteenth century. Recital and recording situations being as they are, it may be difficult for performers to abandon instrumental accompaniment completely, but I express pleasure at noting that percussion instruments seem to be losing ground in recordings of medieval music.

On more than one occasion I have written that medieval performers of chansons must have sung expressively, but that we do not know just how dramatic their renditions were. We may be able to draw one more conclusion from the nature and the number of variants among multiple versions. As mentioned above, the variants in the melodies are not only more numerous but also more significant than the variants in the poems. Perhaps one can conclude that the similarities and differences among multiple versions suggest that medieval singers concentrated on presenting the poetry but were rather free in their treatment of the music. In this respect we may raise a crude question: are troubadour and trouvère chansons poems that happen to have a melody or are they musical compositions that happen to have a text? We may not want to answer either question with a simple "yes" or "no," but we can safely assume that the poet-composers wanted their texts to be understood. Thus, we may have an objective criterion by which to judge authenticity of present-day performances, and hold that, from a historical point of view, something is seriously wrong when a song is performed in a rhythm and with an accompaniment that obscure the words. For modern performers there is a painful irony in this conclusion. A performer who sings without instrumental accompaniment, who makes the pitches more or less equal, and who gives a perfect rendition of the text, may encounter less audience appreciation than the one who sings in jumpy rhythms, who is accompanied by an ensemble of odd-sounding instruments, and who is dressed in medieval garb.

---

37. Christopher Page, *Voices and Instruments*.

Index

(References to diagrams, music examples are in **bold**)

Aarburg, Ursula xiii, xvii, 283, 307
Adam de la Halle
   chansons xvi, 207–26, 311
      aesthetic 207
      diversity 218, 220–1
      formulae, music examples **217**
      high style 214
      isosyllabic transcription 207–8
      manuscripts 207
      melodies 215–21
      nature of 210
      notation 492
   conventions 211
   works
      Adan, mout fu Aristotes sachans
         music example **247–8**
         musical structure 247
         text 248
      Amours m'ont si doucement, popular style 214
      Au repairier en la douce contrée
         craftsmanship 211
         metrical pattern 211
         music example **219**
         text 209–10
         tonality 220
         verbal stresses 212, 213
         versions 208
         words and music 222–3
      Congé 208
      Glorieuse virge Marie 218
      Il ne muet pas 224
         music example **225**
      Jeu de la feuillée 208
      Merchi, Amors, de la douce dolor 210
      On me demande mout souvent k'est Amors 210
      Robin et Marion 208
      Roi de Sezile 208
   Tant me plaist vivre en amoureus dangier 214, 221
      motif, music example **216**
      music example **215**
      notation 215–16
      step movement 216
      structure 215
Adam Puschman, Meistersinger 321, 325–6
Adémar II of Poitiers 353
Adenet le Roi, *Berte aus grans piés*, performance 381
Aimeric de Belenoi 428
Aimeric de Peguilhan 430
Al-Farabi, on rhythm 256, 257
Al-Tifashi, Ahmad 272
Alamanda 115, 418
alba 125, 149
   melody 194
Albertet 429
Albigensian Crusade 34, 440
Aldric del Vilar 32, 36
Alegret 32, 34, 41
   Ara pareisson ll'aubre sec 37
Alexander IV, Pope 86
Alexandre, performance 376–7
Alexandre de Bernay 474
Alfonso II, King of Aragon 37
Alfonso VII, Emperor 32
Alfonso X, King of Castile and León 278, 453
Amis et Amile 406
   performance 380–1
amor de lonh 34
Andalusian music
   character 268–73
   classical repertory 275
   hybridity 254, 273
   oral transmission 274–5
Andalusian song, form 254, 273–8
Anglés, Higinio 253, 255
Anonymous IV 459, 463, 467, 468
Anseïs de Carthage, performance 381, 390
Anselm, St 85
Antonio da Tempo 212

Apel, Willi 225–6
Apocalypsis, Golias (attrib) 59, 65, 75
Arab invasion, Iberian Peninsula 267
Arab world, women musicians 113–14
Aristotle, musical composition 186–7
Arles, Provincial Council of 86
Arnaut Daniel 211, 324
    composition abilities 431–2
Arnaut de Maroill 358
    Las grans beutatz e.ls fis ensenhamens
        music examples **344, 345**
        style 344–5, 347
        text 343–4
Arnaut de Tintinhac 33
Arnulf of St Ghislain, on women singers 123
Arthur, King 8, 15
Aubry, Pierre 312, 313, 469, 476
Aucassin et Nicolette 117
    performance 388
Audefroi li Bastars 295
Augustine, St 491
Aurell, Martin 42
Auziàs March 103
Avempace *see* Ibn Bajja
Aye d'Avignon 29
Azalais de Porcairagues, *vida* 115
azjal see zajal

bagpipes 375–6, 423
ballades 502, 503
ballare 503
ballate, in *Decameron* 126, 127
Barlaam et Josaphat, *bozinas* 441
Barr, Cyrilla xiii
Bartsch, Karl 227, 504
bassas dansas 424
Baum, Richard 354
Bec, Pierre xvi, 95–6, 124
    Chants d'amour des femmes-troubadours 96, 98–100, 103
        criticism of 96–8, 104
    La Lyrique française au moyen âge (XII–XIII) 102
Beck, Eleonora 122–3
Beck, Jean 212, 469, 476
Bede, the Venerable, *De arte metrica* 138
Beheim, Michael 322
Beltrán, Vicente 254, 273
Bernart de la Fon, poems 149, 417
Bernart de Saissac 32

Bernart de Ventadorn 32, 33, 37, 125, 223, 438
    skills 433
Bernart Marti 31, 32, 34, 37, 40, 41
    A, senhor, qui so cuges 38
Berte aus grans piés, musical instruments 395
Bertran Carbonel, *cobla* 183
Bertran de Born 37, 41, 193, 418
    poems 421–2, 425
    Rassa, tan creis e mont'e puoia, melody 193, 194
    son de n'Alamanda 115
Beuve de Hantone, performance 382–3
Bianca de' Medici, performances 123
Bittinger, Werner 283, 286, 312
Blacasset, *dansa*, music example **348**
Blancandin, performance 382
Blondel de Nesle 295, 477, 500
Boccaccio, Giovanni, *Decameron* 126
    ballate in 126, 127
    brigata dances 126, 127
    carole dance in 127
    women singing 126–7
Boefs de Haumtone character 19
Boethius, *De differentiis topiciis* 137–8
Boeve de Haumtone 27, 28
Bogin, Meg 95, 99, 105
bordon 19
Boyde, P. 208
Boynton, Susan xiii, xiv
bozinas
    Barlaam et Josaphat 441
    Flamenca 441
Brakelmann, J. 291
brigata dances, in *Decameron* 126, 127
Brunetto Latini 212, 213, 222
buccina 442
Burk Mangolt 324

Cancionero musical de Palacio 273
canso 98, 104, 125, 149–50, 195, 359
    instrumental accompaniment 423
    meaning 419
Canso de St. Fides 447–8
cantar/chantar, meaning 419, 420
cantigas xi, xvii
Cantigas de Santa Maria 273
    Andalusian *rondeau* 255, 278
    musical styles 262
    muwashshah 255
    notation 255

Ribera's edition, criticism 253
virelai 254–5, 279
zajal 278, 279
cantilena 164, 166, 185
cantus coronatus 163–4, 168, 181, 185–6, 467, 468
    music example **165**
cantus versicularis 168
cantus versualis 164
canzone, Dante on 222, 324
Cardalhac 36
Carmina Burana 53, 319, 321, 325
carole 26–7, 113, 118–19
    in the *Decameron* 127
    in *Effects of Good Government* fresco 127
    see also rondet de carole
Cercamon 31, 32, 34, 38, 39, 40, 426
C'est la gieus en mi les préz (anon) **21**, **346**
Chami, Younes 277
chanson de geste 163, 168, 389, 406, 504, 505
    accompaniment
        fiddle 391
        hurdy-gurdy 391
    Daurel et Beton 351
Chanson de Guillaume 29
chanson de mal-mariée 125
chanson de toile 389, 392
chansons de toile, *Guillaume de Dole* 117–18, 125, 392
chantaire 430
chantar see cantar
Chapelain de Laon, *Un petit devant le jour*
    music example **233–4**
    poetic structure 233
    text 234
Charlemagne 8, 11, 19, 482
Chastelain de Couci 13, 283, 293, 294, 399–400
    A vous, amant plus qu'a nule autre gent 285
        music example **307**
        variants 295, 302, 306
    Bele dame me prie de chanter, variants 303–4
    Bien cuidai vivre sans amour 251, 286
    chansons
        collection 313
        variant melodies 284
    Coment que longue demeure, variants 296
    Je chantasse volentiers liement 285, 287
        variants 295–6, 303
    La douce vois du rossignol salvage, variants 302

Li nouviaus tens et mais et violente, variants 295
Merci clamant de mon fol errement, variants 296–7
Mout m'est bele la douce commençance
    music example **251**
    variants 296, **297**
Quant li rossignols jolis (attrib) 287, 462
    variants **288**, 289, 302, 304
Chatterton, Thomas, Vigny on 41
Chaytor, H.J. 314
chevalier 21, 22
Cheyette, Frederic 115, 116
chivalric fiction
    anti-intellectualism 22–3
    music in 3–4, 5, 17, 23
    polyphony in 7 fn9
chivalry, ethic of 23
Chrétien de Troyes 17, 18, 311
    Chevalier au Lion (Yvain) 120
        manuscript variants 365, 367
        performance 365–8
    Philomena 117
Cicero, Marcus Tullius, *De inventione* 137
Claris et Laris 19, 20, 24, 28
    fiddle accompaniment 391
coblas 36–7
    Bertran Carbonel 183
Coldwell, Maria 96
Comte d'Anjou, performance 373, 390
Comtessa de Dia, *A chantar* 115
confraternities, lay 81–2
Conon de Béthune 13, 14, 283, 294
    Chançon legiere a entendre
        melody variations 285
        musical pattern 241
    chansons, variant melodies 184
    L'autrier un jor après la saint Denise, variants 304
Constantinople 14
contrafact 112, 115
contraposita melodies 284, 286
Cordoba, Emirate of 268, 271
corn 439, 440

dance scenes
    Perceforest 401
    Prison amoureuse 401–2
dancing songs, derivatives 502–3
    see also estampies

dansa 354, 503
    fiddle, relationship 354, 356
    melody 195–6, 197
    poems 355
    structure 355
Dante Alighieri 85, 212
    on the *canzone* 222, 324
    on melodic structure 230
    on poetry 146
    works
        Al poco giorno ed al gran cerchio d'ombra 324
        Convivio 223
        De vulgari eloquentia xiv, 222, 223, 227, 229–30, 319–20
Daude de Pradas 431
Daurel et Beton (anon)
    joglars 442–3
    lais d'amor 351–2, 353
    music references 351, 438–9
    text 351
    vers 351, 353
De musica libellus 458
descort 353
    as anti-*canso* 354
    definition 354
    fiddle, relationship 354
    melodies 191–2
    text of 192
    see also *canso*
dire, meaning 420
Dit de la panthère d'amours
    performance 397
    polyphony 397
Doctrina de compondre dictats 144–5, 189–92, 195, 198
Donatus, *Ars minor* 138
Dorfmüller, Kurt 471
Doss-Quinby, Eglal 96
Dragonetti, Roger xvi, 211, 212, 230, 343
    La Technique poétique des trouvères 228, 469, 475–6
drama, Middle Ages 72
Duby, G. 39
Duchesse de Lorraine
    Par maintes fois aurai estei requise (attrib) 101
    Un petit devant le jor (attrib) 101
ductia 166–7, 172, 173, 175, 181, 457, 462, 467
Durmart le Galois
    performance 396
    polyphony 396

Eberhardini 63, 64
Eble II de Ventadour 349
Eble III de Ventadour 34
Elias Cairel 432
Elias de Barjols 428
eloquence, cult of 13–14
epics, checklist of 24–5
Eracle 29
Erec et Enide 17, 24
Erlanger, Baron Rodolphe d' 256, 271
estampidas 196
    Kalenda maia 197, 198
estampies 197–8, 502
    see also dancing songs

Fadet 35
far, meanings 120, 428, 429
Faral, Edmond 32–3, 34, 39
Fauvel, motet 403
feast
    description 17–18
    elements of 25–6
    language formulae 25–6
    music at 25, 26
Ferrari de Ferrara 432
Ferreira, Manuel Pedro xiii, xiv, xvii, xxiii
Fibonacci, Leonardo 474
Fichtner, E.G. 65
fiddle 391, 392–3, 406–7
    dansa 354, 356
    descort 354
fiddlers 436
flagellant mania (1260) 83–4
    influence 87
Flamenca 415, 437, 438, 447
    bozinas 441
    flutes 441
    joglars 435–6
    Mass references 446
    musical instruments 434–5
Florimont 29
flutes, *Flamenca* 441
Folque de Candie 14, 25
Folquet de Marseilles/Marselha 141, 227
    Chantars mi torn' ad afan 417
    S'al cor plagues be fora huei may sazos a lais, music example **352**, 353

Foster, K. 208
Foulque of Toulouse *see* Folquet de Marseilles
Francesco da Barberino, *Reggimento e costumi di donna* 122
Francis of Assisi, St, *Cantico delle creature* 82
Franciscans, Spiritual 85
Franco of Cologne 235, 255, 492
    Ars cantus mensurabilis 157
Frederick II, Holy Roman Emperor 84
Friedrichs des Siegreichen 322
Froissart, Jean
    Chronicles, performance 382
    Prison amoureuse 401–2

Gace Brulé 294
Gace de la Buigne, *Roman des deduis*, performance 393–5
Galahad character 8
Galeran de Bretagne 117, 125
gamut, Johannes de Grocheio on 161
Ganelon 11
Garin lo Brun
    Ensenhamen de la Donzela, parallelism 448–9
    Ensenhamens 115
Gaucelm Faidit 116, 429
Gaunt, Simon 96
    Gender and Genre... 97–8
Gautier de Coinci, *Miracles*, performance 392–3
Gautier de Dargies
    Autres que je ne suel fas
        music example **249–50**
        musical pattern 249
        text 250
    Chançon ferai mout marris
        music example **244–5**
        musical structure 244
        text 245
    Maintes fois m'a on demandé
        music example **245–6**
        musical pattern 245
        text 246
Gautier d'Espinal, *Ne puet laissier fins cuers c'adès se plaigne* 251
    musical pattern 241
Gautier, Léon 34
Gawayn character 3, 4, 7, 8, 15–16, 22
Gaydon 28
Gennrich, Friedrich 283, 312, 327
    Grundriss 228

Geoffroi de Vinsauf
    on poetry 140–1
    works
        Ars Poetica 25
        Poetria nova 140
Gerard of San Donnino 85, 86
Gerbert de Montreuil, *Roman de la Violette* 117, 125
Gesù Cristo society 86
Ghil, Eliza 34
Gilbert de Montreuil, *Perceval* 390
Gille de Chyn 28
Gillebert de Berneville
    D'Amours me vient li sens dont j'ai chanté
        music example **243**
        musical pattern 242–3
        text 243
Gilles de Chyn 399, 406
    performance 383
Gillingham, Bryan xiii
Giraldus Cambrensis 60
    Speculum Ecclesiae 54, 62, 75
goliard
    dictionary definitions 69–70
    etymology 54, 55–7, 64, 78–9
    hat associations 69, 70–1
    phonological development 64–5
    Wright on 55–6
goliardic poems 65–6
    examples 67–9
goliards 39, 53
    actor-entertainers 71–2, 74
    see also Vaganten
Golias 55, 56, 64, 78, 79
    Apocalypsis (attrib) 59, 65, 75
    extra-biblical use 60–1
    personality of 61, 75
    Peter Abelard as 61–2, 64
    as root of goliard 60
Golias family 62–3
Goliath story, in Jerome 60
Gottfried von Strassburg, *Tristan* 121–2
Gouiran, Gérard 41
graile 439, 440, 441
Gravdal, Kathryn 96–7
Great Hall, atmosphere 4
Gregorian chant 226, 501
Grimbert, Joan xiii
Grimm, Jakob 64
Guerau de Cabrera 35

Gui d'Ussel 116
Guilelma Monja 116, 117
Guilhalmi 38–9, 40
Guilhem Anelier 440
Guilhem de Berguedan 37
Guilhem de la Barra, Mass reference 445–6
Guilhem de la Tor 426, 427
Guilhelm de Poitiers 427
    poem 418
    see also William IX
Guilhem Figueira 427
Guilhem Magret 428
Guillaume d'Amiens 311, 503
Guillaume de Dole, chansons de toile 117–18, 125, 392
Guillaume de Lorris, *Roman de la Rose*, performance 368
Guillaume de Machaut 191, 503
    Fonteinne amoureuse, performance 376
    Joie, plaisence et douce nourriture 373
Guillaume li Viniers 295
Guillem Augier Novella, *Ses alegratge* 191
Guillem de Ribas 422
Guiot de Berguedà, song 355–6
Guiot de Dijon
    Chanterai pour mon corage (attrib) 101
    Quant je plus voi felon rire 235
Guiot de Provins, *Mout me merveil de ma dame et de moi* 239
Guiraut de Bornelh 116, 358, 359, 422, 427–8
    alba tune 437–8
    poems 418, 421
Guiraut de Cabreira, *sirventes* 349–50, 450
Guiraut de Calanson 35, 430
    ensenhamen 451–2
Guiraut de Salignac 426, 427
Guiraut Riquier 36, 195, 453–4
Guiron le Courtois 14, 22, 24
gula 64
    literary references 57–9
    as root of goliard 55, 56, 57, 69

harp playing 3, 4, 5, 9–10, 28–9, 380, 386
    see also lais
Harvey, Ruth xiii
Henderson, John 81, 86
Henry II, King 76
    traveling court 37
Hervis de Metz 26
Higgins, Paula 123

high style songs xx, 343, 344, 346–7, 353
    Adam de la Halle chansons 214
    low style, comparison xv, xvi, 347
hocket 178–9, 180
Hölderlin, Friedrich 320
Hopkins, Gerard Manley 23
Horace, *Ars poetica* 137, 138
Horn 388
    performance 377–8
Horn character, musical abilities 12–13
Hrotsvitha, plays 72–3
Hue de la Ferté, *Je chantasse volentiers liement*
    variants 304
    see also Chastelain de Couci
Hugh Primas 62, 65, 78
Hugh of St-Victor 85
Hughes, Andrew 497
Hugo von Montfort 322, 324
Hugues de Berzé 283, 294
    chansons, variant melodies 284
    works
        Ausi con cil qui cuevre sa pesance, variants 297, 298
        Encor ferai une chançon, variants 295
        Nus hom ne set d'ami qui puet valoir, variants 289, **290**, 301–2
        S'onques nus hom por dure departie 287, 306
Huot, Sylvia xiii, xix
hurdy-gurdy 391
Husmann, Heinrich 477

Iberian Peninsula, Arab invasion 267
    see also Cordoba
Ibn Bajja (Avempace) 272
Ibn Quzman, *zajal* 274
Ich sezte mînen fuoz 331–2
instruments *see* musical instruments
integrity, chivalric 21–2
ioculator 37, 39
Isabella d'Este, musical patronage 124
Iseut/Isolde character, *lai* composing/singing 120–2

J'ai maintes fois chanté de cuer marri 231
Jaufre (anon) 354
    joglars references 353, 437, 444
    performance 444
Jaufre Rudel, prince of Blaye 31, 32, 34, 41, 349, 350, 353, 420, 429, 450, 479, 482–3

Jean Bodel 311
Jean de Garlande
  on melodic structure 147–8
  on poetry 141–3
  works
    De triumphis ecclesiae 141
    Parisiana poetria 141
Jean Renart
  Guillaume de Dole 20, 24, 27, 399
    chansons de toile 117–18, 125, 392
    pastourelle 119
    performance 371
    rondet de carole 118–19, 125
    songs 112–13, 118
    women singing 117–19
Jeffery, Peter 124
Jehan Erart
  En Pascour un jour erroie
    music example **232**
    structure 231–2
  Pastorel 231
Jehan et Blonde 26
Jerome of Moravia, *Tractatus de Musica* 21
Jerome, St, Goliath story 60
Joachim of Fiore 84–5
Joachimism 86
Joachites 84
Jofre de Foixà
  Doctrina de compondre dictats (attrib) 144
  Regles de trobar 144, 189
  on song themes 189
joglaressa 117
joglars 15, 21, 31, 419, 449–50
  Abril issia reference 357
  Daurel et Beton, references 442–3
  disparagement of 421–2, 450
  Ensenhamen de la Donzela 449
  Flamenca reference 435–6
  Jaufre references 353, 437, 444
  lifestyle 32, 428
    sources 40–1
  meaning 34, 36
  praise of 423–4, 451–2
  social
    position 425, 453
    skills 35
  troubadours, distinction 32–3, 36, 42, 426, 453–4
  vidas 33–4, 36, 39
  see also troubadours

Johannes de Garlandia 458, 492
Johannes de Grocheio xv, xx, 276, 456–7, 458–9, 491, 492, 501
  De musica 157, 185, 467
    cantilena 164, 166
    cantus coronatus 163–4, **165**, 168, 181, 185–6, 236–7
    cantus versicularis 168
    cantus versualis 164
    chanson de geste 163, 168
    composition, place of 158
    ductia 166–7, 172, 181
    the gamut 161
    hocket 178–9, 180
    instruments 170–1
    motet 176, 179, 180
    music
      classification 159–61, 185, 457, 459, 463
      composition 186–7
      genres 162
    organum 177, 179
    plainchant 180–1
    puncta 173, **174**, 175
    stantipes 166, 169, 172, 181, 197
    tenor voice 179–80
    textual corrections 159–81
  on music theory 147–8
  Norman family, fiefs 158, **159**
  Paris studies 157–8
John of Salisbury
  parasitus, use of 78
  Policraticus 77–8
jongleurs *see joglars*
Juan del Encina, *Tan buen ganadico*, music example **261**

Kalenda maia 197, 433, 444
Karp, Theodore xiv, xvii
Kasten, Ingrid 33, 38, 40
Kay, Sarah 33
Kippenberg, Burkhard 489
Köhler, E. 42

Lai de l'Epine, performance 384–5
lais xx, 12–13, 15, 22, 28, 191, 352
  Beuve de Hantone 382–3
  Breton 398
  Guigemar 372
  Horn 377–8

Iseult/Isolde performance 120–2
Lai de l'Epine 385
meaning 353
Paris et Vienne 386
Perceforest 378–80
Roman de Brut 368–9
Tristan 387–8
Tristan en prose 385–6
see also harp playing
laisse 439, 504
Lambert, Magister, *Tractatus de Musica* 458
Langfors, Arthur 313
langue d'oc 143
Larkin, Philip 42
laude xi
   manuscripts 82, 87–8
   musical notation 82, 88
   origins 82–3
laudesi 87
Le Gentil, Pierre 273
Lejeune, Rita 34
Les Narbonnais 19, 25, 28
Les Quatre Fils Aymon 19, 25, 28
Liu, Benjamin 254, 276
Livre d'Artus 5, 24
Lorenzetti, Ambrogio, *Effects of Good Government* fresco 127
love, and music 9
low style songs, high style, comparison xv, xvi, 347
Lucius II, Pope 84
Luther, Martin, *Von Himmel hoch* 334
lyric poetry, and women 111, 123

Ma douce souffrance 231
Maddrell, J.E. xx, 461, 462, 464
manuscripts
   Chansonnier Cangé 320, 457, 459, 467, 476, 492, 499
   Chansonnier d'Arras 240, 251, 286
      Rome chansonnier, relationship 295
   Chansonnier de Noailles 233
   Chansonnier de Saint Germain 239
   laude 82, 87–8
   Magliabechiano manuscript 82
   Manuscrit du Roi 235, 467, 476, 503
   Minnesang 326
   Rome chansonnier 286
      Arras chansonnier, relationship 295
   trobador xi, xii, xvii, xviii

trouvère
   classification **291–2**, 293, **299**
   ideal edition 307–8
   variant readings 283, 287, 293, 294–306, 315–17
   women, attributed to 101–2
Marcabru 31, 32, 33, 34, 36, 38, 42, 349, 350, 436–7, 450
   Bel m'es quan la rana chanta 37
   L'autrier jost'una sebissa 116
Margaret of Austria 123
Maria de Ventadorn 116
Marie de France, *Guigemar*, performance 372
Maroie de Diergnau, *Mout m'abelist quant je voi revenir* (attrib) 101
Marquis Lanza 36
Marshall, J.H. 210
Mass for the Dead, Ronsasvals 446
Mass references
   Flamenca 446
   Guilhem de la Barra 445–6
   songs 445–6
Matfre Ermengaud 36
Matthew Paris 72
Maugis 23
Maugis d'Aigremont 22, 25
Meliadus, King 15, 22
melodic form 149–50
melodic structure
   Dante on 230
   Jean de Garlande on 147–8
melody
   alba 194
   dansa 195–6, 197
   descorts 191–2
   Fort m'enoja, so auzes dire 193, 194
   non-repetitive 235–6
   planh 196
   poem, structural correspondence 183–4, 186–8, 198–9, 424–5
   and poetic genre 189–90
   Rassa, tan creis e mont'e puoia 193, 194
   retroncha 194–5
   sirventes 193
   trouvère chansons, variations 312, 314–15
   use of
      so (son) 416–17, 419, 433, 448
      sonu 437
Meneghetti, Maria-Luisa 34, 35, 38
mensura, meaning 457, 458, 459, 467

Mervelles de Rigomer 28
Middle Ages
  drama 72
  performers
    names 73
    types 73–4
Minnesang
  melody 319–37
    reconstruction problems 325–32
    structure 332–7
    music examples **328, 329–30, 333, 335, 336**
Minnesinger xi, 322
minstrelsy, art of, in *Abril issia* 358–9
Mocquereau, André 501
modesty, knightly 22
Molinier, Guilhem, *Las Leys d'Amors* (attrib) 197, 198, 212, 226, 415
Mölk, Ulrich, and Friedrich Wolfzettel, *Répertoire métrique* 469, 470
Monge (Monk) de Montaudon 426
  Fort m'enoja, so auzes dire, melody 193, 194
Moniage Guillaume, performance 371–2
Moniot d'Arras 295
  Amors me fait renvoisier et chanter (attrib) 101
monophonic music xi, 21, 161, 185
  genres, summary table **xii**
  oral tradition 112, 122
  performance xix–xxiv
  status of performers xiii
Monroe, James 254, 276
motets 146, 176, 179, 180, 407, 476, 498–9
  analysis 485–6
  Fauvel 403
  music example **486**
  Roman de la rose 397
music
  at feast 25, 26
  canon 161
  in chivalric fiction 3–4, 5, 17, 23
  classification
    in *De musica* 159–61, 185, 457, 459, 463
    forms, in *De musica* 162
  composition 186–7
  ecclesiastical 161
  immeasurable 160
  instrumental 268–9
  and love 9
  manuscripts, for women 123
  measurability 160, 464–5, 467–8
  notation, *Roman de Tristan en Prose* 121
  in Old French fiction 18
  patronage
    Bianca de' Medici 123
    Isabella d'Este 124
  poetry
    asymmetry 146, 274
    as branch of 145
    historiography 228
    overview xiv–xvii
    symmetry 227, 274
    in the *quadrivium* xv, 146
    secular 146–7, 185
    structures 146
    theory, Johannes de Grocheio on 147–8
    treatises on 146
    see also monophonic music; polyphony; singing
  music references
    didactic works 448–54
    lyric poems 416–26
    Old Occitan literature 415–54
    vidas/razos 426–48
musica
  development 491–2
  meaning 463, 465, 467, 491
musica mensurabilis 458
  see also polyphony
musical form 229
musical instruments 170–1, 369, 374–6, 405, 425–6, 451–2
  Berte aus grans piés 395
  Dit de la panthère d'amours 397
  Flamenca 434–5
  Miracle 392–3
  Roman de Brut 390
  Roman de Eledus et Serene 395
  see also bagpipes; fiddle; harp playing; organs
muwashshah 254
  Cantigas de Santa Maria 255
  origins 269
  performance style 271
  structure 270, 273, 277–8
  see also zajal

Na Tecla de Borja 103
nafil 441
Nantes 445
narcissism 11–13

Neidhart, *Blôzen wir den anger ligen sâhen* 326
neuma 181
Nicole Bozon, *Contes moralisé* 402–3
nota 433
notar 439
notation xii, xiv, xx, xxi–xxiv, 82, 88, 207, 228,
　　235, 253, 255, 260–62, 315, 321, 331,
　　348, 453, 456, 459, 462, 464–5, 467, 474,
　　478, 492–3, 499–500
nova 359
Nus ne porroit de mauvaise raison (anon),
　　contrafactum 285

Old French fiction
　music in 18
　music typologies
　　epics 24–5
　　romances 24
　see also chivalric fiction
Old Occitan literature, music references 415–54
organar 451
organs, portable 407
　Roman de la rose 397
organum 177, 179
Oswald von Wolkenstein 322, 325, 470
Ovide moralisé, performance 375

Pacholczyk, Jozef 277
Paden, William D. 36, 96
Page, Christopher xiii, xiv, xvi, 119, 384, 389,
　　506, 507
　Voices and Instruments xix–xx
Pamphile et Galatée 391
parasitus
　John of Salisbury, use 78
　meanings 75, 75–6, 78
　in Roman drama 76–7
Paris et Vienne, performance 383–4, 386
Paris, Gaston xvi
partimen 353, 354
pastora 195
pastorela 149, 195
pastourelles xx, 374, 375, 377, 504
Peire Cardenal 430
Peire d'Alvernhe 32, 33, 37, 429
　self-praise 422–3
Peire de Corbian, *Tezaur* 451–2
Peire de la Mula 427
Peire de Ladils, poems 420
Peire de Maensac 429

Peire de Valeria 32, 33
Peire Vidal 36, 427
　poem 425
Peirol 428
Perceforest 404
　dance scene 401
　lais 378–80
　performance 378–80, 398–9, 401
Perdigo 353, 427
performance
　Alexandre 376–7
　Amis et Amile 380–1
　Anseïs de Carthage 381, 390
　Aucassin et Nicolette 388
　Berte aus grans piés 381
　Beuve de Hantone 382–3
　Blancandin 382
　Chevalier au Lion (Yvain) 365–8
　Comte d'Anjou 373, 390
　Dit de la panthère d'amours 397
　Durmart le Galois 396
　Fonteinne amoureuse 376
　Froissart's *Chronicles* 382
　Gilles de Chyn 383
　Guigemar 372
　Guillaume de Dole 371
　Horn 377–8
　instruments, use of xix, 12–13, 114, 123,
　　197, 271, 351, 354–5, 369–70, 372–3,
　　375–7, 380–82, 385–6, 387, 390–92
　Jaufre 444
　Lai de l'Epine 384–5
　Miracles 392–3
　Moniage Guillaume 371–2
　monophonic music xix–xxiv
　Ovide moralisé 375
　Paris et Vienne 383–4, 386
　Perceforest 378–80, 398–9, 401
　polyphonic music 393–4
　rhythm xix, 316, 317, 470–471, 479, 489,
　　500–501
　Roman de Brut 368–9
　Roman de la Rose 368
　Roman de la violette 388–9
　Roman de Silence 383, 390
　Roman des deduis 393–5
　rural settings 444–5
　social setting xiii, 4, 16, 20, 359, 394, 405
　Tournois de Chauvency 389
　Tristan 387–8

Tristan en prose 385–6
Tristan ménestral 374
verbs for 369–70, 404, 419–21
Voie d'Enfer et de Paradis 396
women 111–15, 117–18, 119–27
Perrin d'Angecourt 407
Peter Abelard 8
  as Golias 61–2, 64
Peter of Blois 35, 37, 39
Pfeffer, Wendy 96
Philip the Chancellor 53
Philip the Fair 123
Picker, Martin 123
Pidal, Menendez 34
Pierre de Molins 283
  chansons, variant melodies 284
  Quant foillissent li boscage (attrib) 287, 306
    variants 303
Pietro Casella da Pistoia, *Amor che nella mente mi ragiona* 324
Pistoleta 430
Pius II, Pope 123
plainchant 180–1, 185, 492, 501
planh 149
  melody 196
Plenckers, Leo 277
poetic structure, classification 229, 230–1
poetry
  as branch of music 145
  Dante on 146
  debate poems 115–16
  five parts 139–40
  genre, and melody 189–90
  Geoffroi de Vinsauf on 140–1
  as grammatical art 138, 139
  Jean de Garlande on 141–3
  melody, structural correspondence 183–4, 186–7, 198–9, 424–5
  music
    asymmetry 146, 274
    historiography 228
    overview xiv–xvii
    symmetry 227, 274
  Raimon Vidal on 143–4, 358
  treatises on 139–45
  see also versification
polemics, literary 36–7
polyphony 185, 395
  aristocratic performers 398
  in chivalric fiction 7 fn9

court 394
development 465
Dit de la panthère d'amours 397
Durmart le Galois 396
measured rhythm 478
Renart le contrefait 395
Roman de la rose 397
Roman des deduis 393–5
Voie d'Enfer et de Paradis 396
Pons de Capduelh 430
Post, Jennifer 124
Priscian, *Institutiones grammaticae* 138
puncta 173, 175
  music example **174**

quadrivium 145, 447
  music in xv, 146
Quant li dous tens renouvele
  analysis 484–5
  music examples **484**
Quintilian, *Institutio oratoria* 137

Rabanus Maurus 85
Raimbaut d'Aurenga 31, 34, 37, 38, 417
Raimbaut de Vaqueiras 116, 353, 502
  Kalenda maia 197, 433
Raimon Berenguer V 42
Raimon de Cornet, poem 424
Raimon de Miraval 424
  poems 419–20
Raimon Vidal
  on poetry 143–4, 358
  on songs 188–9
  works
    Abril issia 35, 343
      on art of ministrelsy 358–9
      joglar references 357
      text 357
    ensenhamen 449–50
    Las Razos de trobar 143, 188–9
Raniero Fasani 83, 86
Raoul de Ferrières, *Quant li rossignols jolis* (attrib) 287
  variant readings **288**, 289
Rasd ed Dhil, *nawba* 277
Raynaud, Gaston 227
Raynouard, F.J. 451
razos 148, 149, 432–3
regula, meaning 459
Renart le contrefait, polyphony 395

retroncha, melody 194–5
rhetoric
    elements 138, 187
    five parts 138
    function 137, 187
    styles 138
    in *trivium* 146
Rhetorica ad Herennium 137, 140
rhythm xvii, xix–xxiv, 176, 180, 207, 212, 222, 224, 226, 228, 255–62, 277, 316–17, 326, 331–2, 455–9, 462–5, 467–8, 469, 470, 471, 474–9, 481, 484, 487, 489, 490–491, 495, 496–9, 500–502, 505
Ribera, Julián, *Cantigas de Santa Maria* 253
Richard de Berbezilh 429
Richart de Fournival 311
    Onques n'amai tant que jou fui amee (attrib) 101
    Talent avoie d'amer
        music example **240**
        text 241
Rieger, Angelica 96, 99, 100, 116
Riemann, Hugo 469
Riquer, Martin de 31, 33
Robert de Blois, *Chastoiment des Dames* 117
Robert de Castel d'Arras 476
Rohloff, E. 157
Roi de Navarre 284
    Li dous penser et li dous souvenir
        music example **241–2**
        text 242
Roland character 8
Roland le Pettour 37
Roman de Eledus et Serene, musical instruments 395
Roman de Flamenca 119
Roman de Horn 11, 12, 13, 22, 29
Roman de la rose
    motet 397
    organs 397
    polyphony 397
Roman de la violette, performance 388–9
Roman de Silence, performance 383, 390
Roman de Tristan en Prose, music notation 121
romances 504
    checklist of 25
rondeau 20, 184, 502
    Andalusian 255, 276–7, 278, 279, 280
    Cantigas de Santa Maria 255, 278
    definition 276–7
    French 255, 273, 277, 278, 280
    monophonic 503
    polyphonic 207, 236 fn12 396
    structure 273–4
rondet de carole 118–19, 125, 345
    music example **346**
    style 347
    see also carole
Ronsasvals, Mass for the Dead 446
Rosenberg, Samuel 102
Ruodlieb 9
Ruodlieb character 9–10

Sachs, Curt, *The Wellsprings of Music* 481
Salimbene 83
Salinas, Francisco 261, 262
Sancta Aines 437
Sappler, Paul, *Königstein Songbook* 469, 470–1
    music examples 472–3
Sawa, George 268
Schönberg, Arnold 332
Seay, Albert 157, 201, 462
Simon de Montfort 141
singing
    camerale 122
    on horseback 19, 27–8
    improvisation 112
    party 27
    tenor voice 179–80
    women 113, 115
        in *Decameron* 126–7
        in *Guillaume de Dole* 117–19
    see also songs
sirventes 149, 192–3
    Guiraut de Cabreira 349–50, 450
    melody 193
so (son), meaning 416–17, 419, 433, 448
sonar, meaning 420, 438
Sone de Nansay 119–20
sonet, meaning 418, 419
The Song of Roland 8, 11, 13, 14, 439–40
songs
    composer/performer fusion 113, 120, 122–3, 125
    discography 128–9
    German 470–1
    in *Guillaume de Dole* 112–13
    high style xx, 343, 344, 346–7, 353
    low style, comparison xv, xvi, 347
    instrumental accompaniment, role 112

Mass references 445–6
metaphor for community 127
music examples **xxii**
narrative 389–90, 504–5
new 15–16
performance xix–xxiv
Raimon Vidal on 188–9
themes, Jofre de Foixà on 189
transmission xvii–xix
see also trouvère chansons
sonu, meaning 437
Sordello 430
poem 417–18
Southern, R.W. 39
Spanke, Hans 230, 285, 294
Beziehungen 228
Städtler, Katharina 96
stantipes 166, 169, 172, 173, 175, 181, 197
Stevens, John xiv, xvi, 497–8
Stronski, S. 33
Switten, Margaret 115, 116
Symonds, John Addington 56, 64

tenor voice 179–80
tenso 149
authorship 102, 103
Occitan 116
sound recordings 116
Thibaut de Blason 294
Thibaut de Champagne 14, 284
Li dous penser et li dous souvenir, musical pattern 241
Tout autresi con l'ente fait venir, musical pattern 241
Thomas of Britain, *Tristan* 120
Thomas of Chobham 34
Thomas d'Angleterre, *Tristan*, performance 387–8
Thompson, James Westfall 54
Tischler, Hans xx
Tournois de Chauvency, performance 389
Tristan character 15, 506
Tristan en prose 398
performance 385–6
Tristan ménestral, performance 374
trivium 139, 447
rhetoric in 146
trobador xi, xx, 427, 429, 453
see also troubadours
trobaire 427, 430

trobairitz see troubadours, women
trobar, meaning 427, 428, 430, 453
trobar clus, vs *trobar leu* style 417
trompa 440, 441
trompador 440
troubadour songs 188, 353, 359
dotted rhythm 189
high style 356
melodies 189
moral purpose 357–8
in non-mensural notes 474
performance 392, 399, 407 fn24
tenso aristocratisante 102
see also trouvère chansons
troubadours 40
biographies 34
composition
methods 148–50
skills 429–30
joglars, distinction 32–3, 36, 42, 426, 453–4
professional 42
status, evidence for 31–2
trouvères, distinction 311–12
types 31, 33
women 95–105, 115, 117
poems 100–1
studies 96
writing skills 432
see also joglars; *trobador*; trouvères
trouvère chansons 218, 407
chromatic alterations 505–6
classification 229–31, **232**
dancing songs 502–3
editing practices 312–14
editions 469–70
requirements of 470
expressive performance 507
instrumental accompaniment xix, 506–7
melodic variations 312, 314–15, 493
meter 491
multiple versions 493–5
music examples **472–3**
narrative 504–5
narrative function 400–1
notation xxi, xxiii, 492–3
music examples **xxii**
in notationless culture 317
note equality 495–6
oral tradition hypothesis 290–1, 315, 455–6, 493–4

performance 496–7, 500–1, 507
pitch 495–6
   precisely measured 498–500
preservation 490
rhythm
   modal 498, 499, 500
   theories xx–xxii, 456, 459, 471, 474, 475–8, 481–2
roots 474–5
syllable count 490–91
texts 490–91
Van der Werf on 455–6, 462–5, 469, 479, 482–3
see also Minnesang; troubadour songs
trouvères xi, 311
   etymology 218
   examples of 13
   meaning 490 fn2
   status 312
   troubadours, distinction 311–12
   women 96, 97, 101, 103, 104, 106, 117
   see also troubadours
tuba 442
Tyssens, Madeleine 96, 101

Uc Brunet 430
Uc Catola 36
Uc de Saint-Circ 32, 433
   poem 149
Uc Faidit, *Donatz proensals* 143
Ulrich von Lichtenstein 322–3
upar, meaning 451

Vaganten 53, 59, 79
   see also goliards
Van der Werf, Hendrik xvii, xix, xx, 214, 255, 467, 468, 474, 477, 481
   The Chansons of the Troubadours and Trouvères 469, 470
   on trouvère chansons 455–6, 462–5, 469, 479, 482–3
verbs, for performance 369–70, 404, 419–21
vers capcauda, examples 285
versification 138–9
   see also poetry
Vidame de Chartres 283, 294
   chansons, variants 284
   Combien que j'aie demouré
      music example **301**
      variants 299–300

Quant foillissent li boscage (attrib) 287, 306
   variants 303
Tant con je fusse fors de ma contrée, variants 300
viella 171
   see also musical instruments
Vigny, Alfred de, on Chatterton 41
virelai 502, 503
   form
      Cantigas de Santa Maria 254–5, 279
      Prison amoureuse 401–2
   in France 279
   structure 254, 273, 278
Voie d'Enfer et de Paradis
   performance 396
   polyphony 396
Voyage de Charlemange 26

Wace, *Roman de Brut*
   musical instruments 390
   performance 368–9
Waddell, Helen 53
Walter, Archbishop of Sens 60
Walter Map/es 35, 54, 62, 76, 78
Walther von der Vogelweide 321, 334, 471
   Palestine Song 326, 327, 337, 479
   Wol vierzec jâr hab ich gesungen 319
   Zwei minner sehzic doene ich hân 319
William IX, Duke of Aquitaine 31
   histrio playing 32
   red cat poem 34
   see also Guilhem de Poitiers
William X, Duke of Aquitaine 32, 40
Wizlav von Rugen 322
   Nâch der senenden klage môt ik singen 326
Wolf, Ferdinand 227
Wolfger of Ellenbrechstkirchen 63
women
   and lyric poetry 111, 123
   manuscripts, attributed 101–2
   music manuscripts for 123
   musicians xiii–xiv
      Arab world 113–14
      ethnomusicological approach 124
      limits on 122
      professional 123
   performance 111–15, 117–18, 119–27
   singing 113, 115
      Arnulf of St Ghislain on 123
      in *Decameron* 126–7

in *Guillaume de Dole* 117–19
troubadours *see under* troubadours
Wright, Thomas 54–5, 65
   on Goliards 55–6
Wulstan, David 254, 274

Yudkin, Jeremy 127

zajal (pl *azjal*) 254
   Cantigas de Santa Maria 278, 279
   Hebrew 271
   Ibn Quzman 274
   performance style 271
   structure 270–1, 273, 274, 278
   see also muwashshah
Zink, Michael 118
Ziryab, influence 268
Zitzmann, Rudolf 286
Zumthor, Paul xvi, 211